Social and Political Philosophy

READINGS FROM PLATO TO GANDHI

JOHN SOMERVILLE, who received his Ph.D. degree from Columbia University, is the author of six books—including *The Philosophy of Peace* and *Methodology in Social Science*—and co-author of another six. Editor of the translation journal *Soviet Studies in Philosophy* and a frequent contributor to philosophical publications, he has been awarded fellowships and grants by Columbia, Stanford, and the Rockefeller Foundation for special researches in philosophy here and abroad. UNESCO has published his contributions to three of its projects in the field of social philosophy, and he has presented papers before International Congresses of Philosophy at Copenhagen, Harvard, Amsterdam, Brussels, and Venice. Professor Somerville is Professor Emeritus of the City University of New York.

RONALD E. SANTONI holds the Maria Teresa Barney Chair of Philosophy at Denison University in Ohio and is a Life Member of Clare Hall, Cambridge University. He has been Visiting Scholar and a Visiting Lecturer in the Faculty of Philosophy at the University of Cambridge (1990), a Visiting Fellow at Clare Hall, Cambridge (1986), a Royal Society of Canada Fellow at the University of Paris (Sorbonne), and, on three occasions, has been either a Visiting or Research Fellow at Yale University. He is co-editor of *Social and Political Philosophy*, editor of *Religious Language and the Problem of Religious Knowledge*, and contributor to *Current Issues in Philosophy; Towards the Understanding and Prevention of Genocide*; *Nuclear War: Philosophical Perspectives*; *Genocide: A Critical Bibliographic Review*; and *The Institution of War*, among other works. A scholar of the philosophy of Jean-Paul Sartre, he has published over one hundred articles, commentaries, and reviews in professional philosophical journals and national magazines. Long an activist in civil rights, anti-war, and peace activities, he is Vice-President of the American and Japanese Professionals Against Nuclear Omnicide (American Division), a founding officer of International Philosophers for the Prevention of Nuclear Omnicide, and a member of the Board of Directors of the Institute on the Holocaust and Genocide in Jerusalem. He is contributing editor of the *Internet on Genocide and the Holocaust*, and a member of the Board of Editors of the *Journal for Peace and Justice Studies*.

SOCIAL AND
POLITICAL PHILOSOPHY

READINGS FROM PLATO TO GANDHI

Edited by John Somerville and Ronald E. Santoni

ANCHOR BOOKS
A DIVISION OF RANDOM HOUSE, INC.
NEW YORK

Grateful acknowledgment is made to the following for granting permission
to reprint the selections that appear in this book.

BEACON PRESS. Chapter 8 from *Reconstruction in Philosophy* by John
Dewey. (First published in 1920.) Copyright 1948 by Beacon Press. Reprinted by permission of Beacon Press.

HAFNER PUBLISHING COMPANY, INC., and CHARLES FRANKEL. Book I,
Chapters 1–9 and Book II, Chapters 1–8 from *The Social Contract* by Jean
Jacques Rousseau, an 18th century translation, revised and edited by
Charles Frankel. Copyright 1947 by Hafner Publishing Company, Inc. Re-
printed by permission of the publisher and Charles Frankel.

HOGARTH PRESS, LTD. *The Political and Social Doctrine of Fascism* by
Benito Mussolini, translated by Jane Soames (1933). Reprinted by permission of The Hogarth Press, Ltd.

HOLT, RINEHART AND WINSTON, INC. Chapters 16 and 17 (abridged) from
Ethics by John Dewey and James H. Tufts (revised edition). Copyright
1932, 1960. Reprinted by permission of Holt, Rinehart and Winston, Inc.

HOUGHTON MIFFLIN COMPANY. Selections from *Mein Kampf* by Adolf
Hitler. Copyright 1932 by Houghton Mifflin Company. Reprinted by permission of the publisher.

INTERNATIONAL PUBLISHERS COMPANY, INC. Chapters 1, 2, and 5 from
State and Revolution, by V. I. Lenin. Copyright 1943 by International Publishers Company, Inc. in V. I. Lenin, *Selected Works*, Volume VII, and as a
reprint in Little Lenin Library. Reprinted by permission of the publisher.

NAVAJIVAN TRUST. Essays from *Non-Violent Resistance* by M. K. Gandhi
(published by Schocken Books, Inc.). Copyright © 1951 by Navajivan
Trust. Reprinted by permission of Navajivan Trust.

OXFORD UNIVERSITY PRESS. Chapters 5–7, 9, 10, 15–19 from *The Prince*
by Niccolò Machiavelli, translated by Luigi Ricci (1903), revised by
E. R. P. Vincent. Copyright 1940, 1950 by Random House, Inc. Reprinted
by permission of Oxford University Press.

All possible care has been taken to trace the ownership of rights to every
selection included and to make full acknowledgment of its use. If any omission has occurred, it will be corrected in subsequent editions, provided
notification is sent to the publisher.

ISBN 0-385-01238-1
Library of Congress Catalog Card Number 63–18039
www.anchorbooks.com
PRINTED IN THE UNITED STATES OF AMERICA

50 49 48 47 46 45 44 43

CONTENTS[1]

[1] In some instances original titles have been supplemented in the table of contents in order to indicate themes and issues dealt with. Wherever any supplementary headings are used in the text, appropriate identification is supplied. *The Editors.*

INTRODUCTION

This volume is intended to meet an increasing need for a comprehensive source book in the area of social and political philosophy. Although interest in this field has grown markedly, there has been little attempt to provide, for the student's use and convenience, a compilation of substantial representative selections from its major writings.

In preparing such a work we have tried to guide ourselves by certain standards. Undoubtedly the best method of introducing students to social philosophy is by directing them to the "classics" in the area; and the richest aspect or adjunct of any "textbook" in this field is, literally, a collection of its most important *texts*. We have therefore tried to bring together in one volume the best representative selections from the outstanding original sources. Our choices have been guided by a desire to present the major positions in the field, and to provide enough material from each of the authors to allow a penetrating coming-to-grips with each position. For this reason we have made the usual allotment for a given viewpoint about forty pages, and have refrained from trying to represent any position by means of a mere "snippet."

In addition to presenting classic figures like Plato, Aristotle, Hobbes, Locke, Rousseau, Mill, and writers who had a special influence on American developments, like Jefferson, Thoreau, and Dewey, we have tried to keep in view the new need to supply substantial primary material in relation to contemporary trends in social philosophy. The twentieth century has witnessed the sharp growth and clash of movements such as communism, socialism, fascism, nazism, and non-violent resistance. In the political thought, ideological debates, and international relations of today, these newer social philosophies have assumed a degree of concrete importance that makes it quite impossible to take a realistic approach without seriously confronting them. We have thus devoted ample space to authors of the last hundred years such as Marx, Engels, Lenin, Hitler, Mussolini, and Gandhi.

We realize that no possible group of selections will recommend itself equally to all. But we are sure that anyone who reads the work of the authors appearing in this volume, following with reasonable care the argument of each selection, will confront and appreciate the basic issues and chief viewpoints of the past and present in this field. Such a reader will certainly have equipped himself to face the problems of the future with increased understanding and effectiveness.

The Editors

Social and Political Philosophy

READINGS FROM PLATO TO GANDHI

Plato (427–347 B.C.)

THE REPUBLIC

Translated from the Greek by Benjamin Jowett

THE PROBLEM OF JUSTICE[1]
BOOK I

The scene is laid in the house of Cephalus at the Piraeus; and the whole dialogue is narrated by Socrates the day after it actually took place to Timaeus, Hermocrates, Critias, and a nameless person, who are introduced in the Timaeus.

I went down yesterday to the Piraeus with Glaucon the son of Ariston, that I might offer up my prayers to the goddess[2]; and also because I wanted to see in what manner they would celebrate the festival, which was a new thing. I was delighted with the procession of the inhabitants; but that of the Thracians was equally, if not more, beautiful. When we had finished our prayers and viewed the spectacle, we turned in the direction of the city; and at that instant Polemarchus the son of Cephalus chanced to catch sight of us from a distance as we were starting on our way home, and told his servant to run and bid us wait for him. The servant took hold of me by the cloak behind, and said: Polemarchus desires you to wait.

I turned round, and asked him where his master was.

There he is, said the youth, coming after you, if you will only wait.

Certainly we will, said Glaucon; and in a few minutes

---

[1] At the beginning of each selection from *The Republic* (which is 400 pages in its entirety) the editors have inserted a heading to indicate the topics on which basic arguments are presented. *The Editors.* [Note: "The Editors" refers to the editors of the present volume. All footnotes not so credited are from the original works and translations.]

[2] Bendis, the Thracian Artemis.

Polemarchus appeared, and with him Adeimantus, Glaucon's brother, Niceratus the son of Nicias, and several others who had been at the procession.

Polemarchus said to me: I perceive, Socrates, that you and your companion are already on your way to the city.

You are not far wrong, I said.

But do you see, he rejoined, how many we are?

Of course.

And are you stronger than all these? for if not, you will have to remain where you are.

May there not be the alternative, I said, that we may persuade you to let us go?

But can you persuade us, if we refuse to listen to you? he said.

Certainly not, replied Glaucon.

Then we are not going to listen; of that you may be assured.

Adeimantus added: Has no one told you of the torch-race on horseback in honour of the goddess which will take place in the evening?

With horses! I replied: That is a novelty. Will horsemen carry torches and pass them one to another during the race?

Yes, said Polemarchus, and not only so, but a festival will be celebrated at night, which you certainly ought to see. Let us rise soon after supper and see this festival; there will be a gathering of young men, and we will have a good talk. Stay then, and do not be perverse.

Glaucon said: I suppose, since you insist, that we must.

Very good, I replied.

Accordingly we went with Polemarchus to his house; and there we found his brothers Lysias and Euthydemus, and with them Thrasymachus the Chalcedonian, Charmantides the Paeanian, and Cleitophon the son of Aristonymus. There too was Cephalus the father of Polemarchus, whom I had not seen for a long time, and I thought him very much aged. He was seated on a cushioned chair, and had a garland on his head, for he had been sacrificing in the court; and there were some other chairs in the room arranged in a semicircle, upon which we sat down by him. He saluted me eagerly, and then he said:—

You don't come to see me, Socrates, as often as you ought: If I were still able to go and see you I would not ask you to come to me. But at my age I can hardly get to the city, and therefore you should come oftener to the Piraeus. For let me tell you, that the more the pleasures of the body fade away, the greater to me is the pleasure and charm of conversation. Do not then deny my request, but make our house your resort and keep company with these young men; we are old friends, and you will be quite at home with us.

I replied: There is nothing which for my part I like better, Cephalus, than conversing with aged men; for I regard them as travellers who have gone a journey which I too may have to go, and of whom I ought to enquire, whether the way is smooth and easy, or rugged and difficult. And this is a question which I should like to ask of you who have arrived at that time which the poets call the "threshold of old age"—Is life harder towards the end, or what report do you give of it?

I will tell you, Socrates, he said, what my own feeling is. Men of my age flock together; we are birds of a feather, as the old proverb says; and at our meetings the tale of my acquaintance commonly is—I cannot eat, I cannot drink; the pleasures of youth and love are fled away: there was a good time once, but now that is gone, and life is no longer life. Some complain of the slights which are put upon them by relations, and they will tell you sadly of how many evils their old age is the cause. But to me, Socrates, these complainers seem to blame that which is not really in fault. For if old age were the cause, I too being old, and every other old man, would have felt as they do. But this is not my own experience, nor that of others whom I have known. How well I remember the aged poet Sophocles, when in answer to the question, How does love suit with age, Sophocles,—are you still the man you were? Peace, he replied; most gladly have I escaped the thing of which you speak; I feel as if I had escaped from a mad and furious master. His words have often occurred to my mind since, and they seem as good to me now as at the time when he uttered them. For certainly old age has a great sense of calm and freedom; when the passions relax their hold, then, as Sophocles says, we are freed from the grasp not of one mad master only, but of many. The truth is, Socrates, that these regrets, and also the complaints about relations, are to be attributed to the same cause, which is not old age, but men's characters and tempers; for he who is of a calm and happy nature will hardly feel the pressure of age, but to him who is of an opposite disposition youth and age are equally a burden.

I listened in admiration, and wanting to draw him out, that he might go on—Yes, Cephalus, I said: but I rather suspect that people in general are not convinced by you when you speak thus; they think that old age sits lightly upon you, not because of your happy disposition, but because you are rich, and wealth is well known to be a great comforter.

You are right, he replied; they are not convinced: and there is something in what they say; not, however, so much as they imagine. I might answer them as Themistocles answered the Seriphian who was abusing him and saying that he was famous, not for his own merits but because he was an Athenian: "If you had been a native of my country or I of yours, neither of us would have been famous." And to those who are not rich and are impatient of old age, the same reply may be made; for to the good poor man old age cannot be a light burden, nor can a bad rich man ever have peace with himself.

May I ask, Cephalus, whether your fortune was for the most part inherited or acquired by you?

Acquired! Socrates; do you want to know how much I acquired? In the art of making money I have been midway between my father and grandfather: for my grandfather, whose name I bear, doubled and trebled the value of his patrimony, that which he inherited being much what I possess now; but my father Lysanias reduced the property below what it is at present: and I shall be satisfied if I leave to these my sons not less but a little more than I received.

That was why I asked you the question, I replied, because I see that you are indifferent about money, which is a characteristic rather of those who have inherited their fortunes than of those who have acquired them, the makers of fortunes have a second love of money as a creation of their own, resembling the affection of authors for their own poems, or of parents for their children, besides that natural love of it for the sake of use and profit which is common to them and all men. And hence they are very bad company, for they can talk about nothing but the praises of wealth.

That is true, he said.

Yes, that is very true, but may I ask another question?— What do you consider to be the greatest blessing which you have reaped from your wealth?

One, he said, of which I could not expect easily to convince others. For let me tell you, Socrates, that when a man thinks himself to be near death, fears and cares enter into his mind which he never had before; the tales of a world below and the punishment which is exacted there of deeds done here were once a laughing matter to him, but now he is tormented with the thought that they may be true: either from the weakness of age, or because he is now drawing nearer to that other place, he has a clearer view of these things; suspicions and alarms crowd thickly upon him, and he begins to reflect and consider what wrongs he has done to others. And when he finds that the sum of his transgressions is great he will many a time like a child start up in his sleep for fear, and he is filled with dark forebodings. But to him who is conscious of no sin, sweet hope, as Pindar charmingly says, is the kind nurse of his age:

> "Hope," he says "cherishes the soul of him who lives in justice and holiness and is the nurse of his age and the companion of his journey;—hope which is mightiest to sway the restless soul of man."

How admirable are his words! And the great blessing of riches, I do not say to every man, but to a good man, is, that he has had no occasion to deceive or to defraud others, either intentionally or unintentionally; and when he departs to the world below he is not in any apprehension about offerings due to the gods or debts which he owes to men. Now to this peace of mind the possession of wealth greatly contributes; and therefore I say, that, setting one thing against another, of the many advantages which wealth has to give, to a man of sense this is in my opinion the greatest.

Well said, Cephalus, I replied; but as concerning justice, what is it?—to speak the truth and to pay your debts—no more than this? And even to this are there not exceptions? Suppose that a friend when in his right mind has deposited arms with me and he asks for them when he is not in his right mind, ought I to give them back to him? No one would say that I ought or that I should be right in doing so, anymore than they would say that I ought always to speak the truth to one who is in his condition.

You are quite right, he replied.

But then, I said, speaking the truth and paying your debts is not a correct definition of justice.

Quite correct, Socrates, if Simonides is to be believed, said Polemarchus interposing.

I fear, said Cephalus, that I must go now, for I have to look after the sacrifices, and I hand over the argument to Polemarchus and the company.

Is not Polemarchus your heir? I said.

To be sure, he answered, and went away laughing to the sacrifices. . . .[3]

---

[3] Socrates has a mild preliminary skirmish, here omitted, with Polemarchus, before the debate with Thrasymachus. *The Editors.*

THRASYMACHUS' DEFINITION AND SOCRATES' REFUTATION

Several times in the course of the discussion Thrasymachus had made an attempt to get the argument into his own hands, and had been put down by the rest of the company, who wanted to hear the end. But when Polemarchus and I had done speaking and there was a pause, he could no longer hold his peace; and, gathering himself up, he came at us like a wild beast, seeking to devour us. We were quite panic-stricken at the sight of him.

He roared out to the whole company: What folly, Socrates, has taken possession of you all? And why, sillybillies, do you knock under to one another? I say that if you want really to know what justice is, you should not only ask but answer, and you should not seek honour to yourself from the refutation of an opponent, but have your own answer; for there is many a one who can ask and cannot answer. And now I will not have you say that justice is duty or advantage or profit or gain or interest, for this sort of nonsense will not do for me; I must have clearness and accuracy.

I was panic-stricken at his words, and could not look at him without trembling. Indeed I believe that if I had not fixed my eye upon him, I should have been struck dumb: but when I saw his fury rising, I looked at him first, and was therefore able to reply to him.

Thrasymachus, I said, with a quiver, don't be hard upon us. Polemarchus and I may have been guilty of a little mistake in the argument, but I can assure you that the error was not intentional. If we were seeking for a piece of gold, you would not imagine that we were "knocking under to one another," and so losing our chance of finding it. And why, when we are seeking for justice, a thing more precious than many pieces of gold, do you say that we are weakly yielding to one another and not doing our utmost to get at the truth? Nay, my good friend, we are most willing and anxious to do so, but the fact is that we cannot. And if so, you people who know all things should pity us and not be angry with us.

How characteristic of Socrates! he replied, with a bitter laugh;—that's your ironical style! Did I not foresee—have I not already told you, that whatever he was asked he would refuse to answer, and try irony or any other shuffle, in order that he might avoid answering?

You are a philosopher, Thrasymachus, I replied, and well

know that if you ask a person what numbers make up twelve, taking care to prohibit him whom you ask from answering twice six, or three times four, or six times two, or four times three, "for this sort of nonsense will not do for me,"—then obviously, if that is your way of putting the question, no one can answer you. But suppose that he were to retort, "Thrasymachus, what do you mean? If one of these numbers which you interdict be the true answer to the question, am I falsely to say some other number which is not the right one?—is that your meaning?"—How would you answer him?

Just as if the two cases were at all alike! he said.

Why should they not be? I replied; and even if they are not, but only appear to be so to the person who is asked, ought he not to say what he thinks, whether you and I forbid him or not?

I presume then that you are going to make one of the interdicted answers?

I dare say that I may, notwithstanding the danger, if upon reflection I approve of any of them.

But what if I give you an answer about justice other and better, he said, than any of these? What do you deserve to have done to you?

Done to me!—as becomes the ignorant, I must learn from the wise—that is what I deserve to have done to me.

What, and no payment! a pleasant notion!

I will pay when I have the money, I replied.

But you have, Socrates, said Glaucon: and you, Thrasymachus, need be under no anxiety about money, for we will all make a contribution for Socrates.

Yes, he replied, and then Socrates will do as he always does —refuse to answer himself, but take and pull to pieces the answer of some one else.

Why, my good friend, I said, how can any one answer who knows, and says that he knows, just nothing; and who, even if he has some faint notions of his own, is told by a man of authority not to utter them? The natural thing is, that the speaker should be some one like yourself who professes to know and can tell what he knows. Will you then kindly answer, for the edification of the company and of myself?

Glaucon and the rest of the company joined in my request and Thrasymachus, as any one might see, was in reality eager to speak; for he thought that he had an excellent answer, and would distinguish himself. But at first he affected to insist on my answering; at length he consented to begin. Behold, he said, the wisdom of Socrates; he refuses to teach himself, and goes about learning of others, to whom he never even says thank you.

That I learn of others, I replied, is quite true; but that I am ungrateful I wholly deny. Money I have none, and therefore I pay in praise, which is all I have: and how ready I am to praise any one who appears to me to speak well you will very soon find out when you answer; for I expect that you will answer well.

Listen, then, he said; I proclaim that justice is nothing else than the interest of the stronger. And now why do you not praise me? But of course you won't.

Let me first understand you, I replied. Justice, as you say, is the interest of the stronger. What, Thrasymachus, is the meaning of this? You cannot mean to say that because Polydamas, the pancratiast, is stronger than we are, and finds the eating of beef conducive to his bodily strength, that to eat beef is therefore equally for our good who are weaker than he is, and right and just for us?

That's abominable of you, Socrates; you take the words in the sense which is most damaging to the argument.

Not at all, my good sir, I said; I am trying to understand them; and I wish that you would be a little clearer.

Well, he said, have you never heard that forms of government differ; there are tyrannies, and there are democracies, and there are aristocracies?

Yes, I know.

And the government is the ruling power in each state?

Certainly.

And the different forms of government make laws democratical, aristocratical, tyrannical, with a view to their several interests; and these laws, which are made by them for their own interests, are the justice which they deliver to their subjects, and him who transgresses them they punish as a breaker of the law, and unjust. And that is what I mean when I say that in all states there is the same principle of justice, which is the interest of the government; and as the government must be supposed to have power, the only reasonable conclusion is, that everywhere there is one principle of justice, which is the interest of the stronger.

Now I understand you, I said; and whether you are right or not I will try to discover. But let me remark, that in defining justice you have yourself used the word "interest" which you forbade me to use. It is true, however, that in your definition the words "of the stronger" are added.

A small addition, you must allow, he said.

Great or small, never mind about that: we must first enquire whether what you are saying is the truth. Now we are both agreed that justice is interest of some sort, but you go on to say "of the stronger"; about this addition I am not so sure, and must therefore consider further.

Proceed.

I will; and first tell me, Do you admit that it is just for subjects to obey their rulers?

I do.

But are the rulers of states absolutely infallible, or are they sometimes liable to err?

To be sure, he replied, they are liable to err.

Then in making their laws they may sometimes make them rightly, and sometimes not?

True.

When they make them rightly, they make them agreeably to their interest; when they are mistaken, contrary to their interest; you admit that?

Yes.

And the laws which they make must be obeyed by their subjects,—and that is what you call justice?

Doubtless.

Then justice, according to your argument, is not only obedience to the interest of the stronger but the reverse?

What is that you are saying? he asked.

I am only repeating what you are saying, I believe. But let us consider: Have we not admitted that the rulers may be mistaken about their own interest in what they command, and also that to obey them is justice? Has not that been admitted?

Yes.

Then you must also have acknowledged justice not to be for the interest of the stronger, when the rulers unintentionally command things to be done which are to their own injury. For if, as you say, justice is the obedience which the subject renders to their commands, in that case, O wisest of men, is there any escape from the conclusion that the weaker are commanded to do, not what is for the interest, but what is for the injury of the stronger?

Nothing can be clearer, Socrates, said Polemarchus.

Yes, said Cleitophon, interposing, if you are allowed to be his witness.

But there is no need of any witness, said Polemarchus, for Thrasymachus himself acknowledges that rulers may some-

times command what is not for their own interest, and that
for subjects to obey them is justice.

Yes, Polemarchus,—Thrasymachus said that for subjects to
do what was commanded by their rulers is just.

Yes, Cleitophon, but he also said that justice is the interest
of the stronger, and, while admitting both these propositions,
he further acknowledged that the stronger may command the
weaker who are his subjects to do what is not for his own interest; whence follows that justice is the injury quite as much
as the interest of the stronger.

But, said Cleitophon, he meant by the interest of the stronger
what the stronger thought to be his interest,—this was what the
weaker had to do; and this was affirmed by him to be justice.

Those were not his words, rejoined Polemarchus.

Never mind, I replied, if he now says that they are, let us
accept his statement. Tell me, Thrasymachus, I said, did you
mean by justice what the stronger thought to be his interest,
whether really so or not?

Certainly not, he said. Do you suppose that I call him who
is mistaken the stronger at the time when he is mistaken?

Yes, I said, my impression was that you did so, when you
admitted that the ruler was not infallible but might be sometimes mistaken.

You argue like an informer, Socrates. Do you mean, for
example, that he who is mistaken about the sick is a physician
in that he is mistaken? or that he who errs in arithmetic or
grammar is an arithmetician or grammarian at the time when
he is making the mistake, in respect of the mistake? True, we
say that the physician or arithmetician or grammarian has
made a mistake, but this is only a way of speaking; for the
fact is that neither the grammarian nor any other person of
skill ever makes a mistake in so far as he is what his name
implies; they none of them err unless their skill fails them, and
then they cease to be skilled artists. No artist or sage or ruler
errs at the time when he is what his name implies; though he
is commonly said to err, and I adopted the common mode of
speaking. But to be perfectly accurate, since you are such a
lover of accuracy, we should say that the ruler, in so far as he
is the ruler, is unerring, and, being unerring, always commands
that which is for his own interest; and the subject is required
to execute his commands; and therefore, as I said at first and
now repeat, justice is the interest of the stronger.

Indeed, Thrasymachus, and do I really appear to you to
argue like an informer?

Certainly, he replied.

And do you suppose that I ask these questions with any design of injuring you in the argument?

Nay, he replied, "suppose" is not the word—I know it; but you will be found out, and by sheer force of argument you will never prevail.

I shall not make the attempt, my dear man; but to avoid any misunderstanding occurring between us in future, let me ask, in what sense do you speak of a ruler or stronger whose interest, as you were saying, he being the superior, it is just that the inferior should execute—is he a ruler in the popular or in the strict sense of the term?

In the strictest of all senses, he said. And now cheat and play the informer if you can; I ask no quarter at your hands. But you never will be able, never.

And do you imagine, I said, that I am such a madman as to try and cheat, Thrasymachus? I might as well shave a lion.

Why, he said, you made the attempt a minute ago, and you failed.

Enough, I said, of these civilities. It will be better that I should ask you a question: Is the physician, taken in that strict sense of which you are speaking, a healer of the sick or a maker of money? And remember that I am now speaking of the true physician.

A healer of the sick, he replied.

And the pilot—that is to say, the true pilot—is he a captain of sailors or a mere sailor?

A captain of sailors.

The circumstance that he sails in the ship is not to be taken into account; neither is he to be called a sailor; the name pilot by which he is distinguished has nothing to do with sailing, but is significant of his skill and of his authority over the sailors.

Very true, he said.

Now, I said, every art has an interest?

Certainly.

For which the art has to consider and provide?

Yes, that is the aim of art.

And the interest of any art is the perfection of it—this and nothing else?

What do you mean?

I mean what I may illustrate negatively by the example of the body. Suppose you were to ask me whether the body is self-sufficing or has wants, I should reply: Certainly the body has wants; for the body may be ill and require to be cured, and has therefore interests to which the art of medicine ministers; and this is the origin and intention of medicine, as you will acknowledge. Am I not right?

Quite right, he replied.

But is the art of medicine or any other art faulty or deficient in any quality in the same way that the eye may be deficient in sight or the ear fail of hearing, and therefore requires another art to provide for the interests of seeing and hearing—has art in itself, I say, any similar liability to fault or defect, and does every art require another supplementary art to provide for its interests, and that another and another without end? Or have the arts to look only after their own interests? Or have they no need either of themselves or of another?—having no faults or defects, they have no need to correct them, either by the exercise of their own art or of any other; they have only to consider the interest of their subject-matter. For every art remains pure and faultless while remaining true—that is to say, while perfect and unimpaired. Take the words in your precise sense, and tell me whether I am not right.

Yes, clearly.

Then medicine does not consider the interest of medicine, but the interest of the body?

True, he said.

Nor does the art of horsemanship consider the interests of the art of horsemanship, but the interests of the horse; neither do any other arts care for themselves, for they have no needs; they care only for that which is the subject of their art?

True, he said.

But surely, Thrasymachus, the arts are the superiors and rulers of their own subjects?

To this he assented with a good deal of reluctance.

Then, I said, no science or art considers or enjoins the interest of the stronger or superior, but only the interest of the subject and weaker?

He made an attempt to contest this proposition also, but finally acquiesced.

Then, I continued, no physician, in so far as he is a physician, considers his own good in what he prescribes, but the good of his patient; for the true physician is also a ruler having the human body as a subject, and is not a mere money-maker; that has been admitted?

Yes.

And the pilot likewise, in the strict sense of the term, is a ruler of sailors and not a mere sailor?

That has been admitted.

And such a pilot and ruler will provide and prescribe for the interest of the sailor who is under him, and not for his own or the ruler's interest?

He gave a reluctant "Yes."

Then, I said, Thrasymachus, there is no one in any rule who, in so far as he is a ruler, considers or enjoins what is for his own interest, but always what is for the interest of his subject or suitable to his art; to that he looks, and that alone he considers in everything which he says and does.

When we had got to this point in the argument, and every one saw that the definition of justice had been completely upset, Thrasymachus, instead of replying to me, said: Tell me, Socrates, have you got a nurse?

Why do you ask such a question, I said, when you ought rather to be answering?

Because she leaves you to snivel, and never wipes your nose: she has not even taught you to know the shepherd from the sheep.

What makes you say that? I replied.

Because you fancy that the shepherd or neatherd fattens or tends the sheep or oxen with a view to their own good and not to the good of himself or his master; and you further imagine that the rulers of states, if they are true rulers, never think of their subjects as sheep, and that they are not studying their own advantage day and night. Oh, no; and so entirely astray are you in your ideas about the just and unjust as not even to know that justice and the just are in reality another's good; that is to say, the interest of the ruler and stronger, and the loss of the subject and servant; and injustice the opposite; for the unjust is lord over the truly simple and just: he is the stronger, and his subjects do what is for his interest, and minister to his happiness, which is very far from being their own. Consider further, most foolish Socrates, that the just is always a loser in comparison with the unjust. First of all, in private contracts: wherever the unjust is the partner of the just you will find that, when the partnership is dissolved, the unjust man has always more and the just less. Secondly, in their dealings with the State: when there is an income tax, the just man will pay more and the unjust less on the same amount of income; and when there is anything to be received the one gains nothing and the other much. Observe also what happens when they take an office; there is the just man neglecting his affairs and perhaps suffering other losses, and getting nothing out of the public,

because he is just; moreover he is hated by his friends and acquaintance for refusing to serve them in unlawful ways. But
all this is reversed in the case of the unjust man. I am speaking,
as before, of injustice on a large scale in which the advantage
of the unjust is more apparent; and my meaning will be most
clearly seen if we turn to that highest form of injustice in
which the criminal is the happiest of men, and the sufferers or
those who refuse to do injustice are the most miserable—that
is to say tyranny, which by fraud and force takes away the
property of others, not little by little but wholesale; comprehending in one, things sacred as well as profane, private and
public; for which acts of wrong, if he were detected perpe-
trating any one of them singly, he would be punished and incur
great disgrace—they who do such wrong in particular cases
are called robbers of temples, and man-stealers and burglars
and swindlers and thieves. But when a man besides taking
away the money of the citizens has made slaves of them, then,
instead of these names of reproach, he is termed happy and
blessed, not only by the citizens but by all who hear of his
having achieved the consummation of injustice. For mankind
censure injustice, fearing that they may be the victims of it
and not because they shrink from committing it. And thus, as
I have shown, Socrates, injustice, when on a sufficient scale,
has more strength and freedom and mastery than justice; and,
as I said at first, justice is the interest of the stronger, whereas
injustice is a man's own profit and interest.

Thrasymachus, when he had thus spoken, having, like a
bathman, deluged our ears with his words, had a mind to go
away. But the company would not let him; they insisted that
he should remain and defend his position; and I myself added
my own humble request that he would not leave us. Thrasymachus, I said to him, excellent man, how suggestive are
your remarks! And are you going to run away before you
have fairly taught or learned whether they are true or not? Is
the attempt to determine the way of man's life so small a matter in your eyes—to determine how life may be passed by each
one of us to the greatest advantage?

And do I differ from you, he said, as to the importance of
the enquiry?

You appear rather, I replied, to have no care or thought
about us, Thrasymachus—whether we live better or worse from
not knowing what you say you know, is to you a matter of indifference. Prithee, friend, do not keep your knowledge to
yourself; we are a large party; and any benefit which you con-

fer upon us will be amply rewarded. For my own part I openly declare that I am not convinced, and that I do not believe injustice to be more gainful than justice, even if uncontrolled and allowed to have free play. For, granting that there may be an unjust man who is able to commit injustice either by fraud or force, still this does not convince me of the superior advantage of injustice, and there may be others who are in the same predicament with myself. Perhaps we may be wrong; if so, you in your wisdom should convince us that we are mistaken in preferring justice to injustice.

And how am I to convince you, he said, if you are not already convinced by what I have just said; what more can I do for you? Would you have me put the proof bodily into your souls?

Heaven forbid! I said; I would only ask you to be consistent; or, if you change, change openly and let there be no deception. For I must remark, Thrasymachus, if you will recall what was previously said, that although you began by defining the true physician in an exact sense, you did not observe a like exactness when speaking of the shepherd; you thought that the shepherd as a shepherd tends the sheep not with a view to their own good, but like a mere diner or banqueter with a view to the pleasures of the table; or, again, as a trader for sale in the market, and not as a shepherd. Yet surely the art of the shepherd is concerned only with the good of his subjects; he has only to provide the best for them, since the perfection of the art is already ensured whenever all the requirements of it are satisfied. And that was what I was saying just now about the ruler. I conceived that the art of the ruler, considered as ruler, whether in a state or in private life, could only regard the good of his flock or subjects; whereas you seem to think that the rulers in states, that is to say, the true rulers, like being in authority.

Think! Nay, I am sure of it.

Then why in the case of lesser offices do men never take them willingly without payment, unless under the idea that they govern for the advantage not of themselves but of others? Let me ask you a question: Are not the several arts different, by reason of their each having a separate function? And, my dear illustrious friend, do say what you think, that we may make a little progress.

Yes, that is the difference, he replied.

And each art gives us a particular good and not merely a

general one—medicine, for example, gives us health; navigation, safety at sea, and so on?

Yes, he said.

And the art of payment has the special function of giving pay: but we do not confuse this with other arts, any more than the art of the pilot is to be confused with the art of medicine, because the health of the pilot may be improved by a sea voyage. You would not be inclined to say, would you, that navigation is the art of medicine, at least if we are to adopt your exact use of language?

Certainly not.

Or because a man is in good health when he receives pay you would not say that the art of payment is medicine?

I should say not.

Nor would you say that medicine is the art of receiving pay because a man takes fees when he is engaged in healing?

Certainly not.

And we have admitted, I said, that the good of each art is specially confined to the art?

Yes.

Then, if there be any good which all artists have in common, that is to be attributed to something of which they all have the common use?

True, he replied.

And when the artist is benefited by receiving pay the advantage is gained by an additional use of the art of pay, which is not the art professed by him?

He gave a reluctant assent to this.

Then the pay is not derived by the several artists from their respective arts. But the truth is, that while the art of medicine gives health, and the art of the builder builds a house, another art attends them which is the art of pay. The various arts may be doing their own business and benefiting that over which they preside, but would the artist receive any benefit from his art unless he were paid as well?

I suppose not.

But does he therefore confer no benefit when he works for nothing?

Certainly, he confers a benefit.

Then now, Thrasymachus, there is no longer any doubt that neither arts nor governments provide for their own interests; but, as we were before saying, they rule and provide for the interests of their subjects who are the weaker and not the stronger—to their good they attend and not to the good of the superior. And this is the reason, my dear Thrasymachus, why, as I was just now saying, no one is willing to govern; because no one likes to take in hand the reformation of evils which are not his concern without remuneration. For, in the execution of his work, and in giving his orders to another, the true artist does not regard his own interest, but always that of his subjects; and therefore in order that rulers may be willing to rule, they must be paid in one of three modes of payment: money, or honour, or a penalty for refusing. . . .

SOCRATES' DEFINITION OF JUSTICE

BOOK IV

The time then has arrived, Glaucon, when, like huntsmen, we should surround the cover, and look sharp that justice does not steal away, and pass out of sight and escape us; for beyond a doubt she is somewhere in this country: watch therefore and strive to catch a sight of her, and if you see her first, let me know.

Would that I could! but you should regard me rather as a follower who has just eyes enough to see what you show him—that is about as much as I am good for.

Offer up a prayer with me and follow.

I will, but you must show me the way.

Here is no path, I said, and the wood is dark and perplexing; still we must push on.

Let us push on.

Here I saw something: Halloo! I said, I begin to perceive a track, and I believe that the quarry will not escape.

Good news, he said.

Truly, I said, we are stupid fellows.

Why so?

Why, my good sir, at the beginning of our enquiry, ages ago, there was justice tumbling out at our feet, and we never saw her; nothing could be more ridiculous. Like people who go about looking for what they have in their hands—that was the way with us—we looked not at what we were seeking, but at what was far off in the distance; and therefore, I suppose, we missed her.

What do you mean?

I mean to say that in reality for a long time past we have been talking of justice, and have failed to recognise her.

I grow impatient at the length of your exordium.

Well then, tell me, I said, whether I am right or not: You remember the original principle which we were always laying down at the foundation of the State, that one man should practise one thing only, the thing to which his nature was best adapted;—now justice is this principle or a part of it.

Yes, we often said that one man should do one thing only.

Further, we affirmed that justice was doing one's own business, and not being a busybody; we said so again and again, and many others have said the same to us.

Yes, we said so.

Then to do one's own business in a certain way may be assumed to be justice. Can you tell me whence I derive this inference?

I cannot, but I should like to be told.

Because I think that this is the only virtue which remains in the State when the other virtues of temperance and courage and wisdom are abstracted; and, that this is the ultimate cause and condition of the existence of all of them, and while remaining in them is also their preservative; and we were saying that if the three were discovered by us, justice would be the fourth or remaining one.

That follows of necessity.

If we are asked to determine which of these four qualities by its presence contributes most to the excellence of the State, whether the agreement of rulers and subjects, or the preservation in the soldiers of the opinion which the law ordains about the true nature of dangers, or wisdom and watchfulness in the rulers, or whether this other which I am mentioning, and which is found in children and women, slave and freeman, artisan, ruler, subject,—the quality, I mean, of every one doing his own work, and not being a busybody, would claim the palm—the question is not so easily answered.

Certainly, he replied, there would be a difficulty in saying which.

Then the power of each individual in the State to do his own work appears to compete with the other political virtues, wisdom, temperance, courage.

Yes, he said.

And the virtue which enters into this competition is justice?
Exactly.

Let us look at the question from another point of view: Are not the rulers in a State those to whom you would entrust the office of determining suits at law?

Certainly.

And are suits decided on any other ground but that a man may neither take what is another's, nor be deprived of what is his own?

Yes; that is their principle.

Which is a just principle?

Yes.

Then on this view also justice will be admitted to be the having and doing what is a man's own, and belongs to him?

Very true.

Think, now, and say whether you agree with me or not. Suppose a carpenter to be doing the business of a cobbler, or a cobbler of a carpenter; and suppose them to exchange their implements or their duties, or the same person to be doing the work of both, or whatever be the change; do you think that any great harm would result to the State?

Not much.

But when the cobbler or any other man whom nature designed to be a trader, having his heart lifted up by wealth or strength or the number of his followers, or any like advantage, attempts to force his way into the class of warriors, or a warrior into that of legislators and guardians, for which he is unfitted, and either to take the implements or the duties of the other; or when one man is trader, legislator, and warrior all in one, then I think you will agree with me in saying that this interchange and this meddling of one with another is the ruin of the State.

Most true.

Seeing then, I said, that there are three distinct classes, any meddling of one with another, or the change of one into another, is the greatest harm to the State, and may be most justly termed evil-doing?

Precisely.

And the greatest degree of evil-doing to one's own city would be termed by you injustice?

Certainly.

This then is injustice; and on the other hand when the trader, the auxiliary, and the guardian each do their own business, that is justice, and will make the city just.

I agree with you.

We will not, I said, be over-positive as yet; but if, on trial, this conception of justice be verified in the individual as well as in the State, there will be no longer any room for doubt; if it be not verified, we must have a fresh enquiry. First let us

complete the old investigation, which we began, as you remember, under the impression that, if we could previously
examine justice on the larger scale, there would be less difficulty in discerning her in the individual. That larger example
appeared to be the State, and accordingly we constructed as
good a one as we could, knowing well that in the good State
justice would be found. Let the discovery which we made be
now applied to the individual—if they agree, we shall be satisfied; or, if there be a difference in the individual, we will
come back to the State and have another trial of the theory.
The friction of the two when rubbed together may possibly
strike a light in which justice will shine forth, and the vision
which is then revealed we will fix in our souls.

That will be in regular course; let us do as you say.

I proceeded to ask: When two things, a greater and less,
are called by the same name, are they like or unlike in so far
as they are called the same?

Like, he replied.

The just man then, if we regard the idea of justice only,
will be like the just State?

He will.

And a State was thought by us to be just when the three
classes in the State severally did their own business; and also
thought to be temperate and valiant and wise by reason of
certain other affections and qualities of these same classes?

True, he said.

And so of the individual; we may assume that he has the
same three principles in his own soul which are found in the
State; and he may be rightly described in the same terms, because he is affected in the same manner?

Certainly, he said . . .

THE SELECTION OF THE RULING
CLASS IN THE PERFECT STATE
BOOKS III, IV

Therefore, as I was just now saying, we must enquire who
are the best guardians of their own conviction that what they
think the interest of the State is to be the rule of their lives.
We must watch them from their youth upwards, and make
them perform actions in which they are most likely to forget
or to be deceived, and he who remembers and is not deceived

is to be selected, and he who fails in the trial is to be rejected. That will be the way?

Yes.

And there should also be toils and pains and conflicts prescribed for them, in which they will be made to give further proof of the same qualities.

Very right, he replied.

And then, I said, we must try them with enchantments—that is the third sort of test—and see what will be their behavior: like those who take colts amid noise and tumult to see if they are of a timid nature, so must we take our youth amid terrors of some kind, and again pass them into pleasures, and prove them more thoroughly than gold is proved in the furnace, that we may discover whether they are armed against all enchantments, and of a noble bearing always, good guardians of themselves and of the music which they have learned, and retaining under all circumstances a rhythmical and harmonious nature, such as will be most serviceable to the individual and to the State. And he who at every age, as boy and youth and in mature life, has come out of the trial victorious and pure, shall be appointed a ruler and guardian of the State; he shall be honoured in life and death, and shall receive sepulture and other memorials of honour, the greatest that we have to give. But him who fails, we must reject. I am inclined to think that this is the sort of way in which our rulers and guardians should be chosen and appointed. I speak generally, and not with any pretension to exactness.

And, speaking generally, I agree with you, he said.

And perhaps the word "guardian" in the fullest sense ought to be applied to this higher class only who preserve us against foreign enemies and maintain peace among our citizens at home, that the one may not have the will, or the others the power, to harm us. The young men whom we before called guardians may be more properly designated auxiliaries and supporters of the principles of the rulers.

I agree with you, he said.

How then may we devise one of those needful falsehoods of which we lately spoke—just one royal lie which may deceive the rulers, if that be possible, and at any rate the rest of the city?

What sort of lie? he said.

Nothing new, I replied; only an old Phoenician tale of what has often occurred before now in other places (as the poets say, and have made the world believe), though not in our

time, and I do not know whether such an event could ever
happen again, or could now even be made probable, if it did.

How your words seem to hesitate on your lips!

You will not wonder, I replied, at my hesitation when you
have heard.

Speak, he said, and fear not.

Well then, I will speak, although I really know not how to
look you in the face, or in what words to utter the audacious
fiction, which I propose to communicate gradually, first to the
rulers, then to the soldiers, and lastly to the people. They are
to be told that their youth was a dream, and the education
and training which they received from us, an appearance only;
in reality during all that time they were being formed and
fed in the womb of the earth, where they themselves and their
arms and appurtenances were manufactured; when they were
completed, the earth, their mother, sent them up; and so, their
country being their mother and also their nurse, they are
bound to advise for her good, and to defend her against attacks, and her citizens they are to regard as children of the
earth and their own brothers.

You had good reason, he said, to be ashamed of the lie
which you were going to tell.

True, I replied, but there is more coming; I have only told
you half. Citizens, we shall say to them in our tale, you are
brothers, yet God has framed you differently. Some of you
have the power of command, and in the composition of these
he has mingled gold, wherefore also they have the greatest
honour; others he has made of silver, to be auxiliaries; others
again who are to be husbandmen and craftsmen he has composed of brass and iron; and the species will generally be preserved in the children. But as all are of the same original
stock, a golden parent will sometimes have a silver son, or a
silver parent a golden son. And God proclaims as a first
principle to the rulers, and above all else, that there is nothing
which they should so anxiously guard, or of which they are
to be such good guardians, as of the purity of the race. They
should observe what elements mingle in their offspring; for if
the son of a golden or silver parent has an admixture of brass
and iron, then nature orders a transposition of ranks, and the
eye of the ruler must not be pitiful towards the child because
he has to descend in the scale and become a husbandman or
artisan, just as there may be sons of artisans who having an
admixture of gold or silver in them are raised to honour, and
become guardians or auxiliaries. For an oracle says that when

a man of brass or iron guards the State, it will be destroyed. Such is the tale; is there any possibility of making our citizens believe in it?

Not in the present generation, he replied; there is no way of accomplishing this; but their sons may be made to believe in the tale, and their sons' sons, and posterity after them.

I see the difficulty, I replied; yet the fostering of such a belief will make them care more for the city and for one another. Enough, however, of the fiction, which may now fly abroad upon the wings of rumour, while we arm our earthborn heroes, and lead them forth under the command of their rulers. Let them look round and select a spot whence they can best suppress insurrection, if any prove refractory within, and also defend themselves against enemies, who like wolves may come down on the fold from without; there let them encamp, and when they have encamped, let them sacrifice to the proper Gods and prepare their dwellings.

Just so, he said.

And their dwellings must be such as will shield them against the cold of winter and the heat of summer.

I suppose that you mean houses, he replied.

Yes, I said; but they must be the houses of soldiers, and not of shop-keepers.

What is the difference? he said.

That I will endeavour to explain, I replied. To keep watchdogs, who, from want of discipline or hunger, or some evil habit or other, would turn upon the sheep and worry them, and behave not like dogs but wolves, would be a foul and monstrous thing in a shepherd?

Truly monstrous, he said.

And therefore every care must be taken that our auxiliaries, being stronger than our citizens, may not grow to be too much for them and become savage tyrants instead of friends and allies?

Yes, great care should be taken.

And would not a really good education furnish the best safeguard?

But they are well-educated already, he replied.

I cannot be so confident, my dear Glaucon, I said; I am much more certain that they ought to be, and that true education, whatever that may be, will have the greatest tendency to civilize and humanize them in their relations to one another, and to those who are under their protection.

Very true, he replied.

And not only their education, but their habitations, and all that belongs to them, should be such as will neither impair their virtue as guardians, nor tempt them to prey upon the other citizens. Any man of sense must acknowledge that.

He must.

Then let us consider what will be their way of life, if they are to realize our idea of them. In the first place, none of them should have any property of his own beyond what is absolutely necessary; neither should they have a private house or store closed against any one who has a mind to enter; their provisions should be only such as are required by trained warriors, who are men of temperance and courage; they should agree to receive from the citizens a fixed rate of pay, enough to meet the expenses of the year and no more; and they will go to mess and live together like soldiers in a camp. Gold and silver we will tell them that they have from God; the diviner metal is within them, and they have therefore no need of the dross which is current among men, and ought not to pollute the divine by any such earthly admixture; for that commoner metal has been the source of many unholy deeds, but their own is undefiled. And they alone of all the citizens may not touch or handle silver or gold, or be under the same roof with them, or wear them, or drink from them. And this will be their salvation, and they will be the saviours of the State. But should they ever acquire homes or lands or moneys of their own, they will become housekeepers and husbandmen instead of guardians, enemies and tyrants instead of allies of the other citizens; hating and being hated, plotting and being plotted against, they will pass their whole life in much greater terror of internal than of external enemies, and the hour of ruin, both to themselves and to the rest of the State, will be at hand. For all which reasons may we not say that thus shall our State be ordered, and that these shall be the regulations appointed by us for our guardians concerning their houses and all other matters?

Yes, said Glaucon.

Here Adeimantus interposed a question: How would you answer, Socrates, said he, if a person were to say that you are making[4] these people miserable, and that they are the cause of their own unhappiness; the city in fact belongs to them, but

---

[4] Or, "that for their own good you are making these people miserable."

they are none the better for it; whereas other men acquire lands, and build large and handsome houses, and have everything handsome about them, offering sacrifices to the gods on their own account, and practising hospitality; moreover, as you were saying just now, they have gold and silver, and all that is usual among the favourites of fortune; but our poor citizens are no better than mercenaries who are quartered in the city and are always mounting guard?

Yes, I said; and you may add that they are only fed, and not paid in addition to their food, like other men; and therefore they cannot, if they would, take a journey of pleasure; they have no money to spend on a mistress or any other luxurious fancy, which, as the world goes, is thought to be happiness; and many other accusations of the same nature might be added.

But, said he, let us suppose all this to be included in the charge.

You mean to ask, I said, what will be our answer?

Yes.

If we proceed along the old path, my belief, I said, is that we shall find the answer. And our answer will be that, even as they are, our guardians may very likely be the happiest of men; but that our aim in founding the State was not the disproportionate happiness of any one class, but the greatest happiness of the whole; we thought that in a State which is ordered with a view to the good of the whole we should be most likely to find justice, and in the ill-ordered State injustice: and, having found them, we might then decide which of the two is the happier. At present, I take it, we are fashioning the happy State, not piecemeal, or with a view of making a few happy citizens, but as a whole; and by-and-by we will proceed to view the opposite kind of State. Suppose that we were painting a statue, and some one came up to us and said, Why do you not put the most beautiful colours on the most beautiful parts of the body—the eyes ought to be purple, but you have made them black—to him we might fairly answer, Sir, you would not surely have us beautify the eyes to such a degree that they are no longer eyes; consider rather whether, by giving this and the other features their due proportion, we make the whole beautiful. And so I say to you, do not compel us to assign to the guardians a sort of happiness which will make them anything but guardians; for we too can clothe our husbandmen in royal apparel, and set crowns of gold on their heads, and bid them till the ground as much as they like, and

no more. Our potters also might be allowed to repose on
couches, and feast by the fireside, passing round the winecup,
while their wheel is conveniently at hand, and working at pot-
tery only as much as they like; in this way we might make
every class happy—and then, as you imagine, the whole State
would be happy. But do not put this idea into our heads; for,
if we listen to you, the husbandman will be no longer a husbandman, the potter will cease to be a potter, and no one will
have the character of any distinct class in the State. Now this
is not of much consequence where the corruption of society,
and pretension to be what you are not, is confined to cobblers;
but when the guardians of the laws and of the government
are only seemingly and not real guardians, then see how they
turn the State upside down; and on the other hand they alone
have the power of giving order and happiness to the State.
We mean our guardians to be true saviours and not the destroyers of the State, whereas our opponent is thinking of peasants at a festival, who are enjoying a life of revelry, not of
citizens who are doing their duty to the State. But, if so, we
mean different things, and he is speaking of something which
is not a State. And therefore we must consider whether in appointing our guardians we would look to their greatest happiness individually, or whether this principle of happiness does
not rather reside in the State as a whole. But if the latter be
the truth, then the guardians and auxiliaries, and all others
equally with them, must be compelled or induced to do their
own work in the best way. And thus the whole State will
grow up in a noble order, and the several classes will receive
the proportion of happiness which nature assigns to them.

I think that you are quite right. . . .

FORMS OF GOVERNMENT, THEIR EFFECTS
ON PEOPLE, AND HOW ONE FORM BECOMES
CHANGED INTO ANOTHER
BOOKS VIII, IX

I shall particularly wish to hear what were the four constitutions of which you were speaking.

That question, I said, is easily answered: the four governments of which I spoke, so far as they have distinct names,
are, first, those of Crete and Sparta, which are generally applauded; what is termed oligarchy comes next; this is not

equally approved, and is a form of government which teems
with evils: thirdly, democracy, which naturally follows oligarchy, although very different: and lastly comes tyranny,
great and famous, which differs from them all, and is the
fourth and worst disorder of a State. I do not know, do you?
of any other constitution which can be said to have a distinct
character. There are lordships and principalities which are
bought and sold, and some other intermediate forms of government. But these are nondescripts and may be found equally
among Hellenes and among barbarians.

Yes, he replied, we certainly hear of many curious forms
of government which exist among them.

Do you know, I said, that governments vary as the dispositions of men vary, and that there must be as many of the one
as there are of the other? For we cannot suppose that States
are made of "oak and rock," and not out of the human natures
which are in them, and which in a figure turn the scale and
draw other things after them?

Yes, he said, the States are as the men are; they grow out
of human characters.

Then if the constitutions of States are five, the dispositions
of individual minds will also be five?

Certainly.

Him who answers to aristocracy, and whom we rightly call
just and good, we have already described.

We have.

Then let us now proceed to describe the inferior sort of
natures, being the contentious and ambitious, who answer to
the Spartan polity; also the oligarchical, democratical, and tyrannical. Let us place the most just by the side of the most
unjust, and when we see them we shall be able to compare the
relative happiness or unhappiness of him who leads a life
of pure justice or pure injustice. The enquiry will then be completed. And we shall know whether we ought to pursue injustice, as Thrasymachus advises, or in accordance with the conclusions of the argument to prefer justice.

Certainly, he replied, we must do as you say.

Shall we follow our old plan, which we adopted with a view
to clearness, of taking the State first and then proceeding to
the individual, and begin with the government of honour?—I
know of no name for such a government other than timocracy,
or perhaps timarchy. We will compare with this the like character in the individual; and, after that, consider oligarchical
man; and then again we will turn our attention to democracy

and the democratical man; and lastly, we will go and view the
city of tyranny, and once more take a look into the tyrant's
soul, and try to arrive at a satisfactory decision.

That way of viewing and judging of the matter will be very
suitable.

First, then, I said, let us enquire how timocracy (the government of honour) arises out of aristocracy (the government
of the best). Clearly, all political changes originate in divisions
of the actual governing power; a government which is
united, however small, cannot be moved.

Very true, he said.

In what way, then, will our city be moved, and in what
manner will the two classes of auxiliaries and rulers disagree
among themselves or with one another? . . .

. . . In the succeeding generation rulers will be appointed
who have lost the guardian power of testing the metal of your
different races, which, like Hesiod's, are of gold and silver
and brass and iron. And so iron will be mingled with silver,
and brass with gold, and hence there will arise dissimilarity
and inequality and irregularity, which always and in all places
are causes of hatred and war. This the Muses affirm to be the
stock from which discord has sprung, wherever arising; and
this is their answer to us.

Yes, and we may assume that they answer truly.

Why, yes, I said, of course they answer truly; how can the
Muses speak falsely?

And what do the Muses say next?

When discord arose, then the two races were drawn different ways: the iron and brass fell to acquiring money and land
and houses and gold and silver; but the gold and silver races,
not wanting money but having the true riches in their own
nature, inclined towards virtue and the ancient order of things.
There was a battle between them, and at last they agreed to
distribute their land and houses among individual owners; and
they enslaved their friends and maintainers, whom they had
formerly protected in the condition of freemen, and made of
them subjects and servants; and they themselves were engaged
in war and in keeping a watch against them.

I believe that you have rightly conceived the origin of the
change.

And the new government which thus arises will be of a form
intermediate between oligarchy and aristocracy?

Very true.

Such will be the change, and after the change has been made, how will they proceed? Clearly, the new State, being in a mean between oligarchy and the perfect State, will partly follow one and partly the other, and will also have some peculiarities.

True, he said.

In the honour given to rulers, in the abstinence of the warrior class from agriculture, handicrafts, and trade in general, in the institution of common meals, and in the attention paid to gymnastics and military training—in all these respects this State will resemble the former.

True.

But in the fear of admitting philosophers to power, because they are no longer to be had simple and earnest, but are made up of mixed elements; and in turning from them to passionate and less complex characters, who are by nature fitted for war rather than peace; and in the value set by them upon military stratagems and contrivances, and in the waging of everlasting wars—this State will be for the most part peculiar.

Yes.

Yes, I said; and men of this stamp will be covetous of money, like those who live in oligarchies; they will have a fierce secret longing after gold and silver, which they will hoard in dark places, having magazines and treasuries of their own for the deposit and concealment of them; also castles which are just nests for their eggs, and in which they will spend large sums on their wives, or on any others whom they please.

That is most true, he said.

And they are miserly because they have no means of openly acquiring the money which they prize; they will spend that which is another man's on the gratification of their desires, stealing their pleasures and running away like children from the law, their father: they have been schooled not by gentle influences but by force, for they have neglected her who is the true Muse, the companion of reason and philosophy, and have honoured gymnastic more than music.

Undoubtedly, he said, the form of government which you describe is a mixture of good and evil.

Why, there is a mixture, I said; but one thing, and one thing only, is predominantly seen,—the spirit of contention and ambition; and these are due to the prevalence of the passionate or spirited element.

Assuredly, he said. . . .

I believe that oligarchy follows next in order.

And what manner of government do you term oligarchy?

A government resting on a valuation of property, in which the rich have power and the poor man is deprived of it.

I understand, he replied.

Ought I not to begin by describing how the change from timocracy to oligarchy arises?

Yes.

Well, I said, no eyes are required in order to see how the one passes into the other.

How?

The accumulation of gold in the treasury of private individuals is the ruin of timocracy; they invent illegal modes of expenditure; for what do they or their wives care about the law?

Yes, indeed.

And then one, seeing another grow rich, seeks to rival him, and thus the great mass of the citizens become lovers of money.

Likely enough.

And so they grow richer and richer, and the more they think of making a fortune the less they think of virtue; for when riches and virtue are placed together in the scales of the balance, the one always rises as the other falls.

True.

And in proportion as riches and rich men are honoured in the State, virtue and the virtuous are dishonoured.

Clearly.

And what is honoured is cultivated, and that which has no honour is neglected.

That is obvious.

And so at last, instead of loving contention and glory, men become lovers of trade and money; they honour and look up to the rich man, and make a ruler of him, and dishonour the poor man.

They do so.

They next proceed to make a law which fixes a sum of money as the qualification of citizenship; the sum is higher in one place and lower in another, as the oligarchy is more or less exclusive; and they allow no one whose property falls below the amount fixed to have any share in the government. These changes in the constitution they effect by force of arms, if intimidation has not already done their work.

Very true.

And this, speaking generally, is the way in which oligarchy is established.

Yes, he said; but what are the characteristics of this form of government, and what are the defects of which we were speaking?

First of all, I said, consider the nature of the qualification. Just think what would happen if pilots were to be chosen according to their property, and a poor man were refused permission to steer, even though he were a better pilot?

You mean that they would shipwreck?

Yes; and is not this true of the government of anything?

I should imagine so.

Except a city?—or would you include a city?

Nay, he said, the case of a city is the strongest of all, inasmuch as the rule of a city is the greatest and most difficult of all.

This, then, will be the first great defect of oligarchy?

Clearly.

And here is another defect which is quite as bad.

What defect?

The inevitable division: such a State is not one, but two States, the one of poor, the other of rich men; and they are living on the same spot and always conspiring against one another.

That, surely, is at least as bad.

Another discreditable feature is, that, for a like reason, they are incapable of carrying on any war. Either they arm the multitude, and then they are more afraid of them than of the enemy; or, if they do not call them out in the hour of battle, they are oligarchs indeed, few to fight as they are few to rule. And at the same time their fondness for money makes them unwilling to pay taxes.

How discreditable!

And, as we said before, under such a constitution the same persons have too many callings—they are husbandmen, tradesmen, warriors, all in one. Does that look well?

Anything but well.

There is another evil which is, perhaps, the greatest of all, and to which this State first begins to be liable.

What evil?

A man may sell all that he has, and another may acquire his property; yet after the sale he may dwell in the city of which he is no longer a part, being neither trader, nor artisan, nor horseman, nor hoplite, but only a poor, helpless creature.

Yes, that is an evil which also first begins in this State.

The evil is certainly not prevented there; for oligarchies have both the extremes of great wealth and utter poverty.

True. . . .

Let us next proceed to consider the nature and origin of the individual who answers to this State.

By all means.

Does not the timocratical man change into the oligarchical on this wise?

How?

A time arrives when the representative of timocracy has a son: at first he begins by emulating his father and walking in his footsteps, but presently he sees him of a sudden foundering against the State as upon a sunken reef, and he and all that he has is lost; he may have been a general or some other high officer who is brought to trial under a prejudice raised by informers, and either put to death, or exiled, or deprived of the privileges of a citizen, and all his property taken from him.

Nothing more likely.

And the son has seen and known all this—he is a ruined man, and his fear has taught him to knock ambition and passion head-foremost from his bosom's throne; humbled by poverty he takes to money-making and by mean and miserly savings and hard work gets a fortune together. Is not such an one likely to seat the concupiscent and covetous element on the vacant throne and to suffer it to play the great king within him, girt with tiara and chain and scimitar?

Most true, he replied.

And when he has made reason and spirit sit down on the ground obediently on either side of their sovereign, and taught them to know their place, he compels the one to think only of how lesser sums may be turned into larger ones, and will not allow the other to worship and admire anything but riches and rich men, or to be ambitious of anything so much as the acquisition of wealth and the means of acquiring it.

Of all changes, he said, there is none so speedy or so sure as the conversion of the ambitious youth into the avaricious one.

And the avaricious, I said, is the oligarchical youth?

Yes, he said; at any rate the individual out of whom he came is like the State out of which oligarchy came. . . .

Next comes democracy; of this the origin and nature have

still to be considered by us; and then we will enquire into the ways of the democratic man, and bring him up for judgment.

That, he said, is our method.

Well, I said, and how does the change from oligarchy into democracy arise? Is it not on this wise?— The good at which such a State aims is to become as rich as possible, a desire which is insatiable?

What then?

The rulers, being aware that their power rests upon their wealth, refuse to curtail by law the extravagance of the spendthrift youth because they gain by their ruin; they take interest from them and buy up their estates and thus increase their own wealth and importance?

To be sure.

There can be no doubt that the love of wealth and the spirit of moderation cannot exist together in citizens of the same State to any considerable extent; one or the other will be disregarded.

That is tolerably clear.

And in oligarchical States, from the general spread of carelessness and extravagance, men of good family have often been reduced to beggary?

Yes, often.

And still they remain in the city; there they are, ready to sting and fully armed, and some of them owe money, some have forfeited their citizenship; a third class are in both predicaments; and they hate and conspire against those who have got their property, and against everybody else, and are eager for revolution.

That is true.

On the other hand, the men of business, stooping as they walk, and pretending not even to see those whom they have already ruined, insert their sting—that is, their money—into some one else who is not on his guard against them, and recover the parent sum many times over multiplied into a family of children: and so they make drone and pauper to abound in the State.

Yes, he said, there are plenty of them—that is certain.

The evil blazes up like a fire; and they will not extinguish it, either by restricting a man's use of his own property, or by another remedy:

What other?

One which is the next best, and has the advantage of compelling the citizens to look to their characters:—Let there be a

general rule that every one shall enter into voluntary contracts
at his own risk, and there will be less of this scandalous money-
making, and the evils of which we were speaking will be
greatly lessened in the State.

Yes, they will be greatly lessened.

At present the governors, induced by the motives which I
have named, treat their subjects badly; while they and their
adherents, especially the young men of the governing class, are
habituated to lead a life of luxury and idleness both of body
and mind; they do nothing, and are incapable of resisting
either pleasure or pain.

Very true.

They themselves care only for making money, and are as
indifferent as the pauper to the cultivation of virtue.

Yes, quite as indifferent.

Such is the state of affairs which prevails among them. And
often rulers and their subjects may come in one another's way,
whether on a pilgrimage or a march, as fellow-soldiers or
fellow-sailors; aye and they may observe the behaviour of each
other in the very moment of danger—for where danger is,
there is no fear that the poor will be despised by the rich—and
very likely the wiry sunburnt poor man may be placed in battle
at the side of a wealthy one who has never spoilt his complexion and has plenty of superfluous flesh—when he sees such an
one puffing and at his wit's end, how can he avoid drawing the
conclusion that men like him are only rich because no one has
the courage to despoil them? And when they meet in private
will not people be saying to one another "Our warriors are
not good for much"?

Yes, he said, I am quite aware that this is their way of
talking.

And, as in a body which is diseased the addition of a touch
from without may bring on illness, and sometimes even when
there is no external provocation a commotion may arise within
—in the same way wherever there is weakness in the State
there is also likely to be illness, of which the occasions may be
very slight, the one party introducing from without their oligarchical, the other their democratical allies, and then the State
falls sick, and is at war with herself; and may be at times distracted, even when there is no external cause.

Yes, surely.

And then democracy comes into being after the poor have
conquered their opponents, slaughtering some and banishing
some, while to the remainder they give an equal share of free-

dom and power; and this is the form of government in which the magistrates are commonly elected by lot.

Yes, he said, that is the nature of democracy, whether the revolution has been effected by arms, or whether fear has caused the opposite party to withdraw.

And now what is their manner of life, and what sort of a government have they? for as the government is, such will be the man.

Clearly, he said.

In the first place, are they not free; and is not the city full of freedom and frankness—a man may say and do what he likes?

'Tis said so, he replied.

And where freedom is, the individual is clearly able to order for himself his own life as he pleases?

Clearly.

Then in this kind of State there will be the greatest variety of human natures?

There will.

This, then, seems likely to be the fairest of States, being like an embroidered robe which is spangled with every sort of flower. And just as women and children think a variety of colours to be of all things most charming, so there are many men to whom this State, which is spangled with the manners and characters of mankind, will appear to be the fairest of States.

Yes.

Yes, my good Sir, and there will be no better in which to look for a government.

Why?

Because of the liberty which reigns there—they have a complete assortment of constitutions; and he who has a mind to establish a State, as we have been doing, must go to a democracy as he would to a bazaar at which they sell them, and pick out the one that suits him; then, when he has made his choice, he may found his State.

He will be sure to have patterns enough.

And there being no necessity, I said, for you to govern in this State, even if you have the capacity, or to be governed, unless you like, or go to war when the rest go to war, or to be at peace when others are at peace, unless you are so disposed—there being no necessity also, because some law forbids you to hold office or be a dicast, that you should not hold office

or be a dicast, if you have a fancy—is not this a way of life
which for the moment is supremely delightful?

For the moment, yes.

And is not their humanity to the condemned[5] in some cases
quite charming? Have you not observed how, in a democracy,
many persons, although they have been sentenced to death or
exile, just stay where they are and walk about the world—the
gentleman parades like a hero, and nobody sees or cares?

Yes, he replied, many and many a one.

See too, I said, the forgiving spirit of democracy, and the
"don't care" about trifles, and the disregard which she shows
of all the fine principles which we solemnly laid down at the
foundation of the city—as when we said that, except in the case
of some rarely gifted nature, there never will be a good man
who has not from his childhood been used to play amid things
of beauty and make of them a joy and a study—how grandly
does she trample all these fine notions of ours under her feet,
never giving a thought to the pursuits which make a statesman,
and promoting to honour any one who professes to be the
people's friend.

Yes, she is of a noble spirit.

These and other kindred characteristics are proper to democracy, which is a charming form of government, full of
variety and disorder, and dispensing a sort of equality to equals
and unequals alike.

We know her well.

Consider now, I said, what manner of man the individual
is, or rather consider, as in the case of the State, how he comes
into being.

Very good, he said.

Is not this the way—he is the son of the miserly and oligarchical father who has trained him in his own habits?

Exactly.

And, like his father, he keeps under by force the pleasures
which are of the spending and not of the getting sort, being
those which are called unnecessary?

Obviously.

Would you like, for the sake of clearness, to distinguish
which are the necessary and which are the unnecessary
pleasures?

I should.

Are not necessary pleasures those of which we cannot get

[5] Or, "the philosophical temper of the condemned."

rid, and of which the satisfaction is a benefit to us? And they are rightly so, because we are framed by nature to desire both what is beneficial and what is necessary, and cannot help it.

True.

We are not wrong therefore in calling them necessary?

We are not.

And the desires of which a man may get rid, if he takes pains from his youth upwards—of which the presence, moreover, does no good, and in some cases the reverse of good—shall we not be right in saying that all these are unnecessary?

Yes, certainly.

Suppose we select an example of either kind, in order that we may have a general notion of them?

Very good.

Will not the desire of eating, that is, of simple food and condiments, in so far as they are required for health and strength, be of the necessary class?

That is what I should suppose.

The pleasure of eating is necessary in two ways; it does us good and it is essential to the continuance of life?

Yes.

But the condiments are only necessary in so far as they are good for health?

Certainly.

And the desire which goes beyond this, of more delicate food, or other luxuries, which might generally be got rid of, if controlled and trained in youth, and is hurtful to the body, and hurtful to the soul in the pursuit of wisdom and virtue, may be rightly called unnecessary?

Very true.

May we not say that these desires spend, and that the others make money because they conduce to production?

Certainly.

And of the pleasures of love, and all other pleasures, the same holds good?

True.

And the drone of whom we spoke was he who was surfeited in pleasures and desires of this sort, and was the slave of the unnecessary desires, whereas he who was subject to the necessary only was miserly and oligarchical?

Very true.

Again, let us see how the democratical man grows out of the oligarchical: the following, as I suspect, is commonly the process.

What is the process?

When a young man who has been brought up as we were just now describing, in a vulgar and miserly way, has tasted drones' honey and has come to associate with fierce and crafty natures who are able to provide for him all sorts of refinements and varieties of pleasure—then, as you may imagine, the change will begin of the oligarchical principle within him into the democratical?

Inevitably.

And as in the city like was helping like, and the change was effected by an alliance from without assisting one division of the citizens, so too the young man is changed by a class of desires coming from without to assist the desires within him, that which is akin and alike again helping that which is akin and alike?

Certainly.

And if there be any ally which aids the oligarchical principle within him, whether the influence of a father or of kindred, advising or rebuking him, then there arises in his soul a faction and an opposite faction, and he goes to war with himself.

It must be so.

And there are times when the democratical principle gives way to the oligarchical, and some of his desires die, and others are banished; a spirit of reverence enters into the young man's soul and order is restored.

Yes, he said, that sometimes happens.

And then, again, after the old desires have been driven out, fresh ones spring up, which are akin to them, and because he, their father, does not know how to educate them, wax fierce and numerous.

Yes, he said, that is apt to be the way.

They draw him to his old associates, and holding secret intercourse with them, breed and multiply in him.

Very true.

At length they seize upon the citadel of the young man's soul, which they perceive to be void of all accomplishments and fair pursuits and true words, which make their abode in the minds of men who are dear to the gods, and are their best guardians and sentinels.

None better.

False and boastful conceits and phrases mount upwards and take their place.

They are certain to do so.

And so the young man returns into the country of the lotus-eaters, and takes up his dwelling there in the face of all men; and if any help be sent by his friends to the oligarchical part of him, the aforesaid vain conceits shut the gate of the king's fastness; and they will neither allow the embassy itself to enter, nor if private advisers offer the fatherly counsel of the aged will they listen to them or receive them. There is a battle and they gain the day, and then modesty, which they call silliness, is ignominiously thrust into exile by them, and temperance, which they nickname unmanliness, is trampled in the mire and cast forth; they persuade men that moderation and orderly expenditure are vulgarity and meanness, and so, by the help of a rabble of evil appetites, they drive them beyond the border.

Yes, with a will.

And when they have emptied and swept clean the soul of him who is now in their power and who is being initiated by them in great mysteries, the next thing is to bring back to their house insolence and anarchy and waste and impudence in bright array having garlands on their heads, and a great company with them, hymning their praises and calling them by sweet names; insolence they term breeding, and anarchy liberty, and waste magnificence, and impudence courage. And so the young man passes out of his original nature, which was trained in the school of necessity, into the freedom and libertinism of useless and unnecessary pleasures.

Yes, he said, the change in him is visible enough.

After this he lives on, spending his money and labour and time on unnecessary pleasures quite as much as on necessary ones; but if he be fortunate, and is not too much disordered in his wits, when years have elapsed, and the heyday of passion is over—supposing that he then re-admits into the city some part of the exiled virtues, and does not wholly give himself up to their successors—in that case he balances his pleasures and lives in a sort of equilibrium, putting the government of himself into the hands of the one which comes first and wins the turn; and when he has had enough of that, then into the hands of another; he despises none of them but encourages them all equally.

Very true, he said.

Neither does he receive or let pass into the fortress any true word of advice; if any one says to him that some pleasures are the satisfactions of good and noble desires, and others of evil desires, and that he ought to use and honour some and chastise and master the others—whenever this is repeated to him he shakes his head and says that they are all alike, and that one is as good as another.

Yes, he said; that is the way with him.

Yes, I said, he lives from day to day indulging the appetite of the hour; and sometimes he is lapped in drink and strains of the flute; then he becomes a water-drinker, and tries to get thin; then he takes a turn at gymnastics; sometimes idling and neglecting everything, then once more living the life of a philosopher; often he is busy with politics, and starts to his feet and says and does whatever comes into his head; and, if he is emulous of any one who is a warrior, off he is in that direction, or of men of business, once more in that. His life has neither law nor order; and this distracted existence he terms joy and bliss and freedom; and so he goes on.

Yes, he replied, he is all liberty and equality.

Yes, I said; his life is motley and manifold and an epitome of the lives of many;—he answers to the State which we described as fair and spangled. And many a man and many a woman will take him for their pattern, and many a constitution and many an example of manners is contained in him.

Just so.

Let him then be set over against democracy; he may truly be called the democratic man.

Let that be his place, he said.

Last of all comes the most beautiful of all, man and State alike, tyranny and the tyrant; these we have now to consider.

Quite true, he said.

Say then, my friend, in what manner does tyranny arise?—that it has a democratic origin is evident.

Clearly.

And does not tyranny spring from democracy in the same manner as democracy from oligarchy—I mean, after a sort?

How?

The good which oligarchy proposed to itself and the means by which it was maintained was excess of wealth—am I not right?

Yes.

And the insatiable desire of wealth and the neglect of all other things for the sake of money-getting was also the ruin of oligarchy?

True.

And democracy has her own good, of which the insatiable desire brings her to dissolution?

What good?

Freedom, I replied; which, as they tell you in a democracy, is the glory of the State—and that therefore in a democracy alone will the freeman of nature deign to dwell.

Yes; the saying is in everybody's mouth.

I was going to observe, that the insatiable desire of this and the neglect of other things introduces the change in democracy, which occasions a demand for tyranny.

How so?

When a democracy which is thirsting for freedom has evil cupbearers presiding over the feast, and has drunk too deeply of the strong wine of freedom, then, unless her rulers are very amenable and give a plentiful draught, she calls them to account and punishes them, and says that they are cursed oligarchs.

Yes, he replied, a very common occurrence.

Yes, I said; and loyal citizens are insultingly termed by her slaves who hug their chains and men of naught; she would have subjects who are like rulers, and rulers who are like subjects: these are men after her own heart, whom she praises and honours both in private and public. Now, in such a State, can liberty have any limit?

Certainly not.

By degrees the anarchy finds a way into private houses, and ends by getting among the animals and infecting them.

How do you mean?

I mean that the father grows accustomed to descend to the level of his sons and to fear them, and the son is on a level with his father, he having no respect or reverence for either of his parents; and this is his freedom, and the metic is equal with the citizen and the citizen with the metic, and the stranger is quite as good as either.

Yes, he said, that is the way.

And these are not the only evils, I said—there are several lesser ones: In such a state of society the master fears and flatters his scholars, and the scholars despise their masters and tutors; young and old are all alike; and the young man is on a level with the old, and is ready to compete with him in word or deed; and old men condescend to the young and are full of pleasantry and gaiety; they are loth to be thought morose and authoritative, and therefore they adopt the manners of the young.

Quite true, he said.

The last extreme of popular liberty is when the slave bought

with money, whether male or female, is just as free as his or
her purchaser; nor must I forget to tell of the liberty and
equality of the two sexes in relation to each other.

Why not, as Aeschylus says, utter the word which rises to
our lips?

That is what I am doing, I replied; and I must add that no
one who does not know would believe, how much greater is
the liberty which the animals who are under the dominion of
man have in a democracy than in any other State: for truly,
the she-dogs, as the proverb says, are as good as their she-
mistresses, and the horses and asses have a way of marching
along with all the rights and dignities of freemen; and they
will run at anybody who comes in their way if he does not
leave the road clear for them: and all things are just ready to
burst with liberty.

When I take a country walk, he said, I often experience
what you describe. You and I have dreamed the same thing.

And above all, I said, and as the result of all, see how sensitive the citizens become; they chafe impatiently at the least
touch of authority and at length, as you know, they cease to
care even for the laws, written or unwritten; they will have no
one over them.

Yes, he said, I know it too well.

Such, my friend, I said, is the fair and glorious beginning
out of which springs tyranny.

Glorious indeed, he said. But what is the next step?

The ruin of oligarchy is the ruin of democracy; the same
disease magnified and intensified by liberty overmasters democracy—the truth being that the excessive increase of anything often causes a reaction in the opposite direction; and this
is the case not only in the seasons and in vegetable and animal
life, but above all in forms of government.

True.

The excess of liberty, whether in States or individuals, seems
only to pass into excess of slavery.

Yes, the natural order.

And so tyranny naturally arises out of democracy, and the
most aggravated form of tyranny and slavery out of the most
extreme form of liberty?

As we might expect . . .

And now remember the character which we attributed to
the democratic man. He was supposed from his youth upwards to have been trained under a miserly parent, who en-

couraged the saving appetites in him, but discountenanced the unnecessary, which aim only at amusement and ornament?

True.

And then he got into the company of a more refined, licentious sort of people, and taking to all their wanton ways rushed into the opposite extreme from an abhorrence of his father's meanness. At last, being a better man than his corruptors, he was drawn in both directions until he halted midway and led a life, not of vulgar and slavish passion, but of what he deemed moderate indulgence in various pleasures. After this manner the democrat was generated out of the oligarch?

Yes, he said; that was our view of him, and is so still.

And now, I said, years will have passed away, and you must conceive this man, such as he is, to have a son, who is brought up in his father's principles.

I can imagine him.

Then you must further imagine the same thing to happen to the son which has already happened to the father:—he is drawn into a perfectly lawless life, which by his seducers is termed perfect liberty; and his father and friends take part with his moderate desires, and the opposite party assist the opposite ones. As soon as these dire magicians and tyrant-makers find that they are losing their hold on him, they contrive to implant in him a master passion, to be lord over his idle and spendthrift lusts—a sort of monstrous winged drone—that is the only image which will adequately describe him.

Yes, he said, that is the only adequate image of him.

And when his other lusts, amid clouds of incense and perfumes and garlands and wines, and all the pleasures of a dissolute life, now let loose, come buzzing around him, nourishing to the utmost the sting of desire which they implant in his drone-like nature, then at last this lord of the soul, having Madness for the captain of his guard, breaks out into a frenzy; and if he finds in himself any good opinions or appetites in process of formation,[6] and there is in him any sense of shame remaining, to these better principles he puts an end, and casts them forth until he has purged away temperance and brought in madness to the full.

Yes, he said, that is the way in which the tyrannical man is generated.

And is not this the reason why of old love has been called a tyrant?

[6] Or, "opinions or appetites such as are deemed to be good."

I should not wonder.

Further, I said, has not a drunken man also the spirit of a tyrant?

He has.

And you know that a man who is deranged and not right in his mind, will fancy that he is able to rule, not only over men, but also over the gods?

That he will.

And the tyrannical man in the true sense of the word comes into being when, either under the influence of nature, or habit, or both, he becomes drunken, lustful, passionate? O my friend, is not that so?

Assuredly.

Such is the man and such is his origin. And next, how does he live?

Suppose, as people facetiously say, you were to tell me.

I imagine, I said, at the next step in his progress, that there will be feasts and carousals and revellings and courtezans, and all that sort of thing; Love is the lord of the house within him, and orders all the concerns of his soul.

That is certain.

Yes; and every day and every night desires grow up many and formidable, and their demands are many.

They are indeed, he said.

His revenues, if he has any, are soon spent.

True.

Then comes debt and the cutting down of his property.

Of course.

When he has nothing left, must not his desires, crowding in the nest like young ravens, be crying aloud for food; and he, goaded on by them, and especially by love himself, who is in a manner the captain of them, is in a frenzy, and would fain discover whom he can defraud or despoil of his property, in order that he may gratify them?

Yes, that is sure to be the case.

He must have money, no matter how, if he is to escape horrid pains and pangs.

He must.

And as in himself there was a succession of pleasures, and the new got the better of the old and took away their rights, so he being younger will claim to have more than his father and his mother, and if he has spent his own share of the property, he will take a slice of theirs.

No doubt he will.

And if his parents will not give way, then he will try first of all to cheat and deceive them.

Very true.

And if he fails, then he will use force and plunder them.

Yes, probably.

And if the old man and woman fight for their own, what then, my friend? Will the creature feel any compunction at tyrannizing over them?

Nay, he said, I should not feel at all comfortable about his parents.

But, O heavens! Adeimantus, on account of some new-fangled love of a harlot, who is anything but a necessary connection, can you believe that he would strike the mother who is his ancient friend and necessary to his very existence, and would place her under the authority of the other, when she is brought under the same roof with her; or that, under like circumstances, he would do the same to his withered old father, first and most indispensable of friends, for the sake of some newly found blooming youth who is the reverse of indispensable?

Yes, indeed, he said; I believe that he would.

Truly, then, I said, a tyrannical son is a blessing to his father and mother.

He is indeed, he replied.

He first takes their property, and when that fails, and pleasures are beginning to swarm in the hive of his soul, then he breaks into a house, or steals the garments of some nightly wayfarer; next he proceeds to clear a temple. Meanwhile the old opinions which he had when a child, and which gave judgment about good and evil, are overthrown by those others which have just been emancipated, and are now the bodyguard of love and share his empire. These in his democratic days, when he was still subject to the laws and to his father, were only let loose in the dreams of sleep. But now that he is under the dominion of love, he becomes always and in waking reality what he was then very rarely and in a dream only; he will commit the foulest murder, or eat forbidden food, or be guilty of any other horrid act.

THE CRITO

Translated from the Greek by Benjamin Jowett

SCENE: *The Prison of Socrates*

SOCRATES. Why have you come at this hour, Crito? it must be quite early?

CRITO. Yes, certainly.

SOC. What is the exact time?

CR. The dawn is breaking.

SOC. I wonder that the keeper of the prison would let you in.

CR. He knows me, because I often come, Socrates; moreover, I have done him a kindness.

SOC. And are you only just come?

CR. No, I came some time ago.

SOC. Then why did you sit and say nothing, instead of awakening me at once?

CR. Why, indeed, Socrates, I myself would rather not have all this sleeplessness and sorrow. But I have been wondering at your peaceful slumbers, and that was the reason why I did not awaken you, because I wanted you to be out of pain. I have always thought you happy in the calmness of your temperament; but never did I see the like of the easy, cheerful way in which you bear this calamity.

SOC. Why, Crito, when a man has reached my age he ought not to be repining at the prospect of death.

CR. And yet other old men find themselves in similar misfortunes and age does not prevent them from repining.

SOC. That may be. But you have not told me why you come at this early hour.

CR. I come to bring you a message which is sad and painful; not, as I believe, to yourself, but to all of us who are your friends, and saddest of all to me.

SOC. What! I suppose that the ship has come from Delos, on the arrival of which I am to die?

CR. No, the ship has not actually arrived, but she will probably be here to-day, as persons who have come from Sunium tell me that they left her there; and therefore to-morrow, Socrates, will be the last day of your life.

SOC. Very well, Crito; if such is the will of God, I am willing; but my belief is that there will be a delay of a day.

CR. Why do you say this?

SOC. I will tell you. I am to die on the day after the arrival of the ship?

CR. Yes; that is what the authorities say.

SOC. But I do not think that the ship will be here until to-morrow; this I gather from a vision which I had last night, or rather only just now, when you fortunately allowed me to sleep.

CR. And what was the nature of the vision?

SOC. There came to me the likeness of a woman, fair and comely, clothed in white raiment, who called to me and said: O Socrates,

The third day hence to Phthia shalt thou go.

CR. What a singular dream, Socrates!

SOC. There can be no doubt about the meaning, Crito, I think.

CR. Yes; the meaning is only too clear. But, Oh! my beloved Socrates, let me entreat you once more to take my advice and escape. For if you die I shall not only lose a friend who can never be replaced, but there is another evil: people who do not know you and me will believe that I might have saved you if I had been willing to give money, but that I did not care. Now, can there be a worse disgrace than this—that I should be thought to value money more than the life of a friend? For the many will not be persuaded that I wanted you to escape, and that you refused.

SOC. But why, my dear Crito, should we care about the opinion of the many? Good men, and they are the only persons who are worth considering, will think of these things truly as they happened.

CR. But do you see, Socrates, that the opinion of the many must be regarded, as is evident in your own case, because they can do the very greatest evil to any one who has lost their good opinion.

SOC. I only wish, Crito, that they could; for then they could also do the greatest good, and that would be well. But the truth is, that they can do neither good nor evil: they can not

make a man wise or make him foolish; and whatever they do
is the result of chance.

CR. Well, I will not dispute about that; but please to tell
me, Socrates, whether you are not acting out of regard to me
and your other friends: are you not afraid that if you escape
hence we may get into trouble with the informers for having
stolen you away, and lose either the whole or a great part of
our property; or that even a worse evil may happen to us?
Now, if this is your fear, be at ease; for in order to save you,
we ought surely to run this, or even a greater risk; be persuaded, then, and do as I say.

SOC. Yes, Crito, that is one fear which you mention, but
by no means the only one.

CR. Fear not. There are persons who at no great cost are
willing to save you and bring you out of prison; and as for
the informers, you may observe that they are far from being
exorbitant in their demands; a little money will satisfy them.
My means, which, as I am sure, are ample, are at your service,
and if you have a scruple about spending all mine, here are
strangers who will give you the use of theirs; and one of them,
Simmias the Theban, has brought a sum of money for this
very purpose; and Cebes and many others are willing to spend
their money too. I say therefore, do not on that account hesitate about making your escape, and do not say, as you did
in the court, that you will have a difficulty in knowing what
to do with yourself if you escape. For men will love you in
other places to which you may go, and not in Athens only;
there are friends of mine in Thessaly, if you like to go to
them, who will value and protect you, and no Thessalian will
give you any trouble. Nor can I think that you are justified,
Socrates, in betraying your own life when you might be saved;
this is playing into the hands of your enemies and destroyers;
and moreover I should say that you were betraying your children; for you might bring them up and educate them; instead
of which you go away and leave them, and they will have
to take their chance; and if they do not meet with the usual
fate of orphans, there will be small thanks to you. No man
should bring children into the world who is unwilling to per-
severe to the end in their nurture and education. But you are
choosing the easier part, as I think, not the better and man-
lier, which would rather have become one who professes
virtue in all his actions, like yourself. And indeed, I am
ashamed not only of you, but of us who are your friends, when
I reflect that this entire business of yours will be attributed

to our want of courage. The trial need never have come on, or might have been brought to another issue; and the end of all, which is the crowning absurdity, will seem to have been permitted by us, through cowardice and baseness, who might have saved you, as you might have saved yourself, if we had been good for anything (for there was no difficulty in escaping); and we did not see how disgraceful, Socrates, and also miserable all this will be to us as well as to you. Make your mind up then, or rather have your mind already made up, for the time of deliberation is over, and there is only one thing to be done, which must be done, if at all, this very night, and which any delay will render all but impossible; I beseech you therefore, Socrates, to be persuaded by me, and to do as I say.

soc. Dear Crito, your zeal is invaluable, if a right one; but if wrong, the greater the zeal the greater the evil; and therefore we ought to consider whether these things shall be done or not. For I am and always have been one of those natures who must be guided by reason, whatever the reason may be which upon reflection appears to me to be the best; and now that this fortune has come upon me, I can not put away the reasons which I have before given: the principles which I have hitherto honored and revered I still honor, and unless we can find other and better principles on the instant, I am certain not to agree with you; no, not even if the power of the multitude could inflict many more imprisonments, confiscations, deaths, frightening us like children with hobgoblin terrors. But what will be the fairest way of considering the question? Shall I return to your old argument about the opinions of men? some of which are to be regarded, and others, as we were saying, are not to be regarded. Now were we right in maintaining this before I was condemned? And has the argument which was once good now proved to be talk for the sake of talking;—in fact an amusement only, and altogether vanity? That is what I want to consider with your help, Crito: —whether, under my present circumstances, the argument appears to be in any way different or not; and is to be allowed by me or disallowed. That argument, which, as I believe, is maintained by many who assume to be authorities, was to the effect, as I was saying, that the opinions of some men are to be regarded, and of other men not to be regarded. Now you, Crito, are a disinterested person who are not going to die to-morrow—at least, there is no human probability of this, and you are therefore not liable to be deceived by the cir-

cumstances in which you are placed. Tell me then, whether
I am right in saying that some opinions, and the opinions of
some men only, are to be valued, and other opinions, and the
opinions of other men, are not to be valued. I ask you whether
I was right in maintaining this?

CR. Certainly.

SOC. The good are to be regarded, and not the bad?

CR. Yes.

SOC. And the opinions of the wise are good, and the opinions of the unwise are evil?

CR. Certainly.

SOC. And what was said about another matter? Was the
disciple in gymnastics supposed to attend to the praise and
blame and opinion of every man, or of one man only—his
physician or trainer, whoever that was?

CR. Of one man only.

SOC. And he ought to fear the censure and welcome the
praise of that one only, and not of the many?

CR. That is clear.

SOC. And he ought to live and train, and eat and drink in
the way which seems good to his single master who has understanding, rather than according to the opinion of all other
men put together?

CR. True.

SOC. And if he disobeys and disregards the opinion and
approval of the one, and regards the opinion of the many
who have no understanding, will he not suffer evil?

CR. Certainly he will.

SOC. And what will the evil be, whither tending and what
affecting, in the disobedient person?

CR. Clearly, affecting the body; that is what is destroyed
by the evil.

SOC. Very good; and is not this true, Crito, of other things
which we need not separately enumerate? In the matter of
just and unjust, fair and foul, good and evil, which are the
subjects of our present consultation, ought we to follow the
opinion of the many and to fear them; or the opinion of the
one man who has understanding, and whom we ought to fear
and reverence more than all the rest of the world: and whom
deserting we shall destroy and injure that principle in us which
may be assumed to be improved by justice and deteriorated
by injustice;—is there not such a principle?

CR. Certainly there is, Socrates.

SOC. Take a parallel instance:—if, acting under the advice

of men who have no understanding, we destroy that which
is improvable by health and deteriorated by disease—when that
has been destroyed, I say, would life be worth having? And
that is—the body?

CR. Yes.

SOC. Could we live, having an evil and corrupted body?

CR. Certainly not.

SOC. And will life be worth having, if that higher part of
man be depraved, which is improved by justice and deteriorated by injustice? Do we suppose that principle, whatever it
may be in man, which has to do with justice and injustice,
to be inferior to the body?

CR. Certainly not.

SOC. More honored, then?

CR. Far more honored.

SOC. Then, my friend, we must not regard what the many
say of us: but what he, the one man who has understanding
of just and unjust, will say, and what the truth will say. And
therefore you begin in error when you suggest that we should
regard the opinion of the many about just and unjust, good
and evil, honorable and dishonorable.—Well, some one will
say, "but the many can kill us."

CR. Yes, Socrates; that will clearly be the answer.

SOC. That is true: but still I find with surprise that the old
argument is, as I conceive, unshaken as ever. And I should
like to know whether I may say the same of another proposition—that not life, but a good life, is to be chiefly valued?

CR. Yes, that also remains.

SOC. And a good life is equivalent to a just and honorable
one—that holds also?

CR. Yes, that holds.

SOC. From these premisses I proceed to argue the question
whether I ought or ought not to try and escape without the
consent of the Athenians: and if I am clearly right in escaping,
then I will make the attempt; but if not, I will abstain. The
other considerations which you mention, of money and loss of
character and the duty of educating children, are, as I fear,
only the doctrines of the multitude, who would be as ready
to call people to life, if they were able, as they are to put
them to death—and with as little reason. But now, since the
argument has thus far prevailed, the only question which remains to be considered is, whether we shall do rightly either
in escaping or in suffering others to aid in our escape and
paying them in money and thanks, or whether we shall not

do rightly; and if the latter, then death or any other calamity which may ensue on my remaining here must not be allowed to enter into the calculation.

CR. I think that you are right, Socrates; how then shall we proceed?

SOC. Let us consider the matter together, and do you either refute me if you can, and I will be convinced; or else cease, my dear friend, from repeating to me that I ought to escape against the wishes of the Athenians: for I am extremely desirous to be persuaded by you, but not against my own better judgment. And now please to consider my first position, and do your best to answer me.

CR. I will do my best.

SOC. Are we to say that we are never intentionally to do wrong, or that in one way we ought and in another way we ought not to do wrong, or is doing wrong always evil and dishonorable, as I was just now saying, and as has been already acknowledged by us? Are all our former admissions which were made within a few days to be thrown away? And have we, at our age, been earnestly discoursing with one another all our life long only to discover that we are no better than children? Or are we to rest assured, in spite of the opinion of the many, and in spite of consequences whether better or worse, of the truth of what was then said, that injustice is always an evil and dishonor to him who acts unjustly? Shall we affirm that?

CR. Yes.

SOC. Then we must do no wrong?

CR. Certainly not.

SOC. Nor when injured injure in return, as the many imagine; for we must injure no one at all?

CR. Clearly not.

SOC. Again, Crito, may we do evil?

CR. Surely not, Socrates.

SOC. And what of doing evil in return for evil, which is the morality of the many—is that just or not?

CR. Not just.

SOC. For doing evil to another is the same as injuring him?

CR. Very true.

SOC. Then we ought not to retaliate or render evil for evil to any one, whatever evil we may have suffered from him. But I would have you consider, Crito, whether you really mean what you are saying. For this opinion has never been held, and never will be held, by any considerable number of persons; and those who are agreed and those who are not agreed upon this point have no common ground, and can only despise one another when they see how widely they differ. Tell me, then, whether you agree with and assent to my first principle, that neither injury nor retaliation nor warding off evil by evil is ever right. And shall that be the premiss of our argument? Or do you decline and dissent from this? For this has been of old and is still my opinion; but, if you are of another opinion, let me hear what you have to say. If, however, you remain of the same mind as formerly, I will proceed to the next step.

CR. You may proceed, for I have not changed my mind.

soc. Then I will proceed to the next step, which may be put in the form of a question:—Ought a man to do what he admits to be right, or ought he to betray the right?

CR. He ought to do what he thinks right.

soc. But if this is true, what is the application? In leaving the prison against the will of the Athenians, do I wrong any? or rather do I not wrong those whom I ought least to wrong? Do I not desert the principles which were acknowledged by us to be just? What do you say?

CR. I can not tell, Socrates; for I do not know.

soc. Then consider the matter in this way:—Imagine that I am about to play truant (you may call the proceeding by any name which you like), and the laws and the government come and interrogate me: "Tell us, Socrates," they say; "what are you about? are you going by an act of yours to overturn us—the laws and the whole state, as far as in you lies? Do you imagine that a state can subsist and not be overthrown, in which the decisions of law have no power, but are set aside and overthrown by individuals?" What will be our answer, Crito, to these and the like words? Any one, and especially a clever rhetorician, will have a good deal to urge about the evil of setting aside the law which requires a sentence to be carried out; and we might reply, "Yes; but the state has injured us and given an unjust sentence." Suppose I say that?

CR. Very good, Socrates.

soc. "And was that our agreement with you?" the law would say; "or were you to abide by the sentence of the state?" And if I were to express astonishment at their saying this, the law would probably add: "Answer, Socrates, instead of opening your eyes: you are in the habit of asking and answering questions. Tell us what complaint you have to make against us which justifies you in attempting to destroy us and the state? In the first place did we not bring you into existence? Your father married your mother by our aid and begat you. Say whether you have any objection to urge against those of us who regulate marriage?" None, I should reply. "Or against those of us who regulate the system of nurture and education of children in which you were trained? Were not the laws, who have the charge of this, right in commanding your father to train you in music and gymnastic?" Right, I should reply. "Well then, since you were brought into the world and nurtured and educated by us, can you deny in the first place that you are our child and slave, as your fathers were before you? And if this is true you are not on equal terms with us; nor can you think that you have a right to do to us what we are doing to you. Would you have any right to strike or revile or do any other evil to a father or to your master, if you had one, when you have been struck or reviled by him, or received some other evil at his hands?—you would not say this? And because we think right to destroy you, do you think that you have any right to destroy us in return, and your country as far as in you lies? And will you, O professor of true virtue, say that you are justified in this? Has a philosopher like you failed to discover that our country is more to be valued and higher and holier far than mother or father or any ancestor, and more to be regarded in the eyes of the gods and of men of understanding? also to be soothed, and gently and reverently entreated when angry, even more than a father, and if not persuaded, obeyed? And when we are punished by her, whether with imprisonment or stripes, the punishment is to be endured in silence; and if she lead us to wounds or death in battle, thither we follow as is right; neither may any one yield or retreat or leave his rank, but whether in battle or in a court of law, or in any other place, he must do what his city and his country order him; or he must change their view of what is just: and if he may do no violence to his father or mother, much less may he do violence to his country." What answer shall we make to this, Crito? Do the laws speak truly, or do they not?

CR. I think that they do.

SOC. Then the laws will say: "Consider, Socrates, if this is true, that in your present attempt you are going to do us wrong. For, after having brought you into the world, and nurtured and educated you, and given you and every other citizen a share in every good that we had to give, we further proclaim and give the right to every Athenian, that if he does not like us when he has come of age and has seen the ways of the city, and made our acquaintance, he may go where he pleases and take his goods with him; and none of us laws will forbid him or interfere with him. Any of you who does not like us and the city, and who wants to go to a colony or to any other city, may go where he likes, and take his goods with him. But he who has experience of the manner in which we order justice and administer the state, and still remains has entered into an implied contract that he will do as we command him. And he who disobeys us is, as we maintain, thrice wrong; first, because in disobeying us he is disobeying his parents; secondly, because we are the authors of his education; thirdly, because he has made an agreement with us that he will duly obey our commands; and he neither obeys them nor convinces us that our commands are wrong; and we do not rudely impose them, but give them the alternative of obeying or convincing us;—that is what we offer, and he does neither. These are the sort of accusations to which, as we were saying, you, Socrates, will be exposed if you accomplish your intentions; you, above all other Athenians." Suppose I ask, why is this? they will justly retort upon me that I above all other men have acknowledged the agreement. "There is clear proof," they will say, "Socrates, that we and the city were not displeasing to you. Of all Athenians you have been the most constant resident in the city, which, as you never leave, you may be supposed to love. For you never went out of the city either to see the games, except once when you went to the Isthmus, or to any other place unless you were on military service; nor did you travel as other men do. Nor had you any curiosity to know other states or their laws: your affections did not go beyond us and our state; we were your special favorites, and you acquiesced in our government of you; and this is the state in which you begat your children, which is a proof of your satisfaction. Moreover, you might, if you had liked, have fixed the penalty at banishment in the course of the trial—the state which refuses to let you go now would have let you go then. But you pretended that you preferred death to exile, and that you were not grieved at death. And now you have forgotten these fine sentiments, and pay no respect to us the laws, of whom you are the destroyer; and are doing what only a miserable slave would do, running away and turning your back upon the compacts and agreements which you made as a citizen. And first of all answer this very question: Are we right in saying that you agreed to be governed according to us in deed, and not in word only? Is that true or not?" How shall we answer that, Crito? Must we not agree?

CR. There is no help, Socrates.

SOC. Then will they not say: "You, Socrates, are breaking the covenants and agreements which you made with us at your leisure, not in any haste or under any compulsion or deception, but having had seventy years to think of them, during which time you were at liberty to leave the city, if we were not to your mind, or if our covenants appeared to you to be unfair. You had your choice, and might have gone either to Lacedaemon or Crete, which you often praise for their good government, or to some other Hellenic or foreign state. Whereas you, above all other Athenians, seemed to be so fond of the state, or, in other words, of us her laws (for who would like a state that has no laws), that you never stirred out of her; the halt, the blind, the maimed were not more stationary in her than you were. And now you run away and forsake your agreements. Not so, Socrates, if you will take our advice; do not make yourself ridiculous by escaping out of the city.

"For just consider, if you transgress and err in this sort of way, what good will you do either to yourself or to your friends? That your friends will be driven into exile and deprived of citizenship, or will lose their property, is tolerably certain; and you yourself, if you fly to one of the neighboring cities, as, for example, Thebes or Megara, both of which are well-governed cities, will come to them as an enemy, Socrates, and their government will be against you, and all patriotic citizens will cast an evil eye upon you as a subverter of the laws, and you will confirm in the minds of the judges the justice of their own condemnation of you. For he who is a corruptor of the laws is more than likely to be corruptor of the young and foolish portion of mankind. Will you then flee from well-ordered cities and virtuous men? and is existence worth having on these terms? Or will you go to them without shame, and talk to them, Socrates? And what will you say to them? What you say here about virtue and justice and institutions and laws being the best things among men. Would that be decent of you? Surely not. But if you go away from well-governed states

to Crito's friends in Thessaly, where there is a great disorder
and license, they will be charmed to have the tale of your escape from prison, set off with ludicrous particulars of the manner in which you were wrapped in a goatskin or some other
disguise, and metamorphosed as the fashion of runaways is—
that is very likely; but will there be no one to remind you that
in your old age you violated the most sacred laws from a miserable desire of a little more life. Perhaps not, if you keep
them in a good temper; but if they are out of temper you will
hear many degrading things; you will live, but how?—as the
flatterer of all men, and the servant of all men; and doing
what?—eating and drinking in Thessaly, having gone abroad in
order that you may get a dinner. And where will be your fine
sentiments about justice and virtue then? Say that you wish to
live for the sake of your children, that you may bring them up
and educate them—will you take them into Thessaly and deprive them of Athenian citizenship? Is that the benefit which
you would confer upon them? Or are you under the impression that they will be better cared for and educated here if you
are still alive, although absent from them; for that your friends
will take care of them? Do you fancy that if you are an inhabitant of Thessaly they will take care of them, and if you
are an inhabitant of the other world they will not take care of
them? Nay; but if they who call themselves friends are truly
friends, they surely will.

"Listen, then, Socrates, to us who have brought you up.
Think not of life and children first, and of justice afterwards,
but of justice first, that you may be justified before the princes
of the world below. For neither will you nor any that belong
to you be happier or holier or juster in this life, or happier
in another, if you do as Crito bids. Now you depart in inno-
cence, a sufferer and not a doer of evil; a victim, not of the
laws, but of men. But if you go forth, returning evil for evil,
and injury for injury, breaking the covenants and agreements
which you have made with us, and wronging those whom you
ought least to wrong, that is to say, yourself, your friends,
your country, and us, we shall be angry with you while you
live, and our brethren, the laws in the world below, will
receive you as an enemy; for they will know that you have
done your best to destroy us. Listen, then, to us and not to
Crito."

This is the voice which I seem to hear murmuring in my
ears, like the sound of the flute in the ears of the mystic; that

voice, I say, is humming in my ears, and prevents me from hearing any other. And I know that anything more which you may say will be vain. Yet speak, if you have anything to say.

CR. I have nothing to say, Socrates.

SOC. Then let me follow the intimations of the will of God.

Aristotle (384–322 B.C.)

POLITICS

Translated from the Greek by Benjamin Jowett

ORIGIN OF THE STATE, NATURE OF MAN,
INSTITUTION OF SLAVERY[1]

BOOK I

1. Every state is a community of some kind, and every community is established with a view to some good; for mankind always act in order to obtain that which they think good. But, if all communities aim at some good, the state or political community, which is the highest of all, and which embraces all the rest, aims at good in a greater degree than any other, and at the highest good.

Some people think that the qualifications of a statesman, king, householder, and master are the same, and that they differ, not in kind, but only in the number of their subjects. For example, the ruler over a few is called a master; over more, the manager of a household; over a still larger number, a statesman or king, as if there were no difference between a great household and a small state. The distinction which is made between the king and the statesman is as follows: When the government is personal, the ruler is a king; when, according to the rules of the political science, the citizens rule and are ruled in turn, then he is called a statesman.

But all this is a mistake; for governments differ in kind, as will be evident to any one who considers the matter according to the method which has hitherto guided us. As in other departments of science, so in politics, the compound should always be resolved into the simple elements or least parts of the whole. We must therefore look at the elements of which the

[1] Aristotle's chapters are without headings. The headings given here are supplied by the Editors.

state is composed, in order that we may see in what the different kinds of rule differ from one another, and whether any scientific result can be attained about each one of them.

2. He who thus considers things in their first growth and origin, whether a state or anything else, will obtain the clearest view of them. In the first place there must be a union of those who cannot exist without each other; namely, of male and female, that the race may continue (and this is a union which is formed, not of deliberate purpose, but because, in common with other animals and with plants, mankind have a natural desire to leave behind them an image of themselves), and of natural ruler and subject, that both may be preserved. For that which can foresee by the exercise of mind is by nature intended to be lord and master, and that which can with its body give effect to such foresight is a subject, and by nature a slave; hence master and slave have the same interest. Now nature has distinguished between the female and the slave. For she is not niggardly, like the smith who fashions the Delphian knife for many uses; she makes each thing for a single use, and every instrument is best made when intended for one and not for many uses. But among barbarians no distinction is made between women and slaves, because there is no natural ruler among them: they are a community of slaves, male and female. Wherefore the poets say—

It is meet that Hellenes should rule over barbarians;

as if they thought that the barbarian and the slave were by nature one.

Out of these two relationships between man and woman, master and slave, the first thing to arise is the family, and Hesiod is right when he says—

First house and wife and an ox for the plough,

for the ox is the poor man's slave. The family is the association established by nature for the supply of men's everyday wants, and the members of it are called by Charondas "companions of the cupboard," and by Epimenides the Cretan, "companions of the manger." But when several families are united, and the association aims at something more than the supply of daily needs, the first society to be formed is the village. And the most natural form of the village appears to be that of a colony from the family, composed of the children and grand-

children, who are said to be "suckled with the same milk."
And this is the reason why Hellenic states were originally governed by kings; because the Hellenes were under royal rule
before they came together, as the barbarians still are. Every
family is ruled by the eldest, and therefore in the colonies of
the family the kingly form of government prevailed because
they were of the same blood. As Homer says:

Each one gives law to his children and to his wives.

For they lived dispersedly, as was the manner in ancient times.
Wherefore men say that the Gods have a king, because they
themselves either are or were in ancient times under the rule
of a king. For they imagine, not only the forms of the Gods,
but their ways of life to be like their own.

When several villages are united in a single complete community, large enough to be nearly or quite self-sufficing, the
state comes into existence, originating in the bare needs of
life, and continuing in existence for the sake of a good life.
And therefore, if the earlier forms of society are natural, so
is the state, for it is the end of them, and the nature of a thing
is its end. For what each thing is when fully developed, we
call its nature, whether we are speaking of a man, a horse, or
a family. Besides, the final cause and end of a thing is the
best, and to be self-sufficing is the end and the best.

Hence it is evident that the state is a creation of nature, and
that man is by nature a political animal. And he who by
nature and not by mere accident is without a state, is either
a bad man or above humanity; he is like the

Tribeless, lawless, heartless one,

whom Homer denounces—the natural outcast is forthwith a
lover of war; he may be compared to an isolated piece at
draughts.

Now, that man is more of a political animal than bees or
any other gregarious animals is evident. Nature, as we often
say, makes nothing in vain, and man is the only animal whom
she has endowed with the gift of speech. And whereas mere
voice is but an indication of pleasure or pain, and is therefore
found in other animals (for their nature attains to the perception of pleasure and pain and the intimation of them to one
another, and no further), the power of speech is intended to
set forth the expedient and inexpedient, and therefore like-

wise the just and the unjust. And it is a characteristic of man that he alone has any sense of good and evil, of just and unjust, and the like, and the association of living beings who have this sense makes a family and a state.

Further, the state is by nature clearly prior to the family and to the individual, since the whole is of necessity prior to the part; for example, if the whole body be destroyed, there will be no foot or hand, except in an equivocal sense, as we might speak of a stone hand; for when destroyed the hand will be no better than that. But things are defined by their working and power; and we ought not to say that they are the same when they no longer have their proper quality, but only that they have the same name. The proof that the state is a creation of nature and prior to the individual is that the individual, when isolated, is not self-sufficing; and therefore he is like a part in relation to the whole. But he who is unable to live in society, or who has no need because he is sufficient for himself, must be either a beast or a god: he is no part of a state. A social instinct is implanted in all men by nature, and yet he who first founded the state was the greatest of benefactors. For man, when perfected, is the best of animals, but, when separated from law and justice, he is the worst of all; since armed injustice is the more dangerous, and he is equipped at birth with arms, meant to be used by intelligence and virtue, which he may use for the worst ends. Wherefore, if he have not virtue, he is the most unholy and the most savage of animals, and the most full of lust and gluttony. But justice is the bond of men in states, for the administration of justice, which is the determination of what is just, is the principle of order in political society.

3. Seeing then that the state is made up of households, before speaking of the state we must speak of the management of the household. The parts of household management correspond to the persons who compose the household, and a complete household consists of slaves and freemen. Now we should begin by examining everything in its fewest possible elements; and the first and fewest possible parts of a family are master and slave, husband and wife, father and children. We have therefore to consider what each of these three relations is and ought to be:—I mean the relation of master and servant, the marriage relation (the conjunction of man and wife has no name of its own), and thirdly, the procreative relation (this

also has no proper name). And there is another element of a
household, the so-called art of getting wealth, which, according to some, is identical with household management, according to others, a principal part of it; the nature of this art will
also have to be considered by us.

Let us first speak of master and slave, looking to the needs
of practical life and also seeking to attain some better theory
of their relation than exists at present. For some are of opinion that the rule of a master is a science, and that the management of a household, and the mastership of slaves, and the
political and royal rule, as I was saying at the outset, are all
the same. Others affirm that the rule of a master over slaves
is contrary to nature, and that the distinction between slave
and freeman exists by law only, and not by nature; and being
an interference with nature is therefore unjust.

4. Property is a part of the household, and the art of acquiring property is a part of the art of managing the household; for no man can live well, or indeed live at all, unless he
be provided with necessaries. And as in the arts which have a
definite sphere the workers must have their own proper instruments for the accomplishment of their work, so it is in the
management of a household. Now instruments are of various
sorts; some are living, others lifeless; in the rudder, the pilot of
a ship has a lifeless, in the look-out man, a living instrument;
for in the arts the servant is a kind of instrument. Thus, too, a
possession is an instrument for maintaining life. And so, in the
arrangement of the family, a slave is a living possession, and
property a number of such instruments; and the servant is
himself an instrument which takes precedence of all other instruments. For if every instrument could accomplish its own
work, obeying or anticipating the will of others, like the
statues of Daedalus, or the tripods of Hephaestus, which, says
the poet,

of their own accord entered the assembly of the Gods;

if, in like manner, the shuttle would weave and the plectrum
touch the lyre without a hand to guide them, chief workmen
would not want servants, nor masters slaves. Here, however,
another distinction must be drawn; the instruments commonly
so called are instruments of production, whilst a possession is
an instrument of action. The shuttle, for example, is not only
of use; but something else is made by it, whereas of a garment

or of a bed there is only the use. Further, as production and
action are different in kind, and both require instruments, the
instruments which they employ must likewise differ in kind.
But life is action and not production, and therefore the slave
is the minister of action. Again, a possession is spoken of as
a part is spoken of; for the part is not only a part of something else, but wholly belongs to it; and this is also true of a
possession. The master is only the master of the slave; he does
not belong to him, whereas the slave is not only the slave of
his master, but wholly belongs to him. Hence we see what is
the nature and office of a slave; he who is by nature not his
own but another's man, is by nature a slave; and he may be
said to be another's man who, being a human being, is also a
possession. And a possession may be defined as an instrument
of action, separable from the possessor.

5. But is there any one thus intended by nature to be a slave,
and for whom such a condition is expedient and right, or
rather is not all slavery a violation of nature?

There is no difficulty in answering this question, on grounds
both of reason and of fact. For that some should rule and
others be ruled is a thing not only necessary, but expedient;
from the hour of their birth, some are marked out for subjection, others for rule.

And there are many kinds both of rulers and subjects (and
that rule is the better which is exercised over better subjects
—for example, to rule over men is better than to rule over
wild beasts; for the work is better which is executed by better
workmen, and where one man rules and another is ruled, they
may be said to have a work); for in all things which form a
composite whole and which are made up of parts, whether
continuous or discrete, a distinction between the ruling and the
subject element comes to light. Such a duality exists in living
creatures, but not in them only; it originates in the constitution
of the universe; even in things which have no life there is a
ruling principle, as in a musical mode. But we are wandering
from the subject. We will therefore restrict ourselves to the
living creature, which, in the first place, consists of soul and
body: and of these two, the one is by nature the ruler, and the
other the subject. But then we must look for the intentions of
nature in things which retain their nature, and not in things
which are corrupted. And therefore we must study the man

who is in the most perfect state both of body and soul, for in him we shall see the true relation of the two; although in bad or corrupted natures the body will often appear to rule over the soul, because they are in an evil and unnatural condition. At all events we may firstly observe in living creatures both a despotical and a constitutional rule; for the soul rules the body with a despotical rule, whereas the intellect rules the appetites with a constitutional and royal rule. And it is clear that the rule of the soul over the body, and of the mind and the rational element over the passionate, is natural and expedient; whereas the equality of the two or the rule of the inferior is always hurtful. The same holds good of animals in relation to men; for tame animals have a better nature than wild, and all tame animals are better off when they are ruled by man; for then they are preserved. Again, the male is by nature superior, and the female inferior; and the one rules, and the other is ruled; this principle, of necessity, extends to all mankind. Where then there is such a difference as that between soul and body, or between men and animals (as in the case of those whose business is to use their body, and who can do nothing better), the lower sort are by nature slaves, and it is better for them as for all inferiors that they should be under the rule of a master. For he who can be, and therefore is, another's, and he who participates in rational principle enough to apprehend, but not to have, such a principle, is a slave by nature. Whereas the lower animals cannot even apprehend a principle; they obey their instincts. And indeed the use made of slaves and of tame animals is not very different; for both with their bodies minister to the needs of life. Nature would like to distinguish between the bodies of freemen and slaves, making the one strong for servile labour, the other upright, and although useless for such services, useful for political life in the arts both of war and peace. But the opposite often happens—that some have the souls and others have the bodies of freemen. And doubtless if men differed from one another in the mere forms of their bodies as much as the statues of the Gods do from men, all would acknowledge that the inferior class should be slaves of the superior. And if this is true of the body, how much more just that a similar distinction should exist in the soul? but the beauty of the body is seen, whereas the beauty of the soul is not seen. It is clear, then, that some men are by nature free, and others slaves, and that for these latter slavery is both expedient and right.

CONCEPT OF STATE AND CITIZEN
BOOK III, CHAPTER 1

He who would inquire into the essence and attributes of various kinds of governments must first of all determine "What is a state?" At present this is a disputed question. Some say that the state has done a certain act; others, no, not the state, but the oligarchy or the tyrant. And the legislator or statesman is concerned entirely with the state; a constitution or government being an arrangement of the inhabitants of a state. But a state is composite, like any other whole made up of many parts;—these are the citizens, who compose it. It is evident, therefore, that we must begin by asking, Who is the citizen, and what is the meaning of the term? For here again there may be a difference of opinion. He who is a citizen in a democracy will often not be a citizen in an oligarchy. Leaving out of consideration those who have been made citizens, or who have obtained the name of citizen in any other accidental manner, we may say, first, that a citizen is not a citizen because he lives in a certain place, for resident aliens and slaves share in the place; nor is he a citizen who has no legal right except that of suing and being sued; for this right may be enjoyed under the provisions of a treaty. Nay, resident aliens in many places do not possess even such rights completely, for they are obliged to have a patron, so that they do but imperfectly participate in citizenship, and we call them citizens only in a qualified sense, as we might apply the term to children who are too young to be on the register, or to old men who have been relieved from state duties. Of these we do not say quite simply that they are citizens, but add in the one case that they are not of age, and in the other, that they are past the age, or something of that sort; the precise expression is immaterial, for our meaning is clear. Similar difficulties to those which I have mentioned may be raised and answered about deprived citizens and about exiles. But the citizen whom we are seeking to define is a citizen in the strictest sense, against whom no such exception can be taken, and his special characteristic is that he shares in the administration of justice, and in offices. Now of offices some are discontinuous, and the same persons are not allowed to hold them twice, or can only hold them after a fixed interval; others have no limit of time—for example, the office of dicast or ecclesiast. It may, indeed, be argued that these are not magistrates at all, and that their functions give them no share in the government. But surely it is ridiculous to say that those who have the supreme power do not govern. Let us not dwell further upon this, which is a purely verbal question; what we want is a common term including both dicast and ecclesiast. Let us, for the sake of distinction, call it "indefinite office," and we will assume that those who share in such office are citizens. This is the most comprehensive definition of a citizen, and best suits all those who are generally so called.

But we must not forget that things of which the underlying principles differ in kind, one of them being first, another second, another third, have, when regarded in this relation, nothing, or hardly anything, worth mentioning in common. Now we see that governments differ in kind, and that some of them are prior and that others are posterior; those which are faulty or perverted are necessarily posterior to those which are perfect. (What we mean by perversion will be hereafter explained.) The citizen then of necessity differs under each form of government; and our definition is best adapted to the citizen of a democracy; but not necessarily to other states. For in some states the people are not acknowledged, nor have they any regular assembly, but only extraordinary ones; and suits are distributed by sections among the magistrates. At Lacedaemon, for instance, the Ephors determine suits about contracts, which they distribute among themselves, while the elders are judges of homicide, and other causes are decided by other magistrates. A similar principle prevails at Carthage; there certain magistrates decide all causes. We may, indeed, modify our definition of the citizen so as to include these states. In them it is the holder of a definite, not of an indefinite office, who legislates and judges, and to some or all such holders of definite offices is reserved the right of deliberating or judging about some things or about all things. The conception of the citizen now begins to clear up.

He who has the power to take part in the deliberative or judicial administration of any state is said by us to be a citizen of that state; and, speaking generally, a state is a body of citizens sufficing for the purposes of life.

BOOK III, CHAPTER 5

There still remains one more question about the citizen: Is he only a true citizen who has a share of office, or is the mechanic to be included? If they who hold no office are to be deemed citizens, not every citizen can have this virtue of ruling and obeying; for this man is a citizen. And if none of the lower class are citizens, in which part of the state are they to be placed? For they are not resident aliens, and they are not foreigners. May we not reply, that as far as this objection goes there is no more absurdity in excluding them than in excluding slaves and freedmen from any of the above-mentioned classes? It must be admitted that we cannot consider all those to be citizens who are necessary to the existence of the state; for example, children are not citizens equally with grown-up men, who are citizens absolutely, but children, not being grown up, are only citizens on a certain assumption. Nay, in ancient times, and among some nations, the artisan class *were* slaves or foreigners, and therefore the majority of them are so now. The best form of state will not admit them to citizenship; but if they are admitted, then our definition of the virtue of a citizen will not apply to every citizen, nor to every free man as such, but only to those who are freed from necessary services. The necessary people are either slaves who minister to the wants of individuals, or mechanics and labourers who are the servants of the community. These reflections carried a little further will explain their position; and indeed what has been said already is of itself, when understood, explanation enough.

Since there are many forms of government there must be many varieties of citizens, and especially of citizens who are subjects; so that under some governments the mechanic and the labourer will be citizens, but not in others, as, for example, in aristocracy or the so-called government of the best (if there be such an one), in which honours are given according to virtue and merit; for no man can practise virtue who is living the life of a mechanic or labourer. In oligarchies the qualification for office is high, and therefore no labourer can ever be a citizen; but a mechanic may, for an actual majority of them are rich. At Thebes there was a law that no man could hold office who had not retired from business for ten years. But in many states the law goes to the length of admitting aliens; for in some democracies a man is a citizen though his mother only be a citizen; and a similar principle is applied to illegitimate children; the law is relaxed when there is a dearth of population. But when the number of citizens increases, first the children of a male or a female slave are excluded; then those whose mothers only are citizens; and at last the right of citizenship is confined to those whose fathers and mothers are both citizens.

Hence, as is evident, there are different kinds of citizens; and he is a citizen in the highest sense who shares in the honours of the state. Compare Homer's words "like some dishonoured stranger"; he who is excluded from the honours of the state is no better than an alien. But when this exclusion is concealed, then the object is that the privileged class may deceive their fellow inhabitants.

As to the question whether the virtue of the good man is the same as that of the good citizen, the considerations already adduced prove that in some states the good man and the good citizen are the same, and in others different. When they are the same it is not every citizen who is a good man, but only the statesman and those who have or may have, alone or in conjunction with others, the conduct of public affairs.

FORMS OF GOVERNMENT
BOOK III, CHAPTERS 7, 8

7. Having determined these points, we have next to consider how many forms of government there are, and what they are; and in the first place what are the true forms, for when they are determined the perversions of them will at once be apparent. The words constitution and government have the same meaning, and the government, which is the supreme authority in states, must be in the hands of one, or of a few, or of the many. The true forms of government, therefore, are those in which the one, or the few, or the many, govern with a view to the common interest; but governments which rule with a view to the private interest, whether of the one, or of the few, or of the many, are perversions. For the members of a state, if they are truly citizens, ought to participate in its advantages. Of forms of government in which one rules, we call that which regards the common interests, kingship or

royalty; that in which more than one, but not many, rule, aristocracy; and it is so called, either because the rulers are the best men, or because they have at heart the best interests of the state and of the citizens. But when the citizens at large administer the state for the common interest, the government is called by the generic name—a constitution. And there is a reason for this use of language. One man or a few may excel in virtue; but as the number increases it becomes more difficult for them to attain perfection in every kind of virtue, though they may in military virtue, for this is found in the masses. Hence in a constitutional government the fighting-men have the supreme power, and those who possess arms are the citizens.

Of the above-mentioned forms, the perversions are as follows:—of royalty, tyranny; of aristocracy, oligarchy; of constitutional government, democracy. For tyranny is a kind of monarchy which has in view the interest of the monarch only; oligarchy has in view the interest of the wealthy; democracy, of the needy: none of them the common good of all.

8. But there are difficulties about these forms of government, and it will therefore be necessary to state a little more at length the nature of each of them. For he who would make a philosophical study of the various sciences, and does not regard practice only, ought not to overlook or omit anything, but to set forth the truth in every particular. Tyranny, as I was saying, is monarchy exercising the rule of a master over the political society; oligarchy is when men of property have the government in their hands; democracy, the opposite, when the indigent, and not the men of property, are the rulers. And here arises the first of our difficulties, and it relates to the distinction just drawn. For democracy is said to be the government of the many. But what if the many are men of property and have the power in their hands? In like manner oligarchy is said to be the government of the few; but what if the poor are fewer than the rich, and have the power in their hands because they are stronger? In these cases the distinction which we have drawn between these different forms of government would no longer hold good.

Suppose, once more, that we add wealth to the few and poverty to the many, and name the governments accordingly —an oligarchy is said to be that in which the few and the wealthy, and a democracy that in which the many and the poor are the rulers—there will still be a difficulty. For, if the

only forms of government are the ones already ment
how shall we describe those other governments also just mentioned by us, in which the rich are the more numerous and the
poor are the fewer, and both govern in their respective states?

The argument seems to show that, whether in oligarchies
or in democracies, the number of the governing body, whether
the greater number, as in a democracy, or the smaller number, as in an oligarchy, is an accident due to the fact that the
rich everywhere are few, and the poor numerous. But if
so, there is a misapprehension of the causes of the difference
between them. For the real difference between democracy
and oligarchy is poverty and wealth. Wherever men rule by
reason of their wealth, whether they be few or many, that is
an oligarchy, and where the poor rule, that is a democracy.
But as a fact the rich are few and the poor many; for few are
well-to-do, whereas freedom is enjoyed by all, and wealth and
freedom are the grounds on which the oligarchical and
democratical parties respectively claim power in the state.

BOOK IV, CHAPTERS 4–10

. . . Of forms of democracy first comes that which is said to
be based strictly on equality. In such a democracy the law says
that it is just for the poor to have no more advantage than the
rich; and that neither should be masters, but both equal. For
if liberty and equality, as is thought by some, are chiefly to
be found in democracy, they will be best attained when all persons alike share in the government to the utmost. And since
the people are the majority, and the opinion of the majority
is decisive, such a government must necessarily be a democracy. Here then is one sort of democracy. There is another,
in which the magistrates are elected according to a certain
property qualification, but a low one; he who has the required
amount of property has a share in the government, but he who
loses his property loses his rights. Another kind is that in which
all the citizens who are under no disqualification share in the
government, but still the law is supreme. In another, everybody, if he be only a citizen, is admitted to the government,
but the law is supreme as before. A fifth form of democracy,
in other respects, the same, is that in which, not the law, but
the multitude, have the supreme power, and supersede the law
by their decrees. This is a state of affairs brought about by the

demagogues. For in democracies which are subject to the law the best citizens hold the first place, and there are no demagogues; but where the laws are not supreme, there demagogues spring up. For the people becomes a monarch, and is many in one; and the many have the power in their hands, not as individuals, but collectively. Homer says that "it is not good to have a rule of many," but whether he means this corporate rule, or the rule of many individuals, is uncertain. At all events this sort of democracy, which is now a monarch, and no longer under the control of law, seeks to exercise monarchical sway, and grows into a despot; the flatterer is held in honour; this sort of democracy being relatively to other democracies what tyranny is to other forms of monarchy. The spirit of both is the same, and they alike exercise a despotic rule over the better citizens. The decrees of the demos correspond to the edicts of the tyrant; and the demagogue is to the one what the flatterer is to the other. Both have great power;—the flatterer with the tyrant, the demagogue with democracies of the kind which we are describing. The demagogues make the decrees of the people override the laws, by referring all things to the popular assembly. And therefore they grow great, because the people have all things in their hands, and they hold in their hands the votes of the people, who are too ready to listen to them. Further, those who have any complaint to bring against the magistrates say, "let the people be judges"; the people are too happy to accept the invitation; and so the authority of every office is undermined. Such a democracy is fairly open to the objection that it is not a constitution at all; for where the laws have no authority, there is no constitution. The law ought to be supreme over all, and the magistracies should judge of particulars, and only this should be considered a constitution. So that if democracy be a real form of government, the sort of system in which all things are regulated by decrees is clearly not even a democracy in the true sense of the word, for decrees relate only to particulars.

These then are the different kinds of democracy.

5. Of oligarchies, too, there are different kinds:—one where the property qualification for office is such that the poor, although they form the majority, have no share in the government, yet he who acquires a qualification may obtain a share. Another sort is when there is a qualification for office, but a high one, and the vacancies in the governing body are filled

by co-optation. If the election is made out of all the qualified persons, a constitution of this kind inclines to an aristocracy, if out of a privileged class, to an oligarchy. Another sort of oligarchy is when the son succeeds the father. There is a fourth form, likewise hereditary, in which the magistrates are supreme and not the law. Among oligarchies this is what tyranny is among monarchies, and the last-mentioned form of democracy among democracies; and in fact this sort of oligarchy receives the name of a dynasty (or rule of powerful families).

These are the different sorts of oligarchies and democracies. It should however be remembered that in many states the constitution which is established by law, although not democratic, owing to the education and habits of the people may be administered democratically, and conversely in other states the established constitution may incline to democracy, but may be administered in an oligarchical spirit. This most often happens after a revolution: for governments do not change at once; at first the dominant party are content with encroaching a little upon their opponents. The laws which existed previously continue in force, but the authors of the revolution have the power in their hands.

6. From what has been already said we may safely infer that there are so many different kinds of democracies and of oligarchies. For it is evident that either all the classes whom we mentioned must share in the government, or some only and not others. When the class of husbandmen and of those who possess moderate fortunes have the supreme power, the government is administered according to law. For the citizens being compelled to live by their labour have no leisure; and so they set up the authority of the law, and attend assemblies only when necessary. They all obtain a share in the government when they have acquired the qualification which is fixed by the law—the absolute exclusion of any class would be a step towards oligarchy; hence all who have acquired the property qualification are admitted to a share in the constitution. But leisure cannot be provided for them unless there are revenues to support them. This is one sort of democracy, and these are the causes which give birth to it. Another kind is based on the distinction which naturally comes next in order; in this, every one to whose birth there is no objection is eligible, but actually shares in the government only if he can find leisure. Hence in such a democracy the supreme power is vested in the laws, because the state has no means of paying the citizens. A third

kind is when all freemen have a right to share in the government, but do not actually share, for the reason which has been already given; so that in this form again the law must rule. A fourth kind of democracy is that which comes latest in the history of states. In our own day, when cities have far outgrown their original size, and their revenues have increased, all the citizens have a place in the government, through the great preponderance of the multitude; and they all, including the poor who receive pay, and therefore have leisure to exercise their rights, share in the administration. Indeed, when they are paid, the common people have the most leisure, for they are not hindered by the care of their property, which often fetters the rich, who are thereby prevented from taking part in the assembly or in the courts, and so the state is governed by the poor, who are a majority, and not by the laws. So many kinds of democracies there are, and they grow out of these necessary causes.

Of oligarchies, one form is that in which the majority of the citizens have some property, but not very much; and this is the first form, which allows to any one who obtains the required amount the right of sharing in the government. The sharers in the government being a numerous body, it follows that the law must govern, and not individuals. For in proportion as they are further removed from a monarchical form of government, and in respect of property have neither so much as to be able to live without attending to business, nor so little as to need state support, they must admit the rule of law and not claim to rule themselves. But if the men of property in the state are fewer than in the former case, and own more property, there arises a second form of oligarchy. For the stronger they are, the more power they claim, and having this object in view, they themselves select those of the other classes who are to be admitted to the government; but, not being as yet strong enough to rule without the law, they make the law represent their wishes. When this power is intensified by a further diminution of their numbers and increase of their property, there arises a third and further stage of oligarchy, in which the governing class keep the offices in their own hands, and the law ordains that the son shall succeed the father. When, again, the rulers have great wealth and numerous friends, this sort of family despotism approaches a monarchy; individuals rule and not the law. This is the fourth sort of oligarchy, and is analogous to the last sort of democracy.

7. There are still two forms besides democracy and oligarchy; one of them is universally recognized and included among the four principal forms of government, which are said to be (1) monarchy, (2) oligarchy, (3) democracy, and (4) the so-called aristocracy or government of the best. But there is also a fifth, which retains the generic name of polity or constitutional government; this is not common, and therefore has not been noticed by writers who attempt to enumerate the different kinds of government; like Plato, in their books about the state, they recognize four only. The term "aristocracy" is rightly applied to the form of government which is described in the first part of our treatise; for that only can be rightly called aristocracy which is a government formed of the best men absolutely, and not merely of men who are good when tried by any given standard. In the perfect state the good man is absolutely the same as the good citizen; whereas in other states the good citizen is only good relatively to his own form of government. But there are some states differing from oligarchies and also differing from the so-called polity or constitutional government; these are termed aristocracies, and in them magistrates are certainly chosen, both according to their wealth and according to their merit. Such a form of government differs from each of the two just now mentioned, and is termed an aristocracy. For indeed in states which do not make virtue the aim of the community, men of merit and reputation for virtue may be found. And so where a government has regard to wealth, virtue, and numbers, as at Carthage, that is aristocracy; and also where it has regard only to two out of the three, as at Lacedaemon, to virtue and numbers, and the two principles of democracy and virtue temper each other. There are these two forms of aristocracy in addition to the first and perfect state, and there is a third form, viz. the constitutions which incline more than the so-called polity towards oligarchy.

8. I have yet to speak of the so-called polity and of tyranny. I put them in this order, not because a polity or constitutional government is to be regarded as a perversion any more than the above-mentioned aristocracies. The truth is, that they all fall short of the most perfect form of government, and so they are reckoned among perversions, and the really perverted forms are perversions of these, as I said in the original discussion. Last of all I will speak of tyranny, which I place last in

the series because I am inquiring into the constitutions of states, and this is the very reverse of a constitution.

Having explained why I have adopted this order, I will proceed to consider constitutional government; of which the nature will be clearer now that oligarchy and democracy have been defined. For polity or constitutional government may be described generally as a fusion of oligarchy and democracy; but the term is usually applied to those forms of government which incline towards democracy, and the term aristocracy to those which incline towards oligarchy, because birth and education are commonly the accompaniments of wealth. Moreover, the rich already possess the external advantages the want of which is a temptation to crime, and hence they are called noblemen and gentlemen. And inasmuch as aristocracy seeks to give predominance to the best of the citizens, people say also of oligarchies that they are composed of noblemen and gentlemen. Now it appears to be an impossible thing that the state which is governed not by the best citizens but by the worst should be well-governed, and equally impossible that the state which is ill-governed should be governed by the best. But we must remember that good laws, if they are not obeyed, do not constitute good government. Hence there are two parts of good government; one is the actual obedience of citizens to the laws, the other part is the goodness of the laws which they obey; they may obey bad laws as well as good. And there may be a further subdivision; they may obey either the best laws which are attainable to them, or the best absolutely.

The distribution of offices according to merit is a special characteristic of aristocracy, for the principle of an aristocracy is virtue, as wealth is of an oligarchy, and freedom of a democracy. In all of them there of course exists the right of the majority, and whatever seems good to the majority of those who share in the government has authority. Now in most states the form called polity exists, for the fusion goes no further than the attempt to unite the freedom of the poor and the wealth of the rich, who commonly take the place of the noble. But as there are three grounds on which men claim an equal share in the government, freedom, wealth, and virtue (for the fourth or good birth is the result of the two last, being only ancient wealth and virtue), it is clear that the admixture of the two elements, that is to say, of the rich and poor, is to be called a polity or constitutional government; and the union of the three is to be called aristocracy or the government of the best, and more than any other form of government, except the true and ideal, has a right to this name.

Thus far I have shown the existence of forms of states other than monarchy, democracy, and oligarchy, and what they are, and in what aristocracies differ from one another, and polities from aristocracies—that the two latter are not very unlike is obvious.

9. Next we have to consider how by the side of oligarchy and democracy the so-called polity or constitutional government springs up, and how it should be organized. The nature of it will be at once understood from a comparison of oligarchy and democracy; we must ascertain their different characteristics, and taking a portion from each, put the two together, like the parts of an indenture. Now there are three modes in which fusions of government may be effected. In the first mode we must combine the laws made by both governments, say concerning the administration of justice. In oligarchies they impose a fine on the rich if they do not serve as judges, and to the poor they give no pay; but in democracies they give pay to the poor and do not fine the rich. Now (1) the union of these two modes is a common or middle term between them, and is therefore characteristic of a constitutional government, for it is a combination of both. This is one mode of uniting the two elements. Or (2) a mean may be taken between the enactments of the two: thus democracies require no property qualification, or only a small one, from members of the assembly, oligarchies a high one; here neither of these is the common term, but a mean between them. (3) There is a third mode, in which something is borrowed from the oligarchical and something from the democratical principle. For example, the appointment of magistrates by lot is thought to be democratical, and the election of them oligarchical; democratical again when there is no property qualification, oligarchical when there is. In the aristocratical or constitutional state, one element will be taken from each—from oligarchy the principle of electing to offices, from democracy the disregard of qualification. Such are the various modes of combination.

There is a true union of oligarchy and democracy when the same state may be termed either a democracy or an oligarchy; those who use both names evidently feel that the fusion is complete. Such a fusion there is also in the mean; for both extremes appear in it. The Lacedaemonian constitution, for example, is often described as a democracy, because it has many democratical features. In the first place the youth receive a democratical education. For the sons of the poor are brought up with the sons of the rich, who are educated in such a manner as to make it possible for the sons of the poor to be educated like them. A similar equality prevails in the following period of life, and when the citizens are grown up to manhood the same rule is observed; there is no distinction between the rich and poor. In like manner they all have the same food at their public tables, and the rich wear only such clothing as any poor man can afford. Again, the people elect to one of the two greatest offices of state, and in the other they share; for they elect the Senators and share in the Ephoralty. By others the Spartan constitution is said to be an oligarchy, because it has many oligarchical elements. That all offices are filled by election and none by lot, is one of these oligarchical characteristics; that the power of inflicting death or banishment rests with a few persons is another; and there are others. In a well attempered polity there should appear to be both elements and yet neither; also the government should rely on itself, and not on foreign aid, and on itself not through the good will of a majority—they might be equally well-disposed when there is a vicious form of government—but through the general willingness of all classes in the state to maintain the constitution.

Enough of the manner in which a constitutional government, and in which the so-called aristocracies ought to be framed.

10. Of the nature of tyranny I have still to speak, in order that it may have its place in our inquiry (since even tyranny is reckoned by us to be a form of government), although there is not much to be said about it. I have already in the former part of this treatise discussed royalty or kingship according to the most usual meaning of the term, and considered whether it is or is not advantageous to states, and what kind of royalty should be established, and from what source, and how.

When speaking of royalty we also spoke of two forms of tyranny, which are both according to law, and therefore easily pass into royalty. Among Barbarians there are elected monarchs who exercise a despotic power; despotic rulers were also elected in ancient Hellas, called Aesymnetes or dictators. These monarchies, when compared with one another, exhibit certain differences. And they are, as I said before, royal, in so far as the monarch rules according to law over willing subjects; but they are tyrannical in so far as he is despotic and rules according to his own fancy. There is also a third kind of tyranny, which is the most typical form, and is the counterpart of the perfect monarchy. This tyranny is just that arbitrary power of an individual which is responsible to no one, and governs all alike, whether equals or better, with a view to its own advantage, not to that of its subjects, and therefore against their will. No freeman, if he can escape from it, will endure such a government.

REVOLUTIONS

BOOK V, CHAPTERS 1–4

1. The design which we proposed to ourselves is now nearly completed. Next in order follow the causes of revolution in states, how many, and of what nature they are; what modes of destruction apply to particular states, and out of what, and into what they mostly change; also what are the modes of preservation in states generally, or in a particular state, and by what means each state may be best preserved: these questions remain to be considered.

In the first place we must assume as our starting-point that in the many forms of government which have sprung up there has always been an acknowledgement of justice and proportionate equality, although mankind fail in attaining them, as indeed I have already explained. Democracy, for example, arises out of the notion that those who are equal in any respect are equal in all respects; because men are equally free, they claim to be absolutely equal. Oligarchy is based on the notion that those who are unequal in one respect are in all respects unequal; being unequal, that is, in property, they suppose themselves to be unequal absolutely. The democrats think that as they are equal they ought to be equal in all things; while the oligarchs, under the idea that they are unequal, claim too much, which is one form of inequality. All these forms of government have a kind of justice, but, tried by an absolute standard, they are faulty; and, therefore, both parties, whenever their share in the government does not accord with their preconceived ideas, stir up revolution. Those who excel in virtue have the best right of all to rebel (for they alone can with reason be deemed absolutely unequal), but then they are of all men the least inclined to do so. There is also a superiority which is claimed by men of rank; for they are thought noble because they spring from wealthy and virtuous ancestors. Here then, so to speak, are opened the very springs and fountains of revolution; and hence arise two sorts of changes in governments; the one affecting the constitution, when men seek to change from an existing form into some other, for example, from democracy into oligarchy, and from oligarchy into democracy, or from either of them into constitutional government or aristocracy, and conversely; the other not affecting the constitution, when, without disturbing the form of government, whether oligarchy, or monarchy, or any other, they try to get the administration into their own hands. Further, there is a question of degree; an oligarchy, for example, may become more or less oligarchical, and a democracy more or less democratical; and in like manner the characteristics of the other forms of government may be more or less strictly maintained. Or the revolution may be directed against a portion of the constitution only, e. g. the establishment or overthrow of a particular office: as at Sparta it is said that Lysander attempted to overthrow the monarchy, and king Pausanias, the ephoralty. At Epidamnus, too, the change was partial. For instead of phylarchs or heads of tribes, a council was appointed; but to this day the magistrates are the only members of the ruling class who are compelled to go to the Heliaea when an election takes place, and the office of the single archon was another oligarchical feature. Everywhere inequality is a cause of revolution, but an inequality in which there is no proportion—for instance, a perpetual monarchy among equals; and always it is the desire of equality which rises in rebellion.

Now equality is of two kinds, numerical and proportional; by the first I mean sameness or equality in number or size; by the second, equality of ratios. For example, the excess of three over two is numerically equal to the excess of two over one; whereas four exceeds two in the same ratio in which two exceeds one, for two is the same part of four that one is of two, namely, the half. As I was saying before, men agree that justice in the abstract is proportion, but they differ in that some think that if they are equal in any respect they are equal absolutely, others that if they are unequal in any respect they should be unequal in all. Hence there are two principal forms of government, democracy and oligarchy; for good birth and virtue are rare, but wealth and numbers are more common.

In what city shall we find a hundred persons of good birth and of virtue? whereas the rich everywhere abound. That a state should be ordered, simply and wholly, according to either kind of equality, is not a good thing; the proof is the fact that such forms of government never last. They are originally based on a mistake, and, as they begin badly, cannot fail to end badly. The inference is that both kinds of equality should be employed; numerical in some cases, and proportionate in others.

Still democracy appears to be safer and less liable to revolution than oligarchy. For in oligarchies there is the double danger of the oligarchs falling out among themselves and also with the people; but in democracies there is only the danger of a quarrel with the oligarchs. No dissension worth mentioning arises among the people themselves. And we may further remark that a government which is composed of the middle class more nearly approximates to democracy than to oligarchy, and is the safest of the imperfect forms of government.

2. In considering how dissensions and political revolutions arise, we must first of all ascertain the beginnings and causes of them which affect constitutions generally. They may be said to be three in number; and we have now to give an outline of each. We want to know (1) what is the feeling? (2) what are the motives of those who make them? (3) whence arise political disturbances and quarrels? The universal and chief cause of this revolutionary feeling has been already mentioned; viz. the desire of equality, when men think that they are equal to others who have more than themselves; or, again, the desire of inequality and superiority, when conceiving themselves to be superior they think that they have not more but the same or less than their inferiors; pretensions which may and may not be just. Inferiors revolt in order that they may be equal, and equals that they may be superior. Such is the state of mind which creates revolutions. The motives for making them are the desire of gain and honour, or the fear of dishonour and loss; the authors of them want to divert punishment or dishonour from themselves or their friends. The causes and reasons of revolutions, whereby men are themselves affected in the way described, and about the things which I have mentioned, viewed in one way may be regarded as seven, and in another as more than seven. Two of them have been already noticed; but they act in a different manner, for men are excited against one another by the love of gain

and honour—not, as in the case which I have just supposed, in order to obtain them for themselves, but at seeing others, justly or unjustly, engrossing them. Other causes are insolence, fear, excessive predominance, contempt, disproportionate increase in some part of the state; causes of another sort are election intrigues, carelessness, neglect about trifles, dissimilarity of elements.

3. What share insolence and avarice have in creating revolutions, and how they work, is plain enough. When the magistrates are insolent and grasping they conspire against one another and also against the constitution from which they derive their power, making their gains either at the expense of individuals or of the public. It is evident, again, what an influence honour exerts and how it is a cause of revolution. Men who are themselves dishonoured and who see others obtaining honours rise in rebellion; the honour or dishonour when undeserved is unjust; and just when awarded according to merit. Again, superiority is a cause of revolution when one or more persons have a power which is too much for the state and the power of the government; this is a condition of affairs out of which there arises a monarchy, or a family oligarchy. And therefore, in some places, as at Athens and Argos, they have recourse to ostracism. But how much better to provide from the first that there should be no such pre-eminent individuals instead of letting them come into existence and then finding a remedy.

Another cause of revolution is fear. Either men have committed wrong, and are afraid of punishment, or they are expecting to suffer wrong and are desirous of anticipating their enemy. Thus at Rhodes the notables conspired against the people through fear of the suits that were brought against them. Contempt is also a cause of insurrection and revolution; for example, in oligarchies—when those who have no share in the state are the majority, they revolt, because they think that they are the stronger. Or, again, in democracies, the rich despise the disorder and anarchy of the state; at Thebes, for example, where, after the battle of Oenophyta, the bad administration of the democracy led to its ruin. At Megara the fall of the democracy was due to a defeat occasioned by disorder and anarchy. And at Syracuse the democracy aroused contempt before the tyranny of Gelo arose; at Rhodes, before the insurrection.

Political revolutions also spring from a disproportionate increase in any part of the state. For as a body is made up of many members, and every member ought to grow in proportion, that symmetry may be preserved; but loses its nature if the foot be four cubits long and the rest of the body two spans; and, should the abnormal increase be one of quality as well as of quantity, may even take the form of another animal: even so a state has many parts, of which some one may often grow imperceptibly; for example, the number of poor in democracies and in constitutional states. And this disproportion may sometimes happen by an accident, as at Tarentum, from a defeat in which many of the notables were slain in a battle with the Iapygians just after the Persian War, the constitutional government in consequence becoming a democracy; or as was the case at Argos, where the Argives, after their army had been cut to pieces on the seventh day of the month by Cleomenes the Lacedaemonian, were compelled to admit to citizenship some of their perioeci; and at Athens, when, after frequent defeats of their infantry at the time of the Peloponnesian War, the notables were reduced in number, because the soldiers had to be taken from the roll of citizens. Revolutions arise from this cause as well, in democracies as in other forms of government, but not to so great an extent. When the rich grow numerous or properties increase, the form of government changes into an oligarchy or a government of families. Forms of government also change—sometimes even without revolution, owing to election contests, as at Heraea (where, instead of electing their magistrates, they took them by lot, because the electors were in the habit of choosing their own partisans); or owing to carelessness, when disloyal persons are allowed to find their way into the highest offices, as at Oreum, where, upon the accession of Heracleodorus to office, the oligarchy was overthrown, and changed by him into a constitutional and democratical government.

Again, the revolution may be facilitated by the slightness of the change; I mean that a great change may sometimes slip into the constitution through neglect of a small matter; at Ambracia, for instance, the qualification for office, small at first, was eventually reduced to nothing. For the Ambraciots thought that a small qualification was much the same as none at all.

Another cause of revolution is difference of races which do not at once acquire a common spirit; for a state is not the growth of a day, any more than it grows out of a multitude brought together by accident. Hence the reception of strangers in colonies, either at the time of their foundation or afterwards, has generally produced revolution; for example, the Achaeans who joined the Troezenians in the foundation of Sybaris, becoming later the more numerous, expelled them; hence the curse fell upon Sybaris. At Thurii the Sybarites quarrelled with their fellow-colonists; thinking that the land belonged to them, they wanted too much of it and were driven out. At Byzantium the new colonists were detected in a conspiracy, and were expelled by force of arms; the people of Antissa, who had received the Chian exiles, fought with them, and drove them out; and the Zancleans, after having received the Samians, were driven by them out of their own city. The citizens of Apollonia on the Euxine, after the introduction of a fresh body of colonists, had a revolution; the Syracusans, after the expulsion of their tyrants, having admitted strangers and mercenaries to the rights of citizenship, quarrelled and came to blows; the people of Amphipolis, having received Chalcidian colonists, were nearly all expelled by them.

Now, in oligarchies the masses make revolution under the idea that they are unjustly treated, because, as I said before, they are equals, and have not an equal share, and in democracies the notables revolt, because they are not equals, and yet have only an equal share.

Again, the situation of cities is a cause of revolution when the country is not naturally adapted to preserve the unity of the state. For example, the Chytians at Clazomenae did not agree with the people of the island; and the people of Colophon quarrelled with the Notians; at Athens too, the inhabitants of the Piraeus are more democratic than those who live in the city. For just as in war the impediment of a ditch, though ever so small, may break a regiment, so every cause of difference, however slight, makes a breach in a city. The greatest opposition is confessedly that of virtue and vice; next comes that of wealth and poverty; and there are other antagonistic elements, greater or less, of which one is this difference of place.

4. In revolutions the occasions may be trifling, but great interests are at stake. Even trifles are most important when they concern the rulers, as was the case of old at Syracuse; for the Syracusan constitution was once changed by a love-quarrel of two young men, who were in the government. The story is that while one of them was away from home his beloved was gained over by his companion, and he to revenge

himself seduced the other's wife. They then drew the members of the ruling class into their quarrel and so split all the people into portions. We learn from this story that we should be on our guard against the beginnings of such evils, and should put an end to the quarrels of chiefs and mighty men. The mistake lies in the beginning—as the proverb says—"Well begun is half done"; so an error at the beginning, though quite small, bears the same ratio to the errors in the other parts. In general, when the notables quarrel, the whole city is involved, as happened in Hestiaea after the Persian War. The occasion was the division of an inheritance; one of two brothers refused to give an account of their father's property and the treasure which he had found: so the poorer of the two quarrelled with him and enlisted in his cause the popular party, the other, who was very rich, the wealthy classes. . . .

CRITICISM OF PLATO
BOOK V, CHAPTER 12

In the *Republic* of Plato, Socrates treats of revolutions, but not well, for he mentions no cause of change which peculiarly affects the first, or perfect state. He only says that the cause is that nothing is abiding, but all things change in a certain cycle; and that the origin of the change consists in those numbers "of which 4 and 3, married with 5, furnish two harmonies"—(he means when the number of this figure becomes solid); he conceives that nature at certain times produces bad men who will not submit to education; in which latter particular he may very likely be not far wrong, for there may well be some men who cannot be educated and made virtuous. But why is such a cause of change peculiar to his ideal state, and not rather common to all states, nay, to everything which comes into being at all? And is it by the agency of time, which, as he declares, makes all things change, that things which did not begin together, change together? For example, if something has come into being the day before the completion of the cycle, will it change with things that came into being before? Further, why should the perfect state change into the Spartan? For governments more often take an opposite form than one akin to them. The same remark is applicable to the other changes; he says that the Spartan constitution changes into an oligarchy, and this into a democracy, and this again into a tyranny. And yet the contrary happens quite as often; for a democracy is even more likely to change into an oligarchy than into a monarchy. Further, he never says whether tyranny is, or is not, liable to revolutions, and if it is, what is the cause of them, or into what form it changes. And the reason is, that he could not very well have told: for there is no rule; according to him it should revert to the first and best, and then there would be a complete cycle. But in point of fact a tyranny often changes into a tyranny, as that at Sicyon changed from the tyranny of Myron into that of Cleisthenes; into oligarchy, as the tyranny of Antileon did at Chalcis; into democracy, as that of Gelo's family did at Syracuse; into aristocracy, as at Carthage, and the tyranny of Charilaus at Lacedaemon. Often an oligarchy changes into a tyranny, like most of the ancient oligarchies in Sicily; for example, the oligarchy at Leontini changed into the tyranny of Panaetius; that at Gela into the tyranny of Cleander; that at Rhegium into the tyranny of Anaxilaus; the same thing has happened in many other states. And it is absurd to suppose that the state changes into oligarchy merely because the ruling class are lovers and makers of money, and not because the very rich think it unfair that the very poor should have an equal share in the government with themselves. Moreover, in many oligarchies there are laws against making money in trade. But at Carthage, which is a democracy, there is no such prohibition; and yet to this day the Carthaginians have never had a revolution. It is absurd too for him to say that an oligarchy is two cities, one of the rich, and the other of the poor. Is not this just as much the case in the Spartan constitution, or in any other in which either all do not possess equal property, or all are not equally good men? Nobody need be any poorer than he was before, and yet the oligarchy may change all the same into a democracy, if the poor form the majority; and a democracy may change into an oligarchy, if the wealthy class are stronger than the people, and the one are energetic, the other indifferent. Once more, although the causes of the change are very numerous, he mentions only one, which is, that the citizens become poor through dissipation and debt, as though he thought that all, or the majority of them, were originally rich. This is not true: though it is true that when any of the leaders lose their property they are ripe for revolution; but, when anybody else, it is no great matter, and an oligarchy does not even then more often pass into a democracy than into any other form of government. Again, if men are deprived of the

honours of state, and are wronged, and insulted, they make
revolutions, and change forms of government, even although
they have not wasted their substance because they might do
what they liked—of which extravagance he declares excessive
freedom to be the cause.

Finally, although there are many forms of oligarchies and
democracies, Socrates speaks of their revolutions as though
there were only one form of either of them.

DEMOCRACY AND OLIGARCHY

BOOK VI, CHAPTERS 2–7

2. The basis of a democratic state is liberty; which, according to the common opinion of men, can only be enjoyed in
such a state;—this they affirm to be the great end of every
democracy. One principle of liberty is for all to rule and be
ruled in turn, and indeed democratic justice is the application
of numerical not proportionate equality; whence it follows
that the majority must be supreme, and that whatever the majority approve must be the end and the just. Every citizen, it
is said, must have equality, and therefore in a democracy the
poor have more power than the rich, because there are more
of them, and the will of the majority is supreme. This, then, is
one note of liberty which all democrats affirm to be the principle of their state. Another is that a man should live as he
likes. This, they say, is the privilege of a freeman, since, on
the other hand, not to live as a man likes is the mark of a
slave. This is the second characteristic of democracy, whence
has arisen the claim of men to be ruled by none, if possible,
or, if this is impossible, to rule and be ruled in turns; and so it
contributes to the freedom based upon equality.

Such being our foundation and such the principle from
which we start, the characteristics of democracy are as follows:—the election of officers by all out of all; and that all
should rule over each, and each in his turn over all; that the
appointment to all offices, or to all but those which require
experience and skill, should be made by lot; that no property
qualification should be required for offices, or only a very
low one; that a man should not hold the same office twice, or
not often, or in the case of few except military offices: that
the tenure of all offices, or of as many as possible, should be
brief; that all men should sit in judgement, or that judges

selected out of all should judge, in all matters, or in most and in the greatest and most important—such as the scrutiny of accounts, the constitution, and private contracts; that the assembly should be supreme over all causes, or at any rate over the most important, and the magistrates over none or only over a very few. Of all magistracies, a council is the most democratic when there is not the means of paying all the citizens, but when they are paid even this is robbed of its power; for the people then draw all cases to themselves, as I said in the previous discussion. The next characteristic of democracy is payment for services; assembly, law-courts, magistrates, everybody receives pay, when it is to be had; or when it is not to be had for all, then it is given to the law-courts and to the stated assemblies, to the council and to the magistrates, or at least to any of them who are compelled to have their meals together. And whereas oligarchy is characterized by birth, wealth, and education, the notes of democracy appear to be the opposite of these—low birth, poverty, mean employment. Another note is that no magistracy is perpetual, but if any such have survived some ancient change in the constitution it should be stripped of its power, and the holders should be elected by lot and no longer by vote. These are the points common to all democracies; but democracy and demos in their truest form are based upon the recognized principle of democratic justice, that all should count equally; for equality implies that the poor should have no more share in the government than the rich, and should not be the only rulers, but that all should rule equally according to their numbers. And in this way men think that they will secure equality and freedom in their state.

3. Next comes the question, how is this equality to be obtained? Are we to assign to a thousand poor men the property qualifications of five hundred rich men? and shall we give the thousand a power equal to that of the five hundred? or, if this is not to be the mode, ought we, still retaining the same ratio, to take equal numbers from each and give them the control of the elections and of the courts?— Which, according to the democratical notion, is the juster form of the constitution— this or one based on numbers only? Democrats say that justice is that to which the majority agree, oligarchs that to which the wealthier class; in their opinion the decision should be given according to the amount of property. In both principles there is some inequality and injustice. For if justice is the will of

the few, any one person who has more wealth than all the rest
of the rich put together, ought, upon the oligarchical principle,
to have the sole power—but this would be tyranny; or if justice is the will of the majority, as I was before saying, they
will unjustly confiscate the property of the wealthy minority.
To find a principle of equality in which they both agree we
must inquire into their respective ideas of justice.

Now they agree in saying that whatever is decided by the
majority of the citizens is to be deemed law. Granted:—but
not without some reserve; since there are two classes out of
which a state is composed—the poor and the rich—that is to be
deemed law, on which both or the greater part of both agree;
and if they disagree, that which is approved by the greater
number, and by those who have the higher qualification. For
example, suppose that there are ten rich and twenty poor, and
some measure is approved by six of the rich and is disapproved
by fifteen of the poor, and the remaining four of the rich join
with the party of the poor, and the remaining five of the poor
with that of the rich; in such a case the will of those whose
qualifications, when both sides are added up, are the greatest,
should prevail. If they turn out to be equal, there is no greater
difficulty than at present, when, if the assembly or the courts
are divided, recourse is had to the lot, or to some similar expedient. But, although it may be difficult in theory to know
what is just and equal, the practical difficulty of inducing those
to forbear who can, if they like, encroach, is far greater, for
the weaker are always asking for equality and justice, but the
stronger care for none of these things.

4. Of the four kinds of democracy, as was said in the previous discussion, the best is that which comes first in order; it is
also the oldest of them all. I am speaking of them according
to the natural classification of their inhabitants. For the best
material of democracy is an agricultural population; there is
no difficulty in forming a democracy where the mass of the
people live by agriculture or tending of cattle. Being poor, they
have no leisure, and therefore do not often attend the assembly, and not having the necessaries of life they are always at
work, and do not covet the property of others. Indeed, they
find their employment pleasanter than the cares of government
or office where no great gains can be made out of them, for
the many are more desirous of gain than of honour. A proof
is that even the ancient tyrannies were patiently endured by
them, as they still endure oligarchies, if they are allowed to

work and are not deprived of their property; for some of them grow quickly rich and the others are well enough off. Moreover, they have the power of electing the magistrates and calling them to account; their ambition, if they have any, is thus satisfied; and in some democracies, although they do not all share in the appointment of offices, except through representatives elected in turn out of the whole people, as at Mantinea; —yet, if they have the power of deliberating, the many are contented. Even this form of government may be regarded as a democracy, and was such at Mantinea. Hence it is both expedient and customary in the afore-mentioned type of democracy that all should elect to offices, and conduct scrutinies, and sit in the law-courts, but that the great offices should be filled up by election and from persons having a qualification; the greater requiring a greater qualification, or, if there be no offices for which a qualification is required, then those who are marked out by special ability should be appointed. Under such a form of government the citizens are sure to be governed well (for the offices will always be held by the best persons; the people are willing enough to elect them and are not jealous of the good). The good and the notables will then be satisfied, for they will not be governed by men who are their inferiors, and the persons elected will rule justly, because others will call them to account. Every man should be responsible to others, nor should any one be allowed to do just as he pleases; for where absolute freedom is allowed there is nothing to restrain the evil which is inherent in every man. But the principle of responsibility secures that which is the greatest good in states; the right persons rule and are prevented from doing wrong, and the people have their due. It is evident that this is the best kind of democracy, and why? Because the people are drawn from a certain class. Some of the ancient laws of most states were, all of them, useful with a view to making the people husbandmen. They provided either that no one should possess more than a certain quantity of land, or that, if he did, the land should not be within a certain distance from the town or the acropolis. Formerly in many states there was a law forbidding any one to sell his original allotment of land. There is a similar law attributed to Oxylus, which is to the effect that there should be a certain portion of every man's land on which he could not borrow money. A useful corrective to the evil of which I am speaking would be the law of the Aphytaeans, who, although they are numerous, and do not possess much land, are all of them husbandmen. For their properties are reckoned in the census, not entire, but only in such small portions that even the poor may have more than the amount required.

Next best to an agricultural, and in many respects similar, are a pastoral people, who live by their flocks; they, are the best trained of any for war, robust in body and able to camp out. The people of whom other democracies consist are far inferior to them, for their life is inferior; there is no room for moral excellence in any of their employments, whether they be mechanics or traders or labourers. Besides, people of this class can readily come to the assembly, because they are continually moving about in the city and in the agora; whereas husbandmen are scattered over the country and do not meet, or equally feel the want of assembling together. Where the territory also happens to extend to a distance from the city, there is no difficulty in making an excellent democracy or constitutional government; for the people are compelled to settle in the country, and even if there is a town population the assembly ought not to meet, in democracies, when the country people cannot come. We have thus explained how the first and best form of democracy should be constituted; it is clear that the other or inferior sorts will deviate in a regular order, and the population which is excluded will at each stage be of a lower kind.

The last form of democracy, that in which all share alike, is one which cannot be borne by all states, and will not last long unless well regulated by laws and customs. The more general causes which tend to destroy this or other kinds of government have been pretty fully considered. In order to constitute such a democracy and strengthen the people, the leaders have been in the habit of including as many as they can, and making citizens not only of those who are legitimate, but even of the illegitimate, and of those who have only one parent a citizen, whether father or mother; for nothing of this sort comes amiss to such a democracy. This is the way in which demagogues proceed. Whereas the right thing would be to make no more additions when the number of the commonalty exceeds that of the notables and of the middle class—beyond this not to go. When in excess of this point, the constitution becomes disorderly, and the notables grow excited and impatient of the democracy, as in the insurrection at Cyrene; for no notice is taken of a little evil, but when it increases it strikes the eye. Measures like those which Cleisthenes passed when he wanted to increase the power of the democracy at Athens, or such as were taken by the founders of popular government at Cyrene, are useful in the extreme form of democracy. Fresh tribes and brotherhoods should be established; the private rites of families should be restricted and converted into public ones; in short, every contrivance should be adopted which will mingle the citizens with one another and get rid of old connexions. Again, the measures which are taken by tyrants appear all of them to be democratic; such, for instance, as the licence permitted to slaves (which may be to a certain extent advantageous) and also that of women and children, and the allowing everybody to live as he likes. Such a government will have many supporters, for most persons would rather live in a disorderly than in a sober manner.

5. The mere establishment of a democracy is not the only or principal business of the legislator, or of those who wish to create such a state, for any state, however badly constituted, may last one, two, or three days; a far greater difficulty is the preservation of it. The legislator should therefore endeavour to have a firm foundation according to the principles already laid down concerning the preservation and destruction of states; he should guard against the destructive elements, and should make laws, whether written or unwritten, which will contain all the preservatives of states. He must not think the truly democratical or oligarchical measure to be that which will give the greatest amount of democracy or oligarchy, but that which will make them last longest. The demagogues of our own day often get property confiscated in the law-courts in order to please the people. But those who have the welfare of the state at heart should counteract them, and make a law that the property of the condemned should not be public and go into the treasury but be sacred. Thus offenders will be as much afraid, for they will be punished all the same, and the people, having nothing to gain, will not be so ready to condemn the accused. Care should also be taken that state trials are as few as possible, and heavy penalties should be inflicted on those who bring groundless accusations; for it is the practice to indict, not members of the popular party, but the notables, although the citizens ought to be all attached to the constitution as well, or at any rate should not regard their rulers as enemies.

Now, since in the last and worst form of democracy the citizens are very numerous, and can hardly be made to assemble unless they are paid, and to pay them when there are no revenues presses hardly upon the notables (for the money must be obtained by a property-tax and confiscations and corrupt practices of the courts, things which have before now overthrown many democracies); where, I say, there are no revenues, the government should hold few assemblies, and the law-courts should consist of many persons, but sit for a few days only. This system has two advantages: first, the rich do not fear the expense, even although they are unpaid themselves when the poor are paid; and secondly, causes are better tried, for wealthy persons, although they do not like to be long absent from their own affairs, do not mind going for a few days to the law-courts. Where there are revenues the demagogues should not be allowed after their manner to distribute the surplus; the poor are always receiving and always wanting more and more, for such help is like water poured into a leaky cask. Yet the true friend of the people should see that they be not too poor, for extreme poverty lowers the character of the democracy; measures therefore should be taken which will give them lasting prosperity; and as this is equally the interest of all classes, the proceeds of the public revenues should be accumulated and distributed among its poor, if possible, in such quantities as may enable them to purchase a little farm, or, at any rate, make a beginning in trade or husbandry. And if this benevolence cannot be extended to all, money should be distributed in turn according to tribes or other divisions, and in the meantime the rich should pay the fee for the attendance of the poor at the necessary assemblies; and should in return be excused from useless public services. By administering the state in this spirit the Carthaginians retain the affections of the people; their policy is from time to time to send some of them into their dependent towns, where they grow rich. It is also worthy of a generous and sensible nobility to divide the poor amongst them, and give them the means of going to work. The example of the people of Tarentum is also well deserving of imitation, for, by sharing the use of their own property with the poor, they gain their good will. Moreover, they divide all their offices into two classes, some of them being elected by vote, the others by lot; the latter, that the people may participate in them, and the former, that the state may be better administered. A like result may be gained by dividing the same offices, so as to have two classes of magistrates, one chosen by vote, the other by lot.

Enough has been said of the manner in which democracies ought to be constituted.

6. From these considerations there will be no difficulty in seeing what should be the constitution of oligarchies. We have only to reason from opposites and compare each form of oligarchy with the corresponding form of democracy.

The first and best attempered of oligarchies is akin to a constitutional government. In this there ought to be two standards of qualification; the one high, the other low—the lower qualifying for the humbler yet indispensable offices and the higher for the superior ones. He who acquires the prescribed qualification should have the rights of citizenship. The number of those admitted should be such as will make the entire governing body stronger than those who are excluded, and the new citizen should be always taken out of the better class of the people. The principle, narrowed a little, gives another form of oligarchy; until at length we reach the most cliquish and tyrannical of them all, answering to the extreme democracy, which, being the worst, requires vigilance in proportion to its badness. For as healthy bodies and ships well provided with sailors may undergo many mishaps and survive them, whereas sickly constitutions and rotten ill-manned ships are ruined by the very least mistake, so do the worst forms of government require the greatest care. The populousness of democracies generally preserves them (for number is to democracy in the place of justice based on proportion); whereas the preservation of an oligarchy clearly depends on an opposite principle, viz. good order.

7. As there are four chief divisions of the common people —husbandmen, mechanics, retail traders, labourers; so also there are four kinds of military forces—the cavalry, the heavy infantry, the light-armed troops, the navy. When the country is adapted for cavalry, then a strong oligarchy is likely to be established. For the security of the inhabitants depends upon a force of this sort, and only rich men can afford to keep horses. The second form of oligarchy prevails when the country is adapted to heavy infantry; for this service is better suited to the rich than to the poor. But the light-armed and the naval element are wholly democratic; and nowadays, where they are numerous, if the two parties quarrel, the oligarchy are often worsted by them in the struggle. A remedy for this state of things may be found in the practice of generals who combine a proper contingent of light-armed troops with cavalry and heavy-armed. And this is the way in which the poor get the

better of the rich in civil contests; being lightly armed, they
fight with advantage against cavalry and heavy infantry. An
oligarchy which raises such a force out of the lower classes
raises a power against itself. And therefore, since the ages of
the citizens vary and some are older and some younger, the
fathers should have their own sons, while they are still young,
taught the agile movements of light-armed troops; and these,
when they have been taken out of the ranks of the youth,
should become light-armed warriors in reality. The oligarchy
should also yield a share in the government to the people,
either, as I said before, to those who have a property qualification, or, as in the case of Thebes, to those who have abstained
for a certain number of years from mean employments, or, as
at Massalia, to men of merit who are selected for their wor-
thiness, whether previously citizens or not. The magistracies
of the highest rank, which ought to be in the hands of the
governing body, should have expensive duties attached to
them, and then the people will not desire them and will take
no offence at the privileges of their rulers when they see that
they pay a heavy fine for their dignity. It is fitting also that the
magistrates on entering office should offer magnificent sacrifices or erect some public edifice, and then the people who
participate in the entertainments, and see the city decorated
with votive offerings and buildings, will not desire an alteration
in the government, and the notables will have memorials of
their munificence. This, however, is anything but the fashion of
our modern oligarchs, who are as covetous of gain as they are
of honour; oligarchies like theirs may be well described as
petty democracies. Enough of the manner in which democracies and oligarchies should be organized.

THE IDEAL STATE
BOOK VII, CHAPTER 4

4. Thus far by way of introduction. In what has preceded I
have discussed other forms of government, in what remains
the first point to be considered is what should be the conditions
of the ideal or perfect state; for the perfect state cannot exist
without a due supply of the means of life. And therefore we
must pre-suppose many purely imaginary conditions, but nothing impossible. There will be a certain numbers of citizens, a

country in which to place them, and the like. As the weaver
or shipbuilder or any other artisan must have the material
proper for his work (and in proportion as this is better prepared, so will the result of his art be nobler), so the statesman
or legislator must also have the materials suited to him.

First among the materials required by the statesman is population: he will consider what should be the number and character of the citizens, and then what should be the size and
character of the country. Most persons think that a state in
order to be happy ought to be large; but even if they are
right, they have no idea what is a large and what a small state.
For they judge of the size of the city by the number of the
inhabitants; whereas they ought to regard, not their number,
but their power. A city too, like an individual, has a work to
do; and that city which is best adapted to the fulfilment of its
work is to be deemed greatest, in the same sense of the word
great in which Hippocrates might be called greater, not as a
man, but as a physician, than some one else who was taller.
And even if we reckon greatness by numbers, we ought not to
include everybody, for there must always be in cities a multitude of slaves and sojourners and foreigners; but we should
include those only who are members of the state, and who
form an essential part of it. The number of the latter is a proof
of the greatness of a city; but a city which produces numerous
artisans and comparatively few soldiers cannot be great, for
a great city is not to be confounded with a populous one.
Moreover, experience shows that a very populous city can
rarely, if ever, be well governed; since all cities which have a
reputation for good government have a limit of population.
We may argue on grounds of reason, and the same result will
follow. For law is order, and good law is good order; but a
very great multitude cannot be orderly: to introduce order into
the unlimited is the work of a divine power—of such a power
as holds together the universe. Beauty is realized in number
and magnitude, and the state which combines magnitude with
good order must necessarily be the most beautiful. To the
size of states there is a limit, as there is to other things, plants,
animals, implements; for none of these retain their natural
power when they are too large or too small, but they either
wholly lose their nature, or are spoiled. For example, a ship
which is only a span long will not be a ship at all, nor a ship a
quarter of a mile long; yet there may be a ship of a certain
size, either too large or too small, which will still be a ship, but

bad for sailing. In like manner a state when composed of too few is not, as a state ought to be, self-sufficing; when of too many, though self-sufficing in all mere necessaries, as a nation may be, it is not a state, being almost incapable of constitutional government. For who can be the general of such a vast multitude, or who the herald, unless he have the voice of a Stentor?

A state, then, only begins to exist when it has attained a population sufficient for a good life in the political community: it may indeed, if it somewhat exceed this number, be a greater state. But, as I was saying, there must be a limit. What should be the limit will be easily ascertained by experience. For both governors and governed have duties to perform; the special functions of a governor are to command and to judge. But if the citizens of a state are to judge and to distribute offices according to merit, then they must know each other's characters; where they do not possess this knowledge, both the election to offices and the decision of lawsuits will go wrong. When the population is very large they are manifestly settled at haphazard, which clearly ought not to be. Besides, in an overpopulous state foreigners and metics will readily acquire the rights of citizens, for who will find them out? Clearly then the best limit of the population of a state is the largest number which suffices for the purposes of life, and can be taken in at a single view. Enough concerning the size of a state.

BOOK VII, CHAPTERS 8, 9

. . . Now, whereas happiness is the highest good, being a realization and perfect practice of virtue, which some can attain, while others have little or none of it, the various qualities of men are clearly the reason why there are various kinds of states and many forms of government: for different men seek after happiness in different ways and by different means, and so make for themselves different modes of life and forms of government. We must see also how many things are indispensable to the existence of a state, for what we call the parts of a state will be found among the indispensables. Let us then enumerate the functions of a state, and we shall easily elicit what we want:

First, there must be food; secondly, arts, for life requires many instruments; thirdly, there must be arms, for the members of a community have need of them, and in their own hands, too, in order to maintain authority both against disobedient subjects and against external assailants; fourthly, there must be a certain amount of revenue, both for internal needs, and for the purposes of war; fifthly, or rather first, there must be a care of religion, which is commonly called worship; sixthly, and most necessary of all, there must be a power of deciding what is for the public interest, and what is just in men's dealings with one another.

These are the services which every state may be said to need. For a state is not a mere aggregate of persons, but a union of them sufficing for the purposes of life; and if any of these things be wanting, it is as we maintain impossible that the community can be absolutely self-sufficing. A state then should be framed with a view to the fulfilment of these functions. There must be husbandmen to procure food, and artisans, and a warlike and a wealthy class, and priests, and judges to decide what is necessary and expedient.

9. Having determined these points, we have in the next place to consider whether all ought to share in every sort of occupation. Shall every man be at once husbandman, artisan, councillor, judge, or shall we suppose the several occupations just mentioned assigned to different persons? or, thirdly, shall some employments be assigned to individuals and others common to all? The same arrangement, however, does not occur in every constitution; as we were saying, all may be shared by all, or not all by all, but only by some; and hence arise the differences of constitutions, for in democracies all share in all, in oligarchies the opposite practice prevails. Now, since we are here speaking of the best form of government, i. e. that under which the state will be most happy (and happiness, as has been already said, cannot exist without virtue), it clearly follows that in the state which is best governed and possesses men who are just absolutely, and not merely relatively to the principle of the constitution, the citizens must not lead the life of mechanics or tradesmen, for such a life is ignoble, and inimical to virtue. Neither must they be husbandmen, since leisure is necessary both for the development of virtue and the performance of political duties.

Again, there is in a state a class of warriors, and another of councillors, who advise about the expedient and determine matters of law, and these seem in an especial manner parts of a state. Now, should these two classes be distinguished, or are both functions to be assigned to the same persons? Here again there is no difficulty in seeing that both functions will in one way belong to the same, in another, to different persons. To different persons in so far as these employments are suited to different primes of life, for the one requires wisdom and the other strength. But on the other hand, since it is an impossible thing that those who are able to use or to resist force should be willing to remain always in subjection, from this point of view the persons are the same; for those who carry arms can always determine the fate of the constitution. It remains therefore that both functions should be entrusted by the ideal constitution to the same persons, not, however, at the same time, but in the order prescribed by nature, who has given to young men strength and to older men wisdom. Such a distribution of duties will be expedient and also just, and is founded upon a principle of conformity to merit. Besides, the ruling class should be the owners of property, for they are citizens, and the citizens of a state should be in good circumstances; whereas mechanics or any other class which is not a producer of virtue have no share in the state. This follows from our first principle, for happiness cannot exist without virtue, and a city is not to be termed happy in regard to a portion of the citizens, but in regard to them all. And clearly property should be in their hands, since the husbandmen will of necessity be slaves or barbarian Perioeci.

Of the classes enumerated there remain only the priests, and the manner in which their office is to be regulated is obvious. No husbandman or mechanic should be appointed to it; for the Gods should receive honour from the citizens only. Now since the body of the citizens is divided into two classes, the warriors and the councillors, and it is beseeming that the worship of the Gods should be duly performed, and also a rest provided in their service for those who from age have given up active life, to the old men of these two classes should be assigned the duties of the priesthood.

We have shown what are the necessary conditions, and what the parts of a state husbandmen, craftsmen, and labourers of all kinds are necessary to the existence of states, but the parts of the state are the warriors and councillors. And these are distinguished severally from one another, the distinction being in some cases permanent, in others not.

EDUCATION
BOOK VIII, CHAPTER 1

1. No one will doubt that the legislator should direct his attention above all to the education of youth; for the neglect of education does harm to the constitution. The citizen should be moulded to suit the form of government under which he lives. For each government has a peculiar character which originally formed and which continues to preserve it. The character of democracy creates democracy, and the character of oligarchy creates oligarchy; and always the better the character, the better the government.

Again, for the exercise of any faculty or art a previous training and habituation are required; clearly therefore for the practice of virtue. And since the whole city has one end, it is manifest that education should be one and the same for all, and that it should be public, and not private—not as at present, when every one looks after his own children separately, and gives them separate instruction of the sort which he thinks best; the training in things which are of common interest should be the same for all. Neither must we suppose that any one of the citizens belongs to himself, for they all belong to the state, and are each of them a part of the state, and the care of each part is inseparable from the care of the whole. In this particular as in some others the Lacedaemonians are to be praised, for they take the greatest pains about their children, and make education the business of the state.

Niccolò Machiavelli (1469–1527)

THE PRINCE

Translated from the Italian by Luigi Ricci

Revised by E. R. P. Vincent

NICCOLO MACHIAVELLI
TO
LORENZO THE MAGNIFICENT
SON OF PIERO DI MEDICI

It is customary for those who wish to gain the favour of a prince to endeavour to do so by offering him gifts of those things which they hold most precious, or in which they know him to take especial delight. In this way princes are often presented with horses, arms, cloth of gold, gems, and such-like ornaments worthy of their grandeur. In my desire, however, to offer to Your Highness some humble testimony of my devotion, I have been unable to find among my possessions anything which I hold so dear or esteem so highly as that knowledge of the deeds of great men which I have acquired through a long experience of modern events and a constant study of the past.

With the utmost diligence I have long pondered and scrutinised the actions of the great, and now I offer the results to Your Highness within the compass of a small volume: and although I deem this work unworthy of Your Highness's acceptance, yet my confidence in your humanity assures me that you will receive it with favour, knowing that it is not in my power to offer you a greater gift than that of enabling you to understand in a very short time all those things which I have learnt at the cost of privation and danger in the course of many years. I have not sought to adorn my work with long phrases or high-sounding words or any of those superficial attractions and ornaments with which many writers seek to embellish their material, as I desire no honour for my work but such as the novelty and gravity of its subject may justly deserve. Nor will it, I trust, be deemed presumptuous on the part of a man of humble and obscure condition to attempt to discuss and direct the government of princes; for in the same way that landscape painters station themselves in the valleys in order to draw mountains or high ground, and ascend an eminence in order to get a good view of the plains, so it is necessary to be a prince to know thoroughly the nature of the people, and one of the populace to know the nature of princes.

May I trust, therefore, that Your Highness will accept this little gift in the spirit in which it is offered; and if Your Highness will deign to peruse it, you will recognise in it my ardent desire that you may attain to that grandeur which fortune and your own merits presage for you.

And should Your Highness gaze down from the summit of your lofty position towards this humble spot, you will recognise the great and unmerited sufferings inflicted on me by a cruel fate.

CHAPTER V

THE WAY TO GOVERN CITIES OR DOMINIONS THAT,
PREVIOUS TO BEING OCCUPIED, LIVED UNDER THEIR
OWN LAWS

When those states which have been acquired are accustomed to live at liberty under their own laws, there are three ways of holding them. The first is to despoil them; the second is to go and live there in person; the third is to allow them to live under their own laws, taking tribute of them, and creating within the country a government composed of a few who will keep it friendly to you. Because this government, being created by the prince, knows that it cannot exist without his friendship and protection, and will do all it can to keep them. What is more, a city used to liberty can be more easily held by means of its citizens than in any other way, if you wish to preserve it.

There is the example of the Spartans and the Romans. The Spartans held Athens and Thebes by creating within them a government of a few; nevertheless they lost them. The Romans, in order to hold Capua, Carthage, and Numantia, ravaged them, but did not lose them. They wanted to hold Greece in almost the same way as the Spartans held it, leaving it free and under its own laws, but they did not succeed; so that they were compelled to lay waste many cities in that province in order to keep it, because in truth there is no sure method of holding them except by despoiling them. And whoever becomes the ruler of a free city and does not destroy it, can expect to be destroyed by it, for it can always find a motive for rebellion in the name of liberty and of its ancient usages, which are forgotten neither by lapse of time nor by benefits received; and whatever one does or provides, so long as the inhabitants are not separated or dispersed, they do not forget that name and those usages, but appeal to them at once in every emergency, as did Pisa after being so many years held in servitude by the Florentines. But when cities or provinces have been accustomed to live under a prince, and the family of that prince is extinguished, being on the one hand used to obey, and on the other not having their old prince, they cannot unite in choosing one from among themselves, and they do not know how to live in freedom, so that they are slower to take arms, and a prince can win them over with greater facility and establish himself securely. But in republics there is greater life, greater hatred, and more desire for vengeance; they do not and cannot cast aside the memory of their ancient liberty, so that the surest way is either to lay them waste or reside in them.

CHAPTER VI
OF NEW DOMINIONS WHICH HAVE BEEN ACQUIRED BY ONE'S OWN ARMS AND ABILITY

Let no one marvel if in speaking of new dominions both as to prince and state, I bring forward very exalted instances, for men walk almost always in the paths trodden by others, proceeding in their actions by imitation. Not being always able to follow others exactly, nor attain to the excellence of those he imitates, a prudent man should always follow in the path trodden by great men and imitate those who are most excellent, so that if he does not attain to their greatness, at any rate he will get some tinge of it. He will do as prudent archers, who when the place they wish to hit is too far off, knowing how far their bow will carry, aim at a spot much higher than the one they wish to hit, not in order to reach this height with their arrow, but by help of this high aim to hit the spot they wish to.

I say then that in new dominions, where there is a new prince, it is more or less easy to hold them according to the greater or lesser ability of him who acquires them. And as the fact of a private individual becoming a prince presupposes either great ability or good fortune, it would appear that either of these things would in part mitigate many difficulties. Nevertheless those who have been less beholden to good fortune have maintained themselves best. The matter is also facilitated by the prince being obliged to reside personally in his territory, having no others. But to come to those who have become princes through their own merits and not by fortune, I regard as the greatest, Moses, Cyrus, Romulus, Theseus, and their like. And although one should not speak of Moses, he having merely carried out what was ordered him by God, still he deserves admiration, if only for that grace which made him worthy to speak with God. But regarding Cyrus and others who have acquired or founded kingdoms, they will all be found worthy of admiration; and if their particular actions and methods are examined they will not appear very different from those of Moses, although he had so great a Master. And in examining their life and deeds it will be seen that they owed nothing to fortune but the opportunity which gave them matter to be shaped into what form they thought fit; and without that opportunity their powers would have been wasted, and without their powers the opportunity would have come in vain.

It was thus necessary that Moses should find the people of Israel slaves in Egypt and oppressed by the Egyptians, so that they were disposed to follow him in order to escape from their servitude. It was necessary that Romulus should be unable to remain in Alba, and should have been exposed at his birth, in order that he might become King of Rome and founder of that nation. It was necessary that Cyrus should find the Persians discontented with the empire of the Medes, and the Medes weak and effeminate through long peace. Theseus could not have shown his abilities if he had not found the Athenians dispersed. These opportunities, therefore, gave these men their chance, and their own great qualities enabled them to profit by them, so as to ennoble their country and augment its fortunes.

Those who by the exercise of abilities such as these become princes, obtain their dominions with difficulty but retain them easily, and the difficulties which they have in acquiring their dominions arise in part from the new rules and regulations that they have to introduce in order to establish their position securely. It must be considered that there is nothing more difficult to carry out, nor more doubtful of success, nor more dangerous to handle, than to initiate a new order of things. For the reformer has enemies in all those who profit by the old order, and only lukewarm defenders in all those who would profit by the new order, this lukewarmness arising partly from fear of their adversaries, who have the laws in their favour; and partly from the incredulity of mankind, who do not truly believe in anything new until they have had actual experience of it. Thus it arises that on every opportunity for attacking the reformer, his opponents do so with the zeal of partisans, the others only defend him half-heartedly, so that between them he runs great danger. It is necessary, however, in order to investigate thoroughly this question, to examine whether these innovators are independent, or whether they depend upon others, that is to say, whether in order to carry out their designs they have to entreat or are able to compel. In the first case they invariably succeed ill, and accomplish nothing; but when they can depend on their own strength and are able to use force, they rarely fail. Thus it comes about that all armed prophets have conquered and unarmed ones failed; for besides what has been already said, the character of peoples varies, and it is easy to persuade them of a thing, but difficult to keep them in that persuasion. And so it is necessary to order things so that when they no longer believe, they can be made to believe by force. Moses, Cyrus, Theseus, and Romulus would not have been able to keep their constitutions observed for so long had they been disarmed, as happened in our own time with Fra Girolamo Savonarola, who failed entirely in his new rules when the multitude began to disbelieve in him, and he had no means of holding fast those who had believed nor of compelling the unbelievers to believe. Therefore such men as these have great difficulty in making their way, and all their dangers are met on the road and must be overcome by their own abilities; but when once they have overcome them and have begun to be held in veneration, and have suppressed those who envied them, they remain powerful and secure, honoured and happy.

To the high examples given I will add a lesser one, which, however, is in some measure comparable and will serve as an instance of all such cases, that of Hiero of Syracuse, who from a private individual became Prince of Syracuse, without other aid from fortune beyond the opportunity; for the Syracusans being oppressed, elected him as their captain, from which post he rose by ability to be prince; while still in private life his virtues were such that it was written of him, that he lacked nothing to reign but the kingdom. He abolished the old militia, raised a new one, abandoned his old friendships and formed others; and as he had thus friends and soldiers of his own choosing, he was able on this foundation to build securely, so that while he had great trouble in acquiring his position he had little in maintaining it.

CHAPTER VII

OF NEW DOMINIONS ACQUIRED BY THE POWER OF OTHERS OR BY FORTUNE

Those who rise from private citizens to be princes merely by fortune have little trouble in rising but very much in maintaining their position. They meet with no difficulties on the way as they fly over them, but all their difficulties arise when they are established. Such are they who are granted a state either for money, or by favour of him who grants it, as happened to many in Greece, in the cities of Ionia and of the Hellespont, who were created princes by Darius in order to hold these places for his security and glory; such were also those emperors who from private citizens rose to power by bribing the army. Such as these depend absolutely on the good will and fortune of those who have raised them, both of which are extremely inconstant and unstable. They neither know how to, nor are in a position to maintain their rank, for unless he be a man of great genius it is not likely that one who has always lived in a private position should know how to command, and they are unable to maintain themselves because they possess no forces friendly and faithful to them. Moreover, states quickly founded, like all other things of rapid beginnings and growth, cannot have deep roots and wide ramifications, so that the first storm destroys them, unless, as already said, the man who thus becomes a prince is of such great genius as to be able to take immediate steps for maintaining what fortune has thrown into his lap, and lay afterwards those foundations which others make before becoming princes.

With regard to these two methods of becoming a prince, —by ability or by good fortune, I will here adduce two examples which have occurred within our memory, those of Francesco Sforza and Cesare Borgia. Francesco, by appropriate means and through great abilities, from citizen became Duke of Milan, and what he had attained after a thousand difficulties he maintained with little trouble. On the other hand, Cesare Borgia, commonly called Duke Valentine, acquired the state by the influence of his father and lost it when that influence failed, and that although every measure was adopted by him and everything done that a prudent and capable man could do to establish himself firmly in a state that the arms and the favours of others had given him. For, as we have said, he who does not lay his foundations beforehand may by great abilities do so afterwards, although with great trouble to the architect and danger to the building. If, then, one considers the procedure of the duke, it will be seen how firm were the foundations he had laid to his future power, which I do not think it superfluous to examine, as I know of no better precepts for a new prince to follow than may be found in his actions; and if his measures were not successful, it was through no fault of his own but only by the most extraordinary malignity of fortune.

In wishing to aggrandise the duke his son, Alexander VI had to meet very great difficulties both present and future. In the first place, he saw no way of making him ruler of any state that was not a possession of the Church. He knew that the Duke of Milan and the Venetians would not consent in his attempt to take papal cities, because Faenza and Rimini were already under the protection of the Venetians. He saw, moreover, that the military forces of Italy, especially those which might have served him, were in the hands of those who would fear the greatness of the pope, and therefore he could not depend upon them, being all under the command of the Orsini and Colonna and their adherents. It was, therefore, necessary to disturb the existing condition and bring about disorders in the states of Italy in order to obtain secure mastery over a part of them; this was easy, for he found the Venetians, who, actuated by other motives, had invited the French into Italy, which he not only did not oppose, but facilitated by dissolving the first marriage of King Louis. The king came thus into Italy with the aid of the Venetians and the consent of Alexander, and had hardly arrived at Milan before the pope obtained troops from him for his enterprise in the Romagna, which was made possible for him thanks to the reputation of the king. The duke having thus obtained the Romagna and defeated the Colonna, was hindered by two things in maintaining it and proceeding further: the one, his forces, of which he doubted the fidelity; the other the will of France; that is to say, he feared lest the arms of the Orsini of which he had availed himself should fail him, and not only hinder him in obtaining more but take from him what he had already conquered, and he also feared that the king might do the same. He had evidence of this as regards the Orsini when, after taking Faenza, he assaulted Bologna and observed their backwardness in the assault. And as regards the king, he perceived his designs when, after taking the dukedom of Urbino, he attacked Tuscany, and the king made him desist from that enterprise. Whereupon the duke decided to depend no longer on the fortunes and arms of others. The first thing he did was to weaken the parties of the Orsini and Colonna in Rome by gaining all their adherents who were gentlemen and making them his own followers, by granting them large remuneration, and appointing them to commands and offices according to their rank, so that their attachment to their parties was extinguished in a few months, and entirely concentrated on the duke. After this he awaited an opportunity for crushing the chiefs of the Orsini, having already suppressed those of the Colonna family, and when the opportunity arrived he made good use of it, for the Orsini seeing at length that the greatness of the duke and of the Church meant their own ruin, convoked a diet at Magione in the Perugino. Hence sprang the rebellion of Urbino and the tumults in Romagna and infinite dangers to the duke, who overcame them all with the help of the French; and having regained his reputation, neither trusting France nor other foreign forces, in order not to venture on their alliance, he had recourse to stratagem. He dissembled his aims so well that the Orsini made their peace with him, being represented by Signor Paulo whose suspicions the duke disarmed with every courtesy, presenting him with robes, money, and horses, so that in their simplicity they were induced to come to Sinigaglia and fell into his hands. Having thus suppressed these leaders and made their partisans his friends, the duke had laid a very good foundation to his power, having all the Romagna with the duchy of Urbino, and having gained the favour of the inhabitants, who began to feel the benefit of his rule.

And as this part is worthy of note and of imitation by others, I will not omit mention of it. When he took the Romagna, it had previously been governed by weak rulers, who had rather despoiled their subjects than governed them, and given them more cause for disunion than for union, so that the province was a prey to robbery, assaults, and every kind of disorder. He, therefore, judged it necessary to give them a good government in order to make them peaceful and obedient to his rule. For this purpose he appointed Messer Remirro de Orco, a cruel and able man, to whom he gave the fullest authority. This man, in a short time, was highly successful in rendering the country orderly and united, whereupon the duke, not deeming such excessive authority expedient, lest it should become hateful, appointed a civil court of justice in the centre of the province under an excellent president, to which each city appointed its own advocate. And as he knew that the harshness of the past had engendered some amount of hatred, in order to purge the minds of the people and to win them over completely, he resolved to show that if any cruelty had taken place it was not by his orders, but through the harsh disposition of his minister. And having found the opportunity he had him cut in half and placed one morning in the public square at Cesena with a piece of wood and blood-stained knife by his side. The ferocity of this spectacle caused the people both satisfaction and amazement. But to return to where we left off.

The duke being now powerful and partly secured against present perils, being armed himself, and having in a great measure put down those neighbouring forces which might injure him, had now to get the respect of France, if he wished to proceed with his acquisitions, for he knew that the king, who had lately discovered his error, would not give him any help. He began therefore to seek fresh alliances and to vacillate with France on the occasion of the expedition that the French were undertaking towards the kingdom of Naples against the Spaniards, who were besieging Gaeta. His intention was to assure himself of them, which he would soon have succeeded in doing if Alexander had lived.

These were the measures taken by him with regard to the

present. As to the future, he feared that a new successor to the states of the Church might not be friendly to him and might seek to deprive him of what Alexander had given him, and he sought to provide against this in four ways. First, by destroying all who were of the blood of those ruling families which he had despoiled, in order to deprive the pope of any opportunity. Secondly, by gaining the friendship of the Roman nobles, so that he might through them hold as it were the pope in check. Thirdly, by obtaining as great a hold on the College as he could. Fourthly, by acquiring such power before the pope died as to be able to resist alone the first onslaught. Of these four things he had at the death of Alexander accomplished three, and the fourth he had almost accomplished. For of the dispossessed rulers he killed as many as he could lay hands on, and very few escaped; he had gained to his party the Roman nobles; and he had a great influence in the College. As to new possessions, he designed to become lord of Tuscany, and already possessed Perugia and Piombino, and had assumed the protectorate over Pisa; and as he had no longer to fear the French (for the French had been deprived of the kingdom of Naples by the Spaniards in such a way that both parties were obliged to buy his friendship) he seized Pisa. After this, Lucca and Siena at once yielded, partly through hate of the Florentines and partly through fear; the Florentines had no resources, so that, had he succeeded as he had done before, in the very year that Alexander died he would have gained such strength and renown as to be able to maintain himself without depending on the fortunes or strength of others, but solely by his own power and ability. But Alexander died five years after Cesare Borgia had first drawn his sword. He was left with only the state of Romagna firmly established, and all the other schemes in mid-air, between two very powerful and hostile armies, and suffering from a fatal illness. But the valour and ability of the duke were such, and he knew so well how to win over men or vanquish them, and so strong were the foundations that he had laid in this short time, that if he had not had those two armies upon him, or else had been in good health, he would have survived every difficulty. And that his foundations were good is seen from the fact that the Romagna waited for him more than a month; in Rome, although half dead, he remained secure, and although the Baglioni, Vitelli, and Orsini entered Rome they found no followers against him. He was able, if not to make pope whom he wished, at any rate to prevent a pope being created whom he did not wish. But if at the death of Alexander he had been well, everything would have been easy. And he told me on the day that Pope Julius II was elected, that he had thought of everything which might happen on the death of his father, and provided against everything, except that he had never thought that at his father's death he would be dying himself.

Reviewing thus all the actions of the duke, I find nothing to blame, on the contrary, I feel bound, as I have done, to hold him up as an example to be imitated by all who by fortune and with the arms of others have risen to power. For with his great courage and high ambition he could not have acted otherwise, and his designs were only frustrated by the short life of Alexander and his own illness. Whoever, therefore, deems it necessary in his new principality to secure himself against enemies, to gain friends, to conquer by force or fraud, to make himself beloved and feared by the people, followed and reverenced by the soldiers, to destroy those who can and may injure him, introduce innovations into old customs, to be severe and kind, magnanimous and liberal, suppress the old militia, create a new one, maintain the friendship of kings and princes in such a way that they are glad to benefit him and fear to injure him, such a one can find no better example than the actions of this man. The only thing he can be accused of is that in the creation of Julius II he made a bad choice; for, as has been said, not being able to choose his own pope, he could still prevent any one individual being made pope, and he ought never to have permitted any of those cardinals to be raised to the papacy whom he had injured, or who when pope would stand in fear of him. For men commit injuries either through fear or through hate. Those whom he had injured were, among others, San Pietro ad Vincula, Colonna, San Giorgio, and Ascanio. All the others, if elected to the pontificate, would have had to fear him except Rohan and the Spaniards; the latter through their relationship and obligations to him, the former from his great power, being related to the King of France. For these reasons the duke ought above all things to have created a Spaniard pope; and if unable, then he should have consented to Rohan being appointed and not San Pietro ad Vincula. And whoever thinks that in high personages new benefits cause old offences to be forgotten, makes a great mistake. The duke, therefore, erred in this choice, and it was the cause of his ultimate ruin.

CHAPTER IX
OF THE CIVIC PRINCIPALITY

But we now come to the case where a citizen becomes prince not through crime or intolerable violence, but by the favour of his fellow-citizens, which may be called a civic principality. To attain this position depends not entirely on worth or entirely on fortune, but rather on cunning assisted by fortune. One attains it by help of popular favour or by the favour of the aristocracy. For in every city these two opposite parties are to be found, arising from the desire of the populace to avoid the oppression of the great, and the desire of the great to command and oppress the people. And from these two opposing interests arises in the city one of the three effects: either absolute government, liberty, or licence. The former is created either by the populace or the nobility, depending on the relative opportunities of the two parties; for when the nobility see that they are unable to resist the people they unite in exalting one of their number and creating him prince, so as to be able to carry out their own designs under the shadow of his authority. The populace, on the other hand, when unable to resist the nobility, endeavour to exalt and create a prince in order to be protected by his authority. He who becomes prince by help of the nobility has greater difficulty in maintaining his power than he who is raised by the populace, for he is surrounded by those who think themselves his equals, and is thus unable to direct or command as he pleases. But one who is raised to leadership by popular favour finds himself alone, and has no one, or very few, who are not ready to obey him. Besides which, it is impossible to satisfy the nobility by fair dealing and without inflicting injury on others, whereas it is very easy to satisfy the mass of the people in this way. For the aim of the people is more honest than that of the nobility, the latter desiring to oppress, and the former merely to avoid oppression. It must also be added that the prince can never insure himself against a hostile populace on account of their number, but he can against the hostility of the great, as they are but few. The worst that a prince has to expect from a hostile people is to be abandoned, but from hostile nobles he has to fear not only desertion but their active opposition, and as they are more far-seeing and more cunning, they are always in time to save themselves and take sides with the one who they expect will conquer. The prince is, moreover, obliged to live always with the same people, but he can easily do without the same nobility, being able to make and unmake them at any time, and improve their position or deprive them of it as he pleases.

And to throw further light on this part of my argument, I would say, that the nobles are to be considered in two different manners; that is, they are either to be ruled so as to make them entirely dependent on your fortunes, or else not. Those that are thus bound to you and are not rapacious, must be honoured and loved; those who stand aloof must be considered in two ways, they either do this through pusillanimity and natural want of courage, and in this case you ought to make use of them, and especially such as are of good counsel, so that they may honour you in prosperity and in adversity you have not to fear them. But when they are not bound to you of set purpose and for ambitious ends, it is a sign that they think more of themselves than of you; and from such men the prince must guard himself and look upon them as secret enemies, who will help to ruin him when in adversity.

One, however, who becomes prince by favour of the populace, must maintain its friendship, which he will find easy, the people asking nothing but not to be oppressed. But one who against the people's wishes becomes prince by favour of the nobles, should above all endeavour to gain the favour of the people; this will be easy to him if he protects them. And as men, who receive good from whom they expected evil, feel under a greater obligation to their benefactor, so the populace will soon become even better disposed towards him than if he had become prince through their favour. The prince can win their favour in many ways, which vary according to circumstances, for which no certain rule can be given, and will therefore be passed over. I will only say, in conclusion, that it is necessary for a prince to possess the friendship of the people; otherwise he has no resource in times of adversity.

Nabis, prince of the Spartans, sustained a siege by the whole of Greece and a victorious Roman army, and defended his country against them and maintained his own position. It sufficed when the danger arose for him to make sure of a few, which would not have sufficed if the populace had been hostile to him. And let no one oppose my opinion in this by quoting the trite proverb, "He who builds on the people, builds on mud"; because that is true when a private citizen relies upon the people and persuades himself that they will liberate him if he is oppressed by enemies or by the magistrates; in this case he might often find himself deceived, as were in Rome the Gracchi and in Florence Messer Georgio Scali. But when it is a prince who founds himself on this basis, one who can command and is a man of courage, and does not get frightened in adversity, and does not neglect other preparations, and one who by his own valour and measures animates the mass of the people, he will not find himself deceived by them, and he will find that he has laid his foundations well.

Usually these principalities are in danger when the prince from the position of a civil ruler changes to an absolute one, for these princes either command themselves or by means of magistrates. In the latter case their position is weaker and more dangerous, for they are at the mercy of those citizens who are appointed magistrates, who can, especially in times of adversity, with great facility deprive them of their position, either by acting against them or by not obeying them. The prince is not in time, in such dangers, to assume absolute authority, for the citizens and subjects who are accustomed to take their orders from the magistrates are not ready in these emergencies to obey his, and he will always in difficult times lack men whom he can rely on. Such a prince cannot base himself on what he sees in quiet times, when the citizens have need of the state; for then every one is full of promises and each one is ready to die for him when death is far off; but in adversity, when the state has need of citizens, then he will find but few. And this experience is the more dangerous, in that it can only be had once. Therefore a wise prince will seek means by which his subjects will always and in every possible condition of things have need of his government, and then they will always be faithful to him.

CHAPTER X
HOW THE STRENGTH OF ALL STATES SHOULD BE MEASURED

In examining the character of these principalities it is necessary to consider another point, namely, whether the prince has such a position as to be able in case of need to maintain himself alone, or whether he has always need of the protection of others. The better to explain this I would say, that I consider those capable of maintaining themselves alone who can, through abundance of men or money, put together a sufficient army, and hold the field against any one who assails them; and I consider to have need of others, those who cannot take the field against their enemies, but are obliged to take refuge within their walls and stand on the defensive. We have already discussed the former case and will speak of it in future as occasion arises. In the second case there is nothing to be said except to encourage such a prince to provision and fortify his own town, and not to trouble about the surrounding country. And whoever has strongly fortified his town and, as regards the government of his subjects, has proceeded as we have already described and will further relate, will be attacked with great reluctance, for men are always averse to enterprises in which they foresee difficulties, and it can never appear easy to attack one who has his town stoutly defended and is not hated by the people.

The cities of Germany are absolutely free, have little surrounding country, and obey the emperor when they choose, and they do not fear him or any other potentate that they have about them. They are fortified in such a manner that every one thinks that to reduce them would be tedious and difficult, for they all have the necessary moats and bastions, sufficient artillery, and always keep food, drink, and fuel for one year in the public storehouses. Beyond which, to keep the lower classes satisfied, and without loss to the commonwealth, they have always enough means to give them work for one year in these employments which form the nerve and life of the town, and in the industries by which the lower classes live. Military exercises are still held in high reputation, and many regulations are in force for maintaining them.

A prince, therefore, who possesses a strong city and does not make himself hated, cannot be assaulted; and if he were to be so, the assailant would be obliged to retire shamefully; for so many things change, that it is almost impossible for any one to maintain a siege for a year with his armies idle. And to those who urge that the people, having their possessions outside and seeing them burnt, will not have patience, and the long siege and self-interest will make them forget their prince, I reply that a powerful and courageous prince will always overcome those difficulties by now raising the hopes of his subjects that the evils will not last long, now impressing them with fear of the enemy's cruelty, now by dextrously assuring himself of those who appear too bold. Besides which, the enemy would naturally burn and ravage the country on first arriving and at the time when men's minds are still hot and eager to defend themselves, and therefore the prince has still less to fear, for after some time, when people have cooled down, the damage is done, the evil has been suffered, and there is no remedy, so that they are the more ready to unite with their prince, as it appears that he is under an obligation to them, their houses having been burnt and their possessions ruined in his defence.

It is the nature of men to be as much bound by the benefits that they confer as by those they receive. From which it follows that, everything considered, a prudent prince will not find it difficult to uphold the courage of his subjects both at the commencement and during a state of siege, if he possesses provisions and means to defend himself.

CHAPTER XV

OF THE THINGS FOR WHICH MEN, AND ESPECIALLY PRINCES,
ARE PRAISED OR BLAMED

It now remains to be seen what are the methods and rules for a prince as regards his subjects and friends. And as I know that many have written of this, I fear that my writing about it may be deemed presumptuous, differing as I do, especially in this matter, from the opinions of others. But my intention being to write something of use to those who understand, it appears to me more proper to go to the real truth of the matter than to its imagination; and many have imagined republics and principalities which have never been seen or known to exist in reality; for how we live is so far removed from how we ought to live, that he who abandons what is done for what ought to be done, will rather learn to bring about his own ruin than his preservation. A man who wishes to make a profession of goodness in everything must necessarily come to grief among so many who are not good. Therefore it is necessary for a prince, who wishes to maintain himself, to learn how not to be good, and to use this knowledge and not use it, according to the necessity of the case.

Leaving on one side, then, those things which concern only an imaginary prince, and speaking of those that are real, I state that all men, and especially princes, who are placed at a greater height, are reputed for certain qualities which bring them either praise or blame. Thus one is considered liberal, another *misero* or miserly (using a Tuscan term, seeing that *avaro* with us still means one who is rapaciously acquisitive and *misero* one who makes grudging use of his own); one a free giver, another rapacious; one cruel, another merciful; one a breaker of his word, another trustworthy; one effeminate and pusillanimous, another fierce and high-spirited; one humane, another haughty; one lascivious, another chaste; one frank, another astute; one hard, another easy; one serious, another frivolous; one religious, another an unbeliever, and so on. I know that every one will admit that it would be highly praiseworthy in a prince to possess all the above-named qualities that are reputed good, but as they cannot all be possessed or observed, human conditions not permitting of it, it is necessary that he should be prudent enough to avoid the scandal of those vices which would lose him the state, and guard himself if possible against those which will not lose it him, but if not able to, he can indulge them with less scruple. And yet he must not mind incurring the scandal of those vices, without which it would be difficult to save the state, for if one considers well, it will be found that some things which seem virtues would, if followed, lead to one's ruin, and some others which appear vices result in one's greater security and well-being.

CHAPTER XVI

OF LIBERALITY AND NIGGARDLINESS

Beginning now with the first qualities above named, I say that it would be well to be considered liberal; nevertheless liberality such as the world understands it will injure you, because if used virtuously and in the proper way, it will not be known, and you will incur the disgrace of the contrary vice. But one who wishes to obtain the reputation of liberality among men, must not omit every kind of sumptuous display, and to such an extent that a prince of this character will consume by such means all his resources, and will be at last compelled, if he wishes to maintain his name for liberality, to impose heavy taxes on his people, become extortionate, and do everything possible to obtain money. This will make his subjects begin to hate him, and he will be little esteemed being poor, so that having by this liberality injured many and benefited but few, he will feel the first little disturbance and be endangered by every peril. If he recognises this and wishes to change his system, he incurs at once the charge of niggardliness.

A prince, therefore, not being able to exercise this virtue of liberality without risk if it be known, must not, if he be prudent, object to be called miserly. In course of time he will be thought more liberal, when it is seen that by his parsimony his revenue is sufficient, that he can defend himself against those who make war on him, and undertake enterprises without burdening his people, so that he is really liberal to all those from whom he does not take, who are infinite in number, and niggardly to all to whom he does not give, who are few. In our times we have seen nothing great done except by those who have been esteemed niggardly; the others have all been ruined. Pope Julius II, although he had made use of a reputation for liberality in order to attain the papacy, did not seek to retain it afterwards, so that he might be able to wage war. The present King of France has carried on so many wars without imposing an extraordinary tax, because his extra expenses were covered by the parsimony he had so long practised. The present King of Spain, if he had been thought liberal, would not have engaged in and been successful in so many enterprises.

For these reasons a prince must care little for the reputation of being a miser, if he wishes to avoid robbing his subjects, if he wishes to be able to defend himself, to avoid becoming poor and contemptible, and not to be forced to become rapacious; this niggardliness is one of those vices which enable him to reign. If it is said that Cæsar attained the empire through liberality, and that many others have reached the highest positions through being liberal or being thought so, I would reply that you are either a prince already or else on the way to become one. In the first case, this liberality is harmful; in the second, it is certainly necessary to be considered liberal. Cæsar was one of those who wished to attain the mastery over Rome, but if after attaining it he had lived and had not moderated his expenses, he would have destroyed that empire. And should any one reply that there have been many princes, who have done great things with their armies, who have been thought extremely liberal, I would answer by saying that the prince may either spend his own wealth and that of his subjects or the wealth of others. In the first case he must be sparing, but for the rest he must not neglect to be very liberal. The liberality is very necessary to a prince who marches with his armies, and lives by plunder, sack and ransom, and is dealing with the wealth of others, for without it he would not be followed by his soldiers. And you may be very generous indeed with what is not the property of yourself or your subjects, as were Cyrus, Cæsar, and Alexander; for spending the wealth of others will not diminish your reputation, but increase it, only spending your own resources will injure you. There is nothing which destroys itself so much as liberality, for by using it you lose the power of using it, and become either poor and despicable, or, to escape poverty, rapacious and hated. And of all things that a prince must guard against, the most important are being despicable or hated, and liberality will lead you to one or other of these conditions. It is, therefore, wiser to have the name of a miser, which produces disgrace without hatred, than to incur of necessity the name of being rapacious, which produces both disgrace and hatred.

CHAPTER XVII
OF CRUELTY AND CLEMENCY, AND WHETHER IT IS BETTER TO BE LOVED OR FEARED

Proceeding to the other qualities before named, I say that every prince must desire to be considered merciful and not cruel. He must, however, take care not to misuse this mercifulness. Cesare Borgia was considered cruel, but his cruelty had brought order to the Romagna, united it, and reduced it to peace and fealty. If this is considered well, it will be seen that he was really much more merciful than the Florentine people, who, to avoid the name of cruelty, allowed Pistoia to be destroyed. A prince, therefore, must not mind incurring the charge of cruelty for the purpose of keeping his subjects united and faithful; for, with a very few examples, he will be more merciful than those who, from excess of tenderness, allow disorders to arise, from whence spring bloodshed and rapine; for these as a rule injure the whole community, while the executions carried out by the prince injure only individuals. And of all princes, it is impossible for a new prince to escape the reputation of cruelty, new states being always full of dangers. Wherefore Virgil through the mouth of Dido says:

Res dura, et regni novitas me talia cogunt
Moliri, et late fines custode tueri.

Nevertheless, he must be cautious in believing and acting,
and must not be afraid of his own shadow, and must proceed
in a temperate manner with prudence and humanity, so that
too much confidence does not render him incautious, and too
much diffidence does not render him intolerant.

From this arises the question whether it is better to be loved
more than feared, or feared more than loved. The reply is,
that one ought to be both feared and loved, but as it is difficult
for the two to go together, it is much safer to be feared than
loved, if one of the two has to be wanting. For it may be said
of men in general that they are ungrateful, voluble, dissem-
blers, anxious to avoid danger, and covetous of gain; as long
as you benefit them, they are entirely yours; they offer you
their blood, their goods, their life, and their children, as I have
before said, when the necessity is remote; but when it approaches, they revolt. And the prince who has relied solely
on their words, without making other preparations, is ruined;
for the friendship which is gained by purchase and not through
grandeur and nobility of spirit is bought but not secured, and
at a pinch is not to be expended in your service. And men
have less scruple in offending one who makes himself loved
than one who makes himself feared; for love is held by a
chain of obligation which, men being selfish, is broken whenever it serves their purpose; but fear is maintained by a dread
of punishment which never fails.

Still, a prince should make himself feared in such a way
that if he does not gain love, he at any rate avoids hatred;
for fear and the absence of hatred may well go together, and
will be always attained by one who abstains from interfering
with the property of his citizens and subjects or with their
women. And when he is obliged to take the life of any one,
let him do so when there is a proper justification and manifest
reason for it; but above all he must abstain from taking the
property of others, for men forget more easily the death of
their father than the loss of their patrimony. Then also pre-
texts for seizing property are never wanting, and one who
begins to live by rapine will always find some reason for taking
the goods of others, whereas causes for taking life are rarer
and more fleeting.

But when the prince is with his army and has a large number of soldiers under his control, then it is extremely necessary

that he should not mind being thought cruel; for without this reputation he could not keep an army united or disposed to any duty. Among the noteworthy actions of Hannibal is numbered this, that although he had an enormous army, composed of men of all nations and fighting in foreign countries, there never arose any dissension either among them or against the prince, either in good fortune or in bad. This could not be due to anything but his inhuman cruelty, which together with his infinite other virtues, made him always venerated and terrible in the sight of his soldiers, and without it his other virtues would not have sufficed to produce that effect. Thoughtless writers admire on the one hand his actions, and on the other blame the principal cause of them.

And that it is true that his other virtues would not have sufficed may be seen from the case of Scipio (famous not only in regard to his own times, but all times of which memory remains), whose armies rebelled against him in Spain, which arose from nothing but his excessive kindness, which allowed more licence to the soldiers than was consonant with military discipline. He was reproached with this in the senate by Fabius Maximus, who called him a corrupter of the Roman militia. Locri having been destroyed by one of Scipio's officers was not revenged by him, nor was the insolence of that officer punished, simply by reason of his easy nature; so much so, that some one wishing to excuse him in the senate, said that there were many men who knew rather how not to err, than how to correct the errors of others. This disposition would in time have tarnished the fame and glory of Scipio had he persevered in it under the empire, but living under the rule of the senate this harmful quality was not only concealed but became a glory to him.

I conclude, therefore, with regard to being feared and loved, that men love at their own free will, but fear at the will of the prince, and that a wise prince must rely on what is in his power and not on what is in the power of others, and he must only contrive to avoid incurring hatred, as has been explained.

CHAPTER XVIII

IN WHAT WAY PRINCES MUST KEEP FAITH

How laudable it is for a prince to keep good faith and live with integrity, and not with astuteness, every one knows. Still the experience of our times shows those princes to have done great things who have had little regard for good faith, and have been able by astuteness to cónfuse men's brains, and who have ultimately overcome those who have made loyalty their foundation.

You must know, then, that there are two methods of fighting, the one by law, the other by force: the first method is that of men, the second of beasts; but as the first method is often insufficient, one must have recourse to the second. It is therefore necessary for a prince to know well how to use both the beast and the man. This was covertly taught to rulers by ancient writers, who relate how Achilles and many others of those ancient princes were given to Chiron the centaur to be brought up and educated under his discipline. The parable of this semi-animal, semi-human teacher is meant to indicate that a prince must know how to use both natures, and that the one without the other is not durable.

A prince being thus obliged to know well how to act as a beast must imitate the fox and the lion, for the lion cannot protect himself from traps, and the fox cannot defend himself from wolves. One must therefore be a fox to recognize traps, and a lion to frighten wolves. Those that wish to be only lions do not understand this. Therefore, a prudent ruler ought not to keep faith when by so doing it would be against his interest, and when the reasons which made him bind himself no longer exist. If men were all good, this precept would not be a good one; but as they are bad, and would not observe their faith with you, so you are not bound to keep faith with them. Nor have legitimate grounds ever failed a prince who wished to show colourable excuse for the non-fulfilment of his promise. Of this one could furnish an infinite number of modern examples, and show how many times peace has been broken, and how many promises rendered worthless, by the faithlessness of princes, and those that have been best able to imitate the fox have succeeded best. But it is necessary to be able to disguise this character well, and to be a great feigner and dissembler; and men are so simple and so ready to obey present necessities, that one who deceives will always find those who allow themselves to be deceived.

I will only mention one modern instance. Alexander VI did nothing else but deceive men, he thought of nothing else, and found the occasion for it; no man was ever more able to give assurances, or affirmed things with stronger oaths, and no man observed them less; however, he always succeeded in his deceptions, as he well knew this aspect of things.

It is not, therefore, necessary for a prince to have all the above-named qualities, but it is very necessary to seem to have them. I would even be bold to say that to possess them and always to observe them is dangerous, but to appear to possess them is useful. Thus it is well to seem merciful, faithful, humane, sincere, religious, and also to be so; but you must have the mind so disposed that when it is needful to be otherwise you may be able to change to the opposite qualities. And it must be understood that a prince, and especially a new prince, cannot observe all those things which are considered good in men, being often obliged, in order to maintain the state, to act against faith, against charity, against humanity, and against religion. And, therefore, he must have a mind disposed to adapt itself according to the wind, and as the variations of fortune dictate, and, as I said before, not deviate from what is good, if possible, but be able to do evil if constrained.

A prince must take great care that nothing goes out of his mouth which is not full of the above-named five qualities, and, to see and hear him, he should seem to be all mercy, faith, integrity, humanity, and religion. And nothing is more necessary than to seem to have this last quality, for men in general judge more by the eyes than by the hands, for every one can see, but very few have to feel. Everybody sees what you appear to be, few feel what you are, and those few will not dare to oppose themselves to the many, who have the majesty of the state to defend them; and in the actions of men, and especially of princes, from which there is no appeal, the end justifies the means. Let a prince therefore aim at conquering and maintaining the state, and the means will always be judged honourable and praised by every one, for the vulgar is always taken by appearances and the issue of the event; and the world consists only of the vulgar, and the few who are not vulgar are isolated when the many have a rallying point in the prince. A certain prince of the present time, whom it is well not to name, never does anything but preach peace and good faith, but he is really a great enemy to both, and either of them, had he observed them, would have lost him state or reputation on many occasions.

CHAPTER XIX
THAT WE MUST AVOID BEING DESPISED AND HATED

But as I have now spoken of the most important of the qualities in question, I will now deal briefly and generally with the rest. The prince must, as already stated, avoid those things which will make him hated or despised; and whenever he succeeds in this, he will have done his part, and will find no danger in other vices. He will chiefly become hated, as I said, by being rapacious, and usurping the property and women of his subjects, which he must abstain from doing, and whenever one does not attack the property or honour of the generality of men, they will live contented; and one will only have to combat the ambition of a few, who can be easily held in check in many ways. He is rendered despicable by being thought changeable, frivolous, effeminate, timid, and irresolute; which a prince must guard against as a rock of danger, and so contrive that his actions show grandeur, spirit, gravity, and fortitude; and as to the government of his subjects, let his sentence be irrevocable, and let him adhere to his decisions so that no one may think of deceiving or cozening him.

The prince who creates such an opinion of himself gets a great reputation, and it is very difficult to conspire against one who has a great reputation, and he will not easily be attacked, so long as it is known that he is capable and reverenced by his subjects. For a prince must have two kinds of fear: one internal as regards his subjects, one external as regards foreign powers. From the latter he can defend himself with good arms and good friends, and he will always have good friends if he has good arms; and internal matters will always remain quiet, if they are not perturbed by conspiracy and there is no disturbance from without; and even if external powers sought to attack him, if he has ruled and lived as I have described, he will always if he stands firm, be able to sustain every shock, as I have shown that Nabis the Spartan did. But with regard to the subjects, if not acted on from outside, it is still to be feared lest they conspire in secret, from which the prince may guard himself well by avoiding hatred and contempt, and keeping the people satisfied with him, which it is necessary to accomplish, as has been related at length. And one of the most potent remedies that a prince has against conspiracies, is that of not being hated by the mass of the people; for whoever conspires always believes that he will satisfy the people by the death of their prince; but if he thought to offend them by doing this, he would fear to engage in such an undertaking, for the difficulties that conspirators have to meet are infinite. Experience shows that there have been very many conspiracies, but few have turned out well, for whoever conspires cannot act alone, and cannot find companions except among those who are discontented; and as soon as you have disclosed your intention to a malcontent, you give him the means of satisfying himself, for by revealing it he can hope to secure everything he wants; to such an extent that seeing a certain gain by doing this, and seeing on the other hand only a doubtful one and full of danger, he must either be a rare friend to you or else a very bitter enemy to the prince if he keeps faith with you. And to express the matter in a few words, I say, that on the side of the conspirator there is nothing but fear, jealousy, suspicion, and dread of punishment which frightens him; and on the side of the prince there is the majesty of government, the laws, the protection of friends and of the state which guard him. When to these things is added the goodwill of the people, it is impossible that any one should have the temerity to conspire. For whereas generally a conspirator has to fear before the execution of his plot, in this case, having the people for an enemy, he must also fear after his crime is accomplished, and thus he is not able to hope for any refuge.

Numberless instances might be given of this, but I will content myself with one which took place within the memory of our fathers. Messer Annibale Bentivogli, Prince of Bologna, ancestor of the present Messer Annibale, was killed by the Canneschi, who conspired against him. He left no relations but Messer Giovanni, who was then an infant, but after the murder the people rose up and killed all the Canneschi. This arose from the popular goodwill that the house of Bentivogli enjoyed at that time, which was so great that, as there was nobody left after the death of Annibale who could govern the state, the Bolognese hearing that there was one of the Bentivogli family in Florence, who had till then been thought the son of a blacksmith, came to fetch him and gave him the government of the city, and it was governed by him until Messer Giovanni was old enough to assume the government.

I conclude, therefore, that a prince need trouble little about conspiracies when the people are well disposed, but when they are hostile and hold him in hatred, then he must fear everything and everybody. Well-ordered states and wise princes have studied diligently not to drive the nobles to desperation, and to satisfy the populace and keep it contented, for this is one of the most important matters that a prince has to deal with. . . .

DISCOURSES
ON THE
FIRST TEN BOOKS OF TITUS LIVIUS

Translated from the Italian
by Christian E. Detmold

FIRST BOOK

INTRODUCTION

Although the envious nature of men, so prompt to blame
and so slow to praise, makes the discovery and introduction
of any new principles and systems as dangerous almost as the
exploration of unknown seas and continents, yet, animated by
that desire which impels me to do what may prove for the
common benefit of all, I have resolved to open a new route,
which has not yet been followed by any one, and may prove
difficult and troublesome, but may also bring me some reward
in the approbation of those who will kindly appreciate my
efforts.

And if my poor talents, my little experience of the present
and insufficient study of the past, should make the result of
my labors defective and of little utility, I shall at least have
shown the way to others, who will carry out my views with
greater ability, eloquence, and judgment, so that if I do not
merit praise, I ought at least not to incur censure.

When we consider the general respect for antiquity, and
how often—to say nothing of other examples—a great price is
paid for some fragments of an antique statue, which we are
anxious to possess to ornament our houses with, or to give to
artists who strive to imitate them in their own works; and when
we see, on the other hand, the wonderful examples which the
history of ancient kingdoms and republics presents to us, the

prodigies of virtue and of wisdom displayed by the kings, captains, citizens, and legislators who have sacrificed themselves for their country,—when we see these, I say, more admired than imitated, or so much neglected that not the least trace of this ancient virtue remains, we cannot but be at the same time as much surprised as afflicted. The more so as in the differences which arise between citizens, or in the maladies to which they are subjected, we see these same people have recourse to the judgments and the remedies prescribed by the ancients. The civil laws are in fact nothing but decisions given by their jurisconsults, and which, reduced to a system, direct our modern jurists in their decisions. And what is the science of medicine, but the experience of ancient physicians, which their successors have taken for their guide? And yet to found a republic, maintain states, to govern a kingdom, organize an army, conduct a war, dispense justice, and extend empires, you will find neither prince, nor republic, nor captain, nor citizen, who has recourse to the examples of antiquity! This neglect, I am persuaded, is due less to the weakness to which the vices of our education have reduced the world, than to the evils caused by the proud indolence which prevails in most of the Christian states, and to the lack of real knowledge of history, the true sense of which is not known, or the spirit of which they do not comprehend. Thus the majority of those who read it take pleasure only in the variety of the events which history relates, without ever thinking of imitating the noble actions, deeming that not only difficult, but impossible; as though heaven, the sun, the elements, and men had changed the order of their motions and power, and were different from what they were in ancient times.

Wishing, therefore, so far as in me lies, to draw mankind from this error, I have thought it proper to write upon those books of Titus Livius that have come to us entire despite the malice of time; touching upon all those matters which, after a comparison between the ancient and modern events, may seem to me necessary to facilitate their proper understanding. In this way those who read my remarks may derive those advantages which should be the aim of all study of history; and although the undertaking is difficult, yet, aided by those who have encouraged me in this attempt, I hope to carry it sufficiently far, so that but little may remain for others to carry it to its destined end.

CHAPTER I

OF THE BEGINNING OF CITIES IN GENERAL, AND ESPECIALLY
THAT OF THE CITY OF ROME

Those who read what the beginning of Rome was, and what
her lawgivers and her organization, will not be astonished that
so much virtue should have maintained itself during so many
centuries; and that so great an empire should have sprung
from it afterwards. To speak first of her origin, we will premise that all cities are founded either by natives of the country
or by strangers. The little security which the natives found in
living dispersed; the impossibility for each to resist isolated,
either because of the situation or because of their small number, the attacks of any enemy that might present himself; the
difficulty of uniting in time for defence at his approach, and
the necessity of abandoning the greater number of their re-
treats, which quickly became a prize to the assailant,—such
were the motives that caused the first inhabitants of a country
to build cities for the purpose of escaping these dangers. They
resolved, of their own accord, or by the advice of some one
who had most authority amongst them, to live together in some
place of their selection that might offer them greater conveniences and greater facility of defence. Thus, amongst many
others were Athens and Venice; the first was built under the
authority of Theseus, who had gathered the dispersed inhabitants; and the second owed its origin to the fact that several
tribes had taken refuge on the little islands situated at the
head of the Adriatic Sea, to escape from war, and from the
Barbarians who after the fall of the Roman Empire had overrun Italy. These refugees of themselves, and without any prince
to govern them, began to live under such laws as seemed to
them best suited to maintain their new state. In this they succeeded, happily favored by the long peace, for which they
were indebted to their situation upon a sea without issue, where
the people that ravaged Italy could not harass them, being
without any ships. Thus from that small beginning they attained that degree of power in which we see them now.

The second case is when a city is built by strangers; these
may be either freemen, or subjects of a republic or of a prince,
who, to relieve their states from an excessive population, or
to defend a newly acquired territory which they wish to pre-

serve without expense, send colonies there. The Romans
founded many cities in this way within their empire. Sometimes cities are built by a prince, not for the purpose of living
there, but merely as monuments to his glory; such was Alexandria, built by Alexander the Great. But as all these cities are
at their very origin deprived of liberty, they rarely succeed in
making great progress, or in being counted amongst the great
powers. Such was the origin of Florence; for it was built either
by the soldiers of Sylla, or perhaps by the inhabitants of Mount
Fiesole, who, trusting to the long peace that prevailed in the
reign of Octavian, were attracted to the plains along the Arno.
Florence, thus built under the Roman Empire, could in the
beginning have no growth except what depended on the will
of its master.

The founders of cities are independent when they are people who, under the leadership of some prince, or by themselves, have been obliged to fly from pestilence, war, or famine, that was desolating their native country, and are seeking
a new home. These either inhabit the cities of the country of
which they take possession, as Moses did; or they build new
ones, as was done by Æneas. In such case we are able to appreciate the talents of the founder and the success of his work,
which is more or less remarkable according as he, in founding
the city, displays more or less wisdom and skill. Both the one
and the other are recognized by the selection of the place
where he has located the city, and by the nature of the laws
which he establishes in it. And as men work either from necessity or from choice, and as it has been observed that virtue
has more sway where labor is the result of necessity rather
than of choice, it is a matter of consideration whether it
might not be better to select for the establishment of a city
a sterile region, where the people, compelled by necessity to
be industrious, and therefore less given to idleness, would be
more united, and less exposed by the poverty of the country
to occasions for discord; as was the case with Ragusa, and
several other cities that were built upon an ungrateful soil.
Such a selection of site would doubtless be more useful and
wise if men were content with what they possess, and did not
desire to exercise command over others.

Now, as people cannot make themselves secure except by
being powerful, it is necessary in the founding of a city to
avoid a sterile country. On the contrary, a city should be
placed rather in a region where the fertility of the soil affords
the means of becoming great, and of acquiring strength to

repel all who might attempt to attack it, or oppose the development of its power. As to the idleness which the fertility of a country tends to encourage, the laws should compel men to labor where the sterility of the soil does not do it; as was done by those skilful and sagacious legislators who have inhabited very agreeable and fertile countries, such as are apt to make men idle and unfit for the exercise of valor. These by way of an offset to the pleasures and softness of the climate, imposed upon their soldiers the rigors of a strict discipline and severe exercises, so that they became better warriors than what nature produces in the harshest climates and most sterile countries. Amongst these legislators we may cite the founders of the kingdom of Egypt: despite the charms of the climate, the severity of the institutions there formed excellent men; and if great antiquity had not buried their names in oblivion, we should see that they deserved more praise than Alexander the Great and many others of more recent memory. And whoever has examined the government of the Pachas of Egypt and the discipline of their Mameluke militia before it was destroyed by the Sultan Selim of Turkey, will have seen how much they dreaded idleness, and by what variety of exercises and by what severe laws they prevented in their soldiers that effeminacy which is the natural fruit of the softness of their climate.

I say, then, that for the establishment of a city it is wisest to select the most fertile spot, especially as the laws can prevent the ill effects that would otherwise result from that very fertility.

When Alexander the Great wished to build a city that should serve as a monument to his glory, his architect, Dinocrates, pointed out to him how he could build a city on Mount Athos, which place he said, besides being very strong, could be so arranged as to give the city the appearance of the human form, which would make it a wonder worthy of the greatness of its founder. Alexander having asked him what the inhabitants were to live upon, he replied, "That I have not thought of"; at which Alexander smiled, and, leaving Mount Athos as it was, he built Alexandria, where the inhabitants would be glad to remain on account of the richness of the country and the advantages which the proximity of the Nile and the sea afforded them.

If we accept the opinion that Æneas was the founder of Rome, then we must count that city as one of those built by strangers; but if Romulus is taken as its founder, then must it be classed with those built by the natives of the country. Either way it will be seen that Rome was from the first free and independent; and we shall also see (as we shall show further on) to how many privations the laws of Romulus, of Numa, and of others subjected its inhabitants; so that neither the fertility of the soil, nor the proximity of the sea, nor their many victories, nor the greatness of the Empire, could corrupt them during several centuries, and they maintained there more virtues than have ever been seen in any other republic.

The great things which Rome achieved, and of which Titus Livius has preserved the memory, have been the work either of the government or of private individuals; and as they relate either to the affairs of the interior or of the exterior, I shall begin to discourse of those internal operations of the government which I believe to be most noteworthy, and shall point out their results. This will be the subject of the discourses that will compose this First Book, or rather First Part.

CHAPTER II
OF THE DIFFERENT KINDS OF REPUBLICS, AND OF WHAT KIND THE ROMAN REPUBLIC WAS

I will leave aside what might be said of cities which from their very birth have been subject to a foreign power, and will speak only of those whose origin has been independent, and which from the first governed themselves by their own laws, whether as republics or as principalities, and whose constitution and laws have differed as their origin. Some have had at the very beginning, or soon after, a legislator, who, like Lycurgus with the Lacedæmonians, gave them by a single act all the laws they needed. Others have owed theirs to chance and to events, and have received their laws at different times, as Rome did. It is a great good fortune for a republic to have a legislator sufficiently wise to give her laws so regulated that, without the necessity of correcting them, they afford security to those who live under them. Sparta observed her laws for more than eight hundred years without altering them and without experiencing a single dangerous disturbance. Unhappy, on the contrary, is that republic which, not having at the beginning fallen into the hands of a sagacious and skilful legislator, is herself obliged to reform her laws. More unhappy still is that republic which from the first has diverged from a good constitution. And that republic is furthest from it whose vicious institutions impede her progress, and make her leave the right path that leads to a good end; for those who are in that condition can hardly ever be brought into the right road. Those republics, on the other hand, that started without having even a perfect constitution, but made a fair beginning, and are capable of improvement,—such republics, I say, may perfect themselves by the aid of events. It is very true, however, that such reforms are never effected without danger, for the majority of men never willingly adopt any new law tending to change the constitution of the state, unless the necessity of the change is clearly demonstrated; and as such a necessity cannot make itself felt without being accompanied with danger, the republic may easily be destroyed before having perfected its constitution. That of Florence is a complete proof of this: reorganized after the revolt of Arezzo, in 1502, it was overthrown after the taking of Prato, in 1512.

Having proposed to myself to treat of the kind of government established at Rome, and of the events that led to its perfection, I must at the beginning observe that some of the writers on politics distinguished three kinds of government, viz. the monarchical, the aristocratic, and the democratic; and maintain that the legislators of a people must choose from these three the one that seems to them most suitable. Other authors, wiser according to the opinion of many, count six kinds of governments, three of which are very bad, and three good in themselves, but so liable to be corrupted that they become absolutely bad. The three good ones are those which we have just named; the three bad ones result from the degradation of the other three, and each of them resembles its corresponding original, so that the transition from the one to the other is very easy. Thus monarchy becomes tyranny; aristocracy degenerates into oligarchy; and the popular government lapses readily into licentiousness. So that a legislator who gives to a state which he founds, either of these three forms of government, constitutes it but for a brief time; for no precautions can prevent either one of the three that are reputed good, from degenerating into its opposite kind; so great are in these the attractions and resemblances between the good and the evil.

Chance has given birth to these different kinds of governments amongst men; for at the beginning of the world the inhabitants were few in number, and lived for a time dispersed, like beasts. As the human race increased, the necessity for uniting themselves for defence made itself felt; the better to attain this object, they chose the strongest and most courageous from amongst themselves and placed him at their head, promising to obey him. Thence they began to know the good and the honest, and to distinguish them from the bad and vicious; for seeing a man injure his benefactor aroused at once two sentiments in every heart, hatred against the ingrate and love for the benefactor. They blamed the first, and on the contrary honored those the more who showed themselves grateful, for each felt that he in turn might be subject to a like wrong; and to prevent similar evils, they set to work to make laws, and to institute punishments for those who contravened them. Such was the origin of justice. This caused them, when they had afterwards to choose a prince, neither to look to the strongest nor bravest, but to the wisest and most just. But when they began to make sovereignty hereditary and non-elective, the children quickly degenerated from their fathers; and, so far from trying to equal their virtues, they considered that a prince had nothing else to do than to excel all the rest in luxury, indulgence, and every other variety of pleasure. The prince consequently soon drew upon himself the general hatred. An object of hatred, he naturally felt fear; fear in turn dictated to him precautions and wrongs, and thus tyranny quickly developed itself. Such were the beginning and causes of disorders, conspiracies, and plots against the sovereigns, set on foot, not by the feeble and timid, but by those citizens who, surpassing the others in grandeur of soul, in wealth, and in courage, could not submit to the outrages and excesses of their princes.

Under such powerful leaders the masses armed themselves against the tyrant, and, after having rid themselves of him, submitted to these chiefs as their liberators. These, abhorring the very name of prince, constituted themselves a new government; and at first, bearing in mind the past tyranny, they governed in strict accordance with the laws which they had established themselves; preferring public interests to their own, and to administer and protect with greatest care both public and private affairs. The children succeeded their fathers, and ignorant of the changes of fortune, having never experienced its reverses, and indisposed to remain content with this civil equality, they in turn gave themselves up to cupidity, ambition, libertinage, and violence, and soon caused the aristocratic government to degenerate into an oligarchic tyranny, regardless of all civil rights. They soon, however, experienced the same fate as the first tyrant; the people, disgusted with their government, placed themselves at the command of whoever was willing to attack them, and this disposition soon produced an avenger, who was sufficiently well seconded to destroy them. The memory of the prince and the wrongs committed by him being still fresh in their minds, and having overthrown the oligarchy, the people were not willing to return to the government of a prince. A popular government was therefore resolved upon, and it was so organized that the authority should not again fall into the hands of a prince or a small number of nobles. And as all governments are at first looked up to with some degree of reverence, the popular state also maintained itself for a time, but which was never of long duration, and lasted generally only about as long as the generation that had established it; for it soon ran into that kind of license which inflicts injury upon public as well as private interests. Each individual only consulted his own passions, and a thousand acts of injustice were daily committed, so that, constrained by necessity, or directed by the counsels of some good man, or for the purpose of escaping from this anarchy, they returned anew to the government of a prince, and from this they generally lapsed again into anarchy, step by step, in the same manner and from the same causes as we have indicated.

Such is the circle which all republics are destined to run through. Seldom, however, do they come back to the original form of government, which results from the fact that their duration is not sufficiently long to be able to undergo these repeated changes and preserve their existence. But it may well happen that a republic lacking strength and good counsel in its difficulties becomes subject after a while to some neighboring state, that is better organized than itself; and if such is not the case, then they will be apt to revolve indefinitely in the circle of revolutions. I say, then, that all kinds of government are defective; those three which we have qualified as good because they are too short-lived, and the three bad ones because of their inherent viciousness. Thus sagacious legislators, knowing the vices of each of these systems of government by themselves, have chosen one that should partake of all of them, judging that to be the most stable and solid. In fact, when there is combined under the same constitution a prince, a nobility, and the power of the people, then these three powers will watch and keep each other reciprocally in check.

Amongst those justly celebrated for having established such

a constitution, Lycurgus beyond doubt merits the highest praise. He organized the government of Sparta in such manner that, in giving to the king, the nobles, and the people each their portion of authority and duties, he created a government which maintained itself for over eight hundred years in the most perfect tranquillity, and reflected infinite glory upon this legislator. On the other hand, the constitution given by Solon to the Athenians, by which he established only a popular government, was of such short duration that before his death he saw the tyranny of Pisistratus arise. And although forty years afterwards the heirs of the tyrant were expelled, so that Athens recovered her liberties and restored the popular government according to the laws of Solon, yet it did not last over a hundred years; although a number of laws that had been overlooked by Solon were adopted, to maintain the government against the insolence of the nobles and the license of the populace. The fault he had committed in not tempering the power of the people and that of the prince and his nobles, made the duration of the government of Athens very short, as compared with that of Sparta.

But let us come to Rome. Although she had no legislator like Lycurgus, who constituted her government, at her very origin, in a manner to secure her liberty for a length of time, yet the disunion which existed between the Senate and the people produced such extraordinary events, that chance did for her what the laws had failed to do. Thus, if Rome did not attain the first degree of happiness, she at least had the second. Her first institutions were doubtless defective, but they were not in conflict with the principles that might bring her to perfection. For Romulus and all the other kings gave her many and good laws, well suited even to a free people; but as the object of these princes was to found a monarchy, and not a republic, Rome, upon becoming free, found herself lacking all those institutions that are most essential to liberty, and which her kings had not established. And although these kings lost their empire, for the reasons and in the manner which we have explained, yet those who expelled them appointed immediately two consuls in place of the king; and thus it was found that they had banished the title of king from Rome, but not the regal power. The government, composed of Consuls and a Senate, had but two of the three elements of which we have spoken, the monarchical and the aristocratic; the popular power was wanting. In the course of time, however, the insolence of the nobles, produced by the causes which we shall see further on, induced the people to rise against the others. The nobility, to save a portion of their power, were forced to yield a share of it to the people; but the Senate and the Consuls retained sufficient to maintain their rank in the state. It was then that the Tribunes of the people were created, which strengthened and confirmed the republic, being now composed of the three elements of which we have spoken above. Fortune favored her, so that, although the authority passed successively from the kings and nobles to the people, by the same degrees and for the same reasons that we have spoken of, yet the royal authority was never entirely abolished to bestow it upon the nobles; and these were never entirely deprived of their authority to give it to the people; but a combination was formed of the three powers, which rendered the constitution perfect, and this perfection was attained by the disunion of the Senate and the people, as we shall more fully show in the following two chapters.

CHAPTER III

OF THE EVENTS THAT CAUSED THE CREATION OF TRIBUNES
IN ROME; WHICH MADE THE REPUBLIC MORE PERFECT

All those who have written upon civil institutions demonstrate (and history is full of examples to support them) that whoever desires to found a state and give it laws, must start with assuming that all men are bad and ever ready to display their vicious nature, whenever they may find occasion for it. If their evil disposition remains concealed for a time, it must be attributed to some unknown reason; and we must assume that it lacked occasion to show itself; but time, which has been said to be the father of all truth, does not fail to bring it to light. After the expulsion of the Tarquins the greatest harmony seemed to prevail between the Senate and the people. The nobles seemed to have laid aside all their haughtiness and assumed popular manners, which made them supportable even to the lowest of the citizens. The nobility played this role so long as the Tarquins lived, without their motive being divined; for they feared the Tarquins, and also lest the ill-treated people might side with them. Their party therefore assumed all possible gentleness in their manners towards the people. But so soon as the death of the Tarquins had relieved them of their apprehensions, they began to vent upon the people all the venom they had so long retained within their breasts, and lost no opportunity to outrage them in every possible way; which is one of the proofs of the argument we have advanced, that men act right only upon compulsion; but from the moment that they have the option and liberty to commit wrong with impunity, then they never fail to carry confusion and disorder everywhere. It is this that has caused it to be said that poverty and hunger make men industrious, and that the law makes men good; and if fortunate circumstances cause good to be done without constraint, the law may be dispensed with. But when such happy influence is lacking, then the law immediately becomes necessary. Thus the nobles, after the death of the Tarquins, being no longer under the influence that had restrained them, determined to establish a new order of things, which had the same effect as the misrule of the Tarquins during their existence; and therefore, after many troubles, tumults, and dangers occasioned by the excesses which both the nobles and the people committed, they came, for the security of the people, to the creation of the Tribunes, who were endowed with so many prerogatives, and surrounded with so much respect, that they formed a powerful barrier between the Senate and the people, which curbed the insolence of the former.

Thomas Hobbes (1588–1679)

LEVIATHAN
OR
THE MATTER, FORM, AND POWER
OF A
COMMONWEALTH
ECCLESIASTICAL AND CIVIL

INTRODUCTION

Nature, the art whereby God hath made and governs the world, is by the *art* of man, as in many other things, so in this also imitated, that it can make an artificial animal. For seeing life is but a motion of limbs, the beginning whereof is in some principal part within; why may we not say, that all *automata* (engines that move themselves by springs and wheels as doth a watch) have an artificial life? For what is the heart, but a spring; and the nerves, but so many strings, and the joints, but so many wheels, giving motion to the whole body, such as was intended by the artificer? Art goes yet further, imitating that rational and most excellent work of nature, *man*. For by art is created that great *Leviathan* called a *Commonwealth*, or *State*, in Latin *Civitas*, which is but an artificial man; though of greater stature and strength than the natural, for whose protection and defense it was intended; and in which the sovereignty is an artificial soul, as giving life and motion to the whole body; the magistrates, and other officers of judicature and execution, artificial joints; reward and punishment, by which fastened to the seat of the sovereignty every joint and member is moved to perform his duty, are the nerves, that do the same in the body natural; the wealth and riches of all the particular members, are the strength; *salus populi*, the people's safety, its business; counselors, by whom all things needful for it to know are suggested unto it, are the memory; equity and laws, an artificial reason and will; concord, health; sedition, sickness; and civil war, death. Lastly, the pacts and covenants, by which the parts of this body politic were at first made, set together, and united, resemble that *fiat,* or the *let us make man,* pronounced by God in the creation.

To describe the nature of this artificial man, I will consider:

First, the *matter* thereof, and the *artificer;* both which is *man.*

Secondly, *how,* and by what *covenants* it is made; what are the *rights* and just *power* or *authority* of a *sovereign;* and what it is that preserveth or dissolveth it.

Thirdly, what is a *Christian commonwealth.*

Lastly, what is the *kingdom of darkness.*

Concerning the first, there is a saying much usurped of late, that wisdom is acquired, not by reading of books, but of men. Consequently whereunto, those persons that for the most part can give no other proof of being wise, take great delight to show what they think they have read in men, by uncharitable censures of one another behind their backs. But there is another saying not of late understood, by which they might learn truly to read one another if they would take the pains: that is, *nosce teipsum,* Read thyself; which was not meant, as it is now used, to countenance either the barbarous state of men in power towards their inferiors, or to encourage men of low degree to a saucy behavior towards their betters; but to teach us that from the similitude of the thoughts and passions of one man to the thoughts and passions of another, whosoever looketh into himself, and considereth what he doth when he does think, opine, reason, hope, fear, etc. and upon what grounds; he shall thereby read and know what are the thoughts and passions of all other men upon the like occasions. I say the similitude of *passions,* which are the same in all men, desire, fear, hope, etc.; not the similitude of the *objects* of the passions, which are the things desired, feared, hoped, etc.: for these the constitution individual, and particular education, do so vary, and they are so easy to be kept from our knowledge, that the characters of man's heart, blotted and confounded as they are with dissembling, lying, counterfeiting, and erroneous doctrines, are legible only to him that searcheth hearts. And though by men's actions we do discover their design sometimes; yet to do it without comparing them with our own, and distinguishing all circumstances by which the case may come to be altered, is to decipher without a key, and be for the most part deceived, by too much trust or by too much diffidence, as he that reads is himself a good or evil man.

But let one man read another by his actions never so perfectly, it serves him only with his acquaintance, which are but few. He that is to govern a whole nation, must read in himself not this or that particular man, but mankind; which though it be hard to do, harder than to learn any language or science, yet when I shall have set down my own reading orderly and perspicuously, the pains left another will be only to consider if he also find not the same in himself. For this kind of doctrine admitteth no other demonstration. . . .

CHAPTER XIII

OF THE NATURAL CONDITION OF MANKIND AS CONCERNING THEIR FELICITY, AND MISERY

Nature hath made men so equal, in the faculties of the body and mind; as that, though there be found one man sometimes manifestly stronger in body or of quicker mind than another, yet when all is reckoned together, the difference between man and man is not so considerable, as that one man can thereupon claim to himself any benefit, to which another may not pretend as well as he. For as to the strength of body, the weakest has strength enough to kill the strongest, either by secret machination, or by confederacy with others that are in the same danger with himself.

And as to the faculties of the mind—setting aside the arts grounded upon words, and especially that skill of proceeding upon general and infallible rules, called science; which very few have, and but in few things; as being not a native faculty, born with us; nor attained, as prudence, while we look after somewhat else—I find yet a greater equality amongst men, than that of strength. For prudence is but experience, which equal time equally bestows on all men, in those things they equally apply themselves unto. That which may perhaps make such equality incredible, is but a vain conceit of one's own wisdom, which almost all men think they have in a greater degree than the vulgar; that is, than all men but themselves, and a few others, whom by fame, or for concurring with themselves, they approve. For such is the nature of men, that howsoever they may acknowledge many others to be more witty, or more eloquent, or more learned, yet they will hardly believe there be many so wise as themselves; for they see their own wit at hand, and other men's at a distance. But this proveth rather that men are in that point equal, than unequal. For there is not ordinarily a greater sign of the equal distribution of anything, than that every man is contented with his share.

From this equality of ability, ariseth equality of hope in the attaining of our ends. And therefore if any two men desire the same thing, which nevertheless they cannot both enjoy, they become enemies; and in the way to their end, which is principally their own conservation, and sometimes their delectation only, endeavor to destroy, or subdue one another. And from hence it comes to pass that where an invader hath no more to fear than another man's single power; if one plant, sow, build, or possess a convenient seat, others may probably be expected to come prepared with forces united, to dispossess and deprive him, not only of the fruit of his labor, but also of his life or liberty. And the invader again is in the like danger of another.

And from this diffidence of one another, there is no way for any man to secure himself so reasonable as anticipation; that is, by force or wiles to master the persons of all men he can, so long, till he see no other power great enough to endanger him: and this is no more than his own conservation requireth, and is generally allowed. Also because there be some, that taking pleasure in contemplating their own power in the acts of conquest, which they pursue farther than their security requires; if others, that otherwise would be glad to be at ease within modest bounds, should not by invasion increase their power, they would not be able long time, by standing only on their defense, to subsist. And by consequence, such augmentation of dominion over men being necessary to a man's conservation, it ought to be allowed him.

Again, men have no pleasure, but on the contrary a great deal of grief, in keeping company, where there is no power able to overawe them all. For every man looketh that his companion should value him at the same rate he sets upon himself; and upon all signs of contempt, or undervaluing, naturally endeavors, as far as he dares (which amongst them that have no common power to keep them in quiet, is far enough to make them destroy each other), to extort a greater value from his contemners by damage, and from others by the example.

So that in the nature of man, we find three principal causes of quarrel. First, competition; second, diffidence; thirdly, glory.

The first maketh men invade for gain; the second, for safety; and the third, for reputation. The first use violence to make themselves masters of other men's persons, wives, children, and cattle; the second, to defend them; the third, for trifles, as a word, a smile, a different opinion, and any other sign of undervalue, either direct in their persons, or by reflection in their kindred, their friends, their nation, their profession, or their name.

Hereby it is manifest that during the time men live without a common power to keep them all in awe, they are in that condition which is called war; and such a war as is of every man against every man. For *war* consisteth not in battle only, or the act of fighting, but in a tract of time wherein the will to contend by battle is sufficiently known, and therefore the notion of *time* is to be considered in the nature of war, as it is in the nature of weather. For as the nature of foul weather lieth not in a shower or two of rain, but in an inclination thereto of many days together; so the nature of war consisteth not in actual fighting, but in the known disposition thereto, during all the time there is no assurance to the contrary. All other time is *peace*.

Whatsoever therefore is consequent to a time of war, where every man is enemy to every man; the same is consequent to the time, wherein men live without other security than what their own strength and their own invention shall furnish them withal. In such condition there is no place for industry, because the fruit thereof is uncertain: and consequently no culture of the earth; no navigation, nor use of the commodities that may be imported by sea; no commodious building; no instruments of moving, and removing, such things as require much force; no knowledge of the face of the earth; no account of time; no arts; no letters; no society; and which is worst of all, continual fear, and danger of violent death; and the life of man, solitary, poor, nasty, brutish, and short.

It may seem strange to some man that has not well weighed these things, that nature should thus dissociate, and render men apt to invade and destroy one another; and he may therefore, not trusting to this inference, made from the passions, desire perhaps to have the same confirmed by experience. Let him therefore consider with himself, when taking a journey, he arms himself and seeks to go well accompanied;

when going to sleep, he locks his doors; when even in his house he locks his chests; and this when he knows there be laws, and public officers, armed, to revenge all injuries shall be done him: what opinion he has of his fellow-subjects, when he rides armed; of his fellow-citizens, when he locks his doors; and of his children, and servants, when he locks his chests. Does he not there as much accuse mankind by his actions, as I do by my words? But neither of us accuse man's nature in it. The desires, and other passions of man, are in themselves no sin. No more are the actions that proceed from those passions, till they know a law that forbids them: which till laws be made they cannot know; nor can any law be made, till they have agreed upon the person that shall make it.

It may peradventure be thought, there was never such a time nor condition of war as this; and I believe it was never generally so, over all the world: but there are many places where they live so now. For the savage people in many places of America, except the government of small families, the concord whereof dependeth on natural lust, have no government at all; and live at this day in that brutish manner, as I said before. Howsoever, it may be perceived what manner of life there would be, where there were no common power to fear; by the manner of life which men that have formerly lived under a peaceful government, use to degenerate into in a civil war.

But though there had never been any time wherein particular men were in a condition of war one against another; yet in all times, kings, and persons of sovereign authority, because of their independency, are in continual jealousies, and in the state and posture of gladiators; having their weapons pointing, and their eyes fixed on one another; that is, their forts, garrisons, and guns upon the frontiers of their kingdoms; and continual spies upon their neighbors; which is a posture of war. But because they uphold thereby the industry of their subjects, there does not follow from it that misery which accompanies the liberty of particular men.

To this war of every man against every man, this also is consequent: *that nothing can be unjust.* The notions of right and wrong, justice and injustice, have there no place. Where there is no common power, there is no law; where no law, no injustice. Force and fraud are in war the two cardinal virtues. Justice and injustice are none of the faculties neither of the body nor mind. If they were, they might be in a man that were alone in the world, as well as his senses and passions. They are qualities that relate to men in society, not in solitude. It is consequent also to the same condition, that there be no propriety, no dominion, no *mine* and *thine* distinct; but only that to be every man's, that he can get; and for so long as he can keep it. And thus much for the ill condition which man by mere nature is actually placed in; though with a possibility to come out of it, consisting partly in the passions, partly in his reason.

The passions that incline men to peace are fear of death, desire of such things as are necessary to commodious living, and a hope by their industry to obtain them. And reason suggesteth convenient articles of peace, upon which men may be drawn to agreement. These articles are they which otherwise are called the Laws of Nature whereof I shall speak more particularly in the two following chapters.

CHAPTER XIV

OF THE FIRST AND SECOND NATURAL LAWS,

AND OF CONTRACTS

The right of nature, which writers commonly call *jus naturale*, is the liberty each man hath to use his own power, as he will himself, for the preservation of his own nature; that is to say, of his own life; and consequently, of doing anything, which in his own judgment and reason, he shall conceive to be the aptest means thereunto.

By *liberty*, is understood, according to the proper signification of the word, the absence of external impediments: which impediments, may oft take away part of a man's power to do what he would; but cannot hinder him from using the power left him, according as his judgment and reason shall dictate to him.

A *law of nature*, *lex naturalis*, is a precept or general rule, found out by reason, by which a man is forbidden to do that which is destructive of his life, or taketh away the means of preserving the same; and to omit that by which he thinketh it may be best preserved. For though they that speak of this subject, use to confound *jus* and *lex*, *right* and *law*; yet they ought to be distinguished: because *right* consisteth in liberty to do or to forbear, whereas *law* determineth and bindeth to one of them; so that law, and right differ as much as obligation and liberty; which in one and the same matter are inconsistent.

And because the condition of man, as hath been declared in the precedent chapter, is a condition of war of everyone against everyone; in which case everyone is governed by his own reason, and there is nothing he can make use of that may not be a help unto him in preserving his life against his enemies: it followeth, that in such a condition every man has a right to everything; even to one another's body. And therefore, as long as this natural right of every man to everything endureth, there can be no security to any man, how strong or wise soever he be, of living out the time which nature ordinarily alloweth men to live. And consequently it is a precept, or general rule of reason, *that every man ought to endeavor peace, as far as he has hope of obtaining it; and when he cannot obtain it, that he may seek and use all helps and advantages of war.* The first branch of which rule containeth the first and fundamental law of nature; which is, *to seek peace and follow it.* The second, the sum of the right of nature; which is, *by all means we can, to defend ourselves.*

From this fundamental law of nature, by which men are commanded to endeavor peace, is derived this second law: *that a man be willing, when others are so too, as far forth as for peace and defense of himself he shall think it necessary, to lay down this right to all things; and be contented with so much liberty against other men, as he would allow other men against himself.* For as long as every man holdeth this right, of doing anything he liketh, so long are all men in the condition of war. But if other men will not lay down their right, as well as he, then there is no reason for anyone to divest himself of his: for that were to expose himself to prey, which no man is bound to, rather than to dispose himself to peace. This is that law of the Gospel: *whatsoever you require that others should do to you, that do ye to them.* And that law of all men, *quod tibi fieri non, vis, alteri ne feceris.*

To *lay down* a man's *right* to anything, is to *divest* himself of the *liberty,* of hindering another of the benefit of his own right to the same. For he that renounceth or passeth away his right, giveth not to any other man a right which he had not before; because there is nothing to which every man had not right by nature: but only standeth out of his way, that he may enjoy his own original right, without hindrance from him, not without hindrance from another. So that the effect which redoundeth to one man, by another man's defect of right, is but so much diminution of impediments to the use of his own right original.

Right is laid aside, either by simply renouncing it, or by transferring it to another. By *simply renouncing*, when he cares not to whom the benefit thereof redoundeth. By *transferring*, when he intendeth the benefit thereof to some certain person or persons. And when a man hath in either manner abandoned or granted away his right; then is he said to be *obliged*, or bound, not to hinder those to whom such right is granted or abandoned, from the benefit of it; and that he *ought*, and it is his *duty*, not to make void that voluntary act of his own; and that such hindrance is *injustice*, and *injury*, as being *sine jure;* the right being before renounced, or transferred. So that injury, or injustice, in the controversies of the world, is somewhat like to that, which in the disputations of scholars is called *absurdity*. For as it is there called an absurdity to contradict what one maintained in the beginning; so in the world, it is called injustice, and injury, voluntarily to undo that which from the beginning he had voluntarily done. The way by which a man either simply renounceth, or transferreth his right, is a declaration, or signification, by some voluntary and sufficient sign or signs, that he doth so renounce or transfer, or hath so renounced or transferred the same, to him that accepteth it. And these signs are either words only, or actions only, or, as it happeneth most often, both words and actions. And the same are the *bonds*, by which men are bound and obliged—bonds that have their strength, not from their own nature, for nothing is more easily broken than a man's word, but from fear of some evil consequence upon the rupture.

Whensoever a man transferreth his right, or renounceth it; it is either in consideration of some right reciprocally transferred to himself, or for some other good he hopeth for thereby. For it is a voluntary act; and of the voluntary acts of every man, the object is some *good to himself*. And therefor there be some rights which no man can be understood by any words, or other signs, to have abandoned or transferred. As first a man cannot lay down the right of resisting them that assault him by force, to take away his life; because he cannot be understood to aim thereby, at any good to himself. The same may be said of wounds, and chains, and imprisonment: both because there is no benefit consequent to such patience, as there is to the patience of suffering another to be wounded or imprisoned; as also because a man cannot tell, when he seeth men proceed against him by violence, whether they intend his death or not. And lastly the motive, an end for which this renouncing and transferring of right is introduced, is nothing else but the security of a man's person, in his life, and in the means of so preserving life as not to be weary of it. And therefore if a man by words, or other signs, seem to despoil himself of the end for which those signs were intended, he is not to be understood as if he meant it, or that it was his will, but that he was ignorant of how such words and actions were to be interpreted.

The mutual transferring of right, is that which men call *contract*. . . .

CHAPTER XVII
OF THE CAUSES, GENERATIONS, AND
DEFINITION OF A COMMONWEALTH

The final cause, end, or design of men who naturally love liberty and dominion over others, in the introduction of that restraint upon themselves in which we see them live in commonwealths, is the foresight of their own preservation, and of a more contented life thereby; that is to say, of getting themselves out from that miserable condition of war, which is necessarily consequent, as hath been shown in Chapter XIII, to the natural passions of men, when there is no visible power to keep them in awe, and tie them by fear of punishment to the performance of their covenants and observation of those laws of nature set down in the fourteenth and fifteenth chapters.

For the laws of nature, as justice, equity, modesty, mercy, and, in sum, *doing to others as we would be done to*, of themselves, without the terror of some power to cause them to be observed, are contrary to our natural passions, that carry us to partiality, pride, revenge, and the like. And covenants, without the sword, are but words, and of no strength to secure a man at all. Therefore notwithstanding the laws of nature, which everyone hath then kept, when he has the will to keep them when he can do it safely; if there be no power erected, or not great enough for our security, every man will, and may, lawfully rely on his own strength and art, for caution against all other men. And in all places

where men have lived by small families, to rob and spoil one
another has been a trade, and so far from being reputed
against the law of nature, that the greater spoils they gained,
the greater was their honor; and men observed no other laws
therein but the laws of honor; that is, to abstain from cruelty,
leaving to men their lives, and instruments of husbandry. And
as small families did then; so now do cities and kingdoms,
which are but greater families, for their own security enlarge
their dominions, upon all pretenses of danger and fear of
invasion, or assistance that may be given to invaders, and endeavor as much as they can to subdue or weaken their neighbors, by open force and secret arts, for want of other caution,
justly; and are remembered for it in after ages with honor.

Nor is it the joining together of a small number of men,
that gives them this security; because in small numbers, small
additions on the one side or the other make the advantage of
strength so great, as is sufficient to carry the victory, and
therefore gives encouragement to an invasion. The multitude
sufficient to confide in for our security, is not determined by
any certain number, but by comparison with the enemy we
fear; and is then sufficient, when the odds of the enemy is
not of so visible and conspicuous moment, to determine the
event of war, as to move him to attempt.

And be there never so great a multitude, yet if their actions
be directed according to their particular judgments and particular appetites, they can expect thereby no defense nor
protection, neither against a common enemy nor against the
injuries of one another. For being distracted in opinions
concerning the best use and application of their strength,
they do not help but hinder one another; and reduce their
strength by mutual opposition to nothing: whereby they are
easily, not only subdued by a very few that agree together;
but also when there is no common enemy, they make war
upon each other, for their particular interests. For if we
could suppose a great multitude of men to consent in the
observation of justice, and other laws of nature, without a
common power to keep them all in awe, we might as well
suppose all mankind to do the same; and then there neither
would be, nor need to be any civil government or commonwealth at all, because there would be peace without subjection.

Nor is it enough for the security, which men desire should
last all the time of their life, that they be governed and directed by one judgment for a limited time, as in one battle

or one war. For though they obtain a victory by their unanimous endeavor against a foreign enemy; yet afterwards, when either they have no common enemy, or he that by one part is held for an enemy, is by another part held for a friend, they must needs by the difference of their interests dissolve, and fall again into a war amongst themselves.

It is true that certain living creatures, as bees and ants, live sociably one with another, which are therefore by Aristotle numbered amongst political creatures; and yet have no other direction than their particular judgments and appetites; nor speech, whereby one of them can signify to another what he thinks expedient for the common benefit: and therefore some man may perhaps desire to know why mankind cannot do the same. To which I answer:

First, that men are continually in competition for honor and dignity, which these creatures are not; and consequently amongst men there ariseth on that ground, envy and hatred, and finally war; but amongst these not so.

Secondly, that amongst these creatures, the common good differeth not from the private; and being by nature inclined to their private, they procure thereby the common benefit. But man, whose joy consisteth in comparing himself with other men, can relish nothing but what is eminent.

Thirdly, that these creatures, having not, as man, the use of reason, do not see, nor think they see, any fault in the administration of their common business; whereas amongst men, there are very many that think themselves wiser, and able to govern the public better, than the rest; and these strive to reform and innovate, one this way, another that way; and thereby bring it into distraction and civil war.

Fourthly, that these creatures, though they have some use of voice in making known to one another their desires and other affections; yet they want that art of words by which some men can represent to others, that which is good in the likeness of evil, and evil in the likeness of good, and augment or diminish the apparent greatness of good and evil; discontenting men and troubling their peace at their pleasure.

Fifthly, irrational creatures cannot distinguish between *injury* and *damage;* and therefore as long as they be at ease, they are not offended with their fellows: whereas man is then most troublesome when he is most at ease; for then it is that he loves to shew his wisdom, and control the actions of them that govern the commonwealth.

Lastly, the agreement of these creatures is natural; that of men is by covenant only, which is artificial: and therefore it is no wonder if there be somewhat else required, besides covenant, to make their agreement constant and lasting; which is a common power, to keep them in awe, and to direct their actions to the common benefit.

The only way to erect such a common power, as may be able to defend them from the invasion of foreigners and the injuries of one another, and thereby to secure them in such sort as that, by their own industry, and by the fruits of the earth, they may nourish themselves and live contentedly; is, to confer all their power and strength upon one man, or upon one assembly of men, that may reduce all their wills, by plurality of voices, unto one will: which is as much as to say, to appoint one man, or assembly of men, to bear their person; and everyone to own and acknowledge himself to be author of whatsoever he that so beareth their person, shall act or cause to be acted in those things which concern the common peace and safety; and therein to submit their wills, everyone to his will, and their judgments, to his judgment. This is more than consent, or concord; it is a real unity of them all, in one and the same person, made by covenant of every man with every man, in such manner as if every man should say to every man, *"I authorize and give up my right of governing myself to this man, or to this assembly of men, on this condition, that thou give up thy right to him, and authorize all his actions in like manner."* This done, the multitude so united in one person, is called a *commonwealth*, in Latin *civitas*. This is the generation of that great LEVIATHAN, or rather, to speak more reverently, of that *mortal god*, to which we owe under the *immortal God*, our peace and defense. For by this authority, given him by every particular man in the commonwealth, he hath the use of so much power and strength conferred on him, that by terror thereof he is enabled to perform the wills of them all, to peace at home and mutual aid against their enemies abroad. And in him consisteth the essence of the commonwealth; which, to define it, is *one person, of whose acts a great multitude, by mutual covenants one with another, have made themselves every one the author, to the end he may use the strength and means of them all, as he shall think expedient, for their peace and common defense.*

And he that carrieth this person, is called *sovereign,* and said to have sovereign power; and everyone besides, his *subject.*

The attaining to this sovereign power is by two ways. One, by natural force; as when a man maketh his children to submit themselves and their children to his government, as being able to destroy them if they refuse; or by war subdueth his enemies to his will, giving them their lives on that condition. The other, is when men agree amongst themselves to submit to some man, or assembly of men, voluntarily, on confidence to be protected by him against all others. This latter, may be called a political commonwealth, or commonwealth by *institution;* and the former, a commonwealth by *acquisition.* And first, I shall speak of a commonwealth by institution.

CHAPTER XVIII
OF THE RIGHTS OF SOVEREIGNS BY INSTITUTION

A commonwealth is said to be *instituted,* when a multitude of men do agree and covenant, everyone with everyone, that to whatsoever man, or assembly of men, shall be given by the major part the right to present the person of them all, that is to say, to be their *representative;* everyone, as well he that voted for it as he that voted against it, shall authorize all the actions and judgments of that man, or assembly of men, in the same manner as if they were his own, to the end to live peaceably amongst themselves and be protected against other men.

From this institution of a commonwealth are derived all the *rights* and *faculties* of him, or them, on whom sovereign power is conferred by the consent of the people assembled.

First, because they covenant, it is to be understood they are not obliged by former covenant to anything repugnant hereunto. And consequently they that have already instituted a commonwealth, being thereby bound by covenant to own the actions and judgments of one, cannot lawfully make a new covenant amongst themselves, to be obedient to any other, in anything whatsoever, without his permission. And therefore, they that are subject to a monarch, cannot without his leave cast off monarchy, and return to the confusion of a disunited multitude; nor transfer their person from him that beareth it, to another man, or other assembly of men:

for they are bound, every man to every man, to own, and be reputed author of all, that he that already is their sovereign shall do and judge fit to be done; so that any one man dissenting, all the rest should break their covenant made to that man, which is injustice: and they have also every man given the sovereignty to him that beareth their person; and therefore if they depose him, they take from him that which is his own, and so again it is injustice. Besides, if he that attempteth to depose his sovereign, be killed or punished by him for such attempt, he is author of his own punishment, as being by the institution, author of all his sovereign shall do; and because it is injustice for a man to do anything for which he may be punished by his own authority, he is also upon that title, unjust. And whereas some men have pretended for their disobedience to their sovereign, a new covenant, made not with men but with God, this also is unjust: for there is no covenant with God, but by mediation of somebody that representeth God's person; which none doth but God's lieutenant, who hath the sovereignty under God. But this pretense of covenant with God, is so evident a lie, even in the pretenders' own consciences, that it is not only an act of an unjust, but also of a vile and unmanly disposition.

Secondly, because the right of bearing the person of them all, is given to him they make sovereign, by covenant only of one to another, and not of him to any of them; there can happen no breach of covenant on the part of the sovereign; and consequently none of his subjects, by any pretense of forfeiture, can be freed from his subjection. That he which is made sovereign maketh no covenant with his subjects beforehand, is manifest; because either he must make it with the whole multitude, as one party to the covenant, or he must make a several covenant with every man. With the whole, as one party, it is impossible, because as yet they are not one person: and if he makes so many several covenants as there be men, those covenants after he hath the sovereignty are void; because what act soever can be pretended by any one of them for breach thereof, is the act both of himself and of all the rest, because done in the person, and by the right of every one of them in particular. Besides, if any one, or more of them, pretend a breach of the covenant made by the sovereign at his institution; and others, as one other of his subjects, or himself alone, pretend there was no such breach: there is in this case, no judge to decide the controversy; it returns therefore to the sword again; and every man recovereth the right of protecting himself by his own strength, contrary to the design they had in the institution. It is therefore in vain to grant sovereignty by way of precedent covenant. The opinion that any monarch receiveth his power by covenant, that is to say, on condition, proceedeth from want of understanding this easy truth, that covenants being but words and breath, have no force to oblige, contain, constrain, or protect any man, but what it has from the public sword; that is, from the untied hands of that man, or assembly of men that hath the sovereignty, and whose actions are avouched by them all, and performed by the strength of them all, in him united. But when an assembly of men is made sovereign, then no man imagineth any such covenant to have passed in the institution; for no man is so dull as to say, for example, the people of Rome made a covenant with the Romans, to hold the sovereignty on such or such conditions; which not performed, the Romans might lawfully depose the Roman people. That men see not the reason to be alike in a monarchy and in a popular government, proceedeth from the ambition of some that are kinder to the government of an assembly, whereof they may hope to participate, than of monarchy, which they despair to enjoy.

Thirdly, because the major part hath by consenting voices declared a sovereign, he that dissented must now consent with the rest; that is, be contented to avow all the actions he shall do, or else justly be destroyed by the rest. For if he voluntarily entered into the congregation of them that were assembled, he sufficiently declared thereby his will, and therefore tacitly covenanted to stand to what the major part should ordain; and therefore if he refuse to stand thereto, or make protestation against any of their decrees, he does contrary to his covenant, and therefore unjustly. And whether he be of the congregation or not, and whether his consent be asked or not, he must either submit to their decrees, or be left in the condition of war he was in before; wherein he might without injustice be destroyed by any man whatsoever.

Fourthly, because every subject is by this institution author of all the actions and judgments of the sovereign instituted; it follows that whatsoever he doth, it can be no injury to any of his subjects, nor ought he to be by any of them accused of injustice. For he that doth anything by authority from another, doth therein no injury to him by whose authority he acteth: but by this institution of a commonwealth,

every particular man is author of all the sovereign doth: and
consequently he that complaineth of injury from his sovereign,
complaineth of that whereof he himself is author; and therefore ought not to accuse any man but himself; no nor himself of injury, because to do injury to one's self, is impossible.
It is true that they that have sovereign power may commit
iniquity, but not injustice, or injury, in the proper signification.

Fifthly, and consequently to that which was said last, no
man that hath sovereign power can justly be put to death,
or otherwise in any manner by his subjects punished. For
seeing every subject is author of the actions of his sovereign,
he punisheth another for the actions committed by himself.

And because the end of this institution, is the peace and
defense of them all, and whosoever has right to the end has
right to the means; it belongeth of right, to whatsoever man
or assembly that hath the sovereignty, to be judge both of
the means of peace and defense, and also of the hindrances
and disturbances of the same; and to do whatsoever he shall
think necessary to be done, both beforehand, for the preserving of peace and security, by prevention of discord at home
and hostility from abroad, and, when peace and security are
lost, for the recovery of the same. And therefore,

Sixthly, it is annexed to the sovereignty, to be judge of
what opinions and doctrines are averse, and what conducing
to peace; and consequently, on what occasions, how far, and
what men are to be trusted withal, in speaking to multitudes
of people; and who shall examine the doctrines of all books
before they be published. For the actions of men proceed
from their opinions; and in the well-governing of opinions
consisteth the well-governing of men's actions, in order to
their peace and concord. And though in matter of doctrine
nothing ought to be regarded but the truth, yet this is not
repugnant to regulating the same by peace. For doctrine
repugnant to peace can no more be true, than peace and
concord can be against the law of nature. It is true that in a
commonwealth, where, by the negligence or unskillfulness of
governors and teachers, false doctrines are by time generally
received; the contrary truths may be generally offensive. Yet
the most sudden and rough bursting in of a new truth that
can be, does never break the peace, but only sometimes awake
the war. For those men that are so remissly governed, that
they dare take up arms to defend or introduce an opinion,

are still in war; and their condition not peace, but only a cessation of arms for fear of one another; and they live, as it were, in the precincts of battle continually. It belongeth therefore to him that hath the sovereign power, to be judge, or constitute all judges of opinions and doctrines, as a thing necessary to peace; thereby to prevent discord and civil war.

Seventhly, is annexed to the sovereignty, the whole power of prescribing the rules, whereby every man may know what goods he may enjoy, and what actions he may do, without being molested by any of his fellow-subjects; and this is it men call *propriety*. For before constitution of sovereign power, as hath already been shown, all men had right to all things; which necessarily causeth war: and therefore this propriety, being necessary to peace, and depending on sovereign power, is the act of that power, in order to the public peace. These rules of propriety, or *meum* and *tuum*, and of good, evil, lawful, and unlawful in the actions of subjects, are the civil laws; that is to say, the laws of each commonwealth in particular: though the name of civil law be now restrained to the ancient civil laws of the city of Rome; which being the head of a great part of the world, her laws at that time were in these parts the civil law.

Eighthly, is annexed to the sovereignty, the right of judicature; that is to say, of hearing and deciding all controversies which may arise concerning law, either civil or natural, or concerning fact. For without the decision of controversies, there is no protection of one subject against the injuries of another: the laws concerning *meum* and *tuum* are in vain; and to every man remaineth, from the natural and necessary appetite of his own conservation, the right of protecting himself by his private strength, which is the condition of war, and contrary to the end for which every commonwealth is instituted.

Ninthly, is annexed to the sovereignty, the right of making war and peace with other nations and commonwealths; that is to say, of judging when it is for the public good, and how great forces are to be assembled, armed, and paid for that end; and to levy money upon the subjects, to defray the expenses thereof. For the power by which the people are to be defended, consisteth in their armies; and the strength of an army, in the union of their strength under one command: which command the sovereign instituted, therefore hath; because the command of the militia, without other institution, maketh him that hath it sovereign. And therefore whosoever is made general of an army, he that hath the sovereign power is always generalissimo.

Tenthly, is annexed to the sovereignty, the choosing of all counsellors, ministers, magistrates, and offices, both in peace and war. For seeing the sovereign is charged with the end, which is the common peace and defense, he is understood to have power to use such means as he shall think most fit for his discharge.

Eleventhly, to the sovereign is committed the power of rewarding with riches, or honor, and of punishing with corporal or pecuniary punishment, or with ignominy, every subject according to the law he hath formerly made; or if there be no law made, according as he shall judge most to conduce to the encouraging of men to serve the commonwealth, or deterring of them from doing disservice to the same.

Lastly, considering what value men are naturally apt to set upon themselves, what respect they look for from others, and how little they value other men; from whence continually arise amongst them, emulation, quarrels, factions, and at last war, to the destroying of one another and diminution of their strength against a common enemy: it is necessary that there be laws of honor, and a public rate of the worth of such men as have deserved or are able to deserve well of the commonwealth; and that there be force in the hands of some or other, to put those laws in execution. But it hath already been shown, that not only the whole militia, or forces of the commonwealth, but also the judicature of all controversies, is annexed to the sovereignty. To the sovereign therefore it belongeth also to give titles of honor; and to appoint what order of place and dignity each man shall hold; and what signs of respect, in public or private meetings, they shall give to one another.

These are the rights which make the essence of sovereignty, and which are the marks whereby a man may discern in what man, or assembly of men, the sovereign power is placed and resideth. For these are incommunicable and inseparable. The power to coin money, to dispose of the estate and persons of infant heirs, to have pre-emption in markets, and all other statute prerogatives, may be transferred by the sovereign; and yet the power to protect his subjects be retained. But if he transfer the militia, he retains the judicature in vain, for want of execution of the laws; or if he grant away the power of raising money, the militia is in vain; or if he give away the government of doctrines, men will be frighted into rebellion with the fear of spirits. And so if we consider any one of the said rights, we shall presently see that the holding of all the rest will produce no effect in the conservation of peace and justice, the end for which all commonwealths are instituted. And this division is it whereof it is said, *a kingdom divided in itself cannot stand:* for unless this division precede, division into opposite armies can never happen. If there had not first been an opinion received of the greatest part of England, that these powers were divided between the King and the Lords and the House of Commons, the people had never been divided and fallen into this civil war; first between those that disagreed in politics, and after between the dissenters about the liberty of religion: which have so instructed men in this point of sovereign right; and there be few now in England that do not see that these rights are inseparable, and will be so generally acknowledged at the next return of peace; and so continue till their miseries are forgotten; and no longer, except the vulgar be better taught than they have hitherto been.

And because they are essential and inseparable rights, it follows necessarily that in whatsoever words any of them seem to be granted away, yet if the sovereign power itself be not in direct terms renounced, and the name of sovereign no more given by the grantees to him that grants them, the grant is void: for when he has granted all he can, if we grant back the sovereignty, all is restored, as inseparably annexed thereunto.

This great authority being indivisible, and inseparably annexed to the sovereignty, there is little ground for the opinion of them that say of sovereign kings, though they be *singulis majores,* of greater power than every one of their subjects, yet they be *universis minores,* of less power than them all together. For if by "all together" they mean not the collective body as one person, then "all together" and "every one" signify the same, and the speech is absurd. But if by "all together" they understand them as one person, which person the sovereign bears, then the power of all together is the same with the sovereign's power, and so again the speech is absurd: which absurdity they see well enough when the sovereignty is in an assembly of the people, but in a monarch they see it not; and yet the power of sovereignty is the same in whomsoever it be placed.

And as the power, so also the honor of the sovereign, ought to be greater than that of any or all the subjects. For in the sovereignty is the fountain of honor. The dignities of lord, earl, duke, and prince are his creatures. As in the presence of the master, the servants are equal and without any honor at all; so are the subjects, in the presence of the sovereign. And though they shine some more, some less, when they are out of his sight; yet in his presence, they shine no more than the stars in the presence of the sun.

But a man may here object that the condition of subjects is very miserable, as being obnoxious to the lusts, and other irregular passions, of him or them that have so unlimited a power in their hands. And commonly they that live under a monarch, think it the fault of monarchy; and they that live under the government of democracy, or other sovereign assembly, attribute all the inconvenience to that form of commonwealth; whereas the power in all forms, if they be perfect enough to protect them, is the same: not considering that the state of man can never be without some incommodity or other; and that the greatest that in any form of government can possibly happen to the people in general, is scarce sensible, in respect to the miseries and horrible calamities that accompany a civil war, or that dissolute condition of masterless men, without subjection to laws and a coercive power to tie their hands from rapine and revenge: nor considering that the greatest pressure of sovereign governors, proceedeth not from any delight or profit they can expect in the damage or weakening of their subjects, in whose vigor consisteth their own strength and glory; but in the restiveness of themselves, that unwillingly contributing to their own defense, make it necessary for their governors to draw from them what they can in time of peace, that they may have means on any emergent occasion or sudden need, to resist or take advantage on their enemies. For all men are by nature provided of notable multiplying glasses, that is their passions and self-love, through which every little payment appeareth a great grievance; but are destitute of those prospective glasses, namely moral and civil science, to see afar off the miseries that hang over them, and cannot without such payment be avoided.

CHAPTER XXI
OF THE LIBERTY OF SUBJECTS

Liberty, or freedom, signifieth, properly, the absence of opposition: by opposition, I mean external impediments of motion; and may be applied no less to irrational and inanimate creatures, than to rational. For whatsoever is so tied, or environed, as it cannot move but within a certain space, which space is determined by the opposition of some external body, we say it hath not liberty to go further. And so of all living creatures, whilst they are imprisoned or restrained, with walls or chains, and of the water whilst it is kept in by banks or vessels, that otherwise would spread itself into a larger space, we use to say, they are not at liberty to move in such manner, as without those external impediments they would. But when the impediment of motion is in the constitution of the thing itself, we use not to say it wants the liberty, but the *power* to move; as when a stone lieth still, or a man is fastened to his bed by sickness.

And according to this proper and generally received meaning of the word, *a "freeman" is he that in those things which by his strength and wit he is able to do, is not hindered to do what he has a will to.* But when the words "free" and "liberty" are applied to anything but bodies, they are abused; for that which is not subject to motion is not subject to impediment: and therefore, when it is said, for example, the way is free, no liberty of the way is signified, but of those that walk in it without stop. And when we say a gift is free, there is not meant any liberty of the gift, but of the giver, that was not bound by any law or covenant to give it. So when we "speak freely," it is not the liberty of voice or pronunciation, but of the man, whom no law hath obliged to speak otherwise than he did. Lastly, from the use of the word *free-will*, no liberty can be inferred of the will, desire, or inclination, but the liberty of the man; which consisteth in this, that he finds no stop, in doing what he has the will, desire, or inclination to do.

Fear and liberty are consistent; as when a man throweth his goods into the sea for *fear* the ship should sink, he doth it nevertheless very willingly, and may refuse to do it if he will; it is therefore the action of one that was *free:* so a man sometimes pays his debt, only for fear of imprisonment, which because nobody hindered him from detaining, was the action of a man at *liberty*. And generally all actions which men do in commonwealths, for fear of the law, are actions which the doers had liberty to omit.

Liberty and necessity are consistent: as in the water, that hath not only *liberty*, but a *necessity* of descending by the channel; so likewise in the actions which men voluntarily do: which, because they proceed from their will, proceed from *liberty*; and yet, because every act of man's will, and every desire, and inclination proceedeth from some cause, and that from another cause, in a continual chain, whose first link is in the hand of God the first of all causes, proceed from *necessity*. So that to him that could see the connection of those causes, the necessity of all men's voluntary actions, would appear manifest. And therefore God, that seeth and disposeth all things, seeth also that the liberty of man in doing what he will, is accompanied with the necessity of doing that which God will, and no more nor less. For though men may do many things which God does not command, nor is therefore author of them; yet they can have no passion nor appetite to anything of which appetite God's will is not the cause. And did not His will assure the *necessity* of man's will, and consequently of all that on man's will dependeth, the *liberty* of men would be a contradiction, and impediment to the omnipotence and liberty of God. And this shall suffice, as to the matter in hand, of that natural liberty, which only is properly called liberty.

But as men, for the attaining of peace and conservation of themselves thereby, have made an artificial man, which we call a commonwealth; so also have they made artificial chains, called *civil laws*, which they themselves, by mutual covenants, have fastened, at one end, to the lips of that man or assembly to whom they have given the sovereign power, and at the other end to their own ears. These bonds, in their own nature but weak, may nevertheless be made to hold, by the danger, though not by the difficulty, of breaking them.

In relation to these bonds only it is, that I am to speak now of the *liberty of subjects*. For seeing there is no commonwealth in the world wherein there be rules enough set down, for the regulating of all the actions and words of men; as being a thing impossible: it followeth necessarily that in all kinds of actions by the laws pretermitted, men have the liberty of doing what their own reasons shall suggest, for the most profitable to themselves. For if we take liberty in the proper sense for corporal liberty; that is to say, freedom from chains and prison; it were very absurd for men to clamor as they do, for the liberty they so manifestly enjoy. Again, if we take liberty for an exemption from laws, it is no less absurd for men to demand as they do, that liberty by which all other men may be masters of their lives. And yet, as absurd as it is, this is it they demand; not knowing that the laws are of no power to protect them, without a sword in the hands of a man, or men, to cause those laws to be put in execution. The liberty of a subject lieth therefore only in those things which in regulating their actions, the sovereign hath pretermitted: such as is the liberty to buy, and sell, and otherwise contract with one another; to choose their own abode, their own diet, their own trade of life, and institute their children as they themselves think fit; and the like.

Nevertheless we are not to understand that by such liberty, the sovereign power of life and death is either abolished or limited. For it has been already shown that nothing the sovereign representative can do to a subject, on what pretense soever, can properly be called injustice, or injury; because every subject is author of every act the sovereign doth; so that he never wanteth right to anything, otherwise than as he himself is the subject of God, and bound thereby to observe the laws of nature. And therefore it may, and doth often happen in commonwealths, that a subject may be put to death, by the command of the sovereign power, and yet neither do the other wrong; as when Jephtha caused his daughter to be sacrificed: in which, and the like cases, he that so dieth, had liberty to do the action for which he is, nevertheless, without injury put to death. And the same holdeth also in a sovereign prince that putteth to death an innocent subject. For though the action be against the law of nature, as being contrary to equity, as was the killing of Uriah by David; yet it was not an injury to Uriah, but to God. Not to Uriah, because the right to do what he pleased was given him by Uriah himself; and yet to God, because David was God's subject, and prohibited all iniquity by the law of nature: which distinction, David himself, when he repented the fact, evidently confirmed, saying, "To Thee only have I sinned." In the same manner, the people of Athens, when they banished the most potent of their commonwealth for ten years, thought they committed no injustice; and yet they never questioned what crime he had done, but what hurt he would do: nay they commanded the banishment of they knew not whom; and every citizen bringing his oystershell into the market place, written with the name of him he desired should be banished, without actually accusing him, sometimes banished an Aristides, for his reputation of justice, and sometimes a scurrilous jester, as Hyperbolus, to make a jest of it. And yet a man cannot say the sovereign people of Athens wanted right to banish them, or an Athenian the liberty to jest, or to be just.

The liberty whereof there is so frequent and honorable mention in the histories and philosophy of the ancient Greeks and Romans, and in the writings and discourse of those that from them have received all their learning in the politics, is not the liberty of particular men, but the liberty of the commonwealth; which is the same with that which every man then should have, if there were no civil laws nor commonwealth at all. And the effects of it also be the same. For as amongst masterless men, there is perpetual war of every man against his neighbor; no inheritance, to transmit to the son, nor to expect from the father; no propriety of goods or lands; no security; but a full and absolute liberty in every particular man: so in states, and commonwealths not dependent on one another, every commonwealth, not every man, has an absolute liberty, to do what it shall judge—that is to say, what that man, or assembly that representeth it, shall judge—most conducing to their benefit. But withal, they live in the condition of a perpetual war, and upon the confines of battle, with their frontiers armed, and cannons planted against their neighbors round about. The Athenians and Romans were free; that is, free commonwealths: not that any particular men had the liberty to resist their own representative, but that their representative had the liberty to resist or invade other people. There is written on the turrets of the city of Lucca in great characters at this day, the word *libertas;* yet no man can thence infer that a particular man has more liberty or immunity from the service of the commonwealth there than in Constantinople. Whether a commonwealth be monarchical or popular, the freedom is still the same.

But it is an easy thing for men to be deceived by the specious name of liberty; and, for want of judgment to distinguish, mistake that for their private inheritance and birthright, which is the right of the public only. And when the same error is confirmed by the authority of men in reputation for their writings on this subject, it is no wonder if it produce sedition and change of government. In these western parts of the world, we are made to receive our opinions concerning the institution and rights of commonwealths from Aristotle, Cicero, and other men, Greeks and Romans, that living under popular states, derived those rights not from the principles of nature, but transcribed them into their books out of the practice of their own commonwealths, which were popular; as the grammarians describe the rules of language out of the practice of the time, or the rules of poetry out of the poems of Homer and Virgil. And because the Athenians were taught, to keep them from desire of changing their government, that they were freemen, and all that lived under monarchy were slaves; therefore Aristotle puts it down in his *Politics* (Lib. vi, Cap. ii), "In democracy, liberty is to be supposed; for it is commonly held that no man is free in any other government." And as Aristotle, so Cicero and other writers have grounded their civil doctrine on the opinions of the Romans, who were taught to hate monarchy, at first, by them that having deposed their sovereign, shared amongst them the sovereignty of Rome; and afterwards by their successors. And by reading of these Greek and Latin authors, men from their childhood have gotten a habit, under a false show of liberty, of favoring tumults, and of licentious controlling the actions of their sovereigns, and again of controlling those controllers; with the effusion of so much blood, as I think I may truly say, there was never anything so dearly bought as these western parts have bought the learning of the Greek and Latin tongues.

To come now to the particulars of the true liberty of a subject—that is to say, what are the things which, though commanded by the sovereign, he may nevertheless without injustice refuse to do,—we are to consider, what rights we pass away when we make a commonwealth; or, which is all one, what liberty we deny ourselves by owning all the actions, without exception, of the man, or assembly, we make our sovereign. For in the act of our *submission* consisteth both our *obligation* and our *liberty;* which must therefore be inferred by arguments taken from thence: there being no obligation on any man which ariseth not from some act of his own; for all men equally are by nature free. And because such arguments must either be drawn from the express words, "I authorize all his actions," or from the intention of him that submitteth himself to his power, which intention is to be understood by the end for which he so submitteth; the obligation, and liberty of the subject, is to be derived either from those words or others equivalent, or else from the end of the institution of sovereignty, namely, the peace of the subjects within themselves and their defense against a common enemy.

First therefore, seeing sovereignty by institution is by covenant of everyone to everyone; and sovereignty by acquisition, by covenants of the vanquished to the victor, or child to the parent; it is manifest that every subject has liberty in all those things, the right whereof cannot by covenant be transferred. I have shewn before, in the fourteenth chapter, that covenants not to defend a man's own body are void. Therefore:

If the sovereign command a man, though justly condemned, to kill, wound, or maim himself; or not to resist those that assault him; or to abstain from the use of food, air, medicine, or any other thing, without which he cannot live; yet hath that man the liberty to disobey.

If a man be interrogated by the sovereign, or his authority, concerning a crime done by himself, he is not bound, without assurance of pardon, to confess it; because no man, as I have shown in the same chapter, can be obliged by covenant to accuse himself.

Again, the consent of a subject to sovereign power is contained in these words, "I authorize, or take upon me, all his actions"; in which there is no restriction at all of his own former natural liberty: for by allowing him to kill me, I am not bound to kill myself when he commands me. It is one thing to say, "Kill me, or my fellow, if you please"; another thing to say, "I will kill myself, or my fellow." It followeth therefore, that:

No man is bound by the words themselves, either to kill himself or any other man; and consequently, that the obligation a man may sometimes have, upon the command of the sovereign to execute any dangerous or dishonorable office, dependeth not on the words of our submission, but on the intention, which is to be understood by the end thereof. When therefore our refusal to obey, frustrates the end for which the sovereignty was ordained, then there is no liberty to refuse; otherwise there is.

Upon this ground, a man that is commanded as a soldier to fight against the enemy, though his sovereign have right enough to punish his refusal with death, may nevertheless in many cases refuse, without injustice; as when he substituteth a sufficient soldier in his place: for in this case he deserteth not the service of the commonwealth. And there is allowance to be made for natural timorousness; not only to women, of whom no such dangerous duty is expected, but also to men of feminine courage. When armies fight, there is on one side, or both, a running away; yet when they do it not out of treachery, but fear, they are not esteemed to do it unjustly, but dishonorably. For the same reason, to avoid battle is not injustice, but cowardice. But he that enrolleth himself a soldier, or taketh imprest money, taketh away the excuse of a timorous nature; and is obliged not only to go to the battle, but also not run from it, without his captain's leave. And when the defense of the commonwealth requireth at once the help of all that are able to bear arms, everyone is obliged; because otherwise the institution of the commonwealth, which they have not the purpose or courage to preserve, was in vain.

To resist the sword of the commonwealth in defense of another man, guilty or innocent, no man hath liberty; because such liberty takes away from the sovereign the means of protecting us, and is therefore destructive of the very essence of government. But in case a great many men together have already resisted the sovereign power unjustly, or committed some capital crime, for which every one of them expecteth death, whether have they not the liberty then to join together, and assist and defend one another? Certainly they have; for they but defend their lives, which the guilty man may as well do as the innocent. There was indeed injustice in the first breach of their duty; their bearing of arms subsequent to it, though it be to maintain what they have done, is no new unjust act. And if it be only to defend their persons, it is not unjust at all. But the offer of pardon taketh from them, to whom it is offered, the plea of self-defense, and maketh their perseverance in assisting, or defending the rest, unlawful.

As for other liberties, they depend on the silence of the law. In cases where the sovereign has prescribed no rule, there the subject hath the liberty to do, or forbear, according to his own discretion. And therefore such liberty is in some places more, and in some less; and in some times more, in other times less, according as they that have the sovereignty shall think most convenient. As for example, there was a time when in England a man might enter into his own land, and dispossess such as wrongfully possessed it, by force. But in after times, that liberty of forcible entry was taken away, by a statute made, by the king, in parliament. And in some places of the world, men have the liberty of many wives; in other places such liberty is not allowed.

If a subject have a controversy with his sovereign, of debt, or of right of possession of lands or goods, or concerning any service required at his hands, or concerning any penalty, corporal, or pecuniary, grounded on a precedent law; he hath the same liberty to sue for his right as if it were against a subject, and before such judges as are appointed by the sovereign. For seeing the sovereign demandeth by force of a former law and not by virtue of his power, he declareth thereby, that he requireth no more than shall appear to be due by that law. The suit therefore is not contrary to the will of the sovereign; and consequently the subject hath the liberty to demand the hearing of his cause, and sentence, according to that law. But if he demand or take anything by pretense of his power, there lieth, in that case, no action of law; for all that is done by him in virtue of his power, is done by the authority of every subject, and consequently he that brings an action against the sovereign, brings it against himself.

If a monarch, or sovereign assembly, grant a liberty to all or any of his subjects, which grant standing, he is disabled to provide for their safety, the grant is void; unless he directly renounce, or transfer the sovereignty to another. For in that he might openly, if it had been his will, and in plain terms, have renounced or transferred it, and did not; it is to be understood it was not his will, but that the grant proceeded from ignorance of the repugnancy between such a liberty and the sovereign power; and therefore the sovereignty is still retained; and consequently all those powers, which are necessary to the exercising thereof; such as are the power of war, and peace, of judicature, of appointing officers, and councillors, of levying money, and the rest named in the eighteenth chapter.

The obligation of subjects to the sovereign, is understood to last as long, and no longer, than the power lasteth by which he is able to protect them. For the right men have by nature to protect themselves, when none else can protect them, can by no covenant be relinquished. The sovereignty is the soul of the commonwealth; which once departed from the body, the members do no more receive their motion from it. The end of obedience is protection; which, wheresoever a man seeth it, either in his own or in another's sword, nature applieth his obedience to it, and his endeavor to maintain it. And though sovereignty, in the intention of them that make it, be immortal; yet it is in its own nature, not only subject to violent death, by foreign war; but also through the ignorance, and passions of men, it hath in it, from the very institution, many seeds of a natural mortality, by intestine discord.

If a subject be taken prisoner in war, or his person or his

means of life be within the guards of the enemy, and hath his life and corporal liberty given him on condition to be subject to the victor, he hath liberty to accept the condition; and having accepted it, is the subject of him that took him, because he had no other way to preserve himself. The case is the same, if he be detained on the same terms in a foreign country. But if a man be held in prison, or bonds, or is not trusted with the liberty of his body, he cannot be understood to be bound by covenant to subjection; and therefore may, if he can, make his escape by any means whatsoever.

If a monarch shall relinquish the sovereignty both for himself and his heirs, his subjects return to the absolute liberty of nature; because, though nature may declare who are his sons, and who are the nearest of his kin; yet it dependeth on his own will, as hath been said in the precedent chapter, who shall be his heir. If therefore he will have no heir, there is no sovereignty, nor subjection. The case is the same, if he die without known kindred, and without declaration of his heir. For then there can no heir be known, and consequently no subjection be due.

If the sovereign banish his subject; during the banishment, he is not subject. But he that is sent on a message, or hath leave to travel, is still subject; but it is by contract between sovereigns, not by virtue of the covenant of subjection. For whosoever entereth into another's dominion, is subject to all the laws thereof; unless he have a privilege of the amity of the sovereigns, or by special license.

If a monarch subdued by war, render himself subject to the victor; his subjects are delivered from their former obligation, and become obliged to the victor. If he be held prisoner, or have not the liberty of his own body, he is not understood to have given away the right of sovereignty; and therefore his subjects are obliged to yield obedience to the magistrates formerly placed, governing not in their own name, but in his. For, his right remaining, the question is only of the administration; that is to say, of the magistrates and officers; which, if he have not means to name, he is supposed to approve those which he himself had formerly appointed.

John Locke (1632–1704)

AN ESSAY CONCERNING THE TRUE ORIGINAL EXTENT AND END OF CIVIL GOVERNMENT[1]

CHAPTER II
OF THE STATE OF NATURE

4. To understand political power aright, and derive it from its original, we must consider what state all men are naturally in, and that is a state of perfect freedom to order their actions and dispose of their possessions and persons as they think fit, within the bounds of the law of nature, without asking leave, or depending upon the will of any other man.

A state also of equality, wherein all the power and jurisdiction is reciprocal, no one having more than another; there being nothing more evident than that creatures of the same species and rank, promiscuously born to all the same advantages of nature, and the use of the same faculties, should also be equal one amongst another without subordination or subjunction, unless the Lord and Master of them all should by any manifest declaration of His will set one above another, and confer on him by an evident and clear appointment an undoubted right to dominion and sovereignty.

5. This equality of men by nature the judicious Hooker looks upon as so evident in itself and beyond all question, that he makes it the foundation of that obligation to mutual love amongst men on which he builds the duties they owe one another, and from whence he derives the great maxims of justice and charity. His words are:—

"The like natural inducement hath brought men to know that it is no less their duty to love others than themselves; for seeing those things which are equal must needs all have one measure, if I cannot but wish to receive good, even as much at

[1] The second of Locke's "Two Treatises on Government." *The Editors.*

every man's hands as any man can wish unto his own soul,
how should I look to have any part of my desire herein satisfied, unless myself be careful to satisfy the like desire, which
is undoubtedly in other men weak, being of one and the same
nature? To have anything offered them repugnant to this desire, must needs in all respects grieve them as much as me, so
that, if I do harm, I must look to suffer, there being no reason
that others should show greater measures of love to me than
they have by me showed unto them. My desire, therefore,
to be loved of my equals in nature as much as possible may
be, imposeth upon me a natural duty of bearing to themward
fully the like affection; from which relation of equality between ourselves and them that are as ourselves, what several
rules and canons natural reason hath drawn for direction of
life no man is ignorant."—(Eccl. Pol., lib. i).

6. But though this be a state of liberty, yet it is not a state of
license; though man in that state have an uncontrollable liberty
to dispose of his person or possessions, yet he has not liberty
to destroy himself, or so much as any creature in his possession, but where some nobler use than its bare preservation
calls for it. The state of nature has a law of nature to govern
it, which obliges everyone; and reason, which is that law,
teaches all mankind who will but consult it, that, being all
equal and independent, no one ought to harm another in his
life, health, liberty, or possessions. For men being all the workmanship of one omnipotent and infinitely wise Maker—all the
servants of one sovereign Master, sent into the world by His
order, and about His business—they are His property, whose
workmanship they are, made to last during His, not one another's pleasure; and being furnished with like faculties, sharing all in one community of nature, there cannot be supposed
any such subordination among us, that may authorize us to
destroy one another, as if we were made for one another's
uses, as the inferior ranks of creatures are for ours. Everyone, as he is bound to preserve himself, and not to quit his
station willfully, so, by the like reason, when his own preservation comes not in competition, ought he, as much as he can,
to preserve the rest of mankind, and not, unless it be to do
justice on an offender, take away or impair the life, or what
tends to the preservation of the life, the liberty, health, limb,
or goods of another.

7. And that all men may be restrained from invading others'
rights, and from doing hurt to one another, and the law of
nature be observed, which willeth the peace and preservation

of all mankind, the execution of the law of nature is in that state put into every man's hand, whereby everyone has a right to punish the transgressors of that law to such a degree as may hinder its violation. For the law of nature would, as all other laws that concern men in this world, be in vain if there were nobody that, in the state of nature, had a power to execute that law, and thereby preserve the innocent and restrain offenders. And if anyone in the state of nature may punish another for any evil he has done, everyone may do so. For in that state of perfect equality, where naturally there is no superiority or jurisdiction of one over another, what any may do in prosecution of that law, everyone must needs have a right to do.

8. And thus in the state of nature one man comes by a power over another; but yet no absolute or arbitrary power, to use a criminal, when he has got him in his hands, according to the passionate heats or boundless extravagance of his own will; but only to retribute to him so far as calm reason and conscience dictate what is proportionate to his transgression, which is so much as may serve for reparation and restraint. For these two are the only reasons why one man may lawfully do harm to another, which is that we call punishment. In transgressing the law of nature, the offender declares himself to live by another rule than that of common reason and equity, which is that measure God has set to the actions of men, for their mutual security; and so he becomes dangerous to mankind, the tie which is to secure them from injury and violence being slighted and broken by him. Which, being a trespass against the whole species, and the peace and safety of it, provided for by the law of nature, every man upon this score, by the right he hath to preserve mankind in general, may restrain, or, where it is necessary, destroy things noxious to them, and so may bring such evil on anyone who hath transgressed that law, as may make him repent the doing of it, and thereby deter him, and by his example others, from doing the like mischief. And in this case, and upon this ground, every man hath a right to punish the offender, and be executioner of the law of nature.

9. I doubt not but this will seem a very strange doctrine to some men: but before they condemn it, I desire them to resolve me by what right any prince or state can put to death or punish an alien, for any crime he commits in their country. 'Tis certain their laws, by virtue of any sanction they receive from the promulgated will of the legislative, reach not a

stranger: they speak not to him, nor, if they did, is he bound to hearken to them. The legislative authority, by which they are in force over the subjects of that commonwealth, hath no power over him. Those who have the supreme power of making laws in England, France, or Holland, are to an Indian but like the rest of the world—men without authority. And, therefore, if by the law of nature every man hath not a power to punish offenses against it, as he soberly judges the case to require, I see not how the magistrates of any community can punish an alien of another country; since in reference to him they can have no more power than what every man naturally may have over another.

10. Besides the crime which consists in violating the law, and varying from the right rule of reason, whereby a man so far becomes degenerate, and declares himself to quit the principles of human nature, and to be a noxious creature, there is commonly injury done, and some person or other, some other man receives damage by his transgression, in which case he who hath received any damage, has, besides the right of punishment common to him with other men, a particular right to seek reparation from him that has done it. And any other person who finds it just, may also join with him that is injured, and assist him in recovering from the offender so much as may make satisfaction for the harm he has suffered.

11. From these two distinct rights—the one of punishing the crime, for restraint and preventing the like offense, which right of punishing is in everybody; the other of taking reparation, which belongs only to the injured party—comes it to pass that the magistrate, who by being magistrate hath the common right of punishing put into his hands, can often, where the public good demands not the execution of the law, remit the punishment of criminal offenses by his own authority, but yet cannot remit the satisfaction due to any private man for the damage he has received. That he who has suffered the damage has a right to demand in his own name, and he alone can remit. The damnified person has this power of appropriating to himself the goods or service of the offender, by right of self-preservation, as every man has a power to punish the crime, to prevent its being committed again, by the right he has of preserving all mankind, and doing all reasonable things he can in order to that end. And thus it is that every man in the state of nature has a power to kill a murderer, both to deter others from doing the like injury, which no reparation can compensate, by the example of the punishment that at-

tends it from everybody, and also to secure men from the attempts of a criminal who having renounced reason, the common rule and measure God hath given to mankind, hath by the unjust violence and slaughter he hath committed upon one, declared war against all mankind, and therefore may be destroyed as a lion or a tiger, one of those wild savage beasts with whom men can have no society nor security. And upon this is grounded that great law of nature. "Whoso sheddeth man's blood, by man shall his blood be shed." And Cain was so fully convinced that everyone had a right to destroy such a criminal, that after the murder of his brother he cries out, "Every one that findeth me shall slay me;" so plain was it writ in the hearts of mankind.

12. By the same reason may a man in the state of nature punish the lesser breaches of that law. It will perhaps be demanded, With death? I answer, each transgression may be punished to that degree, and with so much severity, as will suffice to make it an ill bargain to the offender, give him cause to repent, and terrify others from doing the like. Every offense that can be committed in the state of nature, may in the state of nature be also punished equally, and as far forth as it may, in a commonwealth. For though it would be beside my present purpose to enter here into the particulars of the law of nature, or its measures of punishment, yet it is certain there is such a law, and that, too, as intelligible and plain to a rational creature and a studier of that law as the positive laws of commonwealths; nay, possibly plainer, as much as reason is easier to be understood than the fancies and intricate contrivances of men, following contrary and hidden interests put into words; for truly so are a great part of the municipal laws of countries, which are only so far right as they are founded on the law of nature, by which they are to be regulated and interpreted.

13. To this strange doctrine—viz., that in the state of nature everyone has the executive power of the law of nature—I doubt not but it will be objected that it is unreasonable for men to be judges in their own cases, that self-love will make men partial to themselves and their friends. And on the other side, that ill-nature, passion, and revenge will carry them too far in punishing others; and hence nothing but confusion and disorder will follow; and that therefore God hath certainly appointed government to restrain the partiality and violence of men. I easily grant that civil government is the proper remedy for the inconveniences of the state of nature, which must cer-

tainly be great where men may be judges in their own case, since 'tis easy to be imagined that he who was so unjust as to do his brother an injury, will scarce be so just as to condemn himself for it. But I shall desire those who make this objection, to remember that absolute monarchs are but men, and if government is to be the remedy of those evils which necessarily follow from men's being judges in their own cases, and the state of nature is therefore not to be endured, I desire to know what kind of government that is, and how much better it is than the state of nature, where one man commanding a multitude, has the liberty to be judge in his own case, and may do to all his subjects whatever he pleases, without the least question or control of those who execute his pleasure; and in whatsoever he doth, whether led by reason, mistake, or passion, must be submitted to, which men in the state of nature are not bound to do one to another? And if he that judges, judges amiss in his own or any other case, he is answerable for it to the rest of mankind.

14. 'Tis often asked as a mighty objection, Where are, or ever were there, any men in such a state of nature? To which it may suffice as an answer at present: That since all princes and rulers of independent governments all through the world are in a state of nature, 'tis plain the world never was, nor ever will be, without numbers of men in that state. I have named all governors of independent communities, whether they are or are not in league with others. For 'tis not every compact that puts an end to the state of nature between men, but only this one of agreeing together mutually to enter into one community, and make one body politic; other promises and compacts men may make one with another, and yet still be in the state of nature. The promises and bargains for truck, etc., between the two men in Soldania, in or between a Swiss and an Indian, in the woods of America, are binding to them, though they are perfectly in a state of nature in reference to one another. For truth and keeping of faith belong to men as men, and not as members of society.

15. To those that say there were never any men in the state of nature, I will not only oppose the authority of the judicious Hooker—(Eccl. Pol., lib. i., sect. 10), where he says, "The laws which have been hitherto mentioned," i.e., the laws of nature, "do bind men absolutely, even as they are men, although they have never any settled fellowship, and never any solemn agreement amongst themselves what to do or not to do; but forasmuch as we are not by ourselves sufficient to furnish

ourselves with competent store of things needful for such a life as our nature doth desire—a life fit for the dignity of man —therefore to supply those defects and imperfections which are in us, as living single and solely by ourselves, we are naturally induced to seek communion and fellowship with others; this was the cause of men's uniting themselves at first in politic societies"—but I moreover affirm that all men are naturally in that state, and remain so, till by their own consents they make themselves members of some politic society; and I doubt not, in the sequel of this discourse, to make it very clear.

CHAPTER V
OF PROPERTY

25. Whether we consider natural reason, which tells us that men being once born have a right to their preservation, and consequently to meat and drink and such other things as nature affords for their subsistence; or revelation, which gives us an account of those grants God made of the world to Adam, and to Noah and his sons, 'tis very clear that God, as King David says, Psalm cxv. 16, "has given the earth to the children of men," given it to mankind in common. But this being supposed, it seems to some a very great difficulty how anyone should ever come to have a property in anything. I will not content myself to answer that if it be difficult to make out property upon a supposition that God gave the world to Adam and his posterity in common, it is impossible that any man but one universal monarch should have any property upon a supposition that God gave the world to Adam and his heirs in succession, exclusive of all the rest of his posterity. But I shall endeavor to show how men might come to have a property in several parts of that which God gave to mankind in common, and that without any express compact of all the commoners.

26. God, who hath given the world to men in common, hath also given them reason to make use of it to the best advantage of life and convenience. The earth and all that is therein is given to men for the support and comfort of their being. And though all the fruits it naturally produces, and beasts it feeds, belong to mankind in common, as they are produced by the spontaneous hand of nature; and nobody has originally a private dominion exclusive of the rest of man-

kind in any of them as they are thus in their natural state; yet being given for the use of men, there must of necessity be a means to appropriate them some way or other before they can be of any use or at all beneficial to any particular man. The fruit or venison which nourishes the wild Indian, who knows no enclosure, and is still a tenant in common, must be his, and so his, i.e., a part of him, that another can no longer have any right to it, before it can do any good for the support of his life.

27. Though the earth and all inferior creatures be common to all men, yet every man has a property in his own person; this nobody has any right to but himself. The labor of his body and the work of his hands we may say are properly his. Whatsoever, then, he removes out of the state that nature hath provided and left it in, he hath mixed his labor with, and joined to it something that is his own, and thereby makes it his property. It being by him removed from the common state nature placed it in, it hath by this labor something annexed to it that excludes the common right of other men. For this labor being the unquestionable property of the laborer, no man but he can have a right to what that is once joined to, at least where there is enough, and as good left in common for others.

28. He that is nourished by the acorns he picked up under an oak, or the apples he gathered from the trees in the wood, has certainly appropriated them to himself. Nobody can deny but the nourishment is his. I ask, then, When did they begin to be his—when he digested, or when he ate, or when he boiled, or when he brought them home, or when he picked them up? And 'tis plain if the first gathering made them not his, nothing else could. That labor put a distinction between them and common; that added something to them more than nature, the common mother of all, had done, and so they became his private right. And will anyone say he had no right to those acorns or apples he thus appropriated, because he had not the consent of all mankind to make them his? Was it a robbery thus to assume to himself what belonged to all in common? If such a consent as that was necessary, man had starved, notwithstanding the plenty God had given him. We see in commons which remain so by compact that 'tis the taking any part of what is common and removing it out of the state nature leaves it in, which begins the property; without which the common is of no use. And the taking of this or that part does not depend on the express consent of all the commoners.

Thus the grass my horse has bit, the turfs my servant has cut, and the ore I have dug in any place where I have a right to them in common with others, become my property without the assignation or consent of anybody. The labor that was mine removing them out of that common state they were in, hath fixed my property in them.

29. By making an explicit consent of every commoner necessary to anyone's appropriating to himself any part of what is given in common. Children or servants could not cut the meat which their father or master had provided for them in common without assigning to everyone his peculiar part. Though the water running in the fountain be everyone's, yet who can doubt but that in the pitcher is his only who drew it out? His labor hath taken it out of the hands of Nature where it was common, and belonged equally to all her children, and hath thereby appropriated it to himself.

30. Thus this law of reason makes the deer that Indian's who hath killed it; it is allowed to be his goods who hath bestowed his labor upon it, though, before, it was the common right of everyone. And amongst those who are counted the civilized part of mankind, who have made and multiplied positive laws to determine property, this original law of nature for the beginning of property, in what was before common, still takes place, and by virtue thereof, what fish anyone catches in the ocean, that great and still remaining common of mankind; or what ambergris anyone takes up here is by the labor that removes it out of that common state nature left it in, made his property who takes that pains about it. And even amongst us, the hare that anyone is hunting is thought his who pursues her during the chase. For being a beast that is still looked upon as common, and no man's private possession, whoever has employed so much labor about any of that kind as to find and pursue her has thereby removed her from the state of nature wherein she was common, and hath began a property.

31. It will perhaps be objected to this, that if gathering the acorns, or other fruits of the earth, etc., makes a right to them, then anyone may engross as much as he will. To which I answer, Not so. The same law of nature that does by this means give us property, does also bound that property too. "God has given us all things richly" (i Tim. vi. 17), is the voice of reason confirmed by inspiration. But how far has He given it us? To enjoy. As much as anyone can make use of to any advantage of life before it spoils, so much he may by his

labor fix .a property in; whatever is beyond this, is more than his share, and belongs to others. Nothing was made by God for man to spoil or destroy. And thus considering the plenty of natural provisions there was a long time in the world, and the few spenders, and to how small a part of that provision the industry of one man could extend itself, and engross it to the prejudice of others—especially keeping within the bounds, set by reason, of what might serve for his use—there could be then little room for quarrels or contentions about property so established.

32. But the chief matter of property being now not the fruits of the earth, and the beasts that subsist on it, but the earth itself, as that which takes in and carries with it all the rest, I think it is plain that property in that, too, is acquired as the former. As much land as a man tills, plants, improves, cultivates, and can use the product of, so much is his property. He by his labor does as it were enclose it from the common. Nor will it invalidate his right to say, everybody else has an equal title to it; and therefore he cannot appropriate, he cannot enclose, without the consent of all his fellow-commoners, all mankind. God, when He gave the world in common to all mankind, commanded man also to labor, and the penury of his condition required it of him. God and his reason commanded him to subdue the earth, i.e., improve it for the benefit of life, and therein lay out something upon it that was his own, his labor. He that, in obedience to this command of God, subdued, tilled, and sowed any part of it, thereby annexed to it something that was his property, which another had no title to, nor could without injury take from him. . . .

CHAPTER VIII
OF THE BEGINNING OF POLITICAL SOCIETIES

95. Men being, as has been said, by nature all free, equal, and independent, no one can be put out of this estate, and subjected to the political power of another, without his own consent, which is done by agreeing with other men to join and unite into a community for their comfortable, safe, and peaceable living one amongst another, in a secure enjoyment of their properties, and a greater security against any that are not of it. This any number of men may do, because it injures not the freedom of the rest; they are left as they were in the

liberty of the state of nature. When any number of men have so consented to make one community or government, they are thereby presently incorporated, and make one body politic, wherein the majority have a right to act and conclude the rest.

96. For when any number of men have, by the consent of every individual, made a community, they have thereby made that community one body, with a power to act as one body, which is only by the will and determination of the majority. For that which acts any community being only the consent of the individuals of it, and it being one body must move one way, it is necessary the body should move that way whither the greater force carries it, which is the consent of the majority; or else it is impossible it should act or continue one body, one community, which the consent of every individual that united into it agreed that it should; and so everyone is bound by that consent to be concluded by the majority. And therefore we see that in assemblies empowered to act by positive laws, where no number is set by that positive law which empowers them, the act of the majority passes for the act of the whole, and of course determines, as having by the law of nature and reason the power of the whole.

97. And thus every man, by consenting with others to make one body politic under one government, puts himself under an obligation to every one of that society, to submit to the determination of the majority, and to be concluded by it; or else this original compact, whereby he with others incorporates into one society, would signify nothing, and be no compact, if he be left free and under no other ties than he was in before in the state of nature. For what appearance would there be of any compact? What new engagement if he were no farther tied by any decrees of the society, than he himself thought fit, and did actually consent to? This would be still as great a liberty as he himself had before his compact, or anyone else in the state of nature hath, who may submit himself and consent to any acts of it if he thinks fit.

98. For if the consent of the majority shall not in reason be received as the act of the whole and conclude every individual, nothing but the consent of every individual can make anything to be the act of the whole, which considering the infirmities of health and avocations of business, which in a number, though much less than that of a commonwealth, will necessarily keep many away from the public assembly, and the variety of opinions, and contrariety of interest, which unavoidably happen in all collections of men, 'tis next to impos-

sible ever to be had. And therefore if the coming into society be upon such terms it will be only like Cato's coming into the theater, *tantum ut exiret*. Such a constitution as this would make the mighty leviathan of a shorter duration than the feeblest creatures, and not let it outlast the day it was born in; which cannot be supposed till we can think that rational creatures should desire and constitute societies only to be dissolved. For where the majority cannot conclude the rest, there they cannot act as one body, and consequently will be immediately dissolved again.

99. Whosoever therefore out of a state of nature unite into a community must be understood to give up all the power necessary to the ends for which they unite into society, to the majority of the community, unless they expressly agreed in any number greater than the majority. And this is done by barely agreeing to unite into one political society, which is all the compact that is, or needs be, between the individuals that enter into or make up a commonwealth. And thus that which begins and actually constitutes any political society is nothing but the consent of any number of freemen capable of a majority to unite and incorporate into such a society. And this is that, and that only, which did or could give beginning to any lawful government in the world.

100. To this I find two objections made.

First: That there are no instances to be found in story of a company of men independent, and equal one amongst another, that met together and in this way began and set up a government.

Secondly: 'Tis impossible of right that men should do so, because all men being born under government, they are to submit to that, and are not at liberty to begin a new one.

101. To the first there is this to answer—That it is not at all to be wondered that history gives us but a very little account of men that lived together in the state of nature. The inconveniences of that condition, and the love and want of society, no sooner brought any number of them together, but they presently united and incorporated if they designed to continue together. And if we may not suppose men ever to have been in the state of nature, because we hear not much of them in such a state, we may as well suppose the armies of Salmanasser or Xerxes were never children, because we hear little of them till they were men, and embodied in armies. Government is everywhere antecedent to records, and letters seldom come in amongst a people, till a long continuation of civil

society has, by other more necessary arts, provided for their safety, ease, and plenty. And then they begin to look after the history of their founders, and search into their original, when they have outlived the memory of it. For 'tis with commonwealths as with particular persons, they are commonly ignorant of their own birth and infancies. And if they know anything of their original, they are beholden for it to the accidental records that others have kept of it. And those that we have of the beginning of any polities in the world, excepting that of the Jews, where God Himself immediately interposed, and which favors not at all paternal dominion, are all either plain instances of such a beginning as I have mentioned, or at least have manifest footsteps of it.

102. He must show a strange inclination to deny evident matter of fact, when it agrees not with his hypothesis, who will not allow that the beginning of Rome and Venice were by the uniting together of several men, free and independent one of another, amongst whom there was no natural superiority or subjection. And if Josephus Acosta's word may be taken, he tells us that in many parts of America there was no government at all. "There are great and apparent conjectures," says he, "that these men (speaking of those of Peru) for a long time had neither kings nor commonwealths, but lived in troops, as they do this day in Florida—the Cheriquanas, those of Brazil, and many other nations, which have no certain kings, but, as occasion is offered in peace or war, they choose their captains as they please" (Lib. i. cap. 25). If it be said, that every man there was born subject to his father, or the head of his family, that the subjection due from a child to a father took not away his freedom of uniting into what political society he thought fit, has been already proved; but be that as it will, these men, it is evident, were actually free; and whatever superiority some politicians now would place in any of them, they themselves claimed it not; but, by consent, were all equal, till, by the same consent, they set rulers over themselves. So that their politic societies all began from a voluntary union, and the mutual agreement of men freely acting in the choice of their governors and forms of government.

103. And I hope those who went away from Sparta, with Palantus, mentioned by Justin, will be allowed to have been freemen independent one of another, and to have set up a government over themselves by their own consent. Thus I have given several examples out of history of people, free and in the state of nature, that, being met together, incorporated and

began a commonwealth. And if the want of such instances be
an argument to prove that government were not nor could not
be so begun, I suppose the contenders for paternal empire
were better let it alone than urge it against natural liberty;
for if they can give so many instances out of history of governments began upon paternal right, I think (though at least
an argument from what has been to what should of right be of
no great force) one might, without any great danger, yield
them the cause. But if I might advise them in the case, they
would do well not to search too much into the original of
governments as they have begun *de facto,* lest they should
find at the foundation of most of them something very little
favorable to the design they promote, and such a power as
they contend for.

104. But, to conclude: reason being plain on our side that
men are naturally free; and the examples of history showing
that the governments of the world, that were begun in peace,
had their beginning laid on that foundation, and were made by
the consent of the people; there can be little room for doubt,
either where the right is, or what has been the opinion or
practice of mankind about the first erecting of governments. . . .

119. Every man being, as has been shown, naturally
free, and nothing being able to put him into subjection to any
earthly power but only his own consent, it is to be considered
what shall be understood to be sufficient declaration of a man's
consent to make him subject to the laws of any government.
There is a common distinction of an express and a tacit consent, which will concern our present case. Nobody doubts but
an express consent of any man entering into any society makes
him a perfect member of that society, a subject of that government. The difficulty is, what ought to be looked upon as a
tacit consent, and how far it binds, i.e., how far anyone shall
be looked on to have consented, and thereby submitted to any
government, where he has made no expressions of it at all.
And to this I say that every man that hath any possession or
enjoyment of any part of the dominions of any government
doth thereby give his tacit consent, and is as far forth obliged
to obedience to the laws of that government during such enjoyment as anyone under it; whether this his possession be of
land to him and his heirs for ever, or a lodging only for a
week; or whether it be barely traveling freely on the highway;

and in effect it reaches as far as the very being of anyone within the territories of that government.

120. To understand this the better, it is fit to consider that every man when he at first incorporates himself into any commonwealth, he, by his uniting himself thereunto, annexed also, and submits to the community those possessions which he has or shall acquire that do not already belong to any other government; for it would be a direct contradiction for anyone to enter into society with others for the securing and regulating of property, and yet to suppose his land, whose property is to be regulated by the laws of the society, should be exempt from the jurisdiction of that government to which he himself, and the property of the land, is a subject. By the same act, therefore, whereby anyone unites his person, which was before free, to any commonwealth, by the same he unites his possessions, which was before free, to it also; and they become, both of them, person and possession, subject to the government and dominion of that commonwealth as long as it hath a being. Whoever therefore from thenceforth by inheritance, purchases, permission, or otherwise, enjoys any part of the land so annexed to, and under the government of that commonwealth, must take it with the condition it is under, that is, of submitting to the government of the commonwealth under whose jurisdiction it is as far forth as any subject of it.

121. But since the government has a direct jurisdiction only over the land, and reaches the possessor of it (before he has actually incorporated himself in the society), only as he dwells upon, and enjoys that: the obligation anyone is under, by virtue of such enjoyment, to submit to the government, begins and ends with the enjoyment; so that whenever the owner, who has given nothing but such a tacit consent to the government, will by donation, sale, or otherwise, quit the said possession, he is at liberty to go and incorporate himself into any other commonwealth, or to agree with others to begin a new one (*in vacuis locis*) in any part of the world they can find free and unpossessed. Whereas he that has once by actual agreement and any express declaration given his consent to be of any commonweal is perpetually and indispensably obliged to be and remain unalterably a subject to it, and can never be again in the liberty of the state of nature; unless, by any calamity, the government he was under comes to be dissolved, or else by some public acts cuts him off from being any longer a member of it.

122. But submitting to the laws of any country, living

quietly and enjoying privileges and protection under them makes not a man a member of that society. This is only a local protection and homage due to and from all those who, not being in the state of war, come within the territories belonging to any government to all parts whereof the force of its law extends. But this no more makes a man a member of that society a perpetual subject of that commonwealth, than it would make a man a subject to another in whose family he found it convenient to abide for some time; though whilst he continued in it he were obliged to comply with the laws, and submit to the government he found there. And thus we see, that foreigners by living all their lives under another government, and enjoying the privileges and protection of it, though they are bound even in conscience to submit to its administration as far forth as any denizen, yet do not thereby come to be subjects or members of that commonwealth. Nothing can make any man so, but his actually entering into it by positive engagement, and express promise and compact. This is that, which I think, concerning the beginning of political societies, and that consent which makes anyone a member of any commonwealth.

CHAPTER IX

OF THE ENDS OF POLITICAL SOCIETY AND GOVERNMENT

123. If man in the state of nature be so free, as has been said, if he be absolute lord of his own person and possessions, equal to the greatest, and subject to nobody, why will he part with his freedom, this empire, and subject himself to the dominion and control of any other power? To which, it is obvious to answer, that though in the state of nature he hath such a right, yet the enjoyment of it is very uncertain, and constantly exposed to the invasions of others. For all being kings as much as he, every man his equal, and the greater part no strict observers of equity and justice, the enjoyment of the property he has in his state is very unsafe, very unsecure. This makes him willing to quit this condition, which, however free, is full of fears and continual dangers; and it is not without reason that he seeks out and is willing to join in society with others, who are already united, or have a mind to unite, for the mutual preservation of their lives, liberties, and estates, which I call by the general name, property.

124. The great and chief end, therefore, of men's uniting into commonwealths, and putting themselves under government, is the preservation of their property; to which is the state of nature there are many things wanting.

First, There wants an established, settled, known law, received and allowed by common consent to be the standard of right and wrong, and the common measure to decide all controversies between them. For though the law of nature be plain and intelligible to all rational creatures; yet men, being biased by their interest, as well as ignorant for want of study of it, are not apt to allow of it as a law binding to them in the application of it to their particular cases.

125. Secondly, In the state of nature there wants a known and indifferent judge, with authority to determine all differences according to the established law. For everyone in that state, being both judge and executioner of the law of nature, men being partial to themselves, passion and revenge is very apt to carry them too far, and with too much heat in their own cases, as well as negligence and unconcernedness, to make them too remiss in other men's.

126. Thirdly, In the state of nature there often wants power to back and support the sentence when right, and to give it due execution. They who by any injustice offend, will seldom fail, where they are able by force to make good their injustice; such resistance many times makes the punishment dangerous, and frequently destructive to those who attempt it.

127. Thus mankind, notwithstanding all the privileges of the state of nature, being but in an ill condition, while they remain in it, are quickly driven into society. Hence it comes to pass that we seldom find any number of men live any time together in this state. The inconveniences that they are therein exposed to by the irregular and uncertain exercise of the power every man has of punishing the transgressions of others, make them take sanctuary under the established laws of government, and therein seek the preservation of their property. It is this makes them so willingly give up everyone his single power of punishing, to be exercised by such alone, as shall be appointed to it amongst them; and by such rules as the community, or those authorized by them to that purpose, shall agree on. And in this we have the original right and rise of both the legislative and executive power, as well as of the governments and societies themselves.

128. For in the state of nature, to omit the liberty he has of innocent delights, a man has two powers.

The first is to do whatsoever he thinks fit for the preservation of himself, and others within the permission of the law of nature, by which law, common to them all, he and all the rest of mankind are of one community, make up one society, distinct from all other creatures. And were it not for the corruption and viciousness of degenerate men there would be no need of any other, no necessity that men should separate from this great and natural community, and associate into lesser combinations.

The other power a man has in the state of nature is the power to punish the crimes committed against that law. Both these he gives up when he joins in a private, if I may so call it, or particular political society, and incorporates into any commonwealth separate from the rest of mankind.

129. The first power, viz., of doing whatsoever he thought fit for the preservation of himself and the rest of mankind, he gives up to be regulated by laws made by the society, so far forth as the preservation of himself and the rest of that society shall require; which laws of the society in many things confine the liberty he had by the law of nature.

130. Secondly, The power of punishing he wholly gives up, and engages his natural force (which he might before employ in the execution of the law of nature, by his own single authority as he thought fit), to assist the executive power of the society, as the law thereof shall require. For being now in a new state, wherein he is to enjoy many conveniences, from the labor, assistance, and society of others in the same community, as well as protection from its whole strength; he has to part also with as much of his natural liberty, in providing for himself, as the good, prosperity and safety of the society shall require; which is not only necessary but just, since the other members of the society do the like.

131. But though men when they enter into society give up the equality, liberty and executive power they had in the state of nature into the hands of the society, to be so far disposed of by the legislative as the good of the society shall require; yet it being only with an intention in everyone the better to preserve himself, his liberty and property (for no rational creature can be supposed to change his condition with an intention to be worse), the power of the society, or legislative constituted by them, can never be supposed to extend farther than the common good, but is obliged to secure everyone's property by providing against those three defects above-mentioned that made the state of nature so unsafe and uneasy.

And so whoever has the legislative or supreme power of any commonwealth is bound to govern by established standing laws, promulgated and known to the people, and not by extemporary decrees; by indifferent and upright judges, who are to decide controversies by those laws; and to employ the force of the community at home only in the execution of such laws, or abroad, to prevent or redress foreign injuries, and secure the community from inroads and invasion. And all this to be directed to no other end but the peace, safety, and public good of the people.

CHAPTER X
OF THE FORMS OF A COMMONWEALTH

132. The majority having, as has been shown, upon men's first uniting into society, the whole power of the community, naturally in them, may employ all that power in making laws for the community from time to time, and executing those laws by officers of their own appointing: and then the form of the government is a perfect democracy; or else may put the power of making laws into the hands of a few select men, and their heirs or successors, and then it is an oligarchy; or else into the hands of one man and then it is a monarchy; if to him and his heirs, it is an hereditary monarchy; if to him only for life, but upon his death the power only of nominating a successor to return to them, an elective monarchy. And so accordingly of these, the community may make compounded and mixed forms of government, as they think good. And if the legislative power be at first given by the majority to one or more persons only for their lives, or any limited time, and then the supreme power to revert to them again; when it is so reverted, the community may dispose of it again anew into what hands they please, and so constitute a new form of government. For the form of government depending upon the placing of the supreme power, which is the legislative, it being impossible to conceive that an inferior power should prescribe to a superior, or any but the supreme make laws, according as the power of making laws is placed, such is the form of the commonwealth.

133. By commonwealth, I must be understood all along to mean, not a democracy, or any form of government, but any independent community which the Latins signified by the word

civitas, to which the word which best answers in our language is commonwealth, and most properly expresses such a society of men, which community does not, for there may be subordinate communities in a government; and city much less. And therefore to avoid ambiguity I crave leave to use the word commonwealth in that sense, in which I find it used by King James himself, which I think to be its genuine signification; which if anybody dislike, I consent with him to change it for a better.

CHAPTER XIII

OF THE SUBORDINATION OF THE POWERS

OF THE COMMONWEALTH

149. Though in a constituted commonwealth, standing upon its own basis, and acting according to its own nature, that is, acting for the preservation of the community, there can be but one supreme power, which is the legislative, to which all the rest are and must be subordinate, yet the legislative being only of fiduciary power to act for certain ends, there remains still in the people a supreme power to remove or alter the legislative when they find the legislative act contrary to the trust reposed in them; for all power given with trust for the attaining an end, being limited by that end, whenever that end is manifestly neglected or opposed, the trust must necessarily be forfeited, and the power devolve into the hands of those that gave it who may place it anew where they shall think best for their safety and security. And thus the community perpetually retains a supreme power of saving themselves from the attempts and designs of anybody, even of their legislators whenever they shall be so foolish or so wicked as to lay and carry on designs against the liberties and properties of the subject; for no man or society of men, having a power to deliver up their preservation, or consequently the means of it to the absolute will and arbitrary dominion of another, whenever anyone shall go about to bring them into such a slavish condition they will always have a right to preserve what they have not a power to part with; and to rid themselves of those who invade this fundamental, sacred and unalterable law of self-preservation for which they entered into society; and thus the community may be said in this respect to be always the supreme power, but not as considered under any form of gov-

ernment, because this power of the people can never take place till the government be dissolved.

150. In all cases whilst the government subsists, the legislative is the supreme power; for what can give laws to another must needs be superior to him, and since the legislative is no otherwise legislative of the society but by the right it has to make laws for all the parts and for every member of the society, prescribing rules to their actions, and giving power of execution where they are transgressed, the legislative must needs be the supreme, and all other powers in any members or parts of the society derived from and subordinate to it.

151. In some commonwealths where the legislative is not always in being, and the executive is vested in a single person who has also a share in the legislative, there that single person, in a very tolerable sense, may also be called supreme; not that he has in himself all the supreme power, which is that of lawmaking, but because he has in him the supreme execution from whom all inferior magistrates derive all their several subordinate powers, or, at least, the greatest part of them; having also no legislative superior to him, there being no law to be made without his consent, which cannot be expected should ever subject him to the other part of the legislative, he is properly enough in this sense supreme. But yet it is to be observed that though oaths of allegiance and fealty are taken to him, it is not to him as supreme legislator, but as supreme executor of the law made by a joint power of him with others, allegiance being nothing but an obedience according to law, which, when he violates, he has no right to obedience, nor can claim it otherwise than as the public person vested with the power of the law, and so is to be considered as the image, phantom, or representative of the commonwealth, acted by the will of the society declared in its laws, and thus he has no will, no power, but that of the law. But when he quits this representation, this public will, and acts by his own private will, he degrades himself, and is but a single private person without power and without will; the members owing no obedience but to the public will of the society.

152. The executive power placed anywhere but in a person that has also a share in the legislative is visibly subordinate and accountable to it, and may be at pleasure changed and displaced; so that it is not the supreme executive power that is exempt from subordination, but the supreme executive power vested in one, who having a share in the legislative, has

no distinct superior legislative to be subordinate and accountable to, farther than he himself shall join and consent, so that
he is no more subordinate than he himself shall think fit, which
one may certainly conclude will be but very little. Of other
ministerial and subordinate powers in a commonwealth we
need not speak, they being so multiplied with infinite variety
in the different customs and constitutions of distinct commonwealths, that it is impossible to give a particular account of
them all. Only thus much which is necessary to our present
purpose we may take notice of concerning them, that they
have no manner of authority, any of them, beyond what is by
positive grant and commission delegated to them, and are all
of them accountable to some other power in the commonwealth.

153. It is not necessary—no, nor so much as convenient—
that the legislative should be always in being; but absolutely
necessary that the executive power should, because there is
not always need of new laws to be made, but always need of
execution of the laws that are made. When the legislative hath
put the execution of the laws they make into other hands,
they have a power still to resume it out of those hands when
they find cause, and to punish for any maladministration
against the laws. The same holds also in regard of the federa-
tive power, that and the executive being both ministerial and
subordinate to the legislative, which, as has been shown, in a
constituted commonwealth is the supreme, the legislative also
in this case being supposed to consist of several persons; for
if it be a single person it cannot but be always in being, and
so will, as supreme, naturally have the supreme executive
power, together with the legislative, may assemble and exercise
their legislative at the times that either their original constitution or their own adjournment appoints, or when they please,
if neither of these hath appointed any time, or there be no
other way prescribed to convoke them. For the supreme
power being placed in them by the people, it is always in them,
and they may exercise it when they please, unless by their
original constitution they are limited to certain seasons, or by
an act of their supreme power they have adjourned to a
certain time, and when that time comes they have a right to
assemble and act again.

154. If the legislative, or any part of it, be of representatives, chosen for that time by the people, which afterwards
return into the ordinary state of subjects, and have no share
in the legislature but upon a new choice, this power of choosing

must also be exercised by the people, either at certain appointed seasons, or else when they are summoned to it; and, in this latter case, the power of convoking the legislative is ordinarily placed in the executive, and has one of these two limitations in respect of time:—that either the original constitution requires their assembling and acting at certain intervals; and then the executive power does nothing but ministerially issue directions for their electing and assembling according to due forms; or else it is left to his prudence to call them by new elections when the occasions or exigencies of the public require the amendment of old or making of new laws, or the redress or prevention of any inconveniencies that lie on or threaten the people.

155. It may be demanded here, what if the executive power, being possessed of the force of the commonwealth, shall make use of that force to hinder the meeting and acting of the legislative, when the original constitution or the public exigencies require it? I say, using force upon the people, without authority, and contrary to the trust put in him that does so, is a state of war with the people, who have a right to reinstate their legislative in the exercise of their power. For having erected a legislative with an intent they should exercise the power of making laws, either at certain set times, or when there is need of it, when they are hindered by any force from what is so necessary to the society, and wherein the safety and preservation of the people consists, the people have a right to remove it by force. In all states and conditions the true remedy of force without authority is to oppose force to it. The use of force without authority always puts him that uses it into a state of war as the aggressor, and renders him liable to be treated accordingly.

156. The power of assembling and dismissing the legislative, placed in the executive, gives not the executive a superiority over it, but is a fiduciary trust placed in him for the safety of the people in a case where the uncertainty and variableness of human affairs could not bear a steady fixed rule. For it not being possible that the first framers of the government should by any foresight be so much masters of future events as to be able to prefix so just periods of return and duration to the assemblies of the legislative, in all times to come, that might exactly answer all the exigencies of the commonwealth, the best remedy could be found for this defect was to trust this to the prudence of one who was always to be present, and whose business it was to watch over the public

good. Constant, frequent meetings of the legislative, and long
continuations of their assemblies, without necessary occasion,
could not but be burdensome to the people, and must necessarily in time produce more dangerous inconveniencies, and
yet the quick turn of affairs might be sometimes such as to
need their present help; any delay of their convening might endanger the public; and sometimes, too, their business might be
so great that the limited time of their sitting might be too short
for their work, and rob the public of that benefit which could
be had only from their mature deliberation. What, then, could
be done in this case to prevent the community from being exposed some time or other to imminent hazard on one side or
the other, by fixed intervals and periods set to the meeting and
acting of the legislative, but to entrust it to the prudence of
some who, being present and acquainted with the state of public affairs, might make use of this prerogative for the public
good? And where else could this be so well placed as in his
hands who was entrusted with the execution of the laws for the
same end? Thus, supposing the regulation of times for the assembling and sitting of the legislative not settled by the original
constitution, it naturally fell into the hands of the executive;
not as an arbitrary power depending on his good pleasure, but
with this trust always to have it exercised only for the public
weal, as the occurrences of times and change of affairs might
require. Whether settled periods of their convening, or a liberty
left to the prince for convoking the legislative, or perhaps a
mixture of both, hath the least inconvenience attending it, it is
not my business here to inquire, but only to show that, though
the executive power may have the prerogative of convoking
and dissolving such conventions of the legislative, yet it is not
thereby superior to it.

157. Things of this world are in so constant a flux that
nothing remains long in the same state. Thus people, riches,
trade, power, change their stations; flourishing mighty cities
come to ruin, and prove in time neglected desolate corners,
whilst other unfrequented places grow into populous countries
filled with wealth and inhabitants. But things not always changing equally, and private interest often keeping up customs
and privileges when the reasons of them are ceased, it often
comes to pass that in governments where part of the legislative consists of representatives chosen by the people, that in
tract of time this representation becomes very unequal and
disproportionate to the reasons it was at first established upon.
To what gross absurdities the following of custom when

reason has left it may lead, we may be satisfied when we see the bare name of a town, of which there remains not so much as the ruins, where scarce so much housing as a sheepcote, or more inhabitants than a shepherd is to be found, send as many representatives to the grand assembly of law-makers as a whole county numerous in people and powerful in riches. This strangers stand amazed at, and everyone must confess needs a remedy; though most think it hard to find one, because the constitution of the legislative being the original and supreme act of the society, antecedent to all positive laws in it, and depending wholly on the people, no inferior power can alter it. And, therefore, the people when the legislative is once constituted, having in such a government as we have been speaking of no power to act as long as the government stands, this inconvenience is thought incapable of a remedy.

158. *Salus populi suprema lex* is certainly so just and fundamental a rule that he who sincerely follows it cannot dangerously err. If therefore the executive, who has the power of convoking the legislative, observing rather the true proportion than fashion of representation, regulates, not by old custom, but true reason, the number of members in all places that have a right to be distinctly represented, which no part of the people however incorporated can pretend to, but in proportion to the assistance which it affords to the public, it cannot be judged to have set up a new legislative, but to have restored the old and true one, and to have rectified the disorders which succession of time had insensibly as well as inevitably introduced. For it being the interest, as well as intention of the people, to have a fair and equal representative, whoever brings it nearest to that is an undoubted friend to and establisher of the government, and cannot miss the consent and approbation of the community. Prerogative being nothing but a power in the hands of the prince to provide for the public good in such cases which, depending upon unforeseen and uncertain occurrences, certain and unalterable laws could not safely direct. Whatsoever shall be done manifestly for the good of the people, and the establishing the government upon its true foundations is, and always will be, just prerogative. The power of erecting new corporations, and therewith new representatives, carries with it a supposition that in time the measures of representation might vary, and those have a just right to be represented which before had none; and by the same reason those cease to have a right, and be too inconsiderable for such a privilege which before had it. It is not a change

from the present state, which perhaps corruption or decay has introduced, that makes an inroad upon the government, but the tendency of it to injure or oppress the people, and to set up one part or party with a distinction from, and an unequal subjection of the rest. Whatsoever cannot but be acknowledged to be of advantage to the society and people in general upon just and lasting measures, will always, when done, justify itself; and whenever the people shall choose their representatives upon just and undeniably equal measures, suitable to the original frame of the government, it cannot be doubted to be the will and act of the society who ever permitted or proposed to them so to do.

CHAPTER XIX

OF THE DISSOLUTION OF GOVERNMENT

211. He that will with any clearness speak of the dissolution of government ought, in the first place, to distinguish between the dissolution of the society and the dissolution of the government. That which makes the community, and brings men out of the loose state of nature into one politic society, is the agreement which everyone has with the rest to incorporate and act as one body, and so be one distinct commonwealth. The usual and almost only way whereby this union is dissolved, is the inroad of foreign force making a conquest upon them. For in that case (not being able to maintain and support themselves as one entire and independent body) the union belonging to that body which consisted therein must necessarily cease, and so everyone return to the state he was in before, with a liberty to shift for himself and provide for his own safety as he thinks fit in some other society. Whenever the society is dissolved, it is certain the government of that society cannot remain. Thus conquerors' swords often cut up governments by the roots, and mangle societies to pieces, separating the subdued or scattered multitude from the protection of and dependence on that society which ought to have preserved them from violence. The world is too well instructed in, and too forward to allow of this way of dissolving of, governments to need any more to be said of it; and there wants not much argument to prove that where the society is dissolved, the government cannot remain—that being as impossible as for the frame of a house to subsist when the ma-

terials of it are scattered and displaced by a whirlwind, or jumbled into a confused heap by an earthquake.

212. Besides this overturning from without, governments are dissolved from within.

First. When the legislative is altered. Civil society being a state of peace amongst those who are of it, from whom the state of war is excluded by the umpirage which they have provided in their legislative for the ending all differences that may arise amongst any of them, it is in their legislative that the members of a commonwealth are united and combined together in one coherent living body. This is the soul that gives form, life, and unity to the commonwealth. From hence the several members have their mutual influence, sympathy, and connection. And, therefore, when the legislative is broken or dissolved, dissolution and death follow. For the essence and union of the society consisting in having one will, the legislative, when once established by the majority, has the declaring and, as it were, keeping of, that will. The constitution of the legislative is the first and fundamental act of the society, whereby provision is made for the continuation of their union, under the direction of persons and bonds of laws made by persons authorized thereunto by the consent and appointment of the people, without which no one man or number of men amongst them can have authority of making laws that shall be binding to the rest. When any one or more shall take upon them to make laws, whom the people have not appointed so to do, they make laws without authority, which the people are not therefore bound to obey; by which means they come again to be out of subjection, and may constitute to themselves a new legislative, as they think best, being in full liberty to resist the force of those who without authority would impose anything upon them. Everyone is at the disposure of his own will when those who had by the delegation of the society the declaring of the public will, are excluded from it, and others usurp the place who have no such authority or delegation.

213. This being usually brought about by such in the commonwealth who misuse the power they have, it is hard to consider it aright, and know at whose door to lay it, without knowing the form of government in which it happens. Let us suppose, then, the legislative placed in the concurrence of three distinct persons.

(1) A single hereditary person having the constant supreme executive power, and with it the power of convoking and dissolving the other two within certain periods of time.

(2) An assembly of hereditary nobility.

(3) An assembly of representatives chosen *pro tempore* by the people. Such a form of government supposed, it is evident,

214. First, That when such a single person or prince sets up his own arbitrary will in place of the laws which are the will of the society, declared by the legislative, then the legislative is changed. For that being in effect the legislative whose rules and laws are put in execution and required to be obeyed when other laws are set up, and other rules pretended and enforced, than what the legislative constituted by the society have enacted, it is plain that the legislative is changed. Whoever introduces new laws, not being thereunto authorized by the fundamental appointment of the society, or subverts the old, disowns and overturns the power by which they were made, and so sets up a new legislative.

215. Secondly, When the prince hinders the legislative from assembling in its due time, or from acting freely, pursuant to those ends for which it was constituted, the legislative is altered. For it is not a certain number of men, no, nor their meeting, unless they have also freedom of debating and leisure of perfecting what is for the good of the society, wherein the legislative consists. When these are taken away or altered so as to deprive the society of the due exercise of their power, the legislative is truly altered. For it is not names that constitute governments, but the use and exercise of those powers that were intended to accompany them; so that he who takes away the freedom, or hinders the acting of the legislative in its due seasons, in effect takes away the legislative, and puts an end to the government.

216. Thirdly, When, by the arbitrary power of the prince, the electors or ways of elections are altered, without the consent and contrary to the common interest of the people, there also the legislative is altered. For if others than those whom the society hath authorized thereunto, do choose, or in another way than what the society hath prescribed, those chosen are not the legislative appointed by the people.

217. Fourthly, The delivery also of the people into the subjection of foreign power, either by the prince, or by the legislative, is certainly a change of the legislative, and so a dissolution of the government. For the end why people entered into society being to be preserved one entire, free, independent society, to be governed by its own laws, this is lost whenever they are given up into the power of another.

218. Why, in such a constitution as this, the dissolution of the government in these cases is to be imputed to the prince is evident, because he, having the force, treasure, and offices of the State to employ, and often persuading himself or being flattered by others, that, as supreme magistrate, he is incapable of control; he alone is in a condition to make great advances towards such changes under pretense of lawful authority, and has it in his hands to terrify or suppress opposers as factious, seditious, and enemies to the government; whereas no other part of the legislative, or people, is capable by themselves to attempt any alteration of the legislative without open and visible rebellion, apt enough to be taken notice of, which, when it prevails, produces effects very little different from foreign conquest. Besides, the prince, in such a form of government, having the power of dissolving the other parts of the legislative, and thereby rendering them private persons, they can never, in opposition to him, or without his concurrence, alter the legislative by a law, his consent being necessary to give any of their decrees that sanction. But yet so far as the other parts of the legislative any way contribute to any attempt upon the government, and do either promote, or not, what lies in them, hinder such designs, they are guilty, and partake in this, which is certainly the greatest crime men can be guilty of one towards another.

219. There is one way more whereby such a government may be dissolved, and that is, when he who has the supreme executive power neglects and abandons that charge, so that the laws already made can no longer be put in execution. This is demonstratively to reduce all to anarchy, and so effectually to dissolve the government. For laws not being made for themselves, but to be by their execution the bonds of the society, to keep every part of the body politic, in its due place and function, when that totally ceases, the government visibly ceases, and the people become a confused multitude without order or connection. Where there is no longer the administration of justice, for the securing of men's rights, nor any remaining power within the community to direct the force, or provide for the necessities of the public, there certainly is no government left. Where the laws cannot be executed, it is all one as if there were no laws; and a government without laws is, I suppose, a mystery in politics, inconceivable to human capacity, and inconsistent with human society.

220. In these and the like cases, when the government is dissolved, the people are at liberty to provide for themselves by

erecting a new legislative, differing from the other, by the
change of persons, or form, or both, as they shall find it most
for their safety and good. For the society can never, by the
fault of another, lose the native and original right it has to
preserve itself, which can only be done by a settled legislative,
and a fair and impartial execution of the laws made by it.
But the state of mankind is not so miserable that they are not
capable of using this remedy, till it be too late to look for any.
To tell people they may provide for themselves by erecting a
new legislative, when by oppression, artifice, or being delivered over to a foreign power, their old one is gone, is only
to tell them they may expect relief when it is too late, and the
evil is past cure. This is in effect no more than to bid them
first be slaves, and then to take care of their liberty; and when
their chains are on tell them they may act like free men.
This, if barely so, is rather mockery than relief; and men can
never be secure from tyranny if there be no means to escape
it till they are perfectly under it. And therefore it is that they
have not only a right to get out of it, but to prevent it.

221. There is therefore secondly another way whereby governments are dissolved, and that is when the legislative or the
prince, either of them, act contrary to their trust.

First, The legislative acts against the trust reposed in them
when they endeavor to invade the property of the subject, and
to make themselves or any part of the community masters or
arbitrary disposers of the lives, liberties, or fortunes of the
people.

222. The reason why men enter into society is the preservation of their property; and the end why they choose and authorize a legislative is that there may be laws made, and rules
set, as guards and fences to the properties of all the members
of the society to limit the power and moderate the dominion
of every part and member of the society. For since it can
never be supposed to be the will of the society that the legislative should have a power to destroy that which everyone designs secure by entering into society, and for which the people
submitted themselves to legislators of their own making, whenever the legislators endeavor to take away and destroy the
property of the people, or to reduce them to slavery under
arbitrary power, they put themselves into a state of war with
the people, who are thereupon absolved from any further
obedience, and are left to the common refuge which God hath
provided for all men against force and violence. Whensoever,
therefore, the legislative shall transgress this fundamental rule

of society, and either by ambition, fear, folly, or corruption, endeavor to grasp themselves or put into the hands of any other an absolute power over the lives, liberties, and estates of the people, by this breach of trust they forfeit the power the people had put into their hands, for quite contrary ends, and it devolves to the people, who have a right to resume their original liberty, and by the establishment of the new legislative (such as they shall think fit) provide for their own safety and security, which is the end for which they are in society. What I have said here concerning the legislative in general, holds true also concerning the supreme executor, who having a double trust put in him, both to have a part in the legislative and the supreme execution of the law, acts against both when he goes about to set up his own arbitrary will as the law of the society. He acts also contrary to his trust when he either employs the force, treasure, and offices of the society, to corrupt the representatives, and gain them to his purposes; or openly pre-engages the electors, and prescribes to their choice such whom he has by solicitations, threats, promises, or otherwise won to his designs, and employs them to bring in such, who have promised beforehand what to vote and what to enact. Thus to regulate candidates and electors, and new-model the ways of election, what is it but to cut up the government by the roots, and poison the very fountain of public security? For the people having reserved to themselves the choice of their representatives as the fence to their properties, could do it for no other end but that they might always be freely chosen, and, so chosen, freely act and advise as the necessity of the commonwealth and the public good should upon examination and mature debate be judged to require. This those who give their votes before they hear the debate, and have weighed the reason on all sides, are not capable of doing. To prepare such an assembly as this, and endeavor to set up the declared abettors of his own will for the true representatives of the people and the law-makers of the society, is certainly as great a breach of trust and as perfect a declaration of a design to subvert the government as is possible to be met with. To which if one shall add rewards and punishments visibly employed to the same end and all the arts of perverted law made use of to take off and destroy all that stand in the way of such a design, and will not comply and consent to betray the liberties of their country, it will be past doubt what is doing. What power they ought to have in the society who thus employ it contrary to the trust that went along with it in its first institution is easy to determine; and one cannot but see that he who has once attempted any such thing as this cannot any longer be trusted.

223. To this perhaps it will be said that, the people being ignorant and always discontented, to lay the foundation of government in the unsteady opinion and uncertain humor of the people is to expose it to certain ruin; and no government will be able long to subsist if the people may set up a new legislative whenever they take offense at the old one. To this I answer: Quite the contrary. People are not so easily got out of their old forms as some are apt to suggest. They are hardly to be prevailed with to amend the acknowledged faults in the frame they have been accustomed to. And if there be any original defects, or adventitious ones introduced by time or corruption, it is not an easy thing to get them changed, even when all the world sees there is an opportunity for it. This slowness and aversion in the people to quit their old constitutions has, in the many revolutions which have been seen in this kingdom, in this and former ages still kept us to, or after some interval of fruitless attempts still brought us back again to, our old legislative of Kings, Lords, and Commons. And whatever provocations have made the crown be taken from some of our princes' heads, they never carried the people so far as to place it in another line.

224. But it will be said, this hypothesis lays a ferment for frequent rebellion. To which I answer:
— First, no more than any other hypothesis. For when the people are made miserable, and find themselves exposed to the ill-usage of arbitrary power, cry up their governors as much as you will for sons of Jupiter, let them be sacred and divine, descended, or authorized from heaven, give them out for whom or what you please, the same will happen. The people generally ill-treated, and contrary to right, will be ready upon any occasion to ease themselves of a burden that sits heavy upon them. They will wish and seek for the opportunity, which in the change, weakness, and accidents of human affairs seldom delays long to offer itself. He must have lived but a little while in the world who has not seen examples of this in his time, and he must have read very little who cannot produce examples of it in all sorts of governments in the world.

225. Secondly, I answer, such revolutions happen not upon every little mismanagement in public affairs. Great mistakes in the ruling part, many wrong and inconvenient laws, and all the slips of human frailty will be borne by the people without mutiny or murmur. But if a long train of abuses, prevarica-

tions and artifices, all tending the same way, make the design visible to the people—and they cannot but feel what they lie under, and see whither they are going—it is not to be wondered that they should then rouse themselves and endeavor to put the rule into such hands which may secure to them the ends for which government was at first erected, and without which ancient names and specious forms are so far from being better that they are much worse than the state of nature or pure anarchy; the inconveniences being all as great and as near, but the remedy farther off and more difficult.

226. Thirdly, I answer that this power in the people of providing for their safety anew by a new legislative when their legislators have acted contrary to their trust by invading their property, is the best fence against rebellion, and the probablest means to hinder it. For rebellion being an opposition, not to persons, but authority, which is founded only in the constitutions and laws of the government, those whoever they be who by force break through, and by force justify their violation of them, are truly and properly rebels. For when men by entering into society and civil government have excluded force, and introduced laws for the preservation of property, peace, and unity amongst themselves, those who set up force again in opposition to the laws do *rebellare*—that is, bring back again the state of war—and are properly rebels; which they who are in power (by the pretense they have to authority, the temptation of force they have in their hands, and the flattery of those about them) being likeliest to do, the properest way to prevent the evil is to show them the danger and injustice of it who are under the greatest temptation to run into it.

227. In both the forementioned cases, when either the legislative is changed or the legislators act contrary to the end for which they were constituted, those who are guilty are guilty of rebellion. For if anyone by force takes away the established legislative of any society, and the laws by them made pursuant to their trust, he thereby takes away the umpirage which everyone had consented to for a peaceable decision of all their controversies, and a bar to the state of war amongst them. They who remove or change the legislative, take away this decisive power, which nobody can have but by the appointment and consent of the people, and so destroying the authority which the people did, and nobody else can, set up; and introducing a power which the people hath not authorized, actually introduce a state of war which is that of force without authority. And thus by removing the legislative established by

the society (in whose decisions the people acquiesced and
united as to that of their own will), they untie the knot and
expose the people anew to the state of war. And if those who
by force take away the legislative are rebels, the legislators
themselves, as has been shown, can be no less esteemed so,
when they who were set up for the protection and preservation
of the people, their liberties and properties, shall by force
invade and endeavor to take them away; and so they, putting
themselves into a state of war with those who made them the
protectors and guardians of their peace, are properly and with
the greatest aggravation *rebellantes* (rebels).

228. But if they who say it lays a foundation for rebellion
mean that it may occasion civil wars or intestine broils, to
tell the people they are absolved from obedience when illegal
attempts are made upon their liberties or properties, and may
oppose the unlawful violence of those who were their magistrates when they invade their properties contrary to the trust
put in them and that therefore this doctrine is not to be allowed, being so destructive to the peace of the world: they
may as well say upon the same ground that honest men may
not oppose robbers or pirates because this may occasion disorder or bloodshed. If any mischief come in such cases, it is
not to be charged upon him who defends his own right, but on
him that invades his neighbor's. If the innocent honest man
must quietly quit all he has for peace's sake to him who will
lay violent hands upon it, I desire it may be considered what
a kind of peace there will be in the world which consists only
in violence and rapine, and which is to be maintained only
for the benefit of robbers and oppressors. Who would not
think it an admirable peace betwixt the mighty and the mean
when the lamb without resistance yielded his throat to be torn
by the imperious wolf? Polyphemus's den gives us a perfect
pattern of such a peace and such a government, wherein
Ulysses and his companions had nothing to do but quietly to
suffer themselves to be devoured. And no doubt Ulysses, who
was a prudent man, preached up passive obedience, and ex-
horted them to a quiet submission by representing to them of
what concernment peace was to mankind, and by showing
the inconveniences which might happen if they should offer to
resist Polyphemus, who had now the power over them.

229. The end of government is the good of mankind, and
which is best for mankind, that the people should be always
exposed to the boundless will of tyranny, or that the rulers
should be sometimes liable to be opposed when they grow

exorbitant in the use of their power, and employ it for the destruction and not the preservation of the properties of their people? . . .

240. Here, it is likely, the common question will be made: Who shall be judge whether the prince or legislative act contrary to their trust? This, perhaps, ill-affected and factious men may spread amongst the people when the prince only makes use of his due prerogative. To this I reply: The people shall be judge; for who shall be judge whether the trustee or deputy acts well and according to the trust reposed in him, but he who deputes him, and must, by having deputed him, have still the power to discard him when he fails in his trust? If this be reasonable in particular cases of private men, why should it be otherwise in that of the greatest moment, where the welfare of millions is concerned, and also where the evil, if not prevented, is greater, and the redress very difficult, dear, and dangerous?

241. But farther, this question, who shall be judge, cannot mean that there is no judge at all; for where there is no judicature on earth to decide controversies amongst men, God in heaven is Judge. He alone, it is true, is Judge of the right; but every man is judge for himself, as in all other cases, so in this, whether another hath put himself into a state of war with him, and whether he should appeal to the Supreme Judge as Jephtha did.

242. If a controversy arise betwixt a prince and some of the people in a matter where the law is silent or doubtful, and the thing be of great consequence, I should think the proper umpire in such a case should be the body of the people; for in cases where the prince hath a trust reposed in him, and is dispensed from the common ordinary rules of the law; there, if any men find themselves aggrieved, and think the prince acts contrary to or beyond that trust, who so proper to judge as the body of the people (who at first lodged that trust in him) how far they meant it should extend? But if the prince or whoever they be in the administration decline that way of determination, the appeal then lies nowhere but to heaven; force between either persons who have no known superior on earth, or which permits no appeal to a judge on earth, being properly a state of war, wherein the appeal lies only to heaven, and in that state the injured party must judge for himself when he will think fit to make use of that appeal and put himself upon it.

243. To conclude: The power that every individual gave the society when he entered into it, can never revert to the individuals again as long as the society lasts, but will always remain in the community, because without this there can be no community, no commonwealth, which is contrary to the original agreement; so also when the society hath placed the legislative in any assembly of men to continue in them and their successors, with direction and authority for providing such successors, the legislative can never revert to the people whilst that government lasts, because having provided a legislative with power to continue forever, they have given up their political power to the legislative and cannot resume it. But if they have set limits to the duration of their legislative, and made this supreme power in any person or assembly only temporary; or else when by the miscarriages of those in authority it is forfeited; upon the forfeiture, or at the determination of the time set, it reverts to the society, and the people have a right to act as supreme, and continue the legislative in themselves; or place it in a new form, or new hands as they think good.

Jean Jacques Rousseau (1712–1778)

THE SOCIAL CONTRACT

BOOK I

CHAPTER I
SUBJECT OF THE FIRST BOOK

Man is born free, and yet we see him everywhere in chains. Those who believe themselves the masters of others cease not to be even greater slaves than the people they govern. How this happens I am ignorant; but, if I am asked what renders it justifiable, I believe it may be in my power to resolve the question.

If I were only to consider force, and the effects of it, I should say, "When a people is constrained to obey, and does obey, it does well; but as soon as it can throw off its yoke, and does throw it off, it does better: for a people may certainly use, for the recovery of their liberty, the same right that was employed to deprive them of it: it was either justifiably recovered, or unjustifiably torn from them." But the social order is a sacred right which serves for the basis of all others. Yet this right comes not from nature; it is therefore founded on conventions. The question is, what those conventions are. But, before I come to that point, I must establish the principles which I have just asserted.

CHAPTER II
OF THE FIRST SOCIETIES

The earliest and the only natural societies are families: yet the children remain attached to the father no longer than they have need for his protection. As soon as that need ceases, the bond of nature is dissolved. The child, exempt from the obedience he owed the father, and the father, from the duties he owed the child, return equally to independence. If they continue to remain together, it is not in consequence of a natural, but a voluntary union; and the family itself is maintained only by a convention.

This common liberty is a consequence of the nature of man. His first law is that of self-preservation, his first cares those which he owes to himself; and as soon as he has attained the age of reason, being the only judge of the means proper to preserve himself, he becomes at once his own master.

It appears therefore that families are the first models of political societies: the chief represents the father of the family, the children the people; and being all born equal, and all free, they in either case only alienate their liberty in order to obtain what is more useful. All the difference between the two societies is that, in the family, the gratification which paternal tenderness derives from a consciousness of benefiting those who are the objects of it makes a full amends to the father for the care he bestows on the children; while, in the State, the pleasure of commanding takes the place of that love which the chief does not feel for his people.

Grotius denies that all human power is established for the benefit of those who are governed; and he instances slavery in proof of his assertion. But his constant manner of reasoning is to establish right by fact. A more satisfactory mode might be employed, but none more favourable to tyrants.

It is therefore doubtful, according to Grotius, whether the whole human race belongs to about one hundred men, or this hundred men to the human race; and he appears throughout his book to incline to the former opinion, which is also the idea of Hobbes: so that, according to them, mankind is divided into herds of cattle, each herd having its master who protects it in order to devour it.

As the herdsman is of a nature superior to that of his cattle, so the herdsmen of men, that is, their chiefs, are of a nature superior to their people. So reasoned, according to Philo's account, the Emperor Caligula, who concluded very justly from analogy that either kings were gods, or men were beasts.

The reasoning of Caligula comes to just the same point as that of Grotius and Hobbes. Aristotle had said, before any of them, that men are not naturally equal, but that some are born for slavery and others for dominion.

Aristotle was right; but he mistook the effect for the cause. Nothing is more certain than that all men who are born in slavery are born for slavery. Slaves become so debased by their chains as to lose even the desire of breaking from them; they love their servitude, even as the companions of Ulysses loved their brutishness. If there are some who are slaves by nature, the reason is that men were made slaves against nature. Force made the first slaves, and slavery, by degrading and corrupting its victims, perpetuated their bondage.

I have not said anything of King Adam, or Emperor Noah, the father of three great monarchs, who parted the universe among them, like the children of Saturn, whom they are by many supposed to be. I expect to be applauded for this moderation; because, as I am descended in a direct line from one of these princes, and perhaps from the eldest branch, who can tell whether, in the verification of titles, I might not find myself the legitimate king of the human race? However it be, we can discover nothing but that Adam was sovereign of the world, as Robinson Crusoe was of his island, because he was its only inhabitant; and the happiest circumstance attending the empire was that the monarch was secure in his throne, having nothing to apprehend from rebellions, wars, or conspiracies.

CHAPTER III

OF THE RIGHT OF THE STRONGEST

The strongest are still never sufficiently strong to ensure them continual mastership, unless they find means of transforming force into right, and obedience into duty. Hence the right of the strongest—a right which seems ironical in appearance, but is really established as a principle. But shall we never have an explanation of this term? Force is a physical power; I do not see what morality can result from its effects. To yield to force is an act of necessity, not of inclination; or it is at best only an act of prudence. In what sense then can it be a duty?

Let us suppose for a moment the existence of this pretended right. I see nothing that can arise from it but inexplicable nonsense. For, if we admit that force constitutes right, the effect changes with the cause: all force which overcomes the first succeeds to its right. As soon as men can disobey with impunity, they can do so justifiably; and because the strongest is always in the right, strength is the only thing men should seek to acquire. But what sort of right is that which perishes with the force that gave it existence? If it is necessary to obey by force, there can be no occasion to obey from duty; and when force is no more, all obligation ceases with it. We see, therefore, that this word "right" adds nothing to force, but is indeed an unmeaning term.

If in saying, "Let us obey the powerful," they mean to say, "Let us yield to force," the precept is good, but it is superfluous, for it never is or can be violated. All power, we are told, comes from God. I grant it does; but all diseases likewise come from the same hand, and yet who ever forbade us to call in a physician? If a robber surprises me in a corner of a wood, is it necessary that I should not only give him my purse when forced to do so, but am I in conscience obliged to give it to him, though I should be in a position to escape? For the fact is, the pistol which he holds is also a power.

We must grant, therefore, that force does not constitute right, and that obedience is only due to legitimate powers. Thus everything goes back to my first question.

CHAPTER IV
OF SLAVERY

Since no man has any natural authority over his fellows, and since force produces no right to any, all justifiable authority among men must be established on the basis of conventions.

If an individual, says Grotius, can alienate his liberty, and become the slave of a master, why may not a whole people alienate theirs, and become the subject of a king? There are some equivocal words in this sentence, which require an explanation; but I will confine myself to the word "alienate." To alienate is to give or sell. But a man who becomes the slave of another, cannot give but must sell himself, at least for a subsistence. But for what do a people sell themselves? A king, so far from furnishing his subjects with subsistence, draws his own from them; and, according to Rabelais, a king does not subsist upon a little. Do subjects therefore give their persons on condition that the prince will condescend to accept their property also? I see nothing, after such a gratuity, that there remains for them to preserve.

We are told that a despot ensures civil tranquillity for his subjects. Be it so; but what do his subjects gain if the wars which his ambition draws them into, if his insatiable avarice, and the vexations of his administration, desolate the country even more than civil dissensions? What do they gain if this very tranquillity is one of their miseries? We find tranquillity also in dungeons; but is that enough to make them enjoyable? The Greeks enjoyed the same kind of tranquillity while they were shut up in the cave of the Cyclops, and were expecting every moment that it would be their turn to be devoured.

To say that a man gives himself gratuitously is absurd and incomprehensible; such an act is unjustifiable and void, because the person who performed it is not in his proper senses. To say the same of a whole people is to suppose the people are all mad; and folly does not make it right.

If each individual could alienate himself, he could not alienate his descendants; for, being born men and free, their liberty is their own, and no person can dispose of it but they themselves. Before they arrive at the age of reason, the father may, in his children's name, stipulate conditions for their preservation and welfare, but not give them up irrevocably, and unconditionally; for such a gift would be contrary to the designs of nature, and exceed the rights of paternal authority. It would therefore be necessary, in order to make an arbitrary government justifiable, that each generation should be at liberty to admit or reject it: but then such a government would not be arbitrary.

To renounce our liberty is to renounce our quality of man, and with it all the rights and duties of humanity. No adequate compensation can possibly be made for a sacrifice so complete. Such a renunciation is incompatible with the nature of man; whose actions, when once he is deprived of his free will, must be destitute of all morality. Finally, a convention which stipulates absolute authority on one side, and unlimited obedience on the other, must be considered as vain and contradictory. Is it not clear that there can be no obligation to a person from whom everything may be justly required? And does not the single circumstance of there being no equivalence and no exchange also annul the act? For what right can my slave have against me, since everything that he has belongs to me, and, his right being mine, this right of mine against myself is absolute nonsense?

Grotius and others derive from war another origin for this pretended right of slavery. The victor having, according to them, a right to kill the vanquished, the latter may purchase his life at the expense of his liberty; a convention which is so much the more justifiable because it tends to benefit both parties.

But it is clear that this pretended right of killing the vanquished results not in any manner from the state of war; because, while men remain in their primitive independence, there is no intercourse between them sufficiently settled to constitute either peace or war; and they are not naturally enemies. It is a concurrence of things, and not of men, that occasions war; and the state of war cannot rise out of simple personal concerns, but only out of real relations; nor can private war between man and man exist either in the state of nature, where there is no settled property, or in a civil state, where everything is under the authority of the laws.

Private combats, duels, and rencontres are acts which do not constitute a state of war; and with regard to the petty wars authorized by the "Establishments" of Louis IX of France, and suspended by the Peace of God, they were abuses of the feudal government, a system so completely absurd that it contradicted the principles of natural right and of every sound polity.

War is therefore not a concern between man and man but between State and State, in which individuals are only enemies accidentally, not as men, or as citizens, but as soldiers; not as members of a country, but as its defenders. In fine, States can only have other States, and not men, for enemies, because there can be no true relation between things of different natures.

This principle is conformable to the established maxims of all times, and the invariable practice of all politically organized peoples. Declarations of war are not so much to inform the powers as their subjects. The stranger, be it a monarch, a private individual, or a whole people, that robs, kills, or detains the subjects of another prince, without previously declaring war against that prince, is not an enemy but a robber. Even in real war, a just prince, while he carries away whatever he can seize upon in an enemy's country that belongs to the public, respects the persons and property of private people, because he respects the right by which he holds his own. The end of war being to subdue the hostile State, the army of one State has a right to kill the defenders of the other while they have arms in their hands; but, as soon as they lay them down and surrender themselves, they cease to be enemies or the instruments of enemies; they become simply men, and the victors have no longer any right over their lives. Sometimes it may be possible for one State to destroy another State without destroying one of its members: and war does not give a right to do anything beyond what is absolutely necessary to its end. These are not the principles of Grotius, neither are they adopted on the authority of the poets; but they are derived from the nature of things, and founded on reason.

With regard to the right of conquest, it has no other foundation than the law of the strongest. If war does not give the conqueror the right to massacre the conquered, then that right does not exist and cannot serve as a basis for the right to enslave the conquered. Men have no right to kill the enemy but at the time when it is impossible to enslave them; the right of enslaving cannot therefore be derived from the right of killing: it is therefore an iniquitous barter to make them purchase, at the price of their liberty, that life over which the conquerors have no right. In establishing the right of life and death on that of slavery, and of slavery on that of life and death, is it not clear that we become involved in a vicious circle?

But supposing that this terrible right of massacring everybody did exist, the slaves made in war, or a conquered people, could be bound by no obligation at all to their master, and would only obey him while they were compelled by force to do so. In taking his service as an equivalent for sparing his life, the victor confers no favour on the man he has vanquished: instead of killing him—from whence he could derive no advantage—he spares him that he may reap the fruits of his labour. So far, therefore, is the conqueror from having acquired, by saving the life of the conquered, any other authority over him to second that of force, that the state of war continues to subsist between them as formerly, and even their union is the effect of it; and, while the rights of war are exercised, no treaty of peace can be supposed to exist. I shall be told perhaps that they have made a convention. Be it so; but this convention is so far from terminating the state of war that it supposes the continuance of it.

Thus, in whatever light we view things, the right of slavery is found to be null, not only because it is unjustifiable but because it is absurd and has no meaning. The terms "slavery" and "right" contradict and exclude each other. Be it from man to man, or from a man to a people, it would be equally nonsensical to say: I make a covenant with you entirely at your expense, and for my benefit; I will observe it as far as my inclination leads me, and you shall observe it as far as I please.

CHAPTER V

THAT WE MUST ALWAYS GO BACK TO A FIRST CONVENTION

Had I granted all which I have refuted, the favourers of despotism would not have found their cause advanced by it. There will always be a great difference between subduing a multitude and governing a society. When unorganized men are successively subjugated by one individual, whatever number there may be of them, they appear to me only as a master and slaves; I cannot regard them as a people and their chief; they are, if you please, an *aggregation,* but they are not as yet an *association;* for there is neither public property, nor a political body, among them. A man may have enslaved half the world, and yet continue only a private individual; his interest is separate from that of others, and confined to himself alone. When such a man falls, his empire remains unconnected and without any bond of union, as an oak dissolves and becomes a mass of ashes when consumed by fire.

"A people," says Grotius, "can give themselves to a king." According to Grotius, then, they are a people before they give themselves to a king. The donation itself is a civil act, and supposes a public consultation. It would therefore be better before we examine the act by which they elected a king, to enquire into that by which they became a people; for that act, being necessarily anterior to the other, is the true foundation of society.

In fact, if there was no prior convention, where would be—unless the election was unanimous—the obligation which should bind the minority to submit to the choice of the majority? And whence would a hundred men, who wish to submit to a master, derive the right of binding by their votes ten other men who were not disposed to acknowledge any chief? The law which gives the majority of votes the power of deciding for the whole body can only be established by a convention, and proves that there must have been unanimity at one time at least.

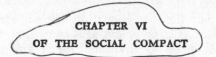

CHAPTER VI
OF THE SOCIAL COMPACT

I will suppose that men in the state of nature are arrived at that crisis when the strength of each individual is insufficient to overcome the resistance of the obstacles to his preservation. This primitive state can therefore subsist no longer; and the human race would perish unless it changed its manner of life.

As men cannot create for themselves new forces, but merely unite and direct those which already exist, the only means they can employ for their preservation is to form by aggregation an assemblage of forces that may be able to overcome the resistance, to be put in motion as one body, and to act in concert.

This assemblage of forces must be produced by the concurrence of many; but as the force and the liberty of each man are the chief instruments of his preservation, how can he engage them elsewhere without danger to himself, and without neglecting the care which is due himself? This difficulty, which leads directly to my subject, may be expressed in these words:

"Where shall we find a form of association which will defend and protect with the whole common force the person and the property of each associate, and by which every person, while uniting himself with all, shall obey only himself and remain as free as before?" Such is the fundamental problem of which the Social Contract gives the solution.

The articles of this contract are so unalterably fixed by the nature of the act that the least modification renders them vain and of no effect; so that they are the same everywhere, and are everywhere tacitly understood and admitted, even though they may never have been formally announced; until, the social compact being violated, each individual is restored to his original rights, and resumes his native liberty, while losing the conventional liberty for which he renounced it.

The articles of the social contract will, when clearly understood, be found reducible to this single point: the total alienation of each associate, and all his rights, to the whole community; for, in the first place, as every individual gives himself up entirely, the condition of every person is alike; and being so, it would not be to the interest of any one to render that condition offensive to others.

Nay, more than this, the alienation being made without any reserve, the union is as complete as it can be, and no associate has any further claim to anything: for if any individual retained rights not enjoyed in general by all, as there would be no common superior to decide between him and the public, each person being in some points his own judge, would soon pretend to be so in everything; and thus would the state of nature be continued and the association necessarily become tyrannical or be annihilated.

Finally, each person gives himself to all, and so not to any one individual; and as there is no one associate over whom the same right is not acquired which is ceded to him by others, each gains an equivalent for what he loses, and finds his force increased for preserving that which he possesses.

If, therefore, we exclude from the social compact all that is not essential, we shall find it reduced to the following terms:

> *Each of us places in common his person and all his power under the supreme direction of the general will; and as one body we all receive each member as an indivisible part of the whole.*

From that moment, instead of as many separate persons as there are contracting parties, this act of association produces a moral and collective body, composed of as many members as there are votes in the assembly, which from this act receives its unity, its common self, its life, and its will. This public person, which is thus formed by the union of all other persons, took formerly the name of "city,"[1] and now takes that of

---

[1] The true sense of this word is almost entirely lost among the moderns: the name of "city" is now generally used to signify a town, and that of "citizen" applied to a burgess. Men do not seem to know that *houses* make a "town," but that *citizens* make a "city." The Carthaginians once paid dearly for a mistake of this kind. I have never seen it mentioned that the title of *cives* was ever given to the subjects of any prince, not even to the Macedonians formerly, or to the English at present, although they are nearer liberty than any other people. The French alone use the name of "citizen" familiarly to all, because they have no true idea of it, as appears from their dictionaries; and without knowing its meaning they are in danger of falling into the crime of lèse majesté, by usurping a title to which they have no just claim. The word "citizen" with them means a virtue, and not a right. Bodin made a very gross

"republic" or "body politic." It is called by its members "State" when it is passive, "Sovereign" when in activity, and, whenever it is compared with other bodies of a similar kind, it is denominated "power." The associates take collectively the name of "people," and separately, that of "citizens," as participating in the sovereign authority, and of "subjects," because they are subjected to the laws of the State. But these terms are frequently confounded and used one for the other; and it is enough that a man understands how to distinguish them when they are employed in all their precision.

CHAPTER VII
OF THE SOVEREIGN

It appears from this formula that the act of association contains a reciprocal engagement between the public and individuals, and that each individual, contracting, as it were, with himself, is engaged under a double character; that is, as a member of the Sovereign engaging with individuals, and as a member of the State engaged with the Sovereign. But we cannot apply here the maxim of civil right, that no person is bound by any engagement which he makes with himself; for there is a material difference between an obligation to oneself individually, and an obligation to a collective body of which oneself constitutes a part.

It is necessary to observe here that public deliberation, which can bind all the subjects to the Sovereign, in consequence of the double character under which the members of that body appear, cannot, for the opposite reason, bind the Sovereign to itself; and consequently that it is against the nature of the body politic for the sovereign power to impose on itself any law which it cannot break. Being able to consider itself as acting under one character only, it is in the situation of an individual forming a contract with himself; and we see

---

mistake, when, in speaking of "citizens" and "burgesses," he mistook the one for the other. M. D'Alembert was better acquainted with the meaning of these terms, and in his article "Genève" he has very properly marked the difference between the four orders of men—indeed I may say five, by including the foreigners—which are found there, and of which two orders only compose the republic. No other French author that I know of has comprehended the true sense of the word "citizen."

therefore that there neither is nor can be any kind of fundamental law obligatory for the body of the people, not even the social contract itself. But this does not mean that this body could not very well engage itself to others in any manner which would not derogate from the contract; for, with respect to what is external to it, it becomes a simple being, an individual. But the body politic, or the Sovereign, which derives its existence from the sacredness of the contract, can never bind itself, even towards outsiders, in anything that would derogate from the original act, such as alienating any portion of itself, or submitting to another Sovereign. To violate the contract by which it exists would be to annihilate itself; and that which is nothing can produce nothing.

As soon as this multitude is united in one body, you cannot offend one of its members without attacking the body; much less can you offend the body without incurring the resentment of all the members. Thus duty and interest equally oblige the two contracting parties to lend aid to each other; and the same men must endeavour to unite under this double character all the advantages which attend it.

Further, the Sovereign, being formed only of the individuals who compose it, neither has, nor can have, any interest contrary to theirs; consequently, the sovereign power need give no guarantee to its subjects, because it is impossible that the body should seek to injure all its members; and we shall see presently that it can do no injury to any individual in particular. The Sovereign, by its nature, is always everything it ought to be.

But this is not so with the relation of subjects towards the Sovereign, which, notwithstanding the common interest, has nothing to make them responsible for the performance of their engagements if some means is not found of ensuring their fidelity.

In fact, each individual may, as a man, have a private will,[2] dissimilar or contrary to the general will which he has as a citizen. His own private interest[3] may dictate to him very differently from the common interest; his absolute and naturally independent existence may make him regard what he owes to the common cause as a gratuitous contribution, the omission of which would be less injurious to others than the payment would be burdensome to himself; and considering the moral

2 [*volonté particulière.*]
3 [*intérêt particulier.*]

person which constitutes the State as a creature of the imagination, because it is not a man, he may wish to enjoy the rights of a citizen without being disposed to fulfil the duties of a subject. Such an injustice would in its progress cause the ruin of the body politic.

In order, therefore, to prevent the social compact from becoming an empty formula, it tacitly comprehends the engagement, which alone can give effect to the others—that whoever refuses to obey the general will shall be compelled to it by the whole body: this in fact only forces him to be free; for this is the condition which, by giving each citizen to his country, guarantees his absolute personal independence, a condition which gives motion and effect to the political machine. This alone renders all civil engagements justifiable, and without it they would be absurd, tyrannical, and subject to the most enormous abuses.

CHAPTER VIII
OF THE CIVIL STATE

The passing from the state of nature to the civil state produces in man a very remarkable change, by substituting justice for instinct in his conduct, and giving to his actions a moral character which they lacked before. It is then only that the voice of duty succeeds to physical impulse, and a sense of what is right, to the incitements of appetite. Man, who had till then regarded none but himself, perceives that he must act on other principles, and learns to consult his reason before he listens to his inclinations. Although he is deprived in this new state of many advantages which he enjoyed from nature, he gains in return others so great, his faculties so unfold themselves by being exercised, his ideas are so extended, his sentiments so exalted, and his whole mind so enlarged and refined, that if, by abusing his new condition, he did not sometimes degrade it even below that from which he emerged, he ought to bless continually the happy moment that snatched him forever from it, and transformed him from a circumscribed and stupid animal to an intelligent being and a man.

In order to draw a balance between the advantages and disadvantages attending his new situation, let us state them in such a manner that they may be easily compared. Man loses by the social contract his *natural* liberty, and an unlimited right to all which tempts him, and which he can obtain; in return he acquires *civil* liberty, and proprietorship of all he possesses. That we may not be deceived in the value of these compensations, we must distinguish natural liberty, which knows no bounds but the power of the individual, from civil liberty, which is limited by the general will; and between possession, which is only the effect of force or of the right of the first occupant, from property, which must be founded on a positive title. In addition we might add to the other acquisitions of the civil state that of moral liberty, which alone renders a man master of himself; for it is *slavery* to be under the impulse of mere appetite, and *freedom* to obey a law which we prescribe for ourselves. But I have already said too much on this head, and the philosophical sense of the word "liberty" is not at present my subject.

CHAPTER IX
OF REAL PROPERTY

Each member of the community, at the moment of its formation, gives himself up to it just as he is: himself and all his forces, of which his wealth forms a part. By this act, however, possession does not change in nature when it changes its master, and become property when it falls into the hands of the Sovereign; but as the forces of the city are infinitely greater than those of an individual, it is better secured when it becomes a public possession, without being more justifiable, at least with respect to foreigners. As to its members, the State is made master of all their wealth by the social contract, which within the State serves as the basis of all rights; but with regard to other powers, it claims only under the title of first occupancy, which it derives from individuals.

The right of the first occupant, though more substantial than that of the strongest, does not become a real right, until after the right of property is established. All men have naturally a right to whatever is necessary for them; but the act which renders a man the positive proprietor of any property excludes him from everything else. This being accomplished, the possessor must confine himself to what is thus made his own, and he can claim no right beyond it against the community. It is by this means that the right of the first occupant, so weak in the state of nature, is respected by every man in civil society. In this right we respect less what is another's than what is not our own.

The following conditions are in general necessary to give validity to the right founded on first occupancy in any domain whatever. In the first place, the land must not yet be inhabited by any person; secondly, the party must not occupy more land than is sufficient to supply him with subsistence; thirdly, he must take possession, not by a vain ceremony, but by labour and cultivation, as they are the only proofs of a man's being a proprietor, which, in default of a legal title, deserve to be respected by others.

Is not the thus granting the right of first occupancy to *want* and to *labour* extending it as far as it can go? Cannot the right have some bounds assigned to it? Is it sufficient to set our foot on a common domain, and pretend from thence a right to possess it? Is there nothing necessary but sufficient force to drive others out for a moment in order to deprive them of their right of ever returning thither? And how can a man, or a people, overrun an immense territory, and prevent all other human beings from participating in it without being guilty of a criminal usurpation, since they deprive by that means the rest of mankind of a place of residence and of the means of subsistence which nature gave in common to all? When Nuñez Balboa took possession, on the shores of the South Sea, of that ocean and of all South America in the name of the crown of Castille, was that act sufficient to dispossess the inhabitants of the country, and exclude all the princes of the world from settling there? At this rate these ceremonies would have been multiplied extravagantly, and the Catholic king might at one stroke have taken possession of the whole universe without going out of his closet, except indeed to have cut off from his empire what had been previously occupied by other princes.

We see how the lands of private persons, contiguous and united, become the public territory, and how the right of sovereignty, extending from the subjects over the lands they occupy, becomes at once real and personal; by which the occupants are rendered more dependent, and their own force made the guarantee of their fidelity; an advantage which does not seem to have been perceived by ancient monarchs, who, styling themselves Kings of the Persians, the Scythians, or the Macedonians, appear to have regarded themselves as the chiefs of men rather than as masters of the country. Those of the present day call themselves more cleverly Kings of France, Spain, England, etc.; and in thus holding the domain, they are sure to hold its inhabitants.

The singular circumstance attending this alienation is that, in accepting the property of individuals, the community is far from despoiling them, and only ensures them justifiable possession, changes usurpation into a true right, and enjoyment into property. By this means, the possessors being considered as depositaries of the public good, their rights are respected by all the members of the State, and protected with all their force against foreigners. So that by a resignation, advantageous to the public, and still more so to the resigners, they may be justly said to have acquired all that they gave up: a paradox which will be easily explained by distinguishing, as I shall do hereafter, between the rights which the Sovereign and the proprietors have in the same property.

It may also happen that men begin to associate before they have any possessions, and that, spreading afterwards over a country sufficient for them all, they may either enjoy it in common, or part it between them equally, or in such proportions as the Sovereign shall direct. In whatever manner the acquisition is made, the right which each individual has over his own property is always subordinate to the right which the community has over all; without which there would be no solidity in the social bond, nor any real force in the exercise of sovereignty.

I shall conclude this chapter and book with a remark which must serve for the basis of the whole social system: it is that, instead of destroying the natural equality of mankind, the fundamental compact substitutes, on the contrary, a moral and legal equality for that physical inequality which nature placed among men, and that, let men be ever so unequal in strength or in genius, they are all equalized by convention and legal right.[4]

4 Under bad governments this equality is but an illusive appearance, which only serves to keep the poor in misery, and support the rich in their usurpations. In fact, laws are always useful to those who have abundance, and injurious to those who have nothing: from whence it follows that the social state is only advantageous to men when every individual has some property, and no one has too much.

BOOK II

CHAPTER I
THAT SOVEREIGNTY IS INALIENABLE

The first and most important consequence of the principles already established is that the general will alone can direct the forces of the State agreeably to the end of its institution, which is the common good; for if the clashing of private interests has rendered the establishing of societies necessary, the agreement of the same interests has made such establishments possible. It is what is common in these different interests that forms the social bond; and if there was not some point in which they all unanimously centered, no society could exist. It is on the basis of this common interest alone that society must be governed.

I say, therefore, that sovereignty, being only the exercise of the general will, can never alienate itself, and that the Sovereign, which is only a collective being, cannot be represented but by itself: the *power* may well be transmitted but not the *will*.

Indeed, if it is not impossible that a private will should accord on some point with the general will, it is at least impossible that such agreement should be regular and lasting; for the private will is inclined by its nature to partiality, and the general will to impartiality.[5] It is even more impossible to guarantee the continuance of this agreement, even if we were to see it always exist; because that existence must be owing not to art but to chance. The Sovereign may indeed say: "My will at present actually agrees with the will of such and such a man, or at least with what he declares to be his will"; but it cannot say, "Our wills shall likewise agree tomorrow"; since it would be absurd for the will to bind itself for the future, and since it does not belong to any will to consent to what might be injurious to the being from whom the will proceeds. If, therefore, the people promise unconditionally to obey, the act of making such a promise dissolves their existence, and they lose their quality of a people; for at the moment that there is a

[5] [*La volonté particulière tend, par sa nature, aux préférences, et la volonté générale à l'égalité.*]

master, there is no longer a Sovereign, and from that moment the body politic is destroyed.

I do not say that the commands of chiefs cannot pass for general wills, so long as the Sovereign, being free to oppose them, does not do so. In such cases we must presume from their silence that the people yield their consent. But I shall explain this more at large presently.

CHAPTER II

THAT SOVEREIGNTY IS INDIVISIBLE

For the same reason that sovereignty is inalienable, it is in-divisible. For the will is general[6] or it is not; it is either the will of the whole body of the people, or only of a part. In the first case, this declared will is an act of sovereignty and consti-tutes law; in the second, it is but a private will or an act of magistracy, and is at most but a decree.

But our political thinkers, not being able to divide sover-eignty in principle, have divided it in its object: into force and will; legislative power and executive power; the rights of levy-ing taxes, of administering justice, and making war; the inter-nal government and the power of treating with foreigners. But by sometimes confounding all these parts, and sometimes sepa-rating them, they make of the sovereign power a fantastical being composed of related pieces; as if man were composed of several bodies, one with eyes, another with arms, another with feet, but none with anything more. The mountebanks of Japan are said to dismember an infant in the sight of the spec-tators, throw its limbs one after another into the air, and make the child come down alive and whole. The tricks of our politi-cal jugglers are very similar, for after dismembering the social body by a sleight worthy of the black art, they bring its parts together again, nobody knows how.

This error arises from our not having formed exact ideas of the sovereign authority, and from our taking for parts of that authority what are only its emanations. For example, the acts of declaring war and making peace are considered as acts of sovereignty, when in fact they are not so, because neither of these acts is a law, but only the application of the law, a par-

[6] To make the will general, it is not always necessary that it should be unanimous; but it is indispensably necessary that every vote should be counted: any formal exclusion destroys generality.

ticular act which determines the application of the law, as we shall clearly perceive when the idea attached to the word "law" is fixed.

By tracing in the same manner the other divisions, we should find that whenever we suppose sovereignty divided we deceive ourselves; that the rights which we take for a part of that sovereignty are all subordinate to it, and always suppose supreme wills of which they only sanction the execution.

It is impossible to express how greatly this want of exactness has obscured the arguments and conclusions of writers on political right, when they have attempted to decide on the respective rights of kings and peoples by the principles which they have themselves laid down. Every person may see in the third and fourth chapters of the First Book of Grotius, how that learned man and his translator, Barbeyrac, have entangled and embarrassed themselves in their sophisms, fearful of saying too much, or of not saying enough to answer their designs, and apprehensive of clashing with those interests which they had to conciliate.

Grotius, discontented with his own country, took refuge in France; and endeavouring to make his court to Louis XIII, to whom his book is dedicated, he has spared no pains to despoil the people of all their rights and transfer them to their kings in the most artful manner. This was also the design of Barbeyrac, who dedicated his translation to George I, King of England. But unfortunately the expulsion of James II, which he calls "abdication," obliged him to proceed very cautiously, to shuffle and evade, that he might avoid making King William appear a usurper. If these two writers had adopted the true principles, all their difficulties would have been removed, and they would have been always consistent; but the task of speaking truth, and recommending themselves to no favour but that of the people, would have been to them a vexatious one. Truth does not lead to fortune, and the people have neither ambassadorships, professorships, nor pensions to bestow.

CHAPTER III

WHETHER THE GENERAL WILL CAN ERR

It follows from what has been said that the general will is always right and tends always to the public advantage; but it does not follow that the deliberations of the people have always the same rectitude. Our will always seeks our own good, but we do not always perceive what it is. The people are never corrupted, but they are often deceived, and only then do they seem to will what is bad.

There is frequently much difference between the *will of all* and the *general will.* The latter regards only the common interest; the former regards private interest, and is indeed but a sum of private wills:[7] but remove from these same wills the pluses and minuses that cancel each other, and then the general will remains as the sum of the differences.[8]

If, when the people, sufficiently informed, deliberated, there was to be no communication among them, from the grand total of trifling differences the general will would always result, and their resolutions be always good. But when cabals and partial associations are formed at the expense of the great association, the will of each such association, though *general* with regard to its members, is *private* with regard to the State: it can then be said no longer that there are as many voters as men, but only as many as there are associations. By this means the differences being less numerous, they produce a result less general. Finally, when one of these associations becomes so large that it prevails over all the rest, you have no longer the sum of many opinions dissenting in a small degree from each other, but one great dictating dissentient; from that moment there is no longer a general will, and the predominating opinion is only an individual one.

It is therefore of the utmost importance for obtaining the expression of the general will, that no partial society should be formed in the State, and that every citizen should speak his opinion entirely from himself:[9] such was the unique and sub-

[7] [*volontés particulières.*]

[8] "Each interest," says the Marquis d'A. [d'Argenson], "has its different principles. The agreement of two private interests is formed by opposition to a third." He might have added that the agreement of all interests is produced by opposition to that of each. If there were no different interests, we should scarcely perceive the common interest, which never finds any opposer; everything would go on regularly of itself, and politics be no longer an art.

[9] "Divisions," says Machiavelli, "sometimes injure and sometimes serve a republic. The injury is done by cabals and factions, the service by a party which maintains itself without cabals or factions. Since, therefore, it is impossible for the founder of a republic to provide against enmities, he must make the best provision he can against factions." (*History of Florence,* Bk. VII.)

lime system of the great Lycurgus. When there are partial societies, it is politic to multiply their number, that they may be all kept on an equality. This method was pursued by Solon, Numa, and Servius. These are the only precautions that can be taken to make the general will always intelligent, and prevent the people from being deceived.

CHAPTER IV
OF THE LIMITS OF THE SOVEREIGN POWER

If the state or city is only a moral person, the existence of which consists in the union of its members, and if its most important care is that of preserving itself, there is a necessity for its possessing a universally compulsive power, for moving and disposing each part in the manner most convenient to the whole. As nature gives to every man absolute command over all his members, the social compact gives to the body politic absolute command over the members of which it is formed; and it is this power, when directed by the general will, that bears, as I have said before, the name of "sovereignty."

But, besides the public person, we have to consider the private persons who compose it, and whose lives and liberty are naturally independent of it. The point here is to distinguish properly between the respective rights of the citizens and the Sovereign,[10] and between the duties which the former have to fulfil in quality of subjects, and the natural rights which they ought to enjoy in quality of men.

It is granted that all which an individual alienates by the social compact is only that part of his power, his property, and his liberty, the use of which is important to the community; but we must also grant that the Sovereign is the only judge of what is important to the community.

All the services which a citizen can render to the State ought to be rendered as soon as the Sovereign demands them; but the Sovereign cannot, on its side, impose any burden on the subject useless to the community; it cannot even have the inclination to do so; for, under the law of reason, nothing is done without a cause, any more than under the law of nature.

[10] Attentive readers, be not too hasty, I beg of you, to accuse me of contradicting myself. I could not avoid doing so terminologically, on account of the poverty of the language; but have patience until I explain my meaning.

The engagements which bind us to the social body are only obligatory because they are mutual; and their nature is such that in fulfilling them we cannot labour for others without labouring at the same time for ourselves. Wherefore is the general will always right, and wherefore do all the wills invariably seek the happiness of every individual among them, if it is not that there is no person who does not appropriate the word "each" to himself, and who does not think of himself when he is voting for all? This proves that the equality of right, and the idea of justice which it inspires, is derived from the preference which each gives to himself, and consequently from the nature of man; that the general will, to be truly such, ought to be so in its object, as well as its essence: that it ought to come from all, if we are to apply it to all; and that it loses its natural rectitude when it tends towards any one individual and determinate object, because then, judging of what is external to us, we have no true principle of equity to guide us.

In fact, as soon as it is a matter of an individual fact or right, on any point which has not been previously regulated by a general convention, the affair becomes contentious. It is a process wherein the persons interested are one of the parties, and the public the other, but where I do not see any law that must be followed, or any judge who ought to decide. It would be ridiculous in such a case to bring the question to an express decision of the general will, which could only be the conclusion of one party, and consequently, which would be, with respect to the other party, but an external and private will, hurried on that occasion into injustice, and subject to error. Thus, in the same manner as a private will cannot represent the general will, the general will, in its turn, changes its nature if its object is private,[11] and cannot, as the general will, pronounce either on a man or a fact. When the people of Athens, for example, nominated or cashiered their chiefs, decreed honours to one, imposed punishments on another, and, by the multitude of their private decrees, exercised indiscriminately all the acts of government, the people, properly speaking, had then no longer a general will; they acted no longer as Sovereign but as magistrate. This will appear contradictory to common ideas; but I must have time to unfold mine.

We should perceive by this that the generality of the will depends less on the number of voters than on the common interest which unites them; for, in this institution, each neces-

11 [*un objet particulier.*]

sarily submits to the conditions which he imposes on others—
an admirable union of interest and justice, which gives to the
common deliberations a character of equity that vanishes in
the discussion of all private affairs for want of a common interest to combine and identify the ruling of the judge with
that of the party.

By whatever path we return to our principle, we always
arrive at the same conclusion—that is, that the social compact
establishes among citizens such an equality that they are all
engaged under the same conditions, and should all enjoy the
same rights. Thus, by the nature of the compact all acts of
sovereignty, that is to say, all authentic acts of the general will,
oblige or favour all citizens alike in such a manner as evinces
that the Sovereign knows no person but the body of the nation, and does not make any distinction among the individuals
who compose it. What, therefore, is properly an act of sovereignty? It is not a convention between a superior and an inferior, but a convention of the body with each of its members
—a justifiable convention because it has the social contract
for its basis; equitable, because it is common to all; beneficial,
because it can have no other object but the general good; and
solid, because it is guaranteed by the public force and the
supreme power. While subjects are under the governance of
such conventions only, they obey no one but only their own
will: and to enquire how far the respective rights of the Sovereign and citizens extend is to ask how far the citizens can
engage with themselves, each towards all, and all towards
each.

We see by this that the sovereign power, all absolute, all
sacred, all inviolable as it is, neither will, nor can, exceed the
bounds of general conventions, and that every man may fully
dispose of what is left to him of his property and his liberty
by these conventions; so that the Sovereign never has any right
to lay a greater charge on one subject than on another, because then the affair would become personal,[12] and in such
cases the power of the Sovereign is no longer competent.

These distinctions once admitted, it is evidently false that
individuals have made any real renunciation by the social contract. On the contrary, they find their situation, by the effect
of that contract, really rendered preferable to what it was before. Instead of making any alienation they have only made an
advantageous transition from a mode of living unsettled and

12 [*l'affaire devenant particulière.*]

precarious to one better and more secure, from a state of natural independence to one of liberty, from possessing the power of injuring others to security for themselves, and from their strength, which others might, by the employment of theirs, overcome, to a right which social union renders invincible. Even their lives, which they have devoted to the State, are continually protected by it; and when they are exposed in its defence, what is it but restoring that which they have received from it? What do they do but what they would do more frequently, and with more danger, in the state of nature, when, living in continual and unavoidable conflicts, they would have to defend at the peril of their lives what was necessary to the preservation of life? All, it is true, must fight for their country when their service is requisite; but then no person has occasion to fight for himself as an individual. And is it not gaining a great advantage to be obliged, for the protection of that to which we owe our security, to incur occasionally only a part of that danger to which we must be again exposed as individuals as soon as we were deprived of it?

CHAPTER V
OF THE RIGHT OF LIFE AND DEATH

It may be asked how individuals, having no right to dispose of their own lives, can transmit to the Sovereign a right which they do not possess. This question appears difficult to solve only because it is improperly stated. Every man has a right to risk his own life for the preservation of it. Was any man ever said to intend suicide when he throws himself from a window to avoid the flames? Is that crime imputed to him who perishes at sea in a tempest because, at the time of his embarkation, he knew of the danger?

The end of the social treaty is the preservation of the contracting parties. Whoever wants to enjoy the end must will the means, and some risks, and even some dangers, are inseparable from these means. The man who would preserve his life at the expense of the lives of others ought in turn to expose his own for their protection when it is necessary. The citizen is not a judge of the peril to which the law may expose him; and when the prince says to him, "It is expedient for the State that thou shouldst die," he ought to die, because it is only on that condition that he has enjoyed his security up to that moment, and because his life is not to be considered simply as the boon of nature, but as a conditional gift from the State.

The punishment of death inflicted on criminals may be considered from the same point of view: it is to secure himself from being the victim of assassins that a man consents to die if he becomes an assassin. In this treaty the parties are so far from disposing of their own lives that they think only of guarding them, and it is not to be supposed that, at the time of contracting, any of the contracting parties intends to deserve the gallows.

Further, every malefactor, by attacking the social right, becomes by his crimes a rebel and a traitor to his country; by violating its laws, he ceases to be a member of it and, in fact, makes war upon it. The existence of the State then becomes incompatible with his; one of the two must therefore perish; and when the criminal is executed he suffers less as a citizen than as an enemy. The proceedings against him, and the judgment pronounced in consequence, are the proofs and the declaration that he has broken the social treaty, and, consequently, that he is no longer a member of the State. But, as he is still considered as such at least while he sojourns there, he must be either removed by exile, as a violator of the pact, or by death, as a public enemy; for such an enemy is not a moral person, he is simply a man: and it is then that it is the right of war to kill the vanquished.

But, it may be asked, is not the condemnation of a criminal an individual act? I grant it: but this condemnation of a criminal does not pertain to the Sovereign; it is a right which the Sovereign can confer, though it cannot itself exercise it. My ideas are consistent, but I cannot explain them all at one time.

It might be added that the frequency of punishments is always a sign of a weak or indolent government. There is no one so vile that he may not be rendered good for something. There is no right to put any one to death, even as an example, except the man whose life cannot be preserved without danger to the State.

In regard to the right of pardon, or exempting a criminal from the sentence directed by the law and pronounced against him by the judge, it pertains only to that which is above the law and the judge, that is, to the Sovereign; but its right in this case is not very clear, and occasions for using it occur but seldom. In a well-governed State there are few punishments, not because there are many pardons, but because there are only a small number of criminals. When the State is declining, the multitude of crimes assures impunity. Under the Roman Republic neither the senate nor the consuls ever attempted to pardon any criminal; nor did even the people, though they sometimes revoked their own sentence. The frequency of pardons announces that crime will soon have no need for them, and it is easy to see what that must lead to. But my heart murmurs and restrains my pen: let us leave the discussion of these questions to the just man who has never erred, nor had himself need for pardon.

CHAPTER VI
OF THE LAW

By the social compact we have given existence and life to the body politic; it now remains to give it motion and will by legislation. For the original act by which the body is formed and united determines none of the measures that ought to be taken for its preservation.

What is good, and conformable to order, is so from the nature of things, and independently of human conventions. All justice flows from God, he alone is the source of it; and if we knew how to receive it from on high, we should require neither government nor laws. This justice is undoubtedly universal and emanates from reason alone; but this justice, to be admitted among us, must be reciprocal. Humanly speaking, the laws of justice, when they have no natural sanction, are vain among men; they are only injurious to the just and advantageous to the wicked part of mankind, for the just man invariably adheres to its rules with respect to everyone, but no one adheres to them towards him. There must therefore be conventions and laws to combine our duties and our rights, and to direct justice to its end. In the state of nature, where everything is in common, I owe nothing to those to whom I have promised nothing; and I do not acknowledge that anything, but what I do not wish to use, can be the property of another person. It is not so in the civil order, where every right is determined by law.

But what, in fine, is a law? While men content themselves with affixing none but metaphysical ideas to this word, they must continue to reason without understanding one another; and when they have said what a law of nature is, they will still be no less ignorant of what a law of the State is.

I have already said that there can be no general will directed towards a private object. That private object is either in the State, or outside the State. If it is outside the State, a will which is alien to it cannot be general with regard to it; and if it is in the State, it makes a part of it, and between the whole and its part there is a relation which proves the existence of two separate beings; of which the said part makes one, and the whole—less that same part—makes the other. But the whole less a part is not the whole; and while this relation subsists, there is no whole, but two unequal parts: from whence it follows that the will of one part cannot in any way be general with respect to the other.

But when the whole people determines for the whole people, it considers only itself; and if a relation is then formed it is only a relation of the whole object from one point of view to the whole object from another point of view, and the whole itself is not divided. Then the affair on which they enact is general, as is the will that enacts. It is this act that I call a "law."

When I say that the object of the laws is always general, I mean that the law views its subjects collectively and their actions abstractly, never a man as individual or an action as private. Thus the law may enact that there shall be certain privileges, but it cannot name the persons who are to enjoy them; the law may divide the citizens into several classes, and specify the qualifications which shall give a right of admission to each class, but it cannot direct such or such a person to be admitted; the law can establish a monarchical government and an hereditary succession, but it cannot elect a king or name a royal family. In a word, all those functions which relate to any individual object pertain not to the legislative power.

Under this idea, we perceive at once how unnecessary it would be to enquire to whom the function of making laws belongs, because the laws are but the acts of the general will; neither need we ask whether the prince is above the laws, since he is a member of the State; nor whether the law can be unjust, as no one is unjust towards himself; nor how we can be free while subjected to the laws, since they are but the registers of our own wills.

We see also that, since the law unites universality of will with universality of object, whatever is ordered of his own accord by any man, whoever he may be, is not law; nay, even that which the Sovereign orders relative to a private object is not a law but a decree; neither is it an act of sovereignty but of magistracy.

I therefore denominate every State a "republic" which is governed by laws, under whatever form of administration it may be; for then only the public interest governs, and the affairs of the public obtain a due regard.[13] All justifiable governments are republican;[14] and I will hereafter explain what government is.

The laws are properly but the conditions of civil association. The people submit themselves to the laws, and ought to enjoy the right of making them; it pertains only to those who associate to regulate the terms of the society. But how do they regulate them? Is it by a common agreement, by a sudden inspiration? Has the body politic an organ for declaring its will? Who gives to that body the necessary foresight to form these acts and publish them beforehand? Or how are they declared at the moment of need? How can an unenlightened multitude, which often does not know what it wants, since it so seldom knows what is good for it, execute, of itself, so great, so difficult an enterprise as a system of legislation? Of themselves the people always will the good, but of themselves they do not always see in what it consists. The general will is always right, but the judgment that guides it is not always enlightened. It is therefore necessary to make the people see things as they are, and sometimes as they ought to appear, to point out to them the right path which they are seeking, to guard them from the seducing voice of private wills, and, helping them to see how times and places are connected, to induce them to balance the attraction of immediate and sensible advantage against the apprehension of unknown and distant evil. Individuals see the good they reject; the public wills the good it does not see. All have equally need for guidance. Some must have their wills made conformable to their reason, and others must be taught what it is they will. From this increase of public knowledge would result the union of judgment and

[13] [*Car alors seulement . . . la chose publique est quelque chose.*]

[14] I do not by the word "republic" mean an aristocracy or democracy only, but in general all governments guided by the general will, which is the law. To be justifiable, the government should not be confounded with the Sovereign, but be considered as its administrator. Then monarchy itself would be a republic. This will be further explained in the following book.

will in the social body; from that union comes the harmony of the parties and the highest power of the whole. From thence is born the necessity of a legislator.

CHAPTER VII
OF THE LEGISLATOR

To discover those happy rules of government which would agree with every nation could only be the work of some superior intelligence, acquainted with all the passions of men, but liable to none of them; who, without bearing any affinity to our nature, knew it perfectly; whose happiness was independent of ours, but who still condescended to make us the object of his care; and who having persevered through a long course of years in the pursuit of distant glory, could enjoy in other ages the reward of his unwearied zeal.[15] In short, gods would be required to give laws to mankind.

The same reasoning which Caligula used with respect to fact Plato employed with respect to right in order to define the civil man or prince in his dialogue, *The Statesman*. But if it be true that a great prince is a rare man, how much more rare must be a good legislator? The first has only to follow the model which the other has to form. One is the scientific mechanician, who invents the machine, the other is the mere mechanic, who winds it up and sets it in motion. "At the birth of societies," says Montesquieu, "the chiefs of the republics form the institutions, but afterwards the institutions form the chiefs."

Those who dare to undertake the institution of a people must feel themselves capable, as it were, of changing human nature, of transforming each individual, who by himself is a perfect and solitary whole, into a part of a much greater whole, from which he in some measure receives his being and his life; of altering the constitution of man for the purpose of strengthening it; of substituting a moral and partial existence instead of the physical and independent existence which we have all received from nature. They must, in a word, remove from man his own proper energies to bestow upon him those

---

[15] A people do not become celebrated until their legislation begins to decline. We do not know during how many ages the Lacedemonians lived happily under the laws of Lycurgus before there was any account made of them by the rest of Greece.

which are strange to him, and which he cannot employ without the assistance of others. The more those natural powers are annihilated, the more august and permanent are those which he acquires, and the more solid and perfect is the institution: so that if each citizen is nothing and can do nothing but when combined with all the other citizens, and the force acquired by the whole from this combination is equal or superior to the sum of all the natural forces of all these individuals, it may be said that legislation is at the highest point of perfection which human talents can attain.

The legislator is in every sense a most extraordinary man in the State. If he must be so from his genius, he is no less so from his employment, which is neither magistracy nor sovereignty. This employment, which constitutes the republic, enters not into its constitution; it is a particular and superior function, which has nothing in common with human empire; because, if he who commands men must not preside over the laws, he who presides over the laws must not have the command over men: otherwise his laws, employed as the ministers of his passions, would frequently merely perpetuate his injustices; and it would be impossible to prevent private aims from defiling the sanctity of his work.

When Lycurgus gave laws to his country, he began by abdicating the royal power. It was the custom with most of the cities of Greece to confide the establishment of their legislation to strangers. The modern republics of Italy have imitated their example; Geneva also did so, and found it to its advantage.[16] Rome in her most glorious days saw all the crimes of tyranny revive within her bosom, and herself on the very eve of perishing, by having united in the same men the legislative authority and the sovereign power.

But even the decemvirs themselves never arrogated the right of making any law by their own authority alone. "Nothing which we propose to you," said they to the people, "can pass into law without your consent. Romans, be you yourselves the authors of the laws which must ensure your happiness."

[16] Those who consider Calvin only as a theologian are little acquainted with the extent of his genius. The compilation of our wise edicts, in which he had so large a part, does him as much honour as his *Institute*. Whatever revolution time may bring about in our religion, while patriotism and the love of liberty are not wholly extinct among us, the memory of that great man will never cease to have the benediction of the Genevans.

He who compiles the laws, therefore, has not, nor ought he to have, any right to legislate, and the people cannot, even if they should be inclined, deprive themselves of that incommunicable right, because, according to the fundamental compact, it is only the general will that can compel individuals, and it can never be known whether a private will is conformable to the general will until it has been submitted to the free vote of the people. I have affirmed this already, but a repetition may not be useless.

Thus we find at the same time in the work of legislation two things which seem incompatible with each other: an enterprise exceeding human power, executed by an authority which is not an authority.

There is also another difficulty which deserves attention. Sages who wish to use their own language in addressing the vulgar instead of vulgar language cannot possibly make themselves understood. For after all, there are a multitude of ideas which it is impossible to express in the language of the people. Views that are too general, and objects that are too remote, are equally beyond their comprehension; and every individual, relishing no scheme of government but that which promotes his own private interest, cannot easily be made sensible of the benefits to be derived from the continual privations imposed upon him by wholesome laws. For a new-born people to relish wise maxims of policy and to pursue the fundamental rules of statecraft, it would be necessary that the effect should become the cause; that the social mind, which should be the product of such institution, should prevail even at the institution of society; and that men should be, before the formation of laws, what those laws alone can make them. The legislator being, from these reasons, unable to employ either force or argument, he must have recourse to an authority of another order, which can bear men away without violence, and persuade without convincing them.

It is this that has, in all ages, obliged the founders of nations to have recourse to the intervention of Heaven and to attribute to the gods what has proceeded from their own wisdom, that the people might submit to the laws of the State as to those of nature and, recognizing that the same power which formed man created the city, obey freely, and contentedly endure that restraint so necessary to the public happiness.

This sublime reason, so far above the comprehension of vulgar men, is that whose decisions legislators put in the mouth of the immortals, that those might be led along under the sanction of divine authority, whom it might be impossible for human prudence to conduct without it.[17] But it belongs not to all men to make the gods speak, nor to gain belief if they pretend to be the interpreters of the divine will. The magnanimous spirit of the legislator is the sole miracle which must prove his mission. Any man may engrave upon tables of stone, purchase an oracle, pretend a secret intercourse with some divinity, teach a bird to whisper in his ear, or find some other means as gross as these to impose upon the people. But whoever depends entirely on such arts, though he may chance to draw a crowd of superstitious fools around him, can never lay the foundation of an empire, and his extravagant undertaking will soon perish with himself. Illusions can form but transitory bonds; it is wisdom alone that renders them permanent. The Jewish law, which still subsists, and that of the child of Ishmæl, which, for ten centuries, has governed half the world, still proclaim the great men by whom they were dictated; and while the pride of philosophy and the blindness of party prejudice will see in these men only fortunate impostures, the true political thinker admires in their institutions that great and comprehensive genius which presides over durable establishments.

After this I should not conclude, with Warburton, that politics and religion have with us one common object, but that, in the origin of nations, the one serves as the instrument of the other.

CHAPTER VIII
OF THE PEOPLE

As an architect, before he begins to erect a large edifice, examines whether the ground is strong enough to support the weight, so the wise lawgiver does not begin by drawing up laws which are good in themselves, but considers whether the people they are designed to govern are likely to carry them into effect. After such an examination, Plato refused to legis-

---

[17] "It is true," says Machiavelli, "there never was, in any country, a promulgator of extraordinary laws who had not recourse to God; because otherwise his system would not have been received; a wise man may know many useful truths, though they are not so self-evident as to carry conviction to the minds of others." (*Discourses on Livy*, Bk. V, chap. II.)

late for the Arcadians and Cyreneans, well knowing that, as these two peoples were wealthy, they could never submit to equality; Minos, though the Cretans were a vicious people, attempted to discipline them; but under excellent laws the people of Crete continued vile.

A thousand nations have made a brilliant appearance on earth who could never have submitted to the governance of good laws; and even those who could have submitted to good laws could have done so for only a very transitory period in their long history. Most peoples, like most human beings, are docile only in their youth, and become more stubborn as their age advances. When once customs are established, and prejudices have taken root, it is idle and dangerous to attempt their reformation; the people, like cowardly and stupid patients who tremble at the sight of their physician, will not even bear to have their evils examined into with a view to removing them.

But just as there are certain diseases incident to men, which derange the reason, and efface all remembrance of the past, so we sometimes find in the history of States that a violent epoch or a revolution has such influence on the minds of the people that the horror which attends the recollection of what has happened produces the same effect as forgetfulness does in the individual; and the State, after being set in flames by civil wars, is born again, as it were, from her own ashes, and recovers all the vigour of youth as it leaves the arms of death. Such was Sparta in the time of Lycurgus, such was Rome after the Tarquins, and, in our time, such have been Holland and Switzerland after the expulsion of the tyrants.

But these events are rare; they are exceptions, the cause of which can only arise from the particular constitution of the State concerned. They can never even happen twice to the same people; because, though men may become free as long as they are still in a state of barbarism, they cannot do so again after civil energy is exhausted. Then troubles may destroy it, but revolutions can never re-establish it; and when the chains of such a people are once broken, it falls asunder, and exists no more: henceforth they need a master, and not a liberator. Oh ye peoples who are free, remember this maxim: "Liberty may be acquired, but never recovered."

Youth is not infancy. There is with nations as with men a period of youth, or, shall I say, maturity, which it is proper they should attain before they are made subject to laws: but it is not always easy to know when a people are sufficiently matured; and, if the moment is anticipated, the work is defeated. One people can be disciplined at birth, another not at the end of ten centuries. The Russians will never be perfectly civilized, because their civilization was attempted too hastily. Peter had a genius for imitation, but he did not possess those great talents which can create and establish everything from nothing. Some of his measures were good, but most of them were ill-timed. He saw that his people were barbarous, but he did not see that they were unripe for civilization; he wanted to civilize them when they needed only to be inured to hardships. Peter was desirous of making them Germans or English, when he should first have made them Russians. By this unwise proceeding, he has forever prevented his subjects from becoming what they might have been, by persuading them that they were what they were not. It is just in the same manner that a French preceptor forms his pupil, so that he shines while in his childish days, and then becomes a nonentity. The Russian empire will want to subjugate all Europe, and will be subjugated herself. The Tartars, now its dependents and neighbours, will soon become its masters, and also ours: this revolution seems to me to be inevitable. All the European princes seem labouring in concert to accelerate the event.

Thomas Jefferson (1743–1826)

THE DECLARATION OF INDEPENDENCE

FROM JEFFERSON'S AUTOBIOGRAPHY

. . . . Congress proceeded the same day to consider the Declaration of Independence, which had been reported and lain on the table the Friday preceding, and on Monday referred to a committee of the whole. The pusillanimous idea that we had friends in England worth keeping terms with, still haunted the minds of many. For this reason, those passages which conveyed censures on the people of England were struck out, lest they should give them offence. The clause too, reprobating the enslaving the inhabitants of Africa, was struck out in complaisance to South Carolina and Georgia, who had never attempted to restrain the importation of slaves, and who, on the contrary, still wished to continue it. Our northern brethren also, I believe, felt a little tender under those censures; for though their people had very few slaves themselves, yet they had been pretty considerable carriers of them to others. The debates, having taken up the greater parts of the 2d, 3d, and 4th days of July, were, on the evening of the last, closed; the Declaration was reported by the committee, agreed to by the House, and signed by every member present, except Mr. Dickinson. As the sentiments of men are known not only by what they receive, but what they reject also, I will state the form of the Declaration as originally reported. The parts struck out by Congress shall be distinguished by a black line drawn under them;[1] and those inserted by them shall be placed in the margin, or in a concurrent column.[2]

[1] Italicized in this edition. *The Editors.*

[2] Printed in capitals in this edition, save the last two paragraphs. *The Editors.*

A DECLARATION BY THE REPRESENTATIVES OF THE UNITED
STATES OF AMERICA, IN GENERAL CONGRESS ASSEMBLED

When, in the course of human events, it becomes necessary
for one people to dissolve the political bands which have connected them with another, and to assume among the powers
of the earth the separate and equal station to which the laws
of nature and of nature's God entitle them, a decent respect
to the opinions of mankind requires that they should declare
the causes which impel them to the separation.

We hold these truths to be self evident: that all men are created equal; that they are endowed by their Creator with CER-
TAIN [*inherent and*] inalienable rights; that among these are
life, liberty, and the pursuit of happiness; that to secure these
rights, governments are instituted among men, deriving their
just powers from the consent of the governed; that whenever
any form of government becomes destructive of these ends, it
is the right of the people to alter or to abolish it, and to institute new government, laying its foundation on such principles, and organizing its powers in such form, as to them shall
seem most likely to effect their safety and happiness. Prudence,
indeed, will dictate that governments long established should
not be changed for light and transient causes; and accordingly
all experience hath shown that mankind are more disposed to
suffer while evils are sufferable, than to right themselves by
abolishing the forms to which they are accustomed. But when
a long train of abuses and usurpations, [*begun at a distinguished period and*] pursuing invariably the same object,
evinces a design to reduce them under absolute despotism, it
is their right, it is their duty to throw off such government,
and to provide new guards for their future security. Such has
been the patient sufferance of these colonies; and such is now
the necessity which constrains them to ALTER [*expunge*]
their former systems of government. The history of the present
king of Great Britain is a history of REPEATED [*unremitting*] injuries and usurpations, ALL HAVING [*among which
appears no solitary fact to contradict the uniform tenor of the
rest, but all have*] in direct object the establishment of an absolute tyranny over these states. To prove this, let facts be submitted to a candid world [*for the truth of which we pledge a
faith yet unsullied by falsehood*].

He has refused his assent to laws the most wholesome and necessary for the public good.

He has forbidden his governors to pass laws of immediate and pressing importance, unless suspended in their operation till his assent should be obtained; and, when so suspended, he has utterly neglected to attend to them.

He has refused to pass other laws for the accommodation of large districts of people, unless those people would relinquish the right of representation in the legislature, a right inestimable to them, and formidable to tyrants only.

He has called together legislative bodies at places unusual, uncomfortable, and distant from the depository of their public records, for the sole purpose of fatiguing them into compliance with his measures.

He has dissolved representative houses repeatedly [*and continually*] for opposing with manly firmness his invasions on the rights of the people.

He has refused for a long time after such dissolutions to cause others to be elected, whereby the legislative powers, incapable of annihilation, have returned to the people at large for their exercise, the state remaining, in the meantime, exposed to all the dangers of invasion from without and convulsions within.

He has endeavored to prevent the population of these states; for that purpose obstructing the laws for naturalization of foreigners, refusing to pass others to encourage their migrations hither, and raising the conditions of new appropriations of lands.

He has OBSTRUCTED [*suffered*] the administration of justice BY [*totally to cease in some of these states*] refusing his assent to laws for establishing judiciary powers.

He has made [*our*] judges dependent on his will alone for the tenure of their offices, and the amount and payment of their salaries.

He has erected a multitude of new offices, [*by a self-assumed power*] and sent hither swarms of new officers to harass our people and eat out their substance.

He has kept among us in times of peace standing armies [*and ships of war*] without the consent of our legislatures.

He has affected to render the military independent of, and superior to, the civil power.

He has combined with others to subject us to a jurisdiction foreign to our constitutions and unacknowledged by our laws, giving his assent to their acts of pretended legislation for quartering large bodies of armed troops among us; for protecting them by a mock trial from punishment for any murders which they should commit on the inhabitants of these states; for cutting off our trade with all parts of the world; for imposing taxes on us without our consent; for depriving us IN MANY CASES of the benefits of trial by jury; for transporting us beyond seas to be tried for pretended offences; for abolishing the free system of English laws in a neighboring province, establishing therein an arbitrary government, and enlarging its boundaries, so as to render it at once an example and fit instrument for introducing the same absolute rule into these COLONIES [*states*]; for taking away our charters, abolishing our most valuable laws, and altering fundamentally the forms of our governments; for suspending our own legislatures, and declaring themselves invested with power to legislate for us in all cases whatsoever.

He has abdicated government here BY DECLARING US OUT OF HIS PROTECTION, AND WAGING WAR AGAINST US [*withdrawing his governors, and declaring us out of his allegiance and protection*].

He has plundered our seas, ravaged our coasts, burnt our towns, and destroyed the lives of our people.

He is at this time transporting large armies of foreign mercenaries to complete the works of death, desolation and tyranny already begun with circumstances of cruelty and perfidy SCARCELY PARALLELED IN THE MOST BARBAROUS AGES, AND TOTALLY unworthy the head of a civilized nation.

He has constrained our fellow citizens taken captive on the high seas, to bear arms against their country, to become the executioners of their friends and brethren, or to fall themselves by their hands.

He has EXCITED DOMESTIC INSURRECTION AMONG US, AND HAS endeavored to bring on the inhabitants of our frontiers, the merciless Indian savages, whose known rule of warfare is an undistinguished destruction of all ages, sexes and conditions [*of existence*].

[*He has incited treasonable insurrections of our fellow citizens, with the allurements of forfeiture and confiscation of our property.*

He has waged cruel war against human nature itself, violating its most sacred rights of life and liberty in the persons of a distant people who never offended him, captivating and carrying them into slavery in another hemisphere, or to incur miserable death in their transportation hither. This piratical warfare, the opprobrium of INFIDEL powers, is the warfare of the CHRISTIAN king of Great Britain. Determined to keep open a market where MEN should be bought and sold, he has prostituted his negative for suppressing every legislative attempt to prohibit or to restrain this execrable commerce. And that this assemblage of horrors might want no fact of distinguished die, he is now exciting those very people to rise in arms among us, and to purchase that liberty of which he has deprived them, by murdering the people on whom he also obtruded them: thus paying off former crimes committed against the LIBERTIES of one people, with crimes which he urges them to commit against the LIVES of another.]

In every stage of these oppressions we have petitioned for redress in the most humble terms: our repeated petitions have been answered only by repeated injuries.

A prince whose character is thus marked by every act which may define a tyrant is unfit to be the ruler of a FREE people [*who mean to be free. Future ages will scarcely believe that the hardiness of one man adventured, within the short compass of twelve years only, to lay a foundation so broad and so undisguised for tyranny over a people fostered and fixed in principles of freedom.*]

Nor have we been wanting in attentions to our British brethren. We have warned them from time to time of attempts by their legislature to extend AN UNWARRANTABLE [*a*] jurisdiction over US [*these our states*]. We have reminded them of the circumstances of our emigration and settlement here, [*no one of which could warrant so strange a pretension: that these were effected at the expense of our own blood and treasure, unassisted by the wealth or the strength of Great Britain: that in constituting indeed our several forms of government, we had adopted one common king, thereby laying a foundation for perpetual league and amity with them: but that submission to their parliament was no part of our constitution, nor ever in idea, if history may be credited: and,*] we HAVE appealed to their native justice and magnanimity AND WE HAVE CONJURED THEM BY [*as well as to*] the ties of our common kindred to disavow these usurpations which WOULD INEVITABLY [*were likely to*] interrupt our connection and correspondence. They too have been deaf to the voice of justice and of consanguinity. WE MUST THEREFORE [*and when occasions have been given them, by*]

the regular course of their laws, of removing from their coun-
cils the disturbers of our harmony, they have, by their free
election, re-established them in power. At this very time too,
they are permitting their chief magistrate to send over not only
soldiers of our common blood, but Scotch and foreign mer-
cenaries to invade and destroy us. These facts have given the
last stab to agonizing affection, and manly spirit bids us to
renounce forever these unfeeling brethren. We must endeavor
to forget our former love for them, and hold them as we
hold the rest of mankind, enemies in war, in peace friends.
We might have a free and a great people together; but a
communication of grandeur and of freedom, it seems, is be-
low their dignity. Be it so, since they will have it. The road to
happiness and to glory is open to us, too. We will tread it
apart from them, and] acquiesce in the necessity which denounces our *[eternal]* separation AND HOLD THEM AS WE
HOLD THE REST OF MANKIND, ENEMIES IN WAR, IN
PEACE FRIENDS!

We therefore the repre-
sentatives of the United States
of America in General Congress assembled, do in the
name, and by the authority
of the good people of these
[*states reject and renounce all*
allegiance and subjection to
the kings of Great Britain and
all others who may hereafter
claim by, through or under
them; we utterly dissolve all
political connection which
may heretofore have subsisted
between us and the people or
parliament of Great Britain:
and finally we do assert and
declare these colonies to be
free and independent states,]
and that as free and independent states, they have full
power to levy war, conclude
peace, contract alliances, establish commerce, and to do
all other acts and things which
independent states may of
right do.

And for the support of
this declaration, we mutually
pledge to each other our lives,
our fortunes, and our sacred
honor.

We, therefore, the repre-
sentatives of the United States
of America in General Congress assembled, appealing to
the supreme judge of the
world for the rectitude of our
intentions, do in the name,
and by the authority of the
good people of these colonies,
solemnly publish and declare,
that these united colonies are,
and of right ought to be free
and independent states; that
they are absolved from all allegiance to the British crown,
and that all political connection between them and the
state of Great Britain is, and
ought to be, totally dissolved;

and that as free and independent states, they have full power to levy war, conclude peace, contract alliances, establish commerce, and to do all other acts and things which independent states may of right do.

And for the support of this declaration, with a firm reliance on the protection of divine providence, we mutually pledge to each other our lives, our fortunes, and our sacred honor.

LETTER TO ROGER C. WEIGHTMAN

Monticello, June 24, 1826

RESPECTED SIR,—The kind invitation I receive from you, on the part of the citizens of the city of Washington, to be present with them at their celebration on the fiftieth anniversary of American Independence, as one of the surviving signers of an instrument pregnant with our own, and the fate of the world, is most flattering to myself, and heightened by the honorable accompaniment proposed for the comfort of such a journey. It adds sensibly to the sufferings of sickness, to be deprived by it of a personal participation in the rejoicings of that day. But acquiescence is a duty, under circum-· stances not placed among those we are permitted to control. I should, indeed, with peculiar delight, have met and exchanged there congratulations personally with the small band, the remnant of that host of worthies, who joined with us on that day, in the bold and doubtful election we were to make for our country, between submission or the sword; and to have enjoyed with them the consolatory fact, that our fellow citizens, after half a century of experience and prosperity, continue to approve the choice we made. May it be to the world, what I believe it will be (to some parts sooner, to others later, but finally to all), the signal of arousing men to burst the chains under which monkish ignorance and superstition had persuaded them to bind themselves, and to assume the blessings and security of self-government. That form which we have substituted, restores the free right to the unbounded exercise of reason and freedom of opinion. All eyes are opened, or opening, to the rights of man. The general spread of the light of science has already laid open to every view the palpable truth, that the mass of mankind has not been born with saddles on their backs, nor a favored few booted and spurred, ready to ride them legitimately, by the grace of God. These are grounds of hope for others. For ourselves, let the annual return of this day forever refresh our recollections of these rights, and an undiminished devotion to them.

I will ask permission here to express the pleasure with which I should have met my ancient neighbors of the city of Washington and its vicinities, with whom I passed so many years of a pleasing social intercourse; an intercourse which so much relieved the anxieties of the public cares, and left impressions so deeply engraved in my affections, as never to be forgotten. With my regret that ill health forbids me the gratification of an acceptance, be pleased to receive for yourself and those for whom you write, the assurance of my highest respect and friendly attachments.

AN ACT FOR ESTABLISHING
RELIGIOUS FREEDOM

AN ACT FOR ESTABLISHING RELIGIOUS FREEDOM [1779], PASSED
IN THE ASSEMBLY OF VIRGINIA IN THE BEGINNING OF THE
YEAR 1786

Well aware that Almighty God hath created the mind free;
that all attempts to influence it by temporal punishments or
burdens, or by civil incapacitations, tend only to beget habits
of hypocrisy and meanness, and are a departure from the plan
of the Holy Author of our religion, who being Lord both of
body and mind, yet chose not to propagate it by coercions on
either, as was in his Almighty power to do; that the impious
presumption of legislators and rulers, civil as well as ecclesiastical, who, being themselves but fallible and uninspired men
have assumed dominion over the faith of others, setting up
their own opinions and modes of thinking as the only true and
infallible, and as such endeavoring to impose them on others,
hath established and maintained false religions over the greatest part of the world, and through all time; that to compel a
man to furnish contributions of money for the propagation of
opinions which he disbelieves, is sinful and tyrannical; that
even the forcing him to support this or that teacher of his own
religious persuasion, is depriving him of the comfortable liberty of giving his contributions to the particular pastor whose
morals he would make his pattern, and whose powers he feels
most persuasive to righteousness, and is withdrawing from the
ministry those temporal rewards, which proceeding from an
approbation of their personal conduct, are an additional in-
citement to earnest and unremitting labors for the instruction
of mankind; that our civil rights have no dependence on our
religious opinions, more than our opinions in physics or geometry; that, therefore, the proscribing any citizen as unworthy
the public confidence by laying upon him an incapacity of
being called to the offices of trust and emolument, unless he

profess or renounce this or that religious opinion, is depriving him injuriously of those privileges and advantages to which in common with his fellow citizens he has a natural right; that it tends also to corrupt the principles of that very religion it is meant to encourage, by bribing, with a monopoly of worldly honors and emoluments, those who will externally profess and conform to it; that though indeed these are criminal who do not withstand such temptation, yet neither are those innocent who lay the bait in their way; that to suffer the civil magistrate to intrude his powers into the field of opinion and to restrain the profession or propagation of principles, on the supposition of their ill tendency, is a dangerous fallacy, which at once destroys all religious liberty, because he being of course judge of that tendency, will make his opinions the rule of judgment, and approve or condemn the sentiments of others only as they shall square with or differ from his own; that it is time enough for the rightful purposes of civil government, for its offices to interfere when principles break out into overt acts against peace and good order; and finally, that truth is great and will prevail if left to herself, that she is the proper and sufficient antagonist to error, and has nothing to fear from the conflict, unless by human interposition disarmed of her natural weapons, free argument and debate, errors ceasing to be dangerous when it is permitted freely to contradict them.

Be it therefore enacted by the General Assembly, That no man shall be compelled to frequent or support any religious worship, place or ministry whatsoever, nor shall be enforced, restrained, molested, or burthened in his body or goods, nor shall otherwise suffer on account of his religious opinions or belief; but that all men shall be free to profess, and by argument to maintain, their opinions in matters of religion, and that the same shall in nowise diminish, enlarge, or affect their civil capacities.

And though we well know this Assembly, elected by the people for the ordinary purposes of legislation only, have no power to restrain the acts of succeeding assemblies, constituted with the powers equal to our own, and that therefore to declare this act irrevocable, would be of no effect in law, yet we are free to declare, and do declare, that the rights hereby asserted are of the natural rights of mankind, and that if any act shall be hereafter passed to repeal the present or to narrow its operation, such act will be an infringement of natural right.

LETTER TO JAMES MADISON

Paris, December 16, 1786

. . . . To make us one nation as to foreign concerns, and keep us distinct in domestic ones, gives the outline of the proper division of powers between the general and particular governments. But, to enable the federal head to exercise the powers given it to best advantage, it should be organized as the particular ones are, into legislative, executive, and judiciary. The first and last are already separated. The second should be. When last with Congress, I often proposed to members to do this, by making of the committee of the States, an executive committee during the recess of Congress, and, during its sessions, to appoint a committee to receive and despatch all executive business, so that Congress itself should meddle only with what should be legislative. But I question if any Congress (much less all successively) can have self-denial enough to go through with this distribution. The distribution, then, should be imposed on them. I find Congress have reversed their division of the western States, and proposed to make them fewer and larger. This is reversing the natural order of things. A tractable people may be governed in large bodies; but, in proportion as they depart from this character, the extent of their government must be less. We see into what small divisions the Indians are obliged to reduce their societies. This measure, with the disposition to shut up the Mississippi, gives me serious apprehensions of the severance of the eastern and western parts of our confederacy. It might have been made the interest of the western States to remain united with us, by managing their interests honestly, and for their own good. But, the moment we sacrifice their interest to our own, they will see it better to govern themselves. The moment they resolve to do this, the point is settled. A forced connection is neither our interest, nor within our power.

The Virginia act for religious freedom has been received with infinite approbation in Europe, and propagated with enthusiasm. I do not mean by the governments, but by the individuals who compose them. It has been translated into French and Italian, has been sent to most of the courts of Europe, and has been the best evidence of the falsehood of those reports which stated us to be in anarchy. It is inserted in the new "Encyclopédie," and is appearing in most of the publications respecting America. In fact, it is comfortable to see the standard of reason at length erected, after so many ages, during which the human mind has been held in vassalage by kings, priests, and nobles; and it is honorable for us, to have produced the first legislature who had the courage to declare, that the reason of man may be trusted with the formation of his own opinions. . . .

FROM HIS "AUTOBIOGRAPHY"

. . . . The bill for establishing religious freedom, the principles of which had, to a certain degree, been enacted before, I had drawn in all the latitude of reason and right. It still met with opposition; but, with some mutilations in the preamble, it was finally passed; and a singular proposition proved that its protection of opinion was meant to be universal. Where the preamble declares, that coercion is a departure from the plan of the holy author of our religion, an amendment was proposed, by inserting the word "Jesus Christ," so that it should read, "a departure from the plan of Jesus Christ, the holy author of our religion;" the insertion was rejected by a great majority, in proof that they meant to comprehend, within the mantle of its protection, the Jew and the Gentile, the Christian and Mahometan, the Hindoo, and Infidel of every denomination . . .

LETTERS

Concept of a Republic[1]

LETTER TO JOHN TAYLOR

Monticello, May 28, 1816

DEAR SIR,—On my return from a long journey and considerable absence from home, I found here the copy of your "Enquiry into the Principles of our Government," which you had been so kind as to send me; and for which I pray you to accept my thanks. The difficulties of getting new works in our situation, inland and without a single bookstore, are such as had prevented my obtaining a copy before; and letters which had accumulated during my absence, and were calling for answers, have not yet permitted me to give to the whole a thorough reading; yet certain that you and I could not think differently on the fundamentals of rightful government, I was impatient, and availed myself of the intervals of repose from the writing-table, to obtain a cursory idea of the body of the work.

I see in it much matter for profound reflection; much which should confirm our adhesion, in practice, to the good principles of our Constitution, and fix our attention on what is yet to be made good. The sixth section on the good moral principles of our government, I found so interesting and replete with sound principles, as to postpone my letter-writing to its thorough perusal and consideration. Besides much other good matter, it settles unanswerably the right of instructing representatives, and their duty to obey. The system of banking we have both equally and ever reprobated. I contemplate it as a

1 Topic headings of Jefferson's letters supplied by the Editors.

blot left in all our Constitutions, which, if not covered, will
end in their destruction, which is already hit by the gamblers
in corruption, and is sweeping away in its progress the fortunes and morals of our citizens. Funding I consider as limited,
rightfully, to a redemption of the debt within the lives of a
majority of the generation contracting it; every generation
coming equally, by the laws of the Creator of the world to
the free possession of the earth He made for their subsistence,
unincumbered by their predecessors, who, like them, were but
tenants for life. You have successfully and completely pul-
verized Mr. Adams' system of orders, and his opening the
mantle of republicanism to every government of laws,
whether consistent or not with natural right. Indeed, it must
be acknowledged, that the term *republic* is of very vague
application in every language. Witness the self-styled republics
of Holland, Switzerland, Genoa, Venice, Poland. Were I to
assign to this term a precise and definite idea, I would say,
purely and simply, it means a government by its citizens in
mass, acting directly and personally, according to rules established by the majority; and that every other government is
more or less republican, in proportion as it has in its composition more or less of this ingredient of the direct action of the
citizens. Such a government is evidently restrained to very
narrow limits of space and population. I doubt if it would be
practicable beyond the extent of a New England township.
The first shade from this pure element, which, like that of
pure vital air, cannot sustain life of itself, would be where the
powers of the government, being divided, should be exercised
each by representatives chosen either *pro hac vice*,[2] or for
such short terms as should render secure the duty of expressing the will of their constituents. This I should consider as the
nearest approach to a pure republic, which is practicable on a
large scale of country or population. And we have examples
of it in some of our State Constitutions, which, if not poisoned
by priest-craft, would prove its excellence over all mixtures
with other elements; and, with only equal doses of poison,
would still be the best. Other shades of republicanism may be
found in other forms of government, where the executive, judiciary and legislative functions, and the different branches of
the latter, are chosen by the people more or less directly, for
longer terms of years, or for life, or made hereditary; or where
there are mixtures of authorities, some dependent on, and

[2] For the occasion.

others independent of the people. The further the departure from direct and constant control by the citizens, the less has the government of the ingredient of republicanism; evidently none where the authorities are hereditary, as in France, Venice, etc., or self-chosen, as in Holland; and little, where for life, in proportion as the life continues in being after the act of election.

The purest republican feature in the government of our own State, is the House of Representatives. The Senate is equally so the first year, less the second, and so on. The Executive still less, because not chosen by the people directly. The Judiciary seriously anti-republican, because for life; and the national arm wielded, as you observe, by military leaders, irresponsible but to themselves. Add to this the vicious constitution of our county courts (to whom the justice, the executive administration, the taxation, police, the military appointments of the county, and nearly all our daily concerns are confided), self-appointed, self-continued, holding their authorities for life, and with an impossibility of breaking in on the perpetual succession of any faction once possessed of the bench. They are in truth, the executive, the judiciary, and the military of their respective counties, and the sum of the counties makes the State. And add, also, that one-half of our brethren who fight and pay taxes, are excluded, like Helots, from the rights of representation, as if society were instituted for the soil, and not for the men inhabiting it; or one-half of these could dispose of the rights and the will of the other half, without their consent.

> "What constitutes a State?
> Not high-raised battlements, or labor'd mound,
> Thick wall, or moated gate;
> Not cities proud, with spires and turrets crown'd;
> No: men, high-minded men;
> Men, who their duties know;
> But know their rights; and knowing, dare maintain.
> These constitute a State."

In the General Government, the House of Representatives is mainly republican; the Senate scarcely so at all, as not elected by the people directly, and so long secured even against those who do elect them; the Executive more republican than the Senate, from its shorter term, its election by the people, in *practice*, (for they vote for A only on an assurance that he will vote for B,) and because, *in practice also*, a principle of rotation seems to be in a course of establishment; the judiciary independent of the nation, their coercion by impeachment being found nugatory.

If, then, the control of the people over the organs of their government be the measure of its republicanism, and I confess I know no other measure, it must be agreed that our governments have much less of republicanism than ought to have been expected; in other words, that the people have less regular control over their agents, than their rights and their interests require. And this I ascribe, not to any want of republican dispositions in those who formed these Constitutions, but to a submission of true principle to European authorities, to speculators on government, whose fears of the people have been inspired by the populace of their own great cities, and were unjustly entertained against the independent, the happy, and therefore orderly citizens of the United States. Much I apprehend that the golden moment is past for reforming these heresies. The functionaries of public power rarely strengthen in their dispositions to abridge it, and an unorganized call for timely amendment is not likely to prevail against an organized opposition to it. We are always told that things are going on well; why change them? *"Chista bene, non si muove,"* said the Italian, "let him who stands well, stand still." This is true; and I verily believe they would go on well with us under an absolute monarch, while our present character remains, of order, industry and love of peace, and restrained, as he would be, by the proper spirit of the people. But it is while it remains such, we should provide against the consequences of its deterioration. And let us rest in the hope that it will yet be done, and spare ourselves the pain of evils which may never happen.

On this view of the import of the term *republic*, instead of saying, as has been said, "that it may mean anything or nothing," we may say with truth and meaning, that governments are more or less republican, as they have more or less of the element of popular election and control in their composition; and believing, as I do, that the mass of the citizens is the safest depository of their own rights and especially, that the evils flowing from the duperies of the people, are less injurious than those from the egoism of their agents, I am a friend to that composition of government which has in it the most of this ingredient. And I sincerely believe, with you, that banking establishments are more dangerous than standing armies; and that the principle of spending money to be paid by posterity, under the name of funding, is but swindling futurity on a large scale.

I salute you with constant friendship and respect.

The Principle of Majority Rule

LETTER TO BARON ALEXANDER VON HUMBOLDT

Monticello, June 13, 1817

. . . . The physical information you have given us of a country [Spain] hitherto so shamefully unknown, has come exactly in time to guide our understandings in the great political revolution now bringing it into prominence on the stage of the world. The issue of its struggles, as they respect Spain, is no longer matter of doubt. As it respects their own liberty, peace and happiness, we cannot be quite so certain. Whether the blinds of bigotry, the shackles of the priesthood, and the fascinating glare of rank and wealth, give fair play to the common sense of the mass of their people, so far as to qualify them for self-government, is what we do not know. Perhaps our wishes may be stronger than our hopes. The first principle of republicanism is, that the *lex majoris partis*[3] is the fundamental law of every society of individuals of equal rights; to consider the will of the society enounced by the majority of a single vote, as sacred as if unanimous, is the first of all lessons in importance, yet the last which is thoroughly learnt. This law once disregarded, no other remains but that of force, which ends necessarily in military despotism. This has been the history of the French Revolution, and I wish the understanding of our Southern brethren may be sufficiently enlarged and firm to see that their fate depends on its sacred observance. . . .

[3] Majority rule.

On Revolutions

LETTER TO EDWARD CARRINGTON

Paris, January 16, 1787

DEAR SIR,— . . . The tumults in America,[4] I expected
would have produced in Europe an unfavorable opinion of our
political state. But it has not. On the contrary, the small effect
of these tumults seems to have given more confidence in the
firmness of our governments. The interposition of the people
themselves on the side of government has had a great effect
on the opinion here. I am persuaded myself that the good sense
of the people will always be found to be the best army. They
may be led astray for a moment, but will soon correct themselves. The people are the only censors of their governors:
and even their errors will tend to keep these to the true principles of their institution. To punish these errors too severely
would be to suppress the only safeguard of the public liberty.
The way to prevent these irregular interpositions of the people
is to give them full information of their affairs thro' the
channel of the public papers, and to contrive that those papers
should penetrate the whole mass of the people. The basis of
our governments being the opinion of the people, the very
first object should be to keep that right; and were it left to
me to decide whether we should have a government without
newspapers or newspapers without a government, I should not
hesitate a moment to prefer the latter. But I should mean
that every man should receive those papers and be capable
of reading them. I am convinced that those societies (as the
Indians) which live without government enjoy in their general
mass an infinitely greater degree of happiness than those who
live under the European governments. Among the former,
public opinion is in the place of law, and restrains morals as
powerfully as laws ever did anywhere. Among the latter,
under pretence of governing they have divided their nations

[4] Jefferson has in view the 1786 uprising of Massachusetts
farmers known as Shays' Rebellion.

into two classes, wolves and sheep. I do not exaggerate. This is a true picture of Europe. Cherish therefore the spirit of our people, and keep alive their attention. Do not be too severe upon their errors, but reclaim them by enlightening them. If once they become inattentive to the public affairs, you and I, and Congress and Assemblies, judges and governors shall all become wolves. It seems to be the law of our general nature, in spite of individual exceptions; and experience declares that man is the only animal which devours his own kind, for I can apply no milder term to the governments of Europe, and to the general prey of the rich on the poor. The want of news has led me into disquisition instead of narration, forgetting you have every day enough of that. I shall be happy to hear from you sometimes, only observing that whatever passes thro' the post is read, and that when you write what should be read by myself only, you must be so good as to confide your letter to some passenger or officer of the packet. I will ask your permission to write to you sometimes, and to assure you of the esteem and respect with which I have honour to be Dear Sir your most obedient and most humble servt.

LETTER TO JAMES MADISON

Paris, January 30, 1787

DEAR SIR,—My last to you was of the 16th of Dec, since which I have received yours of Nov 25, and Dec 4, which afforded me, as your letters always do, a treat on matters public, individual and œconomical. I am impatient to learn your sentiments on the late troubles in the Eastern states. So far as I have yet seen, they do not appear to threaten serious consequences. Those states have suffered by the stoppage of the channels of their commerce, which have not yet found other issues. This must render money scarce, and make the people uneasy. This uneasiness has produced acts absolutely unjustifiable; but I hope they will provoke no severities from their governments. A consciousness of those in power that their administration of the public affairs has been honest, may perhaps produce too great a degree of indignation: and those characters wherein fear predominates over hope may apprehend too much from these instances of irregularity. They may conclude too hastily that nature has formed man insusceptible of any other government but that of force, a conclusion not

founded in truth, nor experience. Societies exist under three
forms sufficiently distinguishable. 1. Without government, as
among our Indians. 2. Under governments wherein the will
of every one has a just influence, as is the case in England in a
slight degree, and in our states, in a great one. 3. Under governments of force: as is the case in all other monarchies and
in most of the other republics. To have an idea of the curse
of existence under these last, they must be seen. It is a government of wolves over sheep. It is a problem, not clear in my
mind, that the first condition is not the best. But I believe it to
be inconsistent with any great degree of population. The second state has a great deal of good in it. The mass of mankind
under that enjoys a precious degree of liberty and happiness.
It has it's evils too: the principal of which is the turbulence to
which it is subject. But weigh this against the oppressions of
monarchy, and it becomes nothing. *Malo periculosam liberta-*
tem quam quietam servitutem. Even this evil is productive of
good. It prevents the degeneracy of government, and nourishes
a general attention to the public affairs. I hold it that a little
rebellion now and then is a good thing, and as necessary in
the political world as storms in the physical. Unsuccessful rebellions indeed generally establish the encroachments on the
rights of the people which have produced them. An observation of this truth should render honest republican governors
so mild in their punishment of rebellions, as not to discourage
them too much. It is a medicine necessary for the sound health
of government. If these transactions give me no uneasiness,
I feel very differently at another piece of intelligence, to wit,
the possibility that the navigation of the Mississippi may be
abandoned to Spain. I never had any interest Westward of the
Alleghaney; and I never will have any. But I have had great
opportunities of knowing the character of the people who
inhabit that country. And I will venture to say that the act
which abandons the navigation of the Mississippi is an act of
separation between the Eastern and Western country. It is a
relinquishment of five parts out of eight of the territory of the
United States, an abandonment of the fairest subject for the
paiment of our public debts, and the chaining those debts on
our own necks *in perpetuum.* I have the utmost confidence in
the honest intentions of those who concur in this measure; but
I lament their want of acquaintance with the character and
physical advantages of the people who, right or wrong, will
suppose their interests sacrificed on this occasion to the contrary interests of that part of the confederacy in possession of

present power. If they declare themselves a separate people, we are incapable of a single effort to retain them. Our citizens can never be induced, either as militia or as souldiers, to go there to cut the throats of their own brothers and sons, or rather to be themselves the subjects instead of the perpetrators of the parricide. Nor would that country requite the cost of being retained against the will of it's inhabitants, could it be done. But it cannot be done. They are able already to rescue the navigation of the Mississippi out of the hands of Spain, and to add New Orleans to their own territory. They will be joined by the inhabitants of Louisiana. This will bring on a war between them and Spain; and that will produce the question with us whether it will not be worth our while to become parties with them in the war, in order to reunite them with us, and thus correct our error? And were I to permit my forebodings to go one step futher, I should predict that the inhabitants of the U S would force their rulers to take the affirmative of that question. I wish I may be mistaken in all these opinions . . .

LETTER TO COLONEL SMITH

Paris, November 13, 1787

. . . . can history produce an instance of rebellion[5] so honorably conducted? I say nothing of its motives. They were founded in ignorance, not wickedness. God forbid we should ever be twenty years without such a rebellion. The people cannot be all, and always, well informed. The part which is wrong will be discontented, in proportion to the importance of the facts they misconceive. If they remain quiet under such misconceptions, it is a lethargy, the forerunner of death to the public liberty. We have had thirteen States independent for eleven years. There has been one rebellion. That comes to one rebellion in a century and a half, for each State. What country before, ever existed a century and a half without a rebellion? And what country can preserve its liberties, if its rulers are not warned from time to time, that this people preserve the spirit of resistance? Let them take arms. The remedy is to set them right as to facts, pardon and pacify

[5] Jefferson refers to "Shays' Rebellion." *The Editors.*

them. What signify a few lives lost in a century or two? The tree of liberty must be refreshed from time to time, with the blood of patriots and tyrants. It is its natural manure. . . .

LETTER TO WILLIAM SHORT

Philadelphia, January 3, 1793

DEAR SIR,— . . . The tone of your letters had for some time given me pain, on account of the extreme warmth with which they censured the proceedings of the Jacobins of France. I considered that sect as the same with the Republican patriots, and the Feuillants as the Monarchical patriots, well known in the early part of the revolution, and but little distant in their views, both having in object the establishment of a free constitution, and differing only on the question whether their chief Executive should be hereditary or not. The Jacobins (as since called) yielded to the Feuillants and tried the experiment of retaining their hereditary Executive. The experiment failed completely, and would have brought on the reestablishment of despotism had it been pursued. The Jacobins saw this, and that the expunging that officer was of absolute necessity. And the Nation was with them in opinion, for however they might have been formerly for the constitution framed by the first assembly, they were come over from their hope in it, and were now generally Jacobins. In the struggle which was necessary, many guilty persons fell without the forms of trial, and with them some innocent. These I deplore as much as any body, and shall deplore some of them to the day of my death. But I deplore them as I should have done had they fallen in battle. It was necessary to use the arm of the people, a machine not quite so blind as balls and bombs, but blind to a certain degree. A few of their cordial friends met at their hands the fate of enemies. But time and truth will rescue and embalm their memories, while their posterity will be enjoying that very liberty for which they would never have hesitated to offer up their lives. The liberty of the whole earth was depending on the issue of the contest and was ever such a prize won with so little innocent blood? My own affections have been deeply wounded by some of the martyrs to this cause, but rather than it should have failed, I would have seen half the earth desolated. Were there but an Adam and an Eve left in every country, and left free, it would be

better than as it now is. I have expressed to you my sentiments because they are really those of 99. in an hundred of our
citizens. The universal feasts, and rejoicings which have lately
been had on account of the successes of the French shewed
the genuine effusions of their hearts. You have been wounded
by the sufferings of your friends, and have by this circumstance been hurried into a temper of mind which would be
extremely disrelished if known to your countrymen.

The Rights of Each Generation

LETTER TO JAMES MADISON

Paris, September 6, 1789

DEAR SIR,—I sit down to write to you without knowing by
what occasion I shall send my letter. I do it because a subject
comes into my head which I would wish to develope a little
more than is practicable in the hurry of the moment of making up general despatches.

The question Whether one generation of men has a right to
bind another, seems never to have been started either on this
or our side of the water. Yet it is a question of such consequences as not only to merit decision, but place also, among
the fundamental principles of every government. The course of
reflection in which we are immersed here on the elementary
principles of society has presented this question to my mind;
and that no such obligation can be transmitted I think very
capable of proof. I set out on this ground which I suppose to
be self evident, *"that the earth belongs in usufruct to the
living;"* that the dead have neither powers nor rights over it.
The portion occupied by any individual ceases to be his when
himself ceases to be, and reverts to the society. If the society
has formed no rules for the appropriation of its lands in
severalty, it will be taken by the first occupants. These will
generally be the wife and children of the decedent. If they
have formed rules of appropriation, those rules may give
it to the wife and children, or to some one of them, or to
the legatee of the deceased. So they may give it to his creditor.

But the child, the legatee or creditor takes it, not by any natural right, but by a law of the society of which they are members, and to which they are subject. Then no man can by *natural right* oblige the lands he occupied, or the persons who succeed him in that occupation, to the paiment of debts contracted by him. For if he could, he might during his own life, eat up the usufruct of the lands for several generations to come, and then the lands would belong to the dead, and not to the living, which would be reverse of our principle. What is true of every member of the society individually, is true of them all collectively, since the rights of the whole can be no more than the sum of the rights of individuals. To keep our ideas clear when applying them to a multitude, let us suppose a whole generation of men to be born on the same day, to attain mature age on the same day, and to die on the same day, leaving a succeeding generation in the moment of attaining their mature age all together. Let the ripe age be supposed of 21. years, and their period of life 34. years more, that being the average term given by the bills of mortality to persons who have already attained 21. years of age. Each successive generation would, in this way, come on and go off the stage at a fixed moment, as individuals do now. Then I say the earth belongs to each of these generations during it's course, fully, and in their own right. The 2d. generation receives it clear of the debts and incumbrances of the 1st., the 3d. of the 2d. and so on. For if the 1st could charge it with a debt, then the earth would belong to the dead and not the living generation. Then no generation can contract debts greater than may be paid during the course of it's own existence. At 21. years of age they may bind themselves and their lands for 34. years to come: at 22. for 33: at 23 for 32. and at 54 for one year only; because these are the terms of life which remain to them at those respective epochs. But a material difference must be noted between the succession of an individual and that of a whole generation. Individuals are parts only of a society, subject to the laws of a whole. These laws may appropriate the portion of land occupied by a decedent to his creditor rather than to any other, or to his child, on condition he satisfies his creditor. But when a whole generation, that is, the whole society dies, as in the case we have supposed, and another generation or society succeeds, this forms a whole, and there is no superior who can give their territory to a third society, who may have lent money to their predecessors beyond their faculty of paying.

What is true of a generation all arriving to self-government on the same day, and dying all on the same day, is true of those on a constant course of decay and renewal, with this only difference. A generation coming in and going out entire, as in the first case, would have a right in the 1st year of their self dominion to contract a debt for 33. years, in the 10th. for 24. in the 20th. for 14. in the 30th. for 4. whereas generations changing daily, by daily deaths and births, have one constant term beginning at the date of their contract, and ending when a majority of those of full age at that date shall be dead. The length of that term may be estimated from the tables of mortality, corrected by the circumstances of climate, occupation &c. peculiar to the country of the contractors. Take, for instance, the table of M. de Buffon wherein he states 23,994 deaths, and the ages at which they happen. Suppose a society in which 23,994 persons are born every year and live to the ages stated in this table. The conditions of that society will be as follows. 1st. it will consist constantly of 617,703 persons of all ages. 2dly. of those living at any one instant of time, one half will be dead in 24. years 8. months. 3dly. 10,675 will arrive every year at the age of 21. years complete. 4thly. it will constantly have 348,417 persons of all ages above 21. years. 5ly. and the half of those of 21. years and upwards living at any one instant of time will be dead in 18. years 8. months, or say 19. years as the nearest integral number. Then 19. years is the term beyond which neither the representatives of a nation, nor even the whole nation itself assembled, can validly extend a debt.

To render this conclusion palpable by example, suppose that Louis XIV. and XV. had contracted debts in the name of the French nation to the amount of 10.000 milliards of livres and that the whole had been contracted in Genoa. The interest of this sum would be 500 milliards, which is said to be the whole rent-roll, or nett proceeds of the territory of France. Must the present generation of men have retired from the territory in which nature produced them, and ceded it to the Genoese creditors? No. They have the same rights over the soil on which they were produced, as the preceding generations had. They derive these rights not from their predecessors, but from nature. They then and their soil are by nature clear of the debts of their predecessors. Again suppose Louis XV. and his contemporary generation had said to the money lenders of Genoa, give us money that we may eat, drink, and be merry in our day; and on condition you will demand no interest till

the end of thirty-four years, you shall then forever after receive
an annual interest of fifteen per cent. The money is lent on
these conditions, is divided among the living, eaten, drank, and
squandered. Would the present generation be obliged to apply
the produce of the earth and of their labour to replace their
dissipations? Not at all.

I suppose that the received opinion, that the public debts
of one generation devolve on the next, has been suggested by
our seeing habitually in private life that he who succeeds to
lands is required to pay the debts of his ancestor or testator,
without considering that this requisition is municipal only,
not moral, flowing from the will of the society which has
found it convenient to appropriate the lands become vacant by
the death of their occupant on the condition of a paiment of his
debts; but that between society and society, or generation and
generation there is no municipal obligation, no umpire but the
law of nature. We seem not to have perceived that, by the
law of nature, one generation is to another as one independant
nation to another.

The interest of the national debt of France being in fact but
a two thousandth part of it's rent-roll, the paiment of it is
practicable enough; and so becomes a question merely of
honor or expediency. But with respect to future debts; would
it not be wise and just for that nation to declare in the constitution they are forming that neither the legislature, nor the
nation itself can validly contract more debt, than they may pay
within their own age, or within the term of 19. years? And that
all future contracts shall be deemed void as to what shall remain unpaid at the end of 19. years from their date? This
would put the lenders, and the borrowers also, on their guard.
By reducing too the faculty of borrowing within its natural
limits, it would bridle the spirit of war, to which too free a
course has been procured by the inattention of money lenders
to this law of nature, that succeeding generations are not
responsible for the preceding.

On similar ground it may be proved that no society can
make a perpetual constitution, or even a perpetual law. The
earth belongs always to the living generation. They may manage it then, and what proceeds from it, as they please, during
their usufruct. They are masters too of their own persons, and
consequently may govern them as they please. But persons and
property make the sum of the objects of government. The
constitution and the laws of their predecessors extinguish
them, in their natural course, with those whose will gave

them being. This could preserve that being till it ceased to be itself, and no longer. Every constitution, then, and every law, naturally expires at the end of 19. years. If it be enforced longer, it is an act of force and not of right.

It may be said that the succeeding generation exercising in fact the power of repeal, this leaves them as free as if the constitution or law had been expressly limited to 19. years only. In the first place, this objection admits the right, in proposing an equivalent. But the power of repeal is not an equivalent. It might be indeed if every form of government were so perfectly contrived that the will of the majority could always be obtained fairly and without impediment. But this is true of no form. The people cannot assemble themselves; their representation is unequal and vicious. Various checks are opposed to every legislative proposition. Factions get possession of the public councils. Bribery corrupts them. Personal interests lead them astray from the general interests of their constituents; and other impediments arise so as to prove to every practical man that a law of limited duration is much more manageable than one which needs a repeal.

This principle that the earth belongs to the living and not to the dead is of very extensive application and consequences in every country, and most especially in France. It enters into the resolution of the questions Whether the nation may change the descent of lands holden in tail? Whether they may change the appropriation of lands given antiently to the church, to hospitals, colleges, orders of chivalry, and otherwise in perpetuity? whether they may abolish the charges and privileges attached on lands, including the whole catalogue ecclesiastical and feudal? it goes to hereditary offices, authorities and jurisdictions; to hereditary orders, distinctions and appellations; to perpetual monopolies in commerce, the arts or sciences; with a long train of *et ceteras:* and it renders the question of reimbursement a question of generosity and not of right. In all these cases the legislature of the day could authorize such appropriations and establishments for their own time, but no longer; and the present holders, even where they or their ancestors have purchased, are in the case of *bona fide* purchasers of what the seller had no right to convey.

Turn this subject in your mind, my Dear Sir, and particularly as to the power of contracting debts, and develope it with that perspicuity and cogent logic which is so peculiarly yours. Your station in the councils of our country gives you an opportunity of producing it to public consideration, of forcing it into discussion. At first blush it may be rallied as a theoretical speculation; but examination will prove it to be solid and salutary. It would furnish matter for a fine preamble to our first law for appropriating the public revenue; and it will exclude, at the threshold of our new government the contagious and ruinous errors of this quarter of the globe, which have armed despots with means not sanctioned by nature for binding in chains their fellow-men. We have already given, in example one effectual check to the Dog of war, by transferring the power of letting him loose from the executive to the Legislative body, from those who are to spend to those who are to pay. I should be pleased to see this second obstacle held out by us also in the first instance. No nation can make a declaration against the validity of long-contracted debts so disinterestedly as we, since we do not owe a shilling which may not be paid with ease principal and interest, within the time of our own lives. Establish the principle also in the new law to be passed for protecting copy rights and new inventions, by securing the exclusive right for 19. instead of 14. years [*a line entirely faded*] an instance the more of our taking reason for our guide instead of English precedents, the habit of which fetters us, with all the political herecies of a nation, equally remarkable for it's enticement from some errors, as long slumbering under others. I write you no news, because when an occasion occurs I shall write a separate letter for that.

Natural Aristocracy

LETTER TO JOHN ADAMS

. . . For I agree with you that there is a natural aristocracy among men. The grounds of this are virtue and talents. Formerly, bodily powers gave place among the aristoi. But since the invention of gunpowder has armed the weak as well as the strong with missile death, bodily strength, like beauty, good humor, politeness and other accomplishments, has become but an auxiliary ground of distinction. There is also an artificial aristocracy, founded on wealth and birth, without either virtue or talents; for with these it would belong to the first class. The natural aristocracy I consider as the most precious gift of nature, for the instruction, the trusts, and government of society. And indeed, it would have been inconsistent in creation to have formed man for the social state, and not to have provided virtue and wisdom enough to manage the concerns of the society. May we not even say, that that form of government is the best, which provides the most effectually for a pure selection of these natural aristoi into the offices of government? The artificial aristocracy is a mischievous ingredient in government, and provision should be made to prevent its ascendency. On the question, what is the best provision, you and I differ; but we differ as rational friends, using the free exercise of our own reason, and mutually indulging its errors. You think it best to put the pseudo-aristoi into a separate chamber of legislation, where they may be hindered from doing mischief by their co-ordinate branches, and where, also, they may be a protection to wealth against the Agrarian and plundering enterprises of the majority of the people. I think that to give them power in order to prevent them from doing mischief, is arming them for it, and increasing instead of remedying the evil. For if the co-ordinate branches can arrest their action, so may they that of the co-ordinates. Mischief may be done negatively as well as positively. Of this, a cabal in the Senate of the United States has furnished many proofs. Nor do I believe them necessary to protect the wealthy; because enough of these will find their way into every branch of the legislation, to protect themselves. From fifteen to twenty legislatures of our own, in action for thirty years past, have proved that no fears of an equalization of property are to be apprehended from them. I think the best remedy is exactly that provided by all our constitutions, to leave to the citizens the free election and separation of the aristoi from the pseudo-aristoi, of the wheat from the chaff. In general they will elect the really good and wise. In some instances, wealth may corrupt, and birth blind them; but not in sufficient degree to endanger the society.

It is probable that our difference of opinion may, in some measure, be produced by a difference of character in those among whom we live. From what I have seen of Massachusetts and Connecticut myself, and still more from what I have heard, and the character given of the former by yourself (vol. I, page 111), who know them so much better, there seems to be in those two States a traditionary reverence for certain families, which has rendered the offices of the government nearly hereditary in those families. I presume that from an early period of your history, members of those families happening to possess virtue and talents, have honestly exercised them for the good of the people, and by their services have endeared their names to them. In coupling Connecticut with you, I mean it politically only, not morally. For having made the Bible the common law of their land, they seem to have modeled their morality on the story of Jacob and Laban. But although this hereditary succession to office with you, may, in some degree, be founded in real family merit, yet in a much higher degree, it has proceeded from your strict alliance of Church and State. These families are canonised in the eyes of the people on common principles, "you tickle me, and I will tickle you." In Virginia we have nothing of this. Our clergy, before the revolution, having been secured against rivalship by fixed salaries, did not give themselves the trouble of acquiring influence over the people. Of wealth, there were great accumulations in particular families, handed down from generation to generation, under the English law of entails. But the only object of ambition for the wealthy was a seat in the King's Council. All their court then was paid to the crown and its creatures; and they Philipised in all collisions between the King and the people. Hence they were unpopular; and that unpopularity continues attached to their names. A Randolph, a Carter, or a Burwell must have great personal superiority over a common competitor to be elected by the people even at this day. At the first session of our-legislature after the Declaration of Independence, we passed a law abolishing entails. And this was followed by one abolishing the privilege primogeniture, and dividing the lands of intestates equally among all their children, or other representatives. These laws, drawn by myself, laid the axe to the foot of pseudo-aristocracy. And had another which I prepared been adopted by the legislature, our work would have been complete. It was a bill for the more general diffusion of learning. This proposed to divide every county into wards of five or six miles square, like your townships; to establish in each ward a free school for reading, writing and common arithmetic; to provide for the annual selection of the best subjects from these schools, who might receive, at the public expense, a higher degree of education at a district school; and from these district schools to select a certain number of the most promising subjects, to be completed at an University, where all the useful sciences should be taught. Worth and genius would thus have been sought out from every condition of life, and completely prepared by education for defeating the competition of wealth and birth for public trusts. My proposition had, for a further object, to impart to these wards those portions of self-government for which they are best qualified, by confiding to them the care of their poor, their roads, police, elections, the nomination of jurors, administration of justice in small cases, elementary exercises of militia; in short, to have made them little republics, with a warden at the head of each, for all those concerns which, being under their eye, they would better manage than the larger republics of the county or State. A general call of ward meetings by their wardens on the same day through the State, would at any time produce the genuine sense of the people on any required point, and would enable the State to act in mass, as your people have so often done, and with so much effect by their town meetings. The law for religious freedom, which made a part of this system, having put down the aristocracy of the clergy, and restored to the citizen the freedom of the mind, and those of entails and descents nurturing an equality of condition among them, this on education would have raised the mass of the people to the high ground of moral respectability necessary to their own safety, and to orderly government; and would have completed the great object of qualifying them to select the veritable aristoi, for the trusts of government, to the exclusion of the pseudalists. . . . Although this law has not yet been acted on but in a small and inefficient degree, it is still considered as before the legislature, with other bills of the revised code, not yet taken up, and I have great hope that some patriotic spirit will, at a favorable moment, call it up, and make it the key-stone of the arch of our government.

With respect to aristocracy, we should further consider, that before the establishment of the American States, nothing was known to history but the man of the old world, crowded within limits either small or overcharged, and steeped in the vices which that situation generates. A government adapted to such men would be one thing; but a very different one, that for the man of these States. Here everyone may have land to labor for himself, if he chooses; or, preferring the exercise of any other industry, may exact for it such compensation as not only to afford a comfortable subsistence, but wherewith to provide for a cessation from labor in old age. Everyone, by his property, or by his satisfactory situation, is interested in the support of law and order. And such men may safely and advantageously reserve to themselves a wholesome control over their public affairs, and a degree of freedom, which, in the hands of the *canaille* of the cities of Europe, would be instantly perverted to the demolition and destruction of everything public and private. The history of the last twenty-five years of France, and of the last forty years in America, nay of its last two hundred years, proves the truth of both parts of this observation.

But even in Europe a change has sensibly taken place in the mind of man. Science had liberated the ideas of those who read and reflect, and the American example had kindled feelings of right in the people. An insurrection has consequently begun, of science, talents, and courage, against rank and birth, which have fallen into contempt. It has failed in its first effort, because the mobs of the cities, the instrument used for its accomplishment, debased by ignorance, poverty, and vice, could not be restrained to rational action. But the world will recover from the panic of this first catastrophe. Science is progressive, and talents and enterprise on the alert. Resort may be had to the people of the country, a more governable power from their principles and subordination; and rank, and birth, and tinsel-aristocracy will finally shrink into insignificance, even there. This, however, we have no right to meddle with. It suffices for us, if the moral and physical condition of our own citizens qualifies them to select the able and good for the direction of their government, with a recurrence of elections at such short periods as will enable them to displace an unfaithful servant, before the mischief he meditates may be irremediable.

The Basis of Rules of Morality

TO THOMAS LAW, ESQ.

Poplar Forest, June 13, 1814

DEAR SIR,—The copy of your Second Thoughts on Instinctive Impulses, with the letter accompanying it, was received just as I was setting out on a journey to this place, two or three days distant from Monticello. I brought it with me and read it with great satisfaction, and with the more as it contained exactly my own creed on the foundation of morality in man. It is really curious that on a question so fundamental, such a variety of opinions should have prevailed among men, and those, too, of the most exemplary virtue and first order of understanding. It shows how necessary was the care of the Creator in making the moral principle so much a part of our constitution as that no errors of reasoning or of speculation might lead us astray from its observation in practice. Of all the theories on this question, the most whimsical seems to have been that of Wollaston, who considers *truth* as the foundation of morality. The thief who steals your guinea does wrong only inasmuch as he acts a lie in using your guinea as if it were his own. Truth is certainly a branch of morality, and a very important one to society. But presented as its foundation, it is as if a tree taken up by the roots, had its stem reversed in the air, and one of its branches planted in the ground. Some have made the love of God the foundation of morality. This, too, is but a branch of our moral duties, which are generally divided into duties to God and duties to man. If we did a good act merely from the love of God and a belief that it is pleasing to Him, whence arises the morality of the Atheist? It is idle to say, as some do, that no such being exists. We have the same evidence of the fact as of most of those we act on, to wit: their own affirmations, and their reasonings in support of them. I have observed, indeed, generally, that while in Protestant countries the defections from the Platonic Christianity of the priests is to Deism, in Catholic countries they are to Atheism. Diderot, D'Alembert, D'Holbach, Condorcet, are known to have been among the most virtuous of men. Their virtue, then, must have had some other foundation than the love of God.

The *kalon*, (the beautiful, Gr.) of others is founded in a different faculty, that of taste, which is not even a branch of morality. We have indeed an innate sense of what we call beautiful, but that is exercised chiefly on subjects addressed to the fancy, whether through the eye in visible forms, as landscape, animal figure, dress, drapery, architecture, the composition of colors, etc., or to the imagination directly, as imagery, style, or measure in prose or poetry, or whatever else constitutes the domain of criticism or taste, a faculty entirely distinct from the moral one. Self-interest, or rather self-love, or *egoism*, has been more plausibly substituted as the basis of morality. But I consider our relations with others as constitut-

ing the boundaries of morality. With ourselves we stand on
the ground of identity, not of relation, which last, requiring
two subjects, excludes self-love confined to a single one. To
ourselves, in strict language, we can owe no duties, obligation
requiring also two parties. Self-love, therefore, is no part of
morality. Indeed it is exactly its counterpart. It is the sole
antagonist of virtue, leading us constantly by our propensities
to self-gratification in violation of our moral duties to others.
Accordingly, it is against this enemy that are erected the bat-
teries of moralists and religionists, as the only obstacle to the
practice of morality. Take from man his selfish propensities,
and he can have nothing to seduce him from the practice of
virtue. Or subdue those propensities by education, instruction
or restraint, and virtue remains without a competitor. Egoism,
in a broader sense, has been thus presented as the source of
moral action. It has been said that we feed the hungry, clothe
the naked, bind up the wounds of the man beaten by thieves,
pour oil and wine into them, set him on our own beast and
bring him to the inn, because we receive ourselves pleasure
from these acts. So Helvetius, one of the best men on earth,
and the most ingenious advocate of this principle, after defining "interest" to mean not merely that which is pecuniary,
but whatever may procure us pleasure or withdraw us from
pain, [*de l'esprit*, 2, 1,] says, [ib. 2, 2,] "the humane man is he
to whom the sight of misfortune is insupportable, and who to
rescue himself from this spectacle, is forced to succor the
unfortunate object." This indeed is true. But it is one step short
of the ultimate question. These good acts give us pleasure, but
how happens it that they give us pleasure? Because nature hath
implanted in our breasts a love of others, a sense of duty to
them, a moral instinct, in short, which prompts us irresistibly
to feel and to succor their distresses, and protests against the
language of Helvetius, [ib. 2, 5,] "what other motive than self-
interest could determine a man to generous actions? It is as
impossible for him to love what is good for the sake of good,
as to love evil for the sake of evil." The Creator would indeed
have been a bungling artist, had he intended man for a social
animal, without planting in him social dispositions. It is true
they are not planted in every man, because there is no rule
without exceptions; but it is false reasoning which converts
exceptions into the general rule. Some men are born without
the organs of sight, or of hearing, or without hands. Yet it
would be wrong to say that man is born without these faculties,

and sight, hearing, and hands may with truth enter into the general definition of man.

The want or imperfection of the moral sense in some men, like the want or imperfection of the senses of sight and hearing in others, is no proof that it is a general characteristic of the species. When it is wanting, we endeavor to supply the defect by education, by appeals to reason and calculation, by presenting to the being so unhappily conformed, other motives to do good and to eschew evil, such as the love, or the hatred, or rejection of those among whom he lives, and whose society is necessary to his happiness and even existence; demonstrations by sound calculation that honesty promotes interest in the long run; the rewards and penalties established by the laws; and ultimately the prospects of a future state of retribution for the evil as well as the good done while here. These are the correctives which are supplied by education, and which exercise the functions of the moralist, the preacher, and legislator; and they lead into a course of correct action all those whose disparity is not too profound to be eradicated. Some have argued against the existence of a moral sense, by saying that if nature had given us such a sense, impelling us to virtuous actions, and warning us against those which are vicious, then nature would also have designated, by some particular ear-marks, the two sets of actions which are, in themselves, the one virtuous and the other vicious. Whereas, we find, in fact, that the same actions are deemed virtuous in one country and vicious in another. The answer is, that nature has constituted *utility* to man, the standard and test of virtue. Men living in different countries, under different circumstances, different habits and regimens, may have different utilities; the same act, therefore, may be useful, and consequently virtuous in one country which is injurious and vicious in another differently circumstanced. I sincerely, then, believe with you in the general existence of a moral instinct. I think it the brightest gem with which the human character is studded, and the want of it as more degrading than the most hideous of the bodily deformities. I am happy in reviewing the roll of associates in this principle which you present in your second letter, some of which I had not before met with. To these might be added Lord Kaims, one of the ablest of our advocates, who goes so far as to say, in his Principles of Natural Religion, that a man owes no duty to which he is not urged by some impulsive feeling. This is correct, if referred to the standard of general feeling in the given case, and not to the feeling of a single individual. Perhaps I may misquote him, it being fifty years since I read his book.

The leisure and solitude of my situation here has led me to the indiscretion of taxing you with a long letter on a subject whereon nothing new can be offered you. I will indulge myself no farther than to repeat the assurances of my continued esteem and respect.

The Place and Value of Social and Political Change

LETTER TO KERCHEVAL

Monticello, July 12, 1816

. . . . I am not among those who fear the people. They, and not the rich, are our dependence for continued freedom. And to preserve their independence, we must not let our rulers load us with perpetual debt. We must make our election between *economy and liberty,* or *profusion and servitude.* If we run into such debts, as that we must be taxed in our meat and in our drink, in our necessaries and our comforts, in our labors and our amusements, for our callings and our creeds, as the people of England are, our people, like them, must come to labor sixteen hours in the twenty-four, give the earnings of fifteen of these to the government for their debts and daily expenses; and the sixteenth being insufficient to afford us bread, we must live, as they now do, on oatmeal and potatoes; have no time to think, no means of calling the mis-managers to account; but be glad to obtain subsistence by hiring ourselves to rivet their chains on the necks of our fellow-sufferers. Our landholders, too, like theirs, retaining indeed the title and stewardship of estates called theirs, but held really in trust for the treasury, must wander, like theirs, in foreign countries, and be contented with penury, obscurity, exile, and the glory of the nation. This example reads to us the salutary lesson, that private fortunes are destroyed by public as well as by private extravagance. And this is the tendency of all human governments. A departure from principle in one instance becomes a precedent for a second; that second for a third; and so on, till the bulk of the society is reduced to be mere automatons of misery, and to have no sensibilities left but for sinning and suffering. Then begins, indeed, the *bellum omnium in omnia,* which some philosophers observing to be so general in this world, have mistaken it for the natural, instead of the abusive state of man. And the fore horse of this frightful team is public debt. Taxation follows that, and in its train wretchedness and oppression.

Some men look at constitutions with sanctimonious reverence, and deem them like the arc of the covenant, too sacred to be touched. They ascribe to the men of the preceding age a wisdom more than human, and suppose what they did to be beyond amendment. I knew that age well; I belonged to it, and labored with it. It deserved well of its country. It was very like the present, but without the experience of the present; and forty years of experience in government is worth a century of book-reading; and this they would say themselves, were they to rise from the dead. I am certainly not an advocate for frequent and untried changes in laws and constitutions. I think moderate imperfections had better be borne with; because, when once known, we accommodate ourselves to them, and find practical means of correcting their ill effects. But I know also, that laws and institutions must go hand in hand with the progress of the human mind. As that becomes more developed, more enlightened, as new discoveries are made, new truths disclosed, and manners and opinions change with the change of circumstances, institutions must advance also, and keep pace with the times. We might as well require a man to wear still the coat which fitted him when a boy, as civilized society to remain ever under the regimen of their barbarous ancestors. It is this preposterous idea which has lately deluged Europe in blood. Their monarchs, instead of wisely yielding to the gradual change of circumstances, of favoring progressive accommodation to progressive improvement, have clung to old abuses, entrenched themselves behind steady habits, and obliged their subjects to seek through blood and violence rash and ruinous innovations, which, had they been referred to the peaceful deliberations and collected wisdom of the nation, would have been put into acceptable and salutary forms. Let us follow no such examples, nor weakly believe that one generation is not as capable as another of taking care of itself, and of ordering its own affairs. Let us, as our sister States have done, avail ourselves of our reason and experience, to correct the crude essays of our first and unexperienced, although wise, virtuous, and well-meaning councils. And lastly, let us provide in our constitution for its revision at stated periods. What these periods should be, nature herself indicates. By the European tables of mortality, of the adults living at any one moment of time, a majority will be dead in about nineteen years. At the end of that period, then, a new majority is come into place; or, in other words, a new generation. Each generation is as independent as the one preceding, as that was of all which had gone before. It has then, like them, a right to choose for itself the form of government it believes most promotive of its own happiness; consequently, to accommodate to the circumstances in which it finds itself, that received from its predecessors; and it is for the peace and good of mankind that a solemn opportunity of doing this every nineteen or twenty years, should be provided by the constitution; so that it may be handed on, with periodical repairs, from generation to generation, to the end of time, if anything human can so long endure. It is now forty years since the constitution of Virginia was formed. The same tables inform us, that, within that period, two-thirds of the adults then living are now dead. Have then the remaining third, even if they had the wish, the right to hold in obedience to their will, and to laws heretofore made by them, the other two-thirds, who, with themselves, compose the present mass of adults? If they have not, who has? The dead? But the dead have no rights. They are nothing; and nothing cannot own something. Where there is no substance, there can be no accident. This corporeal globe, and everything upon it, belong to its present corporeal inhabitants, during their generation. They alone have a right to direct what is the concern of themselves, alone, and to declare the law of that direction; and this declaration can only be made by their majority. That majority, then, has a right to depute representatives to a convention, and to make the constitution what they think will be the best for themselves. But how collect their voice? This is the real difficulty. If invited by private authority, or county or district meetings, these divisions are so large that few will attend; and their voice will be imperfectly, or falsely pronounced. Here, then, would be one of the advantages of the ward divisions I have proposed. The mayor of every ward, on a question like the present, would call his ward together, take the simple yea or nay of its members, convey these to the county court, who would hand on those of all its wards to the proper general authority; and the voice of the whole people would be thus fairly, fully, and peaceably expressed, discussed, and decided by the common reason of the society. If this avenue be shut to the call of sufferance, it will make itself heard through that of force, and we shall go on, as other nations are doing, in the endless circle of oppression, rebellion, reformation; and oppression, rebellion, reformation, again; and so on forever.

These, Sir, are my opinions of the governments we see among men, and of the principles by which alone we may prevent our own from falling into the same dreadful track. I have given them at greater length than your letter called for. But I cannot say things by halves; and I confide them to your honor, so to use them as to preserve me from the gridiron of the public papers. If you shall approve and enforce them, as you have done that of equal representation, they may do some good. If not, keep them to yourself as the effusions of withered age and useless time. I shall, with not the less truth, assure you of my great respect and consideration.

Is It Ever Right to Disobey the Law?

LETTER TO JOHN B. COLVIN[6]

Monticello, September 20, 1810

SIR,— . . . The question you propose, whether circumstances do not sometimes occur, which make it a duty in officers of high trust, to assume authorities beyond the law, is easy of solution in principle, but sometimes embarrassing in practice. A strict observance of the written laws is doubtless *one* of the high duties of a good citizen, but it is not the *highest*. The laws of necessity, of self-preservation, of saving our country when in danger, are of higher obligation. To lose our country by a scrupulous adherence to written law, would be to lose the law itself, with life, liberty, property and all those who are enjoying them with us; thus absurdly sacrificing the end to the means. When, in the battle of Germantown, General Washington's army was annoyed from Chew's house, he did not hesitate to plant his cannon against it, although the property of a citizen. When he besieged Yorktown, he leveled

[6] Editor of the *Republican Advocate*, Fredericktown, Maryland.

the suburbs, feeling that the laws of property must be postponed to the safety of the nation. While the army was before York, the Governor of Virginia took horses, carriages, provisions and even men by force, to enable that army to stay together till it could master the public enemy; and he was justified. A ship at sea in distress for provisions, meets another having abundance, yet refusing a supply; the law of self-preservation authorizes the distressed to take a supply by force. In all these cases, the unwritten laws of necessity, of self-preservation, and of the public safety, control the written laws of *meum* and *tuum*. Further to exemplify the principle, I will state an hypothetical case. Suppose it had been made known to the Executive of the Union in the autumn of 1805, that we might have the Floridas for a reasonable sum, that that sum had not indeed been so appropriated by law, but that Congress were to meet within three weeks, and might appropriate it on the first or second day of their session. Ought he, for so great an advantage to his country, to have risked himself by transcending the law and making the purchase? The public advantage offered, in this supposed case, was indeed immense; but a reverence for law, and the probability that the advantage might still be *legally* accomplished by a delay of only three weeks, were powerful reasons against hazarding the act. But suppose it foreseen that a John Randolph would find means to protract the proceeding on it by Congress, until the ensuing spring, by which time new circumstances would change the mind of the other party. Ought the Executive, in that case, and with that foreknowledge, to have secured the good to his country, and to have trusted to their justice for the transgression of the law? I think he ought, and that the act would have been approved. After the affair of the Chesapeake, we thought war a very possible result. Our magazines were illy provided with some necessary articles, nor had any appropriations been made for their purchase. We ventured, however, to provide them, and to place our country in safety; and stating the case to Congress, they sanctioned the act.

To proceed to the conspiracy of Burr, and particularly to General Wilkinson's situation in New Orleans. In judging this case, we are bound to consider the state of the information, correct and incorrect, which he then possessed. He expected Burr and his band from above, a British fleet from below, and he knew there was a formidable conspiracy within the city. Under these circumstances, was he justifiable, 1st, in seizing notorious conspirators? On this there can be but two opinions; one, of the guilty and their accomplices; the other, that of all honest men. 2d. In sending them to the seat of government, when the written law gave them a right to trial in the territory? The danger of their rescue, of their continuing their machinations, the tardiness and weakness of the law, apathy of the judges, active patronage of the whole tribe of lawyers, unknown disposition of the juries, an hourly expectation of the enemy, salvation of the city, and of the Union itself, which would have been convulsed to its centre, had that conspiracy succeeded; all these constituted a law of necessity and self-preservation, and rendered the *salus populi* supreme over the written law. The officer who is called to act on this superior ground, does indeed risk himself on the justice of the controlling powers of the constitution, and his station makes it his duty to incur that risk. But those controlling powers, and his fellow citizens generally, are bound to judge according to the circumstances under which he acted. They are not to transfer the information of this place or moment to the time and place of his action; but to put themselves into his situation. We knew here that there never was danger of a British fleet from below, and that Burr's band was crushed before it reached the Mississippi. But General Wilkinson's information was very different, and he could act on no other.

From these examples and principles you may see what I think on the questions proposed. They do not go to the case of persons charged with petty duties, where consequences are trifling, and time allowed for a legal course, nor to authorize them to take such cases out of the written law. In these, the example of overleaping the law is of greater evil than a strict adherence to its imperfect provisions. It is incumbent on those only who accept of great charges, to risk themselves on great occasions, when the safety of the nation, or some of its very high interests are at stake. An officer is bound to obey orders; yet he would be a bad one who should do it in cases for which they were not intended, and which involved the most important consequences. The line of discrimination between cases may be difficult; but the good officer is bound to draw it at his own peril, and throw himself on the justice of his country and the rectitude of his motives.

I have indulged freer views on this question, on your assurances that they are for your own eye only, and that they will not get into the hands of newswriters. I met their scurrilities without concern, while in pursuit of the great interests with which I was charged. But in my present retirement, no duty forbids my wish for quiet.

On *"The Politics"* of Aristotle

LETTER TO ISAAC A. TIFFANY

In answer to your inquiry as to the merits of Gillies' translation of the Politics of Aristotle, I can only say that it has the reputation of being preferable to Ellis', the only rival translation into English. I have never seen it myself, and therefore do not speak of it from my own knowledge. But so different was the style of society then, and with those people, from what it is now and with us, that I think little edification can be obtained from their writings on the subject of government. They had just ideas of the value of personal liberty, but none at all of the structure of government best calculated to preserve it. They knew no medium between a democracy (the only pure republic, but impracticable beyond the limits of a town) and an abandonment of themselves to an aristocracy, or a tyranny independent of the people. It seems not to have occurred that where the citizens cannot meet to transact their business in person, they alone have the right to choose the agents who shall transact it; and that in this way a republican, or popular government, of the second grade of purity, may be exercised over any extent of country. The full experiment of a government democratical, but representative, was and is still reserved for us. The idea (taken, indeed, from the little specimen formerly existing in the English constitution, but now lost) has been carried by us, more or less, into all our legislative and executive departments; but it has not yet, by any of us, been pushed into all the ramifications of the system, so far as to leave no authority existing not responsible to the people; whose rights, however, to the exercise and fruits of their own industry, can never be protected against the selfishness of rulers not subject to their control at short periods. The introduction of this new principle of representative democracy has rendered useless almost everything written before on the structure of government; and, in a great measure, relieves our regret, if the political writings of Aristotle, or of any other ancient, have been lost, or are unfaithfully rendered or explained to us. My most earnest wish is to see the republican element of popular control pushed to the maximum of its practicable exercise. I shall then believe that our government may be pure and perpetual.

Henry David Thoreau (1817–1862)

ON THE DUTY OF CIVIL DISOBEDIENCE

I heartily accept the motto,—"That government is best which governs least;" and I should like to see it acted up to more rapidly and systematically. Carried out, it finally amounts to this, which also I believe,—"That government is best which governs not at all;" and when men are prepared for it, that will be the kind of government which they will have. Government is at best but an expedient; but most governments are usually, and all governments are sometimes, inexpedient. The objections which have been brought against a standing army, and they are many and weighty, and deserve to prevail, may also at last be brought against a standing government. The standing army is only an arm of the standing government. The government itself, which is only the mode which the people have chosen to execute their will, is equally liable to be abused and perverted before the people can act through it. Witness the present Mexican war, the work of comparatively a few individuals using the standing government as their tool; for, in the outset, the people would not have consented to this measure.

This American government,—what is it but a tradition, though a recent one, endeavoring to transmit itself unimpaired to posterity, but each instant losing some of its integrity? It has not the vitality and force of a single living man; for a single man can bend it to his will. It is a sort of wooden gun to the people themselves; and, if ever they should use it in earnest as a real one against each other, it will surely split. But it is not the less necessary for this; for the people must have some complicated machinery or other, and hear its din, to satisfy that idea of government which they have. Governments show thus how successfully men can be imposed on, even impose on themselves, for their own advantage. It is excellent, we must all allow; yet this government never of itself furthered any enterprise, but by the alacrity with which it got out of its way. *It* does not keep the country free. *It* does not settle the West. *It* does not educate. The character inherent in the American people has done all that has been accomplished; and it would have done somewhat more, if the government had not sometimes got in its way. For government is an expedient by which men would fain succeed in letting one another alone; and, as has been said, when it is most expedient, the governed are most let alone by it. Trade and commerce, if they were not made of India rubber, would never manage to bounce over the obstacles which legislators are continually putting in their way; and, if one were to judge these men wholly by the effects of their actions, and not partly by their intentions, they would deserve to be classed and punished with those mischievous persons who put obstructions on the railroads.

But, to speak practically and as a citizen, unlike those who call themselves no-government men, I ask for, not at once no government, but *at once* a better government. Let every man make known what kind of government would command his respect, and that will be one step toward obtaining it.

After all, the practical reason why, when the power is once in the hands of the people, a majority are permitted, and for a long period continue, to rule, is not because they are most likely to be in the right, nor because this seems fairest to the minority, but because they are physically the strongest. But a government in which the majority rule in all cases cannot be based on justice, even as far as men understand it. Can there not be a government in which majorities do not virtually decide right and wrong, but conscience?—in which majorities decide only those questions to which the rule of expediency is applicable? Must the citizen ever for a moment, or in the least degree, resign his conscience, to the legislator? Why has every man a conscience, then? I think that we should be men first, and subjects afterward. It is not desirable to cultivate a respect for the law, so much as for the right. The only obligation which I have a right to assume, is to do at any time what I think right. It is truly enough said, that a corporation has no conscience; but a corporation of conscientious men is a corporation *with* a conscience. Law never made men a whit more just; and, by means of their respect for it, even the well-disposed are daily made the agents of injustice. A common and natural result of an undue respect for law is, that you may see a file of soldiers, colonel, captain, corporal, privates, powder-monkeys and all, marching in admirable order over hill and dale to the wars, against their wills, aye, against their common sense and consciences, which makes it very steep marching indeed, and produces a palpitation of the heart. They have no doubt that it is a damnable business in which they are concerned; they are all peaceably inclined. Now, what are they? Men at all? or small moveable forts and magazines, at the service of some unscrupulous man in power? Visit the Navy Yard, and behold a marine, such a man as an American government can make, or such as it can make a man with its black arts, a mere shadow and reminiscence of humanity, a man laid out alive and standing, and already, as one may say, buried under arms with funeral accompaniments, though it may be

> Not a drum was heard, nor a funeral note,
>   As his corpse to the ramparts we hurried;
> Not a soldier discharged his farewell shot
>   O'er the grave where our hero we buried.

The mass of men serve the State thus, not as men mainly, but as machines, with their bodies. They are the standing army, and the militia, jailers, constables, *posse comitatus*, &c. In most cases there is no free exercise whatever of the judgment or of the moral sense; but they put themselves on a level with wood and earth and stones; and wooden men can perhaps be manufactured that will serve the purpose as well. Such command no more respect than men of straw, or a lump of dirt. They have the same sort of worth only as horses and dogs. Yet such as these even are commonly esteemed good citizens. Others, as most legislators, politicians, lawyers, ministers, and office-holders, serve the State chiefly with their heads; and, as they rarely make any moral distinctions, they are as likely to serve the devil, without intending it, as God. A very few, as heroes, patriots, martyrs, reformers in the great sense, and *men,* serve the State with their consciences also, and so necessarily resist it for the most part; and they are commonly treated by it as enemies. A wise man will only be useful as a man, and will not submit to be "clay," and "stop a hole to keep the wind away," but leave that office to his dust at least:—

> I am too high-born to be propertied,
> To be a secondary at control,
> Or useful serving-man and instrument
> To any sovereign state throughout the world.

He who gives himself entirely to his fellow-men appears to them useless and selfish; but he who gives himself partially to them is pronounced a benefactor and philanthropist.

How does it become a man to behave toward this American government to-day? I answer that he cannot without disgrace be associated with it. I cannot for an instant recognize that political organization as *my* government which is the *slave's* government also.

All men recognize the right of revolution; that is, the right to refuse allegiance to and to resist the government, when its tyranny or its inefficiency are great and unendurable. But almost all say that such is not the case now. But such was the case, they think, in the Revolution of '75. If one were to tell me that this was a bad government because it taxed certain foreign commodities brought to its ports, it is most probable that I should not make an ado about it, for I can do without them: all machines have their friction; and possibly this does enough good to counterbalance the evil. At any rate, it is a great evil to make a stir about it. But when the friction comes to have its machine, and oppression and robbery are organized, I say, let us not have such a machine any longer. In other words, when a sixth of the population of a nation which has undertaken to be the refuge of liberty are slaves, and a whole country is unjustly overrun and conquered by a foreign army, and subjected to military law, I think that it is not too soon for honest men to rebel and revolutionize. What makes this duty the more urgent is the fact, that the country so overrun is not our own, but ours is the invading army.

Paley, a common authority with many on moral questions, in his chapter on the "Duty of Submission to Civil Government," resolves all civil obligation into expediency; and he proceeds to say, "that so long as the interest of the whole society requires it, that is, so long as the established government cannot be resisted or changed without public inconveniency, it is the will of God, that the established government be obeyed, and no longer."—"This principle being admitted, the justice of every particular case of resistance is reduced to a computation of the quantity of the danger and grievance on the one side, and of the probability and expense of redressing it on the other." Of this, he says, every man shall judge for himself. But Paley appears never to have contemplated those cases to which the rule of expediency does not apply, in which a people, as well as an individual, must do justice, cost what it may. If I have unjustly wrested a plank from a drowning man, I must restore it to him though I drown myself. This, according to Paley, would be inconvenient. But he that would save his life, in such a case, shall lose it. This people must cease to hold

slaves, and to make war on Mexico, though it cost them their
existence as a people.

In their practice, nations agree with Paley; but does any
one think that Massachusetts does exactly what is right at the
present crisis?

A drab of state, a cloth-o'-silver slut,
To have her train borne up, and her soul trail in the dirt.

Practically speaking, the opponents to a reform in Massachusetts are not a hundred thousand politicians at the South, but
a hundred thousand merchants and farmers here, who are
more interested in commerce and agriculture than they are in
humanity, and are not prepared to do justice to the slave and
to Mexico, *cost what it may*. I quarrel not with far-off foes,
but with those who, near at home, co-operate with, and do
the bidding of those far away, and without whom the latter
would be harmless. We are accustomed to say, that the mass
of men are unprepared; but improvement is slow, because the
few are not materially wiser or better than the many. It is not
so important that many should be as good as you, as that there
be some absolute goodness somewhere; for that will leaven
the whole lump. There are thousands who are *in opinion* opposed to slavery and to the war, who yet in effect do nothing
to put an end to them; who, esteeming themselves children of
Washington and Franklin, sit down with their hands in their
pockets, and say that they know not what to do, and do nothing; who even postpone the question of freedom to the question of free-trade, and quietly read the prices-current along
with the latest advices from Mexico, after dinner, and, it may
be, fall asleep over them both. What is the price-current of an
honest man and patriot to-day? They hesitate, and they regret,
and sometimes they petition; but they do nothing in earnest
and with effect. They will wait, well disposed, for others to
remedy the evil, that they may no longer have it to regret. At
most, they give only a cheap vote, and a feeble countenance
and Godspeed, to the right, as it goes by them. There are nine
hundred and ninety-nine patrons of virtue to one virtuous man;
but it is easier to deal with the real possessor of a thing than
with the temporary guardian of it.

All voting is a sort of gaming, like chequers or backgam-
mon, with a slight moral tinge to it, a playing with right and
wrong, with moral questions; and betting naturally accompanies it. The character of the voters is not staked. I cast my
vote, perchance, as I think right; but I am not vitally concerned

that that right should prevail. I am willing to leave it to the majority. Its obligation, therefore, never exceeds that of expediency. Even voting *for the right* is *doing* nothing for it. It is only expressing to men feebly your desire that it should prevail. A wise man will not leave the right to the mercy of chance, nor wish it to prevail through the power of the majority. There is but little virtue in the action of masses of men. When the majority shall at length vote for the abolition of slavery, it will be because they are indifferent to slavery, or because there is but little slavery left to be abolished by their vote. *They* will then be the only slaves. Only *his* vote can hasten the abolition of slavery who asserts his own freedom by his vote.

I hear of a convention to be held at Baltimore, or elsewhere, for the selection of a candidate for the Presidency, made up chiefly of editors, and men who are politicians by profession; but I think, what is it to any independent, intelligent, and respectable man what decision they may come to, shall we not have the advantage of his wisdom and honesty, nevertheless? Can we not count upon some independent votes? Are there not many individuals in the country who do not attend conventions? But no: I find that the respectable man, so called, has immediately drifted from his position, and despairs of his country, when his country has more reason to despair of him. He forthwith adopts one of the candidates thus selected as the only *available* one, thus proving that he is himself *available* for any purposes of the demagogue. His vote is of no more worth than that of any unprincipled foreigner or hireling native, who may have been bought. Oh for a man who is a *man*, and, as my neighbor says, has a bone in his back which you cannot pass your hand through! Our statistics are at fault: the population has been returned too large. How many *men* are there to a square thousand miles in this country? Hardly one. Does not America offer any inducement for men to settle here? The American has dwindled into an Odd Fellow,—one who may be known by the development of his organ of gregariousness, and a manifest lack of intellect and cheerful self-reliance; whose first and chief concern, on coming into the world, is to see that the alms-houses are in good repair; and, before yet he has lawfully donned the virile garb, to collect a fund for the support of the widows and orphans that may be; who, in short, ventures to live only by the aid of the mutual insurance company, which has promised to bury him decently.

It is not a man's duty, as a matter of course, to devote himself to the eradication of any, even the most enormous wrong; he may still properly have other concerns to engage him; but it is his duty, at least, to wash his hands of it, and, if he gives it no thought longer, not to give it practically his support. If I devote myself to other pursuits and contemplations, I must first see, at least, that I do not pursue them sitting upon another man's shoulders. I must get off him first, that he may pursue his contemplations too. See what gross inconsistency is tolerated. I have heard some of my townsmen say, "I should like to have them order me out to help put down an insurrection of the slaves, or to march to Mexico,—see if I would go;" and yet these very men have each, directly by their allegiance, and so indirectly, at least, by their money, furnished a substitute. The soldier is applauded who refuses to serve in an unjust war by those who do not refuse to sustain the unjust government which makes the war; is applauded by those whose own act and authority he disregards and sets at nought; as if the State were penitent to that degree that it hired one to scourge it while it sinned, but not to that degree that it left off sinning for a moment. Thus, under the name of order and civil government, we are all made at last to pay homage to and support our own meanness. After the first blush of sin, comes its indifference; and from immoral it becomes, as it were, *un*moral, and not quite unnecessary to that life which we have made.

The broadest and most prevalent error requires the most disinterested virtue to sustain it. The slight reproach to which the virtue of patriotism is commonly liable, the noble are most likely to incur. Those who, while they disapprove of the character and measure of a government, yield to it their allegiance and support, are undoubtedly its most conscientious supporters, and so frequently the most serious obstacles to reform. Some are petitioning the State to dissolve the Union, to disregard the requisitions of the President. Why do they not dissolve it themselves,—the union between themselves and the State,—and refuse to pay their quota into its treasury? Do not they stand in the same relation to the State, that the State does to the Union? And have not the same reasons prevented the State from resisting the Union, which have prevented them from resisting the State?

How can a man be satisfied to entertain an opinion merely, and enjoy *it?* Is there any enjoyment in it, if his opinion is that he is aggrieved? If you are cheated out of a single dollar by your neighbor, you do not rest satisfied with knowing that you are cheated or with saying that you are cheated, or even with petitioning him to pay you your due; but you take effectual steps at once to obtain the full amount, and see that you are never cheated again. Action from principle,—the perception and the performance of right,—changes things and relations; it is essentially revolutionary, and does not consist wholly with any thing which was. It not only divides states and churches, it divides families, aye, it divides the *individual*, separating the diabolical in him from the divine.

Unjust laws exist; shall we be content to obey them, or shall we endeavor to amend them, and obey them until we have succeeded, or shall we transgress them at once? Men generally, under such a government as this, think that they ought to wait until they have persuaded the majority to alter them. They think that, if they should resist, the remedy would be worse than the evil. But it is the fault of the government itself that the remedy *is* worse than the evil. *It* makes it worse. Why is it not more apt to anticipate and provide for reform? Why does it not cherish its wise minority? Why does it cry and resist before it is hurt? Why does it not encourage its citizens to be on the alert to point out its faults, and *do* better than it would have them? Why does it always crucify Christ, and excommunicate Copernicus and Luther, and pronounce Washington and Franklin rebels?

One would think, that a deliberate and practical denial of its authority, was the only offense never contemplated by government; else, why has it not assigned its definite, its suitable and proportionate penalty? If a man who has no property refuses but once to earn nine shillings for the State, he is put in prison for a period unlimited by any law that I know, and determined only by the discretion of those who placed him there; but if he should steal ninety times nine shillings from the State, he is soon permitted to go at large again.

If the injustice is part of the necessary friction of the machine of government, let it go, let it go; perchance it will wear smooth,—certainly the machine will wear out. If the injustice has a spring, or a pulley, or a rope, or a crank, exclusively for itself, then perhaps you may consider whether the remedy will not be worse than the evil; but if it is of such a nature that it requires you to be the agent of injustice to another, then, I say, break the law. Let your life be a counter friction to stop the machine. What I have to do is to see, at any rate, that I do not lend myself to the wrong which I condemn.

As for adopting the ways which the State has provided for

remedying the evil, I know not of such ways. They take too much time, and a man's life will be gone. I have other affairs to attend to. I came into this world, not chiefly to make this a good place to live in, but to live in it, be it good or bad. A man has not every thing to do, but something; and because he cannot do *every thing,* it is not necessary that he should do *something* wrong. It is not my business to be petitioning the governor or the legislature any more than it is theirs to petition me; and, if they should not hear my petition, what should I do then? But in this case the State has provided no way: its very Constitution is the evil. This may seem to be harsh and stubborn and unconciliatory; but it is to treat with the utmost kindness and consideration the only spirit that can appreciate or deserve it. So is all change for the better, like birth and death which convulse the body.

I do not hesitate to say, that those who call themselves abolitionists should at once effectually withdraw their support, both in person and property, from the government of Massachusetts, and not wait till they constitute a majority of one, before they suffer the right to prevail through them. I think that it is enough if they have God on their side, without waiting for that other one. Moreover, any man more right than his neighbors, constitutes a majority of one already.

I meet this American government, or its representative the State government, directly, and face to face, once a year, no more, in the person of its tax-gatherer; this is the only mode in which a man situated as I am necessarily meets it; and it then says distinctly, recognize me; and the simplest, the most effectual, and, in the present posture of affairs, the indispensable mode of treating with it on this head, of expressing your little satisfaction with and love for it, is to deny it then. My civil neighbor, the tax-gatherer, is the very man I have to deal with,—for it is, after all, with men and not with parchment that I quarrel,—and he has voluntarily chosen to be an agent of the government. How shall he ever know well what he is and does as an officer of the government, or as a man, until he is obliged to consider whether he shall treat me, his neighbor, for whom he has respect, as a neighbor and well-disposed man, or as a maniac and disturber of the peace, and see if he can get over this obstruction to his neighborliness without a ruder and more impetuous thought or speech corresponding with his action? I know this well, that if one thousand, if one hundred, if ten men whom I could name,—if ten *honest* men only,—aye, if *one* HONEST man, in this State of Massachusetts, *ceasing to hold slaves,* were actually to withdraw from this copartnership, and be locked up in the county jail therefor, it would be the abolition of slavery in America. For it matters not how small the beginning may seem to be: what is once well done is done for ever. But we love better to talk about it: that we say is our mission. Reform keeps many scores of newspapers in its service, but not one man. If my esteemed neighbor, the State's ambassador, who will devote his days to the settlement of the question of human rights in the Council Chamber, instead of being threatened with the prisons of Carolina, were to sit down the prisoner of Massachusetts, that State which is so anxious to foist the sin of slavery upon her sister,—though at present she can discover only an act of inhospitality to be the ground of a quarrel with her,—the Legislature would not wholly waive the subject the following winter.

Under a government which imprisons any unjustly, the true place for a just man is also a prison. The proper place to-day, the only place which Massachusetts has provided for her freer and less despondent spirits, is in her prisons, to be put out and locked out of the State by her own act, as they have already put themselves out by their principles. It is there that the fugitive slave, and the Mexican prisoner on parole, and the Indian come to plead the wrongs of his race, should find them; on that separate, but more free and honorable ground, where the State places those who are not *with* her but *against* her,—the only house in a slave-state in which a free man can abide with honor. If any think that their influence would be lost there, and their voices no longer afflict the ear of the State, that they would not be as an enemy within its walls, they do not know by how much truth is stronger than error, nor how much more eloquently and effectively he can combat injustice who has experienced a little in his own person. Cast your whole vote, not a strip of paper merely, but your whole influence. A minority is powerless while it conforms to the majority; it is not even a minority then; but it is irresistible when it clogs by its whole weight. If the alternative is to keep all just men in prison, or give up war and slavery, the State will not hesitate which to choose. If a thousand men were not to pay their tax-bills this year, that would not be a violent and bloody measure, as it would be to pay them, and enable the State to commit violence and shed innocent blood. This is, in fact, the definition of a peaceable revolution, if any such is possible. If the tax-gatherer, or any other public officer, asks me, as one has done, "But what shall I do?" my answer is, "If you really wish to do any thing, resign your office." When the subject has refused allegiance, and the officer has resigned his office, then the revolution is accomplished. But even suppose blood should flow. Is there not a sort of blood shed when the conscience is wounded? Through this wound a man's real manhood and immortality flow out, and he bleeds to an everlasting death. I see this blood flowing now.

I have contemplated the imprisonment of the offender, rather than the seizure of his goods,—though both will serve the same purpose,—because they who assert the purest right, and consequently are most dangerous to a corrupt State, commonly have not spent much time in accumulating property. To such the State renders comparatively small service, and a slight tax is wont to appear exorbitant, particularly if they are obliged to earn it by special labor with their hands. If there were one who lived wholly without the use of money, the State itself would hesitate to demand it of him. But the rich man—not to make any invidious comparison—is always sold to the institution which makes him rich. Absolutely speaking, the more money, the less virtue; for money comes between a man and his objects, and obtains them for him; and it was certainly no great virtue to obtain it. It puts to rest many questions which he would otherwise be taxed to answer; while the only new question which it puts is the hard but superfluous one, how to spend it. Thus his moral ground is taken from under his feet. The opportunities of living are diminished in proportion as what are called the "means" are increased. The best thing a man can do for his culture when he is rich is to endeavor to carry out those schemes which he entertained when he was poor. Christ answered the Herodians according to their condition. "Show me the tribute-money," said he;—and one took a penny out of his pocket;—If you use money which has the image of Caesar on it, and which he has made current and valuable, that is, *if you are men of the State*, and gladly enjoy the advantages of Caesar's government, then pay him back some of his own when he demands it; "Render therefore to Caesar that which is Caesar's, and to God those things which are God's,"—leaving them no wiser than before as to which was which; for they did not wish to know.

When I converse with the freest of my neighbors, I. perceive that, whatever they may say about the magnitude and seriousness of the question, and their regard for the public tranquillity, the long and the short of the matter is, that they cannot spare the protection of the existing government, and they dread the consequences of disobedience to it to their property and families. For my own part, I should not like to think that I ever rely on the protection of the State. But, if I deny the authority of the State when it presents its tax-bill, it will soon take and waste all my property, and so harass me and my children without end. This is hard. This makes it impossible for a man to live honestly and at the same time comfortably in outward respects. It will not be worth the while to accumulate property; that would be sure to go again. You must hire or squat somewhere, and raise but a small crop, and eat that soon. You must live within yourself, and depend upon yourself, always tucked up and ready for a start, and not have many affairs. A man may grow rich in Turkey even, if he will be in all respects a good subject of the Turkish government. Confucius said,—"If a State is governed by the principles of reason, poverty and misery are subjects of shame; if a State is not governed by the principles of reason, riches and honors are the subjects of shame." No: until I want the protection of Massachusetts to be extended to me in some distant southern port, where my liberty is endangered, or until I am bent solely on building up an estate at home by peaceful enterprise, I can afford to refuse allegiance to Massachusetts, and her right to my property and life. It costs me less in every sense to incur the penalty of disobedience to the State, than it would to obey. I should feel as if I were worth less in that case.

Some years ago, the State met me in behalf of the church, and commanded me to pay a certain sum toward the support of a clergyman whose preaching my father attended, but never I myself. "Pay it," it said, "or be locked up in the jail." I declined to pay. But, unfortunately another man saw fit to pay it. I did not see why the schoolmaster should be taxed to support the priest, and not the priest the schoolmaster: for I was not the State's schoolteacher, but I supported myself by voluntary subscription. I did not see why the lyceum should not present its tax-bill, and have the State to back its demand, as well as the church. However, at the request of the selectmen, I condescended to make some such statement as this in writing:— "Know all men by these presents, that I, Henry Thoreau, do not wish to be regarded as a member of any incorporated society which I have not joined." This I gave to the town-clerk; and he has it. The State, having thus learned that I did not wish to be regarded as a member of that church, has never made a like demand on me since; though it said that it must adhere to its original presumption that time. If I had known

how to name them, I should then have signed off in detail from
all the societies which I never signed on to; but I did not know
where to find a complete list.

I have paid no poll-tax for six years. I was put into a jail
once on this account, for one night; and, as I stood considering the walls of solid stone, two or three feet thick, the door
of wood and iron, a foot thick, and the iron grating which
strained the light, I could not help being struck with the
foolishness of that institution which treated me as if I were
mere flesh and blood and bones, to be locked up. I wondered that it should have concluded at length that this was
the best use it could put me to, and had never thought to
avail itself of my services in some way. I saw that, if there
was a wall of stone between me and my townsmen, there
was a still more difficult one to climb or break through, before they could get to be as free as I was. I did not for a
moment feel confined, and the walls seemed a great waste of
stone and mortar. I felt as if I alone of all my townsmen had
paid my tax. They plainly did not know how to treat me,
but behaved like persons who are underbred. In every threat
and in every compliment there was a blunder; for they
thought that my chief desire was to stand the other side of
that stone wall. I could not but smile to see how industriously
they locked the door on my meditations, which followed
them out again without let or hindrance, and *they* were
really all that was dangerous. As they could not reach me,
they had resolved to punish my body; just as boys, if they
cannot come at some person against whom they have a spite,
will abuse his dog. I saw that the State was half-witted, that it
was timid as a lone woman with her silver spoons, and that
it did not know its friends from its foes, and I lost all my
remaining respect for it, and pitied it.

Thus the State never intentionally confronts a man's sense,
intellectual or moral, but only his body, his senses. It is not
armed with superior wit or honesty, but with superior physical
strength. I was not born to be forced. I will breathe after my
own fashion. Let us see who is the strongest. What force has a
multitude? They only can force me who obey a higher law
than I. They force me to become like themselves. I do not
hear of *men* being *forced* to live this way or that by masses
of men. What sort of life were that to live? When I meet a
government which says to me, "Your money or your life,"
why should I be in haste to give it my money? It may be
in a great strait, and not know what to do: I cannot help

that. It must help itself: do as I do. It is not worth the while
to snivel about it. I am not responsible for the successful
working of the machinery of society. I am not the son of the
engineer. I perceive that, when an acorn and a chestnut fall
side by side, the one does not remain inert to make way for
the other, but both obey their own laws, and spring and
grow and flourish as best they can, till one, perchance, over-
shadows and destroys the other. If a plant cannot live according to its nature, it dies; and so a man.

The night in prison was novel and interesting enough. The
prisoners in their shirt-sleeves were enjoying a chat and the
evening air in the door-way, when I entered. But the jailer
said, "Come, boys, it is time to lock up;" and so they dispersed, and I heard the sound of their steps returning into
the hollow apartments. My roommate was introduced to me
by the jailer, as "a first-rate fellow and a clever man." When
the door was locked, he showed me where to hang my hat,
and how he managed matters there. The rooms were white-
washed once a month; and this one, at least, was the whitest,
most simply furnished, and probably the neatest apartment
in the town. He naturally wanted to know where I came
from, and what brought me there; and, when I had told him,
I asked him in turn how he came there, presuming him to be
an honest man, of course; and, as the world goes, I believe he
was. "Why," said he, "they accuse me of burning a barn; but
I never did it." As near as I could discover, he had probably
gone to bed in a barn when drunk, and smoked his pipe
there; and so a barn was burnt. He had the reputation of
being a clever man, had been there some three months waiting for his trial to come on, and would have to wait as much
longer; but he was quite domesticated and contented, since he
got his board for nothing, and thought that he was well
treated.

He occupied one window, and I the other; and I saw, that,
if one stayed there long, his principal business would be to
look out the window. I had soon read all the tracts that were
left there, and examined where former prisoners had broken
out, and where a grate had been sawed off, and heard the
history of the various occupants of that room; for I found
that even here there was a history and a gossip which never
circulated beyond the walls of the jail. Probably this is the
only house in the town where verses are composed, which
are afterward printed in circular form, but not published. I

was shown quite a long list of verses which were composed
by some young men who had been detected in an attempt to
escape, who avenged themselves by singing them.

I pumped my fellow-prisoner as dry as I could, for fear I
should never see him again; but at length he showed me
which was my bed, and left me to blow out the lamp.

It was like travelling into a far country, such as I had
never expected to behold, to lie there for one night. It seemed
to me that I never had heard the town-clock strike before,
nor the evening sounds of the village; for we slept with the
windows open, which were inside the grating. It was to see
my native village in the light of the middle ages, and our
Concord was turned into a Rhine stream, and visions of
knights and castles passed before me. They were the voices
of old burghers that I heard in the streets. I was an involuntary spectator and auditor of whatever was done and said in
the kitchen of the adjacent village-inn,—a wholly new and
rare experience to me. It was a closer view of my native
town. I was fairly inside of it. I never had seen its institutions before. This is one of its peculiar institutions; for it is
a shire town. I began to comprehend what its inhabitants
were about.

In the morning, our breakfasts were put through the hole
in the door, in small oblong-square tin pans, made to fit, and
holding a pint of chocolate, with brown bread, and an iron
spoon. When they called for the vessels again, I was green
enough to return what bread I had left; but my comrade
seized it, and said that I should lay that up for lunch or dinner. Soon after, he was let out to work at haying in a
neighboring field, whither he went every day, and would
not be back till noon; so he bade me good-day, saying that
he doubted if he should see me again.

When I came out of prison,—for some one interfered, and
paid the tax,—I did not perceive that great changes had taken
place on the common, such as he observed who went in a
youth, and emerged a tottering and gray-headed man; and yet
a change had to my eyes come over the scene,—the town, and
State, and country,—greater than any that mere time could
effect. I saw to what extent the people among whom I lived
could be trusted as good neighbors and friends; that their
friendship was for summer weather only; that they did not
greatly purpose to do right; that they were a distinct race from
me by their prejudices and superstitions, as the Chinamen
and Malays are; that, in their sacrifices to humanity, they ran

no risks, not even to their property; that, after all, they were not so noble but they treated the thief as he had treated them, and hoped, by a certain outward observance and a few prayers, and by walking in a particular straight though useless path from time to time, to save their souls. This may be to judge my neighbors harshly; for I believe that most of them are not aware that they have such an institution as the jail in their village.

It was formerly the custom in our village, when a poor debtor came out of jail, for his acquaintances to salute him, looking through their fingers, which were crossed to represent the grating of a jail window, "How do ye do?" My neighbors did not thus salute me, but first looked at me, and then at one another, as if I had returned from a long journey. I was put into jail as I was going to the shoemaker's to get a shoe which was mended. When I was let out the next morning, I proceeded to finish my errand, and, having put on my mended shoe, joined a huckleberry party, who were impatient to put themselves under my conduct; and in half an hour,—for the horse was soon tackled,—was in the midst of a huckleberry field, on one of our highest hills, two miles off; and then the State was nowhere to be seen.

This is the whole history of "My Prisons."

I have never declined paying the highway tax, because I am as desirous of being a good neighbor as I am of being a bad subject; and, as for supporting schools, I am doing my part to educate my fellow-countrymen now. It is for no particular item in the tax-bill that I refuse to pay it. I simply wish to refuse allegiance to the State, to withdraw and stand aloof from it effectually. I do not care to trace the course of my dollar, if I could, till it buys a man, or a musket to shoot one with,—the dollar is innocent,—but I am concerned to trace the effects of my allegiance. In fact, I quietly declare war with the State, after my fashion, though I will still make what use and get what advantage of her I can, as is usual in such cases.

If others pay the tax which is demanded of me, from a sympathy with the State, they do but what they have already done in their own case, or rather they abet injustice to a greater extent than the State requires. If they pay a tax from a mistaken interest in the individual taxed, to save his going to jail, it is because they have not considered wisely how far they let their private feelings interfere with the public good.

This, then, is my position at present. But one cannot be too much on his guard in such a case, lest his action be biased by obstinacy, or an undue regard for the opinions of men. Let him see that he does only what belongs to himself and to the hour.

I think sometimes, Why, this people mean well; they are only ignorant; they would do better if they knew how; why give your neighbors this pain to treat you as they are not inclined to? But I think, again, this is no reason why I should do as they do, or permit others to suffer much greater pain of a different kind. Again, I sometimes say to myself, when many millions of men, without heat, without ill-will, without personal feeling of any kind, demand of you a few shillings only, without the possibility, such is their constitution, of retracting or altering their present demand, and without the possibility, on your side, of appeal to any other millions, why expose yourself to this overwhelming brute force? You do not resist cold and hunger, the winds and the waves, thus obstinately; you quietly submit to a thousand similar necessities. You do not put your head into the fire. But just in proportion as I regard this as not wholly a brute force, but partly a human force, and consider that I have relations to those millions as to so many millions of men, and not of mere brute or inanimate things, I see that appeal is possible, first and instantaneously, from them to the Maker of them, and, secondly, from them to themselves. But, if I put my head deliberately into the fire, there is no appeal to fire or to the Maker of fire, and I have only myself to blame. If I could convince myself that I have any right to be satisfied with men as they are, and to treat them accordingly, and not according, in some respects, to my requisitions and expectations of what they and I ought to be, then, like a good Mussulman and fatalist, I should endeavor to be satisfied with things as they are, and say it is the will of God. And, above all, there is this difference between resisting this and a purely brute or natural force, that I can resist this with some effect; but I cannot expect, like Orpheus, to change the nature of the rocks and trees and beasts.

I do not wish to quarrel with any man or nation. I do not wish to split hairs, to make fine distinctions, or set myself up as better than my neighbors. I seek rather, I may say, even an excuse for conforming to the laws of the land. I am but too ready to conform to them. Indeed I have reason to suspect myself on this head; and each year, as the tax-gatherer comes

around, I find myself disposed to review the acts and position
of the general and state governments, and the spirit of the
people, to discover a pretext for conformity. I believe that the
State will soon be able to take all my work of this sort out
of my hands, and then I shall be no better a patriot than my
fellow-country-men. Seen from a lower point of view, the
Constitution, with all its faults, is very good; the law and the
courts are very respectable; even this State and this American
government are, in many respects, very admirable and rare
things, to be thankful for, such as a great many have described them; but seen from a point of view a little higher,
they are what I have described them; seen from a higher still,
and the highest, who shall say what they are, or that they are
worth looking at or thinking of at all?

However, the government does not concern me much, and
I shall bestow the fewest possible thoughts on it. It is not
many moments that I live under a government, even in this
world. If a man is thought-free, fancy-free, imagination-free,
that which *is not* never for a long time appearing *to be* to
him, unwise rulers or reformers cannot fatally interrupt him.

I know that most men think differently from myself; but
those whose lives are by profession devoted to the study of
these or kindred subjects, content me as little as any. Statesmen and legislators, standing so completely within the institution, never distinctly and nakedly behold it. They speak of
moving society, but have no resting-place without it. They
may be men of a certain experience and discrimination, and
have no doubt invented ingenious and even useful systems,
for which we sincerely thank them; but all their wit and usefulness lie within certain not very wide limits. They are wont
to forget that the world is not governed by policy and expediency. Webster never goes behind government, and so cannot speak with authority about it. His words are wisdom to
those legislators who contemplate no essential reform in the
existing government; but for thinkers, and those who legislate for all time, he never once glances at the subject. I know
of those whose serene and wise speculations on this theme
would soon reveal the limits of his mind's range and hospitality. Yet, compared with the cheap professions of most
reformers, and the still cheaper wisdom and eloquence of
politicians in general, his are almost the only sensible and
valuable words, and we thank Heaven for him. Comparatively, he is always strong, original, and, above all, practical.
Still his quality is not wisdom, but prudence. The lawyer's

truth is not truth, but consistency, or a consistent expediency.
Truth is always in harmony with herself, and is not concerned
chiefly to reveal the justice that may consist with wrong-doing.
He well deserves to be called, as he has been called, the De-
fender of the Constitution. There are really no blows to be
given by him but defensive ones. He is not a leader, but a
follower. His leaders are the men of '87. "I have never made
an effort," he says, "and never propose to make an effort; I
have never countenanced an effort, and never mean to countenance an effort, to disturb the arrangement as originally
made, by which the various States came into the Union." Still
thinking of the sanction which the Constitution gives to slavery, he says, "Because it was a part of the original compact,
—let it stand." Notwithstanding his special acuteness and
ability, he is unable to take a fact out of its merely political
relations, and behold it as it lies absolutely to be disposed of
by the intellect,—what, for instance, it behoves a man to do
here in America to-day with regard to slavery, but ventures,
or is driven, to make some such desperate answer as the following, while professing to speak absolutely, and as a private
man,—from which what new and singular code of social
duties might be inferred?—"The manner," says he, "in which
the governments of those States where slavery exists are to
regulate it, is for their own consideration, under their responsibility to their constituents, to the general laws of
propriety, humanity, and justice, and to God. Associations
formed elsewhere springing from a feeling of humanity, or
any other cause, have nothing whatever to do with it. They
have never received any encouragement from me, and they
never will."

They who know of no purer sources of truth, who have
traced up its stream no higher, stand, and wisely stand, by
the Bible and the Constitution, and drink at it there with
reverence and humility; but they who behold where it comes
trickling into this lake or that pool, gird up their loins once
more, and continue their pilgrimage toward its fountain-head.

No man with a genius for legislation has appeared in America. They are rare in the history of the world. There are ora-
tors, politicians, and eloquent men, by the thousand; but the
speaker has not yet opened his mouth to speak, who is capable
of settling the much-vexed questions of the day. We love eloquence for its own sake, and not for any truth which it may
utter, or any heroism it may inspire. Our legislators have not
yet learned the comparative value of free-trade and of free-

dom, of union, and of rectitude, to a nation. They have no
genius or talent for comparatively humble questions of taxation and finance, commerce and manufactures and agriculture. If we were left solely to the wordy wit of legislators in
Congress for our guidance, uncorrected by the seasonable experience and the effectual complaints of the people, America
would not long retain her rank among the nations. For eighteen hundred years, though perchance I have no right to say it,
the New Testament has been written; yet where is the legislator who has wisdom and practical talent enough to avail
himself of the light which it sheds on the science of legislation?

The authority of government, even such as I am willing to
submit to,—for I will cheerfully obey those who know and
can do better than I, and in many things even those who
neither know nor can do so well,—is still an impure one: to
be strictly just, it must have the sanction and consent of the
governed. It can have no pure right over my person and
property but what I concede to it. The progress from an absolute to a limited monarchy, from a limited monarchy to a
democracy, is a progress toward a true respect for the individual. Is a democracy, such as we know it, the last improvement possible in government? Is it not possible to take a step
further towards recognizing and organizing the rights of man?
There will never be a really free and enlightened State, until
the State comes to recognize the individual as a higher and independent power, from which all its own power and authority
are derived, and treats him accordingly. I please myself with
imagining a State at last which can afford to be just to all
men, and to treat the individual with respect as a neighbor;
which even would not think it inconsistent with its own repose, if a few were to live aloof from it, not meddling with
it, nor embraced by it, who fulfilled all the duties of neighbors
and fellow-men. A State which bore this kind of fruit, and
suffered it to drop off as fast as it ripened, would prepare the
way for a still more perfect and glorious State, which also I
have imagined, but not yet anywhere seen.

John Stuart Mill (1806–1873)

ON LIBERTY

CHAPTER I
INTRODUCTORY

The subject of this essay is not the so-called liberty of the will, so unfortunately opposed to the misnamed doctrine of philosophical necessity; but civil, or social liberty: the nature and limits of the power which can be legitimately exercised by society over the individual. A question seldom stated and hardly ever discussed in general terms, but which profoundly influences the practical controversies of the age by its latent presence, and is likely soon to make itself recognized as the vital question of the future. It is so far from being new, that, in a certain sense, it has divided mankind almost from the remotest ages; but in the stage of progress into which the more civilized portions of the species have now entered, it presents itself under new conditions, and requires a different and more fundamental treatment.

The struggle between liberty and authority is the most conspicuous feature in the portions of history with which we are earliest familiar, particularly in that of Greece, Rome, and England. But in old times this contest was between subjects, or some classes of subjects, and the government. By liberty, was meant protection against the tyranny of the political rulers. The rulers were conceived (except in some of the popular governments of Greece) as in a necessarily antagonistic position to the people whom they ruled. They consisted of a governing One, or a governing tribe or caste, who derived their authority from inheritance or conquest, who, at all events, did not hold it at the pleasure of the governed, and whose supremacy men did not venture, perhaps did not desire, to contest, whatever precautions might be taken against its oppressive exercise. Their power was regarded as necessary, but also as highly dangerous; as a weapon which they would attempt to use against their subjects, no less than

against external enemies. To prevent the weaker members of
the community from being preyed upon by innumerable vultures, it was needful that there should be an animal of prey
stronger than the rest, commissioned to keep them down. But
as the king of the vultures would be no less bent upon prey-
ing on the flock than any of the minor harpies, it was indispensable to be in a perpetual attitude of defense against
his beak and claws. The aim, therefore, of patriots was to set
limits to the power which the ruler should be suffered to exercise over the community; and this limitation was what they
meant by liberty. It was attempted in two ways. First, by obtaining a recognition of certain immunities, called political
liberties or rights, which it was to be regarded as a breach of
duty in the ruler to infringe, and which if he did infringe,
specific resistance, or general rebellion, was held to be justifiable. A second, and generally a later expedient, was the
establishment of constitutional checks, by which the consent
of the community, or of a body of some sort, supposed to
represent its interests, was made a necessary condition to
some of the more important acts of the governing power. To
the first of these modes of limitation, the ruling power, in
most European countries, was compelled, more or less, to
submit. It was not so with the second; and, to attain this, or
when already in some degree possessed, to attain it more
completely, became everywhere the principal object of the
lovers of liberty. And so long as mankind were content to
combat one enemy by another, and to be ruled by a master,
on condition of being guaranteed more or less efficaciously
against his tyranny, they did not carry their aspirations beyond this point.

A time, however, came, in the progress of human affairs,
when men ceased to think it a necessity of nature that their
governors should be an independent power, opposed in interest to themselves. It appeared to them much better that the
various magistrates of the State should be their tenants or
delegates, revocable at their pleasure. In that way alone, it
seemed, could they have complete security that the powers
of government would never be abused to their disadvantage.
By degrees this new demand for elective and temporary rulers
became the prominent object of the exertions of the popular
party, wherever any such party existed; and superseded, to a
considerable extent, the previous efforts to limit the power of
rulers. As the struggle proceeded for making the ruling power
emanate from the periodical choice of the ruled, some per-

sons began to think that too much importance had been attached to the limitation of the power itself. *That* (it might
seem) was a resource against rulers whose interests were
habitually opposed to those of the people. What was now
wanted was, that the rulers should be identified with the people; that their interest and will should be the interest and will
of the nation. The nation did not need to be protected against
its own will. There was no fear of its tyrannizing over itself.
Let the rulers be effectually responsible to it, promptly re-
movable by it, and it could afford to trust them with power of
which it could itself dictate the use to be made. Their power
was but the nation's own power, concentrated, and in a form
convenient for exercise. This mode of thought, or rather perhaps of feeling, was common among the last generation of
European liberalism, in the Continental section of which it
still apparently predominates. Those who admit any limit to
what a government may do, except in the case of such governments as they think ought not to exist, stand out as brilliant exceptions among the political thinkers of the Continent.
A similar tone of sentiment might by this time have been
prevalent in our own country, if the circumstances which for
a time encouraged it had continued unaltered.

But in political and philosophical theories, as well as in
persons, success discloses faults and infirmities which failure
might have concealed from observation. The notion that the
people have no need to limit their power over themselves,
might seem axiomatic when popular government was a thing
only dreamed about, or read of as having existed at some
distant period of the past. Neither was that notion necessarily
disturbed by such temporary aberrations as those of the
French Revolution, the worst of which were the work of a
usurping few, and which, in any case, belonged not to the
permanent working of popular institutions, but to a sudden
and convulsive outbreak against monarchical and aristocratic
despotism. In time, however, a democratic republic came to
occupy a large portion of the earth's surface, and made itself
felt as one of the most powerful members of the community
of nations; and elective and responsible government became
subject to the observations and criticisms which wait upon a
great existing fact. It was now perceived that such phrases as
"self-government," and "the power of the people over themselves," do not express the true state of the case. The "people" who exercise the power are not always the same people
with those over whom it is exercised; and the "self-govern-

ment" spoken of is not the government of each by himself, but of each by all the rest. The will of the people, moreover, practically means the will of the most numerous or the most active *part* of the people; the majority, or those who succeed in making themselves accepted as the majority: the people, consequently *may* desire to oppress a part of their number, and precautions are as much needed against this as against any other abuse of power. The limitation, therefore, of the power of government over individuals loses none of its importance when the holders of power are regularly accountable to the community, that is, to the strongest party therein. This view of things, recommending itself equally to the intelligence of thinkers and to the inclination of those important classes in European society to whose real or supposed interests democracy is adverse, has had no difficulty in establishing itself; and in political speculations "the tyranny of the majority" is now generally included among the evils against which society requires to be on its guard.

Like other tyrannies, the tyranny of the majority was at first, and is still vulgarly, held in dread chiefly as operating through the acts of the public authorities. But reflecting persons perceived that when society is itself the tyrant—society collectively over the separate individuals who compose it—its means of tyrannizing are not restricted to the acts which it may do by the hands of its political functionaries. Society can and does execute its own mandates; and if it issues wrong mandates instead of right, or any mandates at all in things with which it ought not to meddle, it practices a social tyranny more formidable than many kinds of political oppression, since, though not usually upheld by such extreme penalties, it leaves fewer means of escape, penetrating much more deeply into the details of life, and enslaving the soul itself. Protection, therefore, against the tyranny of the magistrate is not enough: there needs protection also against the tyranny of the prevailing opinion and feeling; against the tendency of society to impose, by other means than civil penalties, its own ideas and practices as rules of conduct on those who dissent from them; to fetter the development, and, if possible, prevent the formation, of any individuality not in harmony with its ways, and compels all characters to fashion themselves upon the model of its own. There is a limit to the legitimate interference of collective opinion with individual independence; and to find that limit, and maintain it against encroachment, is as indispensable to a good condition of human affairs, as protection against political despotism.

But though this proposition is not likely to be contested in general terms, the practical question, where to place the limit —how to make the fitting adjustment between individual independence and social control—is a subject on which nearly everything remains to be done. All that makes existence valuable to anyone, depends on the enforcement of restraints upon the actions of other people. |Some rules of conduct, therefore, must be imposed, by law in the first place, and by opinion on many things which are not fit subjects for the operation of law. What these rules should be is the principal question in human affairs; but if we except a few of the most obvious cases, it is one of those which least progress has been made in resolving. No two ages, and scarcely any two countries, have decided it alike; and the decision of one age or country is a wonder to another. Yet the people of any given age and country no more suspect any difficulty in it, than if it were a subject on which mankind had always been agreed. The rules which obtain among themselves appear to them self-evident and self-justifying. This all but universal illusion is one of the examples of the magical influence of custom, which is not only, as the proverb says, a second nature, but is continually mistaken for the first. The effect of custom, in preventing any misgiving respecting the rules of conduct which mankind impose on one another, is all the more complete because the subject is one on which it is not generally considered necessary that reasons should be given, either by one person to others or by each to himself. People are accustomed to believe, and have been encouraged in the belief by some who aspire to the character of philosophers, that their feelings, on subjects of this nature, are better than reasons, and render reasons unnecessary. The practical principle which guides them to their opinions on the regulation of human conduct, is the feeling in each person's mind that everybody should be required to act as he, and those with whom he sympathizes, would like them to act. No one, indeed, acknowledges to himself that his standard of judgment is his own liking; but an opinion on a point of conduct, not supported by reasons, can only count as one person's preference; and if the reasons, when given, are a mere appeal to a similar preference felt by other people, it is still only many people's liking instead of one. To an ordinary man, however, his own preference, thus supported, is not only a perfectly satisfactory reason, but the only one he generally has for any of his no-

tions of morality, taste, or propriety, which are not expressly
written in his religious creed; and his chief guide in the interpretation even of that. Men's opinions, accordingly, on what
is laudable or blamable, are affected by all the multifarious
causes which influence their wishes in regard to the conduct
of others, and which are as numerous as those which determine their wishes on any other subject. Sometimes their reason, at other times their prejudices or superstitions; often their
social affections, not seldom their antisocial ones, their envy
or jealousy, their arrogance or contemptuousness: but most
commonly their desires or fears for themselves—their legitimate or illegitimate self-interest. Wherever there is an ascendant class, a large portion of the morality of the country
emanates from its class interests, and its feelings of class
superiority. The morality between Spartans and Helots, between planters and Negroes, between princes and subjects,
between nobles and roturiers, between men and women, has
been for the most part the creation of these class interests
and feelings; and the sentiments thus generated react in turn
upon the moral feelings of the members of the ascendant
class, in their relations among themselves. Where, on the
other hand, a class, formerly ascendant, has lost its ascendancy, or where its ascendancy is unpopular, the prevailing
moral sentiments frequently bear the impress of an impatient
dislike of superiority. Another grand determining principle
of the rules of conduct, both in act and forbearance, which
have been enforced by law or opinion, has been the servility
of mankind towards the supposed preferences or aversions of
their temporal masters or of their gods. This servility, though
essentially selfish, is not hypocrisy; it gives rise to perfectly
genuine sentiments of abhorrence; it made men burn magicians and heretics. Among so many baser influences, the
general and obvious interests of society have of course had a
share, and a large one, in the direction of the moral sentiments; less, however, as a matter of reason, and on their own
account, than as a consequence of the sympathies and antipathies which grew out of them; and sympathies and antipathies
which had little or nothing to do with the interests of society,
have made themselves felt in the establishment of moralities
with quite as great force.

The likings and dislikings of society, or of some powerful portion of it, are thus the main thing which has practically
determined the rules laid down for general observance, under
the penalties of law or opinion. And in general, those who

een in advance of society in thought and feeling, have
his condition of things unassailed in principle, however
y may have come into conflict with it in some of its details. They have occupied themselves rather in inquiring what
things society ought to like or dislike, than in questioning
whether its likings or dislikings should be a law to individuals.
They preferred endeavoring to alter the feelings of mankind
on the particular points on which they were themselves heretical, rather than make common cause in defense of freedom, with heretics generally. The only case in which the
higher ground has been taken on principle and maintained
with consistency, by any but an individual here and there,
is that of religious belief: a case instructive in many ways,
and not least so as forming a most striking instance of the
fallibility of what is called the moral sense; for the *odium
theologicum,* in a sincere bigot, is one of the most unequivocal
cases of moral feeling. Those who first broke the yoke of what
called itself the Universal Church, were in general as little
willing to permit difference of religious opinion as that church
itself. But when the heat of the conflict was over, without
giving a complete victory to any party, and each church or
sect was reduced to limit its hopes to retaining possession of
the ground it already occupied; minorities, seeing that they
had no chance of becoming majorities, were under the necessity of pleading to those whom they could not convert,
for permission to differ. It is accordingly on this battlefield,
almost solely, that the rights of the individual against society
have been asserted on broad grounds of principle, and the
claim of society to exercise authority over dissentients openly
controverted. The great writers to whom the world owes what
religious liberty it possesses, have mostly asserted freedom
of conscience as an indefeasible right, and denied absolutely
that a human being is accountable to others for his religious
belief. Yet so natural to mankind is intolerance in whatever
they really care about, that religious freedom has hardly anywhere been practically realized, except where religious indifference, which dislikes to have its peace disturbed by theological quarrels, has added its weight to the scale. In the minds
of almost all religious persons, even in the most tolerant
countries, the duty of toleration is admitted with tacit reserves.
One person will bear with dissent in matters of church government, but not of dogma; another can tolerate everybody,
short of a Papist or a Unitarian; another everyone who believes in revealed religion; a few extend their charity a little

further, but stop at the belief in a God and in a future state. Wherever the sentiment of the majority is still genuine and intense, it is found to have abated little of its claim to be obeyed.

— In England, from the peculiar circumstances of our political history, though the yoke of opinion is perhaps heavier, that of law is lighter, than in most other countries of Europe; and there is considerable jealousy of direct interference, by the legislative or the executive power, with private conduct; not so much from any just regard for the independence of the individual, as from the still subsisting habit of looking on the government as representing an opposite interest to the public. The majority have not yet learnt to feel the power of the government their power, or its opinions their opinions. When they do so, individual liberty will probably be as much exposed to invasion from the government, as it already is from public opinion. But, as yet, there is a considerable amount of feeling ready to be called forth against any attempt of the law to control individuals in things in which they have not hitherto been accustomed to be controlled by it; and this with very little discrimination as to whether the matter is, or is not, within the legitimate sphere of legal control; insomuch that the feeling, highly salutary on the whole, is perhaps quite as often misplaced as well grounded in the particular instances of its application. There is, in fact, no recognized principle by which the propriety or impropriety of government interference is customarily tested. People decide according to their personal preferences. Some, whenever they see any good to be done, or evil to be remedied, would willingly instigate the government to undertake the business; while others prefer to bear almost any amount of social evil, rather than add one to the departments of human interests amenable to governmental control. And men range themselves on one or the other side in any particular case, according to this general direction of their sentiments; or according to the degree of interest which they feel in the particular thing which it is proposed that the government should do, or according to the belief they entertain that the government would, or would not, do it in the manner they prefer; but very rarely on account of any opinion to which they consistently adhere, as to what things are fit to be done by a government. And it seems to me that in consequence of this absence of rule or principle, one side is at present as often wrong as the other: the interference of government is, with about equal frequency, improperly invoked and improperly condemned.

The object of this essay is to assert one very simple principle, as entitled to govern absolutely the dealings of society with the individual in the way of compulsion and control, whether the means used be physical force in the form of legal penalties, or the moral coercion of public opinion. That principle is, that the sole end for which mankind are warranted, individually or collectively, in interfering with the liberty of action of any of their number, is self-protection. That the only purpose for which power can be rightfully exercised over any member of a civilized community, against his will, is to prevent harm to others. His own good, either physical or moral, is not a sufficient warrant. He cannot rightfully be compelled to do or forbear because it will be better for him to do so, because it will make him happier, because, in the opinions of others, to do so would be wise, or even right. These are good reasons for remonstrating with him, or reasoning with him, or persuading him, or entreating him, but not for compelling him, or visiting him with any evil in case he do otherwise. To justify that, the conduct from which it is desired to deter him must be calculated to produce evil to someone else. The only part of the conduct of anyone, for which he is amenable to society, is that which concerns others. In the part which merely concerns himself, his independence is, of right, absolute. Over himself, over his own body and mind, the individual is sovereign.

It is perhaps hardly necessary to say that this doctrine is meant to apply only to human beings in the maturity of their faculties. We are not speaking of children, or of young persons below the age which the law may fix as that of manhood or womanhood. Those who are still in a state to require being taken care of by others, must be protected against their own actions as well as against external injury. For the same reason, we may leave out of consideration those backward states of society in which the race itself may be considered as in its nonage. The early difficulties in the way of spontaneous progress are so great, and there is seldom any choice of means for overcoming them; and a ruler full of the spirit of improvement is warranted in the use of any expedients that will attain an end, perhaps otherwise unattainable. Despotism is a legitimate mode of government in dealing with barbarians, provided the end be their improvement, and the means justified by actually effecting that end. Liberty,

as a principle, has no application to any state of thing
to the time when mankind have become capable
improved by free and equal discussion. Until then, there is
nothing for them but implicit obedience to an Akbar or a
Charlemagne, if they are so fortunate as to find one. But as
soon as mankind have attained the capacity of being guided
to their own improvement by conviction or persuasion (a
period long since reached in all nations with whom we need
here concern ourselves), compulsion, either in the direct form
or in that of pains and penalties for non-compliance, is no
longer admissible as a means to their own good, and justifiable
only for the security of others.

It is proper to state that I forego any advantage which
could be derived to my argument from the idea of abstract
right, as a thing independent of utility. I regard utility as the
ultimate appeal on all ethical questions; but it must be utility
in the largest sense, grounded on the permanent interests of a
man as a progressive being. Those interests, I contend, authorized the subjection of individual spontaneity to external
control, only in respect to those actions of each which concern the interest of other people. If anyone does an act hurtful to others, there is a *prima facie* case for punishing him,
by law, or, where legal penalties are not safely applicable, by
general disapprobation. There are also many positive acts
for the benefit of others, which he may rightfully be compelled to perform: such as to give evidence in a court of
justice; to bear his fair share in the common defense, or in
any other joint work necessary to the interest of the society
of which he enjoys the protection; and to perform certain
acts of individual beneficence, such as saving a fellow-crea-
ture's life, or interposing to protect the defenseless against
ill-usage, things which whenever it is obviously a man's duty
to do, he may rightfully be made responsible to society for
not doing. A person may cause evil to others not only by his
actions but by his inaction, and in either case he is justly
accountable to them for the injury. The latter case, it is true,
requires a much more cautious exercise of compulsion than
the former. To make anyone answerable for doing evil to
others is the rule; to make him answerable for not preventing
evil is, comparatively speaking, the exception. Yet there are
many cases clear enough and grave enough to justify that
exception. In all things which regard the external relations
of the individual, he is *de jure* amenable to those whose interests are concerned, and, if need be, to society as their pro-

tector. There are often good reasons for not holding him to the responsibility; but these reasons must arise from the special expediencies of the case: either because it is a kind of case in which he is on the whole likely to act better, when left to his own discretion, than when controlled in any way in which society have it in their power to control him; or because the attempt to exercise control would produce other evils, greater than those which it would prevent. When such reasons as these preclude the enforcement of responsibility, the conscience of the agent himself should step into the vacant judgment seat, and protect those interests of others which have no external protection; judging himself all the more rigidly, because the case does not admit of his being made accountable to the judgment of his fellow-creatures.

But there is a sphere of action in which society, as distinguished from the individual, has, if any, only an indirect interest; comprehending all that portion of a person's life and conduct which affects only himself, or if it also affects others, only with their free, voluntary, and undeceived consent and participation. When I say only himself, I mean directly, and in the first instance; for whatever affects himself, may affect others through himself; and the objection which may be grounded on this contingency, will receive consideration in the sequel. This, then, is the appropriate region of human liberty. It comprises, *first,* the inward domain of consciousness; demanding liberty of conscience in the most comprehensive sense; liberty of thought and feeling; absolute freedom of opinion and sentiment on all subjects, practical or speculative, scientific, moral, or theological. The liberty of expressing and publishing opinions may seem to fall under a different principle, since it belongs to that part of the conduct of an individual which concerns other people; but, being almost of as much importance as the liberty of thought itself, and resting in great part on the same reasons, is practically inseparable from it. *Secondly,* the principle requires liberty of tastes and pursuits; of framing the plan of our life to suit our own character; of doing as we like, subject to such consequences as may follow: without impediment from our fellow-creatures, so long as what we do does not harm them, even though they should think our conduct foolish, perverse, or wrong. *Thirdly,* from this liberty of each individual, follows the liberty, within the same limits, of combination among individuals; freedom to unite, for any purpose not involving harm to others: the persons combining supposed to be of full age, and not forced or deceived.

No society in which these liberties are not, on the whole, respected, is free, whatever may be its form of government; and none is completely free in which they do not exist absolute and unqualified. The only freedom which deserves the name, is that of pursuing our own good in our own way, so long as we do not attempt to deprive others of theirs, or impede their efforts to obtain it. Each is the proper guardian of his own health, whether bodily, or mental and spiritual. Mankind are greater gainers by suffering each other to live as seems good to themselves, than by compelling each to live as seems good to the rest.

Though this doctrine is anything but new, and, to some persons, may have the air of a truism, there is no doctrine which stands more directly opposed to the general tendency of existing opinion and practice. Society has expended fully as much effort in the attempt (according to its lights) to compel people to conform to its notions of personal as of social excellence. The ancient commonwealths thought themselves entitled to practice, and the ancient philosophers countenanced, the regulation of every part of private conduct by public authority, on the ground that the State had a deep interest in the whole bodily and mental discipline of every one of its citizens: a mode of thinking which may have been admissible in small republics surrounded by powerful enemies, in constant peril of being subverted by foreign attack or internal commotion, and to which even a short interval of relaxed energy and self-command might so easily be fatal that they could not afford to wait for the salutary permanent effects of freedom. In the modern world, the greater size of political communities, and, above all, the separation between spiritual and temporal authority (which placed the direction of men's consciences in other hands than those which controlled their worldly affairs), prevented so great an interference by law in the details of private life; but the engines of moral repression have been wielded more strenuously against divergence from the reigning opinion in self-regarding, than even in social matters; religion, the most powerful of the elements which have entered into the formation of moral feeling, having almost always been governed either by the ambition of a hierarchy, seeking control over every department of human conduct, or by the spirit of Puritanism. And some of those modern reformers who have placed themselves in strongest opposition to the religions of the past, have been no way behind either churches or sects in their assertion of the right of spiritual domination: M. Comte, in particular, whose social system, as unfolded is his *Système de Politique Positive*, aims at establishing (though by moral more than by legal appliances) a despotism of society over the individual, surpassing anything contemplated in the political ideal of the most rigid disciplinarian among the ancient philosophers.

Apart from the peculiar tenets of individual thinkers, there is also in the world at large an increasing inclination to stretch unduly the powers of society over the individual, both by the force of opinion and even by that of legislation; and as the tendency of all the changes taking place in the world is to strengthen society, and diminish the power of the individual, this encroachment is not one of the evils which tend spontaneously to disappear, but, on the contrary, to grow more and more formidable. The disposition of mankind, whether as rulers or as fellow-citizens, to impose their own opinions and inclinations as a rule of conduct on others, is so energetically supported by some of the best and by some of the worst feelings incident to human nature, that it is hardly ever kept under restraint by anything but want of power; and as the power is not declining, but growing, unless a strong barrier of moral conviction can be raised against the mischief, we must expect, in the present circumstances of the world, to see it increase.

It will be convenient for the argument, if, instead of at once entering upon the general thesis, we confine ourselves in the first instance to a single branch of it, on which the principle here stated is, if not fully, yet to a certain point, recognized by the current opinions. This one branch is the *liberty of thought:* from which it is impossible to separate the cognate liberty of speaking and of writing. Although these liberties, to some considerable amount, form part of the political morality of all countries which profess religious toleration and free institutions, the grounds, both philosophical and practical, on which they rest, are perhaps not so familiar to the general mind, nor so thoroughly appreciated by many even of the leaders of opinion, as might have been expected. Those grounds, when rightly understood, are of much wider application than to only one division of the subject, and a thorough consideration of this part of the question will be found the best introduction to the remainder. Those to whom nothing which I am about to say will be new, may therefore,

I hope, excuse me, if on a subject which for now three centuries has been so often discussed, I venture on one discussion more.

The time, it is to be hoped, is gone by, when any defense would be necessary of the "liberty of the press" as one of the securities against corrupt or tyrannical government. No argument, we may suppose, can now be needed against permitting a legislature or an executive, not identified in interest with the people, to prescribe opinions to them, and determine what doctrines or what arguments they shall be allowed to hear. This aspect of the question, besides, has been so often and so triumphantly enforced by preceding writers, that it need not be specially insisted on in this place. Though the law of England, on the subject of the press, is as servile to this day as it was in the time of the Tudors, there is little danger of its being actually put in force against political discussion, except during some temporary panic, when fear of insurrection drives ministers and judges from their propriety;[1]

[1] These words had scarcely been written, when, as if to give them an emphatic contradiction, occurred the Government Press Prosecutions of 1858. That ill-judged interference with the liberty of public discussion has not, however, induced me to alter a single word in the text, nor has it at all weakened my conviction that, moments of panic excepted, the era of pains and penalties for political discussion has, in our own country, passed away. For, in the first place, the prosecutions were not persisted in; and, in the second, they were never, properly speaking, political prosecutions. The offense charged was not that of criticising institutions, or the acts of persons of rulers, but of circulating what was deemed an immoral doctrine, the lawfulness of tyrannicide.

If the arguments of the present chapter are of any validity, there ought to exist the fullest liberty of professing and discussing, as a matter of ethical conviction, any doctrine, however immoral it may be considered. It would, therefore, be irrelevant and out of place to examine here, whether the doctrine of tyrannicide deserves that title. I shall content myself with saying that the subject has been at all times one of the open questions of morals; that the act of a private citizen in striking down a criminal, who, by raising himself above the law, has placed himself beyond the reach of legal punishment or control, has been accounted by whole nations, and, speaking generally, it is not, in constitutional countries, to be apprehended that the government, whether completely responsible to the people or not, will often attempt to control the expression of opinion, except when in doing so it makes itself the organ of the general intolerance of the public. Let us suppose, therefore, that the government is entirely at one with the people, and never thinks of exerting any power of coercion unless in agreement with what it conceives to be their voice. But I deny the right of the people to exercise such coercion, either by themselves or by their government. The power itself is illegitimate. The best government has no more title to it than the worst. It is as noxious, or more noxious, when exerted in accordance with public opinion, than when in opposition to it. If all mankind minus one were of one opinion, and only one person were of the contrary opinion, mankind would be no more justified in silencing that one person, than he, if he had the power, would be justified in silencing mankind. Were an opinion a personal possession of no value except to the owner; if to be obstructed in the enjoyment of it were simply a private injury, it would make some difference whether the injury was inflicted only on a few persons or on many. But the peculiar evil of silencing the expression of an opinion is, that it is robbing the human race: posterity as well as the existing generation; those who dissent from the opinion, still more than those who hold it. If the opinion is right, they are deprived of the opportunity of exchanging error for truth; if wrong, they lose, what is almost as great a benefit, the clearer perception and livelier impression of truth, produced by its collision with error.

It is necessary to consider separately these two hypotheses, each of which has a distinct branch of the argument corresponding to it. We can never be sure that the opinion we are endeavoring to stifle is a false opinion; and if we were sure, stifling it would be an evil still.

---

and by some of the best and wisest of men, not a crime, but an act of exalted virtue; and that, right or wrong, it is not of the nature of assassination, but of civil war. As such, I hold that the instigation to it, in a specific case, may be a proper subject of punishment, but only if an overt act has followed, and at least a probable connection can be established between the act and the instigation. Even then, it is not a foreign government, but the very government assailed, which alone, in the exercise of self-defense, can legitimately punish attacks directed against its own existence.

First: the opinion which it is attempted to suppress by authority may possibly be true. Those who desire to suppress it, of course deny its truth; but they are not infallible. They have no authority to decide the question for all mankind, and exclude every other person from the means of judging. To refuse a hearing to an opinion, because they are sure that it is false, is to assume that *their* certainty is the same thing as *absolute* certainty. All silencing of discussion is an assumption of infallibility. Its condemnation may be allowed to rest on this common argument, not the worse for being common.

Unfortunately for the good sense of mankind, the fact of their fallibility is far from carrying the weight in their practical judgment which is always allowed to it in theory; for while everyone well knows himself to be fallible, few think it necessary to take any precautions against their own fallibility, or admit the supposition that any opinion of which they feel very certain, may be one of the examples of the error to which they acknowledge themselves to be liable. Absolute princes, or others who are accustomed to unlimited deference, usually feel this complete confidence in their own opinions on nearly all subjects. People more happily situated, who sometimes hear their opinions disputed, and are not wholly unused to be set right when they are wrong, place the same unbounded reliance only on such of their opinions as are shared by all who surround them, or to whom they habitually defer; for in proportion to a man's want of confidence in his own solitary judgment, does he usually repose, with implicit trust, on the infallibility of "the world" in general. And the world, to each individual, means the part of it with which he comes in contact—his party, his sect, his church, his class of society; the man may be called, by comparison, almost liberal and large-minded to whom it means anything so comprehensive as his own country or his own age. Nor is his faith in this collective authority at all shaken by his being aware that other ages, countries, sects, churches, classes, and parties have thought, and even now think, the exact reverse. He devolves upon his own world the responsibility of being in the right against the dissentient worlds of other people; and it never troubles him that mere accident has decided which of these numerous worlds is the object of his reliance, and that the same causes which make him a Churchman in London, would have made him a Buddhist or a Confucian in Pekin. Yet it is as evident in itself as any amount of argument can make it, that ages are no more infallible than individuals; every age having held many opinions which subsequent ages have deemed not only false but absurd; and it is as certain that many opinions now general will be rejected by future ages, as it is that many, once general, are rejected by the present.

The objection likely to be made to this argument would probably take some such form as the following. There is no greater assumption of infallibility in forbidding the propagation of error, than in any other thing which is done by public authority on its own judgment and responsibility. Judgment is given to men that they may use it. Because it may be used erroneously, are men to be told that they ought not to use it at all? To prohibit what they think pernicious, is not claiming exemption from error, but fulfilling the duty incumbent on them, although fallible, of acting on their conscientious conviction. If we were never to act on our opinions, because those opinions may be wrong, we should leave all our interests uncared for, and all our duties unperformed. An objection which applies to all conduct can be no valid objection to any conduct in particular. It is the duty of governments, and of individuals, to form the truest opinions they can; to form them carefully, and never impose them upon others unless they are quite sure of being right. But when they are sure (such reasoners may say), it is not conscientiousness but cowardice to shrink from acting on their opinions, and allow doctrines which they honestly think dangerous to the welfare of mankind, either in this life or in another, to be scattered abroad without restraint, because other people, in less enlightened times, have persecuted opinions now believed to be true. Let us take care, it may be said, not to make the same mistake; but governments and nations have made mistakes in other things, which are not denied to be fit subjects for the exercise of authority: they have laid on bad taxes, made unjust wars. Ought we therefore to lay on no taxes, and, under whatever provocation, make no wars? Men, and governments, must act to the best of their ability. There is no such thing as absolute certainty, but there is assurance sufficient for the purposes of human life. We may, and must, assume our opinion to be true for the guidance of our own conduct: and it is assuming no more when we forbid bad men to pervert society by the propagation of opinions which we regard as false and pernicious.

I answer that it is assuming very much more. There is the greatest difference between presuming an opinion to be true because, with every opportunity for contesting it, it has not been refuted, and assuming its truth for the purpose of not permitting its refutation. Complete liberty of contradicting and disproving our opinion is the very condition which justifies us in assuming its truth for purposes of action; and on no other terms can a being with human faculties have any rational assurance of being right.

When we consider either the history of opinion, or the ordinary conduct of human life, to what is it to be ascribed that the one and the other are no worse than they are? Not certainly to the inherent force of the human understanding; for, on any matter not self-evident, there are ninety-nine persons totally incapable of judging of it for one who is capable; and the capacity of the hundredth person is only comparative: for the majority of the eminent men of every past generation held many opinions now known to be erroneous, and did or approved numerous things which no one will now justify. Why is it, then, that there is on the whole a preponderance among mankind of rational opinions and rational conduct? If there really is this preponderance—which there must be unless human affairs are, and have always been, in an almost desperate state—it is owing to a quality of the human mind, the source of everything respectable in man either as an intellectual or as a moral being, namely, that his errors are corrigible. He is capable of rectifying his mistakes, by discussion and experience. Not by experience alone. There must be discussion, to show how experience is to be interpreted. Wrong opinions and practices gradually yield to fact and argument; but facts and arguments, to produce any effect on the mind, must be brought before it. Very few facts are able to tell their own story, without comments to bring out their meaning. The whole strength and value, then, of human judgment, depending on the one property, that it can be set right when it is wrong, reliance can be placed on it only when the means of setting it right are kept constantly at hand. In the case of any person whose judgment is really deserving of confidence, how has it become so? Because he has kept his mind open to criticism of his opinions and conduct. Because it has been his practice to listen to all that could be said against him; to profit by as much of it as was just, and expound to himself, and upon occasion to others, the fallacy of what was fallacious. Because he has felt that the only way in which a human being can make some approach to knowing the whole of a subject,

is by hearing what can be said about it by persons of every
variety of opinion, and studying all modes in which it can
be looked at by every character of mind. No wise man ever
acquired his wisdom in any mode but this; nor is it in the
nature of human intellect to become wise in any other manner. The steady habit of correcting and completing his own
opinion by collating it with those of others, so far from
causing doubt and hesitation in carrying it into practice, is
the only stable foundation for a just reliance on it: for, being cognizant of all that can, at least obviously, be said against
him, and having taken up his position against all gainsayers—
knowing that he has sought for objections and difficulties,
instead of avoiding them, and has shut out no light which
can be thrown upon the subject from any quarter—he has a
right to think his judgment better than that of any person,
or any multitude, who have not gone through a similar
process.

It is not too much to require that what the wisest of mankind, those who are best entitled to trust their own judgment, find necessary to warrant their relying on it, should
be submitted to by that miscellaneous collection of a few
wise and many foolish individuals, called the public. The
most intolerant of churches, the Roman Catholic Church,
even at the canonization of a saint, admits, and listens patiently to, a "devil's advocate." The holiest of men, it appears,
cannot be admitted to posthumous honors, until all that the
devil could say against him is known and weighed. If even
the Newtonian philosophy were not permitted to be questioned, mankind could not feel as complete assurance of its
truth as they now do. The beliefs which we have most warrant for, have no safeguard to rest on but a standing invitation to the whole world to prove them unfounded. If the
challenge is not accepted, or is accepted and the attempt
fails, we are far enough from certainty still; but we have
done the best that the existing state of human reason admits
of; we have neglected nothing that could give the truth a
chance of reaching us: if the lists are kept open, we may
hope that if there be a better truth, it will be found when
the human mind is capable of receiving it; and in the meantime we may rely on having attained such approach to truth
as is possible in our own day. This is the amount of certainty
attainable by a fallible being, and this the sole way of attaining it.

Strange it is that men should admit the validity of the arguments for free discussion, but object to their being "pushed to an extreme"; not seeing that unless the reasons are good for an extreme case, they are not good for any case. Strange that they should imagine that they are not assuming infallibility, when they acknowledge that there should be free discussion on all subjects which can possibly be *doubtful*, but think that some particular principle or doctrine should be forbidden to be questioned because it is so *certain*, that is, because *they are certain* that it is certain. To call any proposition certain while there is anyone who would deny its certainty if permitted, but who is not permitted, is to assume that we ourselves, and those who agree with us, are the judges of certainty, and judges without hearing the other side.

In the present age—which has been described as "destitute of faith, but terrified at scepticism"—in which people feel sure, not so much that their opinions are true, as that they should not know what to do without them—the claims of an opinion to be protected from public attack are rested not so much on its truth, as on its importance to society. There are, it is alleged, certain beliefs so useful, not to say indispensable, to well-being that it is as much the duty of governments to uphold those beliefs, as to protect any other of the interests of society. In a case of such necessity, and so directly in the line of their duty, something less than infallibility may, it is maintained, warrant, and even bind, governments to act on their own opinion, confirmed by the general opinion of mankind. It is also often argued, and still oftener thought, that none but bad men would desire to weaken these salutary beliefs; and there can be nothing wrong, it is thought, in restraining bad men, and prohibiting what only such men would wish to practice. This mode of thinking makes the justification of restraints on discussion not a question of the truth of doctrines, but of their usefulness; and flatters itself by that means to escape the responsibility of claiming to be an infallible judge of opinions. But those who thus satisfy themselves, do not perceive that the assumption of infallibility is merely shifted from one point to another. The usefulness of an opinion is itself matter of opinion: as disputable, as open to discussion, and requiring discussion as much as the opinion itself. There is the same need of an infallible judge of opinions to decide an opinion to be noxious, as to decide it to be false, unless the opinion condemned has full opportunity of defending itself. And it

will not do to say that the heretic may be allowed to maintain the utility or harmlessness of his opinion, though forbidden to maintain its truth. The truth of an opinion is part
of its utility. If we would know whether or not it is desirable
that a proposition should be believed, is it possible to exclude the consideration of whether or not it is true? In the
opinion, not of bad men, but of the best men, no belief
which is contrary to truth can be really useful: and can you
prevent such men from urging that plea, when they are
charged with culpability for denying some doctrine which
they are told is useful, but which they believe to be false?
Those who are on the side of received opinions never fail to
take all possible advantage of this plea: you do not find *them*
handling the question of utility as if it could be completely
abstracted from that of truth; on the contrary, it is, above
all, because their doctrine is "the truth," that the knowledge
or the belief of it is held to be so indispensable. There can
be no fair discussion of the question of usefulness when an
argument so vital may be employed on one side, but not on
the other. And in point of fact, when law or public feeling
do not permit the truth of an opinion to be disputed, they
are just as little tolerant of a denial of its usefulness. The
utmost they allow is an extenuation of its absolute necessity,
or of the positive guilt of rejecting it.

In order more fully to illustrate the mischief of denying a
hearing to opinions because we, in our own judgment, have
condemned them, it will be desirable to fix down the discussion to a concrete case; and I choose, by preference, the
cases which are least favorable to me—in which the argument
against freedom of opinion, both on the score of truth and
on that of utility, is considered the strongest. Let the opinions
impugned be the belief in a God and in a future state, or
any of the commonly received doctrines of morality. To fight
the battle on such ground gives a great advantage to an
unfair antagonist; since he will be sure to say (and many who
have no desire to be unfair will say it internally), "Are these
the doctrines which you do not deem sufficiently certain to
be taken under the protection of law? Is the belief in a God
one of the opinions to feel sure of which you hold to be assuming infallibility?" But I must be permitted to observe
that it is not the feeling sure of a doctrine (be it what it may)
which I call an assumption of infallibility. It is the undertaking to decide that question *for others*, without allowing them
to hear what can be said on the contrary side. And I de-

nounce and reprobate this pretension not the less if put forth
on the side of my most solemn convictions. However positive
anyone's persuasion may be, not only of the falsity but of
the pernicious consequences—not only of the pernicious consequences, but (to adopt expressions which I altogether condemn) the immorality and impiety of an opinion; yet if, in
pursuance of that private judgment, though backed by the
public judgment of his country or his contemporaries, he
prevents the opinion from being heard in its defense, he assumes infallibility. And so far from the assumption being less
objectionable or less dangerous because the opinion is called
immoral or impious, this is the case of all others in which it
is most fatal. These are exactly the occasions on which the
men of one generation commit those dreadful mistakes which
excite the astonishment and horror of posterity. It is among
such that we find the instances memorable in history, when
the arm of the law has been employed to root out the best
men and the noblest doctrines; with deplorable success as to
the men, though some of the doctrines have survived to be
(as if in mockery) invoked in defense of similar conduct
towards those who dissent from *them*, or from their received
interpretation.

Mankind can hardly be too often reminded, that there was
once a man named Socrates, between whom and the legal
authorities and public opinion of his time there took place a
memorable collision. Born in an age and country abounding
in individual greatness, this man has been handed down to
us by those who best knew both him and the age, as the most
virtuous man in it; while *we* know him as the head and
prototype of all subsequent teachers of virtue, the source
equally of the lofty inspiration of Plato and the judicious
utilitarianism of Aristotle, "*i maëstri di color che sanno*," the
two headsprings of ethical as of all other philosophy. This
acknowledged master of all the eminent thinkers who have
since lived—whose fame, still growing after more than two
thousand years, all but outweighs the whole remainder of
the names which make his native city illustrious—was put to
death by his countrymen, after a judicial conviction, for impiety and immorality. Impiety, in denying the gods recognized by the State; indeed his accuser asserted (see the
Apologia) that he believed in no gods at all. Immorality, in
being, by his doctrines and instructions, a "corruptor of
youth." Of these charges the tribunal, there is every ground
for believing, honestly found him guilty, and condemned the

man who probably of all then born had deserved best of mankind to be put to death as a criminal.

To pass from this to the only other instance of judicial iniquity, the mention of which, after the condemnation of Socrates, would not be an anticlimax: the event which took place on Calvary rather more than eighteen hundred years ago. The man who left on the memory of those who witnessed his life and conversation such an impression of his moral grandeur that eighteen subsequent centuries have done homage to him as the Almighty in person, was ignominiously put to death, as what? As a blasphemer. Men did not merely mistake their benefactor; they mistook him for the exact contrary of what he was, and treated him as that prodigy of impiety which they themselves are now held to be for their treatment of him. The feelings with which mankind now regard these lamentable transactions, especially the later of the two, render them extremely unjust in their judgment of the unhappy actors. These were, to all appearance, not bad men—not worse than men commonly are, but rather the contrary; men who possessed in a full, or somewhat more than a full measure, the religious, moral, and patriotic feelings of their time and people: the very kind of men who, in all times, our own included, have every chance of passing through life blameless and respected. The high priest who rent his garments when the words were pronounced which, according to all the ideas of his country, constituted the blackest guilt, was in all probability quite as sincere in his horror and indignation as the generality of respectable and pious men now are in the religious and moral sentiments they profess; and most of those who now shudder at his conduct, if they had lived in his time, and been born Jews, would have acted precisely as he did. Orthodox Christians who are tempted to think that those who stoned to death the first martyrs must have been worse men than they themselves are, ought to remember that one of those persecutors was Saint Paul.

Let us add one more example, the most striking of all, if the impressiveness of an error is measured by the wisdom and virtue of him who falls into it. If ever anyone possessed of power had grounds for thinking himself the best and most enlightened among his contemporaries, it was the Emperor Marcus Aurelius. Absolute monarch of the whole civilized world, he preserved through life not only the most unblemished justice, but what was less to be expected from his Stoical breeding, the tenderest heart. The few failings which are attributed to him were all on the side of indulgence; while his writings, the highest ethical product of the ancient mind, differ scarcely perceptibly, if they differ at all, from the most characteristic teachings of Christ. This man, a better Christian in all but the dogmatic sense of the word than almost any of the ostensibly Christian sovereigns who have since reigned, persecuted Christianity. Placed at the summit of all the previous attainments of humanity, with an open, unfettered intellect, and a character which led him of himself to embody in his moral writings the Christian ideal, he yet failed to see that Christianity was to be a good and not an evil to the world, with his duties to which he was so deeply penetrated. Existing society he knew to be in a deplorable state. But such as it was, he saw, or thought he saw, that it was held together, and prevented from being worse, by belief and reverence of the received divinities. As a ruler of mankind, he deemed it his duty not to suffer society to fall in pieces; and saw not how, if its existing ties were removed, any others could be formed which could again knit it together. The new religion openly aimed at dissolving these ties: unless, therefore, it was his duty to adopt that religion, it seemed to be his duty to put it down. Inasmuch then as the theology of Christianity did not appear to him true or of divine origin; inasmuch as this strange history of a crucified God was not credible to him, and a system which purported to rest entirely upon a foundation to him so wholly unbelievable, could not be foreseen by him to be that renovating agency which, after all abatements, it has in fact proved to be; the gentlest and most amiable of philosophers and rulers, under a solemn sense of duty, authorized the persecution of Christianity. To my mind this is one of the most tragical facts in all history. It is a bitter thought, how different a thing the Christianity of the world might have been, if the Christian faith had been adopted as the religion of the empire under the auspices of Marcus Aurelius instead of those of Constantine. But it would be equally unjust to him and false to truth to deny that no one plea which can be urged for punishing anti-Christian teaching was wanting to Marcus Aurelius for punishing as he did the propagation of Christianity. No Christian more firmly believes that atheism is false, and tends to the dissolution of society, than Marcus Aurelius believed the same things of Christianity; he who, of all men then living, might have been thought the most capable of appreciating it. Unless anyone who approves of pun-

ishment for the promulgation of opinions, flatters himself that
he is a wiser and better man than Marcus Aurelius—more
deeply versed in the wisdom of his time, more elevated in
his intellect above it—more earnest in his search for truth,
or more single-minded in his devotion to it when found; let
him abstain from that assumption of the joint infallibility
of himself and the multitude, which the great Antoninus
made with so unfortunate a result.

Aware of the impossibility of defending the use of punishment for restraining irreligious opinions by any argument
which will not justify Marcus Antoninus, the enemies of religious freedom, when hard pressed, occasionally accept this
consequence, and say, with Dr. Johnson, that the persecutors
of Christianity were in the right; that persecution is an ordeal
through which truth ought to pass, and always passes successfully, legal penalties being, in the end, powerless against truth,
though sometimes beneficially effective against mischievous
errors. This is a form of the argument for religious intolerance sufficiently remarkable not to be passed without notice.

A theory which maintains that truth may justifiably be persecuted because persecution cannot possibly do it any harm,
cannot be charged with being intentionally hostile to the
reception of new truths; but we cannot commend the generosity of its dealing with the persons to whom mankind are
indebted for them. To discover to the world something which
deeply concerns it, and of which it was previously ignorant;
to prove to it that it had been mistaken on some vital point
of temporal or spiritual interest, is as important a service as a
human being can render to his fellow-creatures, and in certain cases, as in those of the early Christians and of the
Reformers, those who think with Dr. Johnson believe it to
have been the most precious gift which could be bestowed
on mankind. That the authors of such splendid benefits should
be requited by martyrdom, that their reward should be to
be dealt with as the vilest of criminals, is not, upon this
theory, a deplorable error and misfortune, for which humanity should mourn in sackcloth and ashes, but the normal
and justifiable state of things. The propounder of a new
truth, according to this doctrine, should stand, as stood, in
the legislation of the Locrians, the proposer of a new law,
with a halter round his neck, to be instantly tightened if the
public assembly did not, on hearing his reasons, then and
there adopt his proposition. People who defend this mode of
treating benefactors cannot be supposed to set much value on

the benefit; and I believe this view of the subject is mostly confined to the sort of persons who think that new truths may have been desirable once, but that we have had enough of them now.

But, indeed, the dictum that truth always triumphs over persecution is one of those pleasant falsehoods which men repeat after one another till they pass into commonplaces, but which all experience refutes. History teems with instances of truth put down by persecution. If not suppressed forever, it may be thrown back for centuries. To speak only of religious opinions: the Reformation broke out at least twenty times before Luther, and was put down. Arnold of Brescia was put down. Fra Dolcino was put down. Savonarola was put down. The Albigeois were put down. The Vaudois were put down. The Lollards were put down. The Hussites were put down. Even after the era of Luther, wherever persecution was persisted in, it was successful. In Spain, Italy, Flanders, the Austrian Empire, Protestantism was rooted out; and, most likely would have been so in England, had Queen Mary lived, or Queen Elizabeth died. Persecution has always succeeded, save where the heretics were too strong a party to be effectually persecuted. No reasonable person can doubt that Christianity might have been extirpated in the Roman Empire. It spread, and became predominant, because the persecutions were only occasional, lasting but a short time, and separated by long intervals of almost undisturbed propagandism. It is a piece of idle sentimentality that truth, merely as truth, has any inherent power denied to error of prevailing against the dungeon and the stake. Men are not more zealous for truth than they often are for error, and a sufficient application of legal or even of social penalties will generally succeed in stopping the propagation of either. The real advantage which truth has, consists in this, that when an opinion is true, it may be extinguished once, twice, or many times, but in the course of ages there will generally be found persons to rediscover it, until some one of its reappearances falls on a time when from favorable circumstances it escapes persecution until it has made such head as to withstand all subsequent attempts to suppress it.

It will be said that we do not now put to death the introducers of new opinions: we are not like our fathers who slew the prophets, we even build sepulchres to them. It is true we no longer put heretics to death; and the amount of penal infliction which modern feeling would probably tolerate, even against the most obnoxious opinions, is not sufficient to extirpate them. But let us not flatter ourselves that we are yet free from the stain even of legal persecution. Penalties for opinion, or at least for its expression, still exist by law; and their enforcement is not, even in these times, so unexampled as to make it at all incredible that they may some day be revived in full force. In the year 1857, at the summer assizes of the county of Cornwall, an unfortunate man,[2] said to be of unexceptionable conduct in all relations of life, was sentenced to twenty-one months' imprisonment, for uttering, and writing on a gate, some offensive words concerning Christianity. Within a month of the same time, at the Old Bailey, two persons, on two separate occasions,[3] were rejected as jurymen, and one of them grossly insulted by the judge and by one of the counsel, because they honestly declared that they had no theological belief; and a third, a foreigner,[4] for the same reason, was denied justice against a thief. This refusal of redress took place in virtue of the legal doctrine, that no person can be allowed to give evidence in a court of justice who does not profess belief in a God (any god is sufficient) and in a future state; which is equivalent to declaring such persons to be outlaws, excluded from the protection of the tribunals; who may not only be robbed or assaulted with impunity, if no one but themselves, or persons of similar opinions, be present, but any one else may be robbed or assaulted with impunity, if the proof of the fact depends on their evidence. The assumption on which this is grounded is that the oath is worthless of a person who does not believe in a future state; a proposition which betokens much ignorance of history in those who assent to it (since it is historically true that a large proportion of infidels in all ages have been persons of distinguished integrity and honor); and would be maintained by no one who had the smallest conception how many of the persons in greatest repute with the world, both for virtues and attainments, are well known, at least to their intimates, to be unbelievers. The rule, besides, is suicidal, and cuts away its own foundation. Under pretense that atheists must be liars, it admits

[2] Thomas Pooley, Bodmin Assizes, July 31, 1857. In December following, he received a free pardon from the Crown.

[3] George Jacob Holyoake, August 17, 1857; Edward Truelove, July, 1857.

[4] Baron de Gleichen, Marlborough Street Police Court, August 4, 1857.

the testimony of all atheists who are willing to lie, and rejects only those who brave the obloquy of publicly confessing a detested creed rather than affirm a falsehood. A rule thus self-convicted of absurdity so far as regards its professed purpose, can be kept in force only as a badge of hatred, a relic of persecution; a persecution, too, having the peculiarity that the qualification for undergoing it is the being clearly proved not to deserve it. The rule, and the theory it implies, are hardly less insulting to believers than to infidels. For if he who does not believe in a future state necessarily lies, it follows that they who do believe are only prevented from lying, if prevented they are, by the fear of hell. We will not do the authors and abettors of the rule the injury of supposing that the conception which they have formed of Christian virtue is drawn from their own consciousness.

These, indeed, are but rags and remnants of persecution, and may be thought to be not so much an indication of the wish to persecute, as an example of that very frequent infirmity of English minds, which makes them take a preposterous pleasure in the assertion of a bad principle, when they are no longer bad enough to desire to carry it really into practice. But unhappily there is no security in the state of the public mind that the suspension of worse forms of legal persecution, which has lasted for about the space of a generation, will continue. In this age the quiet surface of routine is as often ruffled by attempts to resuscitate past evils, as to introduce new benefits. What is boasted of at the present time as the revival of religion, is always, in narrow and uncultivated minds, at least as much the revival of bigotry; and where there is the strong permanent leaven of intolerance in the feelings of a people, which at all times abides in the middle classes of this country, it needs but little to provoke them into actively persecuting those whom they have never ceased to think proper objects of persecution. For it is this— it is the opinions men entertain, and the feelings they cherish, respecting those who disown the beliefs they deem important, which makes this country not a place of mental freedom. For a long time past, the chief mischief of the legal penalties is that they strengthen the social stigma. It is that stigma which is really effective, and so effective is it, that the profession of opinions which are under the ban of society is much less common in England than is, in many other countries, the avowal of those which incur risk of judicial punishment. In respect to all persons but those whose pecuniary

circumstances make them independent of the good will of
other people, opinion, on this subject, is as efficacious as
law; men might as well be imprisoned, as excluded from the
means of earning their bread. Those whose bread is already
secured, and who desire no favors from men in power, or
from bodies of men, or from the public, have nothing to
fear from the open avowal of any opinions, but to be ill-
thought of and ill-spoken of, and this it ought not to require a
very heroic mold to enable them to bear. There is no room
for any appeal *ad misericordiam* in behalf of such persons.
But though we do not now inflict so much evil on those who
think differently from us as it was formerly our custom to
do, it may be that we do ourselves as much evil as ever by
our treatment of them. Socrates was put to death, but the
Socratic philosophy rose like the sun in heaven, and spread
its illumination over the whole intellectual firmament. Christians were cast to the lions, but the Christian church grew
up a stately and spreading tree, overtopping the older and
less vigorous growths, and stifling them by its shade. Our
merely social intolerance kills no one, roots out no opinions, but induces men to disguise them, or to abstain from
any active effort for their diffusion. With us, heretical opinions
do not perceptibly gain, or even lose, ground in each decade
or generation; they never blaze out far and wide, but continue to smolder in the narrow circles of thinking and
studious persons among whom they originate, without ever
lighting up the general affairs of mankind with either a true
or a deceptive light. And thus is kept up a state of things
very satisfactory to some minds, because, without the un-
pleasant process of fining or imprisoning anybody, it maintains all prevailing opinions outwardly undisturbed, while it
does not absolutely interdict the exercise of reason by dissentients afflicted with the malady of thought. A convenient
plan for having peace in the intellectual world, and keeping
all things going on therein very much as they do already!
But the price paid for this sort of intellectual pacification is
the sacrifice of the entire moral courage of the human mind.
A state of things in which a large portion of the most active
and inquiring intellects find it advisable to keep the general
principles and grounds of their convictions within their own
breasts, and attempt, in what they address to the public, to
fit as much as they can of their own conclusions to premises
which they have internally renounced, cannot send forth the
open, fearless characters, and logical, consistent intellects who

once adorned the thinking world. The sort of men who can be looked for under it, are either mere conformers to commonplace, or time-servers for truth, whose arguments on all great subjects are meant for their hearers, and are not those which have convinced themselves. Those who avoid this alternative, do so by narrowing their thoughts and interest to things which can be spoken of without venturing within the region of principles—that is, to small practical matters which would come right of themselves if but the minds of mankind were strengthened and enlarged, and which will never be made effectually right until then; while that which would strengthen and enlarge men's minds, free and daring speculation on the highest subjects, is abandoned.

Those in whose eyes this reticence on the part of heretics is no evil should consider, in the first place, that in consequence of it there is never any fair and thorough discussion of heretical opinions; and that such of them as could not stand such a discussion, though they may be prevented from spreading, do not disappear. But it is not the minds of heretics that are deteriorated most by the ban placed on all inquiry which does not end in the orthodox conclusions. The greatest harm done is to those who are not heretics, and whose whole mental development is cramped, and their reason cowed, by the fear of heresy. Who can compute what the world loses in the multitude of promising intellects combined with timid characters, who dare not follow out any bold, vigorous, independent train of thought, lest it should land them in something which would admit of being considered irreligious or immoral? Among them we may occasionally see some man of deep conscientiousness, and subtle and refined understanding, who spends a life in sophisticating with an intellect which he cannot silence, and exhausts the resources of ingenuity in attempting to reconcile the promptings of his conscience and reason with orthodoxy, which yet he does not, perhaps, to the end succeed in doing. No one can be a great thinker who does not recognize that as a thinker it is his first duty to follow his intellect to whatever conclusions it may lead. Truth gains more even by the errors of one who, with due study and preparation, thinks for himself, than by the true opinions of those who only hold them because they do not suffer themselves to think. Not that it is solely, or chiefly, to form great thinkers, that freedom of thinking is required. On the contrary, it is as much and even more indispensable to enable average human beings to attain the mental stature which they are capable of. There have been, and may again be, great individual thinkers in a general atmosphere of mental slavery. But there never has been, nor ever will be, in that atmosphere an intellectually active people. Where any people has made a temporary approach to such a character, it has been because the dread of heterodox speculation was for a time suspended. Where there is a tacit convention that principles are not to be disputed; where the discussion of the greatest questions which can occupy humanity is considered to be closed, we cannot hope to find that generally high scale of mental activity which has made some periods of history so remarkable. Never when controversy avoided the subjects which are large and important enough to kindle enthusiasm, was the mind of a people stirred up from its foundations, and the impulse given which raised even persons of the most ordinary intellect to something of the dignity of thinking beings. Of such we have had an example in the condition of Europe during the times immediately following the Reformation; another, though limited to the Continent and to a more cultivated class, in the speculative movement of the latter half of the eighteenth century; and a third, of still briefer duration, in the intellectual fermentation of Germany during the Goethean and Fichtean period. These periods differed widely in the particular opinions which they developed; but were alike in this, that during all three the yoke of authority was broken. In each, an old mental despotism had been thrown off, and no new one had yet taken its place. The impulse given at these three periods has made Europe what it now is. Every single improvement which has taken place either in the human mind or in institutions, may be traced distinctly to one or other of them. Appearances have for some time indicated that all three impulses are well nigh spent; and we can expect no fresh start until we again assert our mental freedom.

Let us now pass to the second division of the argument, and dismissing the supposition that any of the received opinions may be false, let us assume them to be true, and examine into the worth of the manner in which they are likely to be held, when their truth is not freely and openly canvassed. However unwillingly a person who has a strong opinion may admit the possibility that his opinion may be false, he ought to be moved by the consideration that, however true it may be, if it is not fully, frequently, and fearlessly discussed, it will be held as a dead dogma, not a living truth.

There is a class of persons (happily not quite so numerous as formerly) who think it enough if a person assents undoubtingly to what they think true, though he has no knowledge whatever of the grounds of the opinion, and could not make a tenable defense of it against the most superficial objections. Such persons, if they can once get their creed taught from authority, naturally think that no good, and some harm, comes of its being allowed to be questioned. Where their influence prevails, they make it nearly impossible for the received opinion to be rejected wisely and considerately, though it may still be rejected rashly and ignorantly; for to shut out discussion entirely is seldom possible, and when it once gets in, beliefs not grounded on conviction are apt to give way before the slightest semblance of an argument. Waiving, however, this possibility—assuming that the true opinion abides in the mind, but abides as a prejudice, a belief independent of, and proof against, argument—this is not the way in which truth ought to be held by a rational being. This is not knowing the truth. Truth, thus held, is but one superstition the more, accidentally clinging to the words which enunciate a truth.

If the intellect and judgment of mankind ought to be cultivated, a thing which Protestants at least do not deny, on what can these faculties be more appropriately exercised by anyone, than on the things which concern him so much that it is considered necessary for him to hold opinions on them? If the cultivation of the understanding consists in one thing more than in another, it is surely in learning the grounds of one's own opinions. Whatever people believe, on subjects on which it is of the first importance to believe rightly, they ought to be able to defend against at least the common objections. But, some one may say, "Let them be *taught* the grounds of their opinions. It does not follow that opinions must be merely parroted because they are never heard controverted. Persons who learn geometry do not simply commit the theorems to memory, but understand and learn likewise the demonstrations; and it would be absurd to say that they remain ignorant of the grounds of geometrical truths, because they never hear anyone deny, and attempt to disprove them." Undoubtedly: and such teaching suffices on a subject like mathematics, where there is nothing at all to be said on the wrong side of the question. The peculiarity of the evidence of mathematical truths is that all the argument is on one side. There are no objections, and no answers to objections. But on every subject on which difference of opinion is possible, the truth depends on a balance to be struck between two sets of conflicting reasons. Even in natural philosophy, there is always some other explanation possible of the same facts—some geocentric theory instead of heliocentric, some phlogiston instead of oxygen—and it has to be shown why that other theory cannot be the true one; and until this is shown, and until we know how it is shown, we do not understand the grounds of our opinion. But when we turn to subjects infinitely more complicated, to morals, religion, politics, social relations, and the business of life, three-fourths of the arguments for every disputed opinion consist in dispelling the appearances which favor some opinion different from it. The greatest orator, save one, of antiquity, has left it on record that he always studied his adversary's case with as great, if not still greater, intensity than even his own. What Cicero practiced as the means of forensic success requires to be imitated by all who study any subject in order to arrive at the truth. He who knows only his own side of the case, knows little of that. His reasons may be good, and no one may have been able to refute them. But if he is equally unable to refute the reasons on the opposite side; if he does not so much as know what they are, he has no ground for preferring either opinion. The rational position for him would be suspension of judgment, and unless he contents himself with that, he is either led by authority, or adopts, like the generality of the world, the side to which he feels most inclination. Nor is it enough that he should hear the arguments of adversaries from his own teachers, presented as they state them, and accompanied by what they offer as refutations. That is not the way to do justice to the arguments, or bring them into real contact with his own mind. He must be able to hear them from persons who actually believe them; who defend them in earnest, and do their very utmost for them. He must know them in their most plausible and persuasive form; he must feel the whole force of the difficulty which the true view of the subject has to encounter and dispose of; else he will never really possess himself of the portion of truth which meets and removes that difficulty. Ninety-nine in a hundred of what are called educated men are in this condition; even of those who can argue fluently for their opinions. Their conclusion may be true, but it might be false for anything they know: they have never thrown themselves into the mental position of those who think differently from them, and considered what such persons may have to say; and consequently they do not, in any proper sense of the word, know the doctrine which they themselves profess. They do not know those parts of it which explain and justify the remainder; the considerations which show that a fact which seemingly conflicts with another is reconcilable with it, or that, of two apparently strong reasons, one and not the other ought to be preferred. All that part of the truth which turns the scale, and decides the judgment of a completely informed mind, they are strangers to; nor is it ever really known but to those who have attended equally and impartially to both sides, and endeavored to see the reasons of both in the strongest light. So essential is this discipline to a real understanding of moral and human subjects, that if opponents of all important truths do not exist, it is indispensable to imagine them, and supply them with the strongest arguments which the most skillful devil's advocate can conjure up.[5] . . .

To what an extent doctrines intrinsically fitted to make the deepest impression upon the mind may remain in it as dead beliefs, without being ever realized in the imagination, the feelings, or the understanding, is exemplified by the manner in which the majority of believers hold the doctrines of Christianity. By Christianity I here mean what is accounted such by all churches and sects—the maxims and precepts contained in the New Testament. These are considered sacred, and accepted as laws, by all professing Christians. Yet it is scarcely too much to say that not one Christian in a thousand guides or tests his individual conduct by reference to those laws. The standard to which he does refer it, is the custom of his nation, his class, or his religious profession. He has thus, on the one hand, a collection of ethical maxims, which he believes to have been vouchsafed to him by infallible wisdom as rules for his government; and on the other a set of every-day judgments and practices, which go a certain length with some of those maxims, not so great a length with others, stand in direct opposition to some, and are, on the whole, a compromise between the Christian creed and the interests and suggestions of worldly life. To the first of these standards he gives his homage; to the other his real allegiance. All Christians believe that the blessed are the poor and humble, and those who are ill-used by

[5] The portion here omitted and the remainder of the chapter are concerned mainly with the application of Mill's position to theological discussions. *The Editors.*

the world; that it is easier for a camel to pass through the eye of a needle than for a rich man to enter the kingdom of heaven; that they should judge not, lest they be judged; that they should swear not at all; that they should love their neighbor as themselves; that if one take their cloak, they should give him their coat also; that they should take no thought for the morrow; that if they would be perfect they should sell all that they have and give it to the poor. They are not insincere when they say that they believe these things. They do believe them, as people believe what they have always heard lauded and never discussed. But in the sense of that living belief which regulates conduct, they believe these doctrines just up to the point to which it is usual to act upon them. The doctrines in their integrity are serviceable to pelt adversaries with; and it is understood that they are to be put forward (when possible) as the reasons for whatever people do that they think laudable. But anyone who reminded them that the maxims require an infinity of things which they never even think of doing, would gain nothing but to be classed among those very unpopular characters who affect to be better than other people. The doctrines have no hold on ordinary believers —are not a power in their minds. They have an habitual respect for the sound of them, but no feeling which spreads from the words to the things signified, and forces the mind to take *them* in, and make them conform to the formula. Whenever conduct is concerned, they look round for Mr. A and B to direct them how far to go in obeying Christ.

Now we may be well assured that the case was not thus, but far otherwise, with the early Christians. Had it been thus, Christianity never would have expanded from an obscure sect of the despised Hebrews into the religion of the Roman empire. When their enemies said, "See how these Christians love one another" (a remark not likely to be made by anybody now), they assuredly had a much livelier feeling of the meaning of their creed than they have ever had since. And to this cause, probably, it is chiefly owing that Christianity now makes so little progress in extending its domain, and after eighteen centuries is still nearly confined to Europeans and the descendants of Europeans. Even with the strictly religious, who are much in earnest about their doctrines, and attach a greater amount of meaning to many of them than people in general, it commonly happens that the part which is thus comparatively active in their minds is that which was made by Calvin, or Knox, or some such person much nearer in character to themselves. The sayings of Christ coexist passively in their minds, producing hardly any effect beyond what is caused by mere listening to words so amiable and bland. There are many reasons, doubtless, why doctrines which are the badge of a sect retain more of their vitality than those common to all recognized sects, and why more pains are taken by teachers to keep their meaning alive; but one reason certainly is, that the peculiar doctrines are more questioned, and have to be oftener defended against open gainsayers. Both teachers and learners go to sleep at their post, as soon as there is no enemy in the field.

CHAPTER IV

OF THE LIMITS TO THE AUTHORITY OF SOCIETY

OVER THE INDIVIDUAL

What, then, is the rightful limit to the sovereignty of the individual over himself? Where does the authority of society begin? How much of human life should be assigned to individuality, and how much to society?

Each will receive its proper share, if each has that which more particularly concerns it. To individuality should belong the part of life in which it is chiefly the individual that is interested; to society, the part which chiefly interests society.

Though society is not founded on a contract, and though no good purpose is answered by inventing a contract in order to deduce social obligations from it, everyone who receives the protection of society owes a return for the benefit, and the fact of living in society renders it indispensable that each should be bound to observe a certain line of conduct towards the rest. This conduct consists, *first*, in not injuring the interests of one another; or rather certain interests, which, either by express legal provision or by tacit understanding, ought to be considered as rights; and *secondly*, in each person's bearing his share (to be fixed on some equitable principle) of the labors and sacrifices incurred for defending the society or its members from injury and molestation. These conditions society is justified in enforcing, at all costs to those who endeavor to withhold fulfillment. Nor is this all that society may do. The acts of an individual may be hurtful to others, or wanting in due consideration for their welfare, without going to the length of violating any of their constituted rights. The offender may then be justly punished by opinion, though not by law. As soon as any part of a person's conduct affects prejudicially the interests of others, society has jurisdiction over it, and the question whether the general welfare will or will not be promoted by interfering with it, becomes open to discussion. But there is no room for entertaining any such question when a person's conduct affects the interests of no persons besides himself, or need not affect them unless they like (all the persons concerned being of full age, and the ordinary amount of understanding). In all such cases, there should be perfect freedom, legal and social, to do the action and stand the consequences.

It would be a great misunderstanding of this doctrine to suppose that it is one of selfish indifference, which pretends that human beings have no business with each other's conduct in life, and that they should not concern themselves about the well-doing or well-being of one another, unless their own interest is involved. Instead of any diminution, there is need of a great increase of disinterested exertion to promote the good of others. But disinterested benevolence can find other instruments to persuade people to their good than whips and scourges, either of the literal or the metaphorical sort. I am the last person to undervalue the self-regarding virtues: they are only second in importance, if even second, to the social. It is equally the business of education to cultivate both. But even education works by conviction and persuasion as well as by compulsion, and it is by the former only that, when the period of education is passed, the self-regarding virtues should be inculcated. Human beings owe to each other help to distinguish the better from the worse, and encouragement to choose the former and avoid the latter. They should be forever stimulating each other to increased exercise of their higher faculties, and increased direction of their feelings and aims towards wise instead of foolish, elevating instead of degrading, objects and contemplations. But neither one person, nor any number of persons, is warranted in saying to another human creature of ripe years, that he shall not do with his life for his own benefit what he chooses to do with it. He is the person most interested in his own well-being: the interest which any other person, except in cases of strong personal attachment, can have in it, is trifling, compared with that which he himself has; the interest which society has in him individually (except as to his conduct to others) is fractional, and altogether indirect; while with respect to his own feelings and circumstances, the most ordinary man or woman has means of knowledge immeasurably surpassing those that can be possessed by anyone else. The interference of society to overrule his judgment and purposes in what only regards himself must be grounded on general presumptions; which may be altogether wrong, and even if right, are as likely as not to be misapplied to individual cases, by persons no better acquainted with the circumstances of such cases than those are who look at them merely from without. In this department, therefore, of human affairs, individuality has its proper field of action. In the conduct of human beings towards one another it is necessary that general rules should for the most part be observed, in order that people may know what they have to expect; but in each person's own concerns his individual spontaneity is entitled to free exercise. Considerations to aid his judgment, exhortations to strengthen his will, may be offered to him, even obtruded on him, by others: but he himself is the final judge. All errors which he is likely to commit against advice and warning are far outweighed by the evil of allowing others to constrain him to what they deem his good.

I do not mean that the feelings with which a person is regarded by others ought not to be in any way affected by his self-regarding qualities or deficiencies. This is neither possible nor desirable. If he is eminent in any of the qualities which conduce to his own good, he is, so far, a proper object of admiration. He is so much the nearer to the ideal perfection of human nature. If he is grossly deficient in those qualities, a sentiment the opposite of admiration will follow. There is a degree of folly, and a degree of what may be called (though the phrase is not unobjectionable) lowness or depravation of taste, which, though it cannot justify doing harm to the person who manifests it, renders him necessarily and properly a subject of distaste, or, in extreme cases, even of contempt: a person could not have the opposite qualities in due strength without entertaining these feelings. Though doing no wrong to anyone, a person may so act as to compel us to judge him, and feel to him, as a fool, or as a being of an inferior order; and since this judgment and feeling are a fact which he would prefer to avoid, it is doing him a service to warn him of it beforehand, as of any other disagreeable consequence to which he exposes himself. It would be well, indeed, if this good office were much more freely rendered than the common notions of politeness at present permit, and if one person could honestly point out to another that he thinks him in fault, without being considered unmannerly or presuming. We have a right, also, in various ways, to act upon our unfavorable opinion of anyone, not to the oppression of his individuality, but in the exercise of ours. We are not bound, for example, to seek his society; we have a right to avoid it (though not to parade the avoidance), for we have a right to choose the society most acceptable to us. We have a right, and it may be our duty, to caution others against him, if we think his example or conversation likely to have a pernicious effect on those with whom he associates. We may give others a preference over him in optional good offices, except those which tend to his improvement. In these various modes a person may suffer very severe penalties at the hands of others for faults which directly concern only himself; but he suffers these penalties only in so far as they are the natural and, as it were, the spontaneous consequences of the faults themselves, not because they are purposely inflicted on him for the sake of punishment. A person who shows rashness, obstinacy, self-conceit—who cannot live within moderate means—who cannot restrain himself from hurtful indulgences—who pursues animal pleasures at the expense of those of feeling and intellect—must expect to be lowered in the opinion of others, and to have a less share of their favorable sentiments; but of this he has no right to complain, unless he has merited their favor by special excellence in his social relations, and has thus established a title to their good offices, which is not affected by his demerits towards himself.

What I contend for is, that the inconveniences which are strictly inseparable from the unfavorable judgment of others, are the only ones to which a person should ever be subjected for that portion of his conduct and character which concerns his own good, but which does not affect the interest of others in their relations with him. Acts injurious to others require a totally different treatment. Encroachment on their rights; infliction on them of any loss or damage not justified by his own rights; falsehood or duplicity in dealing with them; unfair or ungenerous use of advantages over them; even selfish abstinence from defending them against injury—these are fit objects of moral reprobation, and, in grave cases, of moral retribution and punishment. And not only these acts, but the dispositions which lead to them, are properly immoral, and fit subjects of disapprobation which may rise to abhorrence. Cruelty of disposition; malice and ill-nature; that most anti-social and odious of all passions, envy; dissimulation and insincerity, irascibility on insufficient cause, and resentment disproportioned to the provocation; the love of domineering over others; the desire to engross more than one's share of advantages (the πλεονεξία of the Greeks); the pride which derives gratification from the abasement of others; the egotism which thinks self and its concerns more important than everything else, and decides all doubtful questions in its own favor;—these are moral vices, and constitute a bad and odious moral character: unlike the self-regarding faults previously mentioned, which are not properly immoralities, and to whatever pitch they may be carried, do not constitute wickedness. They may be proofs of any amount of folly, or want of personal dignity and self-respect; but they are only a subject of moral reprobation when they involve a breach of duty to others, for whose sake the individual is bound to have care for himself. What are called duties to ourselves are not socially obligatory, unless circumstances render them at the same time duties to others. The term "duty to oneself," when it means anything more than prudence, means self-respect or self-development, and for none of these is anyone accountable to his fellow-creatures, because for none of them is it for the good of mankind that he be held accountable to them. . . .

Karl Marx (1818–1883)
and
Friedrich Engels (1820–1895)

*Engels' Preface (1888) to the Manifesto of
the Communist Party*

. . . The Manifesto being our joint production, I consider
myself bound to state that the fundamental proposition, which
forms its nucleus, belongs to Marx. That proposition is that in
every historical epoch the prevailing mode of economic production and exchange and the social organization necessarily
following from it form the basis upon which is built up, and
from which alone can be explained, the political and intellectual history of that epoch; that consequently the whole history
of mankind (since the dissolution of primitive tribal society,
holding land in common ownership) has been a history of
class struggles, contests between exploiting and exploited, ruling and oppressed classes; that the history of these class struggles forms a series of evolutions in which, nowadays, a stage
has been reached where the exploited and oppressed class—
the proletariat—cannot attain its emancipation from the sway of
the exploiting and ruling class—the bourgeoisie—without, at the
same time, and once and for all, emancipating society at
large from all exploitation, oppression, class distinctions, and
class struggles.

This proposition, which, in my opinion, is destined to do
for history what Darwin's theory has done for biology, we,
both of us, had been gradually approaching for some years
before 1845. How far I had independently progressed towards
it is best shown by my *Condition of the Working Class in
England*. But when I again met Marx at Brussels, in spring
1845, he had it already worked out, and put it before me, in
terms almost as clear as those in which I have stated it here.

From our joint preface to the German edition of 1872, I quote the following:

"However much the state of things may have altered during the last twenty-five years, the general principles laid down in this Manifesto are, on the whole, as correct today as ever. Here and there some detail might be improved. The practical application of the principles will depend, as the Manifesto itself states, everywhere and at all times, on the historical conditions for the time being existing, and for that reason no special stress is laid on the revolutionary measures propoood at the end of Section II. That passage would, in many respects, be very differently worded today. In view of the gigantic strides of modern industry since 1848, and of the accompanying improved and extended organization of the working class, in view of the practical experience gained, first in the February revolution, and then, still more, in the Paris Commune, where the proletariat for the first time held political power for two whole months, this program has in some details become antiquated. One thing especially was proved by the Commune, viz., that "the working class cannot simply lay hold of the ready-made state machinery and wield it for its own purposes." (See *The Civil War in France; Address of the General Council of the International Workingmen's Association*, London, Truelove, 1871, page 15, where this point is further developed.) Further, it is self-evident that the criticism of socialist literature is deficient in relation to the present time, because it comes down only to 1847; also, that the remarks on the relation of the communists to the various opposition parties (Section IV), although in principle still correct, yet in practice are antiquated, because the political situation has been entirely changed and the progress of history has swept from off the earth the greater portion of the political parties there enumerated.

"But then, the Manifesto has become a historical document which we have no longer any right to alter."

The present translation is by Mr. Samuel Moore, the translator of the greater portion of Marx's *Capital*. We have revised it in common, and I have added a few notes explanatory of historical allusions.

Marx and Engels:
MANIFESTO OF THE COMMUNIST PARTY

A specter is haunting Europe—the specter of communism. All the powers of old Europe have entered into a holy alliance to exorcise this specter: Pope and Czar, Metternich and Guizot, French radicals and German police spies.

Where is the party in opposition that has not been decried as communistic by its opponents in power? Where the opposition that has not hurled back the branding reproach of communism against the more advanced opposition parties, as well as against its reactionary adversaries?

Two things result from this fact:

I. Communism is already acknowledged by all European powers to be itself a power.

II. It is high time that communists should openly, in the face of the whole world, publish their views, their aims, their tendencies, and meet this nursery tale of the specter of communism with a Manifesto of the party itself.

To this end, communists of various nationalities have assembled in London and sketched the following Manifesto, to be published in the English, French, German, Italian, Flemish, and Danish languages.

I. BOURGEOIS AND PROLETARIANS[1]

The history of all hitherto existing society[2] is the history of class struggles.

[1] By "bourgeoisie" is meant the class of modern capitalists, owners of the means of social production and employers of wage labor. By proletariat, the class of modern wage laborers who, having no means of production of their own, are reduced to selling their labor power in order to live. [Note by Engels to the English edition of 1888.]

[2] That is, all *written* history. In 1847 the pre-history of society, the social organization existing previous to recorded history, was all but unknown. Since then Haxthausen discovered common ownership of land in Russia, Maurer proved it to be the social founda-

Free man and slave, patrician and plebeian, lord and serf, guild master[3] and journeyman, in a word, oppressor and oppressed, stood in constant opposition to one another, carried on an uninterrupted, now hidden, now open fight, a fight that each time ended either in a revolutionary reconstitution of society at large or in the common ruin of the contending classes.

In the earlier epochs of history we find almost everywhere a complicated arrangement of society into various orders, a manifold gradation of social rank. In ancient Rome we have patricians, knights, plebeians, slaves; in the Middle Ages, feudal lords, vassals, guild masters, journeymen, apprentices, serfs; in almost all of these classes, again, subordinate gradations.

The modern bourgeois society that has sprouted from the ruins of feudal society has not done away with class antagonisms. It has but established new classes, new conditions of oppression, new forms of struggle in place of the old ones.

Our epoch, the epoch of the bourgeoisie, possesses, however, this distinctive feature: it has simplified the class antagonisms. Society as a whole is more and more splitting up into two great hostile camps, into two great classes directly facing each other: bourgeoisie and proletariat.

From the serfs of the Middle Ages sprang the chartered burghers of the earliest towns. From these burgesses the first elements of the bourgeoisie were developed.

The discovery of America, the rounding of the Cape opened up fresh ground for the rising bourgeoisie. The East Indian and Chinese markets, the colonization of America, trade with the colonies, the increase in the means of exchange and in

---

tion from which all Teutonic races started in history, and by and by village communities were found to be, or to have been, the primitive form of society everywhere from India to Ireland. The inner organization of this primitive communistic society was laid bare, in its typical form, by Morgan's crowning discovery of the true nature of the *gens* and its relation to the *tribe*. With the dissolution of these primeval communities society begins to be differentiated into separate and finally antagonistic classes. I have attempted to retrace this process of dissolution in *Der Ursprung der Familie, des Privateigenthums und des Staats* [*The Origin of the Family, Private Property and the State*], second edition, Stuttgart, 1886. [Note by Engels to the English edition of 1888.]

[3] Guild master, that is, a full member of a guild, a master within, not a head of a guild. [Note by Engels to the English edition of 1888.]

commodities generally, gave to commerce, to navigation, to industry an impulse never before known, and thereby, to the revolutionary element in the tottering feudal society, a rapid development.

The feudal system of industry, under which industrial production was monopolized by closed guilds, now no longer sufficed for the growing wants of the new markets. The manufacturing system took its place. The guild masters were pushed on one side by the manufacturing middle class; division of labor between the different corporate guilds vanished in the face of division of labor in each single workshop.

Meantime the markets kept ever growing, the demand ever rising. Even manufacture no longer sufficed. Thereupon steam and machinery revolutionized industrial production. The place of manufacture was taken by the giant, modern industry, the place of the industrial middle class by industrial millionaires, the leaders of whole industrial armies, the modern bourgeois.

Modern industry has established the world market, for which the discovery of America paved the way. This market has given an immense development to commerce, to navigation, to communication by land. This development has, in its turn, reacted on the extension of industry; and in proportion as industry, commerce, navigation, railways extended, in the same proportion the bourgeoisie developed, increased its capital, and pushed into the background every class handed down from the Middle Ages.

We see, therefore, how the modern bourgeoisie is itself the product of a long course of development, of a series of revolutions in the modes of production and of exchange.

Each step in the development of the bourgeoisie was accompanied by a corresponding political advance of that class. An oppressed class under the sway of the feudal nobility, an armed and self-governing association in the medieval commune[4]; here independent urban republic (as in Italy and Germany), there taxable "third estate" of the monarchy (as in France), afterwards, in the period of manufacture proper, serving either the semi-feudal or the absolute monarchy as a

4 "Commune" was the name taken, in France, by the nascent towns even before they had conquered from their feudal lords and masters local self-government and political rights as the "third estate." Generally speaking, for the economic development of the bourgeoisie, England is here taken as the typical country; for its political development, France. [Note by Engels to the English edition of 1888.]

counterpoise against the nobility, and, in fact, cornerstone of the great monarchies in general, the bourgeoisie has at last, since the establishment of modern industry and of the world market, conquered for itself, in the modern representative state, exclusive political sway. The executive of the modern state is but a committee for managing the common affairs of the whole bourgeoisie.

The bourgeoisie, historically, has played a most revolutionary part.

The bourgeoisie, wherever it has got the upper hand, has put an end to all feudal, patriarchal, idyllic relations. It has pitilessly torn asunder the motley feudal ties that bound man to his "natural superiors," and has left remaining no other nexus between man and man than naked self-interest, than callous "cash payment." It has drowned the most heavenly ecstasies of religious fervor, of chivalrous enthusiasm, of Philistine sentimentalism in the icy water of egotistical calculation. It has resolved personal worth into exchange value and, in place of the numberless indefeasible chartered freedoms, has set up that single, unconscionable freedom—free trade. In one word, for exploitation, veiled by religious and political illusions, it has substituted naked, shameless, direct, brutal exploitation.

The bourgeoisie has stripped of its halo every occupation hitherto honored and looked up to with reverent awe. It has converted the physician, the lawyer, the priest, the poet, the man of science into its paid wage laborers.

The bourgeoisie has torn away from the family its sentimental veil, and has reduced the family relation to a mere money relation.

The bourgeoisie has disclosed how it came to pass that the brutal display of vigor in the Middle Ages, which reactionists so much admire, found its fitting complement in the most slothful indolence. It has been the first to show what man's activity can bring about. It has accomplished wonders far surpassing Egyptian pyramids, Roman aqueducts, and Gothic cathedrals; it has conducted expeditions that put in the shade all former exoduses of nations and crusades.

The bourgeoisie cannot exist without constantly revolutionizing the instruments of production, and thereby the relations of production, and with them the whole relations of society. Conservation of the old modes of production in unaltered form was, on the contrary, the first condition of existence for all earlier industrial classes. Constant revolutionizing of production, uninterrupted disturbance of all social conditions, everlasting uncertainty and agitation distinguish the bourgeois epoch from all earlier ones. All fixed, fast-frozen relations, with their train of ancient and venerable prejudices and opinions, are swept away, all new-formed ones become antiquated before they can ossify. All that is solid melts into air, all that is holy is profaned, and man is at last compelled to face with sober senses his real conditions of life and his relations with his kind.

The need of a constantly expanding market for its products chases the bourgeoisie over the whole surface of the globe. It must nestle everywhere, settle everywhere, establish connections everywhere.

The bourgeoisie has through its exploitation of the world market given a cosmopolitan character to production and consumption in every country. To the great chagrin of reactionists, it has drawn from under the feet of industry the national ground on which it stood. All old-established national industries have been destroyed or are daily being destroyed. They are dislodged by new industries, whose introduction becomes a life and death question for all civilized nations, by industries that no longer work up indigenous raw material, but raw material drawn from the remotest zones; industries whose products are consumed not only at home, but in every quarter of the globe. In place of the old wants, satisfied by the productions of the country, we find new wants, requiring for their satisfaction the products of distant lands and climes. In place of the old local and national seclusion and self-sufficiency we have intercourse in every direction, universal interdependence of nations. And as in material, so also in intellectual production. The intellectual creations of individual nations become common property. National one-sidedness and narrow-mindedness become more and more impossible, and from the numerous national and local literatures there arises a world literature.

The bourgeoisie, by the rapid improvement of all instruments of production, by the immensely facilitated means of communication, draws all, even the most barbarian, nations into civilization. The cheap prices of its commodities are the heavy artillery with which it batters down all Chinese walls, with which it forces the barbarians' intensely obstinate hatred of foreigners to capitulate. It compels all nations, on pain of extinction, to adopt the bourgeois mode of production; it compels them to introduce what it calls civilization into their midst, i.e., to become bourgeois themselves. In one word, it creates a world after its own image.

The bourgeoisie has subjected the country to the rule of the towns. It has created enormous cities, has greatly increased the urban population as compared with the rural, and has thus rescued a considerable part of the population from the idiocy of rural life. Just as it has made the country dependent on the towns, so it has made barbarian and semi-barbarian countries dependent on the civilized ones, nations of peasants on nations of bourgeois, the East on the West.

The bourgeoisie keeps more and more doing away with the scattered state of the population, of the means of production, and of property. It has agglomerated population, centralized means of production, and has concentrated property in a few hands. The necessary consequence of this was political centralization. Independent, or but loosely connected provinces, with separate interests, laws, governments and systems of taxation, became lumped together into one nation, with one government, one code of laws, one national class interest, one frontier, and one customs tariff.

The bourgeoisie, during its rule of scarce one hundred years, has created more massive and more colossal productive forces than have all preceding generations together. Subjection of nature's forces to man, machinery, application of chemistry to industry and agriculture, steam navigation, railways, electric telegraphs, clearing of whole continents for cultivation, canalization of rivers, whole populations conjured out of the ground —what earlier century had even a presentiment that such productive forces slumbered in the lap of social labor?

We see then: the means of production and of exchange, on whose foundation the bourgeoisie built itself up, were generated in feudal society. At a certain stage in the development of these means of production and of exchange, the conditions under which feudal society produced and exchanged, the feudal organization of agriculture and manufacturing industry, in one word, the feudal relations of property, became no longer compatible with the already developed productive forces; they became so many fetters. They had to be burst asunder; they were burst asunder.

Into their place stepped free competition, accompanied by a social and political constitution adapted to it, and by the economic and political sway of the bourgeois class.

A similar movement is going on before our own eyes. Modern bourgeois society with its relations of production, of exchange, and of property, a society that has conjured up such gigantic means of production and of exchange, is like the sorcerer who is no longer able to control the powers of the nether world whom he has called up by his spells. For many a decade past, the history of industry and commerce is but the history of the revolt of modern productive forces against modern conditions of production, against the property relations that are the conditions for the existence of the bourgeoisie and of its rule. It is enough to mention the commercial crises that by their periodic return put on its trial, each time more threateningly, the existence of the entire bourgeois society. In these crises a great part not only of the existing products but also of the previously created productive forces are periodically destroyed. In these crises there breaks out an epidemic that in all earlier epochs would have seemed an absurdity—the epidemic of overproduction. Society suddenly finds itself put back into a state of momentary barbarism; it appears as if a famine, a universal war of devastation had cut off the supply of every means of subsistence; industry and commerce seem to be destroyed; and why? Because there is too much civilization, too much means of subsistence, too much industry, too much commerce. The productive forces at the disposal of society no longer tend to further the development of the conditions of bourgeois property; on the contrary, they have become too powerful for these conditions, by which they are fettered, and as soon as they overcome these fetters they bring disorder into the whole of bourgeois society, endanger the existence of bourgeois property. The conditions of bourgeois society are too narrow to comprise the wealth created by them. And how does the bourgeoisie get over these crises? On the one hand, by enforced destruction of a mass of productive forces; on the other, by the conquest of new markets, and by the more thorough exploitation of the old ones. That is to say, by paving the way for more extensive and more destructive crises, and by diminishing the means whereby crises are prevented.

The weapons with which the bourgeoisie felled feudalism to the ground are now turned against the bourgeoisie itself.

But not only has the bourgeoisie forged the weapons that bring death to itself; it has also called into existence the men who are to wield those weapons—the modern working class—the proletarians.

In proportion as the bourgeoisie, i.e., capital, is developed, in the same proportion is the proletariat, the modern working class, developed—a class of laborers, who live only so long as they find work, and who find work only so long as their labor increases capital. These laborers, who must sell themselves piecemeal, are a commodity, like every other article of commerce, and are consequently exposed to all the vicissitudes of competition, to all the fluctuations of the market.

Owing to the extensive use of machinery and to division of labor, the work of the proletarians has lost all individual character and, consequently, all charm for the workman. He becomes an appendage of the machine, and it is only the simplest, most monotonous, and most easily acquired knack that is required of him. Hence the cost of production of a workman is restricted, almost entirely, to the means of subsistence that he requires for his maintenance and for the propagation of his race. But the price of a commodity, and therefore also of labor, is equal to its cost of production. In proportion, therefore, as the repulsiveness of the work increases, the wage decreases. Nay, more, in proportion as the use of machinery and division of labor increases, in the same proportion the burden of toil also increases, whether by prolongation of the working hours, by increase of the work exacted in a given time, or by increased speed of the machinery, etc.

Modern industry has converted the little workshop of the patriarchal master into the great factory of the industrial capitalist. Masses of laborers, crowded into the factory, are organized like soldiers. As privates of the industrial army they are placed under the command of a perfect hierarchy of officers and sergeants. Not only are they slaves of the bourgeois class, and of the bourgeois state; they are daily and hourly enslaved by the machine, by the overlooker, and, above all, by the individual bourgeois manufacturer himself. The more openly this despotism proclaims gain to be its end and aim, the more petty, the more hateful, and the more embittering it is.

The less the skill and exertion of strength implied in manual labor, in other words, the more modern industry becomes developed, the more is the labor of men superseded by that of women. Differences of age and sex have no longer any distinctive social validity for the working class. All are instruments of labor, more or less expensive to use, according to their age and sex.

No sooner is the exploitation of the laborer by the manufacturer over, to the extent that he receives his wages in cash, than he is set upon by the other portions of the bourgeoisie, the landlord, the shopkeeper, the pawnbroker, etc.

The lower strata of the middle class—the small tradespeople, shopkeepers, and retired tradesmen generally, the handicraftsmen and peasants—all these sink gradually into the proletariat, partly because their diminutive capital does not suffice for the scale on which modern industry is carried on, and is swamped in the competition with the large capitalists, partly because their specialized skill is rendered worthless by new methods of production. Thus the proletariat is recruited from all classes of the population.

The proletariat goes through various stages of development. With its birth begins its struggle with the bourgeoisie. At first the contest is carried on by individual laborers, then by the workpeople of a factory, then by the operatives of one trade, in one locality, against the individual bourgeois who directly exploits them. They direct their attacks not against the bourgeois conditions of production, but against the instruments of production themselves; they destroy imported wares that compete with their labor, they smash to pieces machinery, they set factories ablaze, they seek to restore by force the vanished status of the workman of the Middle Ages.

At this stage the laborers still form an incoherent mass scattered over the whole country and broken up by their mutual competition. If anywhere they unite to form more compact bodies, this is not yet the consequence of their own active union, but of the union of the bourgeoisie, which class, in order to attain its own political ends, is compelled to set the whole proletariat in motion, and is moreover yet, for a time, able to do so. At this stage, therefore, the proletarians do not fight their enemies, but the enemies of their enemies, the remnants of absolute monarchy, the landowners, the non-industrial bourgeois, the petty bourgeoisie. Thus the whole historical movement is concentrated in the hands of the bourgeoisie; every victory so obtained is a victory for the bourgeoisie.

But with the development of industry the proletariat not only increases in number; it becomes concentrated in greater masses, its strength grows, and it feels that strength more. The various interests and conditions of life within the ranks of the proletariat are more and more equalized, in proportion as machinery obliterates all distinctions of labor and nearly everywhere reduces wages to the same low level. The growing competition among the bourgeois and the resulting commercial crises make the wages of the workers ever more fluctuating. The unceasing improvement of machinery, ever more rapidly developing, makes their livelihood more and more precarious; the collisions between individual workmen and individual bourgeois take more and more the character of collisions between two classes. Thereupon the workers begin to form combinations (trade unions) against the bourgeois; they club together in order to keep up the rate of wages; they found permanent associations in order to make provision beforehand for these occasional revolts. Here and there the contest breaks out into riots.

Now and then the workers are victorious, but only for a time. The real fruit of their battles lies not in the immediate result, but in the ever expanding union of the workers. This union is helped on by the improved means of communication that are created by modern industry and that place the workers of different localities in contact with one another. It was just this contact that was needed to centralize the numerous local struggles, all of the same character, into one national struggle between classes. But every class struggle is a political struggle. And that union, to attain which the burghers of the Middle Ages, with their miserable highways, required centuries, the modern proletarians, thanks to railways, achieve in a few years.

This organization of the proletarians into a class, and consequently into a political party, is continually being upset again by the competition between the workers themselves. But it ever rises up again, stronger, firmer, mightier. It compels legislative recognition of particular interests of the workers by taking advantage of the divisions among the bourgeoisie itself. Thus the ten-hour bill in England was carried.

Altogether collisions between the classes of the old society further, in many ways, the course of development of the proletariat. The bourgeoisie finds itself involved in a constant battle. At first with the aristocracy; later on, with those portions of the bourgeoisie itself whose interests have become antagonistic to the progress of industry; at all times, with the bourgeoisie of foreign countries. In all these battles it sees itself compelled to appeal to the proletariat, to ask for its help, and thus to drag it into the political arena. The bourgeoisie itself, therefore, supplies the proletariat with its own elements of political and general education: in other words, it furnishes the proletariat with weapons for fighting the bourgeoisie.

Further, as we have already seen, entire sections of the ruling classes are, by the advance of industry, precipitated into the proletariat, or are at least threatened in their conditions of existence. These also supply the proletariat with fresh elements of enlightenment and progress.

Finally, in times when the class struggle nears the decisive hour, the process of dissolution going on within the ruling class, in fact within the whole range of old society, assumes such a violent, glaring character that a small section of the ruling class cuts itself adrift and joins the revolutionary class, the class that holds the future in its hands. Just as, therefore, at an earlier period, a section of the nobility went over to the bourgeoisie, so now a portion of the bourgeoisie goes over to the proletariat, and in particular a portion of the bourgeois ideologists, who have raised themselves to the level of comprehending theoretically the historical movement as a whole.

Of all the classes that stand face to face with the bourgeoisie today, the proletariat alone is a really revolutionary class. The other classes decay and finally disappear in the face of modern industry; the proletariat is its special and essential product.

The lower-middle class, the small manufacturer, the shopkeeper, the artisan, the peasant, all these fight against the bourgeoisie, to save from extinction their existence as fractions of the middle class. They are therefore not revolutionary, but conservative. Nay, more, they are reactionary, for they try to roll back the wheel of history. If by chance they are revolutionary they are so only in view of their impending transfer into the proletariat; they thus defend not their present but their future interests, they desert their own standpoint to place themselves at that of the proletariat.

The "dangerous class," the social scum, that passively rotting mass thrown off by the lowest layers of old society, may, here and there, be swept into the movement by a proletarian revolution; its conditions of life, however, prepare it far more for the part of a bribed tool of reactionary intrigue.

In the conditions of the proletariat those of old society at large are already virtually swamped. The proletarian is without property; his relation to his wife and children has no longer anything in common with the bourgeois family relations; modern industrial labor, modern subjection to capital, the same in England as in France, in America as in Germany, has stripped him of every trace of national character. Law, morality, religion are to him so many bourgeois prejudices, behind which lurk in ambush just as many bourgeois interests.

All the preceding classes that got the upper hand sought to fortify their already acquired status by subjecting society at large to their conditions of appropriation. The proletarians cannot become masters of the productive forces of society, except by abolishing their own previous mode of appropriation, and thereby also every other previous mode of appropriation. They have nothing of their own to secure and to fortify; their mission is to destroy all previous securities for, and insurances of, individual property.

All previous historical movements were movements of minorities, or in the interest of minorities. The proletarian movement is the self-conscious, independent movement of the immense majority, in the interests of the immense majority. The proletariat, the lowest stratum of our present society, cannot stir, cannot raise itself up, without the whole superincumbent strata of official society being sprung into the air.

Though not in substance, yet in form, the struggle of the proletariat with the bourgeoisie is at first a national struggle. The proletariat of each country must, of course, first of all settle matters with its own bourgeoisie.

In depicting the most general phases of the development of the proletariat, we traced the more or less veiled civil war, raging within existing society, up to the point where that war breaks out into open revolution, and where the violent overthrow of the bourgeoisie lays the foundation for the sway of the proletariat.

Hitherto every form of society has been based, as we have already seen, on the antagonism of oppressing and oppressed classes. But in order to oppress a class certain conditions must be assured to it under which it can, at least, continue its slavish existence. The serf, in the period of serfdom, raised himself to membership in the commune, just as the petty bourgeois, under the yoke of feudal absolutism, managed to develop into a bourgeois. The modern laborer, on the contrary, instead of rising with the progress of industry, sinks deeper and deeper below the conditions of existence of his own class. He becomes a pauper, and pauperism develops more rapidly than population and wealth. And here it becomes evident that the bourgeoisie is unfit any longer to be the ruling class in society, and to impose its conditions of existence upon society as an overriding law. It is unfit to rule because it is incompetent to assure an existence to its slave within his slavery, because it cannot help letting him sink into such a state that it has to feed him instead of being fed by him. Society can no longer live under this bourgeoisie: in other words, its existence is no longer compatible with society.

The essential condition for the existence, and for the sway of the bourgeois class, is the formation and augmentation of capital; the condition for capital is wage labor. Wage labor rests exclusively on competition between the laborers. The advance of industry, whose involuntary promoter is the bourgeoisie, replaces the isolation of the laborers, due to competition, by their revolutionary combination, due to association. The development of modern industry, therefore, cuts from under its feet the very foundation on which the bourgeoisie produces and appropriates products. What the bourgeoisie, therefore, produces, above all, is its own gravediggers. Its fall and the victory of the proletariat are equally inevitable.

Engels:
SOCIALISM: UTOPIAN AND SCIENTIFIC[1]

I

Modern socialism is, in its essence, the direct product of the recognition, on the one hand, of the class antagonisms existing in the society of today between proprietors and non-proprietors, between capitalists and wage workers; on the other hand, of the anarchy existing in production. But in its theoretical form modern socialism originally appears ostensibly as a more logical extension of the principles laid down by the great French philosophers of the eighteenth century. Like every new theory, modern socialism had, at first, to connect itself with the intellectual stock in trade ready to its hand, however deeply its roots lay in material economic facts.

The great men, who in France prepared men's minds for the coming revolution, were themselves extreme revolutionists. They recognized no external authority of any kind whatever. Religion, natural science, society, political institutions—everything was subjected to the most unsparing criticism: everything must justify its existence before the judgment seat of reason or give up existence. Reason became the sole measure of everything. It was the time when, as Hegel says, the world stood upon its head;[2] first in the sense that the human head,

[1] A booklet composed of three chapters from Engels' "Anti-Dühring." *The Editors.*

[2] This is the passage on the French Revolution: "Thought, the concept of law, all at once made itself felt, and against this the old scaffolding of wrong could make no stand. In this conception of law, therefore, a constitution has now been established, and henceforth everything must be based upon this. Since the sun had been in the firmament, and the planets circled round him, the sight had never been seen of man standing upon his head—i.e., on the Idea—and building reality after this image. Anaxagoras first said that the nous, reason, rules the world; but now, for the first time, had man come to recognize that the Idea must rule the mental

and the principles arrived at by its thought, claimed to be the basis of all human action and association; but by and by, also, in the wider sense that the reality which was in contradiction to these principles had, in fact, to be turned upside down. Every form of society and government then existing, every old traditional notion was flung into the lumber room as irrational; the world had hitherto allowed itself to be led solely by prejudices; everything in the past deserved only pity and contempt. Now, for the first time, appeared the light of day, the kingdom of reason; henceforth superstition, injustice, privilege, oppression were to be superseded by eternal truth, eternal right, equality based on nature and the inalienable rights of man.

We know today that this kingdom of reason was nothing more than the idealized kingdom of the bourgeoisie; that this eternal right found its realization in bourgeois justice; that this equality reduced itself to bourgeois equality before the law; that bourgeois property was proclaimed as one of the essential rights of man; and that the government of reason, the *contrat social* of Rousseau, came into being, and only could come into being, as a democratic bourgeois republic. The great thinkers of the eighteenth century could, no more than their predecessors, go beyond the limits imposed upon them by their epoch.

But, side by side with the antagonism of the feudal nobility and the burghers, who claimed to represent all the rest of society, was the general antagonism of exploiters and exploited, of rich idlers and poor workers. It was this very circumstance that made it possible for the representatives of the bourgeoisie to put themselves forward as representing not one special class, but the whole of suffering humanity. Still further. From its origin the bourgeoisie was saddled with its antithesis: capitalists cannot exist without wage workers, and, in the same proportion as the medieval burgher of the guild developed into the modern bourgeois, the guild journeyman and the day laborer, outside the guilds, developed into the proletarian. And although, upon the whole, the bourgeoisie, in their

---

reality. And this was a magnificent sunrise. All thinking beings have participated in celebrating this holy day. A sublime emotion swayed men at that time, an enthusiasm of reason pervaded the world, as if now had come the reconciliation of the Divine Principle with the world." [Hegel: *Philosophy of History*, 1840, p. 535.] Is it not high time to set the anti-socialist law in action against such teachings, subversive and to the common danger, by the late Professor Hegel?

struggle with the nobility, could claim to represent at the same time the interests of the different working classes of that period, yet in every great bourgeois movement there were independent outbursts of that class which was the forerunner, more or less developed, of the modern proletariat. For example, at the time of the German Reformation and the Peasants' War, the Anabaptists and Thomas Münzer; in the great English Revolution, the Levelers; in the great French Revolution, Babeuf.

There were theoretical enunciations corresponding with these revolutionary uprisings of a class not yet developed: in the sixteenth and seventeenth centuries, utopian pictures of ideal social conditions; in the eighteenth, actual communistic theories (Morelly and Mably). The demand for equality was no longer limited to political rights; it was extended also to the social conditions of individuals. It was not simply class privileges that were to be abolished, but class distinctions themselves. A communism, ascetic, denouncing all the pleasures of life, Spartan, was the first form of the new teaching. Then came the three great Utopians: St. Simon, to whom the middle-class movement, side by side with the proletarian, still had a certain significance; Fourier; and Owen, who in the country where capitalist production was most developed, and under the influence of the antagonisms begotten of this, worked out his proposals for the removal of class distinction systematically and in direct relation to French materialism.

One thing is common to all three. Not one of them appears as a representative of the interests of that proletariat which historical development had, in the meantime, produced. Like the French philosophers, they do not claim to emancipate a particular class to begin with, but all humanity at once. Like them, they wish to bring in the kingdom of reason and eternal justice, but this kingdom, as they see it, is as far as heaven from earth from that of the French philosophers.

For, to our three social reformers, the bourgeois world, based upon the principles of these philosophers, is quite as irrational and unjust and, therefore, finds its way to the dust hole quite as readily as feudalism and all the earlier stages of society. If pure reason and justice have not hitherto ruled the world, this has been the case only because men have not rightly understood them. What was wanted was the individual man of genius, who has now arisen and who understands the truth. That he has now arisen, that the truth has now been clearly understood, is not an inevitable event, following of necessity in the chain of historical development, but a mere happy accident. He might just as well have been born five hundred years earlier, and might then have spared humanity five hundred years of error, strife, and suffering.

We saw how the French philosophers of the eighteenth century, the forerunners of the Revolution, appealed to reason as the sole judge of all that is. A rational government, rational society were to be founded; everything that ran counter to eternal reason was to be remorselessly done away with. We saw also that this eternal reason was in reality nothing but the idealized understanding of the eighteenth-century citizen, just then evolving into the bourgeois. The French Revolution had realized this rational society and government.

But the new order of things, rational enough as compared with earlier conditions, turned out to be by no means absolutely rational. The state based upon reason completely collapsed. Rousseau's *contrat social* had found its realization in the Reign of Terror, from which the bourgeoisie, who had lost confidence in their own political capacity, had taken refuge first in the corruption of the Directorate, and, finally, under the wing of the Napoleonic despotism. The promised eternal peace was turned into an endless war of conquest. The society based upon reason had fared no better. The antagonism between rich and poor, instead of dissolving into general prosperity, had become intensified by the removal of the guild and other privileges, which had to some extent bridged it, and by the removal of the charitable institutions of the Church. The "freedom of property" from feudal fetters, now veritably accomplished, turned out to be, for the small capitalists and small proprietors, the freedom to sell their small property, crushed under the overmastering competition of the large capitalists and landlords, to these great lords, and thus, as far as the small capitalists and peasant proprietors were concerned, became "freedom *from* property." The development of industry upon a capitalistic basis made poverty and misery of the working masses conditions of existence of society. Cash payment became more and more, in Carlyle's phrase, "the sole nexus between man and man." The number of crimes increased from year to year. Formerly the feudal vices had openly stalked about in broad daylight; though not eradicated, they were now at any rate thrust into the background. In their stead the bourgeois vices, hitherto practiced in secret, began to blossom all the more luxuriantly. Trade became to a greater and greater extent cheating. The "fraternity" of the revolutionary motto was realized in the chicanery and rivalries of the battle of competition. Oppression by force was replaced by corruption; the sword, as the first social lever, by gold. The right of the first night was transferred from the feudal lords to the bourgeois manufacturers. Prostitution increased to an extent never heard of. Marriage itself remained, as before, the legally recognized form, the official cloak of prostitution, and, moreover, was supplemented by rich crops of adultery.

In a word, compared with the splendid promises of the philosophers, the social and political institutions born of the "triumph of reason" were bitterly disappointing caricatures. All that was wanting was the men to formulate this disappointment, and they came with the turn of the century. In 1802, St. Simon's Geneva letters appeared; in 1808 appeared Fourier's first work, although the groundwork of his theory dated from 1799; on January 1, 1800, Robert Owen undertook the direction of New Lanark.

At this time, however, the capitalist mode of production, and with it the antagonism between the bourgeoisie and the proletariat, was still very incompletely developed. Modern industry, which had just arisen in England, was still unknown in France. But modern industry develops, on the one hand, the conflicts which make absolutely necessary a revolution in the mode of production and the doing away with its capitalistic character—conflicts not only between the classes begotten of it, but also between the very productive forces and the forms of exchange created by it. And, on the other hand, it develops, in these very gigantic productive forces, the means of ending these conflicts. If, therefore, about the year 1800 the conflicts arising from the new social order were only just beginning to take shape, this holds still more fully as to the means of ending them. The "have-nothing" masses of Paris, during the Reign of Terror, were able for a moment to gain the mastery, and thus to lead the bourgeois revolution to victory in spite of the bourgeoisie themselves. But in doing so they only proved how impossible it was for their domination to last under the conditions then obtaining. The proletariat, which then for the first time evolved from these "have-nothing" masses as the nucleus of a new class, as yet quite incapable of independent political action, appeared as an oppressed, suffering order, to which, in its incapacity to help itself, help could, at best, be brought in from without or down from above.

This historical situation also dominated the founders of socialism. To the crude conditions of capitalistic production and the crude class conditions corresponded crude theories. The solution of the social problems, which as yet lay hidden in undeveloped economic conditions, the Utopians attempted to evolve out of the human brain. Society presented nothing but wrongs; to remove these was the task of reason. It was necessary, then, to discover a new and more perfect system of social order and to impose this upon society from without by propaganda, and, wherever it was possible, by the example of model experiments. These new social systems were foredoomed as utopian; the more completely they were worked out in detail, the more they could not avoid drifting off into pure fantasies. . . .[8]

III

The materialist conception of history starts from the proposition that the production of the means to support human life—and, next to production, the exchange of things produced —is the basis of all social structure; that in every society that has appeared in history, the manner in which wealth is distributed and society divided into classes or orders is dependent upon what is produced, how it is produced, and how the products are exchanged. From this point of view the final causes of all social changes and political revolutions are to be sought not in men's brains, not in man's better insight into eternal truth and justice, but in changes in the modes of production and exchange. They are to be sought not in the *philosophy,* but in the *economics* of each particular epoch. The growing perception that existing social institutions are unreasonable and unjust, that reason has become unreason and right wrong, is only proof that in the modes of production and exchange changes have silently taken place with which the social order, adapted to earlier economic conditions, is no longer in keep-

[8] The portion here omitted is concerned chiefly with characterizations of the work of St. Simon, Fourier, Owen, and Hegel, treating of these figures as predecessors of Marx. Engels concludes Section II with the statement: "These two great discoveries, the materialist conception of history and the revelation of the secret of capitalistic production through surplus value, we owe to Marx. With these discoveries socialism became a science. The next thing was to work out all its details and relations." *The Editors.*

ing. From this it also follows that the means of getting rid of the incongruities that have been brought to light must also be present, in a more or less developed condition, within the changed modes of production themselves. These means are not to be invented by deduction from fundamental principles, but are to be discovered in the stubborn facts of the existing system of production.

What is, then, the position of modern socialism in this connection?

The present structure of society—this is now pretty generally conceded—is the creation of the ruling class of today, of the bourgeoisie. The mode of production peculiar to the bourgeoisie, known, since Marx, as the capitalist mode of production, was incompatible with the feudal system, with the privileges it conferred upon individuals, entire social ranks, and local corporations, as well as with the hereditary ties of subordination which constituted the framework of its social organization. The bourgeoisie broke up the feudal system and built upon its ruins the capitalist order of society, the kingdom of free competition, of personal liberty, of the equality, before the law, of all commodity owners, of all the rest of the capitalist blessings. Thenceforward the capitalist mode of production could develop in freedom. Since steam, machinery, and the making of machines by machinery transformed the older manufacture into modern industry, the productive forces evolved under the guidance of the bourgeoisie developed with a rapidity and in a degree unheard of before. But just as the older manufacture, in its time, and handicraft, becoming more developed under its influence, had come into collision with the feudal trammels of the guilds, so now modern industry, in its more complete development, comes into collision with the bounds within which the capitalistic mode of production holds it confined. The new productive forces have already outgrown the capitalistic mode of using them. And this conflict between productive forces and modes of production is not a conflict engendered in the mind of man, like that between original sin and divine justice. It exists, in fact, objectively, outside us, independently of the will and actions even of the men who have brought it on. Modern socialism is nothing but the reflex in thought of this conflict in fact; its ideal reflection in the minds, first, of the class directly suffering under it, the working class.

Now in what does this conflict consist?

Before capitalistic production, i.e., in the Middle Ages, the system of petty industry obtained generally, based upon the private property of the laborers in their means of production; in the country, the agriculture of the small peasant, free man, or serf; in the towns, the handicrafts organized in guilds. The instruments of labor—land, agricultural implements, the workshop, the tool—were the instruments of labor of single individuals, adapted for the use of one worker, and, therefore, of necessity, small, dwarfish, circumscribed. But for this very reason they belonged, as a rule, to the producer himself. To concentrate these scattered, limited means of production, to enlarge them, to turn them into the powerful levers of production of the present day—this was precisely the historic role of capitalist production and of its upholder, the bourgeoisie. In the fourth section of *Capital*, Marx has explained in detail how since the fifteenth century this has been historically worked out through the three phases of simple co-operation, manufacture, and modern industry. But the bourgeoisie, as is also shown there, could not transform these puny means of production into mighty productive forces without transforming them, at the same time, from means of production of the individual into *social* means of production workable only by a collectivity of men. The spinning wheel, the hand loom, the blacksmith's hammer were replaced by the spinning machine, the power loom, the steam hammer; the individual workshop, by the factory, implying the co-operation of hundreds and thousands of workmen. In like manner production itself changed from a series of individual into a series of social acts, and the products from individual to social products. The yarn, the cloth, the metal articles that now came out of the factory were the joint product of many workers, through whose hands they successively had to pass before they were ready. No one person could say of them: "I made that; this is *my* product."

But where, in a given society, the fundamental form of production is that spontaneous division of labor which creeps in gradually and not upon any preconceived plan, there the products take on the form of *commodities,* whose mutual exchange, buying and selling, enable the individual producers to satisfy their manifold wants. And this was the case in the Middle Ages. The peasant, e.g., sold to the artisan agricultural products and bought from him the products of handicraft. Into this society of individual producers, of commodity producers, the new mode of production thrust itself. In the midst of the old division of labor, grown up spontaneously and upon *no definite plan,* which had governed the whole of society, now arose division of labor upon a *definite plan,* as organized in the factory; side by side with *individual* production appeared *social* production. The products of both were sold in the same market, and, therefore, at prices at least approximately equal. But organization upon a definite plan was stronger than spontaneous division of labor. The factories working with the combined social forces of a collectivity of individuals produced their commodities far more cheaply than the individual small producers. Individual production succumbed in one department after another. Socialized production revolutionized all 𝑓𝑓𝑌 the old methods of production. But its revolutionary character was, at the same time, so little recognized that it was, on the contrary, introduced as a means of increasing and developing the production of commodities. When it arose it found ready-made, and made liberal use of, certain machinery for the production and exchange of commodities: merchants' capital, handicraft, wage labor. Socialized production thus introducing itself as a new form of the production of commodities, it was a matter of course that under it the old forms of appropriation remained in full swing and were applied to its products as well.

In the medieval stage of evolution of the production of commodities the question as to the owner of the product of labor could not arise. The individual producer, as a rule, had, from raw material belonging to himself and generally his own handiwork, produced it with his own tools, by the labor of his own hands or of his family. There was no need for him to appropriate the new product. It belonged wholly to him, as a matter of course. His property in the product was, therefore, based *upon his own labor*. Even where external help was used, this was, as a rule, of little importance, and very generally was compensated by something other than wages. The apprentices and journeymen of the guilds worked less for board and wages than for education, in order that they might become master craftsmen themselves.

Then came the concentration of the means of production and of the producers in large workshops and manufactories, their transformation into actual socialized means of production and socialized producers. But the socialized producers and means of production and their products were still treated, after this change, just as they had been before, i.e., as the means of production and the products of individuals. Hitherto the owner of the instruments of labor had himself appropriated the product because, as a rule, it was his own product and the assistance of others was the exception. Now the owner of the instruments of labor always appropriated to himself the product, although it was no longer *his* product, but exclusively the product of the *labor of others*. Thus the products now produced socially were not appropriated by those who had actually set in motion the means of production and actually produced the commodities, but by the *capitalists*. The means of production, and production itself, had become in essence socialized. But they were subjected to a form of appropriation which presupposes the private production of individuals, under which, therefore, everyone owns his own product and brings it to market. The mode of production is subjected to this form of appropriation, although it abolishes the conditions upon which the latter rests.[4]

This contradiction, which gives to the new mode of production its capitalistic character, *contains the germ of the whole of the social antagonisms of today*. The greater the mastery obtained by the new mode of production over all important fields of production and in all manufacturing countries, the more it reduced individual production to an insignificant residuum, *the more clearly was brought out the incompatibility of socialized production with capitalistic appropriation*.

The first capitalists found, as we have said, alongside of other forms of labor, wage labor ready-made for them on the market. But it was exceptional, complementary, accessory, transitory wage labor. The agricultural laborer, though upon occasion he hired himself out by the day, had a few acres of his own land on which he could at all events live in a pinch. The guilds were so organized that the journeyman of today became the master of tomorrow. But all this changed as soon as the means of production became socialized and concentrated in the hands of capitalists. The means of production, as well as the product, of the individual producer became more and more worthless; there was nothing left for him but to turn wage worker under the

---

[4] It is hardly necessary in this connection to point out that, even if the form of appropriation remains the same, the *character* of the appropriation is just as much revolutionized as production is by the changes described above. It is, of course, a very different matter whether I appropriate to myself my own product or that of another. Note in passing that wage labor, which contains the whole capitalistic mode of production in embryo, is very ancient; in a sporadic, scattered form it existed for centuries alongside of slave labor. But the embryo could duly develop into the capitalistic mode of production only when the necessary historical preconditions had been furnished.

capitalist. Wage labor, aforetime the exception and accessory, now became the rule and basis of all production; aforetime complementary, it now became the sole remaining function of the worker. The wage worker for a time became a wage worker for life. The number of these permanent wage workers was further enormously increased by the breaking up of the feudal system that occurred at the same time, by the disbanding of the retainers of the feudal lords, the eviction of the peasants from their homesteads, etc. The separation was made complete between the means of production, concentrated in the hands of the capitalists, on the one side, and the producers, possessing nothing but their labor power, on the other. *The contradiction between socialized production and capitalistic appropriation manifested itself as the antagonism of proletariat and bourgeoisie.*

We have seen that the capitalistic mode of production thrust its way into a society of commodity producers, of individual producers, whose social bond was the exchange of their products. But every society based upon the production of commodities has this peculiarity: that the producers have lost control over their own social interrelations. Each man produces for himself with such means of production as he may happen to have, and for such exchange as he may require to satisfy his remaining wants. No one knows how much of his particular article is coming on the market, nor how much of it will be wanted. No one knows whether his individual product will meet an actual demand, whether he will be able to make good his costs of production or even to sell his commodity at all. Anarchy reigns in socialized production. ⟶⟵

But the production of commodities, like every other form of production, has its peculiar, inherent laws inseparable from it; and these laws work, despite anarchy, in and through anarchy. They reveal themselves in the only persistent form of social interrelations, i.e., in exchange, and here they affect the individual producers as compulsory laws of competition. They are, at first, unknown to these producers themselves, and have to be discovered by them gradually and as the result of experience. They work themselves out, therefore, independently of the producers, and in antagonism to them, as inexorable natural laws of their particular form of production. The product governs the producers.

In medieval society, especially in the earlier centuries, production was essentially directed towards satisfying the wants of the individual. It satisfied, in the main, only the wants of the producer and his family. Where relations of personal dependence existed, as in the country, it also helped to satisfy the wants of the feudal lord. In all this there was, therefore, no exchange; the products, consequently, did not assume the character of commodities. The family of the peasant produced almost everything it wanted: clothes and furniture, as well as means of subsistence. Only when it began to produce more than was sufficient to supply its own wants and the payments in kind to the feudal lord, only then did it also produce commodities. This surplus, thrown into socialized exchange and offered for sale, became commodities.

The artisans of the towns, it is true, had from the first to produce for exchange. But they, also, themselves supplied the greatest part of their own individual wants. They had gardens and plots of land. They turned their cattle out into the communal forest, which, also, yielded them timber and firing. The women spun flax, wool, and so forth. Production for the purpose of exchange, production of commodities, was only in its infancy. Hence exchange was restricted, the market narrow, the methods of production stable; there was local exclusiveness without, local unity within; the mark in the country; in the town, the guild.

But with the extension of the production of commodities, and especially with the introduction of the capitalist mode of production, the laws of commodity production, hitherto latent, came into action more openly and with greater force. The old bonds were loosened, the old exclusive limits broken through, the producers were more and more turned into independent, isolated producers of commodities. It became apparent that the production of society at large was ruled by absence of plan, by accident, by anarchy; and this anarchy grew to greater and greater height. But the chief means by aid of which the capitalist mode of production intensified this anarchy of socialized production was the exact opposite of anarchy. It was the increasing organization of production, upon a social basis, in every individual productive establishment. By this the old, peaceful, stable condition of things was ended. Wherever this organization of production was introduced into a branch of industry, it brooked no other method of production by its side. The field of labor became a battleground. The great geographical discoveries, and the colonization following upon them, multiplied markets and quickened the transformation of handicraft into manufacture. The war did not break out simply between the individual producers of particular localities. The local struggles begot in their turn national conflicts, the commercial wars of the seventeenth and the eighteenth centuries.

Finally, modern industry and the opening of the world market made the struggle universal, and at the same time gave it an unheard-of virulence. Advantages in natural or artificial conditions of production now decide the existence or non-existence of individual capitalists, as well as of whole industries and countries. He that falls is remorselessly cast aside. It is the Darwinian struggle of the individual for existence transferred from nature to society with intensified violence. The conditions of existence natural to the animal appear as the final term of human development. The contradiction between socialized production and capitalistic appropriation now presents itself as *an antagonism between the organization of production in the individual workshop and the anarchy of production in society generally*.

The capitalistic mode of production moves in these two forms of the antagonism immanent to it from its very origin. It is never able to get out of that "vicious circle" which Fourier had already discovered. What Fourier could not, indeed, see in his time is that this circle is gradually narrowing; that the movement becomes more and more a spiral, and must come to an end, like the movement of the planets, by collision with the center. It is the compelling force of anarchy in the production of society at large that more and more completely turns the great majority of men into proletarians, and it is the masses of the proletariat again who will finally put an end to anarchy in production. It is the compelling force of anarchy in social production that turns the limitless perfectibility of machinery under modern industry into a compulsory law by which every individual industrial capitalist must perfect his machinery more and more, under penalty of ruin.

But the perfecting of machinery is making human labor superfluous. If the introduction and increase of machinery means the displacement of millions of manual by a few machine workers, improvement in machinery means the displacement of more and more of the machine workers themselves. It means, in the last instance, the production of a number of available wage workers in excess of the average needs of capital, the formation of a complete industrial reserve army, as I called it in 1845,[5] available at the times when industry is

[5] *The Condition of the Working Class in England.*

working at high pressure, to be cast out upon the street when the inevitable crash comes, a constant dead weight upon the limbs of the working class in its struggle for existence with capital, a regulator for the keeping of wages down to the low level that suits the interests of capital. Thus it comes about, to quote Marx, that machinery becomes the most powerful weapon in the war of capital against the working class; that the instruments of labor constantly tear the means of subsistence out of the hands of the laborer; that the very product of the worker is turned into an instrument for his subjugation. Thus it comes about that the economizing of the instruments of labor becomes at the same time, from the outset, the most reckless waste of labor power, and robbery based upon the normal conditions under which labor functions; that machinery, "the most powerful instrument for shortening labor time, becomes the most unfailing means for placing every moment of the laborer's time and that of his family at the disposal of the capitalist for the purpose of expanding the value of his capital." (*Capital*, American edition, page 445.) Thus it comes about that the overwork of some becomes the preliminary condition for the idleness of others, and that modern industry, which hunts after new consumers over the whole world, forces the consumption of the masses at home down to a starvation minimum, and in doing thus destroys its own home market. "The law that always equilibrates the relative surplus population, or industrial reserve army, to the extent and energy of accumulation, this law rivets the laborer to capital more firmly than the wedges of Vulcan did Prometheus to the rock. It establishes an accumulation of misery corresponding with accumulation of capital. Accumulation of wealth at one pole is, therefore, at the same time accumulation of misery, agony of toil, slavery, ignorance, brutality, mental degradation at the opposite pole, i.e., on the side of the class that produces *its own product in the form of capital*." (Marx's *Capital*, American edition, page 661.) And to expect any other division of the products from the capitalistic mode of production is the same as expecting the electrodes of a battery not to decompose acidulated water, not to liberate oxygen at the positive, hydrogen at the negative pole, so long as they are connected with the battery.

We have seen that the ever increasing perfectibility of modern machinery is, by the anarchy of social production, turned into a compulsory law that forces the individual industrial capitalist always to improve his machinery, always to increase its productive force. The bare possibility of extending the field of production is transformed for him into a similar compulsory law. The enormous expansive force of modern industry, compared with which that of gases is mere child's play, appears to us now as a *necessity* for expansion, both qualitative and quantitative, that laughs at all resistance. Such resistance is offered by consumption, by sales, by the markets for the products of modern industry. But the capacity for expansion, extensive and intensive, of the markets is primarily governed by quite different laws that work much less energetically. The expansion of the markets cannot keep pace with the extension of production. The collision becomes inevitable, and as this cannot produce any real solution so long as it does not break into pieces the capitalist mode of production, the collisions become periodic. Capitalist production has begotten another "vicious circle."

As a matter of fact, since 1825, when the first general crisis broke out, the whole industrial and commercial world, production and exchange among all civilized peoples and their more or less barbaric hangers-on, are thrown out of joint about once every ten years. Commerce is at a standstill, the markets are glutted, products accumulate, as multitudinous as they are unsalable, hard cash disappears, credit vanishes, factories are closed, the mass of the workers are in want of the means of subsistence because they have produced too much of the means of subsistence; bankruptcy follows upon bankruptcy, execution upon execution. The stagnation lasts for years; productive forces and products are wasted and destroyed wholesale, until the accumulated mass of commodities finally filters off, more or less depreciated in value, until production and exchange gradually begin to move again. Little by little the pace quickens. It becomes a trot. The industrial trot breaks into a canter, the canter in turn grows into the headlong gallop of a perfect steeplechase of industry, commercial credit, and speculation, which finally, after breakneck leaps, ends where it began—in the ditch of a crisis. And so over and over again. We have now, since the year 1825, gone through this five times, and at the present moment (1877) we are going through it for the sixth time. And the character of these crises is so clearly defined that Fourier hit all of them off when he described the first as *"crise pléthorique,"* a crisis from plethora.

In these crises the contradiction between socialized production and capitalist appropriation ends in a violent explosion. The circulation of commodities is, for the time being, stopped.

Money, the means of circulation, becomes a hindrance to circulation. All the laws of production and circulation of commodities are turned upside down. The economic collision has reached its apogee. *The mode of production is in rebellion against the mode of exchange.*

The fact that the socialized organization of production within the factory has developed so far that it has become incompatible with the anarchy of production in society, which exists side by side with and dominates it, is brought home to the capitalists themselves by the violent concentration of capital that occurs during crises, through the ruin of many large, and a still greater number of small, capitalists. The whole mechanism of the capitalist mode of production breaks down under the pressure of the productive forces, its own creations. It is no longer able to turn all this mass of means of production into capital. They lie fallow, and for that very reason the industrial reserve army must also lie fallow. Means of production, means of subsistence, available laborers, all the elements of production and of general wealth, are present in abundance. But "abundance becomes the source of distress and want" (Fourier), because it is the very thing that prevents the transformation of the means of production and subsistence into capital. For in capitalistic society the means of production can function only when they have undergone a preliminary transformation into capital, into the means of exploiting human labor power. The necessity of this transformation into capital of the means of production and subsistence stands like a ghost between these and the workers. It alone prevents the coming together of the material and personal levers of production; it alone forbids the means of production to function, the workers to work and live. On the one hand, therefore, the capitalistic mode of production stands convicted of its own incapacity to further direct these productive forces. On the other, these productive forces themselves, with increasing energy, press forward to the removal of the existing contradiction, to the abolition of their quality as capital, to the *practical recognition of their character as social productive forces.*

This rebellion of the productive forces, as they grow more and more powerful, against their quality as capital, this stronger and stronger command that their social character shall be recognized, forces the capitalist class itself to treat them more and more as social productive forces, so far as this is possible under capitalist conditions. The period of industrial high pressure, with its unbounded inflation of credit, not less

than the crash itself, by the collapse of great capitalist establishments, tends to bring about that form of the socialization
of great masses of means of production which we meet with
in the different kinds of joint-stock companies. Many of these
means of production and of distribution are, from the outset,
so colossal that, like the railways, they exclude all other forms
of capitalistic exploitation. At a further stage of evolution
this form also becomes insufficient. The producers on a large
scale in a particular branch of industry in a particular country
unite in a "trust," a union for the purpose of regulating production. They determine the total amount to be produced,
parcel it out among themselves, and thus enforce the selling
price fixed beforehand. But trusts of this kind, as soon as business becomes bad, are generally liable to break up, and on
this very account compel a yet greater concentration of association. The whole of the particular industry is turned into one
gigantic joint-stock company; internal competition gives place
to the internal monopoly of this one company. This has happened in 1890 with the English *alkali* production, which is
now, after the fusion of forty-eight large works, in the hands
of one company, conducted upon a single plan and with a
capital of six million pounds.

In the trusts freedom of competition changes into its very
opposite—into monopoly; and the production without any definite plan of capitalistic society capitulates to the production
upon a definite plan of the invading socialistic society. Certainly this is so far still to the benefit and advantage of the
capitalists. But in this case the exploitation is so palpable that
it must break down. No nation will put up with production
conducted by trusts, with so barefaced an exploitation of the
community by a small band of dividend-mongers.

In any case, with trusts or without, the official representative of capitalist society—the state—will ultimately have to undertake the direction of production.[6] This necessity for con-

---

[6] I say "have to." For only when the means of production and
distribution have *actually* outgrown the form of management by
joint-stock companies and when, therefore, the taking them over by
the state has become *economically* inevitable, only then—even if it
is the state of today that effects this—is there an economic advance,
the attainment of another step preliminary to the taking over of all
productive forces by society itself. But of late, since Bismarck went
in for state ownership of industrial establishments, a kind of
spurious socialism has arisen, degenerating, now and again, into
something of flunkyism, that without more ado declares *all* state

version into state property is felt first in the great institutions for intercourse and communication—the post office, the telegraphs, the railways.

If the crises demonstrate the incapacity of the bourgeoisie for managing any longer modern productive forces, the transformation of the great establishments for production and distribution into joint-stock companies, trusts, and state property show how unnecessary the bourgeoisie are for that purpose. All the social functions of the capitalist are now performed by salaried employees. The capitalist has no further social function than that of pocketing dividends, tearing off coupons, and gambling on the stock exchange, where the different capitalists despoil one another of their capital. At first the capitalistic mode of production forces out the workers. Now it forces out the capitalists, and reduces them, just as it reduced the workers, to the ranks of the surplus population, although not immediately into those of the industrial reserve army.

But the transformation, either into joint-stock companies and trusts or into state ownership, does not do away with the capitalistic nature of the productive forces. In the joint-stock companies and trusts this is obvious. And the modern state, again, is only the organization that bourgeois society takes on in order to support the external conditions of the capitalist mode of production against the encroachments as well of the workers as of individual capitalists. The modern state, no matter what its form, is essentially a capitalist machine, the state of the capitalists, the ideal personification of the total national capital. The more it proceeds to the taking over of productive forces, the more does it actually become the national

---

ownership, even of the Bismarckian sort, to be socialistic. Certainly if the taking over by the state of the tobacco industry is socialistic, then Napoleon and Metternich must be numbered among the founders of socialism. If the Belgian state, for quite ordinary political and financial reasons, itself constructed its chief railway lines; if Bismarck, not under any economic compulsion, took over for the state the chief Prussian lines, simply to be the better able to have them in hand in case of war, to bring up the railway employees as voting cattle for the government, and especially to create for himself a new source of income independent of parliamentary votes—this was in no sense a socialistic measure, directly or indirectly, consciously or unconsciously. Otherwise the Royal Maritime Company, the Royal porcelain manufacture, and even the regimental tailor of the army would also be socialistic institutions, or even, as was seriously proposed by a sly dog in Frederick William III's reign, the taking over by the state of the brothels.

capitalist, the more citizens does it exploit. The workers remain wage workers—proletarians. The capitalist relation is not done away with. It is rather brought to a head. But, brought to a head, it topples over. State ownership of the productive forces is not the solution of the conflict, but concealed within it are the technical conditions that form the elements of that solution.

This solution can consist only in the practical recognition of the social nature of the modern forces of production, and therefore in the harmonizing of the modes of production, appropriation, and exchange with the socialized character of the means of production. And this can come about only by society openly and directly taking possession of the productive forces which have outgrown all control except that of society as a whole. The social character of the means of production and of the products today reacts against the producers, periodically disrupts all production and exchange, acts only like a law of nature working blindly, forcibly, destructively. But with the taking over by society of the productive forces, the social character of the means of production and of the products will be utilized by the producers with a perfect understanding of its nature, and instead of being a source of disturbance and periodic collapse will become the most powerful lever of production itself.

Active social forces work exactly like natural forces: blindly, forcibly, destructively, so long as we do not understand, and reckon with, them. But when once we understand them, when once we grasp their action, their direction, their effects, it depends only upon ourselves to subject them more and more to our own will, and by means of them to reach our own ends. And this holds quite especially of the mighty productive forces of today. As long as we obstinately refuse to understand the nature and the character of these social means of action—and this understanding goes against the grain of the capitalist mode of production and its defenders—so long as these forces are at work in spite of us, in opposition to us, so long do they master us, as we have shown above in detail.

But when once their nature is understood, they can, in the hands of the producers working together, be transformed from master demons into willing servants. The difference is as that between the destructive force of electricity in the lightning of the storm and electricity under command in the telegraph and the voltaic arc, the difference between a conflagration and fire working in the service of man. With this recognition, at last, of the real nature of the productive forces of today, the social anarchy of production gives place to a social regulation of production upon a definite plan, according to the needs of the community and of each individual. Then the capitalist mode of appropriation, in which the product enslaves first the producer and then the appropriator, is replaced by the mode of appropriation of the products that is based upon the nature of the modern means of production: upon the one hand, direct social appropriation as means to the maintenance and extension of production; on the other, direct individual appropriation as means of subsistence and of enjoyment.

While the capitalist mode of production more and more completely transforms the great majority of the population into proletarians, it creates the power which, under penalty of its own destruction, is forced to accomplish this revolution. While it forces on more and more the transformation of the vast means of production, already socialized, into state property, it shows itself the way to accomplishing this revolution. *The proletariat seizes political power and turns the means of production into state property.*

But in doing this it abolishes itself as proletariat, abolishes all class distinctions and class antagonisms, abolishes also the state as state. Society thus far, based upon class antagonisms, has had need of the state. That is, of an organization of the particular class which was *pro tempore* the exploiting class, an organization for the purpose of preventing any interference from without with the existing conditions of production, and, therefore, especially for the purpose of forcibly keeping the exploited classes in the condition of oppression corresponding with the given mode of production (slavery, serfdom, wage labor). The state was the official representative of society as a whole; the gathering of it together into a visible embodiment. But it was this only in so far as it was the state of that class which itself represented, for the time being, society as a whole: in ancient times, the state of slave-owning citizens; in the Middle Ages, the feudal lords; in our own time, the bourgeoisie. When at last it becomes the real representative of the whole of society it renders itself unnecessary. As soon as there is no longer any social class to be held in subjection, as soon as class rule and the individual struggle for existence based upon our present anarchy in production, with the collisions and excesses arising from these, are removed, nothing more remains to be repressed, and a special repressive force, a state, is no longer necessary. The first act by virtue of which

the state really constitutes itself the representative of the whole
of society—the taking possession of the means of production
in the name of society—this is, at the same time, its last independent act as a state. State interference in social relations
becomes, in one domain after another, superfluous, and then
dies out of itself; the government of persons is replaced by
the administration of things, and by the conduct of processes
of production. The state is not "abolished." *It dies out.* This
gives the measure of the value of the phrase *"a free state,"*
both as to its justifiable use at times by agitators and as to its
ultimate scientific insufficiency, and also of the demands of the
so-called anarchists for the abolition of the state out of hand.

Since the historical appearance of the capitalist mode of
production, the appropriation by society of all the means of
production has often been dreamed of, more or less vaguely,
by individuals as well as by sects, as the ideal of the future.
But it could become possible, could become a historical necessity, only when the actual conditions for its realization were
there. Like every other social advance, it becomes practicable
not by men understanding that the existence of classes is in
contradiction to justice, equality, etc., not by the mere willingness to abolish these classes, but by virtue of certain new
economic conditions. The separation of society into an exploiting and an exploited class, a ruling and an oppressed class,
was the necessary consequence of the deficient and restricted
development of production in former times. So long as the
total social labor yields only a produce which but slightly
exceeds that barely necessary for the existence of all; so long,
therefore, as labor engages all or almost all the time of the
great majority of the members of society—so long, of necessity,
this society is divided into classes. Side by side with the great
majority, exclusively bond slaves to labor, arises a class freed
from directly productive labor, which looks after the general
affairs of society: the direction of labor, state business, law,
science, art, etc. It is, therefore, the law of division of labor
that lies at the basis of the division into classes. But this does
not prevent this division into classes from being carried out
by means of violence and robbery, trickery and fraud. It does
not prevent the ruling class, once having the upper hand, from
consolidating its power at the expense of the working class,
from turning its social leadership into an intensified exploitation of the masses.

But if, upon this showing, division into classes has a certain historical justification, it has this only for a given period,

only under given social conditions. It was based upon the insufficiency of production. It will be swept away by the complete development of modern productive forces. And, in fact, the abolition of classes in society presupposes a degree of historical evolution at which the existence not simply of this or that particular ruling class, but of any ruling class at all, and, therefore, the existence of class distinction itself, has become an anachronism. It presupposes, therefore, the development of production carried out to a degree at which appropriation of the means of production and of the products, and, with this, of political domination, of the monopoly of culture, and of intellectual leadership by a particular class of society, has become not only superfluous but economically, politically, intellectually a hindrance to development.

This point is now reached.

Marx:
A CONTRIBUTION TO THE CRITIQUE OF POLITICAL ECONOMY[1]
Translated from the German by N. I. Stone

THE BASIC DYNAMIC OF HISTORY

. . . The general conclusion at which I arrived and which, once reached, continued to serve as the leading thread in my studies may be briefly summed up as follows: In the social production which men carry on they enter into definite relations that are indispensable and independent of their will; these relations of production correspond to a definite stage of development of their material powers of production. The sum total of these relations of production constitutes the economic structure of society—the real foundation, on which rise legal and political superstructures and to which correspond definite forms of social consciousness. The mode of production in material life determines the general character of the social, political, and spiritual processes of life. It is not the consciousness of men that determines their existence, but, on the contrary, their social existence determines their consciousness. At a certain stage of their development the material forces of production in society come into conflict with the existing relations of production, or—what is but a legal expression for the same thing—with the property relations within which they had been at work before. From forms of development of the forces of production these relations turn into their fetters. Then comes the period of social revolution. With the change of the economic foundation the entire immense superstructure is more or less rapidly transformed. In considering such transformations the distinction should always be made between the ma-

[1] The brief passage here given has become famous as the most succinct formulation Marx ever made of the basis of his central social theory. *The Editors.*

terial transformation of the economic conditions of production, which can be determined with the precision of natural science, and the legal, political, religious, aesthetic, or philosophic—in short, ideological—forms in which men become conscious of this conflict and fight it out. Just as our opinion of an individual is not based on what he thinks of himself, so can we not judge such a period of transformation by its own consciousness; on the contrary, this consciousness must rather be explained from the contradictions of material life, from the existing conflict between the social forces of production and the relations of production. No social order ever disappears before all the productive forces for which there is room in it have been developed, and new, higher relations of production never appear before the material conditions of their existence have matured in the womb of the old society. Therefore mankind always takes up only such problems as it can solve, since, looking at the matter more closely, we will always find that the problem itself arises only when the material conditions necessary for its solution already exist or are at least in the process of formation. In broad outlines we can designate the Asiatic, the ancient, the feudal, and the modern bourgeois methods of production as so many epochs in the progress of the economic formation of society. The bourgeois relations of production are the last antagonistic form of the social process of production—antagonistic not in the sense of individual antagonism, but of one arising from conditions surrounding the life of individuals in society; at the same time the productive forces developing in the womb of bourgeois society create the material conditions for the solution of that antagonism. This social formation constitutes, therefore, the closing chapter of the prehistoric stage of human society. . . .

Vladimir Ilyich Lenin (1870–1924)

STATE AND REVOLUTION

1. The State as the Product of the Irreconcilability of Class Antagonisms

What is now happening to Marx's doctrine has, in the course of history, often happened to the doctrines of other revolutionary thinkers and leaders of oppressed classes struggling for emancipation. During the lifetime of great revolutionaries, the oppressing classes have visited relentless persecution on them and received their teaching with the most savage hostility, the most furious hatred, the most ruthless campaign of lies and slanders. After their death, attempts are made to turn them into harmless icons, canonise them, and surround their *names* with a certain halo for the "consolation" of the oppressed classes and with the object of duping them, while at the same time emasculating and vulgarising the *real essence* of their revolutionary theories and blunting their revolutionary edge. At the present time, the bourgeoisie and the opportunists within the labour movement are co-operating in this work of adulterating Marxism. They omit, obliterate, and distort the revolutionary side of its teaching, its revolutionary soul. They push to the foreground and extol what is, or seems, acceptable to the bourgeoisie. All the social-chauvinists are now "Marxists" —joking aside! And more and more do German bourgeois professors, erstwhile specialists in the demolition of Marx, speak now of the "national-German" Marx, who, they aver, has educated the labour unions which are so splendidly organised for conducting the present predatory war!

In such circumstances, the distortion of Marxism being so widespread, it is our first task to *resuscitate* the real teachings of Marx on the state. For this purpose it will be necessary to quote at length from the works of Marx and Engels themselves. Of course, long quotations will make the text cumbersome and in no way help to make it popular reading, but we cannot possibly avoid them. All, or at any rate, all the most essential passages in the works of Marx and Engels on the subject of the state must necessarily be given as fully as possible, in order that the reader may form an independent opinion of all the views of the founders of scientific Socialism and of the development of those views, and in order that their distortions by the present predominant "Kautskyism" may be proved in black and white and rendered plain to all.

Let us begin with the most popular of Engels' works, *Der Ursprung der Familie, des Privateigentums und des Staats*,[1] the sixth edition of which was published in Stuttgart as far back as 1894. We must translate the quotations from the German originals, as the Russian translations, although very numerous, are for the most part either incomplete or very unsatisfactory.

Summarising his historical analysis Engels says:

> The state is therefore by no means a power imposed on society from the outside; just as little is it "the reality of the moral idea," "the image and reality of reason," as Hegel asserted. Rather, it is a product of society at a certain stage of development; it is the admission that this society has become entangled in an insoluble contradiction with itself, that it is cleft into irreconcilable antagonisms which it is powerless to dispel. But in order that these antagonisms, classes with conflicting economic interests, may not consume themselves and society in sterile struggle, a power apparently standing above society becomes necessary, whose purpose is to moderate the conflict and keep it within the bounds of "order"; and this power arising out of society, but placing itself above it, and increasingly separating itself from it, is the state.

Here we have, expressed in all its clearness, the basic idea of Marxism on the question of the historical rôle and meaning of the state. The state is the product and the manifestation of the *irreconcilability* of class antagonisms. The state arises when, where, and to the extent that the class antagonisms *cannot* be objectively reconciled. And, conversely, the existence

---

[1] Friedrich Engels, *The Origin of the Family, Private Property, and the State*, London and New York, 1933.—*Ed.* (Footnotes followed by *"Ed."* are those of the editor of the English translation. *The Editors.*)

of the state proves that the class antagonisms *are* irreconcilable.

It is precisely on this most important and fundamental point that distortions of Marxism arise along two main lines.

On the one hand, the bourgeois, and particularly the petty-bourgeois, ideologists, compelled under the pressure of indisputable historical facts to admit that the state only exists where there are class antagonisms and the class struggle, "correct" Marx in such a way as to make it appear that the state is an organ for *reconciling* the classes. According to Marx, the state could neither arise nor maintain itself if a reconciliation of classes were possible. But with the petty-bourgeois and philistine professors and publicists, the state—and this frequently on the strength of benevolent references to Marx!—becomes a conciliator of the classes. According to Marx, the state is an organ of class *domination,* an organ of *oppression* of one class by another; its aim is the creation of "order" which legalises and perpetuates this oppression by moderating the collisions between the classes. But in the opinion of the petty-bourgeois politicians, order means reconciliation of the classes, and not oppression of one class by another; to moderate collisions does not mean, they say, to deprive the oppressed classes of certain definite means and methods of struggle for overthrowing the oppressors, but to practice reconciliation.

For instance, when, in the Revolution of 1917, the question of the real meaning and rôle of the state arose in all its vastness as a practical question demanding immediate action on a wide mass scale, all the Socialist-Revolutionaries and Mensheviks suddenly and completely sank to the petty-bourgeois theory of "reconciliation" of the classes by the "state." Innumerable resolutions and articles by politicians of both these parties are saturated through and through with this purely petty-bourgeois and philistine theory of "reconciliation." That the state is an organ of domination of a definite class which *cannot* be reconciled with its antipode (the class opposed to it)—this petty-bourgeois democracy is never able to understand. Its attitude towards the state is one of the most telling proofs that our Socialist-Revolutionaries and Mensheviks are not Socialists at all (which we Bolsheviks have always maintained), but petty-bourgeois democrats with a near-Socialist phraseology.

On the other hand, the "Kautskyist" distortion of Marx is far more subtle. "Theoretically," there is no denying that the state is the organ of class domination, or that class antagonisms are irreconcilable. But what is forgotten or glossed over is this: if the state is the product of the irreconcilable character of class antagonisms, if it is a force standing *above* society and "increasingly separating itself from it," then it is clear that the liberation of the oppressed class is impossible not only without a violent revolution, *but also without the destruction* of the apparatus of state power, which was created by the ruling class and in which this "separation" is embodied. As we shall see later, Marx drew this theoretically self-evident conclusion from a concrete historical analysis of the problems of revolution. And it is exactly this conclusion which Kautsky —as we shall show fully in our subsequent remarks—has "forgotten" and distorted.

2. *Special Bodies of Armed Men, Prisons, Etc.*

Engels continues:

In contrast with the ancient organisation of the *gens,* the first distinguishing characteristic of the state is the grouping of the subjects of the state *on a territorial basis.* . . .

Such a grouping seems "natural" to us, but it came after a prolonged and costly struggle against the old form of tribal or gentilic society.

. . . The second is the establishment of a *public* force, which is no longer absolutely identical with the population organising itself as an armed power. This special public force is necessary, because a self-acting armed organisation of the population has become impossible since the cleavage of society into classes. . . . This public force exists in every state; it consists not merely of armed men, but of material appendages, prisons and repressive institutions of all kinds, of which gentilic society knew nothing. . . .[2]

Engels develops the conception of that "power" which is termed the state—a power arising from society, but placing itself above it and becoming more and more separated from it. What does this power mainly consist of? It consists of special bodies of armed men who have at their disposal prisons, etc.

We are justified in speaking of special bodies of armed

2 *Ibid.—Ed.*

men, because the public power peculiar to every state is not "absolutely identical" with the armed population, with its "self-acting armed organisation."

Like all the great revolutionary thinkers, Engels tries to draw the attention of the class-conscious workers to that very fact which to prevailing philistinism appears least of all worthy of attention, most common and sanctified by solid, indeed, one might say, petrified prejudices. A standing army and police are the chief instruments of state power. But can this be otherwise?

From the point of view of the vast majority of Europeans at the end of the nineteenth century whom Engels was addressing, and who had neither lived through nor closely observed a single great revolution, this cannot be otherwise. They cannot understand at all what this "self-acting armed organisation of the population" means. To the question, whence arose the need for special bodies of armed men, standing above society and becoming separated from it (police and standing army), the Western European and Russian philistines are inclined to answer with a few phrases borrowed from Spencer or Mikhailovsky, by reference to the complexity of social life, the differentiation of functions, and so forth.

Such a reference seems "scientific" and effectively dulls the senses of the average man, obscuring the most important and basic fact, namely, the break-up of society into irreconcilably antagonistic classes.

Without such a break-up, the "self-acting armed organisation of the population" might have differed from the primitive organisation of a herd of monkeys grasping sticks, or of primitive men, or men united in a tribal form of society, by its complexity, its high technique, and so forth, but would still have been possible.

It is impossible now, because society, in the period of civilisation, is broken up into antagonistic and, indeed, irreconcilably antagonistic classes, which, if armed in a "self-acting" manner, would come into armed struggle with each other. A state is formed, a special power is created in the form of special bodies of armed men, and every revolution, by shattering the state apparatus, demonstrates to us how the ruling class aims at the restoration of the special bodies of armed men at *its* service, and how the oppressed class tries to create a new organisation of this kind, capable of serving not the exploiters, but the exploited.

In the above observation, Engels raises theoretically the

very same question which every great revolution raises practically, palpably, and on a mass scale of action, namely, the question of the relation between special bodies of armed men and the "self-acting armed organisation of the population." We shall see how this is concretely illustrated by the experience of the European and Russian revolutions.

But let us return to Engels' discourse.

He points out that sometimes, for instance, here and there in North America, this public power is weak (he has in mind an exception that is rare in capitalist society, and he speaks about parts of North America in its pre-imperialist days, where the free colonist predominated), but that in general it tends to become stronger:

> It [the public power] grows stronger, however, in proportion as the class antagonisms within the state grow sharper, and with the growth in size and population of the adjacent states. We have only to look at our present-day Europe, where class struggle and rivalry in conquest have screwed up the public power to such a pitch that it threatens to devour the whole of society and even the state itself.[3]

This was written as early as the beginning of the 'nineties of last century, Engels' last preface being dated June 16, 1891. The turn towards imperialism, understood to mean complete domination of the trusts, full sway of the large banks, and a colonial policy on a grand scale, and so forth, was only just beginning in France, and was even weaker in North America and in Germany. Since then the "rivalry in conquest" has made gigantic progress—especially as, by the beginning of the second decade of the twentieth century, the whole world had been finally divided up between these "rivals in conquest," *i.e.*, between the great predatory powers. Military and naval armaments since then have grown to monstrous proportions, and the predatory war of 1914–1917 for the domination of the world by England or Germany, for the division of the spoils, has brought the "swallowing up" of all the forces of society by the rapacious state power nearer to a complete catastrophe.

As early as 1891 Engels was able to point to "rivalry in conquest" as one of the most important features of the foreign policy of the great powers, but in 1914–1917, when this rivalry, many times intensified, has given birth to an imperialist

[3] *Ibid.—Ed.*

war, the rascally social-chauvinists cover up their defence of the predatory policy of "their" capitalist classes by phrases about the "defence of the fatherland," or the "defence of the republic and the revolution," etc.!

3. The State as an Instrument for the Exploitation of the Oppressed Class

For the maintenance of a special public force standing above society, taxes and state loans are needed.

Having at their disposal the public force and the right to exact taxes, the officials now stand as organs of society *above* society. The free, voluntary respect which was accorded to the organs of the gentilic form of government does not satisfy them, even if they could have it. . . .

Special laws are enacted regarding the sanctity and the inviolability of the officials. "The shabbiest police servant . . . has more authority" than the representative of the clan, but even the head of the military power of a civilised state "may well envy the least among the chiefs of the clan the unconstrained and uncontested respect which is paid to him."[4]

Here the question regarding the privileged position of the officials as organs of state power is clearly stated. The main point is indicated as follows: what is it that places them *above* society? We shall see how this theoretical problem was solved in practice by the Paris Commune in 1871 and how it was slurred over in a reactionary manner by Kautsky in 1912.

As the state arose out of the need to hold class antagonisms in check; but as it, at the same time, arose in the midst of the conflict of these classes, it is, as a rule, the state of the most powerful, economically dominant class, which by virtue thereof becomes also the dominant class politically, and thus acquires new means of holding down and exploiting the oppressed class. . . .

Not only the ancient and feudal states were organs of exploitation of the slaves and serfs, but

the modern representative state is the instrument of the exploitation of wage-labour by capital. By way of exception, however, there are periods when the warring classes so nearly attain equilibrium that the state power, ostensi-

4 *Ibid.—Ed.*

bly appearing as a mediator, assumes for the moment a certain independence in relation to both. . . .[5]

Such were, for instance, the absolute monarchies of the seventeenth and eighteenth centuries, the Bonapartism of the First and Second Empires in France, and the Bismarck régime in Germany.

Such, we may add, is now the Kerensky government in republican Russia after its shift to persecuting the revolutionary proletariat, at a moment when the Soviets, thanks to the leadership of the petty-bourgeois democrats, have *already* become impotent, while the bourgeoisie is *not yet* strong enough to disperse them outright.

In a democratic republic, Engels continues, "wealth wields its power indirectly, but all the more effectively," first, by means of "direct corruption of the officials" (America); second, by means of "the alliance of the government with the stock exchange" (France and America).

At the present time, imperialism and the domination of the banks have "developed" to an unusually fine art both these methods of defending and asserting the omnipotence of wealth in democratic republics of all descriptions. If, for instance, in the very first months of the Russian democratic republic, one might say during the honeymoon of the union of the "socialists"—Socialist-Revolutionaries and Mensheviks—with the bourgeoisie, Mr. Palchinsky obstructed every measure in the coalition cabinet, restraining the capitalists and their war profiteering, their plundering of the public treasury by means of army contracts; and if, after his resignation, Mr. Palchinsky (replaced, of course, by an exactly similar Palchinsky) was "rewarded" by the capitalists with a "soft" job carrying a salary of 120,000 rubles per annum, what was this? Direct or indirect bribery? A league of the government with the capitalist syndicates, or "only" friendly relations? What is the rôle played by the Chernovs, Tseretelis, Avksentyevs and Skobelevs? Are they the "direct" or only the indirect allies of the millionaire treasury looters?

The omnipotence of "wealth" is thus more *secure* in a democratic republic, since it does not depend on the poor political shell of capitalism. A democratic republic is the best possible political shell for capitalism, and therefore, once capital has gained control (through the Palchinskys, Chernovs, Tseretelis and Co.) of this very best shell, it establishes its power so

[5] *Ibid.—Ed.*

securely, so firmly that *no* change, either of persons, or institutions, or parties in the bourgeois republic can shake it.

We must also note that Engels quite definitely regards universal suffrage as a means of bourgeois domination. Universal suffrage, he says, obviously summing up the long experience of German Social-Democracy, is "an index of the maturity of the working class; it cannot, and never will, be anything else but that in the modern state."

The petty-bourgeois democrats, such as our Socialist-Revolutionaries and Mensheviks, and also their twin brothers, the social-chauvinists and opportunists of Western Europe, all expect "more" from universal suffrage. They themselves share, and instil into the minds of the people, the wrong idea that universal suffrage "in the *modern* state" is really capable of expressing the will of the majority of the toilers and of assuring its realisation.

We can here only note this wrong idea, only point out that this perfectly clear, exact and concrete statement by Engels is distorted at every step in the propaganda and agitation of the "official" (*i.e.*, opportunist) Socialist parties. A detailed analysis of all the falseness of this idea, which Engels brushes aside, is given in our further account of the views of Marx and Engels on the "modern" state.

A general summary of his views is given by Engels in the most popular of his works in the following words:

> The state, therefore, has not existed from all eternity. There have been societies which managed without it, which had no conception of the state and state power. At a certain stage of economic development, which was necessarily bound up with the cleavage of society into classes, the state became a necessity owing to this cleavage. We are now rapidly approaching a stage in the development of production at which the existence of these classes has not only ceased to be a necessity, but is becoming a positive hindrance to production. They will disappear as inevitably as they arose at an earlier stage. Along with them, the state will inevitably disappear. The society that organises production anew on the basis of a free and equal association of the producers will put the whole state machine where it will then belong: in the museum of antiquities, side by side with the spinning wheel and the bronze axe.[6]

[6] *Ibid.—Ed.*

It is not often that we find this passage quoted in the propaganda and agitation literature of contemporary Social-Democracy. But even when we do come across it, it is generally quoted in the same manner as one bows before an icon, *i.e.*, it is done merely to show official respect for Engels, without any attempt to gauge the breadth and depth of revolutionary action presupposed by this relegating of "the whole state machine . . . to the museum of antiquities." In most cases we do not even find an understanding of what Engels calls the state machine.

4. The "Withering Away" of the State and Violent Revolution

Engels' words regarding the "withering away" of the state enjoy such popularity, they are so often quoted, and they show so clearly the essence of the usual adulteration by means of which Marxism is made to look like opportunism, that we must dwell on them in detail. Let us quote the whole passage from which they are taken.

> The proletariat seizes state power, and then transforms the means of production into state property. But in doing this, it puts an end to itself as the proletariat, it puts an end to all class differences and class antagonisms, it puts an end also to the state as the state. Former society, moving in class antagonisms, had need of the state, that is, an organisation of the exploiting class at each period for the maintenance of its external conditions of production; therefore, in particular, for the forcible holding down of the exploited class in the conditions of oppression (slavery, bondage or serfdom, wage-labour) determined by the existing mode of production. The state was the official representative of society as a whole, its embodiment in a visible corporate body; but it was this only in so far as it was the state of that class which itself, in its epoch, represented society as a whole: in ancient times, the state of the slave-owning citizens; in the Middle Ages, of the feudal nobility; in our epoch, of the bourgeoisie. When ultimately it becomes really representative of society as a whole, it makes itself superfluous. As soon as there is no longer any class of society to be held in subjection; as soon as, along with class domination and the struggle for individual existence based on the former anarchy of production, the collisions and excesses arising from these have also been abolished, there is nothing more to be

repressed, and a special repressive force, a state, is no longer necessary. The first act in which the state really comes forward as the representative of society as a whole —the seizure of the means of production in the name of society—is at the same time its last independent act as a state. The interference of a state power in social relations becomes superfluous in one sphere after another, and then becomes dormant of itself. Government over persons is replaced by the administration of things and the direction of the processes of production. The state is not "abolished," *it withers away*. It is from this standpoint that we must appraise the phrase "people's free state"—both its justification at times for agitational purposes, and its ultimate scientific inadequacy—and also the demand of the so-called Anarchists that the state should be abolished overnight.[7]

Without fear of committing an error, it may be said that of this argument by Engels so singularly rich in ideas, only one point has become an integral part of Socialist thought among modern Socialist parties, namely, that, unlike the Anarchist doctrine of the "abolition" of the state, according to Marx the state "withers away." To emasculate Marxism in such a manner is to reduce it to opportunism, for such an "interpretation" only leaves the hazy conception of a slow, even, gradual change, free from leaps and storms, free from revolution. The current popular conception, if one may say so, of the "withering away" of the state undoubtedly means a slurring over, if not a negation, of revolution.

Yet, such an "interpretation" is the crudest distortion of Marxism, which is advantageous only to the bourgeoisie; in point of theory, it is based on a disregard for the most important circumstances and considerations pointed out in the very passage summarising Engels' ideas, which we have just quoted in full.

In the first place, Engels at the very outset of his argument says that, in assuming state power, the proletariat by that very act "puts an end to the state as the state." One is "not accustomed" to reflect on what this really means. Generally, it is either ignored altogether, or it is considered as a piece of "Hegelian weakness" on Engels' part. As a matter of fact, however, these words express succinctly the experience of one of

[7] Friedrich Engels, *Anti-Dühring*, London and New York, 1933.—*Ed.*

the greatest proletarian revolutions—the Paris Commune of 1871, of which we shall speak in greater detail in its proper place. As a matter of fact, Engels speaks here of the destruction of the bourgeois state by the proletarian revolution, while the words about its withering away refer to the remains of *proletarian* statehood *after* the Socialist revolution. The bourgeois state does not "wither away," according to Engels, but is "put an end to" by the proletariat in the course of the revolution. What withers away after the revolution is the proletarian state or semi-state.

Secondly, the state is a "special repressive force." This splendid and extremely profound definition of Engels' is given by him here with complete lucidity. It follows from this that the "special repressive force" of the bourgeoisie for the suppression of the proletariat, of the millions of workers by a handful of the rich, must be replaced by a "special repressive force" of the proletariat for the suppression of the bourgeoisie (the dictatorship of the proletariat). It is just this that constitutes the destruction of "the state as the state." It is just this that constitutes the "act" of "the seizure of the means of production in the name of society." And it is obvious that such a substitution of one (proletarian) "special repressive force" for another (bourgeois) "special repressive force" can in no way take place in the form of a "withering away."

Thirdly, as to the "withering away" or, more expressively and colourfully, as to the state "becoming dormant," Engels refers quite clearly and definitely to the period *after* "the seizure of the means of production [by the state] in the name of society," that is, *after* the Socialist revolution. We all know that the political form of the "state" at that time is complete democracy. But it never enters the head of any of the opportunists who shamelessly distort Marx that when Engels speaks here of the state "withering away," or "becoming dormant," he speaks of *democracy*. At first sight this seems very strange. But it is "unintelligible" only to one who has not reflected on the fact that democracy is *also* a state and that, consequently, democracy will *also* disappear when the state disappears. The bourgeois state can only be "put an end to" by a revolution. The state in general, *i.e.*, most complete democracy, can only "wither away."

Fourthly, having formulated his famous proposition that "the state withers away," Engels at once explains concretely that this proposition is directed equally against the opportunists and the Anarchists. In doing this, however, Engels puts in the first place that conclusion from his proposition about the "withering away" of the state which is directed against the opportunists.

One can wager that out of every 10,000 persons who have read or heard about the "withering away" of the state, 9,990 do not know at all, or do not remember, that Engels did not direct his conclusions from this proposition against the Anarchists *alone*. And out of the remaining ten, probably nine do not know the meaning of a "people's free state" nor the reason why an attack on this watchword contains an attack on the opportunists. This is how history is written! This is how a great revolutionary doctrine is imperceptibly adulterated and adapted to current philistinism! The conclusion drawn against the Anarchists has been repeated thousands of times, vulgarised, harangued about in the crudest fashion possible until it has acquired the strength of a prejudice, whereas the conclusion drawn against the opportunists has been hushed up and "forgotten"!

The "people's free state" was a demand in the programme of the German Social-Democrats and their current slogan in the 'seventies. There is no political substance in this slogan other than a pompous middle-class circumlocution of the idea of democracy. In so far as it referred in a lawful manner to a democratic republic, Engels was prepared to "justify" its use "at times" from a propaganda point of view. But this slogan was opportunist, for it not only expressed an exaggerated view of the attractiveness of bourgeois democracy, but also a lack of understanding of the Socialist criticism of every state in general. We are in favour of a democratic republic as the best form of the state for the proletariat under capitalism, but we have no right to forget that wage slavery is the lot of the people even in the most democratic bourgeois republic. Furthermore, every state is a "special repressive force" for the suppression of the oppressed class. Consequently, *no* state is either "free" or a "people's state." Marx and Engels explained this repeatedly to their party comrades in the 'seventies.

Fifthly, in the same work of Engels, from which every one remembers his argument on the "withering away" of the state, there is also a disquisition on the significance of a violent revolution. The historical analysis of its rôle becomes, with Engels, a veritable panegyric on violent revolution. This, of course, "no one remembers"; to talk or even to think of the importance of this idea is not considered good form by contemporary Socialist parties, and in the daily propaganda and agitation among the masses it plays no part whatever. Yet it is indissolubly bound up with the "withering away" of the state in one harmonious whole.

Here is Engels' argument:

> . . . That force, however, plays another rôle (other than that of a diabolical power) in history, a revolutionary rôle; that, in the words of Marx, it is the midwife of every old society which is pregnant with the new; that it is the instrument with whose aid social movement forces its way through and shatters the dead, fossilised political forms—of this there is not a word in Herr Dühring. It is only with sighs and groans that he admits the possibility that force will perhaps be necessary for the overthrow of the economic system of exploitation—unfortunately! because all use of force, forsooth, demoralises the person who uses it. And this in spite of the immense moral and spiritual impetus which has resulted from every victorious revolution! And this in Germany, where a violent collision—which indeed may be forced on the people—would at least have the advantage of wiping out the servility which has permeated the national consciousness as a result of the humiliation of the Thirty Years' War. And this parson's mode of thought—lifeless, insipid and impotent—claims to impose itself on the most revolutionary party which history has known?[8]

How can this panegyric on violent revolution, which Engels insistently brought to the attention of the German Social-Democrats between 1878 and 1894, *i.e.*, right to the time of his death, be combined with the theory of the "withering away" of the state to form one doctrine?

Usually the two views are combined by means of eclecticism, by an unprincipled, sophistic, arbitrary selection (to oblige the powers that be) of either one or the other argument, and in ninety-nine cases out of a hundred (if not more often), it is the idea of the "withering away" that is specially emphasised. Eclecticism is substituted for dialectics—this is the most usual, the most widespread phenomenon to be met with in the official Social-Democratic literature of our day in relation to Marxism. Such a substitution is, of course, nothing new; it may be observed even in the history of classic Greek philosophy. When Marxism is adulterated to become oppor-

[8] *Ibid.—Ed.*

tunism, the substitution of eclecticism for dialectics is the best method of deceiving the masses; it gives an illusory satisfaction; it seems to take into account all sides of the process, all the tendencies of development, all the contradictory factors and so forth, whereas in reality it offers no consistent and revolutionary view of the process of social development at all.

We have already said above and shall show more fully later that the teaching of Marx and Engels regarding the inevitability of a violent revolution refers to the bourgeois state. It *cannot* be replaced by the proletarian state (the dictatorship of the proletariat) through "withering away," but, as a general rule, only through a violent revolution. The panegyric sung in its honour by Engels and fully corresponding to the repeated declarations of Marx (remember the concluding passages of the *Poverty of Philosophy* and the *Communist Manifesto,* with its proud and open declaration of the inevitability of a violent revolution; remember Marx's *Critique of the Gotha Programme* of 1875 in which, almost thirty years later, he mercilessly castigates the opportunist character of that programme) —this praise is by no means a mere "impulse," a mere declamation, or a polemical sally. The necessity of systematically fostering among the masses *this* and just this point of view about violent revolution lies at the root of the *whole* of Marx's and Engels' teaching. The neglect of such propaganda and agitation by both the present predominant social-chauvinist and the Kautskyist currents brings their betrayal of Marx's and Engels' teaching into prominent relief.

The replacement of the bourgeois by the proletarian state is impossible without a violent revolution. The abolition of the proletarian state, *i.e.,* of all states, is only possible through "withering away."

Marx and Engels gave a full and concrete exposition of these views in studying each revolutionary situation separately, in analysing the lessons of the experience of each individual revolution. We now pass to this, undoubtedly the most important part of their work.

CHAPTER II

THE EXPERIENCES OF 1848–1851

1. On the Eve of Revolution

The first productions of mature Marxism—the *Poverty of Philosophy* and the *Communist Manifesto*—were created on the very eve of the Revolution of 1848. For this reason we have in them, side by side with a statement of the general principles of Marxism, a reflection, to a certain degree, of the concrete revolutionary situation of the time. Consequently, it will possibly be more to the point to examine what the authors of these works say about the state immediately before they draw conclusions from the experience of the years 1848–1851.

> In the course of its development,—wrote Marx in the *Poverty of Philosophy*—the working class will replace the old bourgeois society by an association which excludes classes and their antagonism, and there will no longer be any real political power, for political power is precisely the official expression of the class antagonism within bourgeois society.

It is instructive to compare with this general statement of the idea of the state disappearing after classes have disappeared, the statement contained in the *Communist Manifesto*, written by Marx and Engels a few months later—to be exact, in November, 1847:

> In depicting the most general phases of the development of the proletariat, we traced the more or less veiled civil war, raging within existing society, up to the point where that war breaks out into open revolution, and where the violent overthrow of the bourgeoisie lays the foundation for the sway of the proletariat. . . .
> We have seen above that the first step in the revolution by the working class is to raise [literally "promote"] the proletariat to the position of ruling class, to establish democracy.
> The proletariat will use its political supremacy to wrest by degrees all capital from the bourgeoisie, to centralise all instruments of production in the hands of the state, *i.e.*, of the proletariat organised as the ruling class; and

to increase the total of productive forces as rapidly as possible.

Here we have a formulation of one of the most remarkable and most important ideas of Marxism on the subject of the state, namely, the idea of the "dictatorship of the proletariat" (as Marx and Engels began to term it after the Paris Commune); and also a definition of the state, in the highest degree interesting, but nevertheless also belonging to the category of "forgotten words" of Marxism: *"the state,* i.e., *the proletariat organised as the ruling class."*

This definition of the state, far from having ever been explained in the current propaganda and agitation literature of the official Social-Democratic parties, has been actually forgotten, as it is absolutely irreconcilable with reformism, and is a slap in the face of the common opportunist prejudices and philistine illusions about the "peaceful development of democracy."

The proletariat needs the state—this is repeated by all the opportunists, social-chauvinists and Kautskyists, who assure us that this is what Marx taught. They "forget," however, to add that, in the first place, the proletariat, according to Marx, needs only a state which is withering away, *i.e.,* a state which is so constituted that it begins to wither away immediately, and cannot but wither away; and, secondly, the workers need "a state, *i.e.,* the proletariat organised as the ruling class."

The state is a special organisation of force; it is the organisation of violence for the suppression of some class. What class must the proletariat suppress? Naturally, the exploiting class only, *i.e.,* the bourgeoisie. The toilers need the state only to overcome the resistance of the exploiters, and only the proletariat can direct this suppression and bring it to fulfilment, for the proletariat is the only class that is thoroughly revolutionary, the only class that can unite all the toilers and the exploited in the struggle against the bourgeoisie, in completely displacing it.

The exploiting classes need political rule in order to maintain exploitation, *i.e.,* in the selfish interests of an insignificant minority, and against the vast majority of the people. The exploited classes need political rule in order completely to abolish all exploitation, *i.e.,* in the interests of the vast majority of the people, and against the insignificant minority consisting of the slave-owners of modern times—the landowners and the capitalists.

The petty-bourgeois democrats, these sham Socialists who

have substituted for the class struggle dreams of harmony between classes, imagined even the transition to Socialism in a dreamy fashion—not in the form of the overthrow of the rule of the exploiting class, but in the form of the peaceful submission of the minority to a majority conscious of its aims. This petty-bourgeois Utopia, indissolubly connected with the idea of the state's being above classes, in practice led to the betrayal of the interests of the toiling classes, as was shown, for example, in the history of the French revolutions of 1848 and 1871, and in the participation of "Socialists" in bourgeois cabinets in England, France, Italy and other countries at the end of the nineteenth and the beginning of the twentieth centuries.

Marx fought all his life against this petty-bourgeois Socialism—now reborn in Russia in the Socialist-Revolutionary and Menshevik Parties. He carried his analysis of the class struggle logically right to the doctrine of political power, the doctrine of the state.

The overthrow of bourgeois rule can be accomplished only by the proletariat, as the particular class, which, by the economic conditions of its existence, is being prepared for this work and is provided both with the opportunity and the power to perform it. While the capitalist class breaks up and atomises the peasantry and all the petty-bourgeois strata, it welds together, unites and organises the town proletariat. Only the proletariat—by virtue of its economic rôle in large-scale production—is capable of leading *all* the toiling and exploited masses, who are exploited, oppressed, crushed by the bourgeoisie not less, and often more, than the proletariat, but who are incapable of carrying on the struggle for their freedom *independently*.

The doctrine of the class struggle, as applied by Marx to the question of the state and of the Socialist revolution, leads inevitably to the recognition of the *political rule* of the proletariat, of its dictatorship, *i.e.*, of a power shared with none and relying directly upon the armed force of the masses. The overthrow of the bourgeoisie is realisable only by the transformation of the proletariat into the *ruling class*, able to crush the inevitable and desperate resistance of the bourgeoisie, and to organise, for the new economic order, *all* the toiling and exploited masses.

The proletariat needs state power, the centralised organisation of force, the organisation of violence, both for the purpose of crushing the resistance of the exploiters and for the purpose of *guiding* the great mass of the population—the peasantry, the petty-bourgeoisie, the semi-proletarians—in the work of organising Socialist economy.

By educating a workers' party, Marxism educates the vanguard of the proletariat, capable of assuming power and of *leading the whole people* to Socialism, of directing and organising the new order, of being the teacher, guide and leader of all the toiling and exploited in the task of building up their social life without the bourgeoisie and against the bourgeoisie. As against this, the opportunism predominant at present breeds in the workers' party representatives of the better-paid workers, who lose touch with the rank and file, "get along" fairly well under capitalism, and sell their birthright for a mess of pottage, *i.e.*, renounce their rôle of revolutionary leaders of the people against the bourgeoisie.

"The state, *i.e.*, the proletariat organised as the ruling class" —this theory of Marx's is indissolubly connected with all his teaching concerning the revolutionary rôle of the proletariat in history. The culmination of this rôle is proletarian dictatorship, the political rule of the proletariat.

But, if the proletariat needs the state, as a *special* form of organisation of violence *against* the capitalist class, the following question arises almost automatically: is it thinkable that such an organisation can be created without a preliminary break-up and destruction of the state machinery created for *its own* use by the bourgeoisie? The *Communist Manifesto* leads straight to this conclusion, and it is of this conclusion that Marx speaks when summing up the experience of the revolution of 1848–1851.

2. Results of the Revolution

On the question of the state which we are concerned with, Marx sums up his conclusions from the revolution of 1848–1851 in the following observations contained in his work, *The Eighteenth Brumaire of Louis Bonaparte:*

. . . But the revolution is thorough. It is still on its way through purgatory. It is completing its task methodically. By December 2nd, 1851 [the day of Louis Bonaparte's *coup d'état*], it had completed one-half of its preparatory work; now it is completing the other half. First, it perfected parliamentary power, so that it could overthrow it. Now, when it has achieved this, it is perfecting *executive power*, reducing it to its purest terms, isolating it, setting it over against itself as the sole object of reproach, so that it can *concentrate against it all its forces of destruction* [the italics are ours]. And when it has completed this second half of its preparatory work, Europe will leap to its feet and shout with joy: well grubbed, old mole!

This executive power with its huge bureaucratic and military organisation, with its extensive and artificial state machinery, a horde of half a million officials in addition to an army of another half a million, this frightful body of parasites wound like a caul about the body of French society and clogging its every pore, arose in the time of the absolute monarchy in the period of the fall of feudalism, which it helped to hasten.

The first French Revolution developed centralisation,

but at the same time it developed the scope, the attributes and the servants of the government power. Napoleon perfected this state machinery. The legitimate monarchy and the July monarchy added nothing to it but a greater division of labour. . . .

Finally, in its struggle against the revolution, the parliamentary Republic found itself compelled to strengthen with its repressive measures, the resources and the centralisation of the government power. *All revolutions brought this machine to greater perfection, instead of breaking it up* [the italics are ours]. The parties which alternately contended for supremacy looked on the capture of this vast state edifice as the chief spoils of the victor.

In this remarkable passage Marxism makes a tremendous step forward in comparison with the position of the *Communist Manifesto*. There the question of the state still is treated extremely in the abstract, in the most general terms and expressions. Here the question is treated in a concrete manner, and the conclusion is most precise, definite, practical and palpable: all revolutions which have taken place up to the present have helped to perfect the state machinery, whereas it must be shattered, broken to pieces.

This conclusion is the chief and fundamental thesis in the Marxist theory of the state. Yet it is this fundamental thesis which has been not only completely *forgotten* by the dominant official Social-Democratic parties, but directly *distorted* (as we shall see later) by the foremost theoretician of the Second International, K. Kautsky.

In the *Communist Manifesto* are summed up the general lessons of history, which force us to see in the state the organ of class domination, and lead us to the inevitable conclusion that the proletariat cannot overthrow the bourgeoisie without first conquering political power, without obtaining political rule, without transforming the state into the "proletariat organised as the ruling class"; and that this proletarian state will begin to wither away immediately after its victory, because in a society without class antagonisms, the state is unnecessary and impossible. The question as to how, from the point of view of historical development, this replacement of the capitalist state by the proletarian state shall take place, is not raised here.

It is precisely this question that Marx raises and solves in 1852. True to his philosophy of dialectical materialism, Marx takes as his basis the experience of the great revolutionary years 1848–1851. Here, as everywhere, his teaching is the *summing up of experience,* illuminated by a profound philosophical world-conception and a rich knowledge of history.

The problem of the state is put concretely: how did the bourgeois state, the state machinery necessary for the rule of the bourgeoisie, come into being? What were its changes, what its evolution in the course of the bourgeois revolutions and in the face of the independent actions of the oppressed classes? What are the tasks of the proletariat relative to this state machinery?

The centralised state power peculiar to bourgeois society came into being in the period of the fall of absolutism. Two institutions are especially characteristic of this state machinery: bureaucracy and the standing army. In their works, Marx and Engels mention repeatedly the thousand threads which connect these institutions with the bourgeoisie. The experience of every worker illustrates this connection in the clearest and most impressive manner. From its own bitter experience, the working class learns to recognise this connection; that is why it so easily acquires, so completely absorbs the doctrine revealing this inevitable connection, a doctrine which the petty-bourgeois democrats either ignorantly and light-heartedly deny, or, still more light-heartedly, admit "in general," forgetting to draw adequate practical conclusions.

Bureaucracy and the standing army constitute a "parasite" on the body of bourgeois society—a parasite born of the internal antagonisms which tear that society asunder, but essentially a parasite, "clogging every pore" of existence. The Kautskyist opportunism prevalent at present within official Social-Democracy considers this view of the state as a *parasitic organism* to be the peculiar and exclusive property of Anarchism. Naturally, this distortion of Marxism is extremely useful to those philistines who have brought Socialism to the unheard-of disgrace of justifying and embellishing the imperialist war by applying to it the term of "national defence"; but none the less it is an absolute distortion.

The development, perfecting and strengthening of the bureaucratic and military apparatus has been going on through all the bourgeois revolutions of which Europe has seen so many since the fall of feudalism. It is particularly the petty bourgeoisie that is attracted to the side of the big bourgeoisie and to its allegiance, largely by means of this apparatus, which provides the upper strata of the peasantry, small artisans and tradesmen with a number of comparatively comfortable, quiet and respectable berths raising their holders *above* the people. Consider what happened in Russia during the six months following March 12, 1917. The government posts which hitherto had been given by preference to members of the Black Hundreds now became the booty of Cadets, Mensheviks and S.-R.'s. Nobody really thought of any serious reform. They were to be put off "until the Constituent Assembly," which, in its turn, was eventually to be put off until the end of the war! But there was no delay, no waiting for a Constituent Assembly in the matter of dividing the spoils, of getting hold of the berths of ministers, Assistant-Ministers, governor-generals, etc., etc.! The game that went on of changing the combination of persons forming the Provisional Government was, in essence, only the expression of this division and re-division of the "spoils," which was going on high and low, throughout the country, throughout the central and local government. The practical results of the six months between March 12 and September 9, 1917, beyond all dispute, are: reforms shelved, distribution of officials' berths accomplished, and "mistakes" in the distribution corrected by a few re-distributions.

But the longer the process of "re-apportioning" the bureaucratic apparatus among the various bourgeois and petty-bourgeois parties (among the Cadets, S.-R.'s and Mensheviks, if we take the case of Russia) goes on, the more clearly the oppressed classes, with the proletariat at their head, realise that they are irreconcilably hostile to the *whole* of bourgeois society. Hence the necessity for all bourgeois parties, even for the most democratic and "revolutionary-democratic" among them, to increase their repressive measures against the revolutionary proletariat, to strengthen the apparatus of repression, *i.e.*, the same state machinery. Such a course of events compels the revolution *"to concentrate all its forces of destruction"* against the state power, and to regard the problem as one, not of perfecting the machinery of the state, but of *breaking up and annihilating it.*

It was not logical theorising, but the actual course of events, the living experience of 1848–1851, that produced such a statement of the problem. To what extent Marx held strictly to the solid ground of historical experience we can see from the fact that, in 1852, he did not as yet deal concretely with the question of *what* was to replace this state machinery that was to be destroyed. Experience had not yet yielded material for the solution of this problem which history placed on the order of the day later on, in 1871. What could be laid down in 1852 with the accuracy of observation characterising the natural sciences, was that the proletarian revolution *had approached* the task of "concentrating all its forces of destruction" against the state, of "breaking up" the governmental machinery.

Here the question may arise: is it correct to generalise the experience, observations and conclusions of Marx, to apply them to a wider field than the history of France during the three years 1848–1851? To analyse this question, let us recall, first of all, a certain remark of Engels, and then proceed to examine the facts.

France—wrote Engels in his introduction to the third edition of the *Eighteenth Brumaire*—is the country where, more than anywhere else, historical class struggles have been always fought through to a decisive conclusion, and therefore where also the changing political forms within which the struggles developed, and in which their results were summed up, were stamped in sharpest outline. The centre of feudalism in the Middle Ages, the model country (since the Renaissance) of a rigidly unified monarchy, in the great revolution France shattered feudalism and established the unadulterated rule of the bourgeoisie in a more classical form than any other European country. And here also the struggle of the rising proletariat against the ruling bourgeoisie appeared in an acute form such as was unknown elsewhere.

The last sentence is out of date, inasmuch as there has been a lull in the revolutionary struggle of the French proletariat since 1871; though, long as this lull may be, it in no way excludes the possibility that, in the coming proletarian revolution, France may once more reveal itself as the traditional home of the struggle of classes to a finish.

Let us, however, cast a general glance over the history of the more advanced countries during the end of the nineteenth and beginning of the twentieth centuries. We shall see that the same process has been going on more slowly, in more varied forms, on a much wider field: on the one hand, a development of "parliamentary power," not only in the republican countries (France, America, Switzerland), but also in the monarchies (England, Germany to a certain extent, Italy, the Scandinavian countries, etc.); on the other hand, a struggle for power of various bourgeois and petty-bourgeois parties distributing and redistributing the "spoils" of officials' berths, the foundations of capitalist society remaining all the while unchanged; finally, the perfecting and strengthening of the "executive power," its bureaucratic and military apparatus.

There is no doubt that these are the features common to the latest stage in the evolution of all capitalist states generally. In the three years, 1848–1851, France showed, in a swift, sharp, concentrated form, all those processes of development which are inherent in the whole capitalist world.

Imperialism in particular—the era of banking capital, the era of gigantic capitalist monopolies, the era of the transformation of monopoly capitalism into state monopoly-capitalism—shows an unprecedented strengthening of the "state machinery" and an unprecedented growth of its bureaucratic and military apparatus, side by side with the increase of repressive measures against the proletariat, alike in the monarchical and the freest republican countries.

At the present time, world history is undoubtedly leading, on an incomparably larger scale than in 1852, to the "concentration of all the forces" of the proletarian revolution for the purpose of "destroying" the state machinery.

As to what the proletariat will put in its place, instructive data on the subject were furnished by the Paris Commune.

3. The Formulation of the Question by Marx in 1852

In 1907 Mehring published in the magazine *Neue Zeit* (Vol. XXV–2, p. 164) extracts from a letter by Marx to

Weydemeyer dated March 5, 1852. In this letter, among other things, is the following noteworthy observation:

As far as I am concerned, the honour does not belong to me for having discovered the existence either of classes in modern society or of the struggle between the classes. Bourgeois historians a long time before me expounded the historical development of this class struggle, and bourgeois economists, the economic anatomy of classes. What was new on my part, was to prove the following: (1) that the existence of classes is connected only with certain historical struggles which arise out of the development of production [*historische Entwicklungskämpfe der Produktion*]; (2) that class struggle necessarily leads to the dictatorship of the proletariat; (3) that this dictatorship is itself only a transition to the abolition of all classes and to a classless society.

In these words Marx has succeeded in expressing with striking clearness, first, the chief and concrete differences between his teachings and those of the most advanced and profound thinkers of the bourgeoisie, and second, the essence of his teachings concerning the state.

The main point in the teaching of Marx is the class struggle. This has very often been said and written. But this is not true. Out of this error, here and there, springs an opportunist distortion of Marxism, such a falsification of it as to make it acceptable to the bourgeoisie. The theory of the class struggle was *not* created by Marx, but by the bourgeoisie *before* Marx and is, generally speaking, *acceptable* to the bourgeoisie. He who recognises *only* the class struggle is not yet a Marxist; he may be found not to have gone beyond the boundaries of bourgeois reasoning and politics. To limit Marxism to the teaching of the class struggle means to curtail Marxism—to distort it, to reduce it to something which is acceptable to the bourgeoisie. A Marxist is one who *extends* the acceptance of class struggle to the acceptance of the *dictatorship of the proletariat*. Herein lies the deepest difference between a Marxist and an ordinary petty or big bourgeois. On this touchstone it is necessary to test a *real* understanding and acceptance of Marxism. And it is not astonishing that, when the history of Europe put before the working class this question in a practical way, not only all opportunists and reformists but all Kautskyists (people who vacillate between reformism and Marxism) turned out to be miserable philistines and petty-bourgeois democrats, *denying* the dictatorship of the proletariat. Kautsky's pamphlet, *Dictatorship of the Proletariat*, published in August, 1918, *i.e.*, long after the first edition of this book, is an example of petty-bourgeois distortion of Marxism and base renunciation of it *in practice*, while hypocritically recognising it *in words* (see my pamphlet, *The Proletarian Revolution and the Renegade Kautsky*, Petrograd and Moscow, 1918).

The present-day opportunism in the person of its main representative, the former Marxist, K. Kautsky, comes wholly under Marx's characterization of the *bourgeois* position as quoted above, for this opportunism limits the field of recognition of the class struggle to the realm of bourgeois relationships. (Within this realm, inside of its framework, not a single educated liberal will refuse to recognise the class struggle "in principle"!) Opportunism *does not lead* the recognition of class struggle up to the main point, up to the period of *transition* from capitalism to Communism, up to the period of *overthrowing* and completely abolishing the bourgeoisie. In reality, this period inevitably becomes a period of unusually violent class struggles in their sharpest possible forms and, therefore, the state during this period inevitably must be a state that is democratic *in a new way* (for the proletariat and the poor in general) and dictatorial *in a new way* (against the bourgeoisie).

Further, the substance of the teachings of Marx about the state is assimilated only by one who understands that the dictatorship of a *single* class is necessary not only for any class society generally, not only for the *proletariat* which has overthrown the bourgeoisie, but for the entire *historic period* which separates capitalism from "classless society," from Communism. The forms of bourgeois states are exceedingly variegated, but their essence is the same: in one way or another, all these states are in the last analysis inevitably a *dictatorship of the bourgeoisie*. The transition from capitalism to Communism will certainly bring a great variety and abundance of political forms, but the essence will inevitably be only one: *the dictatorship of the proletariat*.

CHAPTER V

THE ECONOMIC BASE OF THE WITHERING AWAY

OF THE STATE

A most detailed elucidation of this question is given by
Marx in his *Critique of the Gotha Programme* (letter to
Bracke, May 15, 1875, printed only in 1891 in the *Neue
Zeit*, IX–1, and in a special Russian edition[9]). The polemical
part of this remarkable work, consisting of a criticism of
Lassalleanism, has, so to speak, overshadowed its positive
part, namely, the analysis of the connection between the
development of Communism and the withering away of the
state.

1. Formulation of the Question by Marx

From a superficial comparison of the letter of Marx to
Bracke (May 15, 1875) with Engels' letter to Bebel (March
28, 1875), analysed above, it might appear that Marx was
much more "prostate" than Engels, and that the difference of
opinion between the two writers on the question of the state
is very considerable.

Engels suggests to Bebel that all the chatter about the
state should be thrown overboard; that the word "state"
should be eliminated from the programme and replaced by
"community"; Engels even declares that the Commune was
really no longer a state in the proper sense of the word. And
Marx even speaks of the "future state in Communist society,"
i.e., he is apparently recognising the necessity of a state even
under Communism.

But such a view would be fundamentally incorrect. A
closer examination shows that Marx's and Engels' views on
the state and its withering away were completely identical,
and that Marx's expression quoted above refers merely to this
withering away of the state.

It is clear that there can be no question of defining the
exact moment of the *future* withering away—the more so as
it must obviously be a rather lengthy process. The apparent
difference between Marx and Engels is due to the different

[9] English translation in *Critique of the Social-Democratic Pro-
grammes.—Ed.*

subjects they dealt with, the different aims they were pursuing. Engels set out to show to Bebel, in a plain, bold and broad outline, all the absurdity of the current superstitions concerning the state, shared to no small degree by Lassalle himself. Marx, on the other hand, only touches upon *this* question in passing, being interested mainly in another subject— the *evolution* of Communist society.

The whole theory of Marx is an application of the theory of evolution—in its most consistent, complete, well considered and fruitful form—to modern capitalism. It was natural for Marx to raise the question of applying this theory both to the *coming* collapse of capitalism and to the *future* evolution of *future* Communism.

On the basis of what *data* can the future evolution of future Communism be considered?

On the basis of the fact that *it has its origin* in capitalism, that it develops historically from capitalism, that it is the result of the action of a social force to which capitalism *has given birth*. There is no shadow of an attempt on Marx's part to conjure up a Utopia, to make idle guesses about that which cannot be known. Marx treats the question of Communism in the same way as a naturalist would treat the question of the evolution of, say, a new biological species, if he knew that such and such was its origin, and such and such the direction in which it changed.

Marx, first of all, brushes aside the confusion the Gotha Programme brings into the question of the interrelation between state and society.

> "Contemporary society" is the capitalist society—he writes—which exists in all civilized countries, more or less free of mediaeval admixture, more or less modified by each country's particular historical development, more or less developed. In contrast with this, the "contemporary state" varies with every state boundary. It is different in the Prusso-German Empire from what it is in Switzerland, and different in England from what it is in the United States. The "contemporary state" is therefore a fiction.
>
> Nevertheless, in spite of the motley variety of their forms, the different states of the various civilised countries all have this in common: they are all based on modern bourgeois society, only a little more or less capitalistically developed. Consequently, they also have

certain essential characteristics in common. In this sense, it is possible to speak of the "contemporary state" in contrast to the future, when its present root, bourgeois society, will have perished.

Then the question arises: what transformation will the state undergo in a Communist society? In other words, what social functions analogous to the present functions of the state will then still survive? This question can only be answered scientifically, and however many thousand times the word people is combined with the word state, we get not a flea-jump closer to the problem. . . .

Having thus ridiculed all talk about a "people's state," Marx formulates the question and warns us, as it were, that to arrive at a scientific answer one must rely only on firmly established scientific data.

The first fact that has been established with complete exactness by the whole theory of evolution, by science as a whole—a fact which the Utopians forgot, and which is forgotten by the present-day opportunists who are afraid of the Socialist revolution—is that, historically, there must undoubtedly be a special stage or epoch of *transition* from capitalism to Communism.

2. *Transition from Capitalism to Communism*

Between capitalist and Communist society—Marx continues—lies the period of the revolutionary transformation of the former into the latter. To this also corresponds a political transition period, in which the state can be no other than *the revolutionary dictatorship of the proletariat.*[10]

This conclusion Marx bases on an analysis of the rôle played by the proletariat in modern capitalist society, on the data concerning the evolution of this society, and on the irreconcilability of the opposing interests of the proletariat and the bourgeoisie.

Earlier the question was put thus: to attain its emancipation, the proletariat must overthrow the bourgeoisie, conquer political power and establish its own revolutionary dictatorship.

Now the question is put somewhat differently: the transition from capitalist society, developing towards Communism,

[10] *Ibid.—Ed.*

towards a Communist society, is impossible without a "political transition period," and the state in this period can only be the revolutionary dictatorship of the proletariat.

What, then, is the relation of this dictatorship to democracy?

We have seen that the *Communist Manifesto* simply places side by side the two ideas: the "transformation of the proletariat into the ruling class" and the "establishment of democracy." On the basis of all that has been said above, one can define more exactly how democracy changes in the transition from capitalism to Communism.

In capitalist society, under the conditions most favourable to its development, we have more or less complete democracy in the democratic republic. But this democracy is always bound by the narrow framework of capitalist exploitation, and consequently always remains, in reality, a democracy for the minority, only for the possessing classes, only for the rich. Freedom in capitalist society always remains just about the same as it was in the ancient Greek republics: freedom for the slave-owners. The modern wage-slaves, owing to the conditions of capitalist exploitation, are so much crushed by want and poverty that "democracy is nothing to them," "politics is nothing to them"; that, in the ordinary peaceful course of events, the majority of the population is debarred from participating in social and political life.

The correctness of this statement is perhaps most clearly proved by Germany, just because in this state constitutional legality lasted and remained stable for a remarkably long time—for nearly half a century (1871–1914)—and because Social-Democracy in Germany during that time was able to achieve far more than in other countries in "utilising legality," and was able to organise into a political party a larger proportion of the working class than anywhere else in the world.

What, then, is this largest proportion of politically conscious and active wage-slaves that has so far been observed in capitalist society? One million members of the Social-Democratic Party—out of fifteen million wage-workers! Three million organised in trade unions—out of fifteen million!

Democracy for an insignificant minority, democracy for the rich—that is the democracy of capitalist society. If we look more closely into the mechanism of capitalist democracy, everywhere, both in the "petty"—so-called petty—details of the suffrage (residential qualification, exclusion of women, etc.), and in the technique of the representative institutions, in the actual obstacles to the right of assembly (public buildings are not for "beggars"!), in the purely capitalist organisation of the daily press, etc., etc.—on all sides we see restriction after restriction upon democracy. These restrictions, exceptions, exclusions, obstacles for the poor, seem slight, especially in the eyes of one who has himself never known want and has never been in close contact with the oppressed classes in their mass life (and nine-tenths, if not ninety-nine hundredths, of the bourgeois publicists and politicians are of this class), but in their sum total these restrictions exclude and squeeze out the poor from politics and from an active share in democracy.

Marx splendidly grasped this *essence* of capitalist democracy, when, in analysing the experience of the Commune, he said that the oppressed were allowed, once every few years, to decide which particular representatives of the oppressing class should be in parliament to represent and repress them!

But from this capitalist democracy—inevitably narrow, subtly rejecting the poor, and therefore hypocritical and false to the core—progress does not march onward, simply, smoothly and directly, to "greater and greater democracy," as the liberal professors and petty-bourgeois opportunists would have us believe. No, progress marches onward, *i.e.*, towards Communism, through the dictatorship of the proletariat; it cannot do otherwise, for there is no one else and no other way to *break the resistance* of the capitalist exploiters.

But the dictatorship of the proletariat—*i.e.*, the organisation of the vanguard of the oppressed as the ruling class for the purpose of crushing the oppressors—cannot produce merely an expansion of democracy. *Together* with an immense expansion of democracy which *for the first time* becomes democracy for the poor, democracy for the people and not democracy for the rich folk, the dictatorship of the proletariat produces a series of restrictions of liberty in the case of the oppressors, the exploiters, the capitalists. We must crush them in order to free humanity from wage-slavery; their resistance must be broken by force; it is clear that where there is suppression there is also violence, there is no liberty, no democracy.

Engels expressed this splendidly in his letter to Bebel when he said, as the reader will remember, that "as long as the proletariat still *needs* the state, it needs it not in the interests of freedom, but for the purpose of crushing its antagonists; and as soon as it becomes possible to speak of freedom, then the state, as such, ceases to exist."

Democracy for the vast majority of the people, and suppression by force, *i.e.*, exclusion from democracy, of the exploiters and oppressors of the people—this is the modification of democracy during the *transition* from capitalism to Communism.

Only in Communist society, when the resistance of the capitalists has been completely broken, when the capitalists have disappeared, when there are no classes (*i.e.*, there is no difference between the members of society in their relation to the social means of production), *only then* "the state ceases to exist," and *"it becomes possible to speak of freedom."* Only then a really full democracy, a democracy without any exceptions, will be possible and will be realised. And only then will democracy itself begin to *wither away* due to the simple fact that, freed from capitalist slavery, from the untold horrors, savagery, absurdities and infamies of capitalist exploitation, people will gradually *become accustomed* to the observance of the elementary rules of social life that have been known for centuries and repeated for thousands of years in all school books; they will become accustomed to observing them without force, without compulsion, without subordination, without the *special apparatus* for compulsion which is called the state.

The expression "the state *withers away*," is very well chosen, for it indicates both the gradual and the elemental nature of the process. Only habit can, and undoubtedly will, have such an effect; for we see around us millions of times how readily people get accustomed to observe the necessary rules of life in common, if there is no exploitation, if there is nothing that causes indignation, that calls forth protest and revolt and has to be *suppressed*.

Thus, in capitalist society, we have a democracy that is curtailed, poor, false; a democracy only for the rich, for the minority. The dictatorship of the proletariat, the period of transition to Communism, will, for the first time, produce democracy for the people, for the majority, side by side with the necessary suppression of the minority—the exploiters. Communism alone is capable of giving a really complete democracy, and the more complete it is the more quickly will it become unnecessary and wither away of itself.

In other words: under capitalism we have a state in the proper sense of the word, that is, special machinery for the suppression of one class by another, and of the majority by the minority at that. Naturally, for the successful discharge of such a task as the systematic suppression by the exploiting minority of the exploited majority, the greatest ferocity and savagery of suppression are required, seas of blood are required, through which mankind is marching in slavery, serfdom, and wage-labour.

Again, during the *transition* from capitalism to Communism, suppression is *still* necessary; but it is the suppression of the minority of exploiters by the majority of exploited. A special apparatus, special machinery for suppression, the "state," is *still* necessary, but this is now a transitional state, no longer a state in the usual sense, for the suppression of the minority of exploiters, by the majority of the wage slaves *of yesterday*, is a matter comparatively so easy, simple and natural that it will cost far less bloodshed than the suppression of the risings of slaves, serfs or wage labourers, and will cost mankind far less. This is compatible with the diffusion of democracy among such an overwhelming majority of the population, that the need for *special machinery* of suppression will begin to disappear. The exploiters are, naturally, unable to suppress the people without a most complex machinery for performing this task; but *the people* can suppress the exploiters even with very simple "machinery," almost without any "machinery," without any special apparatus, by the simple *organisation of the armed masses* (such as the Soviets of Workers' and Soldiers' Deputies, we may remark, anticipating a little).

Finally, only Communism renders the state absolutely unnecessary, for there is *no one* to be suppressed—"no one" in the sense of a *class*, in the sense of a systematic struggle with a definite section of the population. We are not Utopians, and we do not in the least deny the possibility and inevitability of excesses on the part of *individual persons*, nor the need to suppress *such* excesses. But, in the first place, no special machinery, no special apparatus of repression is needed for this; this will be done by the armed people itself, as simply and as readily as any crowd of civilised people, even in modern society, parts a pair of combatants or does not allow a woman to be outraged. And, secondly, we know that the fundamental social cause of excesses which consist in violating the rules of social life is the exploitation of the masses, their want and their poverty. With the removal of this chief cause, excesses will inevitably begin to *"wither away."* We do not know how quickly and in what succession, but we know that they will wither away. With their withering away, the state will also *wither away*.

Without going into Utopias, Marx defined more fully what can *now* be defined regarding this future, namely, the difference between the lower and higher phases (degrees, stages) of Communist society.

3. First Phase of Communist Society

In the *Critique of the Gotha Programme*, Marx goes into some detail to disprove the Lassallean idea of the workers' receiving under Socialism the "undiminished" or "full product of their labour." Marx shows that out of the whole of the social labour of society, it is necessary to deduct a reserve fund, a fund for the expansion of production, for the replacement of worn-out machinery, and so on; then, also, out of the means of consumption must be deducted a fund for the expenses of management, for schools, hospitals, homes for the aged, and so on.

Instead of the hazy, obscure, general phrase of Lassalle's —"the full product of his labour for the worker"—Marx gives a sober estimate of exactly how a Socialist society will have to manage its affairs. Marx undertakes a *concrete* analysis of the conditions of life of a society in which there is no capitalism, and says:

> What we are dealing with here [analysing the programme of the party] is not a Communist society which has *developed* on its own foundations, but, on the contrary, one which is just *emerging* from capitalist society, and which therefore in all respects—economic, moral and intellectual—still bears the birthmarks of the old society from whose womb it sprung.[11]

And it is this Communist society—a society which has just come into the world out of the womb of capitalism, and which, in all respects, bears the stamp of the old society— that Marx terms the "first," or lower, phase of Communist society.

The means of production are no longer the private property of individuals. The means of production belong to the whole of society. Every member of society, performing a certain part of socially-necessary work, receives a certificate from society to the effect that he has done such and such a

[11] *Ibid.—Ed.*

quantity of work. According to this certificate, he receives from the public warehouses, where articles of consumption are stored, a corresponding quantity of products. Deducting that proportion of labour which goes to the public fund, every worker, therefore, receives from society as much as he has given it.

"Equality" seems to reign supreme.

But when Lassalle, having in view such a social order (generally called Socialism, but termed by Marx the first phase of Communism), speaks of this as "just distribution," and says that this is "the equal right of each to an equal product of labour," Lassalle is mistaken, and Marx exposes his error.

"Equal right," says Marx, we indeed have here; but it is *still* a "bourgeois right," which, like every right, *presupposes inequality*. Every right is an application of the *same* measure to *different* people who, in fact, are not the same and are not equal to one another; this is why "equal right" is really a violation of equality, and an injustice. In effect, every man having done as much social labour as every other, receives an equal share of the social products (with the above-mentioned deductions).

But different people are not alike: one is strong, another is weak; one is married, the other is not; one has more children, another has less, and so on.

. . . With equal labour—Marx concludes—and therefore an equal share in the social consumption fund, one man in fact receives more than the other, one is richer than the other, and so forth. In order to avoid all these defects, rights, instead of being equal, must be unequal.[12]

The first phase of Communism, therefore, still cannot produce justice and equality; differences, and unjust differences, in wealth will still exist, but the *exploitation* of man by man will have become impossible, because it will be impossible to seize as private property the *means of production*, the factories, machines, land, and so on. In tearing down Lassalle's petty-bourgeois, confused phrase about "equality" and "justice" *in general*, Marx shows the *course of development* of Communist society, which is forced at first to destroy *only* the "injustice" that consists in the means of production having been seized by private individuals, and which *is not capable* of destroying at once the further injustice consisting

[12] *Ibid.—Ed.*

in the distribution of the articles of consumption "according to work performed" (and not according to need).

The vulgar economists, including the bourgeois professors and also "our" Tugan-Baranovsky, constantly reproach the Socialists with forgetting the inequality of people and with "dreaming" of destroying this inequality. Such a reproach, as we see, only proves the extreme ignorance of the gentlemen propounding bourgeois ideology.

Marx not only takes into account with the greatest accuracy the inevitable inequality of men; he also takes into account the fact that the mere conversion of the means of production into the common property of the whole of society ("Socialism" in the generally accepted sense of the word) *does not remove* the defects of distribution and the inequality of "bourgeois right" which *continue to rule* as long as the products are divided "according to work performed."

> But these defects—Marx continues—are unavoidable in the first phase of Communist society, when, after long travail, it first emerges from capitalist society. Justice can never rise superior to the economic conditions of society and the cultural development conditioned by them.[18]

And so, in the first phase of Communist society (generally called Socialism) "bourgeois right" is *not* abolished in its entirety, but only in part, only in proportion to the economic transformation so far attained, *i.e.*, only in respect of the means of production. "Bourgeois right" recognises them as the private property of separate individuals. Socialism converts them into common property. *To that extent,* and to that extent alone, does "bourgeois right" disappear.

However, it continues to exist as far as its other part is concerned; it remains in the capacity of regulator (determining factor) distributing the products and allotting labour among the members of society. "He who does not work, shall not eat"—this Socialist principle is *already* realised; "for an equal quantity of labour, an equal quantity of products"—this Socialist principle is also *already* realised. However, this is not yet Communism, and this does not abolish "bourgeois right," which gives to unequal individuals, in return for an unequal (in reality unequal) amount of work, an equal quantity of products.

This is a "defect," says Marx, but it is unavoidable during

13 *Ibid.—Ed.*

the first phase of Communism; for, if we are not to fall into Utopianism, we cannot imagine that, having overthrown capitalism, people will at once learn to work for society *without any standards of right;* indeed, the abolition of capitalism *does not immediately lay* the economic foundations for *such* a change.

And there is no other standard yet than that of "bourgeois right." To this extent, therefore, a form of state is still necessary, which, while maintaining public ownership of the means of production, would preserve the equality of labour and equality in the distribution of products.

The state is withering away in so far as there are no longer any capitalists, any classes, and, consequently, no *class* can be suppressed.

But the state has not yet altogether withered away, since there still remains the protection of "bourgeois right" which sanctifies actual inequality. For the complete extinction of the state, complete Communism is necessary.

4. *Higher Phase of Communist Society*

Marx continues:

In a higher phase of Communist society, when the enslaving subordination of individuals in the division of labour has disappeared, and with it also the antagonism between mental and physical labour; when labour has become not only a means of living, but itself the first necessity of life; when, along with the all-round development of individuals, the productive forces too have grown, and all the springs of social wealth are flowing more freely—it is only at that stage that it will be possible to pass completely beyond the narrow horizon of bourgeois rights, and for society to inscribe on its banners: from each according to his ability; to each according to his needs!

Only now can we appreciate the full correctness of Engels' remarks in which he mercilessly ridiculed all the absurdity of combining the words "freedom" and "state." While the state exists there is no freedom. When there is freedom, there will be no state.

The economic basis for the complete withering away of the state is that high stage of development of Communism when the antagonism between mental and physical labour disappears, that is to say, when one of the principal sources of modern *social* inequality disappears—a source, moreover, which it is impossible to remove immediately by the mere conversion of the means of production into public property, by the mere expropriation of the capitalists.

This expropriation will make a gigantic development of the productive forces *possible*. And seeing how incredibly, even now, capitalism *retards* this development, how much progress could be made even on the basis of modern technique at the level it has reached, we have a right to say, with the fullest confidence, that the expropriation of the capitalists will inevitably result in a gigantic development of the productive forces of human society. But how rapidly this development will go forward, how soon it will reach the point of breaking away from the division of labour, of removing the antagonism between mental and physical labour, of transforming work into the "first necessity of life"—this we do not and *cannot* know.

Consequently, we have a right to speak solely of the inevitable withering away of the state, emphasising the protracted nature of this process and its dependence upon the rapidity of development of the *higher phase* of Communism; leaving quite open the question of lengths of time, or the concrete forms of withering away, since material for the solution of such questions is *not available*.

The state will be able to wither away completely when society has realised the rule: "From each according to his ability; to each according to his needs," *i.e.*, when people have become accustomed to observe the fundamental rules of social life, and their labour is so productive, that they voluntarily work *according to their ability*. "The narrow horizon of bourgeois rights," which compels one to calculate, with the hard-heartedness of a Shylock, whether he has not worked half an hour more than another, whether he is not getting less pay than another—this narrow horizon will then be left behind. There will then be no need for any exact calculation by society of the quantity of products to be distributed to each of its members; each will take freely "according to his needs."

From the bourgeois point of view, it is easy to declare such a social order "a pure Utopia," and to sneer at the Socialists for promising each the right to receive from society, without any control of the labour of the individual citizen, any quantity of truffles, automobiles, pianos, etc.

Even now, most bourgeois "savants" deliver themselves of such sneers, thereby displaying at once their ignorance and their self-seeking defence of capitalism.

Ignorance—for it has never entered the head of any Socialist to "promise" that the highest phase of Communism will arrive; while the great Socialists, in *foreseeing* its arrival, presupposed both a productivity of labour unlike the present and a person not like the present man in the street, capable of spoiling, without reflection, like the seminary students in Pomyalovsky's book,[14] the stores of social wealth, and of demanding the impossible.

Until the "higher" phase of Communism arrives, the Socialists demand the *strictest* control, *by society and by the state,* of the quantity of labour and the quantity of consumption; only this control must *start* with the expropriation of the capitalists, with the control of the workers over the capitalists, and must be carried out, not by a state of bureaucrats, but by a state of *armed workers.*

Self-seeking defence of capitalism by the bourgeois ideologists (and their hangers-on like Tsereteli, Chernov and Co.) consists in that they *substitute* disputes and discussions about the distant future for the essential imperative questions of present-day policy: the expropriation of the capitalists, the conversion of *all* citizens into workers and employees of *one* huge "syndicate"—the whole state—and the complete subordination of the whole of the work of this syndicate to the really democratic state of the *Soviets of Workers' and Soldiers' Deputies.*

In reality, when a learned professor, and following him some philistine, and following the latter Messrs. Tsereteli and Chernov, talk of the unreasonable Utopias, of the demagogic promises of the Bolsheviks, of the impossibility of "introducing" Socialism, it is the higher stage or phase of Communism which they have in mind, and which no one has ever promised, or even thought of "introducing," for the reason that, generally speaking, it cannot be "introduced."

And here we come to that question of the scientific difference between Socialism and Communism, upon which Engels touched in his above-quoted discussion on the incorrectness of the name "Social-Democrat." The political difference between the first, or lower, and the higher phase of Com-

---

[14] Pomyalovsky's *Seminary Sketches* depicted a group of student-ruffians who engaged in destroying things for the pleasure it gave them.—*Ed.*

munism will in time, no doubt, be tremendous; but it would be ridiculous to emphasise it now, under capitalism, and only, perhaps, some isolated Anarchist could invest it with primary importance (if there are still some people among the Anarchists who have learned nothing from the Plekhanov-like conversion of the Kropotkins, the Graveses, the Cornelis-sens, and other "leading lights" of Anarchism to social-chauvinism or Anarcho-*Jusquaubout*-ism[15] as Ge, one of the few Anarchists still preserving honour and conscience, has expressed it).

But the scientific difference between Socialism and Communism is clear. What is generally called Socialism was termed by Marx the "first" or lower phase of Communist society. In so far as the means of production become *public* property, the word "Communism" is also applicable here, providing we do not forget that it is *not* full Communism. The great significance of Marx's elucidations consists in this: that here, too, he consistently applies materialist dialectics, the doctrine of evolution, looking upon Communism as something which evolves *out of* capitalism. Instead of artificial, "elaborate," scholastic definitions and profitless disquisitions on the meaning of words (what Socialism is, what Communism is), Marx gives an analysis of what may be called stages in the economic ripeness of Communism.

In its first phase or first stage Communism *cannot* as yet be economically ripe and entirely free of all tradition and of all taint of capitalism. Hence the interesting phenomenon of Communism retaining, in its first phase, "the narrow horizon of bourgeois rights." Bourgeois rights, with respect to distribution of articles of *consumption,* inevitably presupposes, of course, the existence of the *bourgeois state,* for rights are nothing without an apparatus capable of *enforcing* the observance of the rights.

Consequently, for a certain time not only bourgeois rights, but even the bourgeois state remains under Communism, without the bourgeoisie!

This may look like a paradox, or simply a dialectical puzzle for which Marxism is often blamed by people who would not make the least effort to study its extraordinarily profound content.

---

[15] *Jusquaubout*—combination of the French words meaning "until the end." Anarcho-*Jusquaubout*-ism—Anarcho-until-the-End-ism.—*Ed.*

But, as a matter of fact, the old surviving in the new confronts us in life at every step, in nature as well as in society. Marx did not smuggle a scrap of "bourgeois" rights into Communism of his own accord; he indicated what is economically and politically inevitable in a society issuing *from the womb* of capitalism.

Democracy is of great importance for the working class in its struggle for freedom against the capitalists. But democracy is by no means a limit one may not overstep; it is only one of the stages in the course of development from feudalism to capitalism, and from capitalism to Communism.

Democracy means equality. The great significance of the struggle of the proletariat for equality, and the significance of equality as a slogan, are apparent, if we correctly interpret it as meaning the abolition of *classes*. But democracy means only *formal* equality. Immediately after the attainment of equality for all members of society *in respect of* the ownership of the means of production, that is, of equality of labour and equality of wages, there will inevitably arise before humanity the question of going further from formal equality to real equality, *i.e.*, to realising the rule, "From each according to his ability; to each according to his needs." By what stages, by means of what practical measures humanity will proceed to this higher aim—this we do not and cannot know. But it is important to realise how infinitely mendacious is the usual bourgeois presentation of Socialism as something lifeless, petrified, fixed once for all, whereas in reality, it is *only* with Socialism that there will commence a rapid, genuine, real mass advance, in which first the *majority* and then the whole of the population will take part—an advance in all domains of social and individual life.

Democracy is a form of the state—one of its varieties. Consequently, like every state, it consists in organised, systematic application of force against human beings. This on the one hand. On the other hand, however, it signifies the formal recognition of the equality of all citizens, the equal right of all to determine the structure and administration of the state. This, in turn, is connected with the fact that, at a certain stage in the development of democracy, it first rallies the proletariat as a revolutionary class against capitalism, and gives it an opportunity to crush, to smash to bits, to wipe off the face of the earth the bourgeois state machinery—even its republican variety: the standing army, the police, and bureaucracy; then it substitutes for all this a *more* democratic, but still a state machinery in the shape of armed masses of workers, which becomes transformed into universal participation of the people in the militia.

Here "quantity turns into quality": *such* a degree of democracy is bound up with the abandonment of the framework of bourgeois society, and the beginning of its Socialist reconstruction. If *every one* really takes part in the administration of the state, capitalism cannot retain its hold. In its turn, capitalism, as it develops, itself creates *prerequisites* for "every one" *to be able* really to take part in the administration of the state. Among such prerequisites are: universal literacy, already realised in most of the advanced capitalist countries, then the "training and disciplining" of millions of workers by the huge, complex, and socialised apparatus of the post-office, the railways, the big factories, large-scale commerce, banking, etc., etc.

With such *economic* prerequisites it is perfectly possible, immediately, within twenty-four hours after the overthrow of the capitalists and bureaucrats, to replace them, in the control of production and distribution, in the business of *control* of labour and products, by the armed workers, by the whole people in arms. (The question of control and accounting must not be confused with the question of the scientifically educated staff of engineers, agronomists and so on. These gentlemen work today, obeying the capitalists; they will work even better tomorrow, obeying the armed workers.)

Accounting and control—these are the *chief* things necessary for the organising and correct functioning of the *first phase* of Communist society. *All* citizens are here transformed into hired employees of the state, which is made up of the armed workers. *All* citizens become employees and workers of *one* national state "syndicate." All that is required is that they should work equally, should regularly do their share of work, and should receive equal pay. The accounting and control necessary for this have been *simplified* by capitalism to the utmost, till they have become the extraordinarily simple operations of watching, recording and issuing receipts, within the reach of anybody who can read and write and knows the first four rules of arithmetic.[16]

16 When most of the functions of the state are reduced to this accounting and control by the workers themselves, then it ceases to be a "political state," and the "public functions will lose their

When the *majority* of the people begin everywhere to keep such accounts and maintain such control over the capitalists (now converted into employees) and over the intellectual gentry, who still retain capitalist habits, this control will really become universal, general, national; and there will be no way of getting away from it, there will be "nowhere to go."

The whole of society will have become one office and one factory, with equal work and equal pay.

But this "factory" discipline, which the proletariat will extend to the whole of society after the defeat of the capitalists and the overthrow of the exploiters, is by no means our ideal, or our final aim. It is but a *foothold* necessary for the radical cleansing of society of all the hideousness and foulness of capitalist exploitation, *in order to advance further.*

From the moment when all members of society, or even only the overwhelming majority, have learned how to govern the state *themselves,* have taken this business into their own hands, have "established" control over the insignificant minority of capitalists, over the gentry with capitalist leanings, and the workers thoroughly demoralised by capitalism—from this moment the need for any government begins to disappear. The more complete the democracy, the nearer the moment when it begins to be unnecessary. The more democratic the "state" consisting of armed workers, which is "no longer a state in the proper sense of the word," the more rapidly does *every* state begin to wither away.

For when *all* have learned to manage, and independently are actually managing by themselves social production, keeping accounts, controlling the idlers, the gentlefolk, the swindlers and similar "guardians of capitalist traditions," then the escape from this national accounting and control will inevitably become so increasingly difficult, such a rare exception, and will probably be accompanied by such swift and severe punishment (for the armed workers are men of practical life, not sentimental intellectuals, and they will scarcely allow any one to trifle with them), that very soon the *necessity* of observing the simple, fundamental rules of every-day social life in common will have become a *habit.*

The door will then be wide open for the transition from the first phase of Communist society to its higher phase, and along with it to the complete withering away of the state.

---

political character and be transformed into simple administrative functions" (*cf.* above, Chap. IV, § 2 on Engels' polemic against the Anarchists).

Benito Mussolini (1883–1945)

THE DOCTRINE OF FASCISM

I

FUNDAMENTAL IDEAS

Like all sound political conceptions, fascism is action and it is thought; action in which doctrine is immanent, and doctrine arising from a given system of historical forces in which it is inserted, and working on them from within. It has therefore a form correlated to contingencies of time and space; but it has also an ideal content which makes it an expression of truth in the higher region of the history of thought. There is no way of exercising a spiritual influence in the world as a human will dominating the will of others unless one has a conception both of the transient and the specific reality on which that action is to be exercised, and of the permanent and universal reality in which the transient dwells and has its being. To know men one must know man; and to know man one must be acquainted with reality and its laws. There can be no conception of the State which is not fundamentally a conception of life: philosophy or intuition, system of ideas evolving within the framework of logic or concentrated in a vision or a faith, but always, at least potentially, an organic conception of the world.

Thus many of the practical expressions of fascism—such as party organization, system of education, discipline—can only be understood when considered in relation to its general attitude toward life, a spiritual attitude. Fascism sees in the world not only those superficial, material aspects in which man appears as an individual, standing by himself, self-centered, subject to natural law which instinctively urges him toward a life of selfish momentary pleasure; it sees not only the individual but the nation and the country; individuals and generations bound together by a moral law, with common traditions and a mission which, suppressing the instinct for life closed in a brief circle of pleasure, builds up a higher life, founded on duty, a life free from the limitations of time and space, in which the individual by self-sacrifice, the renunciation of self-interest, by death itself can achieve that purely spiritual existence in which his value as a man consists.

The conception is therefore a spiritual one, arising from the general reaction of the century against the flaccid materialistic positivism of the nineteenth century. Anti-positivistic but positive; neither skeptical nor agnostic; neither pessimistic nor supinely optimistic as are, generally speaking, the doctrines (all negative) which place the center of life outside man; whereas, by the exercise of his free will, man can and must create his own world.

Fascism wants man to be active and to engage in action with all his energies; it wants him to be manfully aware of the difficulties besetting him and ready to face them. It conceives of life as a struggle in which it behooves a man to win for himself a really worthy place, first of all by fitting himself (physically, morally, intellectually) to become the implement required for winning it. As for the individual, so for the nation and so for mankind. Hence the high value of culture in all its forms (artistic, religious, scientific), and the outstanding importance of education. Hence also the essential value of work, by which man subjugates nature and creates the human world (economic, political, ethical, intellectual).

This positive conception of life is obviously an ethical one. It invests the whole field of reality as well as the human activities which master it. No action is exempt from moral judgment; no activity can be despoiled of the value which a moral purpose confers on all things. Therefore life, as conceived of by the fascist, is serious, austere, religious; all its manifestations are poised in a world sustained by moral forces and subject to spiritual responsibilities. The fascist disdains an "easy" life.

The fascist conception of life is a religious one, in which man is viewed in his immanent relation to a higher law, endowed with an objective will transcending the individual and raising him to conscious membership in a spiritual society. Those who perceive nothing beyond opportunistic considerations in the religious policy of the fascist regime fail to realize that fascism is not only a system of government but also and above all a system of thought.

In the fascist conception of history, man is man only by virtue of the spiritual process to which he contributes as a member of the family, the social group, the nation, and in function of history to which all nations bring their contribution. Hence the great value of tradition in records, in language, in customs, in the rules of social life. Outside history man is a nonentity. Fascism is therefore opposed to all individualistic abstractions based on eighteenth-century materialism; and it is opposed to all Jacobinistic utopias and innovations. It does not believe in the possibility of "happiness" on earth as conceived by the economistic literature of the eighteenth century, and it therefore rejects the teleological notion that at some future time the human family will secure a final settlement of all its difficulties. This notion runs counter to experience which teaches that life is in continual flux and in process of evolution. In politics fascism aims at realism; in practice it desires to deal only with those problems which are the spontaneous product of historic conditions and which find or suggest their own solutions. Only by entering into the process of reality and taking possession of the forces at work within it can man act on man and on nature.

Anti-individualistic, the fascist conception of life stresses the importance of the State and accepts the individual only in so far as his interests coincide with those of the State, which stands for the conscience and the universal will of man as a historic entity. It is opposed to classical liberalism, which arose as a reaction to absolutism and exhausted its historical function when the State became the expression of the conscience and will of the people. Liberalism denied the State in the name of the individual; fascism reasserts the rights of the State as expressing the real essence of the individual. And if liberty is to be the attribute of living men and not of abstract dummies invented by individualistic liberalism, then fascism stands for liberty, and for the only liberty worth having, the liberty of the State and of the individual within the State. The fascist conception of the State is all-embracing; outside of it no human or spiritual values can exist, much less have value. Thus understood, fascism is totalitarian, and the fascist State—a synthesis and a unit inclusive of all values—interprets, develops, and potentiates the whole life of a people.

No individuals or groups (political parties, cultural associations, economic unions, social classes) are outside the State. Fascism is therefore opposed to socialism to which unity within the State (which amalgamates classes into a single economic and ethical reality) is unknown, and which sees in history nothing but the class struggle. Fascism is likewise opposed to trade-unionism as a class weapon. But when brought within the orbit of the State, fascism recognizes the real needs which gave rise to socialism and trade-unionism, giving them due weight in the guild or corporative system in which divergent interests are coordinated and harmonized in the unity of the State.

Grouped according to their several interests, individuals form classes; they form trade-unions when organized according to their several economic activities; but first and foremost they form the State, which is no mere matter of numbers, the sum of the individuals forming the majority. Fascism is therefore opposed to that form of democracy which equates a nation to the majority, lowering it to the level of the largest number; but it is the purest form of democracy if the nation be considered—as it should be—from the point of view of quality rather than quantity, as an idea, the mightiest because the most ethical, the most coherent, the truest, expressing itself in a people as the conscience and will of the few, if not, indeed, of one, and tending to express itself in the conscience and the will of the mass, of the whole group ethnically molded by natural and historical conditions into a nation, advancing, as one conscience and one will, along the self-same line of development and spiritual formation. Not a race, or a geographically defined region, but a people, historically perpetuating itself; a multitude unified by an idea and imbued with the will to live, the will to power, self-consciousness, personality.

In so far as it is embodied in a State, this higher personality becomes a nation. It is not the nation that generates the State; that is an antiquated naturalistic concept which afforded a basis for nineteenth-century publicity in favor of national governments. Rather is it the State that creates the nation, conferring volition and therefore real life on a people made aware of their moral unity.

The right to national independence does not arise from any merely literary and idealistic form of self-consciousness; still less from a more or less passive and unconscious *de facto* situation, but from an active, self-conscious, political will expressing itself in action and ready to prove its rights. It arises, in short, from the existence, at least *in fieri*, of a State. Indeed, it is the State which, as the expressions of a universal ethical will, creates the right to national independence.

A nation, as expressed in the State, is a living, ethical entity only in so far as it is progressive. Inactivity is death. Therefore the State is not only Authority which governs and confers legal form and spiritual value on individual wills, but it is also

Power which makes its will felt and respected beyond its own frontiers, thus affording practical proof of the universal character of the decisions necessary to insure its development. This implies organization and expansion, potential if not actual. Thus the State equates itself to the will of man, whose development cannot be checked by obstacles and which, by achieving self-expression, demonstrates its own infinity.

The fascist State, as a higher and more powerful expression of personality, is a force, but a spiritual one. It sums up all the manifestations of the moral and intellectual life of man. Its functions cannot therefore be limited to those of enforcing order and keeping the peace, as the liberal doctrine had it. It is no mere mechanical device for defining the sphere within which the individual may duly exercise his supposed rights. The fascist State is an inwardly accepted standard and rule of conduct, a discipline of the whole person; it permeates the will no less than the intellect. It stands for a principle which becomes the central motive of man as a member of civilized society, sinking deep down into his personality; it dwells in the heart of the man of action and of the thinker, of the artist and of the man of science: soul of the soul.

Fascism, in short, is not only a lawgiver and a founder of institutions, but an educator and a promoter of spiritual life. It aims at refashioning not only the forms of life but their content—man, his character, and his faith. To achieve this purpose it enforces discipline and uses authority, entering into the soul and ruling with undisputed sway. Therefore it has chosen as its emblem the lictor's rods, the symbol of unity, strength, and justice.

II

THE POLITICAL AND SOCIAL DOCTRINE OF FASCISM

Authorized Translation by Jane Soames

When, in the now distant March of 1919, I summoned a meeting at Milan through the columns of the *Popolo d'Italia* of the surviving members of the Interventionist Party who had themselves been in action, and who had followed me since the creation of the Fascist Revolutionary Party (which took place in January of 1915), I had no specific doctrinal attitude in my mind. I had a living experience of one doctrine only—that of socialism, from 1903–4 to the winter of 1914–that is to say, about a decade: and from socialism itself, even though I had taken part in the movement first as a member of the rank and file and then later as a leader, yet I had no experience of its doctrine in practice. My own doctrine, even in this period, had always been a doctrine of action. A unanimous, universally accepted theory of socialism did not exist after 1905, when the revisionist movement began in Germany under the leadership of Bernstein, while under pressure of the tendencies of the time a Left revolutionary movement also appeared, which though never getting further than talk in Italy, in Russian socialistic circles laid the foundations of bolshevism. Reformation, revolution, centralization–already the echoes of these terms are spent–while in the great stream of fascism are to be found ideas which began with Sorel, Peguy, with Lagardelle in the "Mouvement Socialiste," and with the Italian trades-union movement which throughout the period 1904–14 was sounding a new note in Italian socialist circles (already weakened by the betrayal of Giolitti) through Olivetti's *Pagine Libre,* Orano's *La Lupa,* and Enrico Leone's *Divenire Sociale.*

After the war, in 1919, socialism was already dead as a doctrine: it existed only as a hatred. There remained to it only one possibility of action, especially in Italy–reprisals against those who had desired the war and who must now be made to "expiate" its results. The *Popolo d'Italia* was then given the subtitle of "The newspaper of ex-servicemen and producers," and the word producers was already the expression of a mental attitude. Fascism was not the nursling of a doctrine worked out beforehand with detailed elaboration; it was born of the need for action and it was itself from the beginning practical rather than theoretical; it was not merely another political party but, even in the first two years, in opposition to all political parties as such, and itself a living movement. The name which I then gave to the organization fixed its character. And yet, if one were to reread, in the now dusty columns of that date, the report of the meeting in which the *Fasci Italiana di combattimento* were constituted, one would there find no ordered expression of doctrine, but a series of aphorisms, anticipations, and aspirations which, when refined by time from the original ore, were destined after some years to develop into an ordered series of doctrinal concepts, forming the fascist political doctrine–different from all others either of the past or the present day.

"If the bourgeoisie," I said then, "think that they will find lightning conductors in us, they are the more deceived; we must start work at once . . . We want to accustom the working class to real and effectual leadership, and also to convince them that it is no easy thing to direct an industry or a commercial enterprise successfully . . . We shall combat every retrograde idea, technical or spiritual . . . When the succession to the seat of government is open, we must not be unwilling to fight for it. We must make haste; when the present regime breaks down, we must be ready at once to take its place. It is we who have the right to the succession, because it was we who forced the country into the war and led her to victory. The present method of political representation cannot suffice; we must have a representation direct from the individuals concerned. It may be objected against this program that it is a return to the conception of the corporation, but that is no matter . . . Therefore, I desire that this assembly shall accept the revindication of national trades-unionism from the economic point of view . . ."

Now is it not a singular thing that even on this first day in the "Piazza San Sepolcro" the word "corporation" arose, which later, in the course of the revolution, came to express one of the creations of social legislation at the very foundations of the regime?

The years which preceded the march to Rome were years of great difficulty, during which the necessity for action did not permit of research or any complete elaboration of doctrine. The battle had to be fought in the towns and villages. There was much discussion, but—what was more important and more sacred—men died. They knew how to die. Doctrine, beautifully defined and carefully elucidated, with headlines and paragraphs, might be lacking; but there was to take its place something more decisive—faith. Even so, anyone who can recall the events of the time through the aid of books, articles, votes of congresses, and speeches of great and minor importance—anyone who knows how to research and weigh evidence —will find that the fundamentals of doctrine were cast during the years of conflict. It was precisely in those years that fascist thought armed itself, was refined, and began the great task of organization. The problem of the relation between the individual citizen and the State; the allied problems of authority and liberty; political and social problems as well as those specifically national—a solution was being sought for all these while at the same time the struggle against liberalism, democracy, socialism, and the Masonic bodies was being carried on, contemporaneously with the "punitive expedition." But, since there was inevitably some lack of system, the adversaries of fascism have disingenuously denied that it had any capacity to produce a doctrine of its own, though that doctrine was growing and taking shape under their very eyes, even though tumultuously; first, as happens to all ideas in their beginnings, in the aspect of a violent and dogmatic negation, and then in the aspect of positive construction which has found its realization in the laws and institutions of the regime as enacted successively in the years 1926, 1927, and 1928.

Fascism is now a completely individual thing, not only as a regime but as a doctrine. And this means that today fascism, exercising its critical sense upon itself and upon others, has formed its own distinct and peculiar point of view, to which it can refer and upon which, therefore, it can act in the face of all problems, practical or intellectual, which confront the world.

And above all, fascism, the more it considers and observes the future and the development of humanity quite apart from political considerations of the moment, believes neither in the possibility nor the utility of perpetual peace. It thus repudiates the doctrine of pacifism—born of a renunciation of the struggle and an act of cowardice in the face of sacrifice. War alone brings up to its highest tension all human energy and puts the stamp of nobility upon the peoples who have the courage to meet it. All other trials are substitutes, which never really put men into the position where they have to make the great decision—the alternative of life or death. Thus a doctrine which is founded upon this harmful postulate of peace is hostile to fascism. And thus hostile to the spirit of fascism, though accepted for what use they can be in dealing with particular political situations, are all the international leagues and societies which, as history will show, can be scattered to the winds when once strong national feeling is aroused by any motive—sentimental, ideal, or practical. This anti-pacifist spirit is carried by fascism even into the life of the individual; the proud motto of the "Squadrista," *"Me ne frego,"* written on the bandage of the wound, is an act of philosophy not only stoic, the summary of a doctrine not only political—it is the education to combat, the acceptation of the risks which combat implies, and a new way of life for Italy. Thus the fascist accepts life and loves it, knowing nothing of and despising suicide: he rather conceives of life as a duty and struggle and conquest, life which should be high and full, lived for oneself,

but above all for others—those who are at hand and those who
are far distant, contemporaries, and those who will come after.

This "demographic" policy of the regime is the result of the
above premise. Thus the fascist loves in actual fact his neighbor, but this "neighbor" is not merely a vague and unde-
fined concept, this love for one's neighbor puts no obstacle
in the way of necessary educational severity, and still less to
differentiation of status and to physical distance. Fascism repudiates any universal embrace, and in order to live worthily
in the community of civilized peoples watches its contemporaries with vigilant eyes, takes good note of their state of mind,
and, in the changing trend of their interests, does not allow
itself to be deceived by temporary and fallacious appearances.

Such a conception of life makes fascism the complete opposite of that doctrine, the base of so-called scientific and
Marxian socialism, the materialist conception of history;
according to which the history of human civilization can be
explained simply through the conflict of interests among the
various social groups and by the change and development in
the means and instruments of production. That the changes
in the economic field—new discoveries of raw materials, new
methods of working them, and the inventions of science—have
their importance no one can deny; but that these factors are
sufficient to explain the history of humanity excluding all
others is an absurd delusion. Fascism, now and always, believes
in holiness and in heroism; that is to say, in actions influenced
by no economic motive, direct or indirect. And if the economic
conception of history be denied, according to which theory
men are no more than puppets carried to and fro by the waves
of chance while the real directing forces are quite out of
their control, it follows that the existence of an unchangeable
and unchanging class war is also denied—the natural progeny
of the economic conception of history. And above all fascism
denies that class war can be the preponderant force in the
transformation of society. These two fundamental concepts of
socialism being thus refuted, nothing is left of it but the sentimental aspiration—as old as humanity itself—toward a social
convention in which the sorrows and sufferings of the humblest
shall be alleviated. But here again fascism repudiates the conception of "economic" happiness to be realized by socialism
and, as it were, at a given moment in economic evolution to
assure to everyone the maximum of well-being. Fascism
denies the materialist conception of happiness as a possibility
and abandons it to its inventors, the economists of the first

half of the nineteenth century: that is to say, fascism denies the validity of the equation, well-being = happiness, which would reduce men to the level of animals, caring for one thing only—to be fat and well fed—and would thus degrade humanity to a purely physical existence.

After socialism, fascism combats the whole complex system of democratic ideology, and repudiates it, whether in its theoretical premises or in its practical application. Fascism denies that the majority, by the simple fact that it is a majority, can direct human society; it denies that numbers alone can govern by means of a periodical consultation, and it affirms the immutable, beneficial, and fruitful inequality of mankind, which can never be permanently leveled through the mere operation of a mechanical process such as universal suffrage. The democratic regime may be defined as from time to time giving the people the illusion of sovereignty, while the real effective sovereignty lies in the hands of other concealed and irresponsible forces. Democracy is a regime nominally without a king, but it is ruled by many kings—more absolute, tyrannical, and ruinous than one sole king, even though a tyrant. This explains why fascism, having first in 1922 (for reasons of expediency) assumed an attitude tending toward republicanism, renounced this point of view before the march to Rome; being convinced that the question of political form is not today of prime importance, and after having studied the examples of monarchies and republics past and present reached the conclusion that monarchy or republicanism is not to be judged, as it were, by an absolute standard; but that they represent forms in which the evolution—political, historical, traditional, or psychological—of a particular country has expressed itself. Fascism supersedes the antithesis monarchy or republicanism, while democracy still tarries beneath the domination of this idea, forever pointing out the insufficiency of the first and forever the praising of the second as the perfect regime. Today it can be seen that there are republics innately reactionary and absolutist, and also monarchies which incorporate the most ardent social and political hopes of the future.

"Reason and science," says Renan (one of the inspired pre-fascists) in his philosophical meditations, "are products of humanity, but to expect reason as a direct product of the people and a direct result of their action is to deceive oneself by a chimera. It is not necessary for the existence of reason that everybody should understand it. And in any case, if such a decimation of truth were necessary, it could not be achieved in a low-class democracy, which seems as though it must of its very nature extinguish any kind of noble training. The principle that society exists solely through the well-being and the personal liberty of all the individuals of which it is composed does not appear to be conformable to the plans of nature, in whose workings the race alone seems to be taken into consideration, and the individual sacrificed to it. It is greatly to be feared that the last stage of such a conception of democracy (though I must hasten to point out that the term "democracy" may be interpreted in various ways) would end in a condition of society in which a degenerate herd would have no other preoccupation but the satisfaction of the lowest desires of common men." Thus Renan. Fascism denies, in democracy, the absurd conventional untruth of political equality dressed out in the garb of collective irresponsibility, and the myth of "happiness" and indefinite progress. But if democracy may be conceived in diverse forms—that is to say, taking democracy to mean a state of society in which the populace are not reduced to impotence in the State—fascism may write itself down as "an organized, centralized, and authoritative democracy."

Fascism has taken up an attitude of complete opposition to the doctrines of liberalism, both in the political field and the field of economics. There should be no undue exaggeration (simply with the object of immediate success in controversy) of the importance of liberalism in the last century, nor should what was but one among many theories which appeared in that period be put forward as a religion for humanity for all time, present and to come. Liberalism only flourished for half a century. It was born in 1830 in reaction against the Holy Alliance, which had been formed with the object of diverting the destinies of Europe back to the period before 1789, and the highest point of its success was the year 1848, when even Pius IX was a liberal. Immediately after that date it began to decay, for if the year 1848 was a year of light and hope, the following year, 1849, was a year of darkness and tragedy. The Republic of Rome was dealt a mortal blow by a sister republic—that of France—and in the same year Marx launched the gospel of the socialist religion, the famous Communist Manifesto. In 1851 Napoleon III carried out his far from liberal "coup d'état" and reigned in France until 1870, when he was deposed by a popular movement as the consequence of a military defeat which must be counted as one of the most decisive in history. The victor was Bismarck, who knew nothing of the religion of liberty, or the prophets by which that faith was revealed. And it is symptomatic that such a highly civilized people as the Germans were completely ignorant of the religion of liberty during the whole of the nineteenth century. It was nothing but a parenthesis, represented by that body which has been called "the ridiculous Parliament of Frankfort," which lasted only for a short period. Germany attained her national unity quite outside the doctrines of liberalism—a doctrine which seems entirely foreign to the German mind, a mind essentially monarchic—while liberalism is the logical and, indeed, historical forerunner of anarchy. The stages in the achievement of German unity are the three wars of '64, '66, and '70, which were guided by such "liberals" as Von Moltke and Bismarck. As for Italian unity, its debt to liberalism is completely inferior in contrast to that which it owes to the work of Mazzini and Garibaldi, who were not liberals. Had it not been for the intervention of the anti-liberal Napoleon, we should not have gained Lombardy; and without the help of the again anti-liberal Bismarck at Sadowa and Sedan it is very probable that we should never have gained the province of Venice in '66, or been able to enter Rome in '70. From 1870 to 1914 a period began during which even the very high priests of the religion themselves had to recognize the gathering twilight of their faith—defeated as it was by the decadence of literature and atavism in practice—that is to say, nationalism, futurism, fascism. The era of liberalism, after having accumulated an infinity of Gordian knots, tried to untie them in the slaughter of the World War—and never has any religion demanded of its votaries such a monstrous sacrifice. Perhaps the liberal gods are athirst for blood? But now, today, the liberal faith must shut the doors of its deserted temples, deserted because the peoples of the world realize that its worship—agnostic in the field of economics and indifferent in the field of politics and morals—will lead, as it has already led, to certain ruin. In addition to this, let it be pointed out that all the political hopes of the present day are anti-liberal, and it is therefore supremely ridiculous to try to classify this sole creed as outside the judgment of history, as though history were a hunting ground reserved for the professors of liberalism alone —as though liberalism were the final unalterable verdict of civilization.

But the fascist negation of socialism, democracy, and liberalism must not be taken to mean that fascism desires to lead the world back to the state of affairs before 1789, the date which seems to be indicated as the opening years of the succeeding semi-liberal century: we do not desire to turn back; fascism has not chosen DeMaistre for its high priest. Absolute monarchy has been and can never return, any more than blind acceptance of ecclesiastical authority.

So, too, the privileges of the feudal system "have been," and the division of society into castes impenetrable from outside, and with no intercommunication among themselves: the fascist conception of authority has nothing to do with such a policy. A party which entirely governs a nation is a fact entirely new to history, there are no possible references or parallels. Fascism uses in its construction whatever elements in the liberal, social, or democratic doctrines still have a living value; it maintains what may be called the certainties which we owe to history, but it rejects all the rest—that is to say, the conception that there can be any doctrine of unquestioned efficacy for all times and all peoples. Given that the nineteenth century was the century of socialism, of liberalism, and of democracy, it does not necessarily follow that the twentieth century must also be a century of socialism, liberalism, and democracy: political doctrines pass, but humanity remains; and it may rather be expected that this will be a century of authority, a century of the Left, a century of fascism. For if the nineteenth century was a century of individualism (liberalism always signifying individualism) it may be expected that this will be the century of collectivism, and hence the century of the State. It is a perfectly logical deduction that a new doctrine can utilize all the still-vital elements of previous doctrines.

No doctrine has ever been born completely new, completely defined, and owing nothing to the past; no doctrine can boast a character of complete originality; it must always derive, if only historically, from the doctrines which have preceded it and develop into further doctrines which will follow. Thus the scientific socialism of Marx is the heir of the utopian socialism of Fourier, of the Owens and Saint-Simon; thus again the liberalism of the eighteenth century is linked with all the advanced thought of the seventeenth century, and thus the doctrines of democracy are heirs of the Encyclopedists. Every doctrine tends to direct human activity toward a determined objective; but the action of men also reacts upon the doctrine, transforms it, adapts it to new needs, or supersedes it with something else. A doctrine then must be no mere exercise in words, but a living act; and thus the value of fascism lies in the fact that it is veined with pragmatism, but at the same time has a will to exist and a will to power, a firm front in the face of the reality of "violence."

The foundation of fascism is the conception of the State, its character, its duty, and its aim. Fascism conceives of the State as an absolute, in comparison with which all individuals or groups are relative, only to be conceived of in their relation to the State. The conception of the liberal State is not that of a directing force, guiding the play and development, both material and spiritual, of a collective body, but merely a force limited to the function of recording results: on the other hand, the fascist State is itself conscious, and has itself a will and a personality—thus it may be called the "ethic" State. In 1929, at the first five-year assembly of the fascist regime, I said:

"For us fascists, the State is not merely a guardian, preoccupied solely with the duty of assuring the personal safety of the citizens; nor is it an organization with purely material aims, such as to guarantee a certain level of well-being and peaceful conditions of life; for a mere council of administration would be sufficient to realize such objects. Nor is it a purely political creation, divorced from all contact with the complex material reality which makes up the life of the individual and the life of the people as a whole. The State, as conceived of and as created by fascism, is a spiritual and moral fact in itself, since its political, juridical, and economic organization of the nation is a concrete thing: and such an organization must be in its origins and development a manifestation of the spirit. The State is the guarantor of security both internal and external, but it is also the custodian and transmitter of the spirit of the people, as it has grown up through the centuries in language, in customs, and in faith. And the State is not only a living reality of the present, it is also linked with the past and above all with the future, and thus transcending the brief limits of individual life, it represents the immanent spirit of the nation. The forms in which States express themselves may change, but the necessity for such forms is eternal. It is the State which educates its citizens in civic virtue, gives them a consciousness of their mission, and welds them into unity, harmonizing their various interests through justice and transmitting to future generations the mental conquests of science, of art, of law, and the solidarity of humanity. It leads men from primitive tribal life to that highest expression of human power which is empire: it links up through the centuries the names of its members who have died for its existence and in obedience to its laws, it holds up the memory of the leaders who have increased its territory and the geniuses who have illumined it with glory as an example to be followed by future generations. When the conception of the State declines, and disunifying and centrifugal tendencies prevail, whether of individuals or of particular groups, the nations where such phenomena appear are in their decline."

From 1929 until today, evolution, both political and economic, has everywhere gone to prove the validity of these doctrinal premises. Of such gigantic importance is the State. It is the force which alone can provide a solution to the dramatic contradictions of capitalism, and that state of affairs which we call the crisis can only be dealt with by the State, as between other States. Where is the shade of Jules Simon, who in the dawn of liberalism proclaimed that, "The State must labor to make itself unnecessary, and prepare the way for its own dismissal"? Or of McCulloch, who, in the second half of the last century, affirmed that the State must guard against the danger of governing too much? What would the Englishman, Bentham, say today to the continual and inevitably invoked intervention of the State in the sphere of economics, while according to his theories industry should ask no more of the State than to be left in peace? Or the German Humboldt, according to whom the "lazy" State should be considered the best? It is true that the second wave of liberal economists were less extreme than the first, and Adam Smith himself opened the door—if only very cautiously—which leads to State intervention in the economic field: but whoever says liberalism implies individualism, and whoever says fascism implies the State. Yet the fascist State is unique, and an original creation. It is not reactionary, but revolutionary, in that it anticipates the solution of the universal political problems which elsewhere have to be settled in the political field by the rivalry of parties, the excessive power of the parliamentary regime, and the irresponsibility of political assemblies; while it meets the problems of the economic field by a system of syndicalism which is continually increasing in importance, as much in the sphere of labor as of industry; and in the moral field enforces order, discipline, and obedience to that which is the determined moral code of the country. Fascism desires the State to be a strong and organic body, at the same time reposing upon broad and popular support. The fascist State has drawn into itself even the economic activities of the nation, and, through the corporative social and educational institutions created by it, its influence reaches every aspect of the national life and includes, framed in their respective organizations, all the political, economic, and spiritual forces of the nation. A State which reposes upon the support of millions of individuals who recognize its authority, are continually conscious of its power, and are ready at once to serve it, is not the old tyrannical State of the medieval lord, nor has it anything in common with the absolute governments either before or after 1789. The individual in the fascist State is not annulled but rather multiplied, just in the same way that a soldier in a regiment is not diminished but rather increased by the number of his comrades. The fascist State organizes the nation but leaves a sufficient margin of liberty to the individual; the latter is deprived of all useless and possibly harmful freedom but retains what is essential; the deciding power in this question cannot be the individual, but the State alone.

The fascist State is not indifferent to the fact of religion in general, or to that particular and positive faith which is Italian Catholicism. The State professes no theology, but a morality, and in the fascist State religion is considered as one of the deepest manifestations of the spirit of man, thus it is not only respected but defended and protected. The fascist State has never tried to create its own God, as at one moment Robespierre and the wildest extremists of the convention tried to do; nor does it vainly seek to obliterate religion from the hearts of men as does bolshevism: fascism respects the God of the ascetics, of the saints and heroes, and, equally, God as He is perceived and worshiped by simple people.

The fascist State is an embodied will to power and government: the Roman tradition is here an ideal of force in action. According to fascism, government is not so much a thing to be expressed in territorial or military terms as in terms of morality and the spirit. It must be thought of as an empire—that is to say, a nation which directly or indirectly rules other nations, without the need for conquering a single square yard of territory. For fascism the growth of empire, that is to say the expansion of the nation, is an essential manifestation of vitality, and its opposite a sign of decadence. Peoples which are rising, or rising again after a period of decadence, are always imperialist; any renunciation is a sign of decay and of death. Fascism is the doctrine best adapted to represent the tendencies and the aspirations of a people, like the people of Italy, who are rising again after many centuries of abasement and foreign servitude. But empire demands discipline, the coordination of all forces, and a deeply felt sense of duty and

sacrifice: this fact explains many aspects of the practical working of the regime, the character of many forces in the State,
and the necessarily severe measures which must be taken
against those who would oppose this spontaneous and inevitable movement of Italy in the twentieth century, and would
oppose it by recalling the outworn ideology of the nineteenth
century—repudiated wheresoever there has been courage to
undertake great experiments of social and political transformation: for never before has the nation stood more in need
of authority, of direction, and of order. If every age has its
own characteristic doctrine, there are a thousand signs which
point to fascism as the characteristic doctrine of our time. For
if a doctrine must be a living thing, this is proved by the fact
that fascism has created a living faith; and that this faith is
very powerful in the minds of men is demonstrated by those
who have suffered and died for it.

Fascism has henceforth in the world the universality of all
those doctrines which, in realizing themselves, have represented a stage in the history of the human spirit.

Adolf Hitler (1889-1945)

MEIN KAMPF

RACE, NATION, STATE[1]

There are statements of truth which are so obvious that just
for this reason the common world does not see, or at least
does not recognize, them. At times the world passes these
well-known truisms blindly and it is most astonished if now
suddenly somebody discovers what everybody ought to know.
The "Columbus eggs" are lying about by the hundreds of thousands, only the Columbuses are rarely seen.

Thus, without exception, people wander about in Nature's
garden; they think they know almost everything, and yet, with
few exceptions, they walk blindly by one of the most outstanding principles of Nature's working: the inner seclusion
of the species of all living beings on earth.

Even the most superficial observation shows, as an almost
brazen basic principle of all the countless forms of expression
of Nature's will to live, her limited form of propagation and
increase, limited in itself. Every animal mates only with a representative of the same species. The titmouse seeks the titmouse, the finch the finch, and stork the stork, the field mouse
the field mouse, the common mouse the common mouse, the
wolf the wolf, etc.

Only exceptional circumstances can change this; first of all
the compulsion of captivity, as well as any other impossibility
of mating within the same species. But then Nature begins to
resist this with the help of all visible means, and her most
visible protest consists either of denying the bastards further
procreative faculty, or she limits the fertility of the coming
offspring; but in most cases she takes away the capacity of
resistance against disease or inimical attacks.

[1] Since *Mein Kampf* is a work running to more than 900 pages,
and Hitler's writing is extremely diffuse and repetitious, the best
introduction to his social doctrine is afforded by a variety of brief
selections grouped under the principal themes that he treats. *The
Editors.*

This is then only too natural.

Any crossing between two beings of not quite the same high standard produces a medium between the standards of the parents. That means: the young one will probably be on a higher level than the racially lower parent, but not as high as the higher one. Consequently, it will succumb later on in the fight against the higher level. But such a mating contradicts Nature's will to breed life as a whole towards a higher level. The presumption for this does not lie in blending the superior with the inferior, but rather in a complete victory of the former. The stronger has to rule and he is not to amalgamate with the weaker one, that he may not sacrifice his own greatness. Only the born weakling can consider this as cruel, but at that he is only a weak and limited human being; for, if this law were not dominating, all conceivable development towards a higher level, on the part of all organically living beings, would be unthinkable for man.

The consequence of this purity of the race, generally valid in Nature, is not only the sharp limitation of the races outwardly, but also their uniform character in themselves. The fox is always a fox, the goose a goose, the tiger a tiger, etc., and the difference can lie, at the most, in the different measure of strength, force, cleverness, skill, perseverance, etc., of the various specimens. But there will never be found a fox which, according to its inner nature, would perhaps have humane tendencies as regards the geese, nor will there be a cat with a friendly disposition towards mice.

Therefore also, here the fight amongst one another originates less from reasons of inner aversion than from hunger and love. In both cases, Nature looks calm and even satisfied. The fight for daily bread makes all those succumb who are weak, sickly, and less determined, while the males' fight for the female gives the right of propagation, or the possibility of it, only to the most healthy. But the fight is always a means for the promotion of the species' health and force of resistance, and thus a cause for its development towards a higher level.

If it were different, every further development towards higher levels would stop, and rather the contrary would happen. For, since according to numbers, the inferior element always outweighs the superior element, under the same preservation of life and under the same propagating possibilities, the inferior element would increase so much more rapidly that finally the best element would be forced to step into the background, if no correction of this condition were carried out. But just this is done by Nature, by subjecting the weaker part to such difficult living conditions that even by this the number is restricted, and finally by preventing the remainder, without choice, from increasing, but by making here a new and ruthless choice, according to strength and health.

Just as little as Nature desires a mating between weaker individuals and stronger ones, far less she desires the mixing of a higher race with a lower one, as in this case her entire work of higher breeding, which has perhaps taken hundreds of thousands of years, would tumble at one blow.

Historical experience offers countless proofs of this. It shows with terrible clarity that with any mixing of the blood of the Aryan with lower races the result was the end of the culture-bearer. North America, the population of which consists for the greatest part of Germanic elements—which mix only very little with the lower, colored races—displays a humanity and a culture different from those of Central and South America, where chiefly the Romanic immigrants have sometimes mixed with the aborigines on a large scale. By this example alone one may clearly and distinctly recognize the influence of the race mixture. The Germanic of the North American continent, who has remained pure and less intermixed, has become the master of that continent, he will remain so until he, too, falls victim to the shame of blood-mixing.

The result of any crossing, in brief, is always the following:

(*a*) Lowering of the standard of the higher race,

(*b*) Physical and mental regression, and, with it, the beginning of a slowly but steadily progressive lingering illness.

To bring about such a development means nothing less than sinning against the will of the Eternal Creator.

This action, then, is also rewarded as a sin.

Man, by trying to resist this iron logic of Nature, becomes entangled in a fight against the principles to which alone he, too, owes his existence as a human being. Thus his attack is bound to lead to his own doom.

Of course, now comes the typically Jewish, impudent, but just as stupid, objection by the modern pacifist: "Man conquers Nature!"

Millions mechanically and thoughtlessly repeat this Jewish nonsense, and in the end they imagine that they themselves represent a kind of conqueror of Nature; whereas they have no other weapon at their disposal but an "idea," and such a wretched one at that, so that according to it no world would be conceivable.

But quite apart from the fact that so far man has never conquered Nature in any affair, but that at the most he gets hold
of and tries to lift a flap of her enormous, gigantic veil of
eternal riddles and secrets, that in reality he does not "invent"
anything but only discovers everything, that he does not domi-
nate Nature, but that, based on the knowledge of a few laws
and secrets of Nature, he has risen to the position of master
of those other living beings lacking this knowledge; but quite
apart from this, an idea cannot *conquer* the presumptions for
the origin and the existence of mankind, as the idea itself depends only on man. Without men there is no human "idea"
in this world; thus the idea is always caused by the presence
of men, and, with it, of all those laws which created the presumptions for this existence.

And not only that! Certain ideas are even tied to certain
men. This can be said most of all of just such thoughts the
content of which has its origin, not in an exact scientific truth,
but rather in the world of feeling, or, as one usually expresses
oneself so nicely and "clearly" today, which reflects an "inner
experience." All these ideas, which have nothing to do with
clear logic in itself, but which represent mere expressions of
feelings, ethical conceptions, etc., are tied to the existence of
those men to whose spiritual force of imagination and creation
they owe their own existence. But precisely in this case the
preservation of these certain races and men is the presumption for the existence of these "ideas." For example, he who
actually desires, with all his heart, the victory of the pacifistic
idea in this world would have to stand up, with all available
means, for the conquest of the world by the Germans; for if
it should come about the other way round, then, with the last
German, the last pacifist would die off, as the other part of
the world has hardly ever been taken in so deeply by this
nonsense, adverse to nature and to reason, as unfortunately
our own people. Therefore, whether one wanted to or not, if
one had the serious will, one would have to decide to wage
war in order to arrive at pacifism. This and nothing else was
what the American world-redeemer Wilson wanted to have
done, at least our German visionaries believed in this. With
this, then, the purpose was fulfilled.

Indeed, the pacifist-humane idea is perhaps quite good
whenever the man of the highest standard has previously
conquered and subjected the world to a degree that makes
him the only master of this globe. Thus the idea is more and
more deprived of the possibility of a harmful effect in the

measure in which its practical application becomes rare and finally impossible. Therefore, first fight, and then one may see what can be done. In the other case, mankind has passed the climax of its development, and the end is not the rule of some ethical "idea," but barbarism, and, in consequence, chaos. Naturally, here the one or the other may laugh, but this planet has driven on its course through the ether for millions of years without men, and the day may come when it will do so again, if people forget that they owe their higher existence, not to the ideas of some crazy ideologists, but to the knowledge and the ruthless application of Nature's brazen laws.

Everything that today we admire on this earth—science and art, technique and inventions—is only the creative product of a few peoples and perhaps originally of *one* race. On them now depends also the existence of this entire culture. If they perish, then the beauty of this earth sinks into the grave with them.

No matter how much the soil, for instance, is able to influence the people, the result will always be a different one, according to the races under consideration. The scanty fertility of a living space may instigate one race towards the highest achievements, while with another race this may only become the cause for the most dire poverty and ultimate malnutrition with all its consequences. The inner disposition of the peoples is always decisive for the way in which outward influences work themselves out. What leads one people to starvation, trains the other for hard work.

All great cultures of the past perished only because the originally creative race died off through blood-poisoning.

The ultimate cause of such a decline was always the forgetting that all culture depends on men and not the reverse; that means, that in order to save a certain culture the man who created it has to be saved. But the preservation is bound to the brazen law of necessity and of the right of the victory of the best and the strongest in this world.

He who wants to live should fight, therefore, and he who does not want to battle in this world of eternal struggle does not deserve to be alive.

Even if this were hard, this is the way things are. But it is certain that by far the hardest fate is the fate which meets that man who believes he can "conquer" Nature, and yet, in truth, only seems to mock her. Misery, distress, and diseases are then her answer!

The man who misjudges and disdains the laws of race actually forfeits the happiness that seems destined to be his. He prevents the victorious march of the best race and with it also the presumption for all human progress, and in consequence he will remain in the domain of the animal's helpless misery, burdened with the sensibility of man.

It is a futile enterprise to argue which race or races were the original bearers of human culture and, with it, the actual founders of what we sum up with the word "mankind." It is simpler to put this question to oneself with regard to the present, and here the answer follows easily and distinctly. What we see before us of human culture today, the results of art, science, and techniques, is almost exclusively the creative product of the Aryan. But just this fact admits of the not unfounded conclusion that he alone was the founder of higher humanity as a whole, thus the prototype of what we understand by the word "man." He is the Prometheus of mankind, out of whose bright forehead springs the divine spark of genius at all times, forever rekindling that fire which in the form of knowledge lightened up the night of silent secrets and thus made man climb the path towards the position of master of the other beings on this earth. Exclude him—and deep darkness will again fall upon the earth, perhaps even, after a few thousand years, human culture would perish and the world would turn into a desert.

If one were to divide mankind into three groups: culture-founders, culture-bearers, and culture-destroyers, then, as representative of the first kind, only the Aryan would come in question. It is from him that the foundation and the walls of all human creations originate, and only the external form and color depend on the characteristics of the various peoples involved. He furnishes the gigantic building-stones and also the plans for all human progress, and only the execution corresponds to the character of the people and races in the various instances. In a few decades, for instance, the entire east of Asia will call a culture its own, the ultimate bases of which will be Hellenic spirit and Germanic technique, just as is the case with us. Only the *external* form will (at least partly) bear the features of Asiatic character. It is not the case, as some people claim, that Japan adds European techniques to her culture, but European science and techniques are trimmed with Japanese characteristics. But the basis of actual life is no longer the special Japanese culture, although it determines the color of life (because outwardly, in consequence of its inner difference, it is more visible to European eyes), but it is the enormous scientific and technical work of Europe and America, that is, of Aryan peoples. Based on these achievements alone the East is also able to follow general human progress. This creates the basis for the fight for daily bread, it furnishes weapons and tools for it, and only the external makeup is gradually adapted to Japanese life.

But if, starting today, all further Aryan influence upon Japan should stop, and supposing that Europe and America were to perish, then a further development of Japan's present rise in science and technology could take place for a little while longer; but in the time of a few years the source would dry out, Japanese life would gain, but its culture would stiffen and fall back into the sleep out of which it was startled seven decades ago by the Aryan wave of culture. Therefore, exactly as the present Japanese development owes its life to Aryan origin, thus also in the dim past foreign influence and foreign spirit were the awakener of the Japanese culture. The best proof of this is the fact that the latter stiffened and became completely paralyzed later on. This can only happen to a people when the originally creative race nucleus was lost, or when the external influence, which gave the impetus and the material for the first development in the cultural field, was lacking later on. But if it is ascertained that a people receives, takes in, and works over the essential basic elements of its culture from other races, and if then, when a further external influence is lacking, it stiffens again and again, then one can perhaps call such a race a *"culture-bearing"* one but never a *"culture-creating"* one.

An examination of the various peoples from this viewpoint evidences the fact that in nearly all cases one has to deal, not with originally *culture-creating*, but rather always with *culture-supporting* peoples.

It is always about the following picture of their development that presents itself:

Aryan tribes (often in a really ridiculously small number of their own people) subjugate foreign peoples, and now, stimulated by the special living conditions of the new territory (fertility, climatic conditions, etc.) and favored by the mass of the helping means in the form of people of inferior kind now at their disposal, they develop the mental and organizatory abilities, slumbering in them. Often, in the course of a few millenniums or even centuries, they create cultures which originally completely bear the inner features of their character, adapted to the already mentioned special qualities of the soil as well as of the subjected people. Finally, however, the conquerors deviate from the purity of their blood which they maintained originally, they begin to mix with the subjected inhabitants and thus they end their own existence; for the fall of man in Paradise has always been followed by expulsion from it.

Often, after a thousand and more years, the last visible trace of the one-time overlords is shown in the fairer complexion which their blood has left, in the form of the color, to the subjected race, and in a petrified culture which they had founded as the original creators. For, just as the actual and spiritual conqueror lost himself in the blood of the subjected, thus also the fuel for the torch of human culture progress was lost! As through the blood the color of the former masters keeps a faint glimmer as a memory of them, thus also the night of the cultural life is faintly brightened by the creations that remained of the erstwhile bearers of light. These now shone through all the barbarism that has returned, and in the thoughtless observer of the moment they awaken only too frequently the opinion that he sees the picture of the present people, whereas it is only the mirror of the past at which he is looking.

Then it may happen that such a people for a second time, nay, even more often in the life of its history, comes into touch with the race of its one-time suppliers of culture, without a memory of former meetings necessarily being present. The remainder of the blood of the one-time masters will unconsciously turn to the new apparition, and what first was only possible by compulsion will now succeed with the help of their own will. Then a new culture wave makes its entrance and lasts until its bearers have once more been submerged in the blood of foreign peoples.

It will be the task of a future culture and world history to make researches in this sense and not to suffocate by reflecting external facts, as this is unfortunately only too often the case with our present science of history.

Merely from this sketch of the development of "culture-bearing" nations results also the picture of the origin, the work, and—the decline of the true culture-creators of this globe, the Aryans themselves.

Just as in daily life the so-called genius requires a special cause, often even a real impetus in order to be made conspicuous, the same is also the case with the ingenious race in the life of the peoples. In the monotony of everyday life even important people often seem unimportant and they hardly stand out over the average of their surroundings; but as soon as they are faced by a situation in which others would despair or go wrong, out of the plain average child the ingenious nature grows visibly, not infrequently to the astonishment of all those who hitherto had an opportunity to observe him, who had meanwhile grown up in the smallness of *bourgeois* life, and therefore, in consequence of this process, the prophet has rarely any honor in his own country. Never is there a better opportunity to observe this than during war. In the hours of distress, when others despair, out of apparently harmless children, there shoot suddenly heroes of death-defying determination and icy coolness of reflection. If this hour of trial had never come, then hardly anyone would ever have been able to guess that a young hero is hidden in the beardless boy. Nearly always such an impetus is needed in order to call genius into action. Fate's hammer stroke, which then throws the one to the ground, suddenly strikes steel in another, and while now the shell of everyday life is broken, the erstwhile nucleus lies open to the eyes of the astonished world. The latter now resists and does not want to believe that the apparently "identical" kind is now suddenly supposed to be a "different" being; a process which repeats itself with every eminent human being.

Although an inventor, for instance, establishes his fame only on the day of his invention, one must not think that perhaps his genius in itself had entered the man only just at this hour, but the spark of genius will be present in the forehead of the truly creatively gifted man from the hour of his birth, although for many years in a slumbering condition and therefore invisible to the rest of the world. But some day, through an external cause or impetus of some kind, the spark becomes fire, something that only then begins to stir the attention of other people. The most stupid of them believe now in all sincerity that the person in question has just become "clever," whereas in reality they themselves now begin at last to recognize his greatness; for true genius is always inborn and never acquired by education or, still less, by learning.

This, however, may be said, as already stressed, not only for the individual man, but also for the race. Creatively active peoples are creatively gifted from the very bottom and forever, although this may not be recognizable to the eyes of the superficial observer. Here, too, external recognition is always only possible as a consequence of accomplished facts, as the rest of the world is not able to recognize genius in itself, but sees only its visible expressions in the form of inventions, discoveries, buildings, pictures, etc.; but even here it often takes a long time till it is able to struggle through to this knowledge. Exactly as in the life of the individual important man his genius or extraordinary ability strives towards its practical realization only when urged on by special occasions, thus also in the life of the peoples the real use of creative forces and abilities that are present can take place only when certain presumptions invite to this.

We see this most clearly in that race that cannot help having been, and being, the supporter of the development of human culture—the Aryans. As soon as Fate leads them towards special conditions, their latent abilities begin to develop in a more and more rapid course and to mold themselves into tangible forms. The cultures which they found in such cases are nearly always decisively determined by the available soil, the climate, and—by the subjected people. The latter, however, is the most decisive of all factors. The more primitive the technical presumptions for a cultural activity are, the more necessary is the presence of human auxiliary forces which then, collected and applied with the object of organization, have to replace the force of the machine. Without this possibility of utilizing inferior men, the Aryan would never have been able to take the first steps towards his later culture; exactly as, without the help of various suitable animals which he knew how to tame, he would never have arrived at a technology which now allows him to do without these very animals. The words *"Der Mohr hat seine Schuldigkeit getan, er kann gehen"* [The Moor has done his duty, he may go] has unfortunately too deep a meaning. For thousands of years the horse had to serve man and to help in laying the foundations of a development which now, through the motor-car makes the horse itself superfluous. In a few years it will have ceased its activity, but without its former co-operation man would hardly have arrived at where he stands today.

Therefore, for the formation of higher cultures, the existence of inferior men was one of the most essential presumptions, because they alone were able to replace the lack of technical means without which a higher development is unthinkable. The first culture of mankind certainly depended

less on the tamed animal, but rather on the use of inferior
people.

Only after the enslavement of subjected races, the same
fate began to meet the animals, and not *vice versa*, as many
would like to believe. For first the conquered walked behind
[in later editions read: before] the plow—and after him, the
horse. Only pacifist fools can again look upon this as a sign
of human baseness, without making clear to themselves that
this development had to take place in order to arrive finally at
that place from where today these apostles are able to sputter
forth their drivel into the world.

The progress of mankind resembles the ascent on an endless ladder; one cannot arrive at the top without first having taken the lower steps. Thus the Aryan had to go the
way which reality showed him and not that of which the
imagination of a modern pacifist dreams. The way of reality,
however, is hard and difficult, but it finally ends where the
other wishes to bring mankind by dreaming, but unfortunately removes it from, rather than brings it nearer to, it.

Therefore, it is no accident that the first cultures originated
in those places where the Aryan, by meeting lower peoples,
subdued them and made them subject to his will. They, then,
were the first technical instrument in the service of a growing
culture.

With this the way that the Aryan had to go was clearly
lined out. As a conqueror he subjected the lower peoples
and then he regulated their practical ability according to
his command and his will and for his aims. But while he
thus led them towards a useful, though hard activity, he not
only spared the lives of the subjected, but perhaps he even
gave them a fate which was better than that of their former
so-called "freedom." As long as he kept up ruthlessly the
master's standpoint, he not only really remained "master"
but also the preserver and propagator of the culture. For
the latter was based exclusively on his abilities, and, with it,
on his preservation in purity. But as soon as the subjected
peoples themselves began to rise (probably) and approached
the conqueror linguistically, the sharp separating wall between
master and slave fell. The Aryan gave up the purity of his
blood and therefore he also lost his place in the Paradise
which he had created for himself. He became submerged in
the race-mixture, he gradually lost his cultural ability more
and more, till at last not only mentally but also physically
he began to resemble more the subjected and aborigines

than his ancestors. For some time he may still live on the existing cultural goods, but then petrifaction sets in, and finally oblivion.

In this way cultures and realms collapse in order to make room for new formations.

The blood-mixing, however, with the lowering of the racial level caused by it, is the sole cause of the dying-off of old cultures; for the people do not perish by lost wars, but by the loss of that force of resistance which is contained only in the pure blood.

All that is not race in this world is trash.

All world historical events, however, are only the expression of the races' instinct of self-preservation in its good or in its evil meaning.

The Jew forms the strongest contrast to the Aryan. Hardly in any people of the world is the instinct of self-preservation more strongly developed than in the so-called "chosen people." The fact of the existence of this race alone may be looked upon as the best proof of this. Where is the people that in the past two thousand years has been exposed to so small changes of the inner disposition, of character, etc., as the Jewish people? Which people finally has experienced greater changes than this one—and yet has always come forth the same from the most colossal catastrophes of mankind? What an infinitely persistent will for life, for preserving the race do these facts disclose!

Also the intellectual abilities were schooled in the course of centuries. Today the Jew is looked upon as "clever," and in a certain sense he has been so at all times. But his reason is not the result of his own development, but that of object lessons from without. For also the human mind is not able to climb the heights without steps; for every step forward he needs the foundation of the past, and, moreover, in that comprehensive meaning which can be revealed only through general culture. All thinking will rest only to a very small extent on one's own realization, but to the greater extent on the experiences of the time past. The general level of culture supplies the individual, mostly without his noticing this, with such a profusion of preliminary knowledge that now, armed in this manner, he can set out towards further steps of his own. The young boy of today, for instance, grows up among a truly vast number of technical achievements of the past few centuries that now, as being matters of course, he no longer pays attention to many things which were still a riddle to great minds a hundred years ago, though for the follow-up and the understanding of our progress in this field it is of decisive importance for him. If today even a genius of the twenties of the past century were suddenly to leave his grave, he would find it much harder to make his way about in the present time than this is the case of an average boy of fifteen of today. For he would lack all the infinite prerequisites which the individual takes in, so to speak, unconsciously, during his adolescence in the midst of the general culture of the corresponding time.

As now the Jew (for reasons which will immediately become evident from the following) was never in the possession of a culture of his own, the bases for his spiritual activity have always been furnished by others. At all times his intellect has developed through the culture that surrounds him.

Never did the reverse process take place.

For, even if the Jewish people's instinct of self-preservation is not smaller, but rather greater, than that of other nations, and even if his spiritual abilities very easily create the impression as though they were equal to the intellectual disposition of the other races, yet the most essential presumption for a cultured people is completely lacking, the idealistic disposition.

In the Jewish people, the will to sacrifice oneself does not go beyond the bare instinct of self-preservation of the individual. The seemingly great feeling of belonging together is rooted in a very primitive herd instinct, as it shows itself in a similar way in many other living beings in this world. Thereby the fact is remarkable that in all these cases a common herd instinct leads to mutual support only as long as a common danger makes this seem useful or unavoidable. The same pack of wolves that jointly falls upon its booty dissolves when its hunger abates. The same is true of horses, which try to ward off the attacker in common, and which fly in different directions when the danger is gone.

With the Jew the case is similar. His will to sacrifice is only ostensible. It endures only as long as the existence of the individual absolutely requires this. However, as soon as the common enemy is beaten and the danger threatening all is averted, the booty recovered, the apparent harmony among the Jews themselves ceases to make way again for the inclinations originally present. The Jew remains united only if forced by a common danger or is attracted by a common booty; if both reasons are no longer evident, then the qualities of the crassest egoism come into their own, and, in a moment, the united people becomes a horde of rats, fighting bloodily among themselves.

If the Jews were alone in this world, they would suffocate as much in dirt and filth, as they would carry on a detestable struggle to cheat and to ruin each other, although the complete lack of the will to sacrifice, expressed in their cowardice, would also in this instance make the fight a comedy.

Thus it is fundamentally wrong to conclude, merely from the fact of their standing together in a fight, or, more rightly expressed, in their exploiting their fellow human beings, that the Jews have a certain idealistic will to sacrifice themselves.

Here, too, the Jew is led by nothing but pure egoism on the part of the individual.

Therefore also the Jewish "State" (which is supposed to be the living organism for the preservation and the propagation of the race) is territorially completely unlimited. For a certain limitation of a State formation by space always presupposes an idealistic attitude by the State race, especially above all a correct conception of the notion "work." In the same measure in which this attitude is lacking or absent, every attempt at a formation or even at the preservation of a territorially limited State fails. But with this also the basis on which a culture alone can originate is eliminated.

For this reason, however, the Jewish people, with all its apparent intellectual qualities, is nevertheless without any true culture, especially without a culture of its own. For the sham culture which the Jew possesses today is the property of other peoples, and is mostly spoiled in his hands.

When judging Jewry in its attitude towards the question of human culture, one has to keep before one's eye as an essential characteristic that there never has been and consequently that today also there is no Jewish art; that above all the two queens of all arts, architecture and music, owe nothing original to Jewry. What he achieves in the field of art is either bowdlerization or intellectual theft. With this, the Jew lacks those qualities which distinguish creatively and, with it, culturally blessed races.

In opposition to this, the "folkish" view recognizes the importance of mankind in its racially innate elements. In principle, it sees in the State only a means to an end, and as its end it considers the preservation of the racial existence of men. Thus it by no means believes in an equality of the races, but with their differences it also recognizes their superior and inferior values, and by this recognition it feels the obligation in accordance with the Eternal Will that dominates this universe to promote the victory of the better and stronger, and to demand the submission of the worse and the weaker. Thus in principle it favors also the fundamental aristocratic thought of nature and believes in the validity of this law down to the last individual. It sees not only the different values of the races, but also the different values of individual man. . . .

Thus the highest purpose of the folkish State is the care for the preservation of those racial primal elements which, supplying culture, create the beauty and dignity of a higher humanity. We, as Aryans, are therefore able to imagine a State only to be the living organism of a nationality which not only safeguards the preservation of that nationality, but which, by a further training of its spiritual and ideal abilities, leads it to the highest freedom.

The folkish State has to make up for what is today neglected in this field in all directions. *It has to put the race into the center of life in general. It has to care for its preservation in purity. It has to make the child the most precious possession of a people. It has to take care that only the healthy beget children; that there is only one disgrace: to be sick and to bring children into the world despite one's own deficiencies; but one highest honor: to renounce this. Further, on the other hand this has to be looked upon as objectionable: to keep healthy children from the nation. Thereby the State has to appear as the guardian of a thousand years' future, in the face of which the wish and the egoism of the individual appears as nothing and has to submit. It has to put the most modern medical means at the service of this knowledge. It has to declare unfit for propagation everybody who is visibly ill and has inherited a disease and it has to carry this out in practice. On the other hand, it has to care that the fertility of the healthy woman is not limited by the financial mismanagement of a State régime which makes children a curse for the parents. It has to do away with that foul, nay criminal, indifference with which today the social presumptions of a family with many children is treated, and in its place it has to consider itself the guardian of this precious blessing of a people. Its care belongs more to the child than to the adult.*

He who is not physically and mentally healthy and worthy must not perpetuate his misery in the body of his child. Here the folkish State has to achieve the most enormous work of education. Some day it will appear as a greater deed than the most victorious wars of our present bourgeois era. By education it has to teach the individual that it is not a disgrace but only a regrettable misfortune to be sick and weakly, but that it is a crime and therefore at the same time a disgrace to dishonor this misfortune by one's egoism by burdening it again upon an innocent being; that in the face of this it gives proof of a nobility of the highest mind and of most admirable humaneness if the innocently sick, by renouncing his own child, gives his love and tenderness to an unknown, poor young descendant of his nationality, whose health promises that one day he will become a vigorous member of a powerful community. With this work of education the State has to render the purely spiritual supplement of its practical activity. Without considering understanding or non-understanding, approval or disapproval, it has to act in this sense.

INEQUALITY, DEMOCRACY, PARLIAMENTS

The parliamentary principle of decision by majority, by denying the authority of the person and placing in its stead the number of the crowd in question, sins against the aristocratic basic idea of Nature, whose opinion of aristocracy, however, need in no way be represented by the present-day decadence of our Upper Ten Thousand.

The reader of Jewish newspapers can hardly imagine the devastation which results from this institution of modern democratic parliamentary rule, unless he has learned to think and examine for himself. It is above all the cause of the terrible flooding of the entire political life with the most inferior products of our time. No matter how far the true leader withdraws from political activity, which to a great extent does not consist of creative work and achievement, but rather of bargaining and haggling for the favor of a majority, this very activity, however, will agree with and attract the people of low mentality.

The more dwarfish the mentality and the abilities of such a present-day leather merchant are, the more clearly his knowledge makes him conscious of the wretchedness of his actual appearance, the more will he praise a system that does not demand of him the strength and the genius of a giant, but rather which calls for the cunning of a village chief or which even prefers this kind of wisdom to that of a Pericles. Such a simpleton need never worry about the responsibility of his actions. He is relieved of this care for the reason that he knows, no matter what the result of his "statesmanlike" bungling may be, that his end has long been predicted by the stars; some day he will have to make room for another, an equally great mind. It is, among other things, a symptom of such a decline that the number of great statesmen increases in the measure in which the competence of the individual one decreases. With increasing dependence on parliamentary majorities, he is bound to shrink, for great minds will refuse to serve as bailiff for stupid good-for-nothings and babblers, and on the other hand, the representatives of the majority, that is, of stupidity, hate nothing more ardently than a superior mind.

For such an assembly of wise men of Gotham, it is always a comforting feeling to know that they are headed by a leader whose wisdom corresponds to the mentality of the assembly; for, is it not pleasant to let one's intellect flash forth from time to time, and finally, if Smith can be master, why not Jones also?

This invention of democracy most closely conforms to a quality which lately has developed into a crying shame, that is, the cowardice of a great part of our so-called "leaders." How fortunate to be able to hide, whenever decisions of importance are involved, behind the coat-tails of a so-called majority!

The young movement, according to its structure and its inner organization, is anti-parliamentarian; that means in general, and in its inner construction, it rejects a principle of a decision by the majority, by which the leader is degraded to the position of the executive of the will and the opinion of the others. The movement, in small things as well as big things, represents the principle of a Germanic democracy: choice of the leader, but absolute authority of the latter.

It would be a folly to appraise man's value according to his race, that means to declare war against the Marxist viewpoint, *Man is equal to man,* if on the other hand, one is nevertheless not determined to draw the ultimate consequences from this. The ultimate consequence of the recognition of the importance of the blood, that means the racial basis in general, is, however, the transmission of this evaluation to the individual person. Just as in general I have to evaluate the nations differently on the basis of the race to which they belong, thus also the individuals within a national community. The statement that a people is not equal to a people is then transmitted to the individual within a national community in the sense that a head cannot be equal to a head, because here too the elements of the blood may be the same, in great lines, but in individual cases are nevertheless subject to thousandfold, most minute differentiations.

The first consequence of this realization is at the same time, I would say, the cruder one, that is, the attempt to promote those racial elements that have been recognized as racially most valuable within the national community and to care for their special increase.

This task is cruder for the reason that one can recognize, and solve it almost mechanically. It is more difficult, however, to recognize, in the community of all, those heads that are mentally and ideally most valuable indeed, and to give them that influence which not only is due these superior minds, but which above all is beneficial to the nation. This sieving according to ability and efficiency cannot be carried out mechanically, but it is a work that is done uninterruptedly by the daily struggle for life.

A view of life which, by rejecting the democratic mass idea, endeavors to give this world to the best people, that means to the most superior men, has logically to obey the same aristocratic principle also within this people and has to guarantee leadership and highest influence within the respective people to the best heads. With this it does not build up on the idea of the majority, but on that of the personality.

WAR, PEACE, IMPERIALISM

But one may well believe that this world will still be subject to the fiercest fights for the existence of mankind. In the end, only the urge for self-preservation will eternally succeed. Under its pressure so-called "humanity," as the expression of a mixture of stupidity, cowardice, and an imaginary superior intelligence, will melt like snow under the March sun. Mankind has grown strong in eternal struggles and it will only perish through eternal peace.

State frontiers are man-made and can be altered by man. The reality of a nation having managed a disproportionate acquisition of territory is no superior obligation for its eternal recognition. It proves at most the might of the conqueror and the weakness of the victim. And, moreover, this might alone makes right. If the German people today, penned into an impossible area, face a wretched future, this is as little Fate's command as its rejection would constitute a snub to Fate. Just as little as some superior power has promised another nation more soil and territory than the German, or would be insulted by the fact of this unjust division of territory. Just as our forefathers did not get the land on which we are living today as a gift from Heaven, but had to conquer it by risking their lives, so no folkish grace but only the might of a triumphant sword will in the future assign us territory, and with it life for our nation. . . .

We National Socialists, however, must go further: *the right to soil and territory can become a duty if decline seems to be in store for a great nation unless it extends its territory.* Even more especially if what is involved is not some little negro people or other, but the German mother of all life, which has given its cultural picture to the contemporary world. *Germany will be either a world power or will not be at all.* To be a world power, however, it requires that size which nowadays gives its necessary importance to such a power, and which gives life to its citizens.

With this, we National Socialists consciously draw a line through the foreign-policy trend of our pre-War period. We take up at the halting place of six hundred years ago. We terminate the endless German drive to the south and west of Europe, and direct our gaze towards the lands in the east. We finally terminate the colonial and trade policy of the pre-War period, and proceed to the territorial policy of the future.

But if we talk about new soil and territory in Europe today, we can think primarily only of *Russia* and its vassal border states.

Fate itself seems to seek to give us a tip at this point. In the surrender of Russia to bolshevism, the Russian people was robbed of that intelligentsia which theretofore produced and guaranteed its State stability. For the organization of a Russian State structure was not the result of Russian Slavdom's State-political capacity, but rather a wonderful example of the State-building activity of the German element in an inferior race. Thus have innumerable mighty empires of the earth been created. Inferior nations with German organizers and lords as leaders have more than once expanded into powerful State structures, and endured as long as the racial nucleus of the constructive State-race maintained itself. For centuries Russia drew nourishment from this Germanic nucleus of its superior strata of leaders. Today it is uprooted and obliterated almost without a trace. The Jew has replaced it. Impossible as it is for the Russians alone to shake off the yoke of the Jews through their own strength, it is equally impossible in the long run for the Jews to maintain the mighty empire. Jewry itself is not an organizing element, but a ferment of decomposition. The Persian Empire, once so powerful, is now ripe for collapse; and the end of Jewish dominion in Russia will also be the end of the Russian State itself. We have been chosen by Fate to be the witnesses of a catastrophe which will be the most powerful substantiation of the correctness of the folkish theory of race.

EDUCATION

The folkish State, through this realization, has to direct its entire education primarily not at pumping in mere knowledge, but at the breeding of absolutely healthy bodies. Of secondary importance is the training of the mental abilities. But here again first of all the development of the character, especially the promotion of will power and determination, connected with education for joyfully assuming responsibility, and only as the last thing, scientific schooling.

Thereby the folkish State has to start from the presumption *that a man, though scientifically little educated but physically healthy, who has a sound, firm character, filled with joyful determination and will power, is of greater value to the national community than an ingenious weakling.* A people of scholars, when they are physically degenerated, irresolute and cowardly pacifists, will not conquer heaven, nay it will not even be able to assure its existence on this globe. In the hard struggle of fate he who knows little succumbs most rarely, but always he who draws from his knowledge the weakest consequences and puts them into activity in the poorest manner. Finally, here also a certain harmony must exist. *A rotten body is not in the least made more aesthetic by a brilliant mind,* nay, highest training of the mind could not at all be justified if its bearers were at the same time physically degenerated and crippled beings, irresolute and weak in character, hesitating and cowardly. What makes the Greek ideal of beauty immortal is the wonderful combination of the most glorious physical beauty with a brilliant mind and the noblest soul. . . .

School as such, in a folkish State, has to set apart infinitely more time for physical training. It won't do to burden the young brains with a ballast which they retain, according to experience, only to a fraction, whereby in most cases instead of the essential the unnecessary trifles remain, as the young child is not in a position to carry out a sensible selection of the material that has been infiltrated in him. If today, even in the curriculum of the middle schools, only two hours per week are devoted to gymnastics and the participation in it is optional with the individual, not compulsory, then this is, compared with the purely intellectual training, a gross disparity. Not a day should pass during which the young man is not trained physically for at least one hour in the morning and again in the evening, in every kind of sport and gymnastics. Here especially one kind of sport must not be forgotten which in the eyes of many "nationals" is considered as brutal and undignified: boxing. It is incredible what erroneous opinions are current about this in the circles of the "educated." That the young man learns to fence and then goes about fighting duels is looked upon as natural and honorable, but that he boxes is supposed to be brutal! Why? There is no sport that, like this, promotes the spirit of aggression in the same measure, demands determination quick as lightning, educates the body for steel-like versatility. If two young people fight out a difference of opinion with their fists, it is no more brutal than if they do so with a piece of ground iron. Also, it is not less noble if one who has been attacked wards off his attacker with his fists instead of running away and calling for a policeman. But above all, the young and healthy boy has to learn to be beaten. This, of course, may appear wild in the eyes of our present spiritual fighters. But the folkish State has not the task of breeding a colony of peaceful aesthetes and physical degenerates. Not in the honest petty *bourgeois* or in the virtuous old maid does it see its ideal of humanity, but in the robust incorporation of manly forces and in women who in their turn are able to bring men into the world.

Analogous with the education of the boy, the folkish State can also direct the education of the girl from the same viewpoints. Here too the main stress should be put on physical training, and only after this on the promotion of spiritual and last of all, the intellectual values. The *goal* of female education has invariably to be the future mother.

Also in science the folkish State has to see a means for the promotion of national pride. Not only world history, but the entire culture history must be taught from this viewpoint. An inventor must appear great not only as an inventor, but greater still as a fellow citizen. The admiration for every great deed has to be recast into pride in the fortunate performer of this deed as a member of one's own nation. From the vast number of all the great names of German history the greatest have to be singled out and presented to youth so impressively as to become the pillars of an unshakable national sentiment.

John Dewey (1859–1952)

RECONSTRUCTION IN PHILOSOPHY

How can philosophic change seriously affect social philosophy? As far as fundamentals are concerned, every view and combination appears to have been formulated already. Society is composed of individuals: this obvious and basic fact no philosophy, whatever its pretensions to novelty, can question or alter. Hence these three alternatives: Society must exist for the sake of individuals; or individuals must have their ends and ways of living set for them by society; or else society and individuals are correlative, organic, to one another, society requiring the service and subordination of individuals and at the same time existing to serve them. Beyond these three views, none seems to be logically conceivable. Moreover, while each of the three types includes many subspecies and variations within itself, yet the changes seem to have been so thoroughly rung that at most only minor variations are now possible.

Especially would it seem true that the "organic" conception meets all the objections to the extreme individualistic and extreme socialistic theories, avoiding the errors alike of Plato and Bentham. Just because society is composed of individuals, it would seem that individuals and the associative relations that hold them together must be of coequal importance. Without strong and competent individuals, the bonds and ties that form society have nothing to lay hold on. Apart from associations with one another, individuals are isolated from one another and fade and wither; or are opposed to one another and their conflicts injure individual development. Law, state, church, family, friendship, industrial association, these and other institutions and arrangements are necessary in order that individuals may grow and find their specific capacities and functions. Without their aid and support human life is, as Hobbes said, brutish, solitary, nasty.

We plunge into the heart of the matter, by asserting that these various theories suffer from a common defect. They are all committed to the logic of general notions under which specific situations are to be brought. What we want light upon is this or that group of individuals, this or that concrete human being, this or that special institution or social arrangement. For such a logic of inquiry, the traditionally accepted logic substitutes discussion of the meaning of concepts and their dialectical relationship to one another. The discussion goes on in terms of *the* state, *the* individual; the nature of institutions as such, society in general.

We need guidance in dealing with particular perplexities in domestic life, and are met by dissertations on the Family or by assertions of the sacredness of individual Personality. We want to know about the worth of the institution of private property as it operates under given conditions of definite time and place. We meet with the reply of Proudhon that property generally is theft, or with that of Hegel that the realization of will is the end of all institutions, and that private ownership as the expression of mastery of personality over physical nature is a necessary element in such realization. Both answers may have a certain suggestiveness in connection with specific situations. But the conceptions are not proffered for what they may be worth in connection with special historic phenomena. They are general answers supposed to have a universal meaning that covers and dominates all particulars. Hence they do not assist inquiry. They close it. They are not instrumentalities to be employed and tested in clarifying concrete social difficulties. They are ready-made principles to be imposed upon particulars in order to determine their nature. They tell us about *the* state when we want to know about *some* state. But the implication is that what is said about *the* state applies to any state that we happen to wish to know about.

In transferring the issue from concrete situations to definitions and conceptual deductions, the effect, especially of the organic theory, is to supply the apparatus for intellectual justification of the established order. Those most interested in practical social progress and the emancipation of groups from oppression have turned a cold shoulder to the organic theory. The effect, if not the intention, of German idealism as applied in social philosophy was to provide a bulwark for the maintenance of the political *status quo* against the tide of radical ideas coming from revolutionary France. Although Hegel asserted in explicit form that the end of states and institutions is to further the realization of the freedom of all, his effect was to consecrate the Prussian State and to enshrine bureaucratic absolutism. Was this apologetic tendency accidental, or did it spring from something in the logic of the notions that were employed?

Surely the latter. If we talk about *the* state and *the* individual, rather than about this or that political organization and this or that group of needy and suffering human beings, the tendency is to throw the glamor and prestige, the meaning and value attached to the general notion, over the concrete situation and thereby to cover up the defects of the latter and disguise the need of serious reforms. The meanings which are found in the general notions are injected into the particulars that come under them. Quite properly so if we once grant the logic of rigid universals under which the concrete cases have to be subsumed in order to be understood and explained.

Again, the tendency of the organic point of view is to minimize the significance of specific conflicts. Since the individual and the state or social institution are but two sides of the same reality, since they are already reconciled in principle and conception, the conflict in any particular case can be but apparent. Since in theory the individual and the state are reciprocally necessary and helpful to one another, why pay much attention to the fact that in *this* state a whole group of individuals are suffering from oppressive conditions? In "reality" their interests cannot be in conflict with those of the state to which they belong; the opposition is only superficial and casual. Capital and labor cannot "really" conflict because each is an organic necessity to the other, and both to the organized community as a whole. There cannot "really" be any sex-problem because men and women are indispensable both to one another and to the state. In his day, Aristotle could easily employ the logic of general concepts superior to individuals to show that the institution of slavery was in the interests both of the state and of the slave class. Even if the intention is not to justify the existing order the effect is to divert attention from special situations. Rationalistic logic formerly made men careless in observation of the concrete in physical philosophy. It now operates to depress and retard observation in specific social phenomena. The social philosopher, dwelling in the region of his concepts, "solves" problems by showing the relationship of ideas, instead of helping men solve problems in the concrete by supplying them hypotheses to be used and tested in projects of reform.

Meanwhile, of course, the concrete troubles and evils remain. They are not magically waived out of existence because in theory society is organic. The region of concrete difficulties, where the assistance of intelligent method for tentative plans for experimentation is urgently needed, is precisely where intelligence fails to operate. In this region of the specific and concrete, men are thrown back upon the crudest empiricism, upon short-sighted opportunism and the matching of brute forces. In theory, the particulars are all neatly disposed of; they come under their appropriate heading and category; they are labelled and go into an orderly pigeon-hole in a systematic filing cabinet, labelled political science or sociology. But in empirical fact they remain as perplexing, confused and unorganized as they were before. So they are dealt with not by even an endeavor at scientific method but by blind rule of thumb, citation of precedents, considerations of immediate advantage, smoothing things over, use of coercive force and the clash of personal ambitions. The world still survives; it has therefore got on somehow:—so much cannot be denied. The method of trial and error and competition of selfishnesses has somehow wrought out many improvements. But social theory nevertheless exists as an idle luxury rather than as a guiding method of inquiry and planning. In the question of methods concerned with reconstruction of special situations rather than in any refinements in the general concepts of institution, individuality, state, freedom, law, order, progress, etc., lies the true impact of philosophical reconstruction.

Consider the conception of the individual self. The individualistic school of England and France in the eighteenth and nineteenth centuries was empirical in intent. It based its individualism, philosophically speaking, upon the belief that individuals are alone real, that classes and organizations are secondary and derived. They are artificial, while individuals are natural. In what way then can individualism be said to come under the animadversions that have been passed? To say the defect was that this school overlooked those connections with other persons which are a part of the constitution of every individual is true as far as it goes; but unfortunately it rarely goes beyond the point of just that wholesale justification of institutions which has been criticized.

The real difficulty is that the individual is regarded as something *given*, something already there. Consequently, he can only be something to be catered to, something whose pleasures are to be magnified and possessions multiplied. When the individual is taken as something given already, anything that can be done to him or for him it can only be by way of external impressions and belongings: sensations of pleasure and pain, comforts, securities. Now it is true that social arrangements, laws, institutions are made for man, rather than that man is made for them; that they are means and agencies of human welfare and progress. But they are not means for obtaining something for individuals, not even happiness. They are means of *creating* individuals. Only in the physical sense of physical bodies that to the senses are separate is individuality an original datum. Individuality in a social and moral sense is something to be wrought out. It means initiative, inventiveness, varied resourcefulness, assumption of responsibility in choice of belief and conduct. These are not gifts, but achievements. As achievements, they are not absolute but relative to the use that is to be made of them. And this use varies with the environment.

The import of this conception comes out in considering the fortunes of the idea of self-interest. All members of the empirical school emphasized this idea. It was the sole motive of mankind. Virtue was to be attained by making benevolent action profitable to the individual; social arrangements were to be reformed so that egoism and altruistic consideration of others would be identified. Moralists of the opposite school were not backward in pointing out the evils of any theory that reduced both morals and political science to means of calculating self-interest. Consequently they threw the whole idea of interest overboard as obnoxious to morals. The effect of this reaction was to strengthen the cause of authority and political obscurantism. When the play of interest is eliminated, what remains? What concrete moving forces can be found? Those who identified the self with something ready-made and its interest with acquisition of pleasure and profit took the most effective means possible to reinstate the logic of abstract conceptions of law, justice, sovereignty, freedom, etc.—all of those vague general ideas that for all their seeming rigidity can be manipulated by any clever politician to cover up his designs and to make the worse seem the better cause. Interests are specific and dynamic; they are the natural terms of any concrete social thinking. But they are damned beyond recovery when they are identified with the things of a petty selfishness. They can be employed as vital terms only when the self is seen to be in process, and interest to be a name for whatever is concerned in furthering its movement.

The same logic applies to the old dispute of whether reform should start with the individual or with institutions. When the self is regarded as something complete within itself, then it is readily argued that only internal moralistic changes are of importance in general reform. Institutional changes are said to be merely external. They may add conveniences and comforts to life, but they cannot effect moral improvements. The result is to throw the burden for social improvement upon freewill in its most impossible form. Moreover, social and economic passivity are encouraged. Individuals are led to concentrate in moral introspection upon their own vices and virtues, and to neglect the character of the environment. Morals withdraw from active concern with detailed economic and political conditions. Let us perfect ourselves within, and in due season changes in society will come of themselves is the teaching. And while saints are engaged in introspection, burly sinners run the world. But when self-hood is perceived to be an active process it is also seen that social modifications are the only means of the creation of changed personalities. Institutions are viewed in their educative effect:—with reference to the types of individuals they foster. The interest in individual moral improvement and the social interest in objective reform of economic and political conditions are identified. And inquiry into the meaning of social arrangements gets definite point and direction. We are led to ask what the specific stimulating, fostering and nurturing power of each specific social arrangement may be. The old-time separation between politics and morals is abolished at its root.

Consequently we cannot be satisfied with the general statement that society and the state is organic to the individual. The question is one of specific causations. Just what response does *this* social arrangement, political or economic, evoke, and what effect does it have upon the disposition of those who engage in it? Does it release capacity? If so, how widely? Among a few, with a corresponding depression in others, or in an extensive and equitable way? Is the capacity which is set free also directed in some coherent way, so that it becomes a power, or its manifestation spasmodic and capricious? Since responses are of an indefinite diversity of kind, these inquiries have to be detailed and specific. Are men's senses rendered more delicately sensitive and appreciative, or are they blunted and dulled by this and that form of social organization? Are their minds trained so that the hands are more deft and cunning? Is curiosity awakened or blunted? What is its quality: is it merely esthetic, dwelling on the forms and surfaces of things or is it also an intellectual searching into their meaning? Such questions as these (as well as the more obvious ones about the qualities conventionally labelled moral), become the starting-points of inquiries about every institution of the community when it is recognized that individuality is not originally given but is created under the influences of associated life. Like utilitarianism, the theory subjects every form of organization to continual scrutiny and criticism. But instead of leading us to ask what it does in the way of causing pains and pleasures to individuals already in existence, it inquires what is done to release specific capacities and co-ordinate them into working powers. What sort of individuals are created?

The waste of mental energy due to conducting discussion of social affairs in terms of conceptual generalities is astonishing. How far would the biologist and the physician progress if when the subject of respiration is under consideration, discussion confined itself to bandying back and forth the concepts of organ and organism:—If for example one school thought respiration could be known and understood by insisting upon the fact that it occurs in an individual body and therefore is an "individual" phenomenon, while an opposite school insisted that it is simply one function in organic interaction with others and can be known or understood therefore only by reference to other functions taken in an equally general or wholesale way? Each proposition is equally true and equally futile. What is needed is specific inquiries into a multitude of specific structures and interactions. Not only does the solemn reiteration of categories of individual and organic or social whole not further these definite and detailed inquiries, but it checks them. It detains thought within pompous and sonorous generalities wherein controversy is as inevitable as it is incapable of solution. It is true enough that if cells were not in vital interaction with one another, they could neither conflict nor co-operate. But the fact of the existence of an "organic" social group, instead of answering any questions merely marks the fact that questions exist: Just what conflicts and what co-operations occur, and what are their specific causes and consequences? But because of the persistence within social philosophy of the order of ideas that has been expelled from natural philosophy, even sociologists take conflict or co-operation as general categories upon which to base their science, and condescend to empirical facts only for illustrations. As a rule, their chief "problem" is a purely dialectical one, covered up by a thick quilt of empirical anthropological and historical citations: How do individuals unite to form society? How are individuals socially controlled? And the problem is justly called dialectical because it springs from antecedent conceptions of "individual" and "social."

Just as "individual" is not one thing, but is a blanket term for the immense variety of specific reactions, habits, dispositions and powers of human nature that are evoked, and confirmed under the influences of associated life, so with the term "social." Society is one word, but infinitely many things. It covers all the ways in which by associating together men share their experiences, and build up common interests and aims; street gangs, schools for burglary, clans, social cliques, trades unions, joint stock corporations, villages and international alliances. The new method takes effect in substituting inquiry into these specific, changing and relative facts (relative to problems and purposes, not metaphysically relative) for solemn manipulation of general notions.

Strangely enough, the current conception of the state is a case in point. For one direct influence of the classic order of fixed species arranged in hierarchical order is the attempt of German political philosophy in the nineteenth century to enumerate a definite number of institutions, each having its own essential and immutable meaning; to arrange them in an order of "evolution" which corresponds with the dignity and rank of the respective meanings. The National State was placed at the top as the consummation and culmination, and also the basis of all other institutions.

Hegel is a striking example of this industry, but he is far from the only one. Many who have bitterly quarrelled with him, have only differed as to the details of the "evolution" or as to the particular meaning to be attributed as essential *Begriff* to some one of the enumerated institutions. The quarrel has been bitter only because the underlying premises were the same. Particularly have many schools of thought, varying even more widely in respect to method and conclusion, agreed upon the final consummating position of the state. They may not go as far as Hegel in making the sole meaning of history to be the evolution of National Territorial States, each of which embodies more than the prior form of the essential meaning or conception of *the* State and consequently displaces it, until we arrive at that triumph of historical evolution, the Prussian

State. But they do not question the unique and supreme position of the State in the social hierarchy. Indeed that conception has hardened into unquestionable dogma under the title of sovereignty.

There can be no doubt of the tremendously important rôle played by the modern territorial national state. The formation of these states has been the centre of modern political history. France, Great Britain, Spain were the first peoples to attain nationalistic organization, but in the nineteenth century their example was followed by Japan, Germany and Italy, to say nothing of a large number of smaller states, Greece, Servia, Bulgaria, etc. As everybody knows, one of the most important phases of the recent world war was the struggle to complete the nationalistic movement, resulting in the erection of Bohemia, Poland, etc., into independent states, and the accession of Armenia, Palestine, etc., to the rank of candidates.

The struggle for the supremacy of the State over other forms of organization was directed against the power of minor districts, provinces, principalities, against the dispersion of power among feudal lords as well as, in some countries, against the pretensions of an ecclesiastic potentate. The "State" represents the conspicuous culmination of the great movement of social integration and consolidation taking place in the last few centuries, tremendously accelerated by the concentrating and combining forces of steam and electricity. Naturally, inevitably, the students of political science have been preoccupied with this great historic phenomenon, and their intellectual activities have been directed to its systematic formulation. Because the contemporary progressive movement was to establish the unified state against the inertia of minor social units and against the ambitions of rivals for power, political theory developed the dogma of the sovereignty of the national state, internally and externally.

As the work of integration and consolidation reaches its climax, the question arises, however, whether the national state, once it is firmly established and no longer struggling against strong foes, is not just an instrumentality for promoting and protecting other and more voluntary forms of association, rather than a supreme end in itself. Two actual phenomena may be pointed to in support of an affirmative answer. Along with the development of the larger, more inclusive and more unified organization of the state has gone the emancipation of individuals from restrictions and servitudes previously imposed by custom and class status. But the individuals freed from external and coercive bonds have not remained isolated. Social molecules have at once recombined in new associations and organizations. Compulsory associations have been replaced by voluntary ones; rigid organizations by those more amenable to human choice and purposes—more directly changeable at will. What upon one side looks like a movement toward individualism, turns out to be really a movement toward multiplying all kinds and varieties of associations: Political parties, industrial corporations, scientific and artistic organizations, trade unions, churches, schools, clubs and societies without number, for the cultivation of every conceivable interest that men have in common. As they develop in number and importance, the state tends to become more and more a regulator and adjuster among them; defining the limits of their actions, preventing and settling conflicts.

Its "supremacy" approximates that of the conductor of an orchestra, who makes no music himself but who harmonizes the activities of those who in producing it are doing the thing intrinsically worth while. The state remains highly important —but its importance consists more and more in its power to foster and co-ordinate the activities of voluntary groupings. Only nominally is it in any modern community the end for the sake of which all the other societies and organizations exist. Groupings for promoting the diversity of goods that men share have become the real social units. They occupy the place which traditional theory has claimed either for mere isolated individuals or for the supreme and single political organization. Pluralism is well ordained in present political practice and demands a modification of hierarchical and monistic theory. Every combination of human forces that adds its own contribution of value to life has for that reason its own unique and ultimate worth. It cannot be degraded into a means to glorify the State. One reason for the increased demoralization of war is that it forces the State into an abnormally supreme position.

The other concrete fact is the opposition between the claim of independent sovereignty in behalf of the territorial national state and the growth of international and what have well been called trans-national interests. The weal and woe of any modern state is bound up with that of others. Weakness, disorder, false principles on the part of any state are not confined within its boundaries. They spread and infect other states. The same is true of economic, artistic and scientific advances. Moreover the voluntary associations just spoken of do not coincide with political boundaries. Associations of mathematicians, chemists, astronomers; business corporations, labor organizations, churches are trans-national because the interests they represent are worldwide. In such ways as these, internationalism is not an aspiration but a fact, not a sentimental ideal but a force. Yet these interests are cut across and thrown out of gear by the traditional doctrine of exclusive national sovereignty. It is the vogue of this doctrine, or dogma, that presents the strongest barrier to the effective formation of an international mind which alone agrees with the moving forces of present-day labor, commerce, science, art and religion.

Society, as was said, is many associations not a single organization. Society means association; coming together in joint intercourse and action for the better realization of any form of experience which is augmented and confirmed by being shared. Hence there are as many associations as there are goods which are enhanced by being mutually communicated and participated in. And these are literally indefinite in number. Indeed, capacity to endure publicity and communication is the test by which it is decided whether a pretended good is genuine or spurious. Moralists have always insisted upon the fact that good is universal, objective, not just private, particular. But too often, like Plato, they have been content with a metaphysical universality or, like Kant, with a logical universality. Communication, sharing, joint participation are the only actual ways of universalizing the moral law and end. We insisted at the last hour upon the unique character of every intrinsic good. But the counterpart of this proposition is that the situation in which a good is consciously realized is not one of transient sensations or private appetites but one of sharing and communication—public, social. Even the hermit communes with gods or spirits; even misery loves company; and the most extreme selfishness includes a band of followers or some partner to share in the attained good. Universalization means socialization, the extension of the area and range of those who share in a good.

The increasing acknowledgment that goods exist and endure only through being communicated and that association is the means of conjoint sharing lies back of the modern sense of humanity and democracy. It is the saving salt in altruism and philanthropy, which without this factor degenerate into moral condescension and moral interference, taking the form of trying to regulate the affairs of others under the guise of doing them good or of conferring upon them some right as if it were a gift of charity. It follows that organization is never an end in itself. It is a means of promoting *association,* of multiplying effective points of contact between persons, directing their intercourse into the modes of greatest fruitfulness.

The tendency to treat organization as an end in itself is responsible for all the exaggerated theories in which individuals are subordinated to some institution to which is given the noble name of society. Society is the *process* of associating in such ways that experiences, ideas, emotions, values are transmitted and made common. To this active process, both the individual and the institutionally organized may truly be said to be subordinate. The individual is subordinate because except in and through communication of experience from and to others, he remains dumb, merely sentient, a brute animal. Only in association with fellows does he become a conscious centre of experience. Organization, which is what traditional theory has generally meant by the term Society or State, is also subordinate because it becomes static, rigid, institutionalized whenever it is not employed to facilitate and enrich the contacts of human beings with one another.

The long-time controversy between rights and duties, law and freedom is another version of the strife between the Individual and Society as fixed concepts. Freedom for an individual means growth, ready change when modification is required.

It signifies an active process, that of release of capacity from whatever hems it in. But since society can develop only as new resources are put at its disposal, it is absurd to suppose that freedom has positive significance for individuality but negative meaning for social interests. Society is strong, forceful, stable against accident only when all its members can function to the limit of their capacity. Such functioning cannot be achieved without allowing a leeway of experimentation beyond the limits of established and sanctioned custom. A certain amount of overt confusion and irregularity is likely to accompany the granting of the margin of liberty without which capacity cannot find itself. But socially as well as scientifically the great thing is not to avoid mistakes but to have them take place under conditions such that they can be utilized to increase intelligence in the future.

If British liberal social philosophy tended, true to the spirit of its atomistic empiricism, to make freedom and the exercise of rights ends in themselves, the remedy is not to be found in recourse to a philosophy of fixed obligations and authoritative law such as characterized German political thinking. The latter, as events have demonstrated, is dangerous because of its implicit menace to the free self-determination of other social groups. But it is also weak internally when put to the final test. In its hostility to the free experimentation and power of choice of the individual in determining social affairs, it limits the capacity of many or most individuals to share effectively in social operations, and thereby deprives society of the full contribution of all its members. The best guarantee of collective efficiency and power is liberation and use of the diversity of individual capacities in initiative, planning, foresight, vigor and endurance. Personality must be educated, and personality cannot be educated by confining its operations to technical and specialized things, or to the less important relationships of life. Full education comes only when there is a responsible share on the part of each person, in proportion to capacity, in shaping the aims and policies of the social groups to which he belongs. This fact fixes the significance of democracy. It cannot be conceived as a sectarian or racial thing nor as a consecration of some form of government which has already attained constitutional sanction. It is but a name for the fact that human nature is developed only when its elements take part in directing things which are common, things for the sake of which men and women form groups—families, industrial companies, governments, churches, scientific associations and so on. The principle holds as much of one form of association, say in industry and commerce, as it does in government. The identification of democracy with political democracy which is responsible for most of its failures is, however, based upon the traditional ideas which make the individual and the state ready-made entities in themselves.

As the new ideas find adequate expression in social life, they will be absorbed into a moral background, and will the ideas and beliefs themselves be deepened and be unconsciously transmitted and sustained. They will color the imagination and temper the desires and affections. They will not form a set of ideas to be expounded, reasoned out and argumentatively supported, but will be a spontaneous way of envisaging life. Then they will take on religious value. The religious spirit will be revivified because it will be in harmony with men's unquestioned scientific beliefs and their ordinary day-by-day social activities. It will not be obliged to lead a timid, half-concealed and half-apologetic life because tied to scientific ideas and social creeds that are continuously eaten into and broken down. But especially will the ideas and beliefs themselves be deepened and intensified because spontaneously fed by emotion and translated into imaginative vision and fine art, while they are now maintained by more or less conscious effort, by deliberate reflection, by taking thought. They are technical and abstract just because they are not as yet carried as matter of course by imagination and feelings.

We began by pointing out that European philosophy arose when intellectual methods and scientific results moved away from social traditions which had consolidated and embodied the fruits of spontaneous desire and fancy. It was pointed out that philosophy had ever since had the problem of adjusting the dry, thin and meagre scientific standpoint with the obstinately persisting body of warm and abounding imaginative beliefs. Conceptions of possibility, progress, free movement and infinitely diversified opportunity have been suggested by modern science. But until they have displaced from *imagination* the heritage of the immutable and the once-for-all ordered and systematized, the ideas of mechanism and matter will lie like a dead weight upon the emotions, paralyzing religion and distorting art. When the liberation of capacity no longer seems a menace to organization and established institutions, something that cannot be avoided practically and yet something that is a threat to conservation of the most precious values of the past, when the liberating of human capacity operates as a socially creative force, art will not be a luxury, a stranger to the daily occupations of making a living. Making a living economically speaking, will be at one with making a life that is worth living. And when the emotional force, the mystic force one might say, of communication, of the miracle of shared life and shared experience is spontaneously felt, the hardness and crudeness of contemporary life will be bathed in the light that never was on land or sea.

Poetry, art, religion are precious things. They cannot be maintained by lingering in the past and futilely wishing to restore what the movement of events in science, industry and politics has destroyed. They are an out-flowering of thought and desires that unconsciously converge into a disposition of imagination as a result of thousands and thousands of daily episodes and contact. They cannot be willed into existence or coerced into being. The wind of the spirit bloweth where it listeth and the kingdom of God in such things does not come with observation. But while it is impossible to retain and recover by deliberate volition old sources of religion and art that have been discredited, it is possible to expedite the development of the vital sources of a religion and art that are yet to be. Not indeed by action directly aimed at their production, but by substituting faith in the active tendencies of the day for dread and dislike of them, and by the courage of intelligence to follow whither social and scientific changes direct us. We are weak today in ideal matters because intelligence is divorced from aspiration. The bare force of circumstance compels us onwards in the daily detail of our beliefs and acts, but our deeper thoughts and desires turn backwards. When philosophy shall have co-operated with the course of events and made clear and coherent the meaning of the daily detail, science and emotion will interpenetrate, practice and imagination will embrace. Poetry and religious feeling will be the unforced flowers of life. To further this articulation and revelation of the meanings of the current course of events is the task and problem of philosophy in days of transition.

John Dewey and James H. Tufts:
ETHICS (Revised Edition)

CHAPTER XVI[1]
MORALS AND SOCIAL PROBLEMS

At the present time, almost all important ethical problems arise out of the conditions of associated life. As we have previously noted, in a stationary society, in one dominated by custom, the existing social order seems to be like the order of nature itself; as inevitable, and as necessary or as capricious as the case may be. Any suggestion for change is regarded as "unnatural." Even in present social life, any deep-seated change is opposed as contrary to nature; such was the case, for example, in the case of "votes for women" a short time ago. Such is the case still with proposals for, say, doing away with war, or the elimination of the pecuniary profit motive from industry. Nevertheless, when inventions modify social conditions, when new wants and new satisfactions abound, when dislocations of elements of population through migration take place on a large scale, when cultures once separated mix and influence one another, when new modes of industry invade domestic life, when the emergence of increased leisure time coincides with new opportunities for amusement, when great combinations of capital arise which determine the opportunities of individuals for finding work, attention is forced to note the influence exerted upon individuals by collective conditions. Personal selves are forced, unless they are merely to drift, to consider their own action with respect to social changes. They are forced, if they engage in reflection at all, to determine what social tendencies they shall favor and which ones they shall oppose; which institutions they will strive to conserve and which they will endeavor to modify or abolish.

[1] The first four pages of this chapter, which are introductory in character, are here omitted. *The Editors.*

That the present is a time of social changes such as have been mentioned is a commonplace; the mere existence alone of democratic government, for example, raises social issues for moral decision which did not exist for most men and women so long as government was autocratic and confined to a few.

The change from "personal" to "social" morality concerns then the kind of moral questions which are uppermost. For many individuals it is not now a question of whether they individually will appropriate property belonging to another, but whether existing large-scale economic arrangements operate to effect an equitable distribution of property; and if not, what they as individuals shall do about it. In one sense the change to social morality makes morals more acutely personal than they were when custom ruled. It forces the need of more personal reflection, more personal knowledge and insight, more deliberate and steadfast personal convictions, more resolute personal attitudes in action—more personal in the sense of being more *conscious* in choice and more voluntary in execution. It would then be absurd to suppose that "social morals" meant a swallowing up of individuality in an anonymous mass, or an abdication of personal responsibility in decision and action. It signifies that the social conditions and social consequences of personal action (which always exist in any case), are now brought to explicit consciousness so that they require searching thought and careful judgment in a way practically unprecedented formerly. It indicates that reflection is morally indispensable. It points out the material of reflection: the sort of things to which moral inquiry and judgment must go out.

There are countless illustrations of the way in which a problem of personal conduct is so complicated by social conditions that a person has to decide about the latter in order to reach a conclusion in the former. His problem thus takes the form: What attitude shall I adopt towards an issue which concerns many persons whom I do not know personally, but whose action along with mine will determine the conditions under which we all live? A person may have reached a conclusion satisfactory to himself about his own use or non-use of alcoholic liquors, but he finds that his matter runs out into the question of legislative and constitutional action by the nation as a whole. He may find the comparatively simple problem of his relations to members of his own family running out into problems of marriage and divorce which require collective and conjoint action. An individual who takes regard for hu-

man life as an unquestioned matter of course suddenly finds
that the matter assumes an entirely new face when his nation is
at war. A person engaged in making a livelihood for himself
and his family finds himself out of work for causes over which
he has no personal control, and he may be then called upon to
reach a judgment regarding large matters of economic and
political policy which can be settled only by collective action.
These are but samples of the broadening out of issues of personal conduct till they include the formation of intelligent
judgments upon great social institutions, family, property,
political states. Unless men are to surrender to chance, to ca-
price, to prejudice, they must have some general moral
principles by which to guide themselves in meeting such questions.

2. THE UNDERLYING ISSUE: INDIVIDUAL AND SOCIAL

While the problems themselves are concrete and particular,
experience shows that, in dealing with them, most persons,
from temperament, education, or environment, lean in one
direction or another. Some incline to favor private as against
combined action. They think that the presumption is always
in favor of leaving individuals to themselves, and that collectively organized action is to be looked upon with suspicion,
since to them it involves invasion of the realm of personal
liberty; every such intervention is, according to them, an interference which has to be especially justified. There are others
who incline to reverse the presumption; they place the burden
of evidence *against* the isolated individual. They think of him
as egoistic in the main, seeking his own private gain, lacking in
consideration of the rights of others, and needing to be guided
by the laws of a group if he is not to become a social menace.
Or, they think of an individual as in and of himself an ignorant
barbarian, living on a level deprived of art and science, and
requiring the beneficent activity of society to develop him into
any worthy culture of mind and spirit.

It is easy to verify the existence of these opposite tendencies
in the issues which we cited as samples. There are those who
hail the conscientious objector in war as a moral hero and who
regard any degree of conscription of an individual by the
state for war as moral tyranny of the worst kind. There are
others, doutbless many more in number, who regard such a

person as a moral shirker, ungrateful to the society which has educated and protected him, as one who prefers from cowardice his own personal safety to the values, perhaps the life, of the community. There are those who think the maximum amount of liberty should be accorded to individuals in their sex relations; that marriage should not be a fixed institution but rather a voluntary contract, to be broken at will provided the interests of the offspring are duly protected. There are others who regard such opinions as a form of moral anarchy, entertained only because of desire for satisfaction of lawless appetites, and destructive of the basic stability of social life. With respect to property and the economic situation, the strife between the upholders of private property as sacred and those in favor of communal ownership is too well known to need more than a reference.

The tendency to split into opposed camps concerning the respective moral claims of unrestrained individuality and of social control affects all phases of life, education, politics, economics, art, religion. It also determines the attitude taken toward more imponderable things. On one side, it is asserted that collective action tends toward regimentation into mechanical uniformity; towards a mass production of people turned out in a common mold, with individual differences wiped out; that social influence is leveling, that it obliterates distinction and tends toward an average which spells mediocrity. Democracy, as compared with aristocracy, is condemned for its alleged tendencies in this direction. Organized society, it is contended, favors censorship; it tends to meddle constantly with private affairs; to interfere with what the individual thinks, eats, and drinks; by its nature it is hostile, so it is said, to freedom of inquiry, discussion, criticism, since such freedom almost certainly produces variation of judgment and action. Thinking is sure to bring some phase of the established social order under adverse criticism and hence is suppressed by those who have more concern for society than for individuals.

Thus there develops a definite school of thought which holds that the action of society in its collective and organized capacity should be limited to a minimum; that its action should be mainly negative, restricting privately initiated action only when it operates to harm others. All, except the most extreme, of this school, admit the necessity of occasional interference of this negative sort, but urge that it should be confined to what men do externally and should never be extended to the essentials of individuality, to desire, emotion, thought, belief.

And they support themselves by pointing to a long and disastrous historical persecution of variation in belief; to the fanaticism and intolerance which have been bred in desire for social conformity.

On the other side stands the collectivist school. Some of its members assume that individuals left to themselves are actuated only by "self-love," which is so powerful as to produce, when it is left to itself, a "war of all against all." Others point to the influence of social connection in the culture of individuals who left to themselves are at best raw and crude. They point to the fact that, from the standpoint of original nature, individuals hardly rise above the animal level; that what they possess in the way of civilization comes to them through nurture and not from nature; that culture is transmitted not by means of biological heredity, but by tradition, transmission of education, books, art products, and the influence of enduring institutions. Maintenance and strengthening of these collective social forces is, therefore, the primary duty of all those who are interested in the moralization of individuals. At the present time, the point more emphasized is a practical one. It is claimed that only organized social action can remake the old social institutions which persist because of mere inertia and the self-interest of a privileged few. Hence they are unfitted to serve the needs of the present day, a reconstruction especially of economic and industrial conditions being imperatively demanded. Such a change is obviously upon a large scale and of vast extent. It can be effected, therefore, only by collective organized action.

3. THREE ASPECTS OF THE CONFLICT

While persons incline in one direction or another, only confusion results from lumping together all issues as so many species of a more general issue of individual *versus* social. In fact, there are a number of questions which are distinct, each of which must be met and dealt with on its own merits, and in which the individual and the social are not opposed terms. Indeed, in the strict sense of the terms, *no* question can be reduced to the individual on one side and the social on the other. As is frequently pointed out, society consists of individuals, and the term "social" designates only the fact that individuals are in fact linked together, related to one another in intimate ways. "Society" cannot conflict, it is pointed out, with its own constituents; one might as well put number in general in opposition to integers taken severally. On the other hand, individuals cannot be opposed to the relations which they themselves maintain. Only an unreal and impossible being, one completely isolated, disconnected, can be put in opposition to society.

It is surely a fact that there is nothing called society over and above John Smith, Susan Jones, and other individual persons. Society as something apart from individuals is a pure fiction. On the other hand, nothing in the universe, not even physical things, exists apart from some form of association; there is nothing from the atom to man which is not involved in conjoint action. Planets exist and act in solar systems, and these systems in galaxies. Plants and animals exist and act in conditions of much more intimate and complete interaction and interdependence. Human beings are generated only by union of individuals; the human infant is so feeble in his powers as to be dependent upon the care and protection of others; he cannot grow up without the help given by others; his mind is nourished by contact with others and by intercommunication; as soon as the individual graduates from family life he finds himself taken into other associations, neighborhood, school, village, professional, or business associates. Apart from the ties which bind him to others, he is nothing. Even the hermit and Robinson Crusoe, as far as they live on a plane higher than that of the brutes, continue even in physical isolation to be what they are, to think the thoughts which go through their minds, to entertain their characteristic aspirations, because of social connections which existed in the past and which still persist in their imagination and emotions.

The facts urged are all of them true. They bear *upon false statements of the nature of the problems at issue; they do not in any way resolve the actual and important conflicts which exist.* It is important to bear them in mind because they protect us from misconceiving the nature of the problem. For reasons just stated, there can be no conflict between *the* individual and *the* social. For both of these terms refer to pure abstractions. What do exist are conflicts between *some* individuals and *some* arrangements in social life; between groups and classes of individuals; between nations and races; between old traditions imbedded in institutions and new ways of thinking and acting which spring from those few individuals who depart from and who attack what is socially accepted.

There is also a genuine difference of convictions as to the way in which, at any given time, these conflicts should be met and managed. There are reasons for holding that they are best settled by private and voluntary action and also for holding that they are best settled by means of combined organized action. No general theory about the individual and the social can settle conflicts or even point out the way in which they should be resolved.

But conflicts nevertheless do exist; they are not got rid of by asserting, what is perfectly true, that there can be no wholesale opposition between society and individuals. How are they to be explained, and to what general kinds can they be reduced? In the first place, there is no single thing denominated "society"; there are many societies, many forms of association. These different groups and classes struggle in many ways against one another and have very diverse values. Men associate in friendship and in antagonism; for recreation and for crime; they unite in clubs and fraternities, in cliques and sects, in churches and armies; to promote science and art and to prey upon others; they unite in business partnerships and corporations. Then these social units compete vigorously against one another. They unite in nations and the nations war with one another; workers combine in trade unions and employers in trade associations and association intensifies struggle between opposite interests. Political life is carried on by parties which oppose each other, and within each party there are contending factions or "wings." Struggle within an organization is indeed a common phenomenon; in trade unions the central organization and the local units often pull different ways, just as in politics there is usually a struggle between forces making for centralization and for local autonomy. Economically, individuals form into groups, and the union accentuates struggle between producer, distributor, and consumer. Church has vied with State for supremacy; the scientific group has at times had to contend with both. Different groups try to get hold of the machinery of government. Officials tend to combine to protect their special interests and these interests are contrary to those of private individuals; it is a recurrent phenomenon for rulers to use power to oppress and harass their subjects. Indeed, so common is it that the whole struggle for political liberty has been represented as a struggle of subjects to emancipate themselves from the tyranny of rulers.

There are then a multitude of conflicts not between individuals and society but between groups and other groups, between some individuals and other individuals. Analysis shows that they tend to fall into classes marked by similar traits, and these traits help explain why there arose the idea that the conflict is between individual and society.

1. There is the struggle between the *dominant* group and the group or groups, occupying, at the time, an *inferior* position of power and economic wealth. The superior group under such circumstances always thinks of itself as representing the social interest, and represents other groups which challenge its power as rebels against constituted authority, as seeking for the satisfaction of their personal appetites against the demands of law and order. A somewhat striking example of this phase of the matter is seen at the present time in the split between those who hold up the political state as the supreme social form, the culminating manifestation of the supreme common moral will, the ultimate source and sole guarantor of all social values, and those who regard the state as simply one of many forms of association, and as one which by undue extension of its claims into virtual monopoly has brought evils in its train. The conflict is not, as was believed earlier, between the state and individual but between the state as the dominant group and other groups seeking greater liberty of action. It is similar in principle, though often opposite in point of material constituents, to the earlier struggle of political groups to get free from the dominant authority of the church.

2. At a certain stage of such conflicts, the inferior but growing group is not organized; it is loosely knit; its members often do not speak for a group which has achieved recognition, much less for social organization as a whole. The dominant group on the other hand is not only well established, but it is *accepted,* acknowledged; it is supported by the bulk of opinion and sentiment of that time. A government which at a later period is regarded as thoroughly despotic cannot always have been so regarded. In that case it would have been easily overthrown.

To remain in power a dominant class must at least seem to the mass to represent and to sustain interests which they themselves prize. There is thus added to the conflict of the old and established class with the inferior but developing group, the conflict of values that are generally accepted with those which are coming into being. This for a time takes the form of a struggle between a majority *conserving* the old, and a minority interested in the generation of something new, in *progress.* Since it takes time for an idea to gain recognition and for a value to become appreciated and shared, the new and relatively unorganized, although it may represent a genuinely important social value, is felt to be that of dissenting individuals. The values of a past society which are to be conserved are recognized as social, while those of a future society which has yet to be brought into being are taken to be those of individuals only.

In these two instances, the conflict is commonly thought to be between those interested in order and those concerned in progress, where maintenance of order is interpreted as "social" and the initiation of progress as the function of individuals. Even those whose activity in the end establishes a new social order often feel at the time that the enemy is social organization itself. Moreover, every social order has many defects, and these defects are taken to be signs of evils inhering in every kind of social organization. The latter is felt to be nothing but a system of chains holding individuals in bondage. This feeling grows up particularly when old institutions are decaying and corrupt. As in France in the latter eighteenth century and Russia in the later nineteenth, they then call out an intense moral individualism like that of Rousseau and that of Tolstoi respectively. When organization needs to be changed all organization is likely to be felt oppressive. The temporary phenomenon is taken as an illustration of an eternal truth, and the needs of a particular situation frozen into a universal principle.

3. There are also cases in which the troubles of the present are associated with the breakdown of a past order, while existing evils are capable of being remedied only by organized social action. Then the alignment of so-called individual and social is altered, indeed, is virtually reversed. Those who profit by the existing régime and who wish to have it retained are now the "individualists," and those who wish to see great changes brought about by combined action are the "collectivists." These latter feel that institutions as they exist are a repressive shell preventing social growth. They find disintegration, instability, inner competition to be so great that existing society is such only in outward appearance, being in reality what Carlyle called the "society" of his day, namely, "anarchy plus the constable." On the other hand stand those who are at a special advantage in the situation. They extol it as the product of individual energy, initiative, industry, and freedom; these precious qualities will be imperiled by adoption of a plan of conjoint collective activity. They represent the

social order desired by others to be one of servility which crushes out the incentives to individual effort, and which creates dependence upon an impersonal whole, putting a vicious paternalism in place of self-reliance. "Collectivism" in their mouths is a term of reproach. In short, those who are on the side of keeping the *status quo* intact are now the "individualists," those who want great social changes are the "collectivists," since the changes desired are on so large a scale that they can be effected only through collective action.

We shall accordingly substitute the consideration of definite conflicts, at particular times and places, for a general opposition between social and individual. Neither "social" nor "individual," in general, has any fixed meaning. All morality (including immorality) is both individual and social:—individual in its immediate inception and execution, in the desires, choices, dispositions from which conduct proceeds; social in its occasions, material, and consequences. That which is regarded as anti-social and immoral at one time is hailed later on as the beginning of great and beneficent social reform—as is seen in the fate of those moral prophets who were condemned as criminals only to be honored later as benefactors of the race. Organizations that were punished as conspiracies by despotic governments have been regarded as the authors of a glorious liberty after their work has succeeded. These facts do not signify that there is no enduring criterion for judgment but that this criterion is to be found in consequences, and not in some general conception of individual and social.

The points just made suggest three angles from which a social problem may be analyzed in detail in order to decide upon the moral values involved. First, the struggle between a dominant class and a rising class or group; secondly, between old and new forms and modes of association and organization; thirdly, between accomplishing results by voluntary private effort, and by organized action involving the use of public agencies. In historic terms, there is the struggle between class and mass; between conservative and liberal (or radical); and between the use of private and public agencies, extension or limitation of public action.

An illustration of the first issue is seen in the origin of states organized on a popular instead of upon an autocratic dynastic basis. This origin involved the overthrow of the established institutions which for a long time had regulated social affairs; it emancipated many individuals. But at the same time, it generated new types of social institutions and organizations. It was not in other words a movement toward mere individualism. The second mentioned struggle, that between conservative (or, as his opponents term him, reactionary) and liberal, between those who want to preserve intact what has been already attained and who fear and oppose all social change, and those who aim at social modifications more or less profound, is seen in all phases of life; in religious organizations, with the cleavage into fundamentalist and modernist; in education, with the traditionalist and the "progressive"; in politics, with its divisions into right and left; in industrial society, between capitalism and communism as extreme illustrations. The controversy between believers in private and in public action is manifested in every issue which concerns the extent and area of governmental action. At one extreme, are anarchists shading off into those who believe in *laissez faire* and hold that government is best which governs least, through those who believe in enlargement of governmental functions to serve the general interest, over to state socialists who would have government assume control of all means of production and distribution that are of any great size.

4. THE PROBLEM OF METHOD

The attempt to settle these issues in our discussion of ethics would obviously involve an exhibition of partisanship. But, what is more important, it would involve the adoption of a method which has been expressly criticized and repudiated. It would assume the existence of final and unquestionable knowledge upon which we can fall back in order to settle automatically every moral problem. It would involve the commitment to a dogmatic theory of morals. The alternative method may be called experimental. It implies that reflective morality demands observation of particular situations, rather than fixed adherence to *a priori* principles; that free inquiry and freedom of publication and discussion must be encouraged and not merely grudgingly tolerated; that opportunity at different times and places must be given for trying different measures so that their effects may be capable of observation and of comparison with one another. It is, in short, the method of democracy, of a positive toleration which amounts to sympathetic regard for the intelligence and personality of others, even if they hold views opposed to ours, and of scientific inquiry into facts and testing of ideas.

The opposed method, even when we free it from the extreme traits of forcible suppression, censorship, and intolerant persecution which have often historically accompanied it, is the method of appeal to authority and to precedent. The will of divine beings, supernaturally revealed; of divinely ordained rulers; of so-called natural law, philosophically interpreted; of private conscience; of the commands of the state, or the constitution; of common consent; of a majority; of received conventions; of traditions coming from a hoary past; of the wisdom of ancestors; of precedents set up in the past, have at different times been the authority appealed to. The common feature of the appeal is that there is some voice so authoritative as to preclude the need of inquiry. The logic of the various positions is that while an open mind may be desirable in respect to physical truths, a completely settled and closed mind is needed in moral matters.

Adoption of the experimental method does not signify that there is no place for authority and precedent. On the contrary, precedent is, as we noted in another connection, a valuable *instrumentality*. But precedents are to be *used* rather than to be implicitly followed; they are to be used as tools of analysis of present situations, suggesting points to be looked into and hypotheses to be tried. They are of much the same worth as are personal memories in individual crises; a storehouse to be drawn upon for suggestion. There is also a place for the use of authorities. Even in free scientific inquiry, present investigators rely upon the findings of investigators of the past. They employ theories and principles which are identified with scientific inquirers of the past. They do so, however, only as long *as no evidence is presented calling for a reëxamination of their findings and theories*. They never assume that these findings are so final that under no circumstances can they be questioned and modified. Because of partisanship, love of certainty, and devotion to routine, accepted points of view gain a momentum which for long periods even in science may restrict observation and reflection. But this limitation is recognized to be a weakness of human nature and not a desirable use of the principle of authority.

In moral matters there is also a presumption in favor of principles that have had a long career in the past and that have been endorsed by men of insight; the presumption is especially strong when all that opposes them is the will of some individual for exemption because of an impulse or passion which is temporarily urgent. Such principles are no more to be lightly discarded than are scientific principles worked out in the past. But in one as in the other, newly discovered facts or newly instituted conditions may give rise to doubts and indicate the inapplicability of accepted doctrines. In questions of social morality more fundamental than any particular principle held or decision reached is the attitude of *willingness to reëxamine and if necessary to revise current convictions, even if that course entails the effort to change by concerted effort existing institutions, and to direct existing tendencies to new ends.*

It is a caricature to suppose that emphasis upon the social character of morality leads to glorification of contemporary conditions just as they are. The position does insist that morals, to have vitality, must be related to these conditions or be up in the air. But there is nothing in the bare position which indicates whether the relation is to be one of favor or of opposition. A man walking in a bog must pay even more heed to his surroundings than a man walking on smooth pavement, but this fact does not mean that he is to surrender to these surroundings. The alternative is not between abdication and acquiescence on one side, and neglect and ignoring on the other; it is between a morals which is effective because related to what is, and a morality which is futile and empty because framed in disregard of actual conditions. Against the social consequences generated by existing conditions there always stands the idea of other and better social consequences which a change would bring into being.

5. HISTORIC INDIVIDUALISM

Examination of the special moral problems presented by existing social conditions is reserved for subsequent chapters. We shall here attempt to illustrate what has been said by a reference to the movement termed "individualism" in a particular sense determined by historical causes.

1. In economics, it is the notion that individuals left free to pursue their own advantage in industry and trade will not only best further their own private interests but will also best promote social progress and contribute most effectively to the satisfaction of the needs of others and hence to the general happiness.

2. Since the "left free" in this statement signifies in point of practice freedom from regulation by legislation and govern-

mental administration, the doctrine has its political side. It signifies that the activities of government shall be restricted as closely as possible to policing society; that is, to keeping order, to preventing encroachments by one person upon the lawful rights of others, and to securing redress when such interference with the rights of others has occurred. In current phrases, it signifies "keep government out of business"; at least keep it out as much as possible.

3. Since the doctrine has an "ideological" support, it also signifies a certain general philosophy, which may be called that of the "natural" *versus* "artificial." Economic activities on this view are natural and governed by natural laws. Men naturally seek to satisfy their wants; labor or the expenditure of energy is naturally economized so that there will be the utmost return for the minimum outgo; to make the future secure men naturally abstain from consuming all they produce, thus laying by capital to increase their future productivity. Since the output of work is greatest when there is the skill which comes with restriction of effort to one field, division of labor is inherent in the development and this division brings about exchange and trade. There results a general interdependence in which each is forced to find the line of work in which he is most productive and to do the things which, in order to bring the most return to himself, will best serve the needs of others. In contrast with the "natural laws" of this economic process, political laws are artificial; the first are implanted by nature (often conceived of as vice-regent of God) in the human frame. The second are man-made. The presumption is always in favor of natural laws and their workings and against human "interference."

4. To this idea of natural laws, identical with economic laws, was joined an idea of natural *rights*. According to this view, certain rightful claims belong inherently to individuals apart from civil society and the State. The right to life, to property which one has personally produced, to contract or make agreements with others, are such rights; they contrast with civil and political rights which are dependent upon the civil and political organization of society. Being innate and inalienable, they set fixed limits to the activity of government. Government exists in order to protect them; if it infringes on them, it violates its own function so that citizens are released from an obligation to obedience. At the least, courts must pronounce such action invalid because in violation of natural rights.

5. There was often, although not always, associated with the above mentioned four points, the doctrine of self-interest, taken as a scientific support based on psychology. According to this view, human nature is so constituted as to be averse to all activity involving the sacrifice of abstinence and toil except when an incentive of the prospect of a greater advantage or profit is offered. All individuals are supposed to be on the alert for their own interest and to be skilled in calculating where it lies—provided at least that they are not paralyzed or confused by oppressive laws and artificial social institutions.

These various considerations taken as a whole constitute the doctrine of "individualism" in its narrower historic sense. It was formulated during the eighteenth century. It had immense influence—far from extinct as yet—in shaping legal and political institutions throughout the nineteenth century. There were definite causes for its appearance and its growth. Newly invented machines, run by steam power instead of by hand, were creating a new industrial development, while existing laws and customs expressed an agrarian culture and contained many feudal survivals. They were filled with regulations which obstructed commerce, foreign and domestic, which hampered the development of the new type of industry, and which favored landlords at the expense of the manufacturing and mercantile class. European governments regulated (in fact obstructed) international trade in the interest of accumulation of specie in the governmental treasury, at the expense of industry and commerce. The doctrine of economic *laissez faire* then presented itself as an unshackling of human initiative, energy, and inventive skill, as opening a definite road of progress. Established organization on the other hand represented inertia, sloth, and repression. This temporary historic conflict was generalized into an inherent and absolute opposition between the "individual" and the "social," the "natural" and the "artificial."

The period coincided with the beginnings of what we now term popular and democratic government. Governments in general were either corrupt or oppressive or both. They were felt—and at the time with good reason—to mark arbitrary limitations on the legitimate freedom of individuals. In the United States, this feeling was reënforced by the struggle between the colonists and the home government in Great Britain. It was an easy step from the restrictions imposed on the colonies by Great Britain to the idea that all government by its very nature tends to be repressive, and that the great aim in political life is to limit the encroachments of governments in order to make secure the liberty of citizens. The United States was born in the atmosphere of jealousy and fear of State action; the tradition has persisted; it forms a large part of the present power of individualistic philosophy. This feeling, combined with the personal initiative, independence, and self-help that were so indispensable under pioneer conditions in a country of small population and having seemingly unbounded natural resources, operated to create a moral background for the doctrine of individualism. Although the idea of democracy was that of self-rule, the traditions and emotions generated under conditions of alien rule persisted to such an extent that any conception that the people could use their own instrument, government, as a constructive agency for furthering their own well-being, was confined at most to the administration of local communities. The doctrine of the superiority of "natural laws" to man-made law led to an abdication of effort at intelligent control; economic processes were supposed to work of themselves and to a beneficent end. The idea of natural rights was interpreted by courts to forbid legislation which in any way disturbed the *status quo* in the distribution of property, or which, in the interest of workers, limited the power of free contract—the legal fiction being that all parties to an industrial arrangement were equally free to enter or not into the arrangement.

Meantime the original circumstances, economic and political, under which the philosophy of so-called individualism grew up and had had, upon the whole, a useful effect, changed completely. Industrialism supplanted agrarianism as the ruling force. The machine became the regular instead of the novel and exceptional means of productions. Impersonal corporations, instead of individual employers in personal contact with workmen, became the rule. Accumulations of capital grew large, and then merged into larger units. The doctrine of liberty and contract and of non-interference with the customary rules of industry inured to the benefit of the employer and investor, and to the detriment of the workers—that of the mass of people. Protective legislation began to make its way and was followed by the development of a "collectivist" point of view in opposition to the older "individualism." The rôles were reversed. The accepted, the established, social order came to include the things which earlier had had to be striven for by a minority. The social order was now itself "individualistic" in the sense defined above, and the doctrines and slogans which had been used earlier by dissidents and reformers were now used to defend the *status quo*. "Liberty" meant *in effect* the legally unrestrained action of those advantageously placed in the existing distribution of power, through possession of capital and ownership of the means of production.

The ethical formula of the individualistic philosophy was and still remains: The greatest possible freedom of individuals as long as that freedom is not used to the detriment of equal or *similar* liberty on the part of other individuals. The formula has had great vogue; as already intimated, it once did a useful service in getting rid of laws and institutions that had outlived their value. But there is, as an intellectual statement, a flaw in it, a "catch." What is meant by *like* or *equal* freedom? If it signified materially alike, equal in actual power, it would be difficult to take objection to it. The formula would be compatible with the efforts of organized society to *equalize conditions*. It would, for example, justify public action to secure to all an education which would effect a complete development of their capacities, so that they might meet one another on a plane of knowledge and trained intelligence as nearly even as possible. It would justify legislation to equalize the standing of those now at a disadvantage because of inequality in physical power, in wealth, in command of the machinery of employment. It would justify, in other words, a vast amount of so-called social legislation which the individualistic theory as usually held condemns.

But the interpretation given to the ideal of equality was formal, not material; it was legalistic not realistic. Individuals were said to be equal provided they were equal *before the law*. In legal theory, the individual who has a starving family to support is equal in making a bargain about hours and conditions of labor and wages, with an employer who has large accumulated wealth to fall back on, and who finds that many other workers near the subsistence line are clamoring for an opportunity to earn something with which to support their families.

Morally speaking, individuals cannot be split up into a number of isolated and independent powers, all of which can be compared, one by one, with like powers of others so as to determine their equality. The individual person is a whole; what he labors at and the reward he gets are things which affect all his capacities, desires, and satisfactions—and not only his own but those of the members of his family. Just as we cannot tell what is "due" a man until we have taken his whole self into account, so we cannot tell whether a man's freedom is furthered or is interfered with until we have taken into account not just some single point, formally and legally defined, but the bearing of the factor in question (for example, "freedom" of contract) upon his whole plane of living, his opportunities for development, and his relations to others.

The purpose of this historical survey is not to indicate that some anti-"individualistic" principle is correct, so that we should supplant it by a collectivistic formula and program in order to meet the moral requirements of society. It is, first, to suggest the *relativism* of social formulæ in their ethical aspect. No single formula signifies the same thing, in its consequences, or in practical meaning under different social conditions. That which was on the side of moral progress in the eighteenth and early nineteenth centuries may be a morally reactionary doctrine in the twentieth century; that which is serviceable now may prove injurious at a later time. This fact is but a statement in more definite form of the impossibility of deriving concrete directions for moral action from the general concepts of individual and social.

From this fact follows the second point. We have to consider the probable consequences of any proposed measure with reference to the situation, as it exists at some defined time and place in which it is to apply. There cannot be any universal rule laid down, for example, regarding the respective scopes of private and public action. All but the most extreme "individualists" stop short of the logical conclusion that there should be no public schools supported by taxation. They are aware of how many children might, under a purely voluntary system, fail to get any education, and they know what inequalities in society would thereby be fostered. Yet, it does not follow that public education is always and only good. A ruling class and the government may use the schools to inculcate particular doctrines in plastic minds; to suppress freedom of inquiry; to turn out minds in a common mold, and a mold favorable to their own special interest. Under such conditions, there is justification for upholding, on moral grounds, the claims of other schools than those supported by the state.

Every question for the extension or restriction of public action should, then, be considered on its merits. There was a time when religion and religious worship were public functions. Almost all peoples are now convinced that it is better that they should be a private, a voluntary, affair. There was a time in English history when the courts of law were not indeed exactly private, but were attached to the domain of feudal lords; few there are today who would question the value of the transfer of the judicial function to the State. But even this transfer is not inconsistent with the growth, under the jurisdiction of government, of private arbitration as a method of settling commercial disputes. If we go further back in history we find the administration of justice in savage tribes a matter of "self-help." There may have been those who opposed its transfer to the public on the ground that it would weaken individual initiative and responsibility and create a servile dependence on state paternalism. In general, we can say that many interests have shifted from public to private and *vice versa* in connection with changes in science, industry, and public sentiment. Every proposed measure of public policy should, therefore, be considered on the ground of its own effects on the welfare of the members of a community, and not be disposed of on the basis of some abstract theory of either the individual or the social.

Finally, while we have taken our examples for the most part from the controversy concerning public *versus* private action, the principle that conclusions should be reached by analysis of consequences in definite situations holds good of the whole range of problems that have been mentioned. Take, for example, the respective moral claims of conservatism and radicalism. It is impossible to imagine a situation in which there are no values worked out in the past which need to be conserved. But their conservation may demand a change in the *means* by which they are maintained, a change in laws and habits. It is evident that not all customs and ways of doing things can be changed simultaneously. The inertia of habit renders it impossible in the first place, and any attempt in that direction would simply throw everything into chaos. Some habits must remain intact in order to get a positive leverage by which to effect changes desired in other institutions. The problem is always one of discrimination and emphasis: What social arrangements at any given time and place should be kept relatively stable and what arrangements should be modified, in order that values may be rendered more secure, more equitably distributed, richer and more diversified? As long as the issue is conceived in a wholesale manner, conservatism will tend to be blind and reactionary, and radicalism will tend to be abrupt and violent. In a normal society, there would be no class of professional reformers. Some social institutions, some phase of every institution, would be continually re-forming, in the literal sense of remaking, in order to be better adapted to its contemporary conditions of social life.

To some persons it may seem an academic matter whether their attitude and the method they follow in judging the ethical values of social institutions, customs, and traditions, be experimental or dogmatic and closed; whether they proceed by study of consequences, of the working of condition, or by an attempt to dispose of all questions by reference to performed absolute standards. There is, however, no opening for application of scientific method in social morals unless the former procedure is adopted. There is at least a presumption that the development of methods of objective and impartial inquiry in social affairs would be as significant there as it has proved in physical matters. The alternative to organic inquiry is reliance upon prejudice, partisanship, upon tradition accepted without questioning, upon the varying pressures of immediate circumstance. Adoption of an experimental course of judgment would work virtually a moral revolution in social judgments and practice. It would eliminate the chief causes of intolerance, persecution, fanaticism, and the use of differences of opinion to create class wars. It is for such reasons as these that it is claimed that, at the present time, the question of method to be used in judging existing customs and policies proposed is of greater moral significance than the particular conclusion reached in connection with any one controversy.

CHAPTER XVII[1]
MORALS AND THE POLITICAL ORDER

. . . For democracy signifies, on one side, that every individual is to share in the duties and rights belonging to control of social affairs, and, on the other side, that social arrangements are to eliminate those external arrangements of status, birth, wealth, sex, etc., which restrict the opportunity of each individual for full development of himself. On the individual side, it takes as the criterion of social organization and of law and government release of the potentialities of individuals. On the social side, it demands coöperation in place of coercion, voluntary sharing in a process of mutual give and take, instead

[1] The selection from this chapter is that portion containing a direct expression of Dewey's conception of democracy. *The Editors.*

of authority imposed from above. As an ideal of social life in its political phase it is much wider than any form of government, although it includes government in its scope. As an ideal, it expresses the need for progress beyond anything yet attained; for nowhere in the world are there institutions which in fact operate equally to secure the full development of each individual, and assure to all individuals a share in both the values they contribute and those they receive. Yet it is not "ideal" in the sense of being visionary and utopian; for it simply projects to their logical and practical limit forces inherent in human nature and already embodied to some extent in human nature. It serves accordingly as basis for criticism of institutions as they exist and of plans of betterment. As we shall see, most criticisms of it are in fact criticisms of the imperfect realization it has so far achieved.

Democracy as a moral ideal is thus an endeavor to unite two ideas which have historically often worked antagonistically: liberation of individuals on one hand and promotion of a common good on the other. In the famous motto of the French Revolution "Liberty and Equality" represent the values which belong to individuals in their severalty, their distinction from one another; "Fraternity" represents the value that belongs to them in their relations with one another. All history proves, however, that there is no automatic equation of liberty and fraternity with each other. How can fraternal relations be secured without putting individual freedom under restraint? History proves also that liberty and equality do not automatically tend to generate and support one another. Granting liberty to all has a tendency to produce inequalities, since those who have superior capacities or superior opportunities, rise, while those of inferior capacity remain stationary or sink. It has been frequently remarked that the American nation is more interested in equality than in liberty, and willingly places great restrictions on freedom of action if it thinks thereby to secure a greater amount of social uniformity.

From the ethical point of view, therefore, it is not too much to say that the democratic ideal poses, rather than solves, the great problem: How to harmonize the development of each individual with the maintenance of a social state in which the activities of one will contribute to the good of all the others. It expresses a postulate in the sense of a demand to be realized: That each individual shall have the opportunity for release, expression, fulfillment, of his distinctive capacities, and that the outcome shall further the establishment of a fund of shared values. Like every true ideal, it signifies something to be done rather than something already given, something ready-made. Because it is something to be accomplished by human planning and arrangement, it involves constant meeting and solving of problems—that is to say, the desired harmony never is brought about in a way which meets and forestalls all future developments. There is no short-cut to it, no single predestined road which can be found once for all and which, if human beings continue to walk in it without deviation, will surely conduct them to the goal.

The conditions and the concrete significance of liberty, of equality, of mutual respect, and reciprocal service, change from generation to generation, in some degree from year to year. The change in their significance for thought, purpose, and choice, since this country was founded, is simply enormous. The change from a small population to a large one, from rural to urban, from agricultural to industrial, from hand to machine production, from comparative economic equality to great disparity of fortunes, from free land and unused natural resources to their appropriation—merely to point to some of the larger alterations—has given the terms of the problem a radically new significance, and demands, therefore, new thoughts and new measures if ideals remaining formally and nominally the same, are to be maintained. Because of these facts, the approach must be experimental. The alternative to the adoption of an experimental method is not the attainment of greater security by adoption of fixed method (as dogmatists allege), but is merely to permit things to drift: to abdicate every attempt at direction and mastery. . . .

Mohandas K. Gandhi (1869–1948)

COLLECTED WRITINGS ON NON-VIOLENT RESISTANCE

SATYAGRAHA

Section First: What Satyagraha Is

I
SATYAGRAHA, CIVIL DISOBEDIENCE
PASSIVE RESISTANCE, NON-CO-OPERATION

Satyagraha is literally holding on to Truth and it means, therefore, Truth-force. Truth is soul or spirit. It is, therefore, known as soul-force. It excludes the use of violence because man is not capable of knowing the absolute truth and, therefore, not competent to punish. The word was coined in South Africa to distinguish the non-violent resistance of the Indians of South Africa from the contemporary "passive resistance" of the suffragettes and others. It is not conceived as a weapon of the weak.

Passive resistance is used in the orthodox English sense and covers the suffragette movement as well as the resistance of the Non-conformists. Passive resistance has been conceived and is regarded as a weapon of the weak. Whilst it avoids violence, being not open to the weak, it does not exclude its use if, in the opinion of a passive resister, the occasion demands it. However, it has always been distinguished from armed resistance and its application was at one time confined to Christian martyrs.

Civil Disobedience is civil breach of unmoral statutory enactments. The expression was, so far as I am aware, coined by Thoreau to signify his own resistance to the laws of a slave

State. He has left a masterly treatise on the duty of Civil Disobedience. But Thoreau was not perhaps an out and out champion of non-violence. Probably, also, Thoreau limited his breach of statutory laws to the revenue law, i.e. payment of taxes. Whereas the term Civil Disobedience as practised in 1919 covered a breach of any statutory and unmoral law. It signified the resister's outlawry in a civil, i.e., non-violent manner. He invoked the sanctions of the law and cheerfully suffered imprisonment. It is a branch of Satyagraha.

Non-co-operation predominantly implies withdrawing of co-operation from the State that in the non-co-operator's view has become corrupt and excludes Civil Disobedience of the fierce type described above. By its very nature, non-co-operation is even open to children of understanding and can be safely practised by the masses. Civil Disobedience presupposes the habit of willing obedience to laws without fear of their sanctions. It can, therefore, be practised only as a last resort and by a select few in the first instance at any rate. Non-co-operation, too, like Civil Disobedience is a branch of Satyagraha which includes all non-violent resistance for the vindication of Truth.

Young India, 23-3-'21

SATYAGRAHA[1]

For the past thirty years I have been preaching and practising Satyagraha. The principles of Satyagraha, as I know it today, constitute a gradual evolution.

Satyagraha differs from Passive Resistance as the North Pole from the South. The latter has been conceived as a weapon of the weak and does not exclude the use of physical force or violence for the purpose of gaining one's end, whereas the former has been conceived as a weapon of the strongest and excludes the use of violence in any shape or form.

The term *Satyagraha* was coined by me in South Africa to express the force that the Indians there used for full eight years and it was coined in order to distinguish it from the movement then going on in the United Kingdom and South Africa under the name of Passive Resistance.

Its root meaning is holding on to truth, hence truth-force. I have also called it Love-force or Soul-force. In the applica-

[1] Extract from a statement by Gandhiji to the Hunter Committee.

tion of Satyagraha I discovered in the earliest stages that pursuit of truth did not admit of violence being inflicted on one's opponent but that he must be weaned from error by patience and sympathy. For what appears to be truth to the one may appear to be error to the other. And patience means self-suffering. So the doctrine came to mean vindication of truth not by infliction of suffering on the opponent but on one's self.

But on the political field the struggle on behalf of the people mostly consists in opposing error in the shape of unjust laws. When you have failed to bring the error home to the lawgiver by way of petitions and the like, the only remedy open to you, if you do not wish to submit to error, is to compel him by physical force to yield to you or by suffering in your own person by inviting the penalty for the breach of the law. Hence Satyagraha largely appears to the public as Civil Disobedience or Civil Resistance. It is civil in the sense that it is not criminal.

The lawbreaker breaks the law surreptitiously and tries to avoid the penalty, not so the civil resister. He ever obeys the laws of the State to which he belongs, not out of fear of the sanctions but because he considers them to be good for the welfare of society. But there come occasions, generally rare, when he considers certain laws to be so unjust as to render obedience to them a dishonour. He then openly and civilly breaks them and quietly suffers the penalty for their breach. And in order to register his protest against the action of the law givers, it is open to him to withdraw his co-operation from the State by disobeying such other laws whose breach does not involve moral turpitude.

In my opinion, the beauty and efficacy of Satyagraha are so great and the doctrine so simple that it can be preached even to children. It was preached by me to thousands of men, women and children commonly called indentured Indians with excellent results.[2]

MEANS AND ENDS

Reader: Why should we not obtain our goal, which is good, by any means whatsoever, even by using violence? Shall I think of the means when I have to deal with a thief in the

---

[2] The remaining two pages of this chapter, here omitted, are concerned mainly with local details. *The Editors.*

house? My duty is to drive him out anyhow. You seem to admit that we have received nothing, and that we shall receive nothing by petitioning. Why, then, may we not do so by using brute force? And, to retain what we may receive we shall keep up the fear by using the same force to the extent that it may be necessary. You will not find fault with a continuance of force to prevent a child from thrusting its foot into fire? Somehow or other we have to gain our end.

Editor: Your reasoning is plausible. It has deluded many. I have used similar arguments before now. But I think I know better now, and I shall endeavour to undeceive you. Let us first take the argument that we are justified in gaining our end by using brute force because the English gained theirs by using similar means. It is perfectly true that they used brute force and that it is possible for us to do likewise, but by using similar means we can get only the same thing that they got. You will admit that we do not want that. Your belief that there is no connection between the means and the end is a great mistake. Through that mistake even men who have been considered religious have committed grievous crimes. Your reasoning is the same as saying that we can get a rose through planting a noxious weed. If I want to cross the ocean, I can do so only by means of a vessel; if I were to use a cart for that purpose, both the cart and I would soon find the bottom. "As is the God, so is the votary," is a maxim worth considering. Its meaning has been distorted and men have gone astray. The means may be likened to a seed, the end to a tree; and there is just the same inviolable connection between the means and the end as there is between the seed and the tree. I am not likely to obtain the result flowing from the worship of God by laying myself prostrate before Satan. If, therefore, any one were to say: "I want to worship God; it does not matter that I do so by means of Satan," it would be set down as ignorant folly. We reap exactly as we sow. The English in 1833 obtained greater voting power by violence. Did they by using brute force better appreciate their duty? They wanted the right of voting, which they obtained by using physical force. But real rights are a result of performance of duty; those rights they have not obtained. We, therefore, have before us in England the force of everybody wanting and insisting on his rights, nobody thinking of his duty. And, where everybody wants rights, who shall give them to whom? I do not wish to imply that they do no duties. They don't perform the duties corresponding to those rights; and as they do not perform that particular duty, namely, acquire fitness, their rights have proved a burden to them. In other words, what they have obtained is an exact result of the means they adopted. They used the means corresponding to the end. If I want to deprive you of your watch, I shall certainly have to fight for it; if I want to buy your watch, I shall have to pay for it; and if I want a gift, I shall have to plead for it; and, according to the means I employ, the watch is stolen property, my own property, or a donation Thus we see three different results from three different means. Will you still say that means do not matter?

Now we shall take the example given by you of the thief to be driven out. I do not agree with you that the thief may be driven out by any means. If it is my father who has come to steal I shall use one kind of means. If it is an acquaintance I shall use another; and in the case of a perfect stranger I shall use a third. If it is a white man, you will perhaps say you will use means different from those you will adopt with an Indian thief. If it is a weakling, the means will be different from those to be adopted for dealing with an equal in physical strength; and if the thief is armed from top to toe, I shall simply remain quiet. Thus we have a variety of means between the father and the armed man. Again, I fancy that I should pretend to be sleeping whether the thief was my father or that strong armed man. The reason for this is that my father would also be armed and I should succumb to the strength possessed by either and allow my things to be stolen. The strength of my father would make me weep with pity; the strength of the armed man would rouse in me anger and we should become enemies. Such is the curious situation. From these examples we may not be able to agree as to the means to be adopted in each case. I myself seem clearly to see what should be done in all these cases, but the remedy may frighten you. I therefore hesitate to place it before you. For the time being I will leave you to guess it, and if you cannot, it is clear you will have to adopt different means in each case. You will also have seen that any means will not avail to drive away the thief. You will have to adopt means to fit each case. Hence it follows that your duty is not to drive away the thief by any means you like.

Let us proceed a little further. That well-armed man has stolen your property; you have harboured the thought of his act; you are filled with anger; you argue that you want to punish that rogue, not for your own sake, but for the good of your neighbours; you have collected a number of armed men, you want to take his house by assault; he is duly informed of it, he runs away; he too is incensed. He collects his brother robbers, and sends you a defiant message that he will commit robbery in broad daylight. You are strong, you do not fear him, you are prepared to receive him. Meanwhile, the robber pesters your neighbours. They complain before you. You reply that you are doing all for their sake, you do not mind that your own goods have been stolen. Your neighbours reply that the robber never pestered them before, and that he commenced his depredations only after you declared hostilities against him. You are between Scylla and Charybdis. You are full of pity for the poor men. What they say is true. What are you to do? You will be disgraced if you now leave the robber alone. You, therefore, tell the poor men: "Never mind. Come, my wealth is yours, I will give you arms, I will teach you how to use them; you should belabour the rogue; don't you leave him alone." And so the battle grows; the robbers increase in numbers; your neighbours have deliberately put themselves to inconvenience. Thus the result of wanting to take revenge upon the robber is that you have disturbed your own peace; you are in perpetual fear of being robbed and assaulted; your courage has given place to cowardice. If you will patiently examine the argument, you will see that I have not overdrawn the picture. This is one of the means. Now let us examine the other. You set this armed robber down as an ignorant brother; you intend to reason with him at a suitable opportunity; you argue that he is, after all, a fellow man; you do not know what prompted him to steal. You, therefore, decide that, when you can, you will destroy the man's motive for stealing. Whilst you are thus reasoning with yourself, the man comes again to steal. Instead of being angry with him you take pity on him. You think that this stealing habit must be a disease with him. Henceforth, you, therefore, keep your doors and windows open, you change your sleeping-place, and you keep your things in a manner most accessible to him. The robber comes again and is confused as all this is new to him; nevertheless, he takes away your things. But his mind is agitated. He inquires about you in the village, he comes to learn about your broad and loving heart, he repents, he begs your pardon, returns you your things, and leaves off the stealing habit. He becomes your servant, and you will find for him honourable employment. This is the second method. Thus, you see, different means have brought about totally different results. I do not wish to deduce from this that robbers will act in the above manner or that all will have the same pity and love like you, but I only wish to show that fair means alone can produce fair results, and that, at least in the majority of cases, if not indeed in all, the force of love and pity is infinitely greater than the force of arms. There is harm in the exercise of brute force, never in that of pity.

Now we will take the question of petitioning. It is a fact beyond dispute that a petition, without the backing of force, is useless. However, the late Justice Ranade used to say that petitions served a useful purpose because they were a means of educating people. They give the latter an idea of their condition and warn the rulers. From this point of view, they are not altogether useless. A petition of an equal is a sign of courtesy; a petition from a slave is a symbol of his slavery. A petition backed by force is a petition from an equal and, when he transmits his demand in the form of a petition, it testifies to his nobility. Two kinds of force can back petitions. "We shall hurt you if you do not give this," is one kind of force; it is the force of arms, whose evil results we have already examined. The second kind of force can thus be stated: "If you do not concede our demand, we shall be no longer your petitioners. You can govern us only so long as we remain the governed; we shall no longer have any dealings with you." The force implied in this may be described as love-force, soul-force, or, more popularly but less accurately, passive resistance.[8] This force is indestructible. He who uses it perfectly understands his position. We have an ancient proverb which literally means: "One negative cures thirty-six diseases." The force of arms is powerless when matched against the force of love or the soul.

Now we shall take your last illustration, that of the child thrusting its foot into fire. It will not avail you. What do you really do to the child? Supposing that it can exert so much physical force that it renders you powerless and rushes into fire, then you cannot prevent it. There are only two remedies open to you—either you must kill it in order to prevent it from perishing in the flames, or you must give your own life because you do not wish to see it perish before your very eyes. You will not kill it. If your heart is not quite full of pity, it is possible that you will not surrender yourself by preceding the child and going into the fire yourself. You,

[8] Finding the word misleading Gandhiji later called the same force Satyagraha or non-violent resistance.—Ed.

therefore, helplessly allow it to go to the flames. Thus, at any rate, you are not using physical force. I hope you will not consider that it is still physical force, though of a low order, when you would forcibly prevent the child from rushing towards the fire if you could. That force is of a different order and we have to understand what it is.

Remember that, in thus preventing the child, you are minding entirely its own interest, you are exercising authority for its sole benefit. Your example does not apply to the English. In using brute force against the English you consult entirely your own, that is the national, interest. There is no question here either of pity or of love. If you say that the actions of the English, being evil, represent fire, and that they proceed to their actions through ignorance, and that therefore they occupy the position of a child and that you want to protect such a child, then you will have to overtake every evil action of that kind by whomsoever committed and, as in the case of the evil child, you will have to sacrifice yourself. If you are capable of such immeasurable pity, I wish you well in its exercise.

Hind Swaraj or Indian Home Rule, chap. xvi

SATYAGRAHA OR PASSIVE RESISTANCE

Reader: Is there any historical evidence as to the success of what you have called soul-force or truth-force? No instance seems to have happened of any nation having risen through soul-force. I still think that the evil-doers will not cease doing evil without physical punishment.

Editor: The poet Tulsidas has said: "Of religion, pity, or love, is the root, as egotism of the body. Therefore, we should not abandon pity so long as we are alive." This appears to me to be a scientific truth. I believe in it as much as I believe in two and two being four. The force of love is the same as the force of the soul or truth. We have evidence of its working at every step. The universe would disappear without the existence of that force. But you ask for historical evidence. It is, therefore, necessary to know what history means. The Gujarati equivalent means: "It so happened." If that is the meaning of history, it is possible to give copious evidence. But, if it means the doings of kings and emperors, there can be no evidence of soul-force or passive resistance in such history. You cannot expect silver ore in a tin mine. History, as we know it, is a record of the wars of the world, and so there is a proverb among Englishmen that a nation which has no history, that is, no wars, is a happy nation. How kings played, how they became enemies of one another, how they murdered one another, is found accurately recorded in history, and if this were all that had happened in the world, it would have been ended long ago. If the story of the universe had commenced with wars, not a man would have been found alive today. Those people who had been warred against have disappeared as, for instance, the natives of Australia of whom hardly a man was left alive by the intruders. Mark, please, that these natives did not use soul-force in self-defense, and it does not require much foresight to know that the Australians will share the same fate as their victims. "Those that take the sword shall perish by the Sword." With us the proverb is that professional swimmers will find a watery grave.

The fact that there are so many men still alive in the world shows that it is based not on the force of arms but on the force of truth or love. Therefore, the greatest and most unimpeachable evidence of the success of this force is to be found in the fact that, in spite of the wars of the world, it still lives on.

Thousands, indeed tens of thousands, depend for their existence on a very active working of this force. Little quarrels of millions of families in their daily lives disappear before the exercise of this force. Hundreds of nations live in peace. History does not and cannot take note of this fact. History is really a record of every interruption of the even working of the force of love or of the soul. Two brothers quarrel; one of them repents and re-awakens the love that was lying dormant in him; the two again begin to live in peace; nobody takes note of this. But if the two brothers, through the intervention of solicitors or some other reason, take up arms or go to law—which is another form of the exhibition of brute force—their doing would be immediately noticed in the press, they would be the talk of their neighbours and would probably go down to history. And what is true of families and communities is true of nations. There is no reason to believe that there is one law for families and another for nations. History, then, is a record of an interruption of the course of nature. Soul-force, being natural, is not noted in history.

Reader: According to what you say, it is plain that instances of this kind of passive resistance are not to be found in history. It is necessary to understand this passive resistance more fully. It will be better, therefore, if you enlarge upon it.

Editor: Passive resistance is a method of securing rights by personal suffering; it is the reverse of resistance by arms. When I refuse to do a thing that is repugnant to my conscience, I use soul-force. For instance, the Government of the day has passed a law which is applicable to me. I do not like it. If by using violence I force the Government to repeal the law, I am employing what may be termed body-force. If I do not obey the law and accept the penalty for its breach, I use soul-force. It involves sacrifice of self.

Everybody admits that sacrifice of self is infinitely superior to sacrifice of others. Moreover, if this kind of force is used in a cause that is unjust, only the person using it suffers. He does not make others suffer for his mistakes. Men have before now done many things which were subsequently found to have been wrong. No man can claim that he is absolutely in the right or that a particular thing is wrong because he thinks so, but it is wrong for him so long as that is his deliberate judgment. It is therefore meet that he should not do that which he knows to be wrong, and suffer the consequence whatever it may be. This is the key to the use of soul-force.

Reader: You would then disregard laws—this is rank disloyalty. We have always been considered a law-abiding nation. You seem to be going even beyond the extremists. They say that we must obey the laws that have been passed, but that if the laws be bad, we must drive out the law-givers even by force.

Editor: Whether I go beyond them or whether I do not is a matter of no consequence to either of us. We simply want to find out what is right and to act accordingly. The real meaning of the statement that we are a law-abiding nation is that we are passive resisters. When we do not like certain laws, we do not break the heads of law-givers but we suffer and do not submit to the laws. That we should obey laws whether good or bad is a newfangled notion. There was no such thing in former days. The people disregarded those laws they did not like and suffered the penalties for their breach. It is contrary to our manhood if we obey laws repugnant to our conscience. Such teaching is opposed to religion and means slavery. If the Government were to ask us to go about without any clothing, should we do so? If I were a passive resister, I would say to them that I would have nothing to do with their law. But we have so forgotten ourselves and become so compliant that we do not mind any degrading law.

A man who has realized his manhood, who fears only God, will fear no one else. Man-made laws are not necessarily binding on him. Even the Government does not expect any such thing from us. They do not say: "You must do such and such a thing," but they say: "If you do not do it, we will punish you." We are sunk so low that we fancy that it is our duty and our religion to do what the law lays down. If man will only realize that it is unmanly to obey laws that are unjust, no man's tyranny will enslave him. This is the key to self-rule or home-rule.

It is a superstition and ungodly thing to believe that an act of a majority binds a minority. Many examples can be given in which acts of majorities will be found to have been wrong and those of minorities to have been right. All reforms owe their origin to the initiation of minorities in opposition to majorities. If among a band of robbers a knowledge of robbing is obligatory, is a pious man to accept the obligation? So long as the superstition that men should obey unjust laws exists, so long will their slavery exist. And a passive resister alone can remove such a superstition.

To use brute-force, to use gunpowder, is contrary to passive resistance, for it means that we want our opponent to do by force that which we desire but he does not. And, if such a use of force is justifiable, surely he is entitled to do likewise by us. And so we should never come to an agreement. We may simply fancy, like the blind horse moving in a circle round a mill, that we are making progress. Those who believe that they are not bound to obey laws which are repugnant to their conscience have only the remedy of passive resistance open to them. Any other must lead to disaster.

Hind Swaraj or Indian Home Rule, chap. XVII

EVIDENCE BEFORE THE HUNTER COMMITTEE

(Extracts)

1. Examination by Lord Hunter

Q. I take it, Mr Gandhi, that you are the author of the Satyagraha movement.

A. Yes, Sir.

Q. Will you explain it briefly?

A. It is a movement intended to replace methods of violence and a movement based entirely upon truth. It is, as I have conceived it, an extension of the domestic law on the political field, and my experience has led me to the conclusion that that movement, and that alone, can rid India of the possibility of violence spreading throughout the length and breadth of the land, for the redress of grievances.

Q. It was adopted by you in connection with the opposition to the Rowlatt Act. And in that connection you asked the people to sign the Satyagraha pledge.

A. Yes, Sir.

Q. Was it your intention to enlist as many men as possible in the movement?

A. Yes, consistently with the principle of truth and non-violence. If I got a million men ready to act according to those principles, I would not mind enlisting them all.

Q. Is it not a movement essentially antagonistic to Government because you substitute the determination of the Satyagraha Committee for the will of the Government?

A. That is not the spirit in which the movement has been understood by the people.

Q. I ask you to look at it from the point of view of the Government. If you were a Governor yourself, what would you say to a movement that was started with the object of breaking those laws which your Committee determined?

A. That would not be stating the whole case of the Satyagraha doctrine. If I were in charge of the Government and brought face to face with a body who, entirely in search of truth, were determined to seek redress from unjust laws without inflicting violence, I would welcome it and would consider that they were the best constitutionalists, and, as a Governor I would take them by my side as advisers who would keep me on the right path.

Q. People differ as to the justice or injustice of particular laws?

A. That is the main reason why violence is eliminated and a Satyagrahi gives his opponent the same right of independence and feelings of liberty that he reserves to himself, and he will fight by inflicting injuries on his own person.

Lord Hunter: I was looking at it from the point of view of the continuance of Government. Would it be possible to continue the Government if you had set up against the Government a body of men who would not accept the Government view but the view of an independent Committee?

A. I have found from my experience that it was possible

to do so during the eight years of continuous struggle in South Africa. I found General Smuts, who went through the whole of that campaign, at the end of it saying that if all conducted themselves as the Satyagrahis had done, they should have nothing to fear.

Q. But there was no such pledge in that campaign as is prescribed here?

A. Certainly there was. Every Satyagrahi was bound to resist all those laws which he considered to be unjust and which were not of a criminal character, in order to bend the Government to the will of the people.

Q. I understand your vow contemplates breaking of laws which a Committee may decide.

A. Yes, my Lord. I want to make it clear to the Committee that that part of the vow was meant to be a restraint on individual liberty. As I intended to make it a mass movement, I thought the constitution of some such Committee as we had appointed was necessary, so that no man should become a law unto himself, and, therefore, we conceived the plan that the Committee would be able to show what laws might be broken.

Q. We hear that doctors differ, and, even Satyagrahis might differ?

A. Yes, I found it so to my cost.

Q. Supposing a Satyagrahi was satisfied that a particular law was a just law and that the Committee did not obey this law, what is a Satyagrahi to do?

A. He is not bound to disobey that law. We had such Satyagrahis in abundance.

Q. Is it not rather a dangerous campaign?

A. If you will conceive the campaign as designed in order to rid the country of violence, then you will share with me the same concern for it; I think that at any cost a movement of this character should live in the country in a purified state.

Q. By your pledge are you not binding a man's conscience?

A. Not according to my interpretation of it. If my interpretation of the pledge is found to be incorrect, I shall mend my error if I have to start the movement again. (*Lord Hunter* —No, no, Mr Gandhi, I do not pretend to advise you.)

I wish I could disabuse the Committee of the idea that it is a dangerous doctrine. It is conceived entirely with the object of ridding the country of the idea of violence.

Lord Hunter here briefly detailed the circumstances preceding the passage of the Rowlatt Act, the widespread general

Indian opposition to the Act etc., and asked Mr Gandhi to describe the essence of his objection to the legislation.

A. I have read the Rowlatt Committee's report to the end and the legislation foreshadowed in it, and I came to the conclusion that the legislation was not warranted by the facts produced by the Committee. I thought it was very restrictive of human liberty and that no self-respecting person or nation could allow such legislation. When I saw the debates in the Legislative Council, I felt that the opposition to it was universal. When I found the agitation against it, I felt that for me as a self-respecting individual and a member of a vast Empire, there was no course left open, but to resist that law to the utmost.

Q. So far as the objects of that legislation are concerned, have you any doubt that they are to put down revolutionary and anarchical crimes?

A. They are quite laudable objects.

Q. Your complaint, then, must be as regards the methods adopted?

A. Entirely.

Q. The method is, I understand, that greater power has been given to the executive than they enjoyed before.

A. That is so.

Q. But is it not the same power that the executive enjoyed under the Defence of India Act?

A. That is true, but that was essentially an emergency measure designed to secure the co-operation of everybody in order to put down any violence that may be offered by any section of the community in connection with the successful carrying on of the war. It was assented to with the greatest reluctance. The Rowlatt legislation is of a different character altogether, and now the experience of the working of the former Act has strengthened my objections to the Rowlatt Act.

Q. Mr Gandhi, the Rowlatt legislation is only to operate if the local Government is satisfied that there is anarchy.

A. I would not, as a legislator, leave that power in the hands of an executive whom I have known to run mad in India at times.

Q. Then really, your objection comes to this, that the Government of India, in the prosecution of a laudable object, adopted a wrong method. Therefore, is not the proper method of dealing with that, from a constitutional point of view, to endeavour to get the legislation remedied by satisfying Government of the inexpediency of it?

A. I approached on bended knees Lord Chelmsford, and pleaded with him and with every English officer I had the pleasure of meeting, and placed my views before them, but they said they were helpless, and that the Rowlatt Committee's recommendations had to be given effect to. We had exhausted all the methods open to us.

Q. If an opponent differs from you, you cannot satisfy him all of a sudden. You must do it by degrees. Is it not rather a drastic way of attempting it by refusing to obey the law?

A. I respectfully beg to differ from Your Lordship. If I find that even my father has imposed upon me a law which is repugnant to my conscience, I think it is the least drastic course that I could adopt, to respectfully tell him that I cannot obey it. By that course I do nothing but justice to my father, and, if I may say so without any disrespect to the Committee, I have myself followed that course with the greatest advantage and I have preached that ever since. If it is not disrespectful to say so to my father, it is not so to a friend and for that matter to my Government.

Lord Hunter: In the prosecution of your Satyagraha movement against the Rowlatt legislation you resolved upon a general *hartal* throughout India. That *hartal* was to be a day when no business was to be done and people were generally to indicate by their attitude that they disapproved of the Government's action. A *hartal* means a general cessation throughout the whole country. Would it not create a very difficult situation?

A. Cessation for a great length of time would create a difficult situation.

Mr Gandhi here explained how the observance of the *hartal* in some part of the country on the 30th March, and all over the country on the 6th April came about not on account of any miscalculation, but on account of the people in one part coming to know of the Viceregal assent to the Act earlier than the people in other parts.

Q. You agree that the abstention from work should be entirely voluntary?

A. Yes, entirely voluntary, in the sense that persuasion on the day of the *hartal* would not be allowed, whereas persuasion by means of leaflets and other propaganda work on the other days would be perfectly legitimate, so long as no physical force was employed.

Q. You disapprove of people interfering with *tongas* on the day of the *hartal?*

A. Certainly.

Q. You would not object to the police interfering in the case of such a disapprovable interference on the people's part?

A. I would not if they acted with proper restraint and forbearance.

Q. But you agree that on the day of the *hartal* it was highly improper to jostle with other people and stop *tongas?*

A. From a Satyagrahi standpoint I would hold it to be criminal.

Lord Hunter: Your leading lieutenant in Delhi, Swami Shraddhananda—*Mr Gandhi* interrupting: I would not call him my lieutenant, but an esteemed co-worker.—Did he write you a letter on the subject, and indicate to you that after what had occurred in Delhi and the Punjab, it was manifest that you could not prosecute a general *hartal* without violence inevitably ensuing?

A. I cannot recall the contents of that letter. I think he went much further and said that it was not possible that the law-breaking campaign could be carried on with impunity among the masses. He did not refer to *hartal* proceeding. There was a difference of opinion between me and Swami Shraddhananda when I suspended civil disobedience. I found it necessary to suspend it because I had not obtained sufficient control, to my satisfaction, over the people. What Swami Shraddhananda said was that Satyagraha could not be taken as a mass movement. But I did not agree with his view and I do not know that he is not converted to my view today. The suspension of civil disobedience was as much necessary as prosecution for offences against law. I would like the Committee to draw a sharp distinction between *hartal* and civil disobedience. *Hartal* was designed to strike the imagination of the people and the Government. Civil disobedience was a discipline for those who were to offer disobedience. I had no means of understanding the mind of India except by some such striking movement. *Hartal* was a proper indication to me how far I would be able to carry civil disobedience.

Q. If there is a *hartal* side by side with the preaching of Satyagraha would it not be calculated to promote violence?

A. My experience is entirely to the contrary. It was an amazing scene for me to see people collected in their thousands—men, women and even little children and babies marching peacefully in procession. The peaceful *hartals* would not have been at all possible if Satyagraha was not preached in the right way.

But as I have said a *hartal* is a different thing from civil disobedience in practice.

*   *   *

Lord Hunter: Now, the only matters that we have got to deal with here are as regards Ahmedabad itself. In Ahmedabad, as we have been told, you enjoy great popularity among the mill workers?

Mr Gandhi: Yes.

Lord Hunter: And your arrest seems to have caused great resentment on their part and led to the very unfortunate actions of the mob on April 10, 11 and 12 in Ahmedabad and Viramgam?

Mr Gandhi: Yes.

Lord Hunter: So far as those incidents are concerned you have no personal knowledge of them?

Mr Gandhi: No.

Lord Hunter: I don't know whether there is anything that you can communicate to us in connection with those events to help us to form an opinion.

Mr Gandhi: I venture to present the opinion that I considered that the action of the mob, whether at Ahmedabad or at Viramgam, was totally unjustified, and I think that it was a sad thing that they lost self-control. But, at the same time, I would like to say that the people among whom, rightly or wrongly, I was popular, were put to a severe test by Government. They should have known better. I do not say that the Government committed an unpardonable error of judgment and the mob committed no error. On the contrary, I hold that it was more unpardonable on the part of the mob than on the part of Government.

Proceeding, Mr Gandhi narrated how he endeavoured to do what he could to repair the error. He placed himself entirely at the disposal of the authorities. He had a long interview with Mr Pratt and other officials. He was to have held a meeting of the people on the 13th but he was told that it would not be possible to hold it that day, not on account of Colonel Fraser's order, because he was promised every assistance in connection with the meeting, but that the notice of the meeting would not reach all the people that day. The meeting took place on the 14th. There he adumbrated what had happened. There he had to use the terms *organized* and *educated* both of which terms had been so much quoted against him and against the people. The speech was in Gujarati. Mr Gandhi explained and hoped Sir Chimanlal Setalwad would bear him out on a reference to the Gujarati speech that the word only means those who can read and write, and that he used the word and expressed the opinion as he sensed the thing at that time.

He emphasized it was not a previous organization that he meant; he only meant to say, and there could be no mistaking the actual words in his speech, that the acts were done in an *organized manner*. He further emphasized that he was speaking of Ahmedabad only, that he had then no knowledge of what had happened even at Viramgam, and that he would not retract a single statement from that speech. In his opinion, said Mr Gandhi, violence was done in an organized manner. It cannot be interpreted to mean a deep-laid conspiracy. He laid special emphasis on the fact that while he used these expressions he was addressing the people, and not the police authorities.

If Mr Guider stated that a single name of the offenders was not forthcoming from him, he was entirely mistaken about his mission and had put an improper valuation upon the term *organization*. The crimes committed by the mob were the result of their being deluded by the wicked rumour of the arrest of Miss Anasuya. There was a class of half-educated people who possessed false ideas obtained from sources such as cinematographs and from silly novels and from political leaders. He knew that school. He had mixed with them and endeavoured to wean them. He had so far succeeded in his endeavours that there were today hundreds of people who had ceased to belong to the school of revolution.

Proceeding, Mr Gandhi said he had now given the whole meaning of what he had said. He had never meant that there were University men behind the disturbances. He did not say they were incapable of those acts, but he was not aware of any highly educated man directing the mob.

Lord Hunter: Do you imply that there was a common purpose on the part of the rioters?

Mr Gandhi: I don't say that. It would be exaggerating to say that, but I think the common purpose was restricted to two or three men or parties who instigated the crimes.

Q. Did the agitation take an anti-European character?

A. It was certainly an anti-Government movement. I would fain believe it was not anti-European, but I have not yet made up my mind as to that.

Lord Hunter: I do not know whether you want to answer

this or not. According to the Satyagraha doctrine, is it right
that people who have committed crimes should be punished
by the civil authorities?

Mr Gandhi: It is a difficult question to answer, because
(through punishment) you anticipate pressure from outside.
I am not prepared to say that it is wrong, but there is a better
method. But I think, on the whole, it would be proper to say
that a Satyagrahi cannot possibly quarrel with any punishment that might be meted out to an offender, and therefore
he cannot be anti-Government in that sense.

Lord Hunter: But apparently it is against the doctrine of
Satyagraha to give assistance to Government by way of placing the information that a Satyagrahi has that would lead to
the conviction of offenders?

Mr Gandhi: According to the principle of Satyagraha it is
inconsistent, for the simple reason that a Satyagrahi's business
is not to assist the police in the method which is open to the
police, but he helps the authorities and the police to make the
people more law-abiding and more respectable to authority.

Lord Hunter: Supposing a Satyagrahi has seen one of the
more serious crimes committed in these riots in his own presence. Would there be no obligation on him to inform the
police?

Mr Gandhi: Of course I answered that question to Mr
Guider before and I think I must answer it to Your Lordship.
I don't want to misguide the youth of the country, but even
then he cannot go against his own brother. When I say brother,
I do not, of course, make any distinction of country or nationality. A Satyagrahi is wholly independent of such a distinction.
The Satyagrahi's position is somewhat similar to that of a
counsel defending an accused. I have known criminals of the
deadliest type and I may humbly claim to have been instru-
mental in weaning them from crimes. I should be forfeiting
their confidence if I disclosed the name of a single man. But
supposing I found myself wanting in weaning them I would
surely not take the next step to go and inform the police about
them; I do not hesitate to say that for a Satyagrahi it is the
straightest thing not to give evidence of a crime done even
under his nose. But there can be only the rarest uses of this
doctrine and even today I am not able to say whether I would
not give evidence against a criminal whom I saw caught in the
act.

2. *Examination by Sir Chimanlal Setalwad*

Sir Chimanlal: With regard to your Satyagraha doctrine, so far as I understand it, it involves the pursuit of truth and in that pursuit you invite suffering on yourself and do not cause violence to anybody else.

Mr Gandhi: Yes, Sir.

Q. However honestly a man may strive in his search for truth his notions of truth may be different from the notions of others. Who then is to determine the truth?

A. The individual himself would determine that.

Q. Different individuals would have different views as to truth. Would that not lead to confusion?

A. I do not think so.

Q. Honestly striving after truth is different in every case.

A. That is why the non-violence part was a necessary corollary. Without that there would be confusion and worse.

Q. Must not the person wanting to pursue truth be of high moral and intellectual equipment?

A. No. It would be impossible to expect that from every one. If A has evolved a truth by his own efforts which B, C and others are to accept I should not require them to have the equipment of A.

Q. Then it comes to this that a man comes to a decision and others of lower intellectual and moral equipment would have to blindly follow him.

A. Not blindly. All I wish to urge is that each individual, unless he wants to carry on his pursuit of truth independently, needs to follow someone who has determined truth.

Q. Your scheme involves the determination of truth by people of high moral and intellectual equipment and a large number of people may follow them blindly being themselves unable to arrive at similar conclusions by reason of their lower intellectual equipment.

A. I would exact from them nothing more than I would expect from an ordinary being.

Q. I take it that the strength of the propaganda must depend on the number of its followers.

A. No. In Satyagraha success is possible even if there is only one Satyagrahi of the proper stamp.

Q. Mr Gandhi, you said you do not consider yourself a perfect Satyagrahi yet. The large mass of people are then even less so.

A. No. I do not consider myself an extraordinary man.

There may be people more capable of determining truth than myself. Forty thousand Indians in South Africa, totally uncultured, came to the conclusion that they could be Satyagrahis and if I could take you through those thrilling scenes in the Transvaal you will be surprized to hear what restraint your countrymen in South Africa exhibited.

Q. But there you were all unanimous.

A. I have more solidity of opinion here than in South Africa.

Q. But there you had a clear-cut issue, not here.

A. Here too we have a clear-cut issue, viz. the Rowlatt Act.

Mr Gandhi then explained how he presented Satyagraha as an instrument of infinitely greater power than violence.

Q. Does not suffering and going on suffering require extraordinary self-control?

A. No; no extraordinary self-control is required. Every mother suffers. Your countrymen, I submit, have got such control and they have exhibited that in a very large measure.

Q. Take Ahmedabad. Did they exhibit control here?

A. All I say is, throughout India where you find these isolated instances of violence you will find a very large number of people who exercised self-restraint. Ahmedabad and other places show that we had not attained proper mastery over self. The Kaira people in the midst of grave provocation last year acted with the greatest self-restraint.

Q. Do you mean to say these acts of violence were mere accidents?

A. Not accidents. But they were rare and would be rarer for a clear conception of Satyagraha. The country, I think, has sufficiently well realized the doctrine to warrant a second trial. I do feel sure that the country is all the purer and better for having gone through the fire of Satyagraha.

Q. Ordinarily your doctrine contemplates co-operation with the Government and elimination of race-hatred and inviting self-suffering. Does not suffering create ill-will?

A. It is contrary to my thirty years' experience that people have by suffering been filled with any ill-will against the Government. In South Africa after a bitter struggle the Indians have lived on the best of terms with the Government, and Gen. Smuts was the recipient of an address which was voluntarily voted by the Indians.

Q. Is it possible to take part in the movement without taking the Satyagraha vow?

A. I would ask them to take part in the non-civil-resistance part of the movement. The masses unless they took the pledge were not to do the civil-disobedience part of the pledge. For those who were not civil resisters, therefore, another vow was devised asking people to follow truth at all costs and to refrain from violence. I had suspended civil resistance then, and as it is open to a leader to emphasize one part of the vow, I eliminated the civil-resistance part which was not for that season suited to the people, and placed the truth part before them.

* * *

Q. Is not the underlying idea embarrassment of Government?

A. Certainly not. A Satyagrahi relies not upon embarrassment but upon self-suffering for securing relief.

Q. Would not ordered Government be impossible?

A. Ordered Government cannot be impossible if totally inoffensive people break the laws. But I would certainly make Government impossible if I found it had taken leave of its senses.

Q. In your message you ask people to refrain from violence and still violence occurred. Does it not show that the ordinary mind finds it very difficult to practise the theory of non-violence?

A. After having used methods of violence for years it is difficult for them to practise abstention.

Young India, 21-1-'20

3. *Examination by Pandit Jagatnarain*

Q. It is alleged that the Satyagraha movement would embarrass the Government. Are you not afraid of any such result of your movement?

A. The Satyagraha movement is not started with the intention of embarrassing the Government while ordinary political agitation is often started with that object. If a Satyagrahi finds his activities resulting in embarrassing the Government, he will not hesitate to face it.

Q. But you will agree with me that every political agitation depends for its success on the number of followers?

A. I do not regard the force of numbers as necessary in a just cause, and in such a cause every man, be he high or low, can have his remedy.

Q. But you would certainly try to have as many men in your movement as possible?

A. Not exactly so. A Satyagrahi depends only on truth and his capacity to suffer for truth.

Q. But in politics, Mahatmaji, how can a single man's voice be heard?

A. That is exactly what I have been attempting to disprove.

Q. Do you believe that an English officer will take any notice of isolated attempts?

A. Why, that is my experience. Lord Bentinck became an ordinary Mr at the instance of Keshavachandra Sen.

Q. Oh, you cite an example of an extraordinary man.

A. Men of ordinary abilities also can develop morality. No doubt I regard illiteracy among my people as deplorable and I consider it necessary to educate them, but it is not at all impossible for an absolutely illiterate man to imbibe the Satyagraha principle. This is my long-standing experience.

Here Mr Gandhi briefly cleared the distinction between *hartal* and Satyagraha. *Hartal* was no integral part of Satyagraha. It should be resorted to only when necessary. He tried and tried it successfully in connection with the deportation of Mr Horniman and the Khilafat movement.

Q. You can resort to no other remedy to oppose the irresponsible, foreign officials and that is why you have started this movement. Is it not?

A. I cannot say that with certainty. I can conceive the necessity of Satyagraha in opposition to the would-be full responsible self-government. Our ministers can never claim to defend themselves on the score of their ignorance, whereas such a defence is available today for the English officers.

Q. But with all the rights of self-government we shall be able to dismiss the ministers.

A. I cannot feel on that point so assured for ever. In England it often happens that ministers can continue in the executive even though they lose all the confidence of the public. The same thing may happen here too and therefore I can imagine a state of things in this country which would need Satyagraha even under Home Rule.

Q. Would you think that there should be no unrest coming after the Satyagraha movement?

A. Not only I do not think so, I would be disappointed if there were no unrest in case Anasuyabehn and I were arrested. But that unrest will not take the shape of violence. It pains a

Satyagrahi to see others suffering; Satyagrahis will follow each other to jail. I do wish for such unrest.

Young India, 4-2-'20

THE THEORY AND PRACTICE OF SATYAGRAHA

[The following is taken from an article by Gandhiji contributed to the Golden Number of *Indian Opinion* which was issued in 1914 as a souvenir of the eight years' Satyagraha in South Africa:]

Carried out to its utmost limit, Satyagraha is independent of pecuniary or other material assistance; certainly, even in its elementary form, of physical force or violence. Indeed, violence is the negation of this great spiritual force, which can only be cultivated or wielded by those who will entirely eschew violence. It is a force that may be used by individuals as well as by communities. It may be used as well in political as in domestic affairs. Its universal applicability is a demonstration of its permanence and invincibility. It can be used alike by men, women and children. It is totally untrue to say that it is a force to be used only by the weak so long as they are not capable of meeting violence by violence. This superstition arises from the incompleteness of the English expression, *passive resistance.* It is impossible for those who consider themselves to be weak to apply this force. Only those who realize that there is something in man which is superior to the brute nature in him and that the latter always yields to it, can effectively be Satyagrahis. This force is to violence, and, therefore, to all tyranny, all injustice, what light is to darkness. In politics, its use is based upon the immutable maxim, that government of the people is possible only so long as they consent either consciously or unconsciously to be governed. We did not want to be governed by the Asiatic Act of 1907 of the Transvaal, and it had to go before this mighty force. Two courses were open to us: to use violence when we were called upon to submit to the Act, or to suffer the penalties prescribed under the Act, and thus to draw out and exhibit the force of the soul within us for a period long enough to appeal to the sympathetic chord in the governors or the law-makers. We have taken long to achieve what we set about striving for. That was because our Satyagraha was not of the most complete type. All Satyagrahis do not understand the full value of the force, nor have we men who always from conviction refrain from violence. The use of this force requires the adoption of poverty, in the sense that we must be indifferent whether we have the wherewithal to feed or clothe ourselves. During the past struggle, all Satyagrahis, if any at all, were not prepared to go that length. Some again were only Satyagrahis so called. They came without any conviction, often with mixed motives, less often with impure motives. Some even, whilst engaged in the struggle, would gladly have resorted to violence but for most vigilant supervision. Thus it was that the struggle became prolonged; for the exercise of the purest soul-force, in its perfect form, brings about instantaneous relief. For this exercise, prolonged training of the individual soul is an absolute necessity, so that a perfect Satyagrahi has to be almost, if not entirely, a perfect man. We cannot all suddenly become such men, but if my proposition is correct—as I know it to be correct—the greater the spirit of Satyagraha in us, the better men will we become. Its use, therefore, is, I think, indisputable, and it is a force, which, if it became universal, would revolutionize social ideals and do away with despotisms and the ever-growing militarism under which the nations of the West are groaning and are being almost crushed to death, and which fairly promises to overwhelm even the nations of the East. If the past struggle has produced even a few Indians who would dedicate themselves to the task of becoming Satyagrahis as nearly perfect as possible, they would not only have served themselves in the truest sense of the term, they would also have served humanity at large. Thus viewed, Satyagraha is the noblest and best education. It should come, not after the ordinary education in letters, of children, but it should precede it. It will not be denied, that a child, before it begins to write its alphabet and to gain worldly knowledge, should know what the soul is, what truth is, what love is, what powers are latent in the soul. It should be an essential of real education that a child should learn, that in the struggle of life, it can easily conquer hate by love, untruth by truth, violence by self-suffering.

Young India, 3-11-'27

NEITHER A SAINT NOR A POLITICIAN

A kind friend has sent me the following cutting from the April number of the *East and West*:

Mr Gandhi has the reputation of a saint but it seems that the politician in him often dominates his decisions. He has been making great use of *hartals* and there can be no gainsaying that under his direction *hartal* is becoming a powerful political weapon for uniting the educated and the uneducated on a single question of the day. The *hartal* is not without its disadvantages. It is teaching direct action, and direct action however potent does not work for unity. Is Mr Gandhi quite sure that he is serving the highest behests of *ahimsa*, harmlessness? His proposal to commemorate the shooting at Jalianwala Bagh is not likely to promote concord. It is a tragic incident into which our Government was betrayed, but is the memory of its bitterness worth retaining? Can we not commemorate the event by raising a temple of peace, to help the widows and orphans, to bless the souls of those who died without knowing why? The world is full of politicians and petti-foggers who, in the name of patriotism, poison the inner sweetness of man and, as a result, we have wars and feuds and such shameless slaughter as turned Jalianwala Bagh into a shambles. Shall we not now try for a larger symbiosis such as Buddha and Christ preached, and bring the world to breathe and prosper together? Mr Gandhi seemed destined to be the apostle of such a movement, but circumstances are forcing him to seek the way of raising resistances and group unities. He may yet take up the larger mission of uniting the world.

I have given the whole of the quotation. As a rule I do not notice criticism of me or my methods except when thereby I acknowledge a mistake or enforce still further the principles criticized. I have a double reason for noticing the extract. For, not only do I hope further to elucidate the principles I hold dear, but I want to show my regard for the author of the criticism whom I know and whom I have admired for many years for the singular beauty of his character. The critic regrets to see in me a politician whereas he expected me to be a saint. Now I think that the word *saint* should be ruled out of present life. It is too sacred a word to be lightly applied to anybody, much less to one like myself who claims only to be a humble searcher after truth, knows his limitations, makes mistakes, never hesitates to admit them when he makes them, and frankly confesses that he, like a scientist, is making experiments about some "of the eternal verities" of life, but cannot

even claim to be a scientist because he can show no tangible
proof of scientific accuracy in his methods or such tangible
results of his experiments as modern science demands. But
though by disclaiming sainthood I disappoint the critic's expectations, I would have him to give up his regrets by answering him that the politician in me has never dominated a single
decision of mine, and if I seem to take part in politics, it is
only because politics encircle us today like the coil of a snake
from which one cannot get out, no matter how much one tries.
I wish therefore to wrestle with the snake, as I have been
doing with more or less success consciously since 1894, unconsciously, as I have now discovered, ever since reaching
years of discretion. Quite selfishly, as I wish to live in peace
in the midst of a bellowing storm howling round me, I have
been experimenting with myself and my friends by introducing religion into politics. Let me explain what I mean by religion. It is not the Hindu religion, which I certainly prize above
all other religions, but the religion which transcends Hinduism,
which changes one's very nature, which binds one indissolubly
to the truth within and which ever purifies. It is the permanent
element in human nature which counts no cost too great in
order to find full expression and which leaves the soul utterly
restless until it has found itself, known its Maker and appreciated the true correspondence between the Maker and itself.

It was in that religious spirit that I came upon *hartal*. I
wanted to show that it is not a knowledge of letters that would
give India consciousness of herself, or that would bind the
educated together. The *hartal* illuminated the whole of India
as if by magic on the 6th of April, 1919. And had it not been
for the interruption of the 10th of April, brought about by
Satan whispering fear into the ears of a Government conscious of its own wrong and inciting to anger a people that
were prepared for it by utter distrust of the Government, India
would have risen to an unimaginable height. The *hartal* had
not only been taken up by the great masses of people in a
truly religious spirit but it was intended to be a prelude to a
series of direct actions.

But my critic deplores direct action. For, he says, "it does
not work for unity." I join issue with him. Never has anything
been done on this earth without direct action. I rejected the
word *passive resistance* because of its insufficiency and its
being interpreted as a weapon of the weak. It was direct action in South Africa which told and told so effectively that it
converted General Smuts to sanity. He was in 1906 the most

relentless opponent of Indian aspirations. In 1914, he took pride in doing tardy justice by removing from the Statute Book of the Union a disgraceful measure which, in 1909 he had told Lord Morley, would be never removed, for he then said South Africa would never tolerate repeal of a measure which was twice passed by the Transvaal Legislature. But what is more, direct action sustained for eight years left behind it not only no bitterness but the very Indians who put up such a stubborn fight against General Smuts ranged themselves round his banner in 1915 and fought under him in East Africa. It was direct action in Champaran which removed an agelong grievance. A meek submission when one is chafing under a disability or a grievance which one would gladly see removed, not only does not make for unity, but makes the weak party acid, angry and prepares him for an opportunity to explode. By allying myself with the weak party, by teaching him direct, firm, but harmless action, I make him feel strong and capable of defying the physical might. He feels braced for the struggle, regains confidence in himself and knowing that the remedy lies with himself, ceases to harbour the spirit of revenge and learns to be satisfied with a redress of the wrong he is seeking to remedy.

It is working along the same line that I have ventured to suggest a memorial about Jalianwala Bagh. The writer in *East and West* has ascribed to me a proposal which has never once crossed my mind. He thinks that I want "to commemorate the shooting at Jalianwala Bagh." Nothing can be further from my thought than to perpetuate the memory of a black deed. I dare say that before we have come to our own we shall have a repetition of the tragedy and I will prepare the nation for it by treasuring the memory of the innocent dead. The widows and the orphans have been and are being helped, but we cannot "bless the souls of those who died without knowing why," if we will not acquire the ground which has been hallowed by innocent blood and there erect a suitable memorial for them. It is not to serve, if I can help it, as a reminder of a foul deed, but it shall serve as an encouragement to the nation that it is better to die helpless and unarmed and as victims rather than as tyrants. I would have the future generations remember that we who witnessed the innocent dying did not ungratefully refuse to cherish their memory. As Mrs Jinnah truly remarked when she gave her mite to the fund, the memorial would at least give us an excuse for living. After all it will be the spirit in which the memorial is erected that will decide its character. What was the larger "symbiosis" that Buddha and Christ preached? Buddha fearlessly carried the war into the enemy's camp and brought down on its knees an arrogant priesthood. Christ drove out the money-changers from the temple of Jerusalem and drew down curses from Heaven upon the hypocrites and the pharisees. Both were for intensely direct action. But even as Buddha and Christ chastized they showed unmistakable gentleness and love behind every act of theirs. They would not raise a finger against their enemies, but would gladly surrender themselves rather than the truth for which they lived. Buddha would have died resisting the priesthood, if the majesty of his love had not proved to be equal to the task of bending the priesthood. Christ died on the cross with a crown of thorns on his head defying the might of a whole empire. And if I raise resistances of a non-violent character I simply and humbly follow in the footsteps of the great teachers named by my critic.

Lastly, the writer of the paragraph quarrels with my "grouping unities" and would have me take up "the larger mission of uniting the world." I once told him under a common roof that I was probably more cosmopolitan than he. I abide by that expression. Unless I group unities I shall never be able to unite the whole world. Tolstoy once said that if we would but get off the backs of our neighbours the world would be quite all right without any further help from us. And if we can only serve our immediate neighbours by ceasing to prey upon them, the circle of unities thus grouped in the right fashion will ever grow in circumference till at last it is conterminous with that of the whole world. More than that it is not given to any man to try or achieve. "As the atom, so the universe" is as true today as ages ago when it was first uttered by an unknown *rishi.*

Young India, 12-5-'20

THE DOCTRINE OF THE SWORD

In this age of the rule of brute force, it is almost impossible for any one to believe that any one else could possibly reject the law of the final supremacy of brute force. And so I receive anonymous letters advising me that I must not interfere with the progress of non-co-operation even though popular violence may break out. Others come to me and, assuming that secretly I must be plotting violence, inquire when the happy moment for declaring open violence will arrive. They assure me that the English will never yield to anything but violence secret or open. Yet others, I am informed, believe that I am the most rascally person living in India because I never give out my real intention, and that they have not a shadow of doubt that I believe in violence just as much as most people do.

Such being the hold that the doctrine of the sword has on the majority of mankind, and as success of non-co-operation depends principally on absence of violence during its pendency, and as my views in this matter affect the conduct of a large number of people, I am anxious to state them as clearly as possible.

I do believe that where there is only a choice between cowardice and violence I would advise violence. Thus when my eldest son asked me what he should have done, had he been present when I was almost fatally assaulted in 1908, whether he should have run away and seen me killed or whether he should have used his physical force which he could and wanted to use, and defended me, I told him that it was his duty to defend me even by using violence. Hence it was that I took part in the Boer War, the so-called Zulu rebellion and the late War. Hence also do I advocate training in arms for those who believe in the method of violence. I would rather have India resort to arms in order to defend her honour than that she should in a cowardly manner become or remain a helpless witness to her own dishonour.

But I believe that non-violence is infinitely superior to violence, forgiveness is more manly than punishment. (Forgiveness adorns a soldier). But abstinence is forgiveness only when there is the power to punish; it is meaningless when it pretends to proceed from a helpless creature. A mouse hardly forgives a cat when it allows itself to be torn to pieces by her. I therefore appreciate the sentiment of those who cry out for the condign punishment of General Dyer and his ilk. They would tear him to pieces if they could. But I do not believe India to be helpless. I do not believe myself to be a helpless creature. Only I want to use India's and my strength for a better purpose.

Let me not be misunderstood. Strength does not come from physical capacity. It comes from an indomitable will. An average Zulu is any way more than a match for an average Englishman in bodily capacity. But he flees from an English boy, because he fears the boy's revolver or those who will use it for him. He fears death and is nerveless in spite of his burly figure. We in India may in a moment realize that one hundred thousand Englishmen need not frighten three hundred million human beings. A definite forgiveness would therefore mean a definite recognition of our strength. With enlightened forgiveness must come a mighty wave of strength in us, which would make it impossible for a Dyer and a Frank Johnson to heap affront upon India's devoted head. It matters little to me that for the moment I do not drive my point home. We feel too downtrodden not to be angry and revengeful. But I must not refrain from saying that India can gain more by waiving the right of punishment. We have better work to do, a better mission to deliver to the world.

I am not a visionary. I claim to be a practical idealist. The religion of non-violence is not meant merely for *rishis* and saints. It is meant for the common people as well. Non-violence is the law of our species as violence is the law of the brute. The spirit lies dormant in the brute and he knows no law but that of physical might. The dignity of man requires obedience to a higher law—to the strength of the spirit.

I have therefore ventured to place before India the ancient law of self-sacrifice. For Satyagraha and its offshoots, non-co-operation and civil resistance, are nothing but new names for the law of suffering. The *rishis*, who discovered the law of non-violence in the midst of violence, were greater geniuses than Newton. They were themselves greater warriors than Wellington. Having themselves known the use of arms, they realized their uselessness and taught a weary world that its salvation lay not through violence but through non-violence.

Non-violence in its dynamic condition means conscious suffering. It does not mean meek submission to the will of the evil-doer, but it means the pitting of one's whole soul against the will of the tyrant. Working under this law of our being, it is possible for a single individual to defy the whole might of an unjust empire, to save his honour, his religion, his soul and lay the foundation for that empire's fall or its regeneration.

And so I am not pleading for India to practise non-violence because she is weak. I want her to practise non-violence being conscious of her strength and power. No training in arms is required for realization of her strength. We seem to need it because we seem to think that we are but a lump of flesh. I want India to recognize that she has a soul that cannot perish and that can rise triumphant above every physical weakness and defy the physical combination of a whole world. What is the meaning of Rama, a mere human being, with his host of monkeys, pitting himself against the insolent strength of ten-headed Ravana surrounded in supposed safety by the raging waters on all sides of Lanka? Does it not mean the conquest of physical might by spiritual strength? However, being a practical man, I do not wait till India recognizes the practicability of the spiritual life in the political world. India considers herself to be powerless and paralyzed before the machineguns, the tanks and the aeroplanes of the English. And she takes up non-co-operation out of her weakness. It must still serve the same purpose, namely, bring her delivery from the crushing weight of British injustice if a sufficient number of people practise it.

I isolate this non-co-operation from Sinn Feinism, for, it is so conceived as to be incapable of being offered side by side with violence. But I invite even the school of violence to give this peaceful non-co-operation a trial. It will not fail through its inherent weakness. It may fail because of poverty of response. Then will be the time for real danger. The high-souled men, who are unable to suffer national humiliation any longer, will want to vent their wrath. They will take to violence. So far as I know, they must perish without delivering themselves or their country from the wrong. If India takes up the doctrine of the sword, she may gain momentary victory. Then India will cease to be the pride of my heart. I am wedded to India because I owe my all to her. I believe absolutely that she has a mission for the world. She is not to copy Europe blindly. India's acceptance of the doctrine of the sword will be the hour of my trial. I hope I shall not be found wanting. My religion has no geographical limits. If I have a living faith in it, it will transcend my love for India herself. My life is dedicated to service of India through the religion of non-violence which I believe to be the root of Hinduism.

Meanwhile I urge those who distrust me not to disturb the even working of the struggle that has just commenced, by inciting to violence in the belief that I want violence. I detest secrecy as a sin. Let them give non-violent non-co-operation a trial and they will find that I had no mental reservation whatsoever.

Young India, 11-8-'20

NON-PAYMENT OF FINES

All the readers of *Young India* may not know that Ahmedabad came under a heavy fine for the misdeeds of the April of last year. The fine was collected from the residents of Ahmedabad but some were exempted at the discretion of the Collector. Among those who were called upon to pay fines were income-tax payers. They had to pay a third of the tax paid by them. Mr V. J. Patel, a noted barrister, and Dr Kanuga, a leading medical practitioner, were among those who were unable to pay. They had admittedly helped the authorities to quell the disturbance. No doubt they were Satyagrahis but they had endeavoured to still the mob fury even at some risk to their own persons. But the authorities would not exempt them. It was a difficult thing for them to use discretion in individual cases. It was equally difficult for these two gentlemen to pay any fine when they were not to blame at all. They did not wish to embarrass the authorities and yet they were anxious to preserve their self-respect. They carried on no agitation but simply notified their inability to pay the fines in the circumstances set forth above. Therefore, an attachment order was issued. Dr Kanuga is a very busy practitioner and his cash box is always full. The watchful attaching official attached his cash box and extracted enough money to discharge the writ of execution. A lawyer's business cannot be conducted on those lines. Mr Patel sported no cash box. A sofa of his sitting room was therefore attached and advertised for sale and duly sold. Both these Satyagrahis thus completely saved their consciences.

Wiseacres may laugh at the folly of allowing writs of attachment and paying for the collection of fines. Multiply such instances and imagine the consequence to the authorities of executing thousands of writs. Writs are possible when they are confined to a few recalcitrants. They are troublesome when they have to be executed against many high-souled persons who have done no wrong and who refuse payment to vindicate a principle. They may not attract much notice when isolated individuals resort to this method of protest. But clean examples have a curious method of multiplying themselves. They bear publicity and the sufferers instead of incurring odium receive congratulations. Men like Thoreau brought about the abolition of slavery by their personal examples. Says Thoreau, "I know this well, that if one thousand, if one hundred, if ten men whom I could name,—if ten *honest* men only—aye, if *one honest* man, in this State of Massachusetts *ceasing to hold slaves* were actually to withdraw from this co-partnership and be locked up in the country gaol therefor, it would be the abolition of slavery in America. For it matters not how small the beginning may seem to be, what is once well done is done for ever." Again he says, "I have contemplated the imprisonment of the offender rather than seizure of his goods —though both will serve the same purpose, because they who assert the purest right and consequently are most dangerous to a corrupt State, commonly have not spent much time in accumulating property." We, therefore, congratulate Mr Patel and Dr Kanuga on the excellent example set by them in an excellent spirit and in an excellent cause.

Young India, 7-7-'20

THE RIGHT OF CIVIL DISOBEDIENCE

I wish I could persuade everybody that civil disobedience is the inherent right of a citizen. He dare not give it up without ceasing to be a man. Civil disobedience is never followed by anarchy. Criminal disobedience can lead to it. Every State puts down criminal disobedience by force. It perishes, if it does not. But to put down civil disobedience is to attempt to imprison conscience. Civil disobedience can only lead to strength and purity. A civil resister never uses arms and hence he is harmless to a State that is at all willing to listen to the voice of public opinion. He is dangerous for an autocratic State, for he brings about its fall by engaging public opinion upon the matter for which he resists the State. Civil disobedience therefore becomes a sacred duty when the State has become lawless, or which is the same thing, corrupt. And a citizen that barters with such a State shares its corruption or lawlessness.

It is therefore possible to question the wisdom of applying civil disobedience in respect of a particular act or law; it is possible to advise delay and caution. But the right itself cannot be allowed to be questioned. It is a birthright that cannot be surrendered without surrender of one's self-respect.

At the same time that the right of civil disobedience is insisted upon, its use must be guarded by all conceivable restrictions. Every possible provision should be made against an outbreak of violence or general lawlessness. Its area as well as its scope should also be limited to the barest necessity of the case.

Young India, 5-1-'22

THE JEWS

The German persecution of the Jews seems to have no parallel in history. Can the Jews resist this organized and shameless persecution? Is there a way to preserve their self-respect, and not to feel helpless, neglected and forlorn? I submit there is. No person who has faith in a living God need feel helpless or forlorn. Jehovah of the Jews is a God more personal than the God of the Christians, the Mussalmans or the Hindus, though, as a matter of fact, in essence, He is common to all and one without a second and beyond description. But as the Jews attribute personality to God and believe that He rules every action of theirs, they ought not to feel helpless. If I were a Jew and were born in Germany and earned my livelihood there, I would claim Germany as my home even as the tallest gentile German may, and challenge him to shoot me or cast me in the dungeon; I would refuse to be expelled or to submit to discriminating treatment. And for doing this, I should not wait for the fellow Jews to join me in civil resistance but would have confidence that in the end the rest are bound to follow my example. If one Jew or all the Jews were to accept the prescription here offered, he or they cannot be worse off than now. And suffering voluntarily undergone will bring them an inner strength and joy which no number of resolutions of sympathy passed in the world outside Germany can. Indeed even if Britain, France and America were to declare hostilities against Germany, they can bring no inner joy, no inner strength. The calculated violence of Hitler may even result in a general massacre of the Jews by way of his first answer to the declaration of such hostilities. But if the Jewish mind could be prepared for voluntary suffering, even the massacre I have imagined could be turned into a day of thanksgiving and joy that Jehovah had wrought deliverance of the race even at the hands of the tyrant. For to the God-fearing, death has no terror. It is a joyful sleep to be followed by a waking that would be all the more refreshing for the long sleep.

It is hardly necessary for me to point out that it is easier for the Jews than for the Czechs to follow my prescription. And they have in the Indian Satyagraha campaign in South Africa an exact parallel. There the Indians occupied precisely the same place that the Jews occupy in Germany. The persecution had also a religious tinge. President Kruger used to say that the white Christians were the chosen of God and Indians were inferior beings created to serve the whites. A fundamental clause in the Transvaal Constitution was that there should be no equality between the whites and coloured races including Asiatics. There too the Indians were consigned to ghettoes described as locations. The other disabilities were almost of the same type as those of the Jews in Germany. The Indians, a mere handful, resorted to Satyagraha without any backing from the world outside or the Indian Government. Indeed the British officials tried to dissuade the Satyagrahis from their contemplated step. World opinion and the Indian Government came to their aid after eight years of fighting. And that too was by way of diplomatic pressure not of a threat of war.

But the Jews of Germany can offer Satyagraha under infinitely better auspices than the Indians of South Africa. The Jews are a compact, homogeneous community in Germany. They are far more gifted than the Indians of South Africa. And they have organized world opinion behind them. I am convinced that if someone with courage and vision can arise among them to lead them in non-violent action, the winter of their despair can in the twinkling of an eye be turned into the summer of hope. And what has today become a degrading man-hunt can be turned into a calm and determined stand offered by unarmed men and women possessing the strength of suffering given to them by Jehovah. It will be then a truly religious resistance offered against the godless fury of dehumanized man. The German Jews will score a lasting victory over the German gentiles in the sense that they will have converted the latter to an appreciation of human dignity. They will have rendered service to fellow-Germans and proved their title to be the real Germans as against those who are today dragging, however unknowingly, the German name into the mire.

Harijan, 26-11-'38

ON NON-VIOLENCE

Questions in Paris and Geneva

"In the method we are adopting in India, fraud, lying, deceit and all the ugly brood of violence and untruth have absolutely no room. Everything is done openly and above board, for truth hates secrecy. The more open you are the more truthful you are likely to be. There is no such thing as defeat or despair in the dictionary of a man who bases his life on truth and non-violence. And yet the method of non-violence is not in any shape or form a passive or inactive method. It is essentially an active movement, much more active than the one involving the use of sanguinary weapons. Truth and non-violence are perhaps the activest forces you have in the world. A man who wields sanguinary weapons and is intent upon destroying those whom he considers his enemies, does at least require some rest and has to lay down his arms for a while in every twenty-four hours. He is, therefore, essentially inactive, for a certain part of the day. Not so the votary of truth and non-violence, for the simple reason that they are not external weapons. They reside in the human breast and they are actively working their way whether you are awake or whether you are asleep, whether you are walking leisurely or playing an active game. The panoplied warrior of truth and non-violence is ever and incessantly active."

"How then can one be effectively non-violent? By simply refusing to take up arms?"

"I would say that merely to refuse military service is not enough. To refuse to render military service when the particular time arrives is to do the thing after all the time for combating the evil is practically gone. Military service is only a symptom of the disease which is deeper. I suggest to you that those who are not on the register of military service are equally participating in the crime if they support the State otherwise. He or she who supports a State organized in the military way—whether directly or indirectly—participates in the sin. Each man old or young takes part in the sin by contributing to the maintenance of the State by paying taxes. That is why I said to myself during the war that so long as I ate wheat supported by the army whilst I was doing everything short of being a soldier, it was best for me to enlist in

the army and be shot; otherwise I should retire to the mountains and eat food grown by nature. Therefore, all those who
want to stop military service can do so by withdrawing all
co-operation. Refusal of military service is much more superficial than non-co-operation with the whole system which supports the State. But then one's opposition becomes so swift
and so effective that you run the risk of not only being
marched to jail, but of being thrown into the streets."

"Then may not one accept the non-military services of the
State?"

"Now," said Gandhiji, "you have touched the tenderest
spot in human nature. I was faced with the very question as
author of the non-co-operation movement. I said to myself,
there is no State either run by Nero or Mussolini which has
not good points about it, but we have to reject the whole,
once we decide to non-co-operate with the system. There are
in our country grand public roads, and palatial educational
institutions, said I to myself, but they are part of a system
which crushes the nation. I should not have anything to do
with them. They are like the fabled snake with a brilliant
jewel on its head, but which has fangs full of poison. So I
came to the conclusion that the British rule in India had
crushed the spirit of the nation and stunted its growth, and
so I decided to deny myself all the privileges—services, courts,
titles. The policy would vary with different countries but
sacrifice and self-denial are essential."

"But is there not a big difference between an independent
nation and a subject nation? India may have a fundamental
quarrel with an alien Government, but how can the Swiss
quarrel with their State?"

"Difference there undoubtedly is," said Gandhiji. "As a
member of a subject nation I could best help by shaking
myself rid of my subjection. But here I am asked as to how
best to get out of a military mentality. You are enjoying your
amenities on condition that you render military service to
the State. There you have to get the State rid of its military
mentality."

In answer to a similar question at another meeting Gandhiji
said: "Non-co-operation in military service and service in
non-military matters are not compatible. 'Definitely' military
service is an ill-chosen word. You are all the while giving
military service by deputy because you are supporting a State
which is based on military service. In Transvaal and other
countries some are debarred from military service, but they

have to pay money to the State. You will have to extend the scope of non-co-operation to your taxes."

"How could a disarmed neutral country allow other nations to be destroyed? But for our army which was waiting ready at our frontier during the last war we should have been ruined."

"At the risk of being considered a visionary or a fool I must answer this question in the only manner I know. It would be cowardly of a neutral country to allow an army to devastate a neighbouring country. But there are two ways in common between soldiers of war and soldiers of non-violence, and if I had been a citizen of Switzerland and a President of the Federal State what I would have done would be to refuse passage to the invading army by refusing all supplies. Secondly, by re-enacting a Thermopylae in Switzerland, you would have presented a living wall of men and women and children and invited the invaders to walk over your corpses. You may say that such a thing is beyond human experience and endurance. I say that it is not so. It was quite possible. Last year in Gujarat women stood *lathi* charges unflinchingly and in Peshawar thousands stood hails of bullets without resorting to violence. Imagine these men and women staying in front of an army requiring a safe passage to another country. The army would be brutal enough to walk over them, you might say. I would then say you will still have done your duty by allowing yourself to be annihilated. An army that dares to pass over the corpses of innocent men and women would not be able to repeat that experiment. You may, if you wish, refuse to believe in such courage on the part of the masses of men and women, but then you would have to admit that non-violence is made of sterner stuff. It was never conceived as a weapon of the weak, but of the stoutest hearts."

"Is it open to a soldier to fire in the air and avoid violence?"

"A soldier who having enlisted himself flattered himself that he was avoiding violence by shooting in the air did no credit to his courage or to his creed of non-violence. In my scheme of things such a man would be held to be guilty of untruth and cowardice both—cowardice in that in order to escape punishment he enlisted, and untruth in that he enlisted to serve as soldier and did not fire as expected. Such a thing discredits the cause of waging war against war. The

War Resisters have to be like Caesar's wife—above suspicion. Their strength lies in absolute adherence to the morality of the question."

Young India, 31-12-'31

WHAT ARE BASIC ASSUMPTIONS

An esteemed correspondent, who has for years been following, as a student, the non-violent action of the Congress and who ultimately joined the Congress, expresses certain doubts with lucid argument. Whilst the argument is helpful to me it is unnecessary to reproduce it here. He lays down three basic assumptions and argues that India is hardly able to satisfy these assumptions under all circumstances.

The suggested basic assumptions are:

1. Complete unity of the people in their desire and demand for freedom;

2. Complete appreciation and assimilation of the doctrine in all its implications by the people as a whole with consequent control over one's natural instincts for resort to violence either in revenge or as a measure of self-defence; and (this is the most important of all)

3. Implicit belief that the sight of suffering on the part of multitudes of people will melt the heart of the aggressor and induce him to desist from his course of violence.

For the application of the remedy of non-violence complete unity is not an indispensable condition. If it was, the remedy would possess no special virtue. For complete unity will bring freedom for the asking. Have I not said repeatedly in the columns of *Young India* and these columns that even a few true Satyagrahis would suffice to bring us freedom? I have maintained that we would require a smaller army of Satyagrahis than that of soldiers trained in modern warfare, and the cost will be insignificant compared to the fabulous sums devoted by nations to armaments.

Nor is the second assumption necessary. Satyagraha by the vast mass of mankind will be impossible if they had all to assimilate the doctrine in all its implications. I cannot claim to have assimilated all its implications nor do I claim even to know them all. A soldier of an army does not know the whole

of the military science; so also does a Satyagrahi not know
the whole science of Satyagraha. It is enough if he trusts his
commander and honestly follows his instructions and is ready
to suffer unto death without bearing malice against the so-
called enemy.

The third assumption has to be satisfied. I should word it
differently, but the result would be about the same.

My friend says there is no historical warrant for the third
assumption. He cites Ashoka as a possible exception. For my
purpose, however, Ashoka's instance is unnecessary. I admit
that there is no historical instance to my knowledge. Hence
it is that I have been obliged to claim uniqueness for the
experiment. I have argued from the analogy of what we do
in families or even clans. The humankind is one big family.
And if the love expressed is intense enough it must apply to
all mankind. If individuals have succeeded even with savages, why should not a group of individuals succeed with a
group, say, of savages? If we can succeed with the English,
surely it is merely an extension of faith to believe that we
are likely to succeed with less cultured or less liberally-minded
nations. I hold that if we succeed with the English, with unadulterated non-violent effort, we must succeed with the
others, or which is the same thing as saying that if we achieve
freedom with non-violence, we shall defend it also with the
same weapon. If we have not achieved that faith our non-
violence is a mere expedient, it is alloy, not pure gold.

Harijan, 22-10-'38

THE SERMON ON THE MOUNT

Q. You often refer to the Sermon on the Mount. Do you
believe in the verse, "If any man will take away thy coat, let
him have thy cloak also"? Does it not follow from the principle of non-violence? If so, then do you advise the weak and
poor tenant of a village to submit gladly to the violent encroachment of the zamindar on his "*abadi* land" or tenancy
rights, which so often occurs in a village these days?

A. Yes, I would unhesitatingly advise tenants to evacuate
the land belonging to a tyrant. That would be like giving your
cloak also when only the coat is demanded. To take what is
required may be profitable; to have more given to you is
highly likely to be a burden. To overload a stomach is to

court slow death. A zamindar wants his rent, he does not want his land. It would be a burden on him when he does not want it. When you give more to a robber than he needs, you spring a surprise on him, you give him a shock although agreeable. He has not been used to it. Historical instances are on record to show that such non-violent conduct has produced a wholesome effect upon evil-doers. These acts cannot be done mechanically; they must come out of conviction and love or pity for the other man. Nor need you work out all the apparent implications of my answer. If you do, you will come across blind alleys. Suffice it to say that in the verse quoted by you Jesus put in a picturesque and telling manner the great doctrine of non-violent non-co-operation. Your non-co-operation with your opponent is violent when you give a blow for a blow, and is ineffective in the long run. Your non-co-operation is non-violent when you give your opponent all in the place of just what he needs. You have disarmed him once for all by your apparent co-operation, which in effect is complete non-co-operation.

Harijan, 13-7-'40

NON-VIOLENT NON-CO-OPERATION

Q. There is a report about some new scheme that you want to propound in one of your *Harijan* articles about non-violent non-co-operation if any invader came to India. Could you give us an idea?

A. It is wrong. I have no plan in mind. If I had, I should give it to you. But I think nothing more need be added when I have said that there should be unadulterated non-violent non-co-operation, and if the whole of India responded and unanimously offered it, I should show that without shedding a single drop of blood Japanese arms—or any combination of arms—can be sterilized. That involves the determination of India not to give quarter on any point whatsoever and to be ready to risk loss of several million lives. But I would consider that cost very cheap and victory won at that cost glorious. That India may not be ready to pay that price may be true. I hope it is not true, but some such price must be paid by any country that wants to retain its independence. After all, the sacrifice made by the Russians and the Chinese is enormous, and they are ready to risk all. The same could be said of the other countries also, whether aggressors or defenders. The cost is enormous. Therefore, in the non-violent technique I am asking India to risk no more than other countries are risking and which India would have to risk even if she offered armed resistance.

Harijan, 24-5-'42

MY FAITH IN NON-VIOLENCE

[From a talk after the evening prayer on board the ship at Suez on the way to London for the Round Table Conference.]

I have found that life persists in the midst of destruction and, therefore, there must be a higher law than that of destruction. Only under that law would a well-ordered society be intelligible and life worth living. And if that is the law of life, we have to work it out in daily life. Wherever there are jars, wherever you are confronted with an opponent, conquer him with love. In a crude manner I have worked it out in my life. That does not mean that all my difficulties are solved. I have found, however, that this law of love has answered as the law of destruction has never done. In India we have had an ocular demonstration of the operation of this law on the widest scale possible. I do not claim therefore that non-violence has necessarily penetrated the three hundred millions, but I do claim that it has penetrated deeper than any other message, and in an incredibly short time. We have not been all uniformly non-violent; and with the vast majority, non-violence has been a matter of policy. Even so, I want you to find out if the country has not made phenomenal progress under the protecting power of non-violence.

It takes a fairly strenuous course of training to attain to a mental state of non-violence. In daily life it has to be a course of discipline though one may not like it, like for instance, the life of a soldier. But I agree that, unless there is a hearty co-operation of the mind, the mere outward observance will be simply a mask, harmful both to the man himself and to others. The perfect state is reached only when mind and body and speech are in proper co-ordination. But it is always a case of intense mental struggle. It is not that I am incapable of anger, for instance, but I succeed on almost all occasions to keep my feelings under control. Whatever may be the result, there is always in me a conscious struggle for following the law of non-violence deliberately and ceaselessly. Such a struggle leaves one stronger for it. Non-violence is a weapon of the strong. With the weak it might easily be hypocrisy. Fear and love are contradictory terms. Love is reckless in giving away, oblivious as to what it gets in return. Love wrestles with the world as with the self and ultimately gains a mastery over all other feelings. My daily experience, as of those who are working with me, is that every problem lends itself to solution if we are determined to make the law of truth and non-violence the law of life. For truth and non-violence are, to me, faces of the same coin.

The law of love will work, just as the law of gravitation will work, whether we accept it or not. Just as a scientist will work wonders out of various applications of the law of nature, even so a man who applies the law of love with scientific precision can work greater wonders. For the force of non-violence is infinitely more wonderful and subtle than the material forces of nature, like, for instance, electricity. The men who discovered for us the law of love were greater scientists than any of our modern scientists. Only our explorations have not gone far enough and so it is not possible for every one to see all its working. Such, at any rate, is the hallucination, if it is one, under which I am labouring. The more I work at this law the more I feel the delight in life, the delight in the scheme of this universe. It gives me a peace and a meaning of the mysteries of nature that I have no power to describe.

The Nation's Voice, part II, pp. 109–10

THE FUTURE

A friend writing from America propounds the following two questions:

1. Granted that Satyagraha is capable of winning India's independence, what are the chances of its being accepted as a principle of State policy in a free India? In other words, would a strong and independent India rely on Satyagraha as a method of self-preservation, or would it lapse back to seeking refuge in the age-old institution of war, however defensive its character? To restate the question on the basis of a purely theoretic problem: Is Satyagraha likely to be accepted only in an up-hill battle, when the phenomenon of martyrdom is

fully effective, or is it also to be the instrument of a sovereign authority which has neither the need nor the scope of behaving on the principle of martyrdom?

2. Suppose a free India adopts Satyagraha as an instrument of State policy how would she defend herself against probable aggression by another sovereign State? To restate the question on the basis of a purely theoretic problem: What would be the Satyagrahic action-patterns to meet the invading army at the frontier? What kind of resistance can be offered the opponent before a common area of action, such as the one now existing in India between the Indian nationalists and the British Government, is established? Or should the Satyagrahis withhold their action until after the opponent has taken over the country?

The questions are admittedly theoretical. They are also premature for the reason that I have not mastered the whole technique of non-violence. The experiment is still in the making. It is not even in its advanced stage. The nature of the experiment requires one to be satisfied with one step at a time. The distant scene is not for him to see. Therefore, my answers can only be speculative.

In truth, as I have said before, now we are not having unadulterated non-violence even in our struggle to win independence.

As to the first question, I fear that the chances of non-violence being accepted as a principle of State policy are very slight, so far as I can see at present. If India does not accept non-violence as her policy after winning independence, the second question becomes superfluous.

But I may state my own individual view of the potency of non-violence. I believe that a State can be administered on a non-violent basis if the vast majority of the people are non-violent. So far as I know, India is the only country which has a possibility of being such a State. I am conducting my experiment in that faith. Supposing, therefore, that India attained independence through pure non-violence, India could retain it too by the same means. A non-violent man or society does not anticipate or provide for attacks from without. On the contrary, such a person or society firmly believes that nobody is going to disturb them. If the worst happens, there are two ways open to non-violence. To yield possession but non-co-operate with the aggressor. Thus, supposing that a modern edition of Nero descended upon India, the representatives of the State will let him in but tell him that he will get no assistance from the people. They will prefer death to submission. The second way would be non-violent resistance by the people who have been trained in the non-violent way. They would offer themselves unarmed as fodder for the aggressor's cannon. The underlying belief in either case is that even a Nero is not devoid of a heart. The unexpected spectacle of endless rows upon rows of men and women simply dying rather than surrender to the will of an aggressor must ultimately melt him and his soldiery. Practically speaking there will be probably no greater loss in men than if forcible resistance was offered; there will be no expenditure in armaments and fortifications. The non-violent training received by the people will add inconceivably to their moral height. Such men and women will have shown personal bravery of a type far superior to that shown in armed warfare. In each case the bravery consists in dying, not in killing. Lastly, there is no such thing as defeat in non-violent resistance. That such a thing has not happened before is no answer to my speculation. I have drawn no impossible picture. History is replete with instances of individual non-violence of the type I have mentioned. There is no warrant for saying or thinking that a group of men and women cannot by sufficient training act non-violently as a group or nation. Indeed the sum total of the experience of mankind is that men somehow or other live on. From which fact I infer that it is the law of love that rules mankind. Had violence, i.e. hate, ruled us, we should have become extinct long ago. And yet the tragedy of it is that the so-called civilized men and nations conduct themselves as if the basis of society was violence. It gives me ineffable joy to make experiments proving that love is the supreme and only law of life. Much evidence to the contrary cannot shake my faith. Even the mixed non-violence of India has supported it. But if it is not enough to convince an unbeliever, it is enough to incline a friendly critic to view it with favour.

Harijan, 13-4-'40